CHAPTER/PAGE		NAME	TYPE	DATA FILE	DESCRIPTION
	171	TEMP4	Interactive		Posttest loop with yes/no control
6	228	BCHART[b]	Either		Utility bar chart subprogram
	227	CHART	Batch	CHART.DAT	Simple modular program that prints bar chart using Subroutine BCHART
	242	COMBO	Interactive		Substantive modular program, while structure menu treatment, screen orientation, combinations subroutine, pause subroutine, uses Function FACT
	255	DICE	Interactive		Simulation of dice throws using Function RAND
	236	FACT[b]	Either		Utility factorial function subprogram
	235	FACTOR	Interactive		Simple modular program that demonstrates Function FACT
	246	PAUSE[b]	Interactive		Utility screen pause subroutine
	257	RAND[b]	Either		Utility pseudorandom number function subprogram, SAVE statement
7	280 282 292 294 297, 302, 305, 309	EX2...	Either		Series of programs for array I/O (EX72, EX73, EX78), column averages (EX79), and subprogram use (EX710 - EX713)
	315	LOOKUP	Hybrid	LOOKUP.DAT	Table lookup with two-dimensional array; life insurance application
	335	NERR[b]	Interactive		Utility subscript-out-of-bounds error subroutine
	333	PLOT	Interactive		Inputs, outputs, and plots two-variable functions; uses Subroutines XYPLOT, NERR, and YNERR
	325	SORT	Interactive		Demonstration of insertion sort; uses Subroutine SORT1

CHAPTER/PAGE		NAME	TYPE	DATA FILE	DESCRIPTION
A	497	PLACE	Interactive		Statement function, intrinsic functions
B	512	AEDIT	Either		A descriptor examples
	524	EMBED	Either		Embedded format specification examples
	505	ENG3	Batch	ENG3.DAT	Output formats
	516	FEDIT	Either		F descriptor examples
	514	IEDIT	Either		I descriptor examples
	518	OTHER	Either		D, E, G, L, and T edit descriptor examples
	522	SLASH	Either		Slash descriptor examples
	524	UNBAL	Either		Unbalanced format specification examples
C	552	ADDIN	Interactive		Input formats with slash, embedding, unbalanced conditions
	544	AINPUT	Interactive		A descriptor examples
	539	ENG4	Batch	ENG4.DAT	Input formats with data file
	546	FINPUT	Interactive		F descriptor examples
	544	IINPUT	Interactive		I descriptor examples
	550	MORE	Interactive		More descriptors: E, D, L, X, T, BN, BZ; complex input
	554	STAT	Batch	STAT.DAT	Descriptive statistics: mean, standard deviation; run-time input formats

---

[a] These programs and data files are in the Examples Library on diskette.

[b] These are utility subprograms that reside as separate files in the Examples Library.

FORTRAN 77

FORTRAN 77

Richard Mojena
University of Rhode Island

Roy Ageloff
University of Rhode Island

Wadsworth Publishing Company
A Division of Wadsworth, Inc.
Belmont, California

Data Processing Editor: Frank Ruggirello
Editorial Assistant: Carol Carreon
Production Management: Stacey C. Sawyer, Incline Village, NV
Print Buyer: Randy Hurst
Designer: Vargas/Williams Design
Copy Editor: Elizabeth Judd
Technical Illustrator: Carl Brown
Compositor: G&S Typesetters, Austin, TX
Cover: Vargas/Williams Design
Signing Representative: Maria Tarantino

Printed in the United States of America

2   3   4   5   6   7   8   9   10—94   93   92   91   90

Library of Congress Cataloging in Publication Data

Mojena, Richard.
    Fortran 77 / Richard Mojena, Roy Ageloff.
        p. cm.
    Includes index.
    ISBN 0-534-11742-2
    1. FORTRAN (Computer program language)   I. Ageloff, Roy, 1943–
II. Title.
QA76.73.F25M63   1989
005.262—dc20   89-35557
                                                          CIP

To Mello, for being there . . .   RM

To Shana, with love   RA

This textbook is designed for a first course in FORTRAN 77 programming. There are no prerequisites, other than a willingness to develop problem-solving skills coupled with patience and endurance. (Learning a computer language takes time, practice, and effort.)

WHAT SETS THIS BOOK APART?

The combination of features described below distinguishes this book from others in the field.

FORTRAN 77 IMPLEMENTATION

Full ANSI FORTRAN 77 is the basis of the FORTRAN material, as established by the document labeled ANSI X3.9-1978. **Part 3** on the inside back cover of the text shows the ANSI FORTRAN 77 program composition, and **Part 4** summarizes FORTRAN 77 statements.

STRUCTURED PROGRAMMING

Structured programming concepts are adhered to throughout the book. All programs strictly use defined control structures (sequence, selection, repetition). GOTO less programming is emphasized, although it's not possible to entirely eliminate use of the GO TO statement in ANSI FORTRAN 77.

TOP-DOWN DESIGN

Stepwise refinement is introduced and motivated at a point (Chapter 3) where programs start getting more elaborate. Other top-down design procedures like top-down execution and top-down testing are discussed at strategic points.

MODULAR PROGRAMMING

Modular programs are discussed in Chapter 6 and used from that point on when appropriate. This topic immediately follows selection and repetition structures, to emphasize its place as a top-down/structured programming tool. The traditional placement of modular programs after arrays is discarded in favor of this current design emphasis.

DESIGN AND STYLE

Program design and style is emphasized throughout in keeping with the current (and future) emphases on both reducing software development/maintenance costs and improving the user interface. Each chapter ends with a Programming Tips section that includes the following two subsections: Design and Style and Common Errors.

MODULAR CHAPTERS

The three modules at the end of the text are meant to give the instructor flexibility in the choice and sequencing of certain topics. The earliest assignments of modular chapters are:

Module		Assign anytime after . . .
A	Intrinsic and Statement Functions	Section 2.6
B	Output Formats	Section 3.3
C	Input Formats	Section 3.3
		Module B

Module A introduces intrinsic functions and statement functions, which are first used in Chapter 2. This module also gives a complete intrinsic functions table, which serves as a reference throughout the text.

Format-directed I/O is covered in chapter-length Modules B and C. Instructors who prefer *early coverage* of format-directed I/O can do so as early as Section 3.3; those who prefer *delayed coverage* of this topic can assign Modules B and C any time after Chapter 3. Modules B and C only use the programming syntax found in Chapters 2 and 3. Moreover, Chapters 3 to 9 deemphasize format-directed I/O, both to allow flexibility of just when format-directed I/O is assigned and to focus on the material at hand.

INTERACTIVE PROGRAMMING

Design issues regarding the user interface in interactive processing are discussed throughout. Menus, screen design, and input error trapping are treated where appropriate.

FLOWCHARTS AND PSEUDOCODE

Both flowcharts and pseudocode (program design language) are illustrated. Flowcharts are deemphasized, however, in keeping with their reduced use within commercial environments and their misuse from a "structured" point of view. We primarily use flowcharts to teach control structures. We use pseudocode mainly as a program design and documentation tool.

APPLICATIONS DIVERSITY

Meaningful applications of the computer are emphasized in our choice of sample programs and programming assignments. They are described in a wide variety of contexts, including areas in engineering, the sciences, business, economics, mathematics, and statistics, as well as public sector areas like health care delivery and governmental administration. All sample programs are described in **Part 1** on the inside front cover. **Part 2** on the inside back cover follows with an index of all programming exercises.

Diversity of easily understood applications in a variety of disciplines has several advantages: It accommodates heterogeneous classes having students from several disciplines, it exposes specialized students (for example, engineering students) to interesting applications in other disciplines, and it broadens the educational experience and fosters an appreciation for the problem-solving similarities in different fields.

EXERCISES

The book has a carefully designed set of exercises, many with multiple parts. Exercises include both follow-up exercises (to reinforce, integrate, and extend preceding material) and additional exercises (for complete programming assignments at the end of chapters and modules). *Answers to most follow-up exercises (those without asterisks) are included at the end of the text.* The follow-up exercises with answers give the book a "programmed learning" flavor without the traditional regimentation of such an approach. Additionally, the follow-up exercises are an excellent basis for planning many classroom lectures.

PROGRAMMING EVOLUTION

We often return to preceding examples and exercises as we introduce new programming concepts and syntax. For example, multiple pages for an exercise in **Part 2** inside back cover shows that this programming exercise is revisited. Program names like TEMP4 and ENG2 in **Part 1** inside front cover suggest that applications programs evolve over time. This evolutionary approach to programming problems has several advantages: It mimics program maintenance over time; it's consistent with stepwise refinement; and it shows alternative means of solving the same problem, with attendant pros and cons.

SOFTWARE DEVELOPMENT CYCLE

A four-step software development cycle (Analysis, Design, Code, Test) is first described and illustrated in Chapter 1. Subsequently it's used in all major applications programs throughout the text. As in commercial environments, this stepwise organization facilitates the development of programs. Students are asked to structure each end-of-chapter assignment according to these four steps.

CHARACTER PROCESSING

The processing of character data is emphasized throughout the text, which reflects the enormous extent of information processing applications in practice. Certain specialized and more difficult text processing and editing applications are delayed until Chapter 8.

EXTERNAL FILES

External data files are introduced early in Section 2.7, and are used where appropriate throughout the text. As a formal topic, however, external file processing is a detailed, specialized topic that's delayed until Chapter 9.

CAMERA-READY PROGRAMS

All complete programs and their input/output have been prepared by camera reproduction of printouts rather than by typesetting. This increases the realism of the programming material and ensures the reliability of programs. Moreover, many of the programs include color shading and explanatory labels to enhance student understanding.

EXAMPLES AND SOLUTIONS LIBRARIES

Adopting instructors receive diskettes with two libraries. The **Examples library** contains all programming examples in the text, including data files and utility subprograms. **Part 1** inside front cover is a description of these ASCII files. These sample programs should be available to students as a starting point for solving exercises. The **Solutions Library** contains program and data files that are solutions to selected follow-up exercises and end-of-chapter programming assignments.

OTHER AIDS

Additional learning aids include the following.

- The use of color type (for user input in the computer runs, important terms, program annotations, and notes), color screens (to highlight and draw attention to the topic of interest), and arrowed margin notes in color provide visual advantages.
- Important concepts and explanations are set off from the rest of the text by specially marked Note paragraphs.
- The inside covers of the text include summary tables of examples, exercises, program composition, and statements.

TEXT SUPPLEMENTS

The text is supplemented by an Instructor's Manual with teaching hints, answers not given in the text to follow-up exercises, and solutions to end-of-chapter programming assignments. Adopting instructors also receive the Example Library and Solutions Library diskettes. The latter includes sample test questions.

ACKNOWLEDGMENTS

We wish to express our deep appreciation to many who have contributed to this project: to Frank Ruggirello, our editor, for unique humor, support, and expert advice; to Carol Carreon, the "assistant coach," for keeping us on track; to Stacey Sawyer and Elizabeth Judd for production and editorial magic; to Vargas/Williams Design for the outstanding design and cover; to Robert Clagett, Dean, University of Rhode Island, for administrative support; to the Computer Laboratories at the University of Rhode Island, for obvious reasons; to Allen Schuermann, Oklahoma State University, for a superb review of the manuscript and corrections to answers; to our reviewers

Herbert Berry
Morehead State University

John Cowles
University of Wyoming

George Devens
Virginia Polytechnic Institute
and State University

Kenneth Cooper
Eastern Kentucky University

Charles Davidson
University of Wisconsin

Donald Ewing
University of Toledo

David Feinstein
University of South Alabama

Nancy Jacqmin
Virginia Commonwealth University

James Marr
University of Alabama, Huntsville

Charles Neblock
Western Illinois University

Allen Schuermann
Oklahoma State University

S. Ganeshalingam
University of California, Riverside

John LeDoux
Virginia Polytechnic Institute
and State University

Larry Miller
University of South Florida

Charles Redeker
University of Washington

John Welch
University of Akron

who provided invaluable suggestions and corrections for manuscript revisions; to our students, who always teach us something about teaching; and to our loved ones, who sometimes wonder what we look like.

Kingston, Rhode Island

Richard Mojena
Roy Ageloff

C O N T E N T S

1

ESSENTIAL CONCEPTS

This chapter presents some essential computer concepts for a course in programming using the FORTRAN 77 language. Its primary purpose is to provide concepts and terminology that facilitate an understanding of computers and their programming. It also orients you to the specialized world of computer terminology. You need not be befuddled any longer by computerspeak like "My computer uses 7-bit ASCII codes for each byte" and "My ROM is fine but I need more RAM."

We see one major prerequisite to doing well in this course: a curiosity, or better yet, a desire to learn more about computers and computer programming. By the time this course is over we hope that we (together with your instructor) will have helped you translate that curiosity into a continuing, productive, and rewarding experience.

1.1 ESSENTIAL ESSENTIALS

Let's start by describing the functional organization of a computer, and follow by defining other related terms that are useful in a first computer course.

WHAT'S A COMPUTER?

We can define a **computer** as a device that rapidly processes arithmetic and logical tasks without human intervention. The typical computer that most of us use is best defined by the five components shown in Figure 1.1 and described next. First, however, let's introduce two terms that are often confused.

Instructions are programmer-defined tasks for the computer to accomplish. For example, we might instruct the computer to

- Input and store a student's name and grades
- Calculate and store the grade-point average
- Print the name and grade-point average

A **computer program** is a complete set of instructions for accomplishing defined tasks.

Data are facts or observations that the computer inputs, manipulates, and outputs. A student's name, grades, and grade-point average are all examples of data. Data are acted on or processed by the instructions within computer programs.

Input Units. The input unit brings data and programs from the outside world to the computer's memory. For most of us this is accomplished by the typewriter-like keyboard and accompanying monitor (display screen) of a video display terminal (VDT). The keyboard and monitor of a desktop computer also serves as an input unit. Other input units include optical character readers (OCRs) for processing coded forms like exam answers, sales slips, and other handwritten or typed documents; magnetic ink character readers (MICRs) for processing bank checks; modems for receiving incoming data and instructions from another computer; mice for moving a screen pointer and selecting menu items; and voice rec-

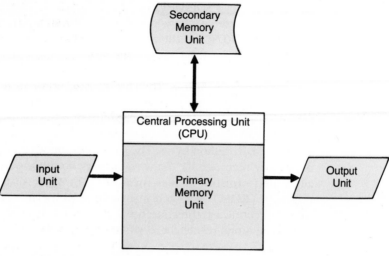

FIGURE 1.1   **Functional organization of a computer**

ognition units for processing human speech. A computer can have more than one input unit.

Output Units.   The function of an output unit is exactly opposite that of an input unit: An output unit receives data from the computer in the form of electronic signals and converts these data into a form that is usable by either humans or computers. The most common output units are monitors (on VDTs and desktop computers) for output that's viewed and line printers for output that's printed on paper. Other output units include modems for sending data and instructions to another computer and voice response (synthesis) units for processing verbal output.

Primary Memory Unit.   This unit temporarily stores programs and data during input, output, and processing operations. The most common primary memory unit is actually a set of tiny memory chips, each smaller than the tip of a finger. A typical memory chip stores roughly 256 thousand (or 256K) bits of data, where a **bit** is a binary digit that assumes one of two possible values: 0 or 1 from a mathematical point of view; off or on from a mechanical perspective; and low voltage or high voltage from an electronic viewpoint.[1] Computers store characters as a packet or series of bits called a **byte.** A common coding scheme abbreviated as

---

[1] Actually, 256K bits really stands for 262,144 bits (or 256 × 1024) instead of 256,000 bits. This is because computers use base 2 arithmetic instead of base 10 (decimal) arithmetic. Two raised to the tenth power gives us the magical number 1024, which is the computer equivalent of Kilo or "one thousand."

ASCII (American Standard Code for Information Interchange) uses seven bits to represent a byte or character. For example, the letter R would be coded and stored as 1010010 and the digit 8 would be coded and stored as 0111000. Most computers enhance the ASCII code to eight bits, which allows additional characters like graphics and foreign language symbols. As a result, the usual assumption is that a *byte is eight bits.* The storage capacity of primary memory is usually expressed as the number of characters (bytes) that can be stored. For example, the IBM PC has a quoted memory capacity of 640K bytes (or 640KB), and the IBM PS/2 Model 70 has up to 16 megabytes (or 16MB) of primary memory where a megabyte is 1 million bytes. The Cray-2 addresses 2 billion bytes (or 2 gigabytes) of primary memory. By the way, primary memory on desktop computers is usually called **random-access memory (RAM)**, to distinguish it from **read-only memory (ROM)**. Data and instructions are permanently placed in ROM at the factory. In contrast, the contents in RAM are temporary in the sense that our data and instructions reside there while we are online (connected) to the computer.

Secondary Memory Units.   Primary memory is said to be volatile because it retains our data and programs only while we are online. In contrast, secondary memory units allow us to "permanently" (is anything permanent?) store data and instructions in external memory for later recall. Computer programs and data not currently in use are stored on media like magnetic tape and disks, and read into primary memory when needed. Common secondary memory units are tape drives and disk drives. Compared with primary memory, secondary memory has greater capacity (many gigabytes) at much less cost per byte, but the amount of time it takes to access data is greater. We can also view secondary memory units as input/output (I/O) units.

Central Processing Unit (CPU).   The CPU, or simply the **processor,** directs the operation of all other units. Its function is to repetitively perform the following three steps:

1. Fetch or obtain an instruction from the program in primary memory
2. Interpret this instruction
3. Execute the instruction by transmitting directions to the appropriate computer component

The processor, together with primary memory, is what most professionals think of as *the* computer. Input, output, and secondary memory units are called **peripherals.** These are not thought of as the "computer" since they are peripheral or external to the computer. We can think of the processor, primary memory, and peripherals as forming a computer system. Current technology can place a CPU on a logic chip that's about one-quarter of an inch square. These are called **microprocessors.** The pace of technology is such that the microprocessor we can balance on the tip of our finger is more powerful than the large computers that filled a room in the early 1970s.[2]

MORE TERMINOLOGY

Computer Types.   Computers are often distinguished by size, which generally translates into storage capacity, speed, and cost. **Mainframe** computers are physically large, process huge amounts of data at incredible speeds on the order of 100 mips (million instructions per second), and strain computer budgets. **Minicomputers** generally range in size from a filing cabinet to a closet. They contain less primary memory, work more slowly, and are cheaper than mainframe computers. **Microcomputers** or **Personal Computers** (PCs) come in sizes that fit pockets to desktops, with correspondingly lower storage capacities, processing speeds, and prices. Microcomputers are often further classified by the number of bits that their logic chips can process. For example, the Apple II is an 8-bit microcomputer, the IBM PC is a 16-bit microcomputer, and the Macintosh is (partly) a 32-bit microcomputer.

Supercomputers are in a class by themselves with respect to memory capacities (in gigabytes) and speed (above 100 mips). For example, the Cray-2 supercomputer has two gigabytes of primary memory and a speed in the neighborhood of 1000 mips, or 1 bip (billion instructions per second).

Parallel Processing.   Many computers include parallel processing, whereby separate processors are linked to work simultaneously or "in parallel" on separate parts of a problem. For example, a Sandia computer has 1024 parallel processors that increase computational speed for certain problems by three orders of magnitude (by a factor of 1000) over single-processor machines.

On Speed.   The speed of a computer is primarily a function of several key factors: processor design—for example, 32-bit logic chips are faster than 16-bit logic chips; parallel processing; clock speed, or the frequency of vibration of the quartz crystal that synchronizes the operation of logical elements within the computer (expressed as megahertz, MHz, or millions of cycles per second—for example, a desktop computer operating at 10 MHz is half as fast as one operating at 20 MHz, all other things equal); number and types of coprocessors, as in using specialized logic chips for mathematical calculations and graphics applications; bus bandwidth, or the number of bits transmitted at once along data paths; and other factors like degree of miniaturization, type of memory technology (for example, dynamic RAM, or DRAM, chips are slower than static RAM, or SRAM, chips) and memory management techniques for moving data in and out of primary memory.

---

[2]The ENIAC, an early *electronic* computer, was completed in 1946. It covered 1500 square feet of floor space, weighed in at 30 tons, sported about 18,000 vacuum tubes, and failed about every 7 minutes. We've come a long way!

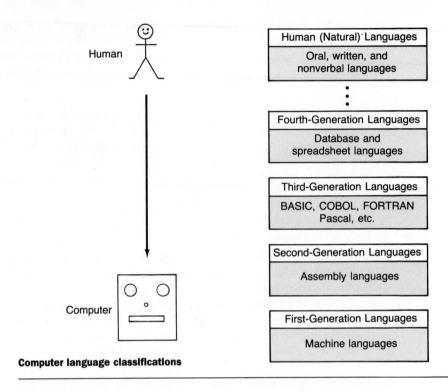

FIGURE 1.2   **Computer language classifications**

Computer Languages.   We communicate our instructions to the computer by writing programs in a computer language. Figure 1.2 indicates one way of classifying computer languages. Any language can be distinguished from any other language by its syntax—that is, by the rules for arranging a specified set of symbols into recognizable patterns. At the computer level the machine only understands **machine language,** which is in a binary syntax for compatibility with electronic circuitry. Instructions in this first-generation language can be written as a series of bits (0s and 1s), although other forms are available, including hard-wired instructions at the factory. As you can imagine, this language is tedious and difficult for us humans, and so second-generation languages were born. These are usually called **assembly languages.** Unlike machine languages, assembly languages use human-like syntax such as S for subtract. Thus, it's easier and faster to program in an assembly language than in a machine language. To a nonspecialist, however, assembly language syntax is cryptic, and is wedded or specific to the particular processor being used.

In the late 1950s the first third-generation language was invented by developers at IBM. Called FORTRAN, this language is particularly popular in scientific and engineering applications. Other third-generation languages include BASIC, the most popular language on microcomputers; COBOL, the traditional language of choice in commercial data processing environments; and Pascal, a more recent language with a wide following in computer science circles. Compared to assembly languages, the third-generation languages are easier to program and reasonably portable from computer to computer. Assembly languages, however, require less cpu time to process and have more detailed control of computer resources than do third-generation languages.

Fourth-generation languages are the latest attempt at getting closer to human language syntax. The most popular of these are database languages such as *Focus* and *dBASE* for creating, maintaining, querying, and generating reports from personnel, airline reservations, student, and other databases. Spreadsheet software like *Lotus 1-2-3* is another example of fourth-generation languages. As time goes on we can expect computer languages to continue the evolution toward human language syntax, since this promotes greater use of computer technology among the masses (and more profits for the computer industry).

Interpreters and Compilers.   A computer program that's written in a third-generation language like FORTRAN cannot be understood directly by the computer, since the computer itself only communicates in machine language. Interpreters and compilers are specialized computer programs that translate third-generation language instructions to machine-language instructions, much as a foreign language interpreter would translate from English into, say, Spanish.

An **interpreter** first translates a single instruction into its machine-language equivalent and then immediately executes or carries out, this instruction. Then it goes on to the next instruction and repeats the translation and execution tasks. This process continues until all instructions have been translated and executed. If any one instruction violates syntax, then a correction is requested before continuing with the next instruction.

A **compiler** is like an interpreter, except all instructions in the program (called the **source program**) are first translated but not executed. If there are no syntax errors, then the translated program (called the **object program**) is executed. Interpreters facilitate the process of correcting programs, but they are slower than compilers once programs are correct. Moreover, object programs can be stored as separate programs (in machine language) and reexecuted without retranslation, which is cost efficient for large programs.

Computer Hardware and Software.   The term computer hardware, of course, refers to the physical equipment, whereas software refers to computer programs. Software itself has two useful classifications: systems software and applications software.

Systems software is designed for tasks that facilitate the use of hardware. The **Operating System (OS)** is the most important piece of systems software. On microcomputers this is usually called the **Disk Operating System (DOS)**. Among other things, operating systems supply the appropriate compiler or interpreter, allocate storage for programs and data, store and retrieve programs from secondary memory units, and display the contents of programs.

Applications software is programs that solve specific problems or conduct specific tasks for end users. For example, applications programs are common for problems and tasks such as engineering analysis, payroll, tracking inventories, billing, class scheduling, simulation of traffic flows, games, airline scheduling, and tax preparation. The types of programs that you will be writing as part of this course (and all programs in this book) are examples of applications programs.

Processing Environments.   There are two major approaches to computing activity: batch processing and interactive processing. There is also a process related to both of these, called distributed processing.

Batch processing periodically accumulates programs (jobs) in groups, or batches, to await execution. Each program is then run or executed according to job priorities established by computing-center personnel. It may take from a few minutes to several hours before the results of a program are available. Typical batch jobs include weekly payrolls, monthly billings, elaborate scientific analyses, and other jobs that require many computations and/or large amounts of input and output.

In **interactive processing** the user directly interacts or conducts a dialog with the program while it executes. This type of processing is usually implemented on either a microcomputer or a time-sharing system, whereby many users working at terminals share the computer. Interactive processing is common in automated banking systems, in airline reservation and other inquiry systems, and in decision-oriented applications that implement "What if . . . ?" interactive analyses. This textbook emphasizes interactive processing.

Communications networks that link various computers and automated office equipment (such as word processors, copying machines, electronic mail, and teleconferencing equipment) at scattered locations are called **distributed processing systems.** A typical system at universities includes a centralized mainframe computer linked to satellite minicomputers and microcomputers at different locations on and off campus. Distributed processing systems usually include both batch and interactive processing. For example, jobs that transmit different sets of data from a computer in San Francisco to a computer in Boston might be batched for transmission during the "graveyard" shift; a student might interactively access the university's mainframe computer first and its minicomputer next to accomplish two different tasks either from home or campus, using either a terminal or a microcomputer.

1.2 SOFTWARE DEVELOPMENT CYCLE

As you know, a computer program is an organized set of instructions written in a computer language; its purpose is to solve a problem that has been defined. This problem is solved when the computer program is correctly executed by the computer.

Writing a computer program involves the following four-step procedure:

1. Problem analysis (understanding the problem and requirements)
2. Program design (the algorithm expressed as a flowchart or pseudocode)
3. Program code (FORTRAN version)
4. Program test (getting out the "bugs")

These four steps are the basis of the **software development cycle.** Thus the act of writing a program includes a step-by-step process, beginning with an analysis of the problem and ending with a program that executes as intended. In actual environments, the software development cycle also includes steps for implementing the newly developed software on an ongoing basis, evaluating its usefulness, and maintaining or modifying it over time.

This four-step process is not a rigid, lock-step procedure. In practice, the development of software cycles through these four steps until the program executes correctly. This means, for example, that the test in Step 4 may indicate a change in design (which takes us back to Step 2) or even a change in the analysis (which takes us to Step 1). By the way, within commercial environments, the software development cycle never really ends throughout the life cycle of a program; new bugs, changes in the environment, and additional requirements are facts of computerized life that promote continued cycling through these steps.

STEP 1: PROBLEM ANALYSIS

First, it's essential to completely understand the structure of the problem and the requirements or needs of the user (or group of users) who will benefit from the program. A common approach is to specify:

a. The output we wish to receive as the solution to the problem
b. The data we will provide the computer
c. The computations and/or logical processes by which the computer will convert the provided data to the output data

As an illustration, suppose that Harvey CORE, the Chief Executive Officer (CEO) of **HC ENGINEering Corporation,** wishes an interactive program that prints a sales report for any one of the firm's automotive engines, as described in Table 1.1. As you can see, Harvey likes to build BIG engines. (He's also a principal stockholder in a gasoline refining company.) The "Two," "Four," and "Six" refer to the number of valves per cylinder. (Harvey's engines are all eight-cylinders.) The data in Table 1.1 provide the necessary input data. The output report is to include the engine's name, its size in cubic inches (the old-timers don't think metric), and sales revenue. Sample output for Baby Two might look like the output that follows Table 1.1 on the next page.

TABLE 1.1   **HC ENGINEering Data**

Engine Name	Size (cc)	Price per Unit	Units Sold
Baby Two	7000	$3000	1500
Momma Four	8500	4000	2000
Poppa Six	10000	5500	1000

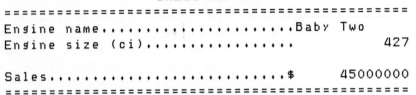

```
                    SALES REPORT
==================================================
Engine name......................Baby Two
Engine size (ci)................          427

Sales........................$      45000000
==================================================
```

In our problem analysis, we need to clearly specify the following.

Data output
Engine name
Engine size (cubic inches, or ci)
Engine sales ($)

Data input
Engine name
Engine size (cubic centimeters, or cc)
Engine price ($/unit)
Engines sold (units)

Parameters
Metric conversion (= 0.06102 ci/cc)

Computations
Size in ci = metric conversion * size in cc
     =   0.06102   * size in cc
     =   0.06102 ci/cc * 7000 cc   (for Baby Two)
     = 427.14 ci

Sales   =   price   *   units
        = $3,000/unit * 1,500 units   (for Baby Two)
        = $4,500,000

NOTE 1   When specifying the data input, we need to ask ourselves: Do the input data provide the necessary items to generate the required output?

NOTE 2   We should specify *units of measure* (like cc, ci, $) for data items, to ensure clarity in the requirements and computations.

NOTE 3   The metric conversion data item given by 0.06102 is an example of a **parameter,** a data item that does not change value from computer run to computer run, as does input data. Generally, its value is provided within the program itself, rather than entered through input.

NOTE 4   The problem analysis in Step 1 often includes a sample problem worked out by hand, as done above. Get in the habit of doing this, which better ensures that you understand the requirements and computations.

In practice (the "real world"), the requirements for output include not only *what* is to be output but also *where* (VDT, line printer, and so on), *when* (daily, weekly, on demand, and so forth), and *how* (design of the display, document, or report). Similar requirements apply to the provided data.

Other considerations in the problem analysis include how the proposed program fits into the organization's computer-based goals, the projected benefits and costs, the needs for additional hardware and software, and future expectations with respect to modifications, enhancements, and extensions.

For us, the analysis in Step 1 is fairly brief. In practice, however, this step is elaborate and can take many months to complete, especially for large applications programs that integrate within a complex system of programs and users.

STEP 2: PROGRAM DESIGN (ALGORITHM)

It's best to design a computer program before it is actually written, much as a building is designed before it is constructed. A program design identifies the necessary processing tasks and spells out the exact sequence or logic by which these tasks are to be carried out. The description of this design is often called an **algorithm.** The manner in which we specify the algorithm, however, is closer to the problem-solving logic of the computer than to the type of prose statement in our preceding step. Throughout this textbook we use flowcharts and/or pseudocode to specify the algorithm.

A **flowchart** is a drawing of the algorithm. It has two primary uses: to help us write the computer program by serving as a blueprint and to document the logic of the computer program for future review.

Flowcharts use specific symbols to represent different activities and a written message within each symbol to explain each activity. Table 1.2 shows the "traditional" flowcharting symbols we use in this textbook, and Figure 1.3 (left) illustrates the flowchart for the HC ENGINEering problem.

Note that this flowchart uses only the first four symbols of Table 1.2. The other symbols are introduced in later chapters, as our programming becomes more sophisticated.

In general, a flowchart must indicate a *Start* and must have an *End.* The flow generally runs from top to bottom and from left to right. As an option, you can use arrowheads to indicate the direction of flow, which is our preference.

TABLE 1.2   **Flowcharting Symbols**

Symbol	Name	Meaning
	Terminal	Indicates the start or end of the program.
	Input/output	Indicates when an input or output operation is to be performed.
	Process	Indicates calculations or data manipulation.
	Flowline	Represents the flow of logic.
	Decision	Represents a decision point or question that requires a choice of which logical path to follow.
	Connector	Connects parts of the flowchart.
	Preparation	Indicates a preparation step as in describing a DO-loop (Chapter 3).
	Predefined process	Indicates a predefined process or step where the details are not shown in this flowchart, as in calling a subprogram (Chapter 6).

A flowchart is one way of diagramming the logic of a program. Many professional programmers and systems analysts use them regularly; others do not. One reason for not using flowcharts is the difficulty in revising them once a program has been modified.

An increasingly popular alternative to flowcharts is called **pseudocode** or **program design language.** Pseudocode expresses the logic of the algorithm using English-like phrases. A key reason for the growing acceptance of pseudocode is its compatibility with the thinking processes of the programmer. The terms and expressions in this false (pseudo) code are often defined by the person doing the programming, and as a result there are many variations in writing pseudocode. The pseudocode in Figure 1.3 (right) should give you some idea of the syntax and structure of pseudocode.

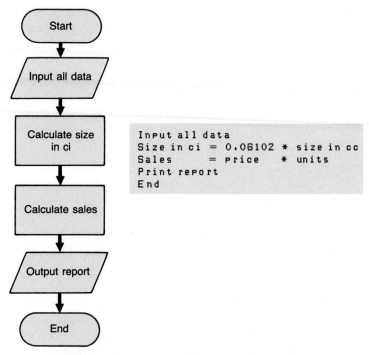

```
Input all data
Size in ci = 0.06102 * size in cc
Sales      = price   * units
Print report
End
```

FIGURE 1.3   **Algorithm for the HC ENGINEering program; *left*—flowchart; *right*—pseudocode**

A program written in pseudocode is similar to a program written in a computer language like FORTRAN. The major difference is the emphasis placed on content versus syntax. Pseudocode primarily concentrates on mapping out the algorithmic logic of a program, with little regard for the syntax of the actual programming language to be used. Thus we are free to concentrate on the design of the program by expressing its logic or structure in ordinary English, including abbreviations, symbols, and formulas.

Either flowcharts or pseudocode can be used to design and document programs, but the simplicity and compactness of pseudocode may tip the balance in its favor, particularly for documenting programs that are likely to undergo frequent modification.

A significant drop in the commercial sales of programs that generate flowcharts suggests the declining popularity of flowcharts as a design and documentation tool. Moreover, experimental research indicates that informal program design languages are more effective than flowcharts for program design and designer-programmer communication.[3]

---

[3]H. R. Ramsey, M. E. Atwood, and J. R. Van Doren, "Flowcharts Versus Program Design Languages: An Experimental Comparison," *Communications of the acm,* June 1983, pp. 445–449.

We prefer pseudocode to flowcharts in designing and documenting programs but believe that flowcharts are useful tools for teaching certain programming concepts. Thus, in this textbook, we will use either flowcharts or pseudocode, whichever is more appropriate.

NOTE 1   Although the example of a flowchart and pseudocode in Figure 1.3 is rather simple, and you may be tempted not to use these aids for such an easy problem, we strongly suggest that you get in the habit of using either pseudocode or flowcharts now. As programs become more complex, you will find these design tools increasingly helpful.

NOTE 2   In Chapter 3 we illustrate two algorithmic design approaches: *control structures* and *top-down design.* These are especially useful in the design of long, elaborate algorithms.

STEP 3: PROGRAM CODE

Coding is the translation of our problem-solving logic from the design phase into a computer program. We use the flowchart or pseudocode as a guide for writing instructions to the computer.

The computer language that our instructions are to be written in must be decided by this step in the procedure. (Quite often the same flowchart or pseudocode can be used with any computer language.) Some languages are more suitable than others, depending on the application.

We use **FORTRAN** in this textbook, which stands for **FOR**mula **TRAN**slation. FORTRAN is widely used in practice for several reasons: it's the first of the third-generation languages; it is (relatively) easy to learn; it has excellent mathematical capabilities, which makes it especially attractive to engineers and scientists; it is a highly efficient language in its compiled form, especially for large-scale (number-crunching) applications; a tremendous inventory of FORTRAN programs is in current commercial use, with an estimated value of over $4 billion; and the language is highly portable, which means that the same program can be used across a wide variety of computers.

FORTRAN compilers are developed and sold by computer hardware companies, universities, and software companies. Most FORTRAN compilers conform to a standard form of FORTRAN approved by the American National Standards Institute, abbreviated **ANSI.** In many cases, compilers include extensions and enhancements of ANSI FORTRAN that differ from the prescribed standard. In 1978 ANSI finalized its latest version of FORTRAN, and named it **FORTRAN 77.** This is the basis of the FORTRAN material in this text, although we will simply use the term FORTRAN.

FORTRAN code for the HC ENGINEering example is shown in Figure 1.4. Note the general correspondence between the program and its flowchart or pseudocode predecessor.

At this point you need not worry about the exact meaning of each instruction in the program. These will be discussed in (excruciating) detail in the next chapter. The program, however, should make some sense to you. (If it doesn't, then we think you might be in trouble.)

Position 1
Position 7 — Defines name of program

PROGRAM ENG1 ◄— Defines name of program

```
* * * * * * * * * * * * * * * * * * * * * * * * * * * * *
*                                                         *
*       Harvey CORE ENGINEering Corporation:  Version 1.0 *
*                                                         *
*          Inputs engine name, size (cc), price, units sold *
*          Calculates engine size (ci) and sales revenue  *
*          Outputs engine name, size (ci), and sales revenue *
*                                                         *
*          Key:                                           *
*             METCON... Metric conversion parameter (cc = 0.06102 ci) *
*             NAME..... Engine name                       *
*             PRICE.... Engine price in $ per unit        *
*             SALES.... Sales in $                        *
*             SIZECC... Engine size in cubic centimeters (cc) *
*             SIZECI... Engine size in cubic inches (ci)  *
*             UNITS.... Number of engines sold in units   *
*                                                         *
* * * * * * * * * * * * * * * * * * * * * * * * * * * * *
```

* Type variables
```
      CHARACTER NAME*20
      INTEGER   PRICE, SALES, UNITS
      REAL      METCON, SIZECC, SIZECI
```
— Define type of data storage (text characters, integer values, real or decimal values)

* Declare parameters
```
      PARAMETER (METCON = 0.06102)
```
— Defines parameter value

* Input data
```
      PRINT *, 'Enter engine name'
      READ *,  NAME

      PRINT *, 'Enter engine size (cc)'
      READ *,  SIZECC

      PRINT *, 'Enter engine price'
      READ *,  PRICE

      PRINT *, 'Enter engines sold'
      READ *,  UNITS
```
— Print prompts that request input data and read input data

* Calculate data
```
      SIZECI = METCON * SIZECC
      SALES  = PRICE  * UNITS
```
— Calculate size in ci and sales

* Output data
```
      PRINT *
      PRINT *, '              SALES REPORT'
      PRINT *, '===================================',
      PRINT *, 'Engine name............', NAME
      PRINT *, 'Engine size (ci).......', INT(SIZECI)
      PRINT *
      PRINT *, 'Sales.................$', SALES
      PRINT *, '===================================',
```
— Print report

END ◄— End program

FIGURE 1.4   **FORTRAN program for the HC ENGINEering problem**

Typically, we first design and then write our code on an ordinary sheet of paper (napkins will do in a pinch). After we're reasonably sure that the program is correct, we enter the code through the appropriate input medium for our system, either a terminal or a microcomputer.

NOTE Your instructor will describe in detail the procedure for entering and storing programs on your particular system. In the material below, we describe the *general procedure* and related concepts for entering programs into the computer.

Login Procedure. On a PC this procedure includes inserting the DOS diskette and our program/data diskette in disk drives and turning on the machine. On a time-sharing system, it includes turning on the terminal, establishing contact with the computer (usually by hitting the "Enter" key), and providing valid identification in the form of a user ID and password.

OS Commands. Assuming a successful login (not always guaranteed), we are now interacting with the Operating System (**OS**), which has its own set of **OS commands** (**DOS commands** on a PC). Besides causing us occasional grief, OS commands allow us, among other things, to edit programs, invoke the appropriate compiler for translating our source (ASCII) program into an object (machine language) program, execute the object program, and list or display the source program either on the screen or on paper.

Workspace Versus Library. After logging in, we're assigned (by the OS) a portion of primary memory called the **workspace** or **foreground.** The workspace stores both the program and the data used by the program. When we exit or log out from the computer, our workspace is erased. If we wish to retrieve a program at a later date, then it must be placed in an area of secondary storage (typically a hard disk or diskette) called a **library** or **background.** A program within a library is usually called a **program file.** We can also store data within libraries for use as input to one or more programs. A set of data stored within a file is called a **data file.** A listing of a user's library files is usually called a **directory.**

Editor or Wordprocessor. **Editors** and **wordprocessors** are commercial programs that we use to enter, alter, and store program and data files. This means that we have to learn yet another set of commands peculiar to the editor or wordprocessor we will use. For example, wordprocessors differ with respect to how they move the cursor around the screen; how they insert, delete, move, or copy portions of text; and how they store files. The primary difference between editors and wordprocessors is that the latter are designed for general text files that will subsequently be printed in a prespecified format, as in a letter, report, memo, or thesis. Consequently, wordprocessors place a lot of emphasis on the hardcopy look of documents, and in supporting the special features of specific printers. Will you be using an editor or a wordprocessor?

Program Lines. A program is a set of separate lines. For example, the program in Figure 1.4 has 61 lines. Program lines are officially classified (by ANSI) as follows:

1. Initial lines are those that initiate a statement A **statement** is an instruction that either directs the computer to perform a specific task (like PRINT in Figure 1.4) or declares certain information that the computer needs (like PARAMETER in Figure 1.4). *Statements are placed in positions 7–72 of the line.* The program in Figure 1.4 has 24 initial lines or statements; these are in the shaded boxes.

2. Continuation lines are needed whenever statements are too long to fit on their initial lines. *Continuation lines are those having any character other than blank or zero in the sixth position of the line. The partial statement is then placed within positions 7–72.* The program in Figure 1.4 has no continuation lines. Initial lines and continuation lines are simply statement lines A statement line that begins a statement is the initial line; if the statement is too long to fit on this line, then the next line is a continuation line.

3. Comment lines are used to document programs for human readability. *Comment lines are either entirely blank or those having either the character * or the character C at the beginning of the line. Comment lines can use all 80 positions in a line.* The program in Figure 1.4 has 37 comment lines (34 begin with an * and 3 are entirely blank).

NOTE Pay attention to the cursor position within a line. Think of a program line as having a length of 80 positions or columns (the width of a screen). Where you can type characters on this line depends on the type of line, as follows:

Comment line..... We can use all 80 positions. Make sure there's an * or a C in position 1 (unless the entire line is blank).

Statement line..... Statement lines break down as follows:

Position	Use for . . .
1–5	Statement labels *
6	Line continuation
7–72	The statement itself

*A statement label is a one- to five-digit number that identifies a statement; we will illustrate these in Chapter 3.

Logout Procedure. In a time-sharing system, we log out by typing a logout command and turning off the terminal (and cleaning up any mess we might have made). When using a PC, we simply turn off the PC and monitor, and remove our diskettes.

STEP 4: PROGRAM TEST

The next step is to run, or execute, the program on the computer. By **run** or **execute** we mean that the instructions that make up the program code are processed (carried out) by the processor. Our purpose, in this case, is to test the program to ensure that it contains no errors. Testing involves running the program with test data to verify that the correct output is produced.

Let's assume that the program from Step 3 has been loaded into primary memory, compiled (without error, of course), and executed. Input and output for

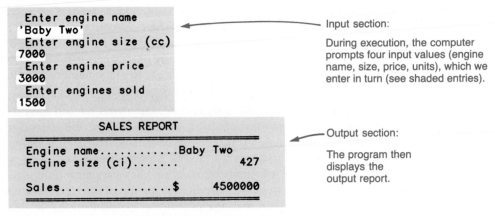

```
Enter engine name
'Baby Two'
Enter engine size (cc)
7000
Enter engine price
3000
Enter engines sold
1500
```

Input section:

During execution, the computer prompts four input values (engine name, size, price, units), which we enter in turn (see shaded entries).

```
              SALES REPORT
 ═══════════════════════════════════════
 Engine name...........Baby Two
 Engine size (ci).......        427

 Sales................$       4500000
```

Output section:

The program then displays the output report.

FIGURE 1.5   Run of HC ENGINEering program

this run are shown in Figure 1.5. Don't worry (just yet) about how this is done. *Your instructor will illustrate the specific steps for your system.*

From our analysis in Step 1, we see that the output is correct; that is, 427 cubic inches (the integer part of 427.14) is equivalent to 7000 cubic centimeters, and $4,500,000 is the product of price ($3000 per unit) and engines sold (1500 units).

You will often write programs that fail to run or that run improperly. (It happens to all of us.) **Debugging** is the process of locating and correcting errors, or "getting out the bugs."[4]

We have three types of errors.

1. **Compile-time (syntax) errors.** These occur when FORTRAN statements violate the rules (*syntax*) of the FORTRAN language. For example, mistyping PRINT as PRONT will cause a compile-time error. When we make this type of error, our program will not execute, and the compiler will identify the incorrect statement by an appropriate (but often befuddling) diagnostic message. At this time, we have to figure out the exact problem, accordingly change our program using the editor, and recompile. Once our program is free of syntax errors, we might have to look forward to . . .

2. **Run-time (execution) errors.** These are errors that take place while the program is running. For example, an attempt to divide some number by

---

[4]According to computer lore, the term bug was born when the Mark I computer at Harvard University stopped working one day in 1945. It seems that a moth got crushed between a set of relay contacts, thereby causing the malfunction. The computer was debugged by removing the moth with tweezers. The Mark I computer, by the way, was the first digital (binary) computer for solving general-purpose problems. Unlike electronic computers, however, it was a mechanical computer that operated by a system of telephone relays, mechanized wheels, and tabulating equipment. (Can you imagine the sounds?)

zero would cause a run-time error. Typically, when an execution error is committed, the system prints an error message or code and terminates execution. If we escape run-time errors, we might still run into . . .

3. **Logic errors.** If our program runs but gives us unexpected, unwanted, or erroneous output, then we have logic errors. For example, we might have incorrectly programmed a formula, or misunderstood the way a particular output feature works, or misplaced a particular statement. These can be the most difficult to debug because they're often subtle.

To help you with errors, we always end each chapter with a description of common errors relating to the material just covered. Read these carefully and you might avoid some unnecessary grief. In the exercises at the end of this chapter, we have you explore some errors on your system.

ADVICE   Just because your program runs (that is, you get output) doesn't mean your program is correct. *Always* validate your program under varying conditions using a set of test data for which you already know the correct results.

1.3 PROGRAMMING TIPS

Each chapter ends with programming tips that summarize and reinforce program design and style considerations and highlight common errors.

DESIGN AND STYLE

1. Use of spaces. Spaces are ignored in FORTRAN, except when they appear within quotation marks (see the PRINT statements in Figure 1.4). In general, we use spaces to improve the readability and visual appeal of programs. For example, the statement

```
SALES = PRICE * UNITS  ☺
```

is more readable than the equivalent statement

```
SALES=PRICE*UNITS  ☹
```

2. Capitalization. The FORTRAN character set (the official set of legitimate characters) is defined by the following 49 characters:

- **CAPITAL letters** (26)
- **Numeric digits** (10)

```
0 1 2 3 4 5 6 7 8 9
```

- **Special characters** (13)

```
+ - * / = ( ) , . ' $ : blank space
```

Modern implementations of FORTRAN expand the character set to include lowercase letters and other special symbols like double quotation marks, underscores, and so on. The expanded characters are not legitimate in the official (ANSI) version of FORTRAN. A strict ANSI FORTRAN compiler might flag any illegitimate character as a syntax error, although we are generally safe using expanded characters within single quotation marks (as in printing output labels) and in comment lines. To improve readability, we will use upper- and lowercase letters within comment lines and in I/O (Input/Output), as illustrated in Figures 1.4 and 1.5.

3. **The paradox.** There's an interesting paradox in programming. On the one hand, good programming requires the type of scientific method outlined in the four-step software development cycle; on the other hand, art and creativity distinguish great programs from average programs. Approach your program as you might a written composition, and let your creative energies loose (you should get a higher grade too).

COMMON ERRORS

1. **Incorrect positioning within line.** Remember that FORTRAN statements must be placed in positions 7−72 within a line. Comment lines, however, can use all 80 positions . . . but don't forget that the first position must have a * or C.

2. **Capitalization.** Don't be a "loose cannon" with lowercase letters. Use them only within single quotation marks and in comment lines. For example, typing

> print ☹

instead of

> PRINT ☺

within the program in Figure 1.4 will violate ANSI FORTRAN syntax. Capitalize all keywords like PROGRAM, CHARACTER, INTEGER, REAL, PARAMETER, PRINT, READ, and END. To further maintain conformity with ANSI FORTRAN, capitalize all variable names (NAME, SIZECC, and so on in Figure 1.4).

Are you ready for some exercises?

FOLLOW-UP EXERCISES

1. **HC ENGINEering.** Try entering and executing the program in Figure 1.4 on your system. Save yourself some typing by omitting most of the comment lines. (You're not being graded here.) Use the test data in Figure 1.5. Also, check out the other test data in Table 1.1. Validate the output by confirming the results with hand calculations (we don't mind your using a calculator).

2. **HC ENGINEering.** Introduce some deliberate syntax errors within the program of the preceding exercise and ponder the compiler's diagnostic messages, if any. (You didn't have any errors when you initially entered it, right?) Try, but don't necessarily restrict yourself, to the following.

   a. Change a `PRINT` to `PRONT`.
   b. Change a `PRINT` to `print`.
   c. Move a `PRINT` to the fifth or sixth position in the line.
   d. Omit the asterisk in one of the `PRINT` statements.
   e. Omit the right quote mark in one of the `PRINT` statements.
   f. Omit the comma in one of the `READ` statements.
   g. Try reversing the second algebraic expression to

   ```
   PRINT * UNITS = SALES
   ```

   h. Try using `name` instead of `NAME`. Do you get a syntax error?
   i. Try using `ENGINENAME` instead of `NAME`. Syntax error?

ADDITIONAL EXERCISES

3. **Temperatures.** Try entering and executing the program below. Use the Fahrenheit temperatures 32, 212, and 0 to validate the program.

```
PROGRAM TEMP1
* * * * * * * * * * * * * * * * * * * * * * * * * * * * * * * * * *
*                                                                 *
*       Temperature Conversions:   Version 1.0                    *
*                                                                 *
*          Inputs degrees Fahrenheit                              *
*          Calculates degrees Celsius                             *
*          Outputs degrees Celsius                                *
*                                                                 *
*          Key:                                                   *
*            C... Degrees Celsius                                 *
*            F... Degrees Fahrenheit                              *
*                                                                 *
* * * * * * * * * * * * * * * * * * * * * * * * * * * * * * * * * *
*─────────────────────────────────────────────────────────────────
      REAL C,F
*─────────────────────────────────────────────────────────────────
      PRINT *, 'Enter degrees Fahrenheit'
      READ *,  F
*─────────────────────────────────────────────────────────────────
      C = 5.0/9.0 * (F - 32.0)
*─────────────────────────────────────────────────────────────────
      PRINT *
      PRINT *, '    Fahrenheit temperature...', F
      PRINT *, '    Celsius equivalent.......', C
*─────────────────────────────────────────────────────────────────
      END
```

4. **Temperatures.** Introduce some deliberate syntax errors within the program of the preceding exercise and check out the compiler's diagnostic messages. (Of

course, you didn't have any errors when you initially entered it!) Try, but don't necessarily restrict yourself, to the following.

a. Change REAL to REEL.

b. Change REAL to reel.

c. Move REAL to the fifth or sixth position in the line.

d. Omit the asterisk in the READ statement.

e. Omit the quotes in the PRINT statement.

f. Omit the comma in the PRINT statement.

g. Omit the parentheses in the algebraic statement. What type of error is this?

h. Change the 9 to 0 in the algebraic statement. What type of error is this?

i. Change the variable C to c. Do you get a syntax error?

j. Change the variable F to FAHRENHEIT. Syntax error?

k. Change the variable F to F_TEMP. Syntax error?

2

FORTRAN FUNDAMENTALS

This chapter introduces certain fundamental elements of the FORTRAN language. By the end of it, you will be writing and running complete, though simple, programs of the type presented in Chapter 1.

The HC ENGINEering problem will be used as a key example throughout this chapter. For your convenience, we reproduce its I/O and listing on pages 25 and 26.

2.1 DATA TYPES

Computers essentially manipulate data, so it's useful to first understand the six types of data that FORTRAN allows.

Integer Type. This type represents an integer (integral or whole-number) numeric value. In Figure 2.1, the data item 1500 (number of engines sold) is type integer. Other integer data types include 0 and −305. Integer data types can be positive, negative, or zero.

Real Type. This type expresses a real (decimal) numeric value, such as 0.06102 for the metric conversion parameter in Figure 2.1. Other examples include 0.0 and −8000.319. These also can be positive, negative, or zero.

Character Type. This type handles a **string,** or sequence of characters. In Figure 2.1, the string Baby Two is a character type data item. The length of a character datum is the number of characters in the string. In our example, Baby Two has a length of 8 (including the blank character between the two words). In general, character data can include any character supported by the computer system. Examples include strings of upper- and lowercase letters of the alphabet; numeric digits like 0, 5, and 9; and special characters like the comma, colon, semicolon, and plus sign.

```
         PROGRAM ENG1
* * * * * * * * * * * * * * * * * * * * * * * * * * * * * * * * *
*                                                               *
*          Harvey CORE ENGINEering Corporation:   Version 1.0   *
*                                                               *
*             Inputs engine name, size (cc), price, units sold  *
*             Calculates engine size (ci) and sales revenue     *
*             Outputs engine name, size (ci), and sales revenue *
*                                                               *
*          Key:                                                 *
*             METCON... Metric conversion parameter (cc = 0.06102 ci)  *
*             NAME..... Engine name                             *
*             PRICE.... Engine price in $ per unit              *
*             SALES.... Sales in $                              *
*             SIZECC... Engine size in cubic centimeters (cc)   *
*             SIZECI... Engine size in cubic inches (ci)        *
*             UNITS.... Number of engines sold in units         *
*                                                               *
* * * * * * * * * * * * * * * * * * * * * * * * * * * * * * * * *
*--------------------------------------------------------------
*  Type variables
*-----------------
      CHARACTER NAME*20
      INTEGER   PRICE, SALES, UNITS
      REAL      METCON, SIZECC, SIZECI
*--------------------------------------------------------------
*  Declare parameters
*--------------------
      PARAMETER (METCON = 0.06102)
*--------------------------------------------------------------
*  Input data
*------------
      PRINT *, 'Enter engine name'
      READ *,   NAME

      PRINT *, 'Enter engine size (cc)'
      READ *,   SIZECC

      PRINT *, 'Enter engine price'
      READ *,   PRICE

      PRINT *, 'Enter engines sold'
      READ *,   UNITS
*--------------------------------------------------------------
*  Calculate data
*----------------
      SIZECI = METCON * SIZECC
      SALES  = PRICE  * UNITS
*--------------------------------------------------------------
*  Output data
*-------------
      PRINT *
      PRINT *, '         SALES REPORT'
      PRINT *, '==============================='
      PRINT *, 'Engine name............', NAME
      PRINT *, 'Engine size (ci).......', INT(SIZECI)
      PRINT *
      PRINT *, 'Sales.................$', SALES
      PRINT *, '==============================='
*--------------------------------------------------------------
      END
```

FIGURE 2.1   **I/O and listing for the HC ENGINEering problem** (*continued on next page*)

```
 Enter engine name
'Baby Two'
 Enter engine size (cc)
7000
 Enter engine price
3000
 Enter engines sold
1500

                  SALES REPORT
       ═══════════════════════════════════════
       Engine name...........Baby Two
       Engine size (ci).......        427

       Sales................$     4500000
       ═══════════════════════════════════════
```

FIGURE 2.1   *(continued)*

Double-Precision Type.   This data type increases the number of digits stored in a real data value. It's used when we need to increase the precision of calculations, which we illustrate later in this chapter.

Logical Data Type.   This data type processes logical values that represent true and false conditions. .TRUE. and .FALSE. are the two logical values defined in FORTRAN. We illustrate their use in Chapter 4.

Complex Data Type.   This numeric type represents complex numbers, which are used in many engineering and scientific applications. A complex number is an ordered pair of real values, where the first value is the real part and the second value is the imaginary part. For example, the complex number $-8.3 + 3.21i$ is written in FORTRAN as $(-8.3, 3.21)$. The real value -8.3 is the real part, and the real value 3.21 is the imaginary part. The symbol i represents $\sqrt{-1}$, so i^2 is -1.

2.2 CONSTANTS

A **constant** is a value that explicitly appears within a program; hence, its value does not change during execution of that program. FORTRAN supports numeric constants, character constants, and logical constants.

NUMERIC CONSTANTS

The types of **numeric constants** correspond to the numeric data types discussed earlier: integer, real, double precision, and complex. Table 2.1 shows some sample numeric constants.

TABLE 2.1   **Sample Numeric Constants**

FORTRAN Representation	Algebraic Representation	Type
0	0	Integer
0.0	0.0	Real
-5001	-5001	Integer
-5001.67	-5001.67	Real
3.141593	3.141593	Real
3.1415926536D+00	3.1415926536	Double precision
(10.015,-6.78)	$10.015 - 6.78i$	Complex
-7.845E+06	-7.845×10^6 or -7845000	Real
5.1E-10	5.1×10^{-10} or 0.00000000051	Real

E-Notation.   The last two examples in Table 2.1 illustrate **exponential notation** (**E-notation**), or the FORTRAN representation of scientific notation. E-notation is useful for stating very small or very large real numeric constants. Note that E+06 is equivalent to $\times 10^6$, and E-10 represents $\times 10^{-10}$. You will often see this type of notation when viewing the output of real values. We might note that the computer stores all real values in E-notation, called floating point representation.

D-Notation.   The double-precision example in Table 2.1 illustrates how we express double-precision constants. The syntax is just like that for E-notation, except the E is replaced by D.

NOTE   Commas and other special characters are not permissible within numeric constants. For example, the representations 7,845,000 and $67.54 would provoke syntax errors.

Precision.   All computers have a limit on the number of digits used to represent a numeric value. This is called the **precision** of the computer. For example, the VAX computers store 7 significant digits, whereas CRAY supercomputers store 13 significant digits. Double-precision representations increase these limits further. The population of the United States in 1980 was 223,324,111. Let's assume we wish to store this value as a real constant. On the VAX this would be stored as 0.2233241E+09, which represents a loss of precision; on the CRAY it would be stored in its entirety as 0.223324111E+09. If we wish to retain 9-digit precision on the VAX, we would have to use the double-precision representation 0.223324111D+09.

Range.   The range of values allowed for integer and real values also varies from system to system. For example, the VAX handles E-notation exponents in the range -38 to 38, while the CRAY takes exponents in the range -2465 to 2465. This means that the real value 0.66E$+100$ exceeds the range of the VAX, but not the CRAY. Similarly, the VAX has an upper limit of 2,147,483,647 for integer values; the corresponding limit for the CRAY is 280,000,000,000,000. Integer or real values that exceed the upper limit cause an **overflow** condition; values smaller than the lower limit cause an **underflow** condition. Systems normally print an execution error message whenever an overflow condition occurs. An underflow condition typically yields a value of zero for the stored number. *What's the precision and range on your system for integer and real values?*

CHARACTER AND LOGICAL CONSTANTS

A **character constant** is a string enclosed within apostrophes (single quotation marks). For example, `'Baby Two'` is a character constant in the input illustration in Figure 2.1. The portion `'Enter engine size (cc)'` within the `PRINT` statement in Figure 2.1 is another character constant. We use character constants for input (as in Figure 2.1); for printing labels, report headings, messages, and other text (see the `PRINT` statements in Figure 2.1); and as expressions within assignment statements (Section 2.6 and Chapter 8) and logic statements (Chapters 4 and 8). By the way, systems do have limitations on the length of a character constant. For example, the VAX has a 255-character limitation. *What's the maximum length of a character data item on your system?*

A **logical constant** is either `.TRUE.` or `.FALSE.` These are used to assign logical values and to carry out certain logical comparisons, as we illustrate in Chapters 4 and 5.

2.3 VARIABLES

We can store data items within identifiable storage locations in primary memory. These storage locations are referenced or addressed by names, called **variable names** or simply **variables.** A variable thus identifies a location in memory where a particular data item is stored (found). For example, in the HC ENGINEering program, the variable name `PRICE` represents the price of an engine. In the sample run in Figure 2.1, 3000 is entered or stored within the memory location called `PRICE`.

It's often useful to visualize memory locations and their contents. For example, we might describe the storage location addressed as `PRICE`, together with its contents, by the following representation.

PRICE
3000

We will use these "memory boxes" throughout the book to explain the execution behavior of programs by tracking the contents of storage locations.

RULES FOR NAMING VARIABLES

1. How many characters? **A variable name must have** 6 characters or less.

2. The first character? **The first character must be a** capital letter.

3. The remaining characters? **The remaining characters can be** capital letters, digits, or a combination of both. **No special characters such as plus (+), slash (/), asterisk (*), or dash (−) are permitted.** Blanks are ignored. **For example,** SIZE CC **is equivalent to** SIZECC. Some programmers prefer the use of embedded blanks to improve readability; others believe the practice may cause confusion when variables appear within arithmetic expressions (Section 2.6) and PRINT lists (Section 2.5). We belong to the latter group.

Table 2.2 gives examples of both acceptable and unacceptable variable names.

NOTE 1   Many compilers enhance variable names over the rather restrictive ANSI FORTRAN rules. For example, the FORTRAN 77 compiler on the Prime Computer allows up to 32 characters, lowercase letters, and the special characters for dollar sign ($) and underscore (_). These extensions, however, are not universal across compilers and computers. They increase the readability of programs, but at the expense of **portability,** or the ability to transport programs from one computer or compiler to another. In this text, we will stay with the ANSI FORTRAN 77 naming conventions.

NOTE 2   A good programming practice is to select variable names that have descriptive meaning (to us humans) within the context of the problem. To illustrate, the variable key in Figure 2.1 shows that the chosen names for the variables suggest the

TABLE 2.2   Variable Names in FORTRAN

Variable Name	Acceptable?
VELOCITY	No . . . Too many characters
vel	No . . . Lowercase letters
VEL	Yes . . .
1 EXAM	No . . . Does not begin with a letter
EXAM1	Yes . . .
MALE SEX	No . . . Too long
M- SEX	No . . . No special characters
M SEX	Yes . . . But we don't recommend embedded blanks

nature of their contents. For example, the variable SIZECC indicates the storage of a *size* value in cubic centimeters (cc).

NUMERIC VARIABLES

The four possible numeric variables correspond to the four numeric data types discussed earlier: integer, real, double precision, and complex. Are you ready for this?

- **Integer variables** store integer values
- **Real variables** store real values
- **Double-precision** variables store double-precision values
- **Complex variables** store complex values

How does the computer know what type of numeric variable it's dealing with? We data type the numeric variable either by implicit or explicit typing. In the absence of explicit typing, **implicit typing** determines the numeric data types integer or real by the *first letter* of the variable name. If the first letter begins with any of the letters I through N, then the system assumes it's an integer variable; otherwise, it assumes it's a real variable. **Explicit typing** declares the type of each variable through type statements, which we present in Section 2.4. Double-precision variables and complex variables must be typed explicitly.

NOTE 3   We don't recommend the use of implicit typing. We say this because implicit typing degrades the readability of variable names (see Note 2 above). All programs in this text will use explicit typing. For instance, the program in Figure 2.1 explicitly typed PRICE, UNITS, and SALES as integer variables; SIZECC, SIZECI, and METCON were explicitly typed as real variables.

CHARACTER AND LOGICAL VARIABLES

Character variables store character data. These variables are primarily used to store names, addresses, text, descriptive engineering specifications, and other non-numeric data. Character variables are typed explicitly, as shown in Section 2.4. The program in Figure 2.1 typed NAME as a character variable of length 20.

Logical variables store logical data. These are typed explicitly, as described in the next section.

NOTE 4   ANSI FORTRAN defines a **keyword** as a specified sequence of letters. Keywords have specific meaning with respect to FORTRAN instructions. For example, the keywords in the program of Figure 2.1 are PROGRAM, CHARACTER, INTEGER, REAL, PARAMETER, PRINT, READ, and END. In selecting variable names, it's best not to use a name that is also a keyword, since it degrades program readability. (Some languages don't permit the use of keywords as variable names; FOR-TRAN allows it.)

2.4 STATEMENTS

In the first chapter we defined a statement as an instruction that either directs the computer to perform a specific task or declares certain information that the computer needs. This section explains these two uses of a statement, and introduces the most common statements.

EXECUTABLE VERSUS NONEXECUTABLE STATEMENTS

An **executable statement** causes activity within the CPU during *execution* of the program. We have five types of executable statements:

1. Input. These statements tell the appropriate input unit to accept input data for storage in primary memory. The READ statements in the program of Figure 2.1 illustrate this type of executable statement. We discuss input statements in Section 2.5 and Module C.

2. Output. These statements instruct the appropriate output unit to print stored data. The PRINT statements in Figure 2.1 serve as examples. We discuss output statements in Section 2.5 and Module B.

3. Assignment. These statements compute and/or store data. See the statements that store values for SIZECI and SALES in Figure 2.1. All assignment statements have = signs. We discuss these in Section 2.6.

4. Termination. These statements terminate program execution. The END statement in Figure 2.1 would be an example. We present these statements later in this section.

5. Transfer of control. These statements alter the sequence of execution in a program. We take these up in Chapters 3 through 6.

A **nonexecutable statement** declares or provides certain information to the compiler during *compilation* of the program. This information is then used by the compiler when generating machine code for the executable statements. The PROGRAM, CHARACTER, INTEGER, REAL, and PARAMETER statements in Figure 2.1 are all examples of nonexecutable statements. We present these later in this section.

NOTE   The book's inside covers summarize the statements used in this book, and indicate whether or not each statement is executable. Check this out now.

PROGRAM STATEMENT

The PROGRAM statement has the following form.

PROGRAM Statement

Syntax:

        PROGRAM *name*

Example:

        PROGRAM ENG1

This nonexecutable statement is optional; if used, it must be the first statement in the program. The name identifies the name of the program. The same rules that apply to variable names (one to six characters, first character a letter, no special characters) apply here. Select a name that suggests the purpose of the program, and make sure this name is not used elsewhere in the program.

We recommend its use for two reasons: It's an example of good programming style, since it documents the name of the program for us humans; and depending on the system, it identifies the program to the operating system, which can be useful for run-time error messages and certain kinds of memory management procedures called overlays (which are beyond the scope of this text).

END AND STOP STATEMENTS

The statement

END Statement

END

is an executable statement that terminates the execution of a program. It also defines the last physical line in a program. It simply tells the compiler that this is the last statement in the program. Don't forget to include the END statement in every program you write.[1]

The following executable statement also terminates program execution.

---

[1] More generally, the END statement is a transfer of control statement that defines the end of a program unit. We discuss this in Chapter 6.

STOP Statement

```
STOP
```

Unlike the END statement, one or more STOP statements can be placed anywhere in the program, as we illustrate later in the text.

TYPE STATEMENTS

A **type statement** is used to explicitly type names, which overrides the implicit
typing discussed earlier. There are six type statements, which correspond to the
six data types defined in Section 2.1. All type statements are nonexecutable, and
must appear in the program before all executable statements and the DATA statement (discussed later in this section).

Type Statements

Syntax:
```
        INTEGER list of names
```
Example:
```
        INTEGER PRICE, UNITS, SALES
```

Syntax:
```
        REAL list of names
```
Example:
```
        REAL SIZECC, SIZECI, METCON
```

Syntax:
```
        DOUBLE PRECISION list of names
```
Example:
```
        DOUBLE PRECISION PI, USAPOP
```

Syntax:
```
        COMPLEX list of names
```
Example:
```
        COMPLEX ROOT1, ROOT2
```

Syntax:

    CHARACTER *list of name*length*

Example:

    CHARACTER NAME*20, SSN*11, CODE

⎸— Length of 1
        assumed

Syntax:

    CHARACTER*length *list of names*

Example:

    CHARACTER*15 FIRST, LAST, MIDDLE

All names have length 15

Syntax:

    LOGICAL *list of names*

Example:

    LOGICAL OFF

NOTE   In deciding on variable names and their type, first select a descriptive variable name—one that would have meaning to the reader of the program; then select its type on the basis of the data needs of the problem. Use type statements for all variables.

For example, in the program of Figure 2.1, we typed PRICE, UNITS, and SALES as integer, since these stored numeric values were to be manipulated and expressed as whole numbers. We typed SIZECC and SIZECI as real, to allow decimal values in the calculation and storage of engine sizes. METCON necessarily had to be typed real, since its value is expressed as a decimal.

As discussed in the last two sections, numeric variables whose values need to be calculated and/or stored with greater precision should be typed double precision. The double-precision irrational π-value in Table 2.1 and the U.S. population example on page 27 illustrate this idea. These are typed double precision in the example above. We will return to the selective use of double-precision variables in Sections 2.6 and 3.6.

In the character variable example above, we typed NAME as a character variable with declared length 20, assuming we need not store names longer than 20 characters. In the same example, social security number (SSN) was typed character with declared length 11. This allows nine digits and two dashes in the usual representation of social security numbers.

PARAMETER STATEMENT

It's often useful to reference a constant by name. For example, a program that uses the constant π, or $3.141592\ldots$, might use the name PI. Constants referenced by names are called **named constants,** and are defined by using the following statement.

PARAMETER Statement

Syntax:

> PARAMETER (*list of named constant = constant expression*)

Example:

> PARAMETER (METCON = 0.06102, PI = 3.1415926536D+00)

Named constants are named in the same manner as variable names, and preferably are typed explicitly. Named constants are also used like variable names (for instance, in PRINT lists or the arithmetic expressions presented in the next section). Unlike variable names, however, they must not be redefined (assigned another value) within the program. The program in Figure 2.1 used one constant, 0.06102, which was given the symbolic name METCON (for METric CONversion). Note that its value is not changed during execution of the program.

The PARAMETER statement is nonexecutable, and must precede all executable and DATA statements; however, it must follow type statements that use named constants within their lists. In Figure 2.1, the PARAMETER statement follows the type statements.

In our example, we used constants to the right of equal signs in the PARAMETER statement, but more generally constant expressions are permitted. We discuss expressions in Section 2.6.

DATA STATEMENTS

The nonexecutable DATA statement instructs the compiler to place initial values in specified memory locations. A simplified form of this statement is given by:

DATA Statement: Form 1

Syntax:

> DATA *list of names* / *list of constants* /

Example:

> DATA SUM, REPLY / 0.0, 'yes' /

In the example, the compiler initializes the location SUM to 0.0 and the location REPLY to the character string yes.

If more than one variable needs to be initialized to the same value, then we can use the following form.

DATA Statement: Form 2

Syntax:

DATA *list of names* / number in list * constant /

Example:

DATA SUM1, SUM2, SUM3 / 3 * 0.0 /

In this case, the three variables SUM1, SUM2, and SUM3 are initialized to the constant 0.0. Both forms may be mixed in one DATA statement.

NOTE   If DATA statements are used, they must follow type and PARAMETER statements.

2.5 LIST-DIRECTED INPUT/OUTPUT

Input/Output (**I/O**) statements are used to move data between storage locations and external devices like printers and screens. The I/O statements in this section are termed **list-directed** because data movement does not use format specifications to specify the placement and display of data. Instead, data are represented according to rules described below. In Modules B and C at the back of the book, we illustrate the more detailed **format-directed I/O.** You can study these modules anytime after Chapter 3. **List-directed I/O** is simpler to use than format-directed I/O, but it is more restrictive with respect to I/O design.

READ STATEMENTS

The READ statement enables the transfer of data from an external location to memory locations. Typical external locations include the keyboard of a PC or terminal and data files that reside in external memory media like hard disks and diskettes.

A common form of the list-directed READ statement is

READ Statement: List Directed, Form 1

Syntax:

READ *, *input list*

Example:

READ *, NAME, SIZECC, PRICE, UNITS

where input list contains one or more variable names.[2] If more than one name appears in the list, then names are delimited or separated by commas.

The following list-directed READ statement is an alternative.

READ Statement: List Directed, Form 2

Syntax:

READ (*external unit identifier ,* *) *input list*

Example:

READ (*,*) NAME, SIZECC, PRICE, UNITS

The external unit identifier refers to the numeric designations used by a particular system for its input units (terminal, disk drive, tape drive, and so on). If * is used for the external unit identifier, as in the example, then the system's "standard input unit" is assumed (usually the keyboard). This alternative READ statement is preferred by many programmers because it's similar to the standard form used in format-directed input (Module C).

Before going on to some examples, we need to be clear on the two modes of processing data and on the external media where data reside. We make a distinction between interactive and batch processing, as described in Chapter 1.

In interactive processing we directly interact with the program while it executes. In our current context, we supply the data interactively from the keyboard when so requested by the program. The sample run in Figure 2.1 illustrates this style of processing. Note that each READ statement in the program is preceded by a PRINT statement that tells the user what data to input (see the sample run for how it looks to the user on the screen). This style of data input is often called **conversational input,** since it appears that a dialog transpires between the computer and the user.

NOTE   In designing and writing programs, it's useful to take the perspective that others (users) will be using your programs. (This could be true someday!) When you write interactive programs, always use conversational input, because this clearly communicates to the user the data items that are requested.

In batch processing we supply the data within an external storage medium, typically a data file in external memory. In this case, all of the input data are placed by themselves in a file using our editor or wordprocessor. A line in the data file is called a **record.** We now have two distinct files: the data file containing the input data in one or more records and the program file containing the program itself.[3] The use of data files is desirable when we're dealing with large amounts of

---

[2]The input list can also include array element names (Chapter 7), array names (Chapter 7), character substring names (Chapter 8), and implied-DO lists (Chapter 7).

[3]On some systems we can place the data after the END statement. Typically, the END statement is followed by an OS command line (to signal that data records follow next), which is followed by the

data. In practice, the manipulation of data files is common. We look at this special-ized topic in Chapter 9. In Section 2.7 we illustrate a data file implementation.

MATCHUP OF NAMES AND DATA ITEMS

The names in the input list are matched with corresponding data items in the input line or record, as the following illustrates.

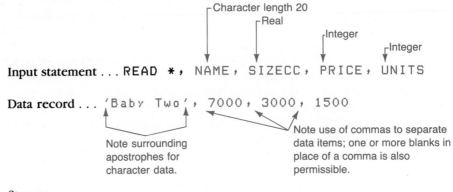

Input statement . . . READ *, NAME, SIZECC, PRICE, UNITS

Data record . . . 'Baby Two', 7000, 3000, 1500

Note surrounding apostrophes for character data.

Note use of commas to separate data items; one or more blanks in place of a comma is also permissible.

Storage . . .

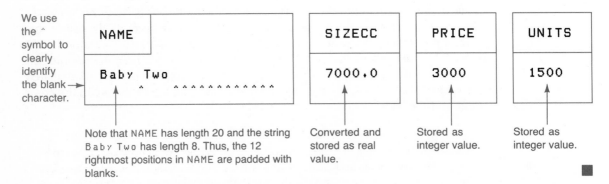

We use the ˆ symbol to clearly identify the blank character.

Note that NAME has length 20 and the string Baby Two has length 8. Thus, the 12 rightmost positions in NAME are padded with blanks.

Converted and stored as real value.

Stored as integer value.

Stored as integer value.

Adjacent data items within an input record must be separated by one or more of the following **delimiters:**

1. Comma. A single comma separates two adjacent data items. Two successive commas with no intervening characters except blanks leave the corre-

---

data records, which is followed by one or more OS command lines that signal the end of the data and run. Can you do this on your system? If we have both choices, our preference is to use separate program and data files, since this more clearly decouples the program from its data. The separation of a program from its data is desirable because changes in the data don't affect the program file itself, thereby simplifying the process of changing the data and simultaneously avoiding unneces-sary changes to the program (which can introduce errors).

sponding storage location in the input list unchanged. To illustrate, if the data record in Example 2.1 were written as

```
'Baby Two'  '' 3000, 1500
```

then execution of the given `READ` statement would have no effect on the storage contents of `SIZECC`.

2. **Blank**. One or more blanks also separate two adjacent data items. Consecutive blanks are equivalent to a single blank, and blanks following a comma are ignored (use these for readability). In Example 2.1, we could have written the data record as

```
'Baby Two' 7000 3000 1500
```

3. **Slash**. A slash terminates read-in of the data record. For example, the data record

```
'Baby Two' 7000  /
```

would leave the contents of `PRICE` and `UNITS` unchanged.

EXAMPLE 2.2

INPUT MEDLEY

Suppose we have the type statements

```
CHARACTER          STRING*5
INTEGER            INT1
REAL               REAL1
DOUBLE PRECISION   DP1
COMPLEX            CPLEX1
LOGICAL            LOGIC1
```

Study the following input variations, and the resulting storage.

Statements	Input Data	Variables	Contents
1. `READ *, INT1, REAL1, DP1`	1 2 3	INT1	1
		REAL1	0.2E+01
		DP1	0.3D+01
2. `READ *, INT1`	1 4	INT1	1
`READ *, REAL1`	2 5	REAL1	0.2E+01
`READ *, DP1`	3 6	DP1	0.3D+01
3. `READ *, STRING`	'12345'	STRING	12345
4. `READ *, STRING`	'123'	STRING	123 ʌ ʌ
5. `READ *, STRING`	'1234567'	STRING	12345
6. `READ *, CPLEX1`	(-8.3, 3.21)	CPLEX1	(-8.3,3.21)
7. `READ *, LOGIC1`	.TRUE.	LOGIC1	T

NOTE 1   If a particular real or double-precision data item doesn't have a decimal part, then we don't have to include a decimal point, since the processor *converts* to the proper type. For example, the input data item for REAL1 is 2, which gets converted to real type and stored as 0.2E+01.

NOTE 2   If the number of data items in the data record is greater than the number of variables in the input list, then the excess data items are ignored. In the second example, note that execution of the READ statement for INT1 stored 1 and ignored the 4. This was also true for REAL1 and DP1.

NOTE 3   The execution of a READ statement processes a new data record. In the second example, the three READ statements processed three separate data records. Thus, INT1 stored 1, REAL1 stored 2.0, and DP1 stored 3.0.

NOTE 4   If the length of a character data item is less than the declared length of the character variable, then the excess positions in the memory storage location are *padded* with blanks; if the length of the character data item exceeds the declared length of the character variable, then the excess characters in the data item are *truncated*. For instance, see the storage of the data items 123 and 1234567 in examples 4 and 5 in the table.

NOTE 5   Complex data input includes the parenthetical expression and the comma separating the real and imaginary parts; logical data input includes the periods surrounding the word TRUE. See examples 6 and 7 in the table.   ■

PRINT AND WRITE STATEMENTS

Output statements move data from storage locations to external media-like computer screens and printer paper. In this section we show two equivalent statements for list-directed output.

The list-directed PRINT statement has the form

PRINT Statement: List Directed

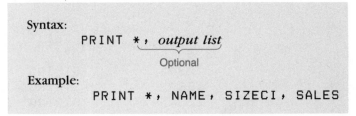

Syntax:

            PRINT *, *output list*
                    ⎵⎵⎵⎵⎵⎵⎵⎵⎵⎵⎵
                       Optional

Example:

            PRINT *, NAME, SIZECI, SALES

where the output list includes one or more of the following:

- Constant
- Variable
- Expression (Section 2.6)
- Array name (Chapter 7)
- Array element name (Chapter 7)
- Character substring name (Chapter 8)

If the optional portion of the PRINT statement is omitted (as in PRINT *), then the computer simply prints a blank line.

The list-directed WRITE statement is equivalent to the list-directed PRINT statement.

WRITE Statement: List Directed

Syntax:

WRITE (*external unit identifier* , *) *output list*

Optional

Example:

WRITE (*,*) NAME, SIZECI, SALES

The external unit identifier is either an integer expression for a system's output units (screen, printer, and so on) or an asterisk. If an * is used for the external unit identifier, as in the example, then the system's "standard output unit" is assumed (usually the screen). This alternative WRITE statement is preferred by many programmers because it's similar to the standard form used in format-directed output (Module B).

In the above PRINT and WRITE examples, the stored values in NAME, SIZECI, and SALES are displayed on one line of a video screen. Other examples are shown in the program and run of Figure 2.1. In particular, note that the PRINT output lists for the Sales Report include the extensive use of character constants for the title and output labels.

NOTE   Good program design includes good output design at the user interface (screen or paper). Take care in designing output that clearly communicates . . . Avoid clutter, unlabeled output, and otherwise UGLY output. The latter, of course, is in the "eye of the beholder" (probably your instructor).

EXAMPLE 2.3

INPUT/OUTPUT MEDLEY

The following program and run reinforce and extend the examples in Example 2.2.

```
PROGRAM MEDLEY
*-------------------------------------------------------------
*      I/O Medley
*-------------------------------------------------------------
       CHARACTER          STRING*5
       INTEGER            INT1
       REAL               REAL1
       DOUBLE PRECISION   DP1
       COMPLEX            CPLEX1
       LOGICAL            LOGIC1

       WRITE (*,*) 'Enter integer, real, and double-precision values'
       READ  (*,*) INT1, REAL1, DP1

       WRITE (*,*) 'Enter string value'
       READ  (*,*) STRING

       WRITE (*,*) 'Enter complex value'
       READ  (*,*) CPLEX1

       WRITE (*,*) 'Enter logical value'
       READ  (*,*) LOGIC1

       WRITE (*,*)
       WRITE (*,*) 'Integer, real, double precision...', INT1, REAL1, DP1
       WRITE (*,*)
       WRITE (*,*) 'String.............................', STRING
       WRITE (*,*)
       WRITE (*,*) 'Complex............................', CPLEX1
       WRITE (*,*)
       WRITE (*,*) 'Logical............................', LOGIC1
*-------------------------------------------------------------
       END
```

Prints blank line → (arrows pointing to the two `WRITE (*,*)` blank lines)

```
 Enter integer, real, and double-precision values
1,2,3
 Enter string value
'1234567'
 Enter complex value
(-8.3, 3.21)
 Enter logical value
.TRUE.

 Integer, real, double precision...         1     2.00000      3.00000000000

 String.............................12345

 Complex............................ (-8.30000,3.21000)

 Logical............................  T
```

NOTE 1　The execution of a PRINT or WRITE statement starts a new output line. The 12 WRITE statements in the program printed 12 lines of output: 4 lines requesting input, 4 blank lines, and 4 lines with labeled value output. If the printed values are too long to fit on one output line, then the system will *wrap* output to the next line.

NOTE 2　If the output list in a PRINT or WRITE statement is omitted, then a *blank line* gets printed. Use blank output lines to make output more attractive, as in the example.

NOTE 3　Numeric output is consistent with *data types* in the output list: An integer variable prints an integer value, a real variable prints a single-precision real value, a double-precision variable prints a double-precision value, and a complex variable prints a complex value in parenthetical form. See the example.

NOTE 4　String values are printed exactly as stored, but logical values are printed as a *T* or an *F.* See the example.　■

2.6 ASSIGNMENT STATEMENTS

An **assignment statement** assigns or stores a value in a memory location.

STRUCTURE

The assignment statement is structured as follows.

Assignment Statement

Syntax:

　　name = *expression*

Example:

　　SALES = PRICE * UNITS

A single variable name identifies a storage location to the left of the equal sign. The right member is an expression having type logical, character, or arithmetic, as we explain below.

---

†The only other name permitted to the left of the equal sign is an array element name (Chapter 7).

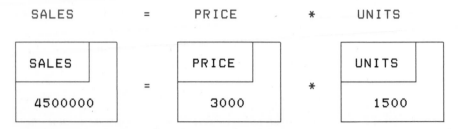

If PRICE stores 3000 and UNITS stores 1500 (which are the values stored in the run of Figure 2.1), then SALES will store 4500000 when this assignment statement is executed.

NOTE   Take care with the meaning of the equal sign in FORTRAN: It means "place the *value* indicated by the expression to the right into the storage location indicated by the *variable* to the left." Because of this meaning, an assignment statement like

    COUNT = COUNT + 1

makes sense in FORTRAN, but not in algebra. Each time this statement is executed, the location COUNT gets increased by 1. In other words, this statement instructs the computer to "add the content of COUNT and 1, and place the result in COUNT." This type of statement is called a **counter** in programming. Some writers prefer the name **assignment operator** instead of equal sign, since this better describes the function of the equal sign in FORTRAN.

TYPES OF EXPRESSIONS

The types of expressions for the right member of the assignment statement correspond to the data types defined earlier: logical, character, and numeric (integer, real, double precision, complex).

Logical Expressions. In its simplest form, the logical expression is either a logical constant (.TRUE. or .FALSE.) or a logical variable. The most commonly used logical expressions, however, are related to the decision logic we consider in Chapter 4. We will describe logical expressions in detail at that time.

Character Expressions. In its simplest form, a character expression is either a character constant or a character variable.[5] To illustrate, suppose we declare two character variables as follows

    CHARACTER FIRST*20, SECOND*15

and we use the following assignment statement.

---

[5] More generally, a character expression can also include a named character constant, a character array element (Chapter 7), a character substring (Chapter 8), a character function (Chapter 8), and expressions that use character operators and parentheses (Chapter 8).

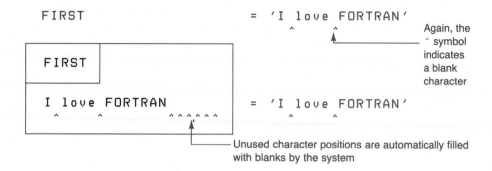

In this example, the character expression is the character constant ′I love FORTRAN′ with length 14 characters, including the two blank characters surrounding love but excluding the apostrophes. Note that the length of 14 for the character constant is 6 characters less than the declared length of 20 in the CHARACTER statement. The computer thus left-justifies the value I love FORTRAN within FIRST, and pads the rightmost unused character positions with blanks. If the CHARACTER statement had declared a length of 6 for the character variable FIRST, then I love would have been stored. In this case, the remaining portion of the character value is **truncated.**

Now suppose the computer next executes the following assignment statement.

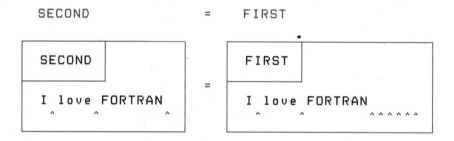

In this case the character expression to the right of the equal sign is the character variable FIRST. Note that this assignment statement simply copied the contents of FIRST into SECOND, leaving the contents of FIRST unaffected. Also notice that SECOND has a length of 15 (see the CHARACTER statement above). Thus, the last 5 blanks in FIRST get truncated within SECOND.

NOTE   Remember that if the number of characters we attempt to store in the character variable is less than the length specified in the CHARACTER statement, then the computer pads the remaining (rightmost) character storage positions with blanks. Alternatively, if we attempt to store more characters than the length we have specified, then the computer fills up storage beginning with the leftmost character and truncates the excess characters.

The manipulation of character expressions is a rather specialized topic that we take up in detail in Chapter 8. Until then, our work in character processing is restricted to I/O, decisions (Chapter 4), and yes/no user responses (Chapter 5).

Arithmetic Expressions. An arithmetic expression describes a numeric computation and can include numeric constants, numeric variables, arithmetic operators, and parentheses.[6] An **arithmetic operator** indicates the desired arithmetic operation, as described in Table 2.3.

TABLE 2.3   **Arithmetic Operators**

Arithmetic Operation	Arithmetic Operator	Algebraic Example	FORTRAN Example
Addition	+	$x + 1$	X + 1
Subtraction	−	$x - 2$	X − 2
Division	/	x/y	X / Y
Multiplication	*	$x*y$	X * Y
Exponentiation	**	x^y	X ** Y

We must avoid the following illegal operations when forming arithmetic expressions.

1. Don't place two arithmetic operators next to each other.

```
SPEED * - 6      ← Not permitted . . . compile-time error
  -6 * SPEED     ← OK
SPEED * (-6)     ← OK
```

2. Don't raise a negative value to a nonintegral or real power.

```
(-25.36)**3.0    ← Not permitted . . . run-time error [7]
(-25.36)**3      ← OK
```

As you might guess by now, arithmetic expressions come in four flavors:

- **Integer expressions** operate on integer values.
- **Real expressions** operate on real values.
- **Double-precision expressions** operate on double-precision values.
- **Complex expressions** operate on complex values.

---

[6]More generally, arithmetic expressions also can include named numeric constants, numeric intrinsic functions (introduced below and in Module A), and numeric array elements (Chapter 7).

[7]This is an execution error because the processor attempts to evaluate this as antilog 3.0*log (-25.36), and the log of a negative value is undefined. Note, however, that $(-25.36)^3$ *is* defined as the permissible product $(-25.36) * (-25.36) * (-25.36)$.

To make life more interesting, we also have:

- **Mixed-type** (or **mixed-mode**) **expressions** operate on a mixture of types—integer, real, double precision, and complex (except that double precision and complex cannot be mixed).

We illustrate the types of arithmetic expressions by the next series of examples.

EXAMPLE 2.4

INTEGER EXPRESSION WITH TRUNCATION

Consider the type statement

```
INTEGER FIRST, SECOND, THIRD
```

the assignment statement

```
THIRD =      FIRST/SECOND        ←Integer expression
```

and the following stored values.

FIRST	SECOND	THIRD	Comment
50	10	5	No problem
57	10	5	5 is the integer part of 57/10 = 5.7 5.7 is truncated to 5
8	10	0	The integer part of 0.8 is 0, so 0.8 is truncated to 0

EXAMPLE 2.5

REAL EXPRESSION: COMPOUNDING PROBLEM

A simple compounding formula is given by

$$\text{Future} = \text{Start} * (1 + \text{Rate}/100)^{\text{Years}}$$

where Future = amount of money at end of time horizon
   Start = amount of money at start of time horizon
   Rate = percent annual rate of return or gain
   Years = number of years in time horizon

For example, if we start with $1000 and gain 10% per year, then after 5 years we end up with

$$\text{Future} = 1000.00 * (1.0 + 10.0/100.0)^5$$
$$= \$1610.51$$

More dramatically, if a government agency borrows $1 billion by issuing bonds at 10% for 30 years, then it must pay back the following amount.

$$\text{Future} = 1000000000.00 * (1.0 + 10.0/100.0)^{30}$$
$$= \$17.44929 \text{ billion}$$

The program below illustrates this compounding application. Note that the variables FUTURE, START, and RATE are typed real, since the necessary calculations and stored values are nonintegral. It follows that the arithmetic expression is a real expression, since all of its constituent elements are real. (The integer power stored in YEARS doesn't alter this fact because it simply indicates that the real expression within parentheses is multiplied by itself; see footnote 7.)

```
      PROGRAM COMP1
*-----------------------------------------------------------
*        Compounding...Single precision version
*-----------------------------------------------------------
      INTEGER YEARS
      REAL    FUTURE, RATE, START

      PRINT *, 'Enter starting amount'
      READ *, START

      PRINT *, 'Enter % interest rate'
      READ *, RATE

      PRINT *, 'Enter number of years'
      READ *, YEARS                               ──── Real expression

      FUTURE = START * (1.0 + RATE/100.0)**YEARS

      PRINT *
      PRINT *, '   Future amount......$', FUTURE
*-----------------------------------------------------------
      END


  Enter starting amount
1000000000
  Enter % interest rate
10
  Enter number of years
30

      Future amount......$    1.744929E+10
```

EXAMPLE 2.6

DOUBLE-PRECISION EXPRESSION: COMPOUNDING PROBLEM

The program below is the double-precision version of the program in the preceding example. Note that FUTURE, START, and RATE are now typed double precision; the subsequent arithmetic expression is thus a double-precision expression The real version of the program gave 1.744929E+10 for the stored 7-digit real value in FUTURE. The run below shows 17449402268.9 for the stored 12-digit double-precision value in FUTURE. In dollar terms, this amounts to a difference of $17,449,290,000 versus $17,449,402,269, or $112,269.

This problem demonstrates the need for greater precision for certain types of calculations, although the percent error in using single precision is small in this case. In Section 3.6 we will show how this type of error is magnified for certain kinds of applications.

```
        PROGRAM COMP2
*————————————————————————————————————————————————
*           Compounding . . . Double-precision version
*————————————————————————————————————————————————
        INTEGER          YEARS
        DOUBLE PRECISION   FUTURE, RATE, START

        PRINT *, 'Enter starting amount'
        READ *, START

        PRINT *, 'Enter % interest rate'
        READ *, RATE

        PRINT *, 'Enter number of years'          Double-precision expression
        READ *, YEARS

        FUTURE = START * (1.0D+00 + RATE/100.0D+00)**YEARS

        PRINT *
        PRINT *, '    Future amount......$', FUTURE
*————————————————————————————————————————————————
        END


 Enter starting amount
1000000000
 Enter % interest rate
10
 Enter number of years
30

        Future amount......$        17449402268.9
```

EXAMPLE 2.7

COMPLEX EXPRESSION: ADDITION

Consider the following complex numbers:

$X = (-8.30, 3.21)$
$Y = (10.015, -6.700)$

The sum of two complex numbers is defined as the sum of their two respective parts (real and imaginary), as follows:

$Z = (1.715, -3.49)$

The following program illustrates this application. Notice that the arithmetic operators also apply to operations on complex numbers, although the operations of division and multiplication are defined differently from scalar arithmetic. We take these up in Exercise 16.

```
        PROGRAM CPLEX
*----------------------------------------------------
*        Complex Numbers... Addition
*----------------------------------------------------
        COMPLEX X, Y, Z

        PRINT *, 'Enter first complex number'
        READ *, X

        PRINT *, 'Enter second complex number'
        READ *, Y

        Z = X + Y  ◄──────────── Complex expression

        PRINT *
        PRINT *, '   The sum is ===> ', Z
*----------------------------------------------------
        END
```

```
 Enter first complex number
(-8.3,3.21)
 Enter second complex number
(10.015,-6.7)

    The sum is ===>   (1.71500,-3.49000)
```

EXAMPLE 2.8

MIXED-TYPE EXPRESSIONS

Numeric data types can also be mixed in an arithmetic expression. In evaluating this type of expression, it's useful to focus on the fact that processors perform one arithmetic operation at a time, called **pairwise arithmetic.** In evaluating a mixed pairwise expression, the processor *favors double precision over real, and real over integer.* For example, a mixed pairwise expression involving a real value and an integer value will be evaluated to a real value, as this example illustrates.

```
INTEGER INT1, INT2, INT3
REAL     REAL1, RESULT
DATA INT1, INT2, INT3, REAL1 / 6, 10, 3, 2.1 /
RESULT = REAL1 * INT1 + INT2 / INT3
```

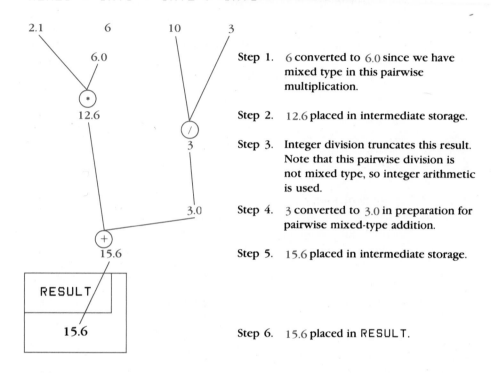

Step 1. 6 converted to 6.0 since we have mixed type in this pairwise multiplication.

Step 2. 12.6 placed in intermediate storage.

Step 3. Integer division truncates this result. Note that this pairwise division is not mixed type, so integer arithmetic is used.

Step 4. 3 converted to 3.0 in preparation for pairwise mixed-type addition.

Step 5. 15.6 placed in intermediate storage.

Step 6. 15.6 placed in RESULT.

It's best to avoid mixed-type expressions, since results unintended by the programmer could "sneak through." For instance, the integer division "10 divided by 3" above gives the integer result 3. If a real result were intended, then we have a logic error.

The product of an integer type and a real type (as in REAL1 * INT1 above) does not present a problem. Some programmers, however, avoid mixed-type expressions altogether (they were illegal on some of the older compilers). In this case, we could rewrite the expression as follows.

```
RESULT = REAL1 * REAL(INT1) + REAL(INT2/INT3)
```

This uses the intrinsic function REAL (see Table 2.4 . . . we discuss these next) to convert an integer value to a real value. The expression still evaluates to 15.6, but it is now a real expression. Note that INT2/INT3 still is an integer pairwise computation yielding the truncated result 10/3 = 3. It's the integer result 3 that's converted to 3.0 by the REAL function. The REAL function isn't really needed because the processor does this integer to real conversion anyway (see Step 4 above).   ■

NOTE   Did you notice that multiplication and division were performed before addition and subtraction? FORTRAN uses *arithmetic hierarchy* rules when evaluating arithmetic expressions, which we will discuss shortly.

INTRINSIC FUNCTIONS

Mathematical operations like square roots, logarithms, and exponentiation are so common that FORTRAN compilers provide **intrinsic functions** for their calculation. Table 2.4 illustrates several, and Table A.1 in Module A at the back of the book gives a complete list.

TABLE 2.4   **Selected Intrinsic Functions**[a]

Name	Description	Algebraic Example	FORTRAN Example
COS	Cosine	$y = \cos \pi/3$ $= 0.5$	Y = COS(PI/3.0)
EXP	Exponentiation	$y = e^{-2}$ $= 0.1353353$	Y = EXP(-2.0)
INT	Conversion to integer value or integer part of	$y = [a/b]$ $= [11/3]$ $= [3.666666 \ldots]$ $= 3$	Y = INT(A/B)
LEN	Length of string	Length of HC $= 2$	L = LEN("HC")
LOG	Natural logarithm	$y = \ln 0.1353353$ $= -2$	Y = LOG(0.1353353)
MAX	Maximum value	$k = \max(3,6,4)$ $= 6$	K = MAX(3,6,4)
MIN	Minimum value	$k = \min(3,6,4)$ $= 3$	K = MIN(3,6,4)
NINT	Rounded integer part	$y = [x + 0.5] \quad x \geq 0$ $= [x - 0.5] \quad x < 0$ $= [3.7 + 0.5]$ $= 4$	Y = NINT(X)
REAL	Conversion to real value	$y = \text{real}(8)$ $= 8.0$	Y = REAL(8)
SQRT	Square root	$y = \sqrt{x}$ $= \sqrt{9}$ $= 3$	Y = SQRT(X)

[a]See Table A.1 in Module A in the back of the book for a complete list of intrinsic functions.

The form of an intrinsic function is given by

Intrinsic Function

Syntax:

function name   (argument list)

Example:

SQRT (B**2 - 4.0*A*C)

The function name is a FORTRAN keyword that identifies the purpose of the function. The argument list is either a single expression or a list of expressions separated by commas. Expressions in the argument list can be character, logical, or any of the four numerics, depending on the function. Each expression in the argument list is called an argument.

In the example, the function name is SQRT; its function is to take the square root of the argument. The single argument is first evaluated; then the square root of the value of the argument is taken.

Intrinsic functions are mostly used within expressions, although there are other appropriate uses. For example, the PRINT statement for SIZECI in Figure 2.1 uses the INT function to print the integer portion of a real value.

Intrinsic functions are commonly used to improve readability, simplify coding, increase computational efficiency, and obtain accurate results. We will use intrinsic functions as needed throughout the book.

ORDER OF EVALUATING NUMERIC EXPRESSIONS

Computers do arithmetic on only one   operation at a time (pairwise arithmetic). Therefore, a numeric expression involving several computations must be computed in a certain sequence.

Arithmetic Hierarchy. The sequence for performing pairwise numeric operations is based on the following **arithmetic hierarchy:**

- *First priority:*   All exponentiation is performed.
- *Second priority:*   All multiplication and division is completed.
- *Third priority:*   All addition and subtraction is performed.

Left-to-Right Rule. The exact order of computation when two or more computations are at the same level of arithmetic hierarchy will be consistent with a *left-to-right scan* of the arithmetic expression.

Use of Parentheses. The insertion of parentheses into arithmetic expressions changes the order of computation according to the following rules.

1. The operations inside parentheses are computed before operations that are not inside parentheses.

2. Parentheses can be embedded inside other parentheses in complicated expressions.

3. The innermost set of parentheses contains the computations done first. Note that within parentheses the hierarchy and left-to-right rules apply.

The following set of examples illustrates these evaluation rules.

EXAMPLE 2.9

POLYNOMIAL FUNCTION: ARITHMETIC HIERARCHY AND LEFT-TO-RIGHT RULES

Consider the following third-degree polynomial function.

$$y = x^3 - 6x^2 + 250$$

The expression in the following assignment statement would be evaluated as described, given that both X and Y are typed real, and X stores 20.0.

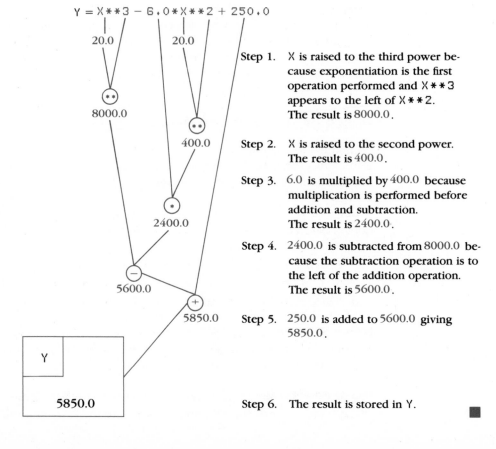

Step 1. X is raised to the third power because exponentiation is the first operation performed and X**3 appears to the left of X**2. The result is 8000.0.

Step 2. X is raised to the second power. The result is 400.0.

Step 3. 6.0 is multiplied by 400.0 because multiplication is performed before addition and subtraction. The result is 2400.0.

Step 4. 2400.0 is subtracted from 8000.0 because the subtraction operation is to the left of the addition operation. The result is 5600.0.

Step 5. 250.0 is added to 5600.0 giving 5850.0.

Step 6. The result is stored in Y.

EXAMPLE 2.10

TEMPERATURE CONVERSIONS: USE OF PARENTHESES

Conversion of temperatures from Fahrenheit to Celsius is given by the formula

$$\text{Celsius} = \frac{5}{9}(\text{Fahrenheit} - 32)$$

Given that both F and C are typed real and F stores 212.0, the following assignment statement would be evaluated as described.

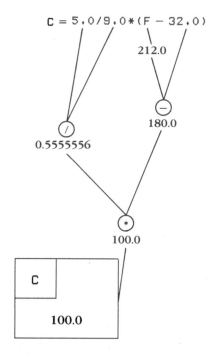

Step 1.   32.0 is subtracted from F because this operation is enclosed in parentheses. The result is 180.0.

Step 2.   5.0 is divided by 9.0 because division is to the left of multiplication.

Step 3.   0.5555556 is multiplied by 180.0. The result is 100.0.

Step 4.   The result is stored in C.

Note that the elimination of parentheses in the expression (F - 32.0) would give the following assignment statement.

        C = 5.0 / 9.0 * F - 32.0

Its evaluation would give 85.77778, a logic error. (Check it out!)

In the temperature example, we used parentheses to simplify the expression, thereby increasing readability. For example, we could have written the mathematically equivalent but less readable expression given by

        C = 5.0 / 9.0 * F - 5.0 / 9.0 * 32.0

In many cases, however, parentheses must be used. For example, an expression for a statistic called variance is given by

$$\frac{s^2}{p-1}$$

In FORTRAN we would write this as

```
S**2/(P - 1.0)
```

The square root of variance, called the standard deviation, is algebraically given by

$$\left(\frac{s^2}{p-1}\right)^{1/2} \quad \text{or} \quad \sqrt{\frac{s^2}{p-1}}$$

In FORTRAN we would write this as follows:

```
SQRT(S**2/(P - 1.0))
```

One final point: *When nesting parentheses, take care that the number of left parentheses equals the number of right parentheses, since a mismatch in these numbers is a common compile-time error.* ■

2.7 ANOTHER APPLICATION: DATA FILE AND STATEMENT FUNCTION

Let's work with another application, to reinforce the software development cycle, illustrate a batch program that processes a data file, and demonstrate the use of a statement function.[8]

PROBLEM ANALYSIS

Harvey CORE, the CEO of HC ENGINEoil Corporation, wishes to locate an off-shore support facility for three of its oil-drilling platforms.[9]

Figure 2.2 shows the coordinate system for the platforms labeled *A, B,* and *C.* The coordinate *H* is the "Home Base" proposed location for the support facility. The coordinates are given in miles from the Origin (0,0) of the system. For example, the coordinate (21,5) for Platform A means that this platform's relative location from the Origin is 21 miles along the *x*-axis and 5 miles along the *y*-axis.

---

[8]Statement functions are similar to intrinsic functions, except they're provided by the programmer instead of the compiler. If you haven't already done so, you might want to read Section A.2 in Module A before going on.

[9]Yes, this is the same Harvey CORE who also heads up the HC ENGINEering Corporation. (Those BIG engines use up a lot of oil. . . .) Actually, it's Harvey CORE, Jr. Corporate folklore has it that his father, Harvey CORE, Sr., changed his surname from Abacus to CORE after claiming that he invented the computer memory used in early computers. Primary memory used to be called magnetic core storage; it was made up of thousands of "doughnut" shaped magnetic cores strung like beads on wire. You heard it here first . . .

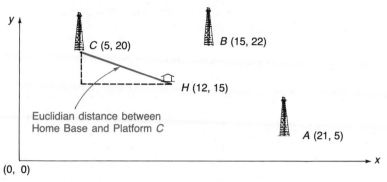

FIGURE 2.2   Cartesian coordinate system for Euclidian distance problem

Sample output might appear as follows.

```
HC ENGINEoil Platform Distances
================================================
Facility    X-Coordinate  Y-Coordinate  Distance
================================================
Home Base       12.0          15.0
Platform A      21.0           5.0        13.5
Platform B      15.0          22.0         7.6
Platform C       5.0          20.0         8.6
================================================
                    Total distance...... 29.7
================================================
                    Minimum distance...   7.6
                    Maximum distance...  13.5
```

Thus, the proposed Home Base location in Figure 2.2 yields a total one-way traveling distance of 29.7 miles; the shortest distance is 7.6 miles, from the Home Base to Platform B; the greatest distance is 13.5 miles, from the Home Base to Platform A.

The following further describes the I/O, and illustrates the computational details for the distance between the Home Base and Platform C.

- Data Output
  Title
  Coordinate of Home Base in miles from Origin
  For each platform:
     Coordinate in miles from Origin
     Distance from Home Base in miles

Sum of distances from Home Base in miles
Minimum distance in miles
Maximum distance in miles

- Data input (from data file)
Title
Coordinate of Home Base in miles from Origin
Coordinates for platforms in miles from Origin

- Computations
The distance between the Home Base at H and Platform C is defined by the Euclidian distance formula given by

$$d_{hc} = \sqrt{(x_h - x_c)^2 + (y_c - y_h)^2}$$
$$= \sqrt{(12 - 5)^2 + (20 - 15)^2}$$
$$= \sqrt{74}$$
$$= 8.60 \text{ miles}$$

where (x_h, y_h) is the coordinate of the Home Base and (x_c, y_c) is the coordinate of Platform C.[10]

NOTE   Output reports often include a display of the input data, for the following reasons.

To confirm that the input data are correct.

To summarize key data in one place.

In our example, the input data (title and all coordinates) are also part of the output report.

PROGRAM DESIGN

The algorithm for this program is straightforward, as expressed by the following pseudocode.

```
Initialize report table line
Input all data
Calculate each distance
Print report
End
```

---

[10] A distance formula based on polar coordinates is best when measuring distance over a sphere like the earth. We've simplified the problem by calculating the distances in a Cartesian (rectangular) coordinate system in a plane, instead of the more appropriate polar coordinate system over a surface. The distance between two points on a sphere is defined by the length of the arc connecting the two points, which requires integral calculus for its evaluation.

Note that the focus of the algorithm is on action tasks that require executable statements in programs. We generally don't express nonexecutable actions like data typing.

PROGRAM CODE

Figure 2.3 shows the program for this application. Note the following:

1. A statement function (Section A.2 in Module A) is used to calculate distances. The statement function itself (DIST) and the dummy arguments (X1, Y1, X2, Y2) are all typed in the REAL statements. Just how this statement function works is described below under "Program Test."

2. The READ statements use input unit number 5; on this particular system it refers to data input through a data file that resides in external memory on a hard disk drive. *Check out what input unit number would have to be used on your system.*

3. The program uses four continuation lines (the ones with + signs in position 6 of the program line). This means that four of the program lines did not fit (within columns 7–72 inclusive) on their initial lines. This is common for PRINT or WRITE statements. As mentioned in Chapter 1, we identify a continuation line by typing any character other than blank or 0 in position 6 of the line. We like to use a + sign for one continuation line and the digits 1, 2, and so on when we need two or more continuation lines for a statement.

PROGRAM TEST

Figure 2.4 shows the data file and Figure 2.5 shows the test run for this problem. Make sure that you understand the following points.

1. This is a batch program rather than an interactive program. Executions of the READ statements move data from an external data file to primary memory locations. We can process a data file in one of two ways, assuming that we have already created a data file called EUCLID.DAT (as in Figure 2.4).
   a. The data file name and input unit number are specified through an OS command. For example, on the Prime computer system, we issue the command

Data File Linkup: Prime System

Syntax:

    FTN77 program name -LGO -DATA input unit number data name

Example:

    FTN77 EUCLID -LGO -DATA 5 EUCLID.DAT

```
      PROGRAM EUCLID
* * * * * * * * * * * * * * * * * * * * * * * * * * * * * * * * * *
*                                                                 *
*        Euclidian Distances:  HC ENGINEoil Corporation           *
*                                                                 *
*           Inputs title, coordinates of Home Base and Platforms  *
*           Calculates distances to each Platform, total, min, max*
*           Outputs title, all coordinates, calculated distances  *
*                                                                 *
*           Note:  All input data in a data file                  *
*                                                                 *
*           Key:                                                  *
*               DIST..... Name for Euclidian distance statement function *
*               DISTA.... Distance from Home Base to Platform A in miles *
*               DISTB.... Distance from Home Base to Platform B in miles *
*               DISTC.... Distance from Home Base to Platform C in miles *
*               LINE..... Table line in output report             *
*               TITLE.... Report title                            *
*               XA, YA... Coordinate of Platform A in miles       *
*               XB, YB... Coordinate of Platform B in miles       *
*               XC, YC... Coordinate of Platform C in miles       *
*               XH, YH... Coordinate of Home Base in miles        *
*               X1, Y1... First dummy coordinate in statement function *
*               X2, Y2... Second dummy coordinate in statement function *
*                                                                 *
* * * * * * * * * * * * * * * * * * * * * * * * * * * * * * * * * *
*-----------------------------------------------------------------
* Type names
*-----------
      CHARACTER LINE*80, TITLE*80
      REAL      XA, YA, XB, YB, XC, YC, XH, YH, X1, Y1, X2, Y2
      REAL      DIST, DISTA, DISTB, DISTC
*-----------------------------------------------------------------
* Statement function                — Statement functions are described in Module A.
*-------------------
      DIST (X1, Y1, X2, Y2) = SQRT( (X1 - X2)**2 + (Y1 - Y2)**2 )
*-----------------------------------------------------------------
* Assign table line                 — We could also use a PARAMETER statement in place of the assignment
*------------------                   statement.
      LINE = '================================================='
*-----------------------------------------------------------------
* Input from data file
*---------------------                See the data file in Figure 2.4, which is external to the program. We use input
      READ (5,*) TITLE                 unit number 5 on our system to specify that our data file resides on a disk drive.
      READ (5,*) XH, YH                Find out what number you would use on your system and how you would go
      READ (5,*) XA, YA                about specifying which particular data file is to be used. See item 1 in our
      READ (5,*) XB, YB                discussion under Program Test.
      READ (5,*) XC, YC
*-----------------------------------------------------------------
* Calculate distances
*--------------------
      DISTA = DIST (XH, YH, XA, YA)   — These assignment statements reference the
      DISTB = DIST (XH, YH, XB, YB)     statement function above.
      DISTC = DIST (XH, YH, XC, YC)
```

FIGURE 2.3   Program for Euclidian distance problem

```
*------------------------------------------------------------
*  Print report
*--------------
      WRITE (*,*)
      WRITE (*,*) TITLE
      WRITE (*,*) LINE
      WRITE (*,*) 'Facility     X-Coordinate     Y-Coordinate     Distanc
     +e'
      WRITE (*,*) LINE
      WRITE (*,*) 'Home Base ', XH, YH
      WRITE (*,*) 'Platform A', XA, YA, DISTA
      WRITE (*,*) 'Platform B', XB, YB, DISTB
      WRITE (*,*) 'Platform C', XC, YC, DISTC
      WRITE (*,*) LINE
      WRITE (*,*) '               Total distance......',
     +               DISTA + DISTB + DISTC
      WRITE (*,*) LINE
      WRITE (*,*) '            Minimum distance...',
     +               MIN( DISTA, DISTB, DISTC )
      WRITE (*,*) '            Maximum distance...',
     +               MAX( DISTA, DISTB, DISTC )
*------------------------------------------------------------
      END
```

Note how dashed lines in report table are printed by these statements. See Figure 2.5.

Distances are summed here.

Note use of intrinsic functions from Module A.

Indicate continuation of statement.

FIGURE 2.3   **continued**

```
'HC ENGINEoil Platform Distances'
12, 15
21,  5
15, 22
 5, 20
```

We created this data file using an editor or word processor and named it EUCLID.DAT. Find out how to do this on your system.

FIGURE 2.4   **Data file EUCLID.DAT for Euclidian distance problem**

HC ENGINEoil Platform Distances

Facility	X-Coordinate	Y-Coordinate	Distance
Home Base	12.0000	15.0000	
Platform A	21.0000	5.00000	13.4536
Platform B	15.0000	22.0000	7.61577
Platform C	5.00000	20.0000	8.60232
		Total distance.....	29.6717
		Minimum distance...	7.61577
		Maximum distance...	13.4536

FIGURE 2.5   **Test run for Euclidian distance problem**

When the operating system executes this command, program EUCLID gets compiled and executed. Moreover, the data file called EUCLID. DAT is associated with input unit number 5, and processed by the READ statements in the program (since they specify input unit number 5, as seen in Figure 2.3). Do you have a corresponding OS command for your system? If so, write it down in the box below.

Data File Linkup: Your System

Syntax:

Example:

b. Alternatively, we can link up the input unit number and data file through an OPEN statement within the program.

Data File Linkup: Simplified OPEN Statement

Syntax:

OPEN (UNIT = *input unit number*, FILE = *'data file name'*)

Example:

OPEN (UNIT = 5, FILE = 'EUCLID.DAT')

In this case we place the OPEN statement within the program just before the READ statements. Execution of the OPEN statement thus links the input unit number in the READ statements to the data file name specified in the OPEN statement. We present the full version of the OPEN statement in Chapter 9.

It's also best to close a data file after it is processed, and before execution terminates; otherwise, we may not have access to the data file should we rerun the program.

CLOSE Statement: Simplified Version

Syntax:

CLOSE (*input unit number*)

Example:

CLOSE (5)

We typically place this statement just before the END statement. We show the full version of the CLOSE statement in Chapter 9.

The following is another statement that we may have to use.

REWIND Statement: Simple Form

Syntax:

REWIND *input unit number*

Example:

REWIND 5

This statement rewinds the file to the beginning, much like rewinding a musical cassette to the beginning of the first cut. We need the REWIND statement whenever we have to process a file more than once during a given run.

2. The program line where the statement function itself appears is not executed; rather the function is executed whenever it's called or referenced in the expressions that calculate the values for DISTA, DISTB, and DISTC. We can describe execution of the DISTC assignment statement as follows.

```
DISTC = DIST (XH,    YH,    XC,    YC)      ← Actual arguments
      = DIST (12.0,  15.0,  5.0,   20.0)    ← Stored values
      = DIST (X1,    Y1,    X2,    Y2)      ← Dummy arguments
      = SQRT((X1    - X2 )**2 + (Y1    - Y2   )**2)
      = SQRT((12.0 - 5.0)**2 + (15.0 - 20.0)**2)
      = SQRT(74.0)
      = 8.60232
```

Note how the proper coordinate values are used through the pairings of dummy and actual arguments.

3. Check out the initialization of variable LINE, its use in the WRITE section of the program, and its output in Figure 2.5. Its use not only saves coding but also increases the program's flexibility and readability.

4. Note that the WRITE statements that print total distance, minimum distance, and maximum distance also calculate these values within their output lists. We didn't need to store these values in a named memory location, so we simply included their calculations as expressions in the output lists.

5. Finally, note the convenience and readability of using the intrinsic functions SQRT, MIN, and MAX.

As you might imagine, Harvey is quite interested in an *optimal* location for his Home Base. The proposed placement of the Home Base at (12,15) yields a total travel distance of 29.6717 miles. In Exercise 18 we ask you to explore better placements for the Home Base.

2.8 PROGRAMMING TIPS

DESIGN AND STYLE

Methods for improving the design and style of programs are important in commercial applications for two reasons: First, good design and readability increase the reliability and facilitate the development, testing, and subsequent maintenance of programs—all of which reduce software costs. Second, programs that are easier to use because of good I/O design are more effective (and sell better!) than programs that pay scant attention to this so-called user interface. In your program writing for this course, you should take this commercial perspective to appreciate what's happening in practice.

The following suggestions should improve the readability and reliability (and the grades!) of your programs.

1. Name selection. Choose descriptive names for variables, named constants, and statement functions (if used). Programs are easier to follow (for us humans) when names suggest function.

2. Explicit typing. Use type statements to data type names. It improves program understanding and avoids unintended implicit typing. It also forces us to think about how we want to type variables (numeric versus character, real versus integer, and so on). We use alphabetical ordering of names in the type lists to improve readability.

3. Input design. Decide whether interactive input or batch input is best for the particular application. For example, data files are usually best for large amounts of input data (we'll show this in the next chapter); interactive input is usually best if we need to "what if . . . ?" the input data ("What if the Home Base were located at coordinate . . . ?"). Many programs are best designed as a combination of batch and interactive input (see Exercise 18). If you use interactive input, make sure it's conversational. In interactive input, it's usually best to request only one data item per input line. This reduces the likelihood of input errors.

4. Output design. Pay attention to output design. Facilitate its readability and understanding by well-chosen labels, alignment, and spacing. Avoid clutter and unlabeled output. Use natural capitalization (upper- and lowercase letters as we're accustomed to in written English). Before actually writing your PRINT or WRITE statements, you should map out your output design on a sheet of paper. This is especially important when you start using the material in Module B.

5. Documentation. Do a good job of documenting programs. We include a title, description, and variable key for all but our small examples. We use alphabetical ordering of names in the variable key, to improve readability. We also segment sections of the program with dashed lines, which gives better visual and functional focus to program listings. If you hand in a program for grading, include your name in the documentation (and any other information your instructor requires). Commercial programs also include documentation in different executable sections of the program as explanatory notes. In addition, the PROGRAM statement documents the name of the program.

6. Program files. Most of us who have been around computers for a while develop (slight) paranoia about losing program files. Disk-head "crashes" that render program files unusable are common occurrences. Make sure you save a program file that you finish editing. In a long session at the keyboard, it's best to periodically save the file (say, every half hour). Also, back up your program file by having a duplicate under another name. For example, if your program file is called PROG1, back it up under the name PROG1.BAK. So, if you had a bad night and the next morning you inadvertently delete a large section of your program (or, worse yet, you delete the program altogether), then you can fall back on the "cloned" backup. You can back up your programs either through the word-processor (editor) or a system command. Check it out! It's also helpful if the name of the program in the PROGRAM statement is consistent with the name of the program file that stores your program.

7. Arithmetic expressions. Break up long, complicated arithmetic expressions into subparts that are evaluated and stored separately under variable names. This improves readability and cuts down on errors. (See Exercise 12g.) If the same expression is used in different parts of the program, assign it a variable name, or use a statement function (as done in the Euclidian distance program).

8. On providing data. Before designing and writing programs, we need to think carefully about the treatment of provided data. There are five choices:

1. As constants
2. As named constants in PARAMETER statements
3. As variables in DATA statements
4. As variables in the left member of assignment statements
5. As variables in READ statements

For example, consider the data items 3.141593 for π and 5 for diameter d in the expression for the circumference of a circle, πd. The value for π is best provided as the named constant PI in a PARAMETER statement. We could also treat π as a constant within the expression itself, or as a variable initialized through a DATA statement or an assignment statement. Since this value does not change over time, it simplifies program maintenance to treat it under one of the first four options. In this case we prefer the named-constant option, since the name PI has descriptive meaning, and its naming through the PARAMETER statement ensures that the compiler treats it as a parameter (a value that can't be changed elsewhere in the program).

Values that are likely to change over time, however, are best treated as variables that store these values through the last three options. In particular, data input through READ statements is best in interactive environments where the user can experiment with different values based on a dialog with the computer. For example, we might ask a question such as "What if the diameter were 6 instead of 5?" This type of "What if . . . ?" analysis is common in practice.

9. Optimization notes. Many applications are computationally burdensome, requiring large amounts of computer time. In these cases, we can get programs to run faster by paying attention to proven methods that increase the computational efficiency of programs. In fact, most compilers are programmed to recognize methods that are computationally efficient. These considerations generally fall under the heading **optimization.** Where appropriate, we will summarize efficiency considerations as optimization notes at the end of each chapter. In the material we have covered thus far, we offer two notes.

a. Group algebraic expressions. For example, use

```
(X - Y) * (A + B)
```

instead of

```
X * (A + B) - Y * (A + B)
```

b. Assign repeat expressions. If the same expression appears more than once, then assign its value to a variable name. For example, if we have the two statements

```
PRINT *, A * B**(N-1), C
PRINT *, A * B**(N-1), D
```

then rewrite these as

```
PROD = A * B**(N - 1)
PRINT *, PROD, C
PRINT *, PROD, D
```

COMMON ERRORS

1. Typing errors. Watch the spelling of keywords. Typos will get flagged as compile-time errors. A more subtle problem: Mistyped variable names appearing in more than one place. For example, on our system (Prime computer using the Salford compiler) we mistyped DISTC as DISTD in the WRITE statement of Figure 2.3, with the following results: the warning "DISTD has not been given an initial value;" DISTD was set to zero; and the output for "Total distance" only included the sums of distances for Platforms A and B.

2. Incorrect names. Take care with the naming rules. In ANSI FORTRAN we're restricted to six characters maximum, all letters capitalized, first character a letter, and optional digits elsewhere. A syntax violation here will earn you a compile-time error message for each program line that contains the variable.

3. Incorrect placement on program line. Remember that all statements must be placed anywhere in positions 7–72 of a statement line (a restriction from "punched card days" that will be eliminated in the next ANSI FORTRAN standard). Also, don't forget to type a character other than blank or zero in position 6 of a continuation line. Finally, remember to type a C or * in position 1 of a comment line.

4. Inattention to syntax. FORTRAN lives by the rules, and so must we. Pay attention to the syntax rules that govern a particular statement. For example, carefully note the special characters that are used in many statements. Examples include parentheses in the PARAMETER statement, asterisks in READ and PRINT/WRITE statements, and commas in many statements.

5. Incorrect assignment statements. Pay close attention to hierarchy, left-to-right, and parentheses rules when forming arithmetic expressions. Two especially common syntax errors are unmatched parentheses and missing arithmetic operators.

6. Incorrect output statements. Don't forget to include the surrounding quotes for character constants in output lists (very common syntax error). Also, make sure each item in the output list is delimited (computer talk for separated) by a comma.

7. Input errors. Make sure to enter the exact number of values required by the input list in the READ statement, and that they match by type (especially numeric values paired with numeric variables, and character values paired with character variables). Don't forget to include the surrounding apostrophes for a character data item (this gives a run-time error). When using a data file, a common run-time error is an end-of-file (eof) condition, whereby the computer attempts to execute a READ statement and one or more data items are missing from the data file.

8. Initialization errors. The act of storing an initial value within a variable name is called **initialization.** To illustrate some potential errors, consider the counter

```
COUNT = COUNT + 1
```

where COUNT is typed integer. Now suppose that before this statement appears in the program we have not *explicitly* initialized COUNT. One of three things will happen when this statement gets executed, depending on the system.

   a. An arbitrary (wrong) value is used for COUNT to the right of the assignment operator.

   b. A value of zero (which could be wrong) is used for COUNT on the right side.

   c. A run-time error terminates execution because COUNT is undefined.

Thus, the use of a name in an expression or output list requires its initialization through PARAMETER, DATA, assignment, or READ statements. In our example, if we wish COUNT to start with a value of 1, then earlier in the program it should be initialized to this value.

9. Logic errors. Most beginning programmers breathe a BIG sigh of relief once their program compiles without errors, and executes without run-time errors. But it's not over yet . . . Always validate your program by checking your output data against results that you know are correct. Common logic errors include not paying attention to units of measure (like mixing meters and yards), missing or incomplete output statements, incorrect data input, misunderstanding how arithmetic expressions are evaluated (like hierarchy rules), mistyped variable names, and statements out of logical sequence (like a PRINT before a needed READ).

   10. Program composition errors. Take care with the ordering of statements, since compile-time errors occur when certain statements are out of order. We suggest the ordering below; a more detailed program composition is diagramed inside the back cover.

Suggested Program Composition

Comment lines can
go anywhere before
END statement

> PROGRAM statement
>
> Type statements
> PARAMETER statements
> DATA statements
> Statement function statements
> Executable statements
>
> END statement

FOLLOW-UP EXERCISES

PLEASE NOTE   Follow-up exercises are meant to reinforce, integrate, and extend the examples in the chapter. Try working these out on your own. Answers to all but the starred (*) exercises are given at the back of the book.

1. Tell whether each of the following variable names is acceptable or unacceptable. If a name is unacceptable, indicate why.

    a. X
    b. x
    c. 3Y
    d. Y3
    e. $RATE

    f. ACCELERATION
    g. ACCEL
    h. SET-UPCOST
    i. SU COST
    j. SUCOST

2. Identify each of the following as integer constant, real constant, or unacceptable constant.

    a. 5,000
    b. 5000
    c. 5000.0

    d. −0.05
    e. +0.05
    f. 0.050

    g. 7.351E03
    h. 7,351
    i. 7351

3. Express the following real constants using E-notation.

    a. -6.142×10^{15}
    b. -6142×10^{12}
    c. 0.0000000007

d. 7×10^{-10}

e. 0.167×10^{123}

4. Identify what is wrong, if anything, with each of the following character constants.
    a. `'DELTA WING`
    b. `"ENCOUNTERS OF THE 3RD KIND "`
    c. `'YOU'RE OK, I'M OK'`

5. Indicate what is wrong, if anything, with the following program.
    ```
    PARAMETER LATHE = 4,178, PRESS = 7042
    CHARACTER 15*FOIL, LEVEL*5
    REAL       LATHE,COST,X
    :} Series of executable statements
    INTEGER I,PRESS
    END
    ```

6. Write down the necessary statements to store the string `CLARK S. KENT` within the 20-character memory location called `NAME`. Draw the memory box and clearly indicate its contents. How would the memory box look if only 15 characters were reserved in `NAME`? Only 10 characters?

7. Identify what is wrong (if anything) with each of the following assignment statements (variables `A, B, C, D, X, Y`, and `Z` are typed real; `K` and `J` are typed integer).
    a. `B + C = A`
    b. `D = 4.0* - X`
    c. `5.0 = AGE`
    d. `X = Y = Z = 5.3`
    e. `K = J**3.2` where `J` stores a negative value
    f. `K = J**3` where `J` stores a negative value

8. Consider the following sequence of instructions, where `K` is integer and `A, B,` and `C` are real,
    ```
    A = 37 / K
    B = A + 1.6 * C
    C = SQRT(B)
    ```
    and the current contents of the specified storage locations given below.

    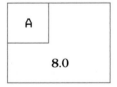
    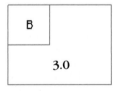
    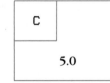
    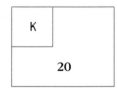

A	B	C	K
8.0	3.0	5.0	20

    Indicate the new contents following the execution of the above instructions.

9. For each of the following expressions, identify the type of result and state its value.

a. I / J, where 4 is in I and 10 is in J.

b. A / B, where 4.0 is in A and 10.0 is in B.

c. I * J, where 12345678901 is in I and 10987654321 is in J. (Any potential problems here?)

d. A * B, where 2.0E+50 is in A and 4.0E+70 is in B. (Any potential problems here?)

e. A * B, where 3.1415926536D+00 is in A and 2.0E+05 is in B.

10. In Example 2.10, what would be stored in C for each case below?

a. C = 5.0/9.0*F − 32.0   (C and F real)

b. C = 5.0/9.0*(F − 32)   (C and F integer)

c. C = 5/9*(F − 32)   (C and F integer)

11. Indicate what would be stored in real A for each of the following, given that 3.0 is in real B and 2.0 is in real C.

a. A = (4.0 + B**3 − C)*C**2

b. A = (4.0 + B**(3.0 − C))*C**2

c. A = (4.0 + B**(3.0 − C))*(C**2)

d. A = 9.0/B*C + 5.0/C

e. A = 9.0/(B*C) + 5.0/C

f. A = 9.0/B/C + 5.0/C

12. Write arithmetic expressions for each of the following algebraic expressions. Assume all variables are real except for K. Avoid mixed typing.

a. x^{k+1}

b. $x^k + 1$

c. $\dfrac{(x - a)^2}{s + 4}$

d. $\sqrt{\dfrac{(x - a)^2}{s + 4}}$

e. $(7 - x)^{1/2}$

f. $(y - 3^{x-1} + 2)^3$

g. $\left(\dfrac{x - y}{100}\right) \cdot \left(\dfrac{1}{a + b}\right) + \left(y - \dfrac{5}{x \cdot t} + 2\right) \cdot (-4)$

13. a. Specify a DATA statement to initialize A, B, C, D, and E to 0.0, F to 100.0, and R1, R2, R3 to YES.

b. Initialize the variables in part a using assignment statements.

How do these approaches differ?

*14. **Debugging problem.** Run the program below on your system *exactly* as shown. On the first run let the compiler identify syntax errors and then make the necessary corrections. On the second run let the operating system identify execution errors and then make the necessary corrections. Finish with an error-free run. Use the following data input: First try 4.2 for X and 0.0 for Y; next try −4.2 for X and 0.1 for Y; finally, try 4.2 for X and 0.1 for Y.

Program that adds, subtracts, multiplies, divides, and exponen-
tiates two numbers

```
REAL X Y
READ X, Y
SUMMATION = X + Y
SUB = X - Y
X * Y = MULT
DIV + X / Y
EXP = X ** Y
PRINT, SUMMATION, SUB, MULT, DIV, EXP
```

*15.   **Precision.** Determine your system's precision by solving the exercises below.

a. Write a simple program to determine how accurately you can express the value for π (3.141592654 . . .) on your system. In the same program, store and output P I 1 as a real variable and P I 2 as a double-precision variable.

b. Run the following program on your system using the following values for X: 38, 39, and 90; and for N: 15, 31, and 47.

```
PROGRAM E215B
*───────────────────────────────────────────────────
*       Chapter 2  Exercise 15B... Precision
*
*       Key:
*           N........ An integer variable
*           X........ A real variable
*───────────────────────────────────────────────────
    INTEGER N
    REAL    X

    PRINT *, 'Enter N'
    READ  *, N
    PRINT *, '2 to the (N-1) power...', 2**(N-1)
    PRINT *
    PRINT *, 'Enter X'
    READ  *, X
    PRINT *, '10 to the X power......', 10.0**X
*───────────────────────────────────────────────────
    END
```

What are your system's limits for real and integer values?

c. Run the following program on your system:

```
PROGRAM E215C
*————————————————————————————————————————
*       Chapter 2  Exercise 15C... Precision
*
*       Key:
*         A, B, C... Real variables
*         D, E, F... Double precision variables
*         J......... Integer variable
*————————————————————————————————————————
      REAL A, B, C
      DOUBLE PRECISION D, E, F
      INTEGER J

      A = 500.6182
      B = 500.618273
      C = 9876543.26

      PRINT *, 'A   =', A
      PRINT *, 'B   =', B
      PRINT *, 'C   =', C
      PRINT *, 'B*C =', B*C

      D = 5.006182D+02
      E = 5.00618273D+02
      F = 9.87654326D+06

      PRINT *, 'D   =', D
      PRINT *, 'E   =', E
      PRINT *, 'F   =', F
      PRINT *, 'E*F =', E*F

      J = 1234567890

      PRINT *, 'J   =', J
      PRINT *, 'J*J =', J*J
*————————————————————————————————————————
      END
```

Comment on the roundoff error associated with real arithmetic versus double-precision arithmetic. Did you get integer overflow on your system?

ADDITIONAL EXERCISES

PLEASE NOTE   Additional exercises are usually given as programming assignments that are turned in for grades. Your instructor will describe the program's documentation requirements and how to obtain *hardcopy listings* and *test runs* on your system.

ON THE RIGHT PERSPECTIVE   You might find it useful to take the perspective that applications programs you develop are to be actually used by others. This will increase your awareness and appreciation of the issues that face the developers of applications software (and should improve your grade . . .).

**ON USING THE
EXAMPLES
LIBRARY** The sample programs in each chapter are available on disk. The names of program and data files are shown inside the front cover (the Part 1 table). Your instructor will describe how you can access these. Use this library of sample programs as a starting point for solving exercises that refer to our examples. Simply edit the existing program according to the exercise, save it under a new name (for example, EXER2.16 for Exercise 16 in this chapter), and run it.

16. **Revisit: Complex expressions.** Modify and run the program in Example 2.7 to calculate and output X*Y, X/Y, and 2.0*X. Based on your output results, complete the following set of pairwise arithmetic operation rules for complex numbers.

    Given

    $$x = (a,b)$$
    $$y = (c,d)$$

    Then

    $$z = x + y = (a + c, b + d)$$
    $$z = x - y =$$
    $$z = x * y =$$
    $$z = x / y =$$
    $$z = k * x = \qquad \text{(where } k \text{ is a scalar number)}$$

17. **Revisit: HC ENGINEering.** Revise and run the program in Figure 2.1 based on the following changes: Read all input data from a data file (use OPEN and CLOSE statements if needed); include the output of engine size in cc, price, and engines sold, in addition to the original output. Do a nice job of designing the output report.

18. **Revisit: HC ENGINEoil.** Modify the program in Figure 2.3 to input the Home Base coordinates interactively. All other input stays in the data file (use OPEN and CLOSE statements if needed). Use the program to explore a better Home Base location than the one proposed. Can you find the location that minimizes total distance? The winner wins a free case of CORE Motor Oil! Send your entry and optimal coordinate to Harvey CORE, c/o R. Mojena, Ballentine Hall, University of Rhode Island, Kingston, RI 02881. (We handle Harvey's mail while he's on location.)

19. **Metric conversion.** Write and debug a program that inputs the volume and weight of a container in U.S. units (gallons and ounces) and outputs the corresponding volume and weight in metric units (liters and kilograms). A gallon is 3.7853 liters and an ounce is 0.0283495 kilogram. For test data use a 6-gallon container weighing 150 ounces.

20. **Blood bank inventory.** Decision making relating to the management of physical inventories is an established area in the management sciences, which in recent years has been applied increasingly in semiprivate and public organizations.

    Suppose that whenever a hospital replenishes its supply of a certain type of blood, it orders from a regional blood bank the amount indicated by the formula

$$q = \sqrt{2 \cdot c \cdot d / h}$$

where q is the number of pints of blood to order, c is the administrative and shipping cost (in dollars) of placing the order, d is the average weekly demand (usage in pints) for this type of blood, and h is the cost (dollars per pint per week) of holding (refrigerating) the blood.

Also, it can be shown that the cost per week of this inventory policy is given by the formula

$$e = \sqrt{2 \cdot c \cdot h \cdot d}$$

where e is the expected cost (dollars) per week. Write a computer program that inputs values of c, h, and d and determines how much blood to order and the cost of such a policy.

Run your program and answer the following questions: How many units of blood should be ordered if it costs $50 to place an order, weekly demand averages 3000 pints, and it costs $0.20 per week per pint of blood to refrigerate? How much should be ordered if the refrigeration cost increases to $0.30? What is the expected cost per week for each of the above?

21. **Electronic failures.** Suppose the probability of annual failures of electronic components in a computer is described by the following *Poisson* distribution.

$$p = \frac{a^x e^{-a}}{x!}$$

where p is the probability of x failures in one year, a is the average number of failures in one year, e is the irrational number 2.71818 . . . (the base of natural logarithms), and $x!$ reads "x factorial," the product $1 \cdot 2 \cdot 3 \cdot \ldots \cdot x$. For example, if the average number of failures per year is 0.2, then the probability of three failures in a year ($x = 3$) is given by

$$p = \frac{(0.2)^3 e^{-0.2}}{3!}$$

$$= 0.00109$$

or about one in one thousand. Write a program that inputs the average number of failures per year, the number of failures, and the factorial of failures (in Exercise 11 of the next chapter the program will calculate the factorial), and outputs the probability of those failures. Run the program to evaluate the probability of 0, 1, 2, 3, 4, and 5 failures when the average number of failures is 0.2 per year. (Note: 0! is 1.) Look at your output and answer the following question: What's the probability that the computer fails in a year?

22. **Projectile range.** The range (horizontal distance) of a large projectile is given by the following formula

$$\text{Range} = \frac{\text{Velocity}^2}{\text{Gravity}} \sin (2*\text{Angle})$$

where Velocity is the initial velocity, Angle is the initial angle of the projectile, and Gravity is the acceleration due to gravity (32 feet/sec/sec or 9.8 meters/second/second). For example, an artillery piece with a muzzle velocity of 2000 feet/second and angled at 30 degrees has a range of

$$\text{Range} = \frac{(2000)^2}{32} \sin 60°$$

$$= 108{,}253 \text{ feet}$$

or about 20.5 miles (at 5280 feet in a mile). Write and debug a program that inputs initial velocity and angle and outputs the range. Assume velocity input is in feet per second and angle input is in degrees. Output the range in the following units: feet, miles, and kilometers. There are 1.60935 kilometers in a mile and $\pi/180$ radians per degree. Check out the sine function in Module A. Run the following test data through the program:

Velocity	Angle
2000	30
2000	45
2000	50
3000	45

At what angle do we get the maximum range?

23. **Drag races.** Consider the following formulas for the speed and distance of an object undergoing constant acceleration in a straight line.

$$\text{Speed} = v_0 + at$$
$$\text{Distance} = v_0 t + 0.5at^2$$

where v_0 is the initial velocity, a is the constant acceleration, and t is the elapsed time. For example, a drag racer starting from rest and constantly accelerating at 25 miles per hour per second ($mi/h/s$) will achieve in 10 seconds a speed of 250 miles per hour and a distance of just over one third of a mile. Take care with units of measure here, as the following calculation illustrates:

$$\text{Distance} = \frac{(0 \text{ mi/h})(10 \text{ s})}{(3600 \text{ s/h})} + \frac{0.5(25 \text{ mi/h/s})(10 \text{ s})^2}{(3600 \text{ s/h})}$$

$$= 0 \text{ mi} \qquad + \qquad 0.347222 \text{ mi}$$
$$= 0.35 \text{ mi}$$

That is, we need to account for mixed units of measure (hours and seconds) by converting hours to seconds. Write and debug a program that inputs initial velocity, acceleration, and elapsed time, and outputs speed and distance. Use the same units of measure as the example. Run the following test data. Who wins the 10-second race? The dragster starting from rest but accelerating at 25 mi/h/s or the dragster getting a running start at a speed of 30 mi/h but with the slower acceleration of 20 mi/h/s? What would be a fair initial velocity for the slower dragster? (Find the initial velocity that puts both dragsters even at the 10-second finish.)

v_0	a	t
0	25	10
0	30	10
0	40	10
0	25	20
30	20	10

24. **Blood flow.**[11] We can estimate the flow of blood in the human circulatory system by the same laws that govern the flow of fluid through pipes. For example, flow through the *aorta* (main artery that carries blood from the heart to all other organs and parts except the lungs) in meters cubed per second (m^3/s) is given by

$$\text{Flow} = 2500 \, \pi r^4$$

where radius r is expressed in meters (m). An average, healthy *aorta* has a radius of approximately 0.01m. Notice that flow is very sensitive to radius. For example, a reduction in the radius by 33% drastically reduces blood flow by about 80%. This can cause *angina pectoris,* a form of heart disease that's characterized by pains in the chest. Hardening of the arteries and deposits of *plaque* (possibly from diet) are leading causes of constricted blood vessels. Write and debug a program that inputs the percent reduction in the radius of the *aorta* and outputs the following: the flow for a healthy *aorta* (one where $r = 0.01$ m); the flow for the constricted *aorta;* the percent reduction in the radius (the input value); and the percent reduction in the flow of the constricted *aorta.* By hand, you should confirm that flow in a healthy *aorta* is about 7.8×10^{-5} m^3/s; if the radius is constricted by 33% to a value of 0.0067 m, then flow in the constricted *aorta* is about 1.6×10^{-5} m^3/s, or about an 80% reduction. Run the program to evaluate the effects of 10%, 33%, and 50% reductions in the radius of a healthy *aorta.*

25. **Automobile financing.** Many consumer automobile loans require the borrower to pay the same amount of money to the lending institution each month throughout the life of the loan. The monthly payment is based on the amount borrowed (purchase price − trade-in of used car − down payment), the time required for repayment, and the interest rate. A lending institution uses the following formula to determine the car buyer's monthly payment:

$$a = i \cdot (p - d - t) \cdot \left(\frac{(1 + i)^m}{(1 + i)^m - 1} \right)$$

---

[11] Adapted from Jerry B. Marion, *General Physics with Bioscience Essays* (New York: Wiley, 1979).

where a = monthly payments
       p = purchase price of car
       d = down payment
       t = trade-in allowance
       i = monthly interest rate
      m = total number of monthly payments

If the interest rate is expressed on an annual basis, then i in the above formula is replaced by $i/12$. Note that $(p - d - t)$ is the amount to be borrowed.

a. Write a program that determines monthly payments, given purchase price, down payment, trade-in allowance, *annual* interest rate, and total number of monthly payments as input data. Include amount borrowed, total number of months, and annual *percent* interest rate in your output, along with the monthly payment. Also include the make of the automobile as part of your I/O. Process the following data:

Make	Price	Down	Trade-in	Annual Interest	Months
Lotus	$12,000	$2,000	$1,000	0.12	60
Lotus	12,000	4,000	1,000	0.12	60
Lotus	12,000	2,000	1,000	0.12	48
Lotus	12,000	2,000	1,000	0.10	48
Packard	30,000	3,000	0	0.14	36

b. Design your program also to calculate and print:
total amount paid over the life of the loan
total interest paid over the life of the loan
the ratio of total interest to total amount paid

How sensitive is the total amount paid to the annual interest rate? To the size of the down payment? To the number of months in the loan?

3

DO-LOOPS

This chapter lays the foundation for a style of programming called structured programming, and then presents a type of loop called the DO-loop.

3.1 STRUCTURED PROGRAMMING

Structured programming is an approach to designing, coding, and testing programs that is based on a body of principles selected to promote well-thought-out, readable code and reliable execution. The basis of structured programming is that any program can be written using only three logical structures:

1. Sequence structure
2. Selection (decision) structure
3. Repetition (loop) structure

These so-called **control structures** can be used to describe the logic of any program completely, as we illustrate in the next four sections.

SEQUENCE STRUCTURES

A **sequence structure** is a sequence of statements that occur one after the other *without* any transfer of control. When transfer of control or branching occurs, the computer interrupts the normal sequential execution of a program and branches (jumps or transfers control) to some other *executable* statement in the program that is not necessarily the next statement in the normal sequence.

Figure 3.1 illustrates a sequence structure for the HC ENGINEering problem. The sequence structure is the only type of control structure we have presented so far.

SELECTION STRUCTURES

Decision or **selection structures** express the logic by which one or more conditions are tested to determine which group of statements, from among alternatives, is to be executed next. In the two-alternative case, either a particular

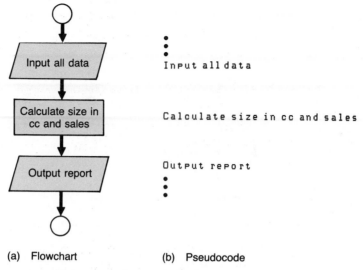

(a)   Flowchart   (b)   Pseudocode

FIGURE 3.1   **Sample sequence structure for HC ENGINEering problem** *

block (set of one or more executable statements) is to be selected (executed) if a condition is true, or an alternative block is to be selected if it is false. Figure 3.2 (a and b) illustrates the two-alternative **if-then-else structure.** Note that the pseudocode version directly incorporates the terms if, then, and else; the flowchart version uses the diamond symbol to represent the test of a stated condition.

Sometimes we have a situation in which, if a condition is true, we select a particular block, otherwise we continue in the program sequence. This is called the single selection or **if-then structure,** as illustrated in Figure 3.2 (c and d).

One example of an if-then structure is price discounting in the HC ENGI-NEering problem: If more than 1500 engines are sold, then discount the price by 5%; else don't discount. The flowchart and pseudocode representations are shown in Figure 3.3. Note that the pseudocode version indents the then block to improve readability.

We will present FORTRAN implementations of these simple single- and two-selection structures in Chapter 4. More complicated selection structures are possible when there are more than two selections to be made or more than one condition to be tested. We will also discuss these selection structures in Chapter 4.

---

* The connectors (circle symbols) in the flowchart allow us to focus on the structure of interest. *The first connector defines the beginning of or entry point to the structure; the second connector defines the end of or exit point from the structure.*

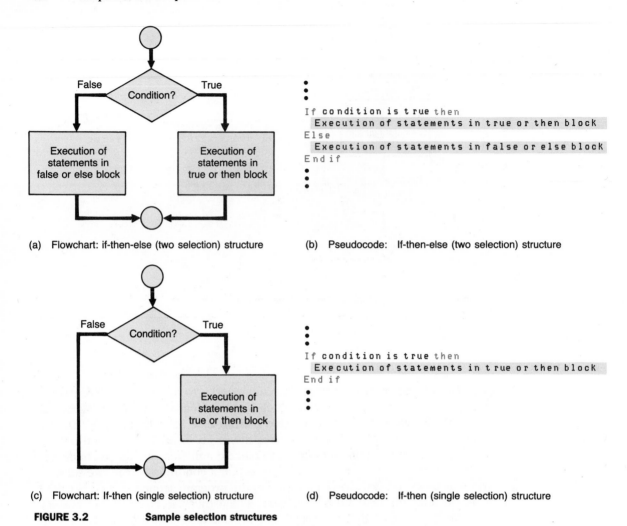

(a) Flowchart: if-then-else (two selection) structure

(b) Pseudocode: If-then-else (two selection) structure

```
⋮
If condition is true then
  Execution of statements in true or then block
Else
  Execution of statements in false or else block
End if
⋮
```

(c) Flowchart: If-then (single selection) structure

(d) Pseudocode: If-then (single selection) structure

```
⋮
If condition is true then
  Execution of statements in true or then block
End if
⋮
```

FIGURE 3.2   **Sample selection structures**

REPETITION STRUCTURES

The **loop** or **repetition structure** results in the repeated execution of a set of executable statements. This structure consists of two parts.

1. A **loop body,** which is the set of executable statements that is to be repeatedly executed

2. A **loop control,** which specifies either the number of times a loop is to be executed or the test (exit) condition under which the loop is to be terminated

Figure 3.4 shows the logic of the loop structure. Part (a) is an example of a **pretest structure.** In this structure, the first action on entering the loop struc-

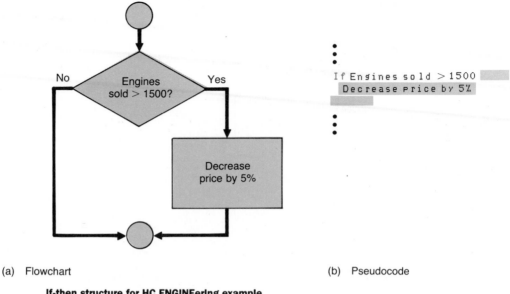

(a) Flowchart   (b) Pseudocode

FIGURE 3.3   **If-then structure for HC ENGINEering example**

ture is to test whether or not the body of the loop is to be executed. If the loop body is to be executed, control passes to the group of statements that make up the loop body. After these statements have been executed, control returns to the test statement. When the test indicates that the body is not to be executed, control passes to the first executable statement following the loop structure. The **while structure** is a common pretest loop that continues looping while the exit condition tests true.

Another repetition structure is the **posttest structure.** As seen in Figure 3.4b, this loop structure executes the loop body first. After each execution of the body, the loop control condition that *follows* the body is tested to determine whether or not the body should be reexecuted. The **until structure** is a common posttest loop that continues looping until the condition tests true.

Figure 3.5 shows sample pretest and posttest structures for the HC ENGINEering problem. In this example, the loop inputs data, performs calculations, and prints a report for each engine type that needs to be processed. In the original example from Chapter 1 there were three engine types, so this loop would repeat three times. In other words, one computer run would process all three engine types, instead of the three separate runs that would be needed without looping.

The particular choice of a repetition structure from among alternatives depends on the characteristics of the problem and the preferences of the programmer. We will return to this issue when we show actual loop implementations.

NOTE 1   Use *indentation* in pseudocodes and programs to enhance the readability of selection and repetition structures. In Figures 3.2 to 3.5, indentation better identifies then blocks, else blocks, and loop bodies.

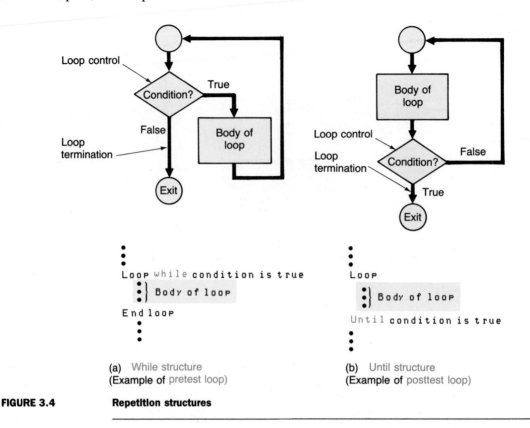

(a)   While structure
(Example of pretest loop**)**

(b)   Until structure
(Example of posttest loop**)**

FIGURE 3.4   **Repetition structures**

NOTE 2   Loop structures are the most powerful features of programming languages, since they make the automatic processing (I/O and computation) of large amounts of *similar* data possible. Without looping, computers would not be cost effective.

3.2 SINGLE DO-LOOPS

In this section we define a common type of repetition structure called the DO-loop. Looping by this method is most often used when we know beforehand the number of loop iterations, or the number of times the body of the loop is to be repeated. In this case, the DO and CONTINUE statements are used to implement all looping details.

DO AND CONTINUE STATEMENTS

A **DO-loop** is best defined by a **DO statement** at the beginning of the loop and a **CONTINUE statement** at the end of the loop. All executable statements in between are the loop body. Loop control details are expressed in the DO statement,

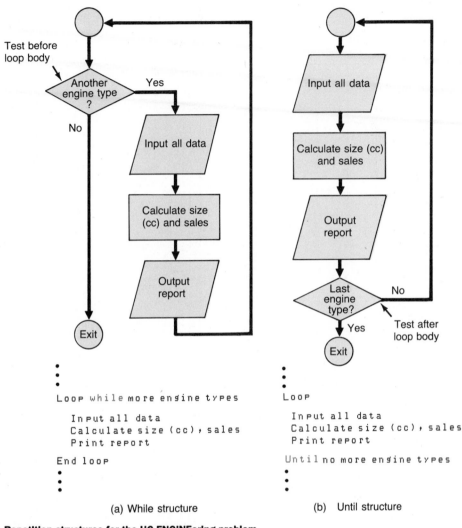

FIGURE 3.5   **Repetition structures for the HC ENGINEering problem**

as illustrated in Figure 3.6. The DO-loop's design and a specific example are shown in Figure 3.7.

In the DO statement we supply information that determines the **iteration count,** that is, the number of times the body of the loop is to be repeatedly executed.

1. **Specify the range with a statement label.** The range is the set of *executable* statements beginning with the statement just under the DO statement

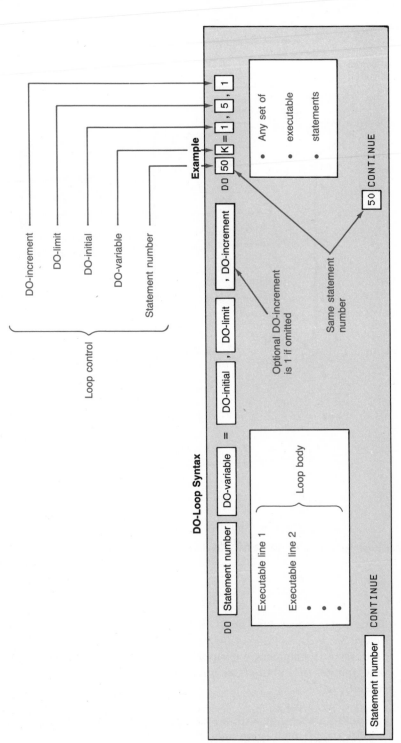

FIGURE 3.6 The DO-loop

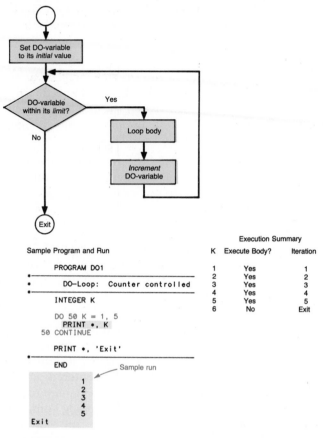

Sample Program and Run

```
        PROGRAM DO1
*
*          DO-Loop:   Counter controlled
*
        INTEGER K

        DO 50 K = 1, 5
          PRINT *, K
     50 CONTINUE

        PRINT *, 'Exit'
*
        END
```

Sample run

```
           1
           2
           3
           4
           5
Exit
```

Execution Summary

K	Execute Body?	Iteration
1	Yes	1
2	Yes	2
3	Yes	3
4	Yes	4
5	Yes	5
6	No	Exit

FIGURE 3.7   **DO-loop design and example**

and ending with the statement labeled by the statement label used in the DO statement. In Figure 3.7, the range includes the PRINT and CONTINUE statements, since the latter is labeled by the statement label 50, the same label found in the DO statement. A **statement label** is a sequence of one to five digits. When it's used to label a statement, as in

    50 CONTINUE

it must precede the statement in positions 1–5 of the same line. For better readability, align statement labels right-justified in positions 1–5. In our example, the 50 is placed in positions 4–5.

2. **Specify the DO-variable.** This can be an integer, real, or double-precision variable. In Figure 3.7, K is the DO-variable. This variable changes as the loop iterates. In our example, K starts with an initial value of 1, then gets changed to 2, 3, 4, 5, and 6.

3. **Specify the DO-initial expression.** The DO-variable must be given an initial value through an arithmetic expression. For example, K is initially set to 1 in our example.

4. **Specify the DO-limit expression.** The value of the DO-variable must be given a limit in the DO statement by using an arithmetic expression. The value of the DO-variable must exceed (when the DO-increment is positive) or be less than (when the DO-increment is negative) its limit before the loop is terminated. In our example, looping continues while the value in K is 5 or less.

5. **Specify the DO-increment expression.** The value in the DO-variable changes by the DO-increment, an arithmetic expression, at each iteration of the DO-loop. In our example, the value in K increases by 1 each time the loop iterates.

NOTE 1   If we omit the DO-increment, FORTRAN assumes it has a value of 1. For example, compare the two versions of the DO statement in Figures 3.6 and 3.7. The first *explicitly* specifies a DO-increment of 1; the second *implicitly* specifies a DO-increment of 1.

     Take a look at the program, sample run, flowchart, and description in Figure 3.7. When the DO statement is executed, the DO-loop is active. K gets initialized to 1, its value is tested against its limit (1 is less than or equal to 5, so "yes" do execute the body), the body is entered, and the value in K gets printed. At the CONTINUE statement K gets incremented to 2, and execution loops back to the loop test in the DO statement. Looping continues while the DO-variable is 5 or less. When K gets incremented to 6, the loop control test yields a "No" response. Now control is transferred to the next executable statement following the CONTINUE statement, or the statement that prints "Exit." At this time the DO-loop becomes inactive. Note that the loop iterates 5 times, which means that the body is sequentially processed 5 times.

NOTE 2   The number of iterations in a DO-loop is given by the DO-limit when both the DO-initial and DO-increment values are 1. In this case the DO-variable is a **counter** and the loop is called a **counter-controlled loop.** Figure 3.7 shows a counter-controlled loop that iterates 5 times, since both the DO-initial and DO-increment values are 1 and the DO-limit is 5.

NOTE 3   The range of the DO-loop need not end with a CONTINUE statement. We always use a CONTINUE statement (whose execution has no effect other than to continue execution) to end a DO-loop for several reasons: It visually facilitates DO-loop identification; it neatly bypasses our having to remember what statements may *not* end a DO-loop (you don't want to know); and it facilitates adding additional statements at the end of DO-loop bodies sometime in the future (should we need to). Note that the **DO-loop body** consists of all executable statements between the DO and CONTINUE statements. Also note how *indentation* better isolates the DO-loop body, thereby improving the readability of DO-loops.

To make sure you understand how loop iterations work, study the examples in Table 3.1 on the next page.

NOTE 4   The FORTRAN 77 DO-loop is a *while structure,* since it's a pretest loop and the body is executed *while* the condition tests true. See the flowchart in Figure 3.7 and compare it to the flowchart in Figure 3.4a.[1]

TEMPERATURES PROGRAM

Let's return to the temperature problem illustrated in Exercises 3 and 4 of Chapter 1 and discussed in Example 2.10.

Problem Analysis.   Suppose we wish a table of temperatures, where the first column is degrees F, the second column is corresponding degrees C, and all temperatures are printed as whole numbers. For example, the following table illustrates corresponding Fahrenheit and Celsius temperatures, where the Fahrenheit temperatures run from 0 to 100 degrees, in increments of 10 degrees. Celsius temperatures are expressed to the nearest integer.

---

[1] In reality, the loop control test is based on what is called an *iteration count,* as given either by the integer part of the expression

$$\left[\frac{\text{DO-terminal value} - \text{DO-initial value} + \text{DO-increment value}}{\text{DO-increment value}} \right]$$

or by zero, whichever is greater. For example, the number of iterations for the loop in Figure 3.7 is

$$\left[\frac{5 - 1 + 1}{1} \right] = [5]$$

or five. The number of iterations for the loop in example b of Table 3.1 is

$$\left[\frac{1 - 3 + (-1)}{-1} \right] = [3]$$

or three. With respect to Figure 3.6, the iteration count is computed just after the DO-variable is set to its initial value, the loop control test is actually "Iteration count > 0?," and the iteration count is decremented (reduced) by 1 just after the value of the DO-variable is changed.

TABLE 3.1　　　　　**DO-Loop Mechanics**

Example	DO-Variable	Execute Body?	Iteration	Remark
a.　PROGRAM DO2 　• 　•　DO-Loop: Table 3.1a 　INTEGER K 　DO 50 K = 3, 10, 2 　　PRINT •, K 　50 CONTINUE 　PRINT •, 'Exit' 　• 　END 　　3 　　5 　　7 　　9 Exit	3 5 7 9 11	Yes Yes Yes Yes No	1 2 3 4 Exit	DO-initial and DO-increment values need not be 1. The loop iterates 4 times.
b.　PROGRAM DO3 　• 　•　DO-Loop: Table 3.1b 　INTEGER K 　DO 50 K = 3, 1, −1 　　PRINT •, K 　50 CONTINUE 　PRINT •, 'Exit' 　• 　END 　　3 　　2 　　1 Exit	3 2 1 0	Yes Yes Yes No	1 2 3 Exit	The DO-increment is negative. Note how K decreases. The loop iterates 3 times.
c.　PROGRAM DO4 　• 　•　DO-Loop: Table 3.1c 　INTEGER K 　DO 50 K = 3, 1 　　PRINT •, K 　50 CONTINUE 　PRINT •, 'Exit' 　• 　END Exit	3	No	Exit	The loop never iterates (is inactive) since DO-initial value exceeds DO-limit right off and the DO-increment is +1.
d.　PROGRAM DO5 　• 　•　DO-Loop: Table 3.1d 　REAL X 　DO 50 X = 1.5, 2.5, 0.5 　　PRINT •, X 　50 CONTINUE 　PRINT •, 'Exit' 　• 　END 　1.50000 　2.00000 　2.50000 Exit	1.5 2.0 2.5 3.0	Yes Yes Yes No	1 2 3 Exit	The DO-variable X is real. The loop iterates 3 times.
e.　PROGRAM DO6 　• 　•　DO-Loop: Table 3.1e 　INTEGER K, M 　M = 1 　DO 50 K = M, 5•M, M + 1 　　PRINT •, K 　50 CONTINUE 　PRINT •, 'Exit' 　• 　END 　　1 　　3 　　5 Exit	1 3 5 7	Yes Yes Yes No	1 2 3 Exit	This shows more general arithmetic expressions to define DO-initial, DO-terminal, and DO-increment expressions. The loop iterates 3 times.

Temperature Table

Fahrenheit	Celsius
0	−17
10	−12
20	− 6
30	− 1
40	4
50	9
60	15
70	21
80	26
90	32
100	37

The following describes specific I/O items and the calculation of degree C based on degree F.

- *Output data*
  The described temperature table

- *Input data*
  First degree F in table
  Last degree F in table
  Change in degree F

- *Computations*

$$C = \frac{5}{9}(F - 32)$$

For example, given F = 10, then

$$C = \frac{5}{9}(10 - 32)$$

$$= \frac{5}{9}(-22)$$

$$= (0.555555)(-22)$$
$$= -12.2222$$

or −12 to the nearest integer.

Program Design.   We might write pseudocode as follows for this problem.

```
Initialize table title, headings, line
Input temperature range
Print table head                        ⟍ Loop
Do for each temperature          ←
  Calculate degree C
  Print degrees F and C
Continue
Print table foot
End
```

Notice that printing a table generally requires the following three distinct sections:

Table head . . .   Title, headings, dashed lines
Table body . . .   The lines of data that make up the table
Table foot . . .   Dashed lines, sums, averages, and other summary statistics

The pseudocode explicitly treats each of these sections, where the body of the table is calculated and printed from within the body of the loop.

Also note that the description of a loop in pseudocode does not use standard notation. For example, we could have written the following.

```
                                   ⟋ Loop
While temperatures remain  ←
  Calculate degree C
  Print degrees F and C
End loop
```

What's important in describing a loop is:

```
                                      ⟋ Loop
Show the beginning of the loop  ←
  Indent the body of the loop
Show the end of the loop
```

Since we're anticipating a DO-loop in this program, we have a preference for using the words Do and Continue in the pseudocode version. But that's all it is . . . a preference.

Program Code and Test.   Figure 3.8 shows the listing and test run for this application. Study the program and its I/O . . . it should be self-explanatory. In particular, notice the treatment of the table head, body, and foot.

NOTE 5   The DO-loop is uniquely suited to processing tables that include a variable whose value changes *systematically,* from an *initial* value to a *terminal* value by a fixed

```
      PROGRAM TEMP2
* * * * * * * * * * * * * * * * * * * * * * * * * * * * * * * * *
*
*          Temperature Conversions:  Version 2.0
*
*            Inputs degrees Fahrenheit table range
*            Calculates degrees Celsius
*            Outputs degrees Fahrenheit and Celsius table
*
*            Key:
*               C........ Degrees Celsius
*               F........ Degrees Fahrenheit
*               FDELTA... Change in degree F
*               FFIRST... First degree F
*               FLAST.... Last degree F
*               HEAD..... Table heading
*               LINE..... Print line
*               TITLE.... Table title
*
* * * * * * * * * * * * * * * * * * * * * * * * * * * * * * * * *
*
* Type names
*————————————————
      CHARACTER HEAD*50, LINE*50, TITLE*50
      REAL      C, F, FDELTA, FFIRST, FLAST
*————————————————————————————————————————
* Initialize
*————————————
      TITLE = 'TEMPERATURE TABLE'
      LINE  = '——————————————————————————'
      HEAD  = '      Fahrenheit    Celsius'
*————————————————————————————————————————
* Input data
*————————————
      PRINT *
      PRINT *, 'Enter first degree F'
      READ *,  FFIRST

      PRINT *
      PRINT *, 'Enter last degree F'
      READ *,  FLAST

      PRINT *
      PRINT *, 'Enter change in degree F'
      READ *,  FDELTA
*————————————————————————————————————————
* Print table head
*——————————————————
      PRINT *
      PRINT *, TITLE
      PRINT *, LINE
      PRINT *, HEAD
      PRINT *, LINE
*————————————————————————————————————————
* Calculate/print table body
*————————————————————————————
      DO 100 F = FFIRST, FLAST, FDELTA

         C = 5.0/9.0 * (F - 32.0)
         PRINT *, INT(F), INT(C)

  100 CONTINUE
*————————————————————————————————————————
* Print table foot
*——————————————————
      PRINT *, LINE
*————————————————————————————————————————
      END
```

FIGURE 3.8   **Listing and run of Temperatures Program (*continued next page*)**

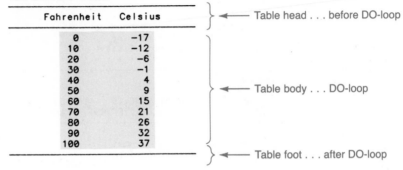

```
    Enter first degree F
  0

    Enter last degree F
  100.

    Enter change in degree F
  10

  TEMPERATURE TABLE
  ─────────────────────────
    Fahrenheit    Celsius
  ─────────────────────────
           0        -17
          10        -12
          20         -6
          30         -1
          40          4
          50          9
          60         15
          70         21
          80         26
          90         32
         100         37
  ─────────────────────────
```

Table head . . . before DO-loop

Table body . . . DO-loop

Table foot . . . after DO-loop

FIGURE 3.8　　　(*continued*)

increment. Whenever your problem analysis detects this variable behavior, "DO-loop bells should be going off in your head."

3.3 DATA FILE PROCESSING, INITIALIZATIONS, AND SUMS

Let's illustrate the batch processing of a data file using a DO-loop, and the initialization and calculation of a sum.

EXAMPLE 3.1

HC ENGINEERING WITH DATA FILE AND SUM

Problem Analysis.　The analysis is similar to that described in Section 1.2, except for the following:

- All of the data in Table 1.1 are placed in a data file.[2] Each line in the data file is called a **record;** each record but the first contains four **fields,** or data

---

[2]You might want to review our discussion of data files in Section 2.7.

items. Except for the first record, records in the data file correspond to the lines in Table 1.1, as follows.

Data file

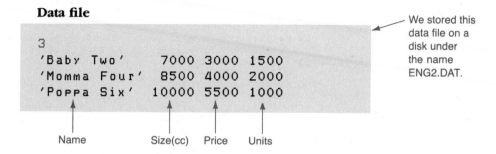

We stored this data file on a disk under the name ENG2.DAT.

Name	Size(cc)	Price	Units

The first record indicates the number of records that follow in the data file, as given by 3 in the above data file.

- All three engine types are to be processed in one computer run, as opposed to the three computer runs that were required in Chapter 1.
- The output report now includes the total sales for all engine types.

Program Design. The following pseudocode describes the algorithm.

```
Initialize table head
Initialize total sales summer to zero
Print report table head
Input number of engine types (records)
Do for each engine type
  Input name, size (cc), price, units
  Calculate size in ci
  Calculate sales
  Total sales = total sales + sales
  Print table body: name, size (ci), sales
Continue
Print report table foot, including total sales
End
```

Repetition structure

Note that a repetition structure is used to process the data. In this case, the loop body inputs a record, performs the required calculations for size and sales, accumulates sales using a total sales summer, and prints the required output for that engine type.

By **summer** we mean a variable that stores a running sum, as in total sales. The summer is initialized before the loop, accumulated within the loop, and printed following the loop. It works like a "running sum." If sales are $4,500,000, $8,000,000, and $5,500,000, then the total sales summer takes on the values $0, $4,500,000, $12,500,000, and $18,000,000.

Program Code and Test. Figure 3.9 shows the listing, data file, and run for this application. Study the program and its I/O, and then note the following.

```
            PROGRAM ENG2
  * * * * * * * * * * * * * * * * * * * * * * * * * * * * * * * * * *
  *                                                                  *
  *        Harvey CORE ENGINEering Corporation:   Version 2.0        *
  *                                                                  *
  *          Inputs engine name, size (cc), price, units from data file
  *          Calculates engine size (ci), sales, total sales         *
  *          Outputs engine name, size (ci), sales, total sales      *
  *          Uses DO-loop to process all data in one run             *
  *                                                                  *
  *          Data file structure:                                    *
  *            Number of engine types                                *
  *            Name  size(cc)  price  units   <=== 1st engine type   *
  *            Name  size(cc)  price  units   <=== 2nd engine type   *
  *            ...                                                    *
  *                                                                  *
  *          Key:                                                    *
  *            LINE..... Dashed line                                 *
  *            METCON... Metric conversion parameter (cc = 0.06102 ci) *
  *            NAME..... Engine name                                 *
  *            NUMBER... Number of engine types processed            *
  *            PRICE.... Engine price in $ per unit                  *
  *            SALES.... Sales in $                                  *
  *            SIZECC... Engine size in cubic centimeters (cc)       *
  *            SIZECI... Engine size in cubic inches (ci)            *
  *            TITLE.... Report title                                *
  *            TOTAL.... Total sales in $                            *
  *            TYPE..... Engine type DO-variable                     *
  *            UNITS.... Number of engines sold in units             *
  *                                                                  *
  * * * * * * * * * * * * * * * * * * * * * * * * * * * * * * * * * *
  *-----------------------------------------------------------------
  * Type variables
  *-----------------
        CHARACTER LINE*50, NAME*20, TITLE*50
        INTEGER   NUMBER, PRICE, SALES, TOTAL, TYPE, UNITS
        REAL      METCON, SIZECC, SIZECI
  *-----------------------------------------------------------------
  * Declare parameters
  *-----------------
        PARAMETER (METCON = 0.06102)
  *-----------------------------------------------------------------
  * Initialize
  *-----------------
        TITLE = '              SALES REPORT'
        LINE  = '=================================='
        TOTAL = 0
  *-----------------------------------------------------------------
  * Print report head
  *-----------------
        PRINT *, TITLE
        PRINT *, LINE
```

FIGURE 3.9   **Listing, data file, and output for revised HC ENGINEering application (*continued next page*)**

```
*------------------------------------------
*  Process data file
*------------------------------------------
        READ (5,*) NUMBER

        DO 100 TYPE = 1, NUMBER

          READ (5,*) NAME, SIZECC, PRICE, UNITS

          SIZECI = METCON * SIZECC

          SALES  = PRICE  * UNITS

          TOTAL  = TOTAL  + SALES

          PRINT *
          PRINT *, 'Engine name............', NAME
          PRINT *, 'Engine size (ci).......', INT(SIZECI)
          PRINT *
          PRINT *, 'Sales.................$', SALES
          PRINT *

  100 CONTINUE
*------------------------------------------
*  Print report foot
*------------------------------------------
        PRINT *, LINE
        PRINT *, 'Total sales...........$', TOTAL
*------------------------------------------
        END
```

We linked the input unit number 5 to the data file name ENG2.DAT through an OS command on our system. Can you? If not, see our discussion of the OPEN statement in Section 2.7.

Data file ENG2.DAT

```
3
'Baby Two'     7000   3000   1500
'Momma Four'   8500   4000   2000
'Poppa Six'   10000   5500   1000
```

Output

```
              SALES REPORT
    ========================================

    Engine name............Baby Two
    Engine size (ci).......       427

    Sales.................$    4500000


    Engine name............Momma Four
    Engine size (ci).......       518

    Sales.................$    8000000


    Engine name............Poppa Six
    Engine size (ci).......       610

    Sales.................$    5500000


    ========================================
    Total sales...........$   18000000
```

Table head: printed before loop

Table body: printed within loop

Table foot: printed after loop

FIGURE 3.9   (*continued*)

1. Variable NUMBER stores 3, the number of engine types or records in the data file. This is the first item in the data file. This variable is used as the DO-limit in the counter-controlled DO-loop. Thus, the DO-loop iterates exactly 3 times, which is to say it processes 3 records (engine types).

2. TYPE, SALES and TOTAL store the following values as the DO-loop iterates.

Storage Contents

TYPE	SALES	TOTAL	
		0	← Initialized before DO-loop
1	4500000	4500000	← After 1st iteration
2	8000000	12500000	← After 2nd iteration
3	5500000	18000000	← After 3rd iteration

NOTE 1   Use of the *variable* NUMBER instead of the *constant* 3 as the DO-limit on the DO-variable illustrates a style of programming that promotes *generality*. For example, if more engine types were to be added, the program itself would not change. We would only need to change the data file. This simplifies program maintenance, thereby reducing software costs in actual programming environments.

NOTE 2   Although many systems initialize all numeric variables to zero, it's a good programming practice to initialize explicitly all summers. In certain applications, it's necessary to initialize summers with assignment statements to avoid logic errors. We illustrate this issue in Example 3.3.

NOTE 3   It's a good idea to describe the *data file structure* as part of the program's documentation, as done in Program ENG2. Now that data file structures are more involved, this reduces the likelihood of incorrectly placing data in the data file.

NOTE 4   It's useful to think of the report as a table with a *head, body,* and *foot,* as shown in the output of Figure 3.9. Remember that a table head is necessarily printed before the loop; a table body is printed from within the loop's body; and a table foot is printed after the loop. We show a variation of this report table in Figure B.1 at the back of the text.

3.4 NESTED DO-LOOPS

Many programming problems require two DO-loops, where one DO-loop is entirely inside the other DO-loop. The inside DO-loop is said to be **nested** within the outside DO-loop. For every iteration of the outside DO-loop, the inside DO-loop iterates through a complete cycle (that is, becomes active and then inactive).

In more complex nesting, we can nest two or more DO-loops within another DO-loop. For example, with three nested DO-loops, we can have an outer DO-loop an inner DO-loop nested within the outer DO-loop, and an innermost DO-loop nested within the inner DO-loop. The only requirement is that each inside DO-loop lie entirely inside (within the body) of its corresponding outside DO-loop.

EXAMPLE 3.2

NESTED DO-LOOPS

The key to understanding nested DO-loops is careful attention to iterations and the values stored within DO-variables. Consider the following program and its output.

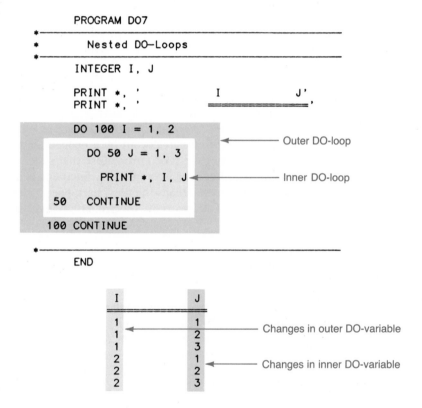

```
    PROGRAM DO7
*------------------------------------------------
*       Nested DO-Loops
*------------------------------------------------
    INTEGER I, J

    PRINT *, '           I              J'
    PRINT *, '           ===============' 

    DO 100 I = 1, 2                              ←——— Outer DO-loop

        DO 50 J = 1, 3

            PRINT *, I, J   ←——— Inner DO-loop
50      CONTINUE
100 CONTINUE

*------------------------------------------------
    END
```

I	J
1	1
1	2	←——— Changes in outer DO-variable
1	3
2	1	←——— Changes in inner DO-variable
2	2
2	3

Note that I is the DO-variable for the outer DO-loop and J is the DO-variable for the inner DO-loop. Now look at the output, and notice that the inner DO-loop is "exhausted" for each value in the outer DO-loop's DO-variable; that is, J changes from 1 to 2 to 3 before I is incremented to its next value. Thus, the inner DO-loop "varies the fastest," or goes through a complete cycle for each iteration of the outer DO-loop.

NOTE   Make sure that the inner DO-loop is entirely within the body of the outer DO-loop; otherwise, it's a compile-time error.

3.5 TOP-DOWN DESIGN AND STEPWISE REFINEMENT

Top-down design is a process that simplifies and systematizes the design and development of complex programs. Strictly speaking, it is not a specific technique, but rather a philosophy that translates into a personalized process for writing programs.

Top-down design starts with an overall look at the entire problem, that is, a look from the "top." Subsequently, the problem is refined further by working "down" through successive levels of greater detail. To illustrate what we mean, consider the process of writing a textbook. First we decide the topic of the book. This is the least level of detail and the highest level of abstraction. Then we write the titles of chapters, the next level of detail. Next we specify the main headings in each chapter, a further refinement in the level of detail. Next we state the subheadings under each main heading, and finally, we provide the greatest level of detail: each word in the body of the text.

The *implementation* of top-down design at either the design or the programming stage is often carried out by a process called **stepwise refinement,** which is an iterative (stepwise) procedure that successively refines the problem at each step. In other words, stepwise refinement is a step-by-step process that continually expands or refines the flowchart, pseudocode, or program, starting at a low level of detail and working toward a high level of detail.

EXAMPLE 3.3

STUDENT AVERAGES

This example illustrates stepwise refinement of pseudocode, nested DO-loops, and the need to reinitialize a summer.

Problem Analysis.   We wish to develop a program that calculates the average score for each student. For example, given the data

Student	Scores		
Joshua Clay	95	90	100
J. K. Dunn	50	90	68
Rick Jardon	88	72	87
Cynthia Mello	85	92	95

the program would compute and print averages (to the nearest integer) of 95, 69, 82, and 91.

Output data
- Name of each student
- Average for each student

Input data (Data file)
- Number of students
- Number of scores
- Name and scores for 1st student
- Name and scores for 2nd student
- . . .

Computations
- Student average = sum of scores for student ÷ number scores for student

Program Design. The following pseudocode illustrates stepwise refinement.

```
Print table head
Input number of students, number of scores
Process students
Print table foot
End
```

Refine outer loop

```
Do each student
  Student sum = 0
  Input name of student
  Input and sum scores
  Student average = student sum/number of scores
  Print name of student, student average
Continue
```

Refine inner loop

```
Do all scores of a student
  Read score
  Student sum = student sum + score
Continue
```

Program Code and Test. Figure 3.10 is the listing, data file, and test run for this application. Study the program and its I/O, and pay attention to the following points.

1. The outer DO-loop processes different students and the inner DO-loop processes the different scores for a particular student. Thus, scores must be summed within the inner DO-loop.

2. The sum must be reinitialized to zero each time a new student is processed. Thus, the executable statement

```
SUM = 0.0
```

```
              PROGRAM AVE1
*  *  *  *  *  *  *  *  *  *  *  *  *  *  *  *  *  *  *  *  *  *  *  *  *  *  *
*                                                                           *
*           Student Averages:   Version 1.0                                 *
*                                                                           *
*           Inputs name and scores for each student                         *
*           Calculates average for each student                             *
*           Outputs name and average for each student                       *
*                                                                           *
*           Data file structure:                                            *
*             Number of students                                            *
*             Number of scores                                              *
*             1st name                                                      *
*                1st score                                                  *
*                2nd score                                                  *
*                ...                                                         *
*             2nd name                                                      *
*                1st score                                                  *
*                2nd score                                                  *
*                ...                                                         *
*             ...                                                           *
*                                                                           *
*           Key:                                                            *
*             AVE...... Student's average score                             *
*             HEAD..... Table heading                                       *
*             LINE..... Dashed line                                         *
*             NAME..... Student's name                                      *
*             NUMSCO... Number of scores                                    *
*             NUMSTU... Number of students                                  *
*             SCO...... Score DO-variable                                   *
*             SCORE.... Student's score                                     *
*             STU...... Student DO-variable                                 *
*             SUM...... Student's sum of scores                             *
*             TITLE.... Report title                                        *
*                                                                           *
*  *  *  *  *  *  *  *  *  *  *  *  *  *  *  *  *  *  *  *  *  *  *  *  *  *  *
*---------------------------------------------------------------------------
*  Type variables
*------------
      CHARACTER HEAD*40, LINE*40, NAME*20, TITLE*40
      INTEGER   NUMSCO, NUMSTU, SCO, STU
      REAL      AVE, SCORE, SUM
*---------------------------------------------------------------------------
*  Initialize
*------------
      TITLE = '             AVERAGE SCORES'
      LINE  = '----------------------------------------',
      HEAD  = 'Student                        Average'
*---------------------------------------------------------------------------
*  Print table head
*------------
      WRITE (*,*) TITLE
      WRITE (*,*) LINE
      WRITE (*,*) HEAD
      WRITE (*,*) LINE
```

FIGURE 3.10   **Listing, data file, and run of student averages application (*continued next page*)**

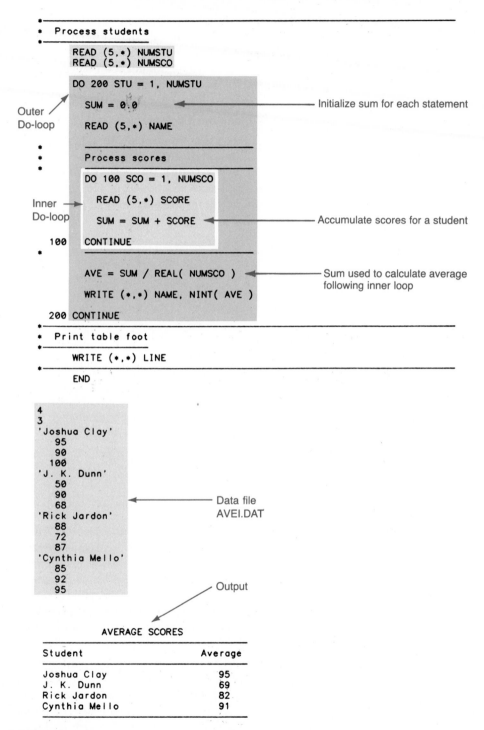

```
*-------------------------------------------------------------
*  Process students
*-------------------------------------------------------------
        READ (5,*) NUMSTU
        READ (5,*) NUMSCO

     DO 200 STU = 1, NUMSTU                          ◄──────── Initialize sum for each statement

        SUM = 0.0

        READ (5,*) NAME
*
*         Process scores
*      ──────────────────────────────────
        DO 100 SCO = 1, NUMSCO

          READ (5,*) SCORE

          SUM = SUM + SCORE                          ◄──────── Accumulate scores for a student

   100  CONTINUE
*      ──────────────────────────────────
        AVE = SUM / REAL( NUMSCO )                   ◄──────── Sum used to calculate average
                                                              following inner loop
        WRITE (*,*) NAME, NINT( AVE )

   200 CONTINUE
*-------------------------------------------------------------
*  Print table foot
*-------------------------------------------------------------
        WRITE (*,*) LINE
*-------------------------------------------------------------
        END
```

Outer / Do-loop

Inner → Do-loop

```
4
3
'Joshua Clay'
   95
   90
  100
'J. K. Dunn'
   50
   90
   68                    ◄──────── Data file
'Rick Jardon'                    AVEl.DAT
   88
   72
   87
'Cynthia Mello'
   85
   92
   95
```

Output

AVERAGE SCORES

Student	Average
Joshua Clay	95
J. K. Dunn	69
Rick Jardon	82
Cynthia Mello	91

FIGURE 3.10   (*continued*)

must be within the outer DO-loop (to be reinitialized) and just before the inner DO-loop (which will calculate a fresh sum). Note that a nonexecutable reinitialization statement like the DATA statement would give a logic error, since the sum would not get reset to zero for each new student (that would be good news for students late in the alphabet!).

3. The average is calculated and printed following the inner DO-loop, since the inner DO-loop must be completed for the needed value in SUM.

4. The first two records in the data file contain the DO-limit for the outer DO-variable (4 students) and the limit for the inner DO-variable (3 scores). These are input just before the nested DO-loop (NUMSTU stores 4 and NUMSCO stores 3). As mentioned in Example 3.1, this treatment of DO-variable limits promotes the generality of programs. ∎

3.6 PROGRAMMING TIPS

DESIGN AND STYLE

1. **Indentation.** Indent the body of the DO-loop, to visually isolate the body and better identify the beginning and end of the DO-loop.

2. **Generalized DO-expressions.** Generalize DO-initial, DO-limit, and DO-increment expressions that are likely to change. For example, in Program TEMP2 in Figure 3.8 we used

```
DO 100 F = FFIRST, FLAST, FDELTA  ☺
```

instead of

```
DO 100 F =     0.0, 100.0, 10.0   ☹
```

where the DO-expressions are input variables. This means we can use the same program to generate different temperature tables, *without changing the program itself.* This reduces software maintenance costs, an important consideration in practice. Of course, if this program's purpose in life is to *always* generate temperature tables that run Fahrenheit degrees from 0.0 to 100.0 in increments of 10.0, then we would want to use parameters for the DO-expressions (why force the poor user to forever input the same temperature range?).

3. **Documentation.** Now that programs are getting more elaborate, you might want to "beef up" your documentation by including pseudocode. Also, data files with more than one record are best described in the program's documentation. A description of the data file structure reduces the likelihood of data input errors. For example, see Program AVE1 in Figure 3.10 and program ENG2 in Figure 3.9.

4. **Optimization notes.** We have two common computational efficiencies regarding DO-loops.

   a. **Nesting efficiency.** Nest long DO-loops (those with more iterations) within short DO-loops, if feasible. Each time an outer DO-loop iterates, the inner DO-expressions get reinitialized, which takes time. If the outer DO-loop is the short DO-loop, then we have fewer reinitializations.

   b. **Calculating efficiency.** Avoid unnecessary calculations within loop bodies to improve the execution efficiency of programs. For example, many beginning programmers place the calculation of an average just after the summer within the loop body, rather than following the loop itself. (See Program AVE1 in Figure 3.10.)

COMMON ERRORS

1. **Incorrect placement of statement label.** Make sure you place statement labels in positions $1-5$ of the program line; otherwise, it's a compile-time error.

2. **Redefined DO-variable.** Don't redefine the value of a DO-variable within its DO-loop, since this gives a compile-time error. Also, it's not a good practice to redefine variables that act as DO-initial, DO-limit, or DO-increment expressions. It would be confusing to anyone reading a listing of the DO-loop. Compilers allow this because their values are used only to calculate the iteration count (see footnote 1).

3. **Improper DO-expression values.** Avoid the following pitfalls with DO-expression values.

   DO 100 K = 1, LIMIT   ← Execution error or inactive loop if LIMIT not initialized and system stores 0 in LIMIT.

   DO 200 L = 1, LIMIT, STEP   ← Execution error or **infinite loop** (one that doesn't stop iterating unless we "pull the plug" or hit the keyboard's break key) if STEP not initialized and system stores 0 in STEP.

   DO 300 M = 50, 1   ← Inactive loop; use a negative value like -1 for DO-increment.

4. **DO-loop nesting errors.** Crossovers and identical DO-variables will give compile-time errors.

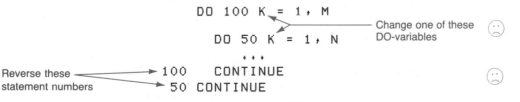

5. **End of file (eof) condition.** An **eof condition** occurs when the computer attempts to input more data than available in a data file. This can happen in one of two ways (or both): We incorrectly specified too many loop iterations or we placed too little data in the data file. In either case, we get a run-time error, and processing terminates.

6. **Reinitialization errors.** In the last chapter we discussed initialization errors. In some cases, we remember to initialize, but forget that *reinitialization during execution is necessary.* See Program AVE1 in Figure 3.10 and item 2 on page 101.

7. **Roundoff errors.** As mentioned in the last chapter, binary computers introduce roundoff error when decimal values are stored. For example, a decimal value like 0.2 is not represented exactly in a binary system; it's only *approximated.*[3] This can cause intolerable inaccuracy in certain kinds of problems, such as space-trajectory estimates and certain financial calculations.

The following contrived program shows how roundoff error gets compounded in repetition structures that have recursive calculations, or calculations whose succeeding values depend in part on preceding values.

```
      PROGRAM DOERR5
*-------------------------------------------------------------
*        Roundoff error: Recursive calculations
*-------------------------------------------------------------
      INTEGER K, M
      REAL SUM

      PRINT *, 'Enter loop iterations'
      READ *, M

      SUM = 0.0

      DO 100 K = 1, M
         SUM = SUM + 2.0/3.0   ◄——— SUM recursively calculated
100   CONTINUE

      PRINT *, 'Sum =', SUM
*-------------------------------------------------------------
      END
```

```
Enter loop iterations
48000
  Sum =        31926.2   ◄——— Intended value is 32,000 (or 48,000 × ⅔)
                              giving a roundoff error of 73.8, or 0.2%
```

```
Enter loop iterations
192000
  Sum =        126822.   ◄——— Intended value is 128,000 (or 192,000 × ⅔)
                              giving a roundoff error of 1.178, or 0.9%
```

---

[3]Decimal values given by $\frac{1}{2}$ to an integer power are represented *exactly,* such as $\frac{1}{2}$, $\frac{1}{4}$, $\frac{1}{8}$, and $\frac{1}{16}$. So are sums of powers of $\frac{1}{2}$. For example, $\frac{3}{4}$ (or $\frac{1}{2} + \frac{1}{4}$) has an exact binary representation.

Note that the roundoff error increases as the number of iterations increases. In some applications, particularly in engineering and the sciences, roundoff errors of this magnitude can render the results useless. For such cases, special algorithmic procedures must be implemented that reduce the magnitude of roundoff errors.[4] A simple way of *postponing* roundoff error is to use double-precision values. We ask you to look at this in Exercise 8.

8. **Classic debugging techniques.** Debugging gets more complex (and "entertaining") as we move into more elaborate programs. In your efforts to debug execution and logic errors, you might try the following time-tested debugging techniques.

  a. **Roleplaying the computer.** Pretend that you're the computer and begin "executing" your program line by line. As you do this, enter data into boxes or tables that represent storage locations. You will be surprised at how many errors you can find this way. Really. You should do this with every program you write. In practice, roleplaying is carried out by small groups of programmers and is called the **group walkthrough,** or **structured walkthrough.**

  b. **Data validation techniques.** To check your data for input errors, place a PRINT statement immediately after each READ statement. The paired statements must have identical variable lists. Once you have confirmed that the data are correct, remove these statements. This technique is called **mirror,** or **echo, printing.** Other data validation techniques include **error routines** that trap user input errors and otherwise check for incorrect data types and values. We take a look at these approaches in Chapters 4 to 6.

  c. **Diagnostic PRINT (trace) statements.** Place temporary PRINT statements at strategic points in your program. These should print the values of important variables as the calculating sequence evolves. In other words, these PRINT statements provide intermediate results that may be helpful in tracing what, where, and when something went wrong. When the error is corrected, remove these PRINT statements.

  d. **Programming technique.** You will avoid many errors if you carefully practice the first three steps of our four-step software development cycle. Get in the habit now.

  e. **Experience.** Learn by your mistakes. Experience is the classic teacher.

  f. **Attitude.** Time and again we have seen students become frustrated and upset during the process of correcting errors. This is a good time to practice detachment. Actually, debugging can be fun. Finding and correcting errors can be a very satisfying experience. Maybe you will become the greatest debugging sleuth in computer history.

---

[4] These procedures are treated in a field of study called numerical analysis.

1. What values get printed for each of the following DO-loops, and how many times does each iterate?

   a.
   ```
        DO 50 K = 2, 7, 3
           PRINT *, K
     50 CONTINUE
   ```

   b. Same as part a except
   ```
        DO 50 K = 2, 2
   ```

   c. Same as part a except
   ```
        DO 50 K = 2, 1
   ```

   d. Given VOL and SPEC are typed real and SPEC stores 10.0.
   ```
        DO 100 VOL = SPEC, 2 * SPEC, SPEC / 4.0
           PRINT *, VOL
    100 CONTINUE
   ```

   e.
   ```
        DO 400 J = 1, 2
          DO 300 K = 4, 2, -1
            PRINT *, J, K
    300     CONTINUE
    400 CONTINUE
   ```

   f. Same as part e, except replace the PRINT statement with
   ```
          DO 200 L = 1, 8, 2
            PRINT *, J, K, L
    200     CONTINUE
   ```

2. **Roleplay.** Roleplay computer for the sample run in Figure 3.10 by filling in values in the following memory locations as if a "snapshot" of memory were taken just before each execution of the first CONTINUE statement.

   ```
   -------------------------------------------------------
   STU    SCO    NAME             SCORE    SUM    AVE
   -------------------------------------------------------
   ```

3. **Temperatures.** Modify Program TEMP2 in Figure 3.8 as follows:
   a. Print temperatures *rounded* to the nearest integer. Currently they are *truncated.*
   *b. Have the program print multiple copies of the *same* table in one run. Input the value for the number of copies desired and store it in the variable COPIES.
   *c. Same as part b, except print *different* tables in one computer run based on different input ranges for degrees F.
   *d. Run the revised program in part a or b on your system.
4. **HC ENGINEering.** Modify Program ENG2 in Figure 3.9 as follows.
   a. Calculate and print average sales.
   *b. Suppose Harvey wants to keep track of two separate sales regions in the country, East and West. The original data are for the East. The name and size of engine types is the same in both regions, but prices and units sold in the Western region differ as follows. (Our West Coast neighbors like *big* engines, and so are willing to pay more . . . and buy more.)

Name	Price ($)	Units
Baby Two	3500	2200
Momma Four	4700	3000
Poppa Six	6500	4000

   Process both sets of data in one computer run. Also, input the number of regions (Harvey might expand in the future) and the name of each region. Print the name of each region as part of the report title above each region's report. Include total sales for each region, and overall total sales for all regions combined. Clearly define the revised data file structure.
   *c. Run the revised program on your system.
5. **Student averages.** Modify Program AVE1 in Figure 3.10 as follows.
   a. Roleplay the output if we had used the statement

   DATA SUM / 0.0 /

   to initialize SUM.
   *b. Allow the processing of a different number of scores for each student. Modify the data by deleting the third score for the third student (the 87). Take care in redefining the data file structure.
   *c. Run the revised program in part b on your system.
*6. **Standard deviation.** Modify program AVE1 in Figure 3.10 as follows:
   a. Compute and print the standard deviation (a measure of variation about the mean) for each student, in addition to the average.

$$s = \sqrt{\frac{n \Sigma x^2 - (\Sigma x)^2}{n(n-1)}}$$

---

*Follow-up exercises with stars (*) don't have answers in the back of the book. Check with your instructor.

where n = number of scores

x = score

Σx = sum of scores for a section

Σx^2 = sum of squared scores for a section

b. Run the revised program on your system.

*7. **Mean absolute deviation.** Modify Program AVE1 in Figure 3.10 as follows.

a. Compute and print the mean absolute deviation (MAD, a measure of variation about the mean) for each section, in addition to the average.

$$\text{MAD} = \frac{\Sigma |x - \bar{x}|}{n}$$

where n = number of scores

x = score

$\bar{x}$ = mean score for section

$|x - \bar{x}|$ = absolute difference between x and $\bar{x}$

$\Sigma |x - \bar{x}|$ = sum of the absolute differences

Hint: Check out the ABS function in Module A.

b. Run the revised program on your system.

*8. **Roundoff errors.** Check out Program DOERR5 on page 106 as follows.

a. Run the program on your system and compare the magnitude and percent roundoff error between your system and our system.

b. Change SUM to a double-precision variable, run the revised program, and compare the results to part a.

ADDITIONAL EXERCISES

---

9. **Revisit: HC ENGINEoil.** Rework Exercise 18 in Chapter 2 as follows.

a. Use nested DO-loops to systematically vary x- and y-coordinates for the proposed Home Base. Interactively input separate ranges, 10 to 20 for x_b and 8 to 22 for y_b, in increments of 1. Redesign the output to print a table with the following headings: X-Home, Y-Home, Min Dist, Max Dist, Total Dist. What Home Base coordinate gives minimum total distance (to the nearest mile)?

b. Use a DO-loop to process the data file platform coordinates. Now we don't need separate variable names for the coordinates and distances of each platform. The program is further simplified by printing the body of the report table from within the DO-loop. *Hint:* Check out the OPEN, REWIND, and CLOSE statements.

10. **Revisit: Blood bank inventory.** Rework Exercise 20 in Chapter 2 as follows.

a. Interactively input a range of demands that runs from 2500 to 3500 pints in increments of 100 pints. Use a DO-loop to print a table of demands, number of pints to order, and expected cost.

b. Interactively input a range of refrigeration costs that runs from $0.20 to $0.40 in increments of $0.05. Use a second DO-loop to process separate tables from part a. For the given refrigeration range, five separate tables will be printed. Give each table a title that includes the specific refrigeration cost for that table.

c. Interactively input a range of ordering costs that runs from $45 to $55 in increments of $5. Use a third DO-loop to process separate tables from part a. For the given data, we now have 15 separate tables. Include the ordering cost in the title of each table, along with the refrigeration cost.

11. **Revisit: Electronic failures.** Rework Exercise 21 in Chapter 2 as follows.

a. Use a DO-loop to calculate the factorial of x. *Hint:* Define a variable PROD that stores a running product within the DO-loop. This is analogous to a summer. Initialize this variable to 1 just before the DO-loop.

b. Interactively input a range of failures that runs from 0 to 10 in increments of 1. Use a DO-loop to print a table of x and p.

c. Interactively input a range of average failures (a) that runs from 0.10 to 0.30 in increments of 0.05. Use a second DO-loop to process separate tables from part b, one for each value of a. Include the value for a in the title of each table. For the given data, we have five separate tables.

12. **Revisit: Projectile range.** Rework Exercise 22 in Chapter 2 as follows.

a. Interactively input a range of angles that runs from 5 to 50 degrees in increments of 5 degrees. Use a DO-loop to print a table of angle and range values, where range values are expressed in feet, miles, and kilometers.

b. Interactively input a range of velocities that runs from 2000 fps to 3000 fps in increments of 500 fps. Use a second DO-loop to process separate tables from part a, one for each value of velocity. Include the value for velocity in the title of each table. For the given data, we have three separate tables.

13. **Revisit: Drag races.** Rework Exercise 23 in Chapter 2 as follows.

a. Interactively input a range of times that runs from 10 to 20 seconds in increments of 1 second. Use a DO-loop to print a table of times, speeds, and distances.

b. Interactively input a range of accelerations that runs from 20 to 40 mi/h/s in increments of 5 mi/h/s. Use a second DO-loop to process separate tables from part a. For the given acceleration range, five separate tables will be printed. Give each table a title that includes the specific acceleration for that table.

c. Interactively input a range of initial velocities that runs from 20 mi/h to 30 mi/h in increments of 5 mi/h. Use a third DO-loop to process separate tables from part a. For the given data, we now have 15 separate tables. Include the initial velocity in the title of each table, along with the acceleration.

14. **Revisit: Blood flow.** Rework Exercise 24 in Chapter 2 to process the required output as a table that ranges from a 1% to a 75% reduction in the radius of a healthy *aorta*. Use an increment of 1%. Interactively input the percent range.

15. **Revisit: Automobile financing.** Rework Exercise 25 in Chapter 2 as follows. Treat the input data as a data file that gets processed by a DO-loop. In the output table include all input data as well as the monthly payment and the three items described in part b.

16. **Exponential Cumulative Distribution Function.** The function

$$p = 1 - e^{-x/a}$$

describes the probability (p) that a random (chance) variable takes on a value less than or equal to x, where a is the expected (average) value of the random variable and e is the base of natural logarithms (see Table A.1). For example, if the random variable "number of hours an electronic component operates until failure (life)" is distributed exponentially and average life is known to be 8000 hours, then the probability this component lasts 5000 hours or less is

$$p = 1 - e^{-5000/8000}$$
$$= 1 - e^{-0.625}$$
$$= 1 - 0.5352614$$
$$= 0.4647386$$

that is, approximately 46% of these components will last 5000 hours or less.

a. Design a program that interactively inputs average life (a), initial value for x, terminal value for x, and incremental value for x, and outputs a table of x-values and corresponding probabilities. In your sample run, try x from 1000 to 12,000 in increments of 1000.

b. Interactively input a range for average life, from 7900 hours to 8100 hours in increments of 100 hours. For each average life, print the corresponding table described in part a. Include a title for each table that includes the average life that corresponds to that table. For the given data, we have five tables.

17. **Bank savings.** Consider the formula

$$A = P \cdot (1 + R/M)^{N \cdot M}$$

where A = accumulated funds
    P = principal (amount we first invest)
    R = annual interest rate
    N = number of years
    M = number of times per year the account is compounded (for example, if the account is compounded quarterly, then $M = 4$, or interest is added in four times a year)

To illustrate, if we start with $1000 ($P = 1000$) at 6% per year ($R = 0.06$) compounded once a year ($M = 1$), then after two years ($N = 2$) we end up with

$$A = 1000 \cdot (1 + 0.06/1)^{2 \cdot 1}$$
$$= \$1123.60$$

However, if we compound quarterly ($M = 4$), then in two years we end up with

$$A = 1000 \cdot (1 + 0.06/4)^{2 \cdot 4}$$
$$= \$1126.49$$

which is $2.89 better than under annual compounding.

In recent years banks have competitively increased the number of compounding periods to attract customers. For example, under daily compounding ($M =$

365) your account earns interest daily, which is preferred to, say, monthly compounding ($M = 12$).

a. Design and run a program that processes the following input data in one run.

P	R	N	M
1000	0.06	10	1
1000	0.06	10	4
1000	0.06	10	12
1000	0.06	10	52
1000	0.06	10	365

As output, print the above table together with a new column for A. Comment on the behavior of A. *Hint:* Watch out for roundoff error.

b. The "ultimate" account compounds continuously according to the formula

$$A = P \cdot e^{R \cdot N}$$

where e is the base of natural logarithms (see Table A.1). For example, if we start with \$1000 and compound continuously at 6% per year, then after two years we end up with

$$A = 1000 \cdot e^{(0.06) \cdot (2)}$$
$$= 1000 \cdot e^{0.12}$$
$$= (1000) \cdot (1.127496)$$
$$= \$1127.50$$

which is \$1.01 better than under quarterly compounding. Wouldn't you rather earn money even as you read this? Modify the output in part a to include a last row in the table for continuous compounding. Comment on the behavior of A.

c. Manhattan Island purchase. In 1626 Peter Minuit, the first Director General of the Dutch Province of New Netherland, bought Manhattan Island from the Indians for a dollar equivalent of about \$22. If the Indians had invested this amount at 7% per year and let it ride, how much would it be worth today?

18. **Econometric model.** Econometrics is a field of study that applies mathematical models to describe the behavior of economic systems. To illustrate a simple econometric model, suppose that the cost per credit charged by a college directly affects student enrollment according to the following demand curve.

$$s = d_1 - d_2 c$$

where s = student enrollment (students)
c = cost per credit (\$/credit)
d_1 = first parameter in demand curve (students)
d_2 = second parameter in demand curve (students/\$/credit)

For example, if the tuition charge is \$80 per credit and the demand curve parameters are 14,000 and 100, then enrollment is estimated by

$$s = 14,000 \text{ students} - (100 \text{ students/\$/credit})(80 \text{ \$/credit})$$
$$= 6000 \text{ students}$$

If the cost per credit is increased to $90, then estimated enrollment drops to 5000 students. The average balance due the college is given by the price function

$$b = ac + f$$

where b = average balance due the college ($/student)
a = average number of credit hours (credits/student)
f = fee ($/student)

and c is defined as before. For example, if the average number of credit hours taken by students is 14, the cost per credit is $80, and fees are $250, then the average bill is

$$b = (14 \text{ credits/student})(80 \text{ $/credit}) + 250 \text{ $/student}$$
$$= \$1370 \text{ per student}$$

The revenue function is given by

$$r = bs$$

where

$$r = \text{projected revenue ($)}$$

and b and s are defined as before. Continuing our example, we have a projected revenue for the college of

$$r = (1370 \text{ $/student})(6000 \text{ students})$$
$$= \$8,220,000$$

a. Design and run a program for this econometric model. Use a DO-loop that varies c over a range. Process the following input data.

d_1	d_2	a	f	..... c-range		
14000	100	14	250	50	80	1

Input the c-range interactively, and the other data items through a data file. Print an output table headed by four columns: Cost per Credit, Average Bill, Expected Enrollment, and Expected Revenue. What cost per credit maximizes expected revenue for the college?

b. Add an outer DO-loop that processes all colleges in a statewide system. Use the following test data.

College name	d_1	d_2	a	f	... c-range ...		
OK State U	14000	100	14	250	50	80	1
AOK State U	14000	25	14	250	200	300	5
NotOK State U	30000	250	13.5	500	10	60	1

Input the c-range interactively, and all other data through a data file. Use the same output design as in part a, except just before each table print the name of the college. What tuition (cost per credit) should be charged at each college

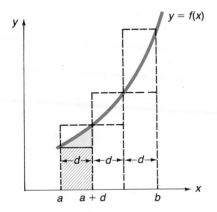

(a)   Monotonically Increasing Function

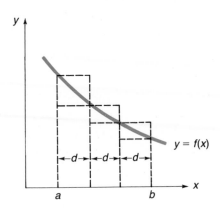

(b)   Monotonically Decreasing Function

FIGURE 3.11   **Continuous monotonic functions (Exercise 19)**

to maximize revenue? Would you say there's a flaw in the econometric model if students freely change colleges within the state system on the basis of tuition?

c. Solve this problem by calculus. Do your analytic and computer results agree?

19. **Numerical integration.** A continuous monotonic function

$$y = f(x)$$

plots as a smooth curve (no breaks) and either continually rises (monotonically increases) or continually falls (monotonically decreases). Figure 3.11 illustrates two such functions in the interval $x = a$ to $x = b$. *Numerical integration* is the process of computing areas under curves of functions, a process that has widespread applicability in engineering and the sciences.[5] The trapezoid method described below applies only to continuous monotonic functions.

The rectangles of width d in Figure 3.11 suggest one method of estimating area under $f(x)$ in the interval a to b. Focusing on Figure 3.11a, note that the leftmost rectangle is divided into a lower area given by the hatched portion and a triangular shaded area. The hatched area is calculated by

$$\text{Hatched area} = (\text{width}) \cdot (\text{height})$$
$$= d \cdot f(a)$$

where $f(a)$ is the value of the function when $x = a$. The shaded area is the triangular lower half of the upper rectangle, or

---

[5] Those who have had calculus should recognize this as equivalent to evaluating the definite integral

$$\int_a^b f(x)\ dx$$

$$\text{Shaded area} = \left(\frac{1}{2}\right) \cdot (\text{width of triangle}) \cdot (\text{height of triangle})$$

$$= \left(\frac{1}{2}\right) \cdot (d) \cdot [f(a + d) - f(a)]$$

The estimated area under the curve from $x = a$ to $x = a + d$ is the sum of these two areas, or

$$\text{Area from } a \text{ to } a + d = \text{hatched area} + \text{shaded area}$$

$$= d \cdot f(a) + \frac{1}{2} \cdot d \cdot [f(a + d) - f(a)]$$

$$= d/2 \cdot [f(a) + f(a + d)]$$

which is equivalent to the area of a trapezoid. If the interval from a to b contains n of these trapezoids, each of width d, it follows that

$$\text{Area from } a \text{ to } b = d/2 \sum_{k=1}^{n} [f(a + (k - 1) \cdot d) + f(a + k \cdot d)]$$

is an approximation to the actual area under $f(x)$ from a to b. It should make sense to you that the greater the number of trapezoids between a and b (that is, the smaller the width d), the better is the approximation to the actual area. Note that the width of each trapezoid is given by

$$d = \frac{b - a}{n}$$

a. Suppose we wish to find the area under

$$y = 2^x$$

from $x = 1$ to $x = 4$. By hand, estimate this area by using three trapezoids. Next, double the number of trapezoids to six and compare results. The actual area is 20.19773. Which approximation has the least error?

b. Design and write an interactive program that inputs a, b, and number of trapezoids, and outputs an approximation to the area. Use the following test data. Note that each function requires a change in the program itself. Use a statement function within the program.

Function[a]	a	b	Number of Trapezoids
2^x	1.0	4.0	3; 6; 100; 211; 1000
$-1 + 2x$	1.0	10.0	100
	0.5	10.0	2; 10
$(1/8000)e^{-x/8000}$	0.0	5000.0	100

[a]The symbol e is the base of natural logarithms.

c. The number of trapezoids n needed for the approximation to be within a specified error E of the actual area is given by the formula

$$n = \text{int}\left[\frac{(b - a) \cdot |f(a) - f(b)|}{2E}\right] + 1$$

where int stands for "integer part of" and $|f(a) - f(b)|$ is the absolute value of the difference. For example, if we want our estimated area for the first function in part b to be within 0.1 of the actual area, then we need 211 trapezoids.

$$n = \text{int}\left[\frac{(4 - 1) \cdot |2^1 - 2^4|}{2 \cdot (0.1)}\right] + 1 = 211$$

Was the estimated area within 0.1 of the actual area 20.19773 when you used 211 trapezoids in part (b)?

Modify your program to input E instead of number of trapezoids, and process the following data.

Function	a	b	E
$(1/8000)e^{-x/8000}$	0.0	1000.0	0.001
	0.0	5000.0	0.001
	0.0	12000.0	0.001
	5000.0	12000.0	0.001

These data are consistent with the scenario outlined in Exercise 16 of this chapter. What is the meaning of the area for the range 5000 to 12000?

4

SELECTION STRUCTURES

As stated in the last chapter, we can write any program as a set of sequence, selection, and repetition structures. Sequence structures were introduced in Chapter 2, a type of repetition structure called the DO-loop was presented in the last chapter, and this chapter begins and concludes the treatment of selection structures. We come back to and finish repetition structures in the next chapter.

4.1 IF-THEN-ELSE STRUCTURE

The **if-then-else structure** is the two-selection structure described in Figure 4.1. It's the *most fundamental* selection structure because one or more if-then-else structures can solve any possible selection or decision problem, although other selection structures more "cleanly" model certain types of selection problems (as shown in Sections 4.2 and 4.4). In this section we show how FORTRAN 77 implements the if-then-else structure.

BLOCK IF, ELSE, AND END IF STATEMENTS

The following statements are used to implement the if-then-else structure.

If-Then-Else Structure

	Syntax:	Example:
Block IF → statement	IF (*logical expression*) THEN	IF (SIZE .LT. BREAK) THEN
	· ⎫ · ⎬ Statements executed if logical · ⎭ expression is *true* (**THEN-** or **IF-block**)	COST = PRICE1 * SIZE
ELSE → statement	ELSE	ELSE
	· ⎫ · ⎬ Statements executed if logical · ⎭ expression is *false* (**ELSE-**block)	COST = PRICE2 * SIZE
END IF → statement	END IF	END IF

The logical expression illustrated by SIZE .LT. BREAK is tested when the block IF statement is executed (Is SIZE less than BREAK?). If the logical expression evaluates as true, then the statements within the IF-block are exe-

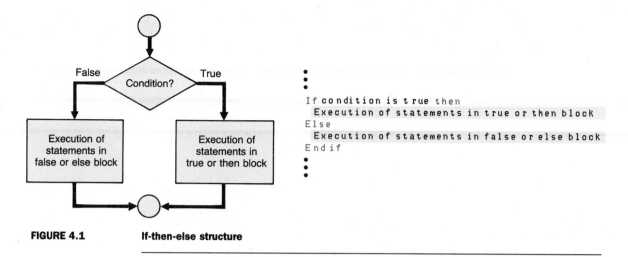

FIGURE 4.1   **If-then-else structure**

cuted. Execution control then passes to the first executable statement following the END IF statement, which defines the end of the if-then-else structure. In the example, if the value in SIZE is in fact less than the value in BREAK, then the first COST statement is executed, after which execution passes to the next executable statement following the END IF statement. Whenever the logical expression evaluates to false, statements within the ELSE-block are executed (the IF-block is skipped over), and control then passes out the bottom of the if-then-else structure. In the example, the second COST statement would be executed whenever the logical expression is false. Note that the described behavior of execution logic is identical to that described by Figure 4.1.

NOTE 1   The if-then-else structure is like a *building block* within a program, where execution enters at the top of the block, behaves within the block as described in Figure 4.1, and exits out the bottom. We can think of sequence and selection structures in the same way. Thus, we can view a program as a set of these building blocks (control structures), which simplifies the conceptualization of programs, thereby reducing developmental and maintenance costs.

NOTE 2   It's good programming style to indent IF-blocks and ELSE-blocks, since it improves the identification of the if-then-else structure and its two separate blocks.

SIMPLE LOGICAL EXPRESSIONS

A **logical expression** describes a logical computation whose evaluation is either true or false. The forms of a logical expression include a logical constant (.TRUE. or .FALSE.), a logical variable (as declared in a LOGICAL statement), a logical named constant (as assigned in a PARAMETER statement), a logical array element (**Chapter 7**), a logical function reference (**Module A and Chapter 6**), a relational expression (**as defined below**), and forms that include logical operators (**Section 4.3**). All forms but the last we call simple logical expressions, to distinguish them from the more complicated compound logical expressions presented in Section 4.3.

The most commonly used simple logical expression is a **relational expression,** which compares the values of either two arithmetic expressions or two character expressions, as follows.

Relational Expression

Syntax:

Arithmetic expression   relational operator   arithmetic expression

Example:

```
B**2 - 4.0 * A * C          .LT.                   0.0
```

Syntax:

Character expression   relational operator   character expression

Example:

```
        CHOICE             .EQ.                    'E'
```

In the first example, suppose B stores 2.0, A stores 1.0, and C stores 3.0. The arithmetic expression to the left evaluates to −8.0. The relational operator .LT. stands for "less than." The relational expression thus reads "Is −8.0 less than zero?" This evaluates as true. In the second example, suppose CHOICE stores M. Noting that .EQ. is the relational operator for "equal," the relational expression says "Does M equal E?" This evaluates as false.

The complete set of **relational operators** is given in Table 4.1, together with examples. Note that the third and fifth examples compare character expressions, while the other examples compare arithmetic expressions.

NOTE   Take care in comparing real, double-precision, or complex expressions when using the .EQ. relational operator. The two arithmetic expressions may have equal values (in theory), but *roundoff error* yields a false rather than true evaluation. It's best to avoid this kind of comparison; in cases where we must use .EQ. between noninteger arithmetic expressions, we need to take the precaution described in item 6 on page 153.

As illustrated, a relational expression can compare the value of one character expression to the value of another character expression. From a simple perspective, we can view this comparison between two strings alphabetically; for example, A is less than B, and g is greater than c. As you know, however, the com-

TABLE 4.1   **Relational Operators and Expressions**

Relational Operator	Meaning	Sample Relational Expression
.EQ.	Equal to	SPEED1 .EQ. SPEED2
.NE.	Not Equal to	CODE .NE. 1
.LT.	Less Than	NAME .LT. 'M'
.LE.	Less than or Equal to	X + Y .LE. SQRT(Z − 1.2)
.GT.	Greater Than	NAME1 .GT. NAME2
.GE.	Greater than or Equal to	SPEED1 .GE. SPEED2

TABLE 4.2   **Collating Sequence of Selected Characters**[a]

ASCII Code Values	Characters[b]
032	space
033−047	! " # $ % & ' ( ) * + , − ./
048−057	0 1 2 3 4 5 6 7 8 9
065−090	A B C ... X Y Z
097−122	abc ... xyz

[a]Based on ASCII codes.
[b]Numeric digits are less than alphabetic characters, and uppercase letters are less than lowercase letters.

puter internally stores all characters as coded binary numbers. Thus we can view the comparison of two strings as a comparison between the values of two coded binary numbers, in which one value (string) is less than, equal to, or greater than the other value (string).

The comparison of two strings is carried out from left to right, one character at a time. This comparison ends in one of three ways: (1) The character in one string has a lower value than the corresponding character in the other string; (2) the end of one string is reached but not the end of the other, in which case the shorter string has a lower value; or (3) the end of each string is reached, in which case the two strings have equal value.

The ordering of characters by value is called the **collating sequence.** Implementations on minicomputers and microcomputers typically base the collating sequence on the **American Standard Code for Information Interchange** (**ASCII,** pronounced ask-key), which officially uses 7 bits to code each of 128 characters in the sequence shown in Table 4.2. For example, the code value is 48 for the digit 0, 66 for the letter *B,* and 98 for the letter *b.* An 8th bit is a common enhancement to the ASCII coding scheme. This gives the ability to code 256 characters, including foreign language, graphics, and mathematical characters.

IBM mainframes and plug-compatibles (mainframes from other manufacturers that clone IBM mainframes) use a different collating sequence called **Extended Binary Coded Decimal Interchange Code** (**EBCDIC,** pronounced ebb-c-dick). This coding scheme uses 8 bits; in contrast to the ASCII scheme, lowercase letters precede uppercase letters, and the 9 digits "bring up the rear" in the collating sequence.

NOTE   The value of a relational expression that compares two character expressions when using the relational operators ‧GE‧, ‧GT‧, ‧LE‧, or ‧LT‧ can differ depending on the coding scheme. For example, the digit *9* is less than the letter *A* in the ASCII scheme, but greater in the EBCDIC scheme. Programs that make such comparisons should use the intrinsic logical functions **LGE, LGT, LLE,** and **LLT** (see Module A), for greater generality across systems. To illustrate, the fifth example in Table 4.1 would be rewritten as LGT(NAME1, NAME2), which ensures that the strings in NAME1 and NAME2 would be compared using the ASCII scheme, regardless of what coding scheme is used by the computer itself.

EXAMPLE 4.1

MICROCOMPUTER PRICE QUOTATIONS WITH IF-THEN-ELSE STRUCTURE

Problem Analysis. A computer store chain, Microland, is pricing its microcomputers according to the price table below. For example, an order for 500 micros would cost $1300 per micro, or $650,000; an order for 10 micros would cost $1500 per micro, or $15,000.

Price Table

Order Size	Price per Microcomputer
Under 100	$1500
100 or more	$1300

Microland currently gives price quotations over the telephone, as computed by an operator using a hand calculator. They would like us to write a program that interactively records the name, address, and order size of all pricing requests, and then prints quotations on the screen. The operator then uses screen output to relay the quotation over the telephone. Later, the program will be modified to print quotations on special forms that are mailed to those who request it. Also, other products and more price breaks may be added later (see Exercise 8).

Output data
Quotation showing:
  Name
  Address
  Order size
  Cost

Input data
Number of quotations
For each quotation:
　　Name
　　Street
　　City
　　Order size

Parameters
Price break (100 units)
First price ($1500)
Second price ($1300)

Computations
If order size < 100 then Cost = $1500 * order size
　　　　　　　　　　　　　else Cost = $1300 * order size

Program Design. The following top-down pseudocode describes the program.

```
Initialize price table data and output title and line
Process quotes ──────┐ Refine
Print farewell       │
End                  │
                     │
                     ▼
        ┌──────────────────────────────────────────────┐
        │  Input number of quotes                       │
        │  Do quote                                     │
        │     Input name, street, city, order size      │
        │     Compute cost ─────────────────────────────┼──── Refine
        │     Print quote                               │
        │  Continue                                     │
        └──────────────────────────────────────────────┘
                                                        │
                                                        ▼
                         ┌─────────────────────────────────────┐
                         │  If order size < 100 then            │
                         │     Cost = $1500 * order size        │
                         │  Else                                │
                         │     Cost = $1300 * order size        │
                         │  End if                              │
                         └─────────────────────────────────────┘
```

An overall look at the program shows that we need to initialize certain variables, process quotes, and print a farewell message just before ending execution.

The bulk of the program relates to processing quotes, which we refine in the second step above. We must use a loop to process quotes, since we're processing more than one quote within a single computer run. The body of this loop necessarily describes the tasks that we need to carry out for each quote: input the name, city, street, and order size; compute the cost; print the quote.

How we compute the cost represents our final refinement. The price per computer is either $1500 or $1300, depending on whether the order size is below 100 units. This suggests an if-then-else structure for computing cost. The test compares the order size to the price break of 100, and routes execution to the proper cost branch, as shown in the pseudocode.

Program Code and Test. Figure 4.2 shows the code and test run for Program MICRO. Try roleplaying the input data to its relevant output, paying special attention to the execution logic within the if-then-else structure. Also note the following:

1. We used an unbalanced input format for NAME, STREET, and CITY (see Sections C.3 and C.4 in Module C). This allows us to interactively enter character data without having to type surrounding quotes, which is more natural to our way of everyday writing.

2. Prices and the break point in the price table are stored in the parameters PRICE1, PRICE2, and BREAK. This simplifies program maintenance whenever these values change in practice.

3. The program prints a farewell message at the end, which is common in many interactive commercial programs; it indicates that the program is terminating execution, often based on an action taken by the user. ■

4.2 IF-THEN STRUCTURE

The **if-then structure** is the single-selection structure illustrated in Figure 4.3. This structure is a special case of the if-then-else structure, where the ELSE-block is omitted. Its implementation uses the block IF and END IF statements, as shown below.

If-Then Structure

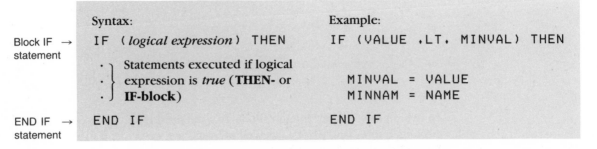

	Syntax:	Example:
Block IF → statement	IF (*logical expression*) THEN	IF (VALUE .LT. MINVAL) THEN
	· ⎱ Statements executed if logical · ⎰ expression is *true* (**THEN-** or · ⎰ **IF-block**)	MINVAL = VALUE MINNAM = NAME
END IF → statement	END IF	END IF

The logical expression within parentheses is tested when the block IF statement is executed. If the logical expression evaluates as true, then the state-

```
PROGRAM MICRO
* * * * * * * * * * * * * * * * * * * * * * * * * * * * * * * *
*                                                            *
*        Microcomputer Price Quotations                      *
*                                                            *
*           Inputs number of quotes, order name, address, and size *
*           Calculates order cost                            *
*           Outputs order name, address, size, and cost      *
*                                                            *
*           Key:                                             *
*              BREAK.... Price break point based on order size *
*              CITY..... City, State, and ZIP code part of address *
*              COST..... Cost of order (nearest dollar)      *
*              LINE..... Line in printed quotation           *
*              NAME..... Name part of address                *
*              NUMBER... Number of quotes or orders          *
*              PRICE1... First (highest) price per microcomputer *
*              PRICE2... Second price per microcomputer      *
*              QUOTE.... Quote number (DO-variable)          *
*              SIZE..... Size of order (number of micros)    *
*              SPACE.... Space over in printed quotation     *
*              STREET... Number and street part of address   *
*              TITLE.... Title in printed quotation          *
*                                                            *
* * * * * * * * * * * * * * * * * * * * * * * * * * * * * * * *
*------------------------------------------------------------
* Type names
*------------------------------------------------------------
      CHARACTER*50  CITY, LINE, NAME, SPACE*22, STREET, TITLE
      INTEGER       BREAK, COST, NUMBER, PRICE1, PRICE2, QUOTE, SIZE
*------------------------------------------------------------
* Parameters
*------------------------------------------------------------
      PARAMETER ( BREAK  = 100,
     +            PRICE1 = 1500,
     +            PRICE2 = 1300 )
*------------------------------------------------------------
* Initialize printed quote parts
*------------------------------------------------------------
      TITLE = 'Microcomputer:  MacManzana'
      LINE  = '============================'
      SPACE = '   '
*------------------------------------------------------------
* Process quotes
*------------------------------------------------------------
      PRINT *, 'Enter number of quotes'
      READ *, NUMBER

      DO 100 QUOTE = 1, NUMBER

        PRINT *
        PRINT *,'Enter name and address'
        READ '( A )', NAME, STREET, CITY
        PRINT *
        PRINT *,'Enter order size'
        READ *, SIZE

        IF ( SIZE .LT. BREAK ) THEN          If-then-else structure
          COST = PRICE1 * SIZE
        ELSE
          COST = PRICE2 * SIZE
        END IF
```

FIGURE 4.2   **Microcomputer price quotations (*continued next page*)**

```
          PRINT *
          PRINT *, SPACE, NAME
          PRINT *, SPACE, STREET
          PRINT *, SPACE, CITY
          PRINT *
          PRINT *
          PRINT *, SPACE, TITLE
          PRINT *, SPACE, LINE
          PRINT *, SPACE, 'Order size:   ', SIZE
          PRINT *, SPACE, '      cost:  $', COST
          PRINT *, SPACE, LINE
          PRINT *

     100 CONTINUE
*————————————————————————————————————
*  Print farewell message
*—————————————————————————
          PRINT *
          PRINT *, 'Another day, another $...  Have a nice night!'
*————————————————————————————————————
          END
```

```
     Enter number of quotes
     2

     Enter name and address
EBM
Box 1328
Boca Raton, FL  33432

     Enter order size
500
```

```
                         EBM
                         Box 1328
                         Boca Raton, FL  33432


                         Microcomputer:  MacManzana
                         ════════════════════════════════
                         Order size:           500
                              cost:  $      650000
                         ════════════════════════════════
```

```
     Enter name and address
Harvey CORE
57 Wandsworth St.
Narragansett, RI  02882

     Enter order size
10
```

```
                         Harvey CORE
                         57 Wandsworth St.
                         Narragansett, RI  02882


                         Microcomputer:  MacManzana
                         ════════════════════════════════
                         Order size:            10
                              cost:  $       15000          ⟵ Farewell message
                         ════════════════════════════════


     Another day, another $...  Have a nice night!
```

FIGURE 4.2   *(continued)*

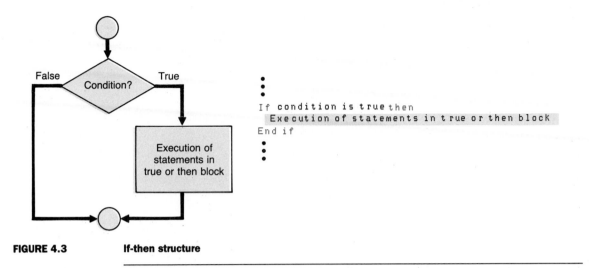

```
If condition is true then
    Execution of statements in true or then block
End if
```

FIGURE 4.3   If-then structure

ments within the IF-block are executed. Execution control then passes to the first executable statement following the END IF statement, which defines the end of the if-then structure. In the example, if the value in VALUE is less than the value in MINVAL, then the two statements within the IF-block are executed, after which execution passes to the next executable statement following the END IF statement. Whenever the logical expression evaluates to false, statements within the IF-block are skipped over, and control passes out the bottom of the if-then structure. Note that the described behavior of execution logic is identical to that described by Figure 4.3.

EXAMPLE 4.2

MINIMUM VALUE

The program and run in Figure 4.4 illustrate the determination of a minimum real value from a set of data stored in a data file. Each record in the data file has a record description (microcomputer in the example) and a real value (processing time in the example). The program finds the minimum (best) processing speed, and prints it together with the associated microcomputer name. The benchmark test in the sample data measured processor speed in seconds by looping through a series of real calculations.

The minimum value algorithm has the following design.

```
         PROGRAM MIN
•  •  •  •  •  •  •  •  •  •  •  •  •  •  •  •  •  •  •  •  •  •  •  •  •  •
•                                                                        •
•       Minimum Value                                                    •
•                                                                        •
•          Inputs data set title, names and associated real values       •
•          Determines minimum value and its associated name              •
•          Outputs minimum value and its associated name                 •
•                                                                        •
•          Data file structure:                                          •
•             Title in quotes                                            •
•             Number of items                                            •
•             1st name in quotes          value                          •
•             2nd name in quotes          value                          •
•             ...                                                        •
•                                                                        •
•          Key:                                                          •
•             ITEM..... Item number (DO-variable)                        •
•             MINNAM... Name of item whose value is the minimum          •
•             MINVAL... Minimum value                                    •
•             NAME..... Descriptive name of item                         •
•             NUMBER... Number of items                                  •
•             TITLE.... Title of data set                               •
•             VALUE.... Value of item                                    •
•                                                                        •
•  •  •  •  •  •  •  •  •  •  •  •  •  •  •  •  •  •  •  •  •  •  •  •  •  •
•
•  Type names
•
       CHARACTER MINNAM*40, NAME*40, TITLE*80
       INTEGER   ITEM, NUMBER
       REAL      MINVAL, VALUE
•
•  Process data file
•
       READ (5,*) TITLE
       READ (5,*) NUMBER

       READ (5,*) MINNAM, MINVAL        ◄─────── Initialize minima

       DO 100 ITEM = 1, NUMBER

         READ (5,*) NAME, VALUE

         IF (VALUE .LT. MINVAL) THEN    ◄─────── If-then structure for finding new minima
            MINVAL = VALUE
            MINNAM = NAME
         END IF

   100 CONTINUE
•
•  Print results
•
       PRINT *, TITLE
       PRINT *
       PRINT *, ' Minimum value............',      MINVAL
       PRINT *, ' Associated description...      ', MINNAM

       END                              ⌐Data file
```

```
'Benchmark test speeds in seconds, PC Magazine, 10/13/87, p. 332'
9
'IBM PC AT (8 MHz)'               35.60
'Mitsubishi MP 286'               28.12
'FiveStar FS-286'                 27.98
'Wong 280'                        28.01
'IndTech 5191'                    22.23
'ARC Turbo 12'                    23.56
'PC Designs GV-286'               18.82
'Standard 286/12'                 23.16
'Compaq Deskpro 386 (16 MHz)'     15.50
```

⌐Output

```
Benchmark test speeds in seconds, PC Magazine, 10/13/87, p. 332

   Minimum value............       15.5000
   Associated description...       Compaq Deskpro 386 (16 MHz)
```

FIGURE 4.4   **Minimum value**

TABLE 4.3   **Roleplay of Test Run In Figure 4.4**

ITEM	VALUE	MINVAL	VALUE .LT. MINVAL	NAME	MINNAM
		35.60			IBM PC AT (8 MHz)
2	28.12	28.12	True	Mitsubishi MP 286	Mitsubishi MP 286
3	27.98	27.98	True	FiveStar FS-286	FiveStar FS-286
4	28.01	27.98	False	Wang 280	FiveStar FS-286
5	22.23	22.23	True	IndTech 5191	IndTech 5191
6	23.56	22.23	False	ARC Turbo 12	IndTech 5191
7	18.82	18.82	True	PC Designs GV-286	PC Designs GV-286
8	23.16	18.82	False	Standard 286/12	PC Designs GV-286
9	15.50	15.50	True	Compaq Deskpro 386 (16 MHz)	Compaq Deskpro 386 (16 MHz)

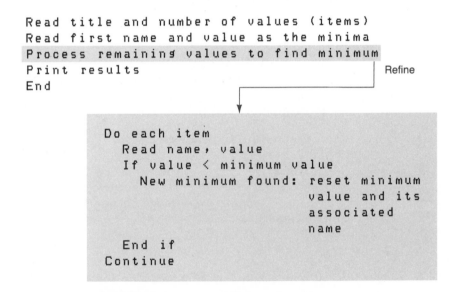

```
Read title and number of values (items)
Read first name and value as the minima
Process remaining values to find minimum
Print  results                                    Refine
End
```

```
Do each item
   Read name, value
   If value < minimum value
      New minimum found: reset minimum
                         value and its
                         associated
                         name

      End if
   Continue
```

The logic is best understood by roleplaying the test run, as described by Table 4.3. The memory contents shown are those that describe memory as if a snapshot were taken just before the CONTINUE statement is executed.

Note the following in the test run and Table 4.3.

1. The variable that stores the minimum value (MINVAL) is initialized to the first value in the data file, or 35.60 in our example. This ensures that the first candidate value for the minimum is the first data item. In addition, also note that the name that corresponds to the current minimum value (MINNAM) is also read in at this time.

2. The if-then structure in the program ensures the storage of the current minimum value and its associated description; that is, a true value for the logical expression

```
VALUE .LT. MINVAL
```

gives us a new value for the current minimum (MINVAL) and its associated description (MINNAM). We also can use the intrinsic function MIN to find minimum values, but without also storing any associated data items (see Exercise 7).

By the way, the odds were stacked in favor of the Compaq computer; all other things being equal, a processor with a 16-MHz clock speed will be twice as fast as one with an 8-MHz clock speed. Moreover, the Compaq in the benchmark test has the 32-bit INTEL 80386 processor; all other machines in the test had 16-bit processors. Realizing these factors, the PC Designs machine stacks up well, doesn't it? (It runs at 12 MHz.) ∎

4.3 COMPOUND LOGICAL EXPRESSIONS

Up to now we have worked with simple logical expressions. In many applications it's best to combine one or more simple logical expressions. This is accomplished by using logical operators like .AND. and .OR. to connect simple logical expressions into a **compound logical expression** that has the following form.

Compound Logical Expression

Syntax:

First simple	*Logical*	*Second simple*	Other logical operators and simple logical expressions (if any)
logical expression	*operator*	*logical expression* . . .	↓

Example:

```
SEX .EQ. 'F'    .AND.    AGE .GE. 25
```

As with simple logical expressions, the test of a compound logical expression yields either a true or false logical value. In the example, if the current value in SEX is F (a female) and the current value in AGE is 28 (28 years old), then the first logical expression is true (we have a female) and the second logical expression is true (over 25 years old). Thus, we have the compound condition true AND true, which evaluates to true (we have a female AND she's over 25); however, if M were in SEX, then we would have false AND true, which evaluates to false.

LOGICAL OPERATORS

The five **logical operators** are defined in Table 4.4. **Truth tables** are an alternative way of defining logical operators by showing all possible combinations of T and F logical values for the logical expressions operated on by the logical

TABLE 4.4   **Logical Operators**[a]

Logical Operator	Logical Expression	Definition
.AND.	L1 .AND. L2	Logical conjunction: true if both L1 and L2 are true; false otherwise.
.OR.	L1 .OR. L2	Logical disjunction: true if either L1, or L2, or both are true; false otherwise.
.NOT.	.NOT. L	Logical negation: true if L is false; false if L is true.
.EQV.	L1 .EQV. L2	Logical equivalence: true if both L1 and L2 are true or both are false; false otherwise.
.NEQV.	L1 .NEQV. L2	Logical nonequivalence: true if one of L1 or L2 is true and the other is false; false otherwise.

[a]L, L1, and L2 represent any logical expressions.

TABLE 4.5   **Truth Table for .NOT. Operator**[a]

Value of L	Value of .NOT. L
T	F
F	T

[a]L is any logical expression.

TABLE 4.6   **Truth Table for Other Logical Operators**[a]

Value of...					
L1	L2	L1 .AND. L2	L1 .OR. L2	L1 .EQV. L2	L1 .NEQV. L2
T	T	T	T	T	F
T	F	F	T	F	T
F	T	F	T	F	T
F	F	F	F	T	F

[a]L1 and L2 are any logical expressions.

operators. Table 4.5 shows the truth table for the .NOT. operator, and Table 4.6 is the truth table for the other logical operators.

For example, in the first line of Table 4.5, if a logical expression like X .GT. Y evaluates as true, then .NOT. (X .GT. Y) evaluates as false. In the third line of Table 4.6, if the logical expression represented by L1 is false and the logical expression represented by L2 is true, then the compound expression:

```
false                    true      ← Values for L1 and L2 in the 3rd line of Table 4.6
  ↓                       ↓
 L1  .AND.  L2  is false   (It's false that both L1 and L2 are true)
 L1  .OR.   L2  is true    (It's true that either L1 or L2 is true)
 L1  .EQV.  L2  is false   (It's false that L1 and L2 are equivalent)
 L1 .NEQV.  L2  is true    (It's true that L1 and L2 are not
                            equivalent)
```

HIERARCHY

The following hierarchy rule applies when using more than one logical operator within a compound logical expression.

Hierarchy Rule

Operator	Priority
.NOT.	Highest
.AND.	
.OR.	↓
.EQV. or .NEQV.	Lowest

In general, a compound logical expression is evaluated as follows:

- Logical expressions within parentheses are evaluated first.
- Relational expressions are evaluated before any logical expression acted on by a logical operator.
- Logical operations are performed according to the above hierarchy rule.

Let's explain this evaluation procedure by example.

EXAMPLE 4.3

HIERARCHY RULE AND USE OF PARENTHESES

If the following values are stored

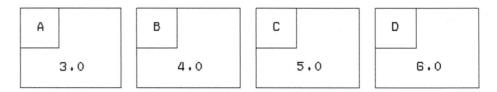

A	B	C	D
3.0	4.0	5.0	6.0

then the logical expression in

```
IF (A .LT. B .OR. A .GT. C .AND. D .LE. 5.1) THEN
    SUM = SUM + A
END IF
```

is true and the IF-block

```
SUM = SUM + A
```

is executed. This logical expression is evaluated in the following manner.

1. According to the hierarchy, .AND. is evaluated before .OR., which means that we should focus on the shaded portion below.

```
A .LT. B .OR. A .GT.    C .AND. D    .LE. 5.1
                                ↓
            3.0 .GT. 5.0 .AND. 6.0 .LE. 5.1
                                ↓
                     false .AND. false
                                ↓
                             false
```

2. We are now left with

```
            A .LT. B .OR. false
                        ↓
    3.0 .LT. 4.0 .OR. false
                        ↓
           true .OR. false
                        ↓
                     true
```

Thus the logical expression itself has the value true.

As in arithmetic expressions, parentheses can be used to modify the order of evaluation within logical expressions. For example, assuming the same values in A, B, C, and D, the logical expression in

```
IF ( (A .LT. B .OR. A .GT. C ) .AND. D .LE. 5.1) THEN
   SUM = SUM + A
END IF
```

is false and control goes directly to the END IF statement without executing the IF-block. Now the expression is evaluated in the following manner.

1. Expressions enclosed within parentheses are evaluated before expressions not enclosed within parentheses. Thus the shaded portion below is evaluated first as true.

$$(A \text{ .LT. } B \text{ .OR. } A \text{ .GT. } C) \text{ .AND. } D \text{ .LE. } 5.1$$
$$\downarrow$$
$$3.0 \text{ .LT. } 4.0 \text{ .OR. } 3.0 \text{ .GT. } 5.0$$
$$\downarrow$$

true .OR. false

$$\downarrow$$

true

2. We are now left with

true .AND. D   .LE. 5.1
$$\downarrow$$
true .AND. 6.0 .LE. 5.1
$$\downarrow$$
true .AND. false
$$\downarrow$$
false

The logical expression, therefore, is false.

Improving readability is an alternative use of parentheses within logical expressions, as it is in arithmetic expressions. For instance, the clarity of the original block IF statement in this example can be improved as follows.

```
IF ((A .LT. B) .OR. (A .GT. C .AND. D .LE. 5.1)) THEN
```

The value of this logical expression is true, as before; however, it is now quite clear that the operator .AND. is considered before the operator .OR., since .AND. is within parentheses.   ■

4.4 MULTIPLE SELECTIONS

Many problems require that the computer select one from among multiple courses of action. In this section we illustrate three approaches to multiple selections else-if structure sequential if-then structures and nested-selection structures

ELSE-IF STRUCTURE

The **else-if structure** is illustrated in Figure 4.5. This structure evaluates a series of conditions from top to bottom until one (if any) is true. The block of statements corresponding to the first true condition is executed, after which control passes out through the bottom of the structure. If all the conditions are false, control drops to a special block that usually includes an error routine. An **error routine** is a segment of the program that detects errors in either entered data or

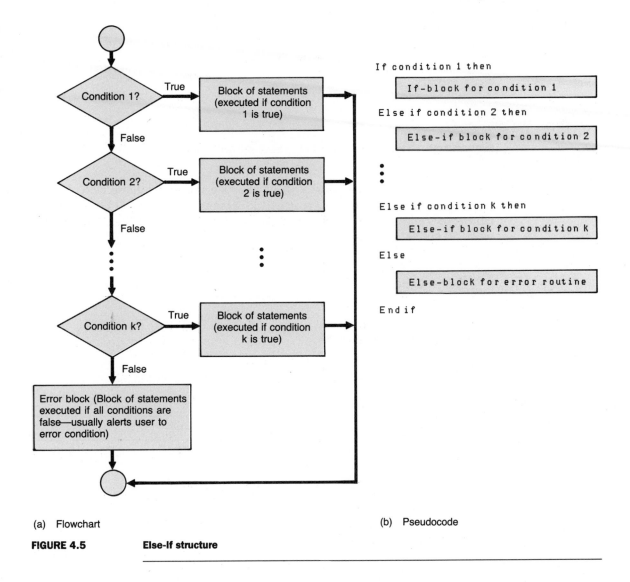

(a) Flowchart   (b) Pseudocode

FIGURE 4.5   **Else-If structure**

computational results. Typically, an error routine prints a message that alerts the user to the problem and then either continues with the normal execution sequence or terminates program execution.[1]

---

[1]We might mention, just in case you run across it, that the **case structure** is another common multiple-selection structure. In its most general implementation, it looks the same as the else-if structure described in Figure 4.5; in its most restrictive implementation, the test condition (case) is based on numeric codes, where code 1 executes the first case (block), code 2 executes the second case, and so on. FORTRAN 77 has no need for a case structure implementation because the else-if structure implementation handles "case-type" problems. (See Exercise 10b.)

In FORTRAN 77 the else-if structure is best implemented by a combination of the block IF, ELSE IF, ELSE, and END IF statements. Of these, the **ELSE IF statement** is new, as shown on the next page.

EXAMPLE 4.4

MICROCOMPUTER PRICE QUOTATIONS WITH ELSE-IF STRUCTURE

The else-if structure example above illustrates a multiple pricing table for the price quotation problem first presented in Example 4.1. In this case, the price table shows multiple prices ($1500, $1300, $1100, $1000) and price breaks (100 units, 500 units, 1000 units), as follows.

Price Table

Order Size	Price per Microcomputer
Under 100	$1500
100 but less than 500	$1300
500 but less than 1000	$1100
1000 or more	$1000

The price table variables in the program would store the following:

Price Table Variables

Variable	Value	Variable	Value
BREAK1	100	PRICE1	1500
BREAK2	500	PRICE2	1300
BREAK3	1000	PRICE3	1100
		PRICE4	1000

For example, if 700 is stored in SIZE, then the else-if structure would execute as follows:

1. The test in   — 700 > 0 and 700 < 100 is false

```
IF (SIZE .GT. 0 .AND. SIZE .LT. BREAK1) THEN
```

is false. Execution proceeds to the first ELSE IF statement.

2. The test in   700 ≥ 100 and 700 < 500 is false

```
ELSE IF (SIZE .GE. BREAK1 .AND. SIZE .LT. BREAK2) THEN
```

is false. Execution proceeds to the next ELSE IF statement.

3. The test in   700 ≥ 500 and 700 < 1000 is true

```
ELSE IF (SIZE .GE. BREAK2 .AND. SIZE .LT. BREAK3) THEN
```

ELSE-IF Structure

```
                                  Example:
Block IF →        Syntax:         IF (SIZE .GT. 0 .AND. SIZE .LT. BREAK1) THEN
statement         IF (logical expression 1) THEN
                  .  } IF-block for condition 1
                  .                  COST = PRICE1 * SIZE

ELSE IF →         ELSE IF (logical expression 2) THEN    ELSE IF (SIZE .GE. BREAK1 .AND. SIZE .LT. BREAK2) THEN
statement         .  } ELSE-IF block for condition 2
                  .                  COST = PRICE2 * SIZE

ELSE IF →         ELSE IF (logical expression 3) THEN    ELSE IF (SIZE .GE. BREAK2 .AND. SIZE .LT. BREAK3) THEN
statement         .  } IF-block for condition 1
                  .                  COST = PRICE3 * SIZE

                  . . .                                  ELSE IF (SIZE .GE. BREAK3) THEN
                                                             COST = PRICE4 * SIZE

ELSE →            ELSE                                   ELSE
statement         .  } ELSE-block executed if all conditions    PRINT *, 'Wrong order size'
                  .       false

END IF →          END IF                                 END IF
statement
```

is true. Execution now enters this ELSE-IF block, the statement

```
COST = PRICE3 * SIZE
```

is executed (storing 770000 in COST), and execution immediately exits the else-if structure (as defined by the END IF statement).

This type of selection structure is so common in computerized applications that it's called the **table lookup problem.** In Chapter 7 we will show another approach to solving table lookup problems. ◼

SEQUENTIAL IF-THEN STRUCTURES

We can solve multiple-selection problems by using a sequence of if-then structures, as the following example illustrates.

EXAMPLE 4.5

MICROCOMPUTER PRICE QUOTATIONS WITH SEQUENTIAL IF-THEN STRUCTURES

Let's return to the preceding example by using the following sequential if-then structures instead of the else-if structure.

700 > 0 and 700 < 100 is false

```
IF (SIZE .GT. 0 .AND. SIZE .LT. BREAK1) THEN
   COST = PRICE1 * SIZE
END IF
```

700 ≥ 100 and 700 < 500 is false

```
IF (SIZE .GE. BREAK1 .AND. SIZE .LT. BREAK2) THEN
   COST = PRICE2 * SIZE
END IF
```

700 ≥ 500 and 700 < 1000 is true

```
IF (SIZE .GE. BREAK2 .AND. SIZE .LT. BREAK3) THEN
   COST = PRICE3 * SIZE
END IF
```

700 ≥ 1000 is false

```
IF (SIZE .GE. BREAK3) THEN
   COST = PRICE4 * SIZE
END IF
```

700 ≤ 0 is false

```
IF (SIZE .LE. 0) THEN
   PRINT *, 'Wrong order size'
END IF
```

For example, if SIZE stores 700, then the first IF-test ($700 > 0$ and $700 < 100$?) is false, and control passes to the second if-then structure. This IF-test ($700 \geq 100$ and $700 < 500$?) is also false, so control passes to the third if-then structure. This IF-test ($700 \geq 500$ and $700 < 1000$?) is true, so PRICE3 is correctly used to calculate COST. Note that, so far, the execution logic parallels the else-if structure. In our present example, unlike the else-if structure, IF-tests continue through the last if-then structure. In our current example, the fourth and fifth IF-tests are also conducted (both false). In our earlier else-if example, execution exits the structure once the proper else-if block is executed. ◼

NOTE   In general, the computational efficiency (not to mention simplicity) of the else-if structure is preferred to sequential if-then structures. To appreciate this, consider a problem with 50 selections (say, one for each state in the United States). If the proper selection for a particular run is the 20th, then the else-if implementation exits the structure after 20 IF-tests, whereas the sequential if-then implementation performs all 50 IF-tests.

NESTED-SELECTION STRUCTURES

A **nested-selection structure** is one where one or more if-then-else, if-then, or else-if structures appear *within* or *inside* other if-then-else, if-then, or else-if structures. To illustrate, let's return to our last two examples.

EXAMPLE 4.6

MICROCOMPUTER PRICE QUOTATIONS WITH NESTED IF-THEN-ELSE STRUCTURES

Let's implement the table lookup logic for our price quotation example as a nested if-then-else structure.

```
IF (SIZE .GT. 0 .AND. SIZE .LT. BREAK1) THEN
   COST = PRICE1 * SIZE
ELSE
   IF (SIZE .GE. BREAK1 .AND. SIZE .LT. BREAK2) THEN
      COST = PRICE2 * SIZE
   ELSE
      IF (SIZE .GE. BREAK2 .AND. SIZE .LT. BREAK3) THEN
         COST = PRICE3 * SIZE
      ELSE
         IF (SIZE .GE. BREAK3) THEN
            COST = PRICE4 * SIZE
         ELSE
            PRINT *, 'Wrong order size'
         END IF
      END IF
   END IF
END IF
```

Outer if-then-else structure

Second-level inner if-then-else structure

Third-level inner if-then-else structure

Fourth-level inner if-then-else structure

Try roleplaying the logic to confirm that, when SIZE stores 700, the price in PRICE3 is used to calculate cost. As before, BREAK1, BREAK2, and BREAK3 store 100, 500, and 1000, respectively. ■

NOTE   Avoid nested-selection structures if possible, since they increase the difficulty of reading programs. Can you picture the use of 49 nested if-then-else structures to model a 50-selection problem? In some applications, however, we need to nest selection structures (see Exercise 8b).

MENUS

Interactive software is frequently designed as **menu-driven programs.** These programs present the user with a list of options (the **menu**) and then take appropriate actions based on the user's choice. Menus are very common in commercial interactive programs, since they facilitate the training of users and reduce the likelihood that users will commit errors. For example, many game programs include menus of available games, and spreadsheet programs like Lotus 1-2-3 not only have extensive main menus but also have submenus that give further options once main menu items are selected.

Figure 4.6 illustrates a sample menu for a wordprocessing package. There are four processing options: retrieve a file, store a file, print a file, and delete a file. In addition, the user can exit the system if desired. In general, good menu design pays attention to clearly communicating the choices through text layout, mean-

MENU

```
 |                                      |
 |  R      Retrieve file                |
 |  S      Store file                   |
 |  P      Print file                   |
 |  D      Delete file                  |
 |                                      |
 |  X      eXit program                 |
 |                                      |
```

Enter choice ===›

FIGURE 4.6   **Sample wordprocessing menu**

ingful choices, and use of color. Good menu design also calls for an error routine that traps incorrect choices.

The else-if structure is ideal for implementing menu choices, as the following example illustrates.

EXAMPLE 4.7

SYNCHRONOUS SATELLITE ORBITS

Problem Analysis. Satellites that remain in fixed positions over the earth's equator are commonly used by the military, communications networks, and meteorologists. The height at which these satellites are placed into orbit is determined by the earth's rotational period (24 hours), gravitational acceleration (32 feet per second-squared or 9.8 meters per second-squared), and radius (about 3964 miles or 6380 kilometers). If the rotational period (time for one complete revolution) of the satellite equals the rotational period of the earth, then the satellite and earth will rotate together (synchronously), and the satellite will remain fixed relative to the earth.

Let's write an interactive program that offers the user a menu of planets over which we can (theoretically) place synchronous orbiting satellites. The program computes and prints the required altitude over the equator.

Output data
Name of planet
Altitude of satellite in kilometers
Altitude of satellite in miles

Input data
Menu choice based on the following menu:
E   Earth
M   Mars
O   Other
Q   Quit.

The following when choice Other is selected:

Name of planet
Gravitational acceleration in meters/second/second (m/s/s)
Rotational period in seconds
Radius in kilometers (km)

Parameters
π (= 3.141593)
For earth:
Name (= earth)
Gravitational acceleration (= 9.8 m/s/s)
Rotational period (= 86,400 s)
Radius (= 6380 km)

For Mars:
Name (= Mars)
Gravitational acceleration (= 3.7 m/s/s)
Rotational period (= 88,560 s)
Radius (= 3401 km)

Computations
The altitude (km) for a synchronous orbit over the equator is given by

$$A = \left(\frac{gp^2R^2}{4000\ \pi^2} \right)^{1/3} - R$$

where A = altitude in km
g = gravitational acceleration in m/s/s
p = rotational period in s
R = radius in km

Also, A in km is converted to A in miles by the conversion factor 0.62137 mile/km.
For example, a synchronous satellite over the earth would have to be placed at the following altitude over the equator:

$$A = \left[\frac{(9.8)(86400)^2(6380)^2}{4000(3.141593)^2} \right]^{1/3} - 6380$$
$$= 42252 - 6380$$
$$= 35,872 \text{ km} \quad \text{or} \quad 22,290 \text{ miles}$$

Program Design. The following stepwise-refined pseudocode expresses the program's execution logic. Note how the else-if structure is tailor-made for branching based on a menu selection.

```
Print menu
Input choice
Select choice ──────────── Refine
Print results
End
```

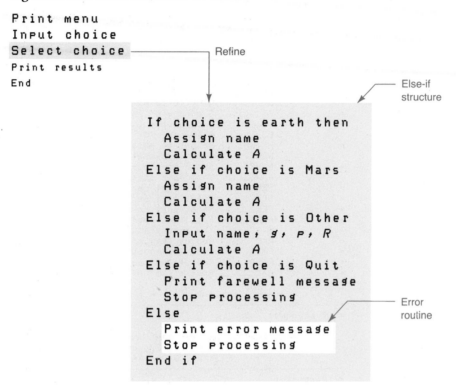

```
If choice is earth then
    Assign name
    Calculate A
Else if choice is Mars
    Assign name
    Calculate A
Else if choice is Other
    Input name, g, p, R
    Calculate A
Else if choice is Quit
    Print farewell message
    Stop processing
Else
        Print error message
    Stop processing
End if
```

Program Code and Test. Figure 4.7 shows the listing and sample runs for Program ORBIT. Study the figure and note the following:

1. The statement function (see Module A) named ALT is an efficient and readable way of implementing the altitude calculations.

2. The else-if structure is an efficient and "clean" way to implement menu choices. Other alternatives include sequential if-then structures and nested if-then-else structures.

3. The STOP statement is used within two blocks in the else-if structure. In the first instance, it stops execution based on the menu choice Quit; in the second, it stops execution whenever an incorrect menu choice is selected.

4. The ELSE-block shows a simple error routine, where an error message is printed indicating an incorrect menu choice, and execution stops. In practice, execution would continue with a reoffering of the menu, as described in item 5 next.

```
            PROGRAM ORBIT
* * * * * * * * * * * * * * * * * * * * * * * * * * * * * * * * * * * *
*                                                                     *
*          Synchronous Satellite Orbits                               *
*                                                                     *
*          Inputs menu choice for planet; if choice is "Other planet" *
*             then also inputs g acceleration, period, and radius     *
*          Calculates altitude over equator of synchronous satellite  *
*          Outputs planet's name and altitude in km and miles         *
*                                                                     *
*          Key:                                                       *
*            ALT...... Altitude (km) statement function               *
*            CHOICE... Menu choice for planet (E, M, O) or Quit (Q)   *
*            G........ Gravitational acceleration (m/s/s) for planet  *
*            G1....... G parameter (m/s/s) for Earth                  *
*            G2....... G parameter (m/s/s) for Mars                   *
*            G3....... G (m/s/s) for other planet                     *
*            HEIGHT... Height of satellite (km) for planet            *
*            NAME..... Name of planet                                 *
*            NAME1.... Earth name parameter                           *
*            NAME2.... Mars name parameter                            *
*            PER...... Rotational period (s) of planet                *
*            PER1..... Rotational period (s) parameter of Earth       *
*            PER2..... Rotational period (s) parameter of Mars        *
*            PER3..... Rotational period (s) of other planet          *
*            PI....... The parameter 3.141593                         *
*            RAD...... Radius (km) of planet                          *
*            RAD1..... Radius (km) parameter of Earth                 *
*            RAD2..... Radius (km) parameter of Mars                  *
*            RAD3..... Radius (km) of other planet                    *
*                                                                     *
* * * * * * * * * * * * * * * * * * * * * * * * * * * * * * * * * * * *
*---------------------------------------------------------------------
*  Type names
*-------------
      CHARACTER*10 CHOICE*1, NAME, NAME1, NAME2
      REAL         ALT, G, G1, G2, G3, HEIGHT, PER, PER1, PER2, PER3,
     +             PI, RAD, RAD1, RAD2, RAD3
*---------------------------------------------------------------------
*  Parameters
*-------------
      PARAMETER ( PI = 3.141593 )
      PARAMETER ( NAME1 = 'Earth', G1 = 9.8, PER1 = 86400, RAD1 = 6380 )
      PARAMETER ( NAME2 = 'Mars',  G2 = 3.7, PER2 = 88560, RAD2 = 3401 )
*---------------------------------------------------------------------
*  Statement function
*---------------------
      ALT(G,PER,RAD) = (G/4000.0/PI**2 *PER**2 *RAD**2)**(1.0/3.0) - RAD
*---------------------------------------------------------------------
*  Print menu and enter choice
*------------------------------
      PRINT *, 'PLANETARY SYNCHRONOUS SATELLITE ALTITUDES'
      PRINT *
      PRINT *, '   MENU CHOICES   '
      PRINT *, ' _____ '
      PRINT *, '|               |'
      PRINT *, '|  E  Earth     |'
      PRINT *, '|  M  Mars      |'
      PRINT *, '|  O  Other     |'
      PRINT *, '|               |'
      PRINT *, '|  Q  Quit      |'
      PRINT *, '|_____|'
      PRINT *
      PRINT *, 'Enter choice'

      READ '( A )', CHOICE
```

FIGURE 4.7   **Synchronous satellite orbits (*continued on next page*)**

```
*-------------------------------------------------------------------
* Select based on choice                          Else-if structure
*-------------------------------------------------------------------
      IF ( CHOICE .EQ. 'E' ) THEN
         NAME   = NAME1
         HEIGHT = ALT ( G1, PER1, RAD1 )

      ELSE IF (CHOICE .EQ. 'M' ) THEN
         NAME   = NAME2
         HEIGHT = ALT ( G2, PER2, RAD2 )

      ELSE IF (CHOICE .EQ. 'O' ) THEN
         PRINT *
         PRINT *,'Enter name of other planet'
         READ '( A )', NAME
         PRINT *,'Enter gravitational acceleration (meter/second/second)'
         READ *, G3
         PRINT *,'Enter rotational period (seconds)'
         READ *, PER3
         PRINT *,'Enter radius (kilometers)'
         READ *, RAD3
         HEIGHT = ALT ( G3, PER3, RAD3 )

      ELSE IF (CHOICE .EQ. 'Q' ) THEN
         PRINT *
         PRINT *, 'Have a nice orbit...'
         STOP
                                                   Error routine
      ELSE
         PRINT *
         PRINT *, 'Wrong menu choice... Please enter E, M, O, or Q.'
         STOP

      END IF
*-------------------------------------------------------------------
* Output data
*-------------------------------------------------------------------
      PRINT *
      PRINT *, '     Planet............  ', NAME
      PRINT *, '     Altitude (km)......',   HEIGHT
      PRINT *, '     Altitude (miles)...',   HEIGHT * 0.62137
*-------------------------------------------------------------------
      END
```

```
PLANETARY SYNCHRONOUS SATELLITE ALTITUDES

    MENU CHOICES

    _____
   |                   |
   |   E   Earth       |
   |   M   Mars        |
   |   O   Other       |
   |                   |
   |   Q   Quit        |
   |_____|

  Enter choice
  E

        Planet............   Earth
        Altitude (km)......     35871.7
        Altitude (miles)...     22289.6
```

FIGURE 4.7   *(continued)*

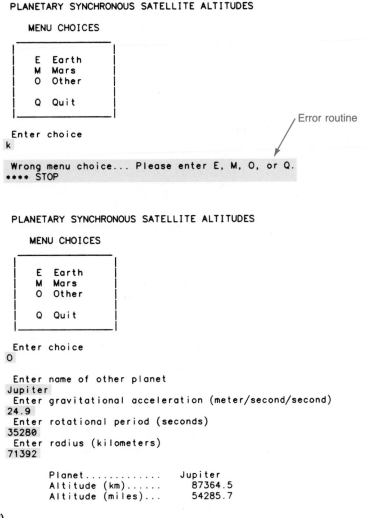

```
        PLANETARY SYNCHRONOUS SATELLITE ALTITUDES

           MENU CHOICES
           _____
          |               |
          |   E   Earth   |
          |   M   Mars    |
          |   O   Other   |
          |               |
          |   Q   Quit    |
          |_____|

        Enter choice
        k
```

                                                                        Error routine

```
        Wrong menu choice... Please enter E, M, O, or Q.
        **** STOP
```

```
        PLANETARY SYNCHRONOUS SATELLITE ALTITUDES

           MENU CHOICES
           _____
          |               |
          |   E   Earth   |
          |   M   Mars    |
          |   O   Other   |
          |               |
          |   Q   Quit    |
          |_____|

        Enter choice
        O

        Enter name of other planet
        Jupiter
        Enter gravitational acceleration (meter/second/second)
        24.9
        Enter rotational period (seconds)
        35280
        Enter radius (kilometers)
        71392

                Planet.............   Jupiter
                Altitude (km)......     87364.5
                Altitude (miles)...     54285.7
```

FIGURE 4.7   *(continued)*

5. The Quit option in a menu is usually controlled (implemented) by a test in either a pretest or a posttest loop. In our current example, each new menu offering required a new run of the program. In practice, programs loop back to reoffer the menu. The DO-loop is not a good implementation for interactive menu programs (see Exercise 10d) . . . so we'll delay this approach until the next chapter.

```
          PLANETARY SYNCHRONOUS SATELLITE ALTITUDES

              MENU CHOICES

             ┌─────────────────┐
             │                 │
             │   E   Earth     │
             │   M   Mars      │
             │   O   Other     │
             │                 │
             │   Q   Quit      │
             │                 │
             └─────────────────┘

          Enter choice
            M

                      Planet.............    Mars
                      Altitude (km)......    17009.0
                      Altitude (miles)...    10568.9


          PLANETARY SYNCHRONOUS SATELLITE ALTITUDES

              MENU CHOICES

             ┌─────────────────┐
             │                 │
             │   E   Earth     │
             │   M   Mars      │
             │   O   Other     │
             │                 │
             │   Q   Quit      │
             │                 │
             └─────────────────┘

          Enter choice
            Q

          Have a nice orbit...
          **** STOP
```

FIGURE 4.7   *(continued)*

4.5 PROGRAMMING TIPS

DESIGN AND STYLE

1. **Keep on spacing.** Indent statements within IF-blocks, ELSE-blocks, and ELSE-IF blocks. Also, align corresponding block-IF, ELSE, ELSE IF, and END IF statements. It helps to identify the blocks, and improves readability. To convince yourself, try visualizing the nested-selection structure in Example 4.6 without indentation and proper alignment.

2. **Optimization note: Else-if structure versus sequential if-then structures.** Use the else-if structure over sequential if-then structures. It's more efficient and readable. See the note on page 141.

3. **Nested-selection structures.** If possible avoid these, since they can be difficult to follow, especially if there are many nesting levels (see the note on page 142). Some applications, however, require nested selections (see Exercise 8b).

4. **Error routines.** Reserve the ELSE-block of an else-if structure for an error routine whenever appropriate. In Example 4.7 it's appropriate as a means to "capture" incorrect menu selections; in Example 4.4 the error routine detects zero and negative order sizes.

COMMON ERRORS

1. **Logical expression lapses.** Logical expressions are great for trying out your debugging skills. Watch out for the following mental lapses:

   a. Missing periods around relational and logical operators, as in writing `AND` instead of `,AND,`   ☹

   b. Missing apostrophes around character constants, as in writing `CHOICE ,EQ, M` instead of `CHOICE ,EQ, 'M'`

   c. Using algebraic symbols in place of relational operators, as in writing `<` instead of `,LT,`   ☹

   d. Missing parentheses around logical expressions, as in

   ```
   IF A ,GT, B THEN
   ```
   ────── Missing parentheses   ☹

   instead of

   ```
   IF (A ,GT, B) THEN
   ```
   ☺

   Each of these gives a compile-time error.

2. **Incomplete compound logical expressions.** We can't tell you how often we've seen this compile-time error.

   ```
   IF (OPTION ,GE, 1 ,AND, ,LE, 5) THEN
   ```
   ────── Missing OPTION   ☹

   We tend to make this error because of the way we're accustomed to verbalizing this kind of algebraic relationship:

   ```
   1 ≤ OPTION ≤ 5
   ```

   "Option greater than or equal to 1 and less than or equal to 5."

3. **Hierarchy errors.** Pay attention to the hierarchy rule outlined on page 134. Inattention to this may give a logic error.

4. **Missing or extra END IF statement.** Remember that each block IF statement is "married" to a corresponding `END IF` statement. "Divorcing" these earns us a compile-time error.

5. **Nesting errors.** An inner selection structure nested within an outer selection structure must lie entirely within a block of the outer selection struc-

ture; otherwise, it's a compile-time error. You can pretty much avoid this problem by proper indentation and the alignment of ELSE, ELSE IF, and END IF statements with corresponding block IF statements. For instance, see the nested structure in Example 4.6.

6. **The ,EQ, hazard.** Take care in using the relational operator ,EQ, for comparing noninteger numeric values. Remember that the processor stores values as binary numbers; hence, many decimal values are stored as approximate rather than exact values. For example, the test described by

```
IF (A + B .EQ. C) THEN
```

may test false even when A stores 9.0, B stores 0.31, and C stores 9.31. We can account for this type of inexact representation by rewriting the logical expression as follows:

```
IF (ABS(A + B - C) ,LT, 1,0E-06) THEN
```

where   is the intrinsic function (Module A) that takes absolute values. As long as the error tolerance is less than 1.0×10^{-6}, the rewritten logical expression ensures "equality." If possible, avoid use of the ,EQ, operator with noninteger numeric values altogether. Use of an operator like ,GE,, however, may require the error tolerance "fixup."

7. **Test data selection.** When debugging, deliberately select test data that ensure execution flows through all IF-blocks, ELSE-blocks, and ELSE-IF blocks. For example, see our test run in Figure 4.7. This guarantees that all segments in the program are tested. The test data we give in the programming exercises at the end of the chapter are designed to push you in this debugging direction. Also, always confirm the correctness of test output by parallel hand calculations.

FOLLOW-UP EXERCISES

---

1. Indicate whether a true or false condition exists for each relational expression.

K	L	M	N
17	170	-57	33

a. K ,LT, L   d. N ,EQ, 33
b. L ,LE, N   e. K + N ,GE, L - M
c. M ,GT, -58   f. L/K ,NE, M + N

2. Suppose L stores 1, M stores 2, and N stores 3. Indicate true or false logical values for the following logical expressions.

a. .NOT. (L .LT. M)

b. L .GT. M .AND. M .EQ. N .OR. L .LE. N .AND. M .LT. N

c. L .GT. M .AND. (M .EQ. N .OR. L .LE. N) .AND. M .LT. N

d. L .GT. M .EQV. (M .EQ. N .OR. L .LE. N) .EQV. M .LT. N

e. L .GT. M .NEQV. (M .EQ. N .OR. L .LE. N) .NEQV. M .LT. N

3. Write code for each of the pseudocode-like descriptions below.

   a. If credits (CREDIT) taken are 12 or more, then tuition (TUIT) is $1200, update the full-time tuition sum (SUMFUL), and update the full-time student counter (KOUNTF); else tuition is $100 per credit, update the part-time tuition sum (SUMPAR), and update the part-time student counter (KOUNTP).

   b. If the last name (LAST) is CORE, then print "Harvey is my kind of guy."; else update the counter COUNT.

   c. If the last name is not CORE, then print "Where's Harvey?"; otherwise continue with execution.

   d. If $b^2 - 4ac$ is positive, then print "Two real roots exist"; if zero, then print "One repeated real root exists"; if negative, then print "No real roots exist".

   *e. If the reply is *not* Y or y or YES or yes or N or n or NO or no then print "Incorrect response; please try again"; otherwise continue with execution.

   *f. Print "Flight information (y/n)?"
   Input reply
   If reply is Y or y then
       Input date in form mm, dd where mm is a 2-digit
       month and dd is a 2-digit day of the month
       Input flight number as an integer value
   Else if reply is N or n
       Continue with execution
   Else
       Print "Please enter Y, y, N, or n."
   End if

4. **Logical variables and assignment statements.** As you might recall from Chapter 2, a logical variable is typed by using the LOGICAL statement, and stores either the logical value T or the logical value F. Moreover, we can assign logical values to logical variables using an assignment statement:

Logical Assignment Statement

Syntax:
> *Logical variable = logical expression*

Example:

```
GOOD = SEX .EQ. 'M' .OR. SEX .EQ. 'F'
```

One use of a logical variable is the simplification of IF-tests or ELSE-IF tests. For example, the IF- test in

```
IF (SEX .EQ. 'M' .OR. SEX .EQ. 'F') THEN
```

could be rewritten as

```
IF (GOOD) THEN
```

where the logical variable GOOD is assigned a value according to the sample assignment statement above.

Use this idea to rewrite the following.

a. Exercise 3d.

*__b.__ Exercise 3e.

*__c.__ Exercise 3f.

*__5.__ **Grade table lookup.** Students are assigned grades according to the following rule.

Score	Grade
90 or above	A
80 but less than 90	B
70 but less than 80	C
60 but less than 70	D
below 60	F

Write a program segment that prints the student's name (NAME), and grade (GRADE) based on the score (SCORE). Use the following selection structures for the table lookup.

a. Else-if structure

b. Sequential if-then structures

c. Nested if-then-else structures

Which approach do you prefer, and why?

*__6.__ **The .EQ. fixup.** Check out the problem with comparing real values as equals, as follows. (Remember the discussion in item 6 on page 151?)

a. Write a short program that inputs real values for A, B, and C, and prints according to the following design.

```
If A + B = C then
   Print "First logical expression equal"
Else
   Print "First logical expression not equal"
End if
If abs(A + B - C) < 1 x 10⁻⁶ then
   Print "Second logical expression equal"
Else
   Print "Second logical expression not equal"
End if
```

Try the following values for A, B, and C.

A	B	C
9.00	0.31	9.31
0.50	0.50	1.00
0.25	0.25	0.50
9.31	9.31	1.00

    b. Repeat part a for the logical expression A/B = C.

7. **Minimum value.** Let's try the following changes to Program MIN in Figure 4.4.
    a. How might we use the MIN function in Module A to find the minimum value?
    *b. Change the program to also print the maximum value and its associated description.

*8. **Microcomputer price quotations.** Let's try the following changes to Program MICRO in Figure 4.2.
    a. Incorporate the price table and else-if structure given in Example 4.4. Input the price table from a data file. Why is this hybrid design (both batch and inter-active) better than a strictly batch or strictly interactive design?
    b. Offer the user a menu with the following options.

        E   price quote for EBM micros
        M price quote for MacManzana micros
        S   price quote for Sol Microsystems micros
        X eXit

    Use the same order size breaks for these micros (as in Example 4.4). The price breaks are: $2500, $2200, $2000, and $1800 for EBM; $1500, $1300, $1100, and $1000 for MacManzana; and $5000, $4500, $4200, and $3900 for Sol.

9. **Microcomputer price quotations, once more.** Suppose we need not worry about an entry less than zero for order size. How can we simplify the else-if struc-ture in Example 4.4? Can we simplify as well in Example 4.5? Example 4.6?

10. **Synchronous satellite orbits.** Let's try the following changes to Program ORBIT in Figure 4.7.
    a. Change the program to allow both uppercase and lowercase menu choices.
    b. What changes would we need to make to offer numeric menu choices?

        1 Earth
        2 Mars
        3 Other
        9 Quit

    *c. Add Jupiter to the menu, and make any other needed changes in the program. Does ordering within the menu or in the else-if structure matter?
    *d. Add a DO-loop so that the menu is reoffered after the output report for each planet. Assume we never have more than 10 menu selections in any one run.

11. **Revisit: HC ENGINEering.** Rework Program ENG1 in Figure 2.1 by letting the program determine engine size (cc) based on the engine name. The program inputs all three engine names and corresponding sizes (cc) from a data file, and then inputs the desired engine name, price, and units sold interactively. Output is the same. Engine size (ci) is still calculated from its metric equivalent, but the latter is now determined by a selection structure that uses engine names in the test conditions. For example, given the desired engine name Baby Two, the program executes a selection structure, thereby selecting 7000 cc as the relevant engine size.

12. **Revisit: HC ENGINEoil.** Rework Exercise 9 in Chapter 3 to print a report of the coordinate of the Home Base that minimizes total distance. Don't print results for nonoptimal coordinates. We just get one report . . . the optimal one.

13. **Revisit: Bank savings.** Rework Exercise 17 in Chapter 3 as follows. Offer a menu with three choices: the first compounding formula, the second compounding formula, and quit. For each choice, interactively input appropriate data, and print the accumulated funds. Use the same test data as the original problem.

14. **Revisit: Econometric model.** Rework Exercise 18 in Chapter 3 as follows. Use the same DO-loops described in parts a and b, but omit the output tables. Instead, print a summary table that gives the name of each college, its maximum revenue, and the corresponding enrollment. In the table foot, print total maximum revenue and enrollment for the entire state system.

15. **SAT report.** Write and debug a program that uses the data file shown below to generate the described SAT report.

Data File

Name	Class Code[a]	Math SAT	Verbal SAT
Test 1	2	550	630
Test 2	1	500	590
Test 3	1	620	750
Test 4	3	575	520
Test 5	2	620	530
Test 6	1	750	710
Test 7	4	470	420
Test 8	4	450	490
Test 9	2	520	550
Test 10	3	540	520

[a] 1 = Freshman   2 = Sophomore   3 = Junior   4 = Senior

SAT Report

Class	Students		Math	Mean SAT........... Verbal	Combined
Freshman	xxxx		xxx	xxx	xxxx
Sophomore	↓		↓	↓	↓
Junior					
Senior					
All Classes	xxxxx		xxx	xxx	xxxx

16. **Quality control.** In recent years industrial engineering applications in the factory have stressed quality control as a means of regaining a competitive edge in the marketplace. Consider the mass manufacturing of memory chips by three types of robots: R2D2, R2D3, and R2D4. Suppose random batches of chips manufactured by each of these robots are selected for failure tests. A sample data file for 5 batches is given below. For example, 1000 memory chips were tested in the first batch (processed by R2D3), and 4 were found defective.

Data File

Robot	Batch Size	Defects
R2D3	1000	4
R2D2	3000	15
R2D2	500	7
R2D4	300	0
R2D3	2000	6

a. Write and debug a program that inputs the given data file and prints the following quality control report.

Quality Control Report

Robot	Total Chips	Total Defective	Percent Defective
R2D2	xxxxxx	xxxxx	xx.xx
R2D3	↓	↓	↓
R2D4			
Overall	xxxxxxxx	xxxxxx	xx.xx

b. Suppose that results are graded according to the following criteria: Excellent if 0% defective; Good if less than 0.5% defective; Poor if 0.5% and above defective. Add another column to the output report that grades each robot, as well as the overall results.

17. **Epidemiological forecasting.** Epidemiology is a branch of medicine that specializes in the causes, prediction, and control of epidemics. Epidemics due to communicable diseases, if left unchecked, can grow in ways that are often predictable by one or more mathematical models in statistics, biology, and diffusion models with differential equations (systems of equations having derivatives or instantaneous rates of change that describe the behavior of diffusion or spreading processes). Write and debug a program that offers a menu of growth formulas, as follows.

> 1 Simple compound growth
> 2 Simple exponential growth
> 3 Limited exponential growth
> 4 Quit

Simple compound growth is given by

$$F = S(1 + r)^t$$

simple exponential growth by

$$F = Se^{rt}$$

and limited exponential growth by the logistic equation

$$F = \frac{ke^{rt}}{k/S - 1 + e^{rt}}$$

where F = Forecast of number infected at time t
S = Starting number infected (at $t = 0$)
r = Rate of growth in the infected population
t = Time units from starting time, where starting time is $t = 0$
k = Carrying capacity, or upper limit (asymptote) on size of infected
 population as $t \to \infty$

Write and debug a program that offers the menu, inputs appropriate data based on the menu selection, and prints the forecast table shown below, where T is an upper limit on time (as input by the user).

Forecast Table

Time	Number Infected
0	xxxxxxxx
1	
2	
.	
.	
.	
T	

Use the following test data: $S = 35{,}000$; $r = 1.15$ (115% per year); $k = 200{,}000{,}000$; $T = 20$ years.[2]

18. **Fibonacci numbers.** In 1202 Leonardo of Pisa (nicknamed Fibonacci, or Son of Bonacci) solved the following theoretical problem. Consider a starting pair of rabbits (male and female, of course) that produces a new pair at the end of one month. Allowing one month for maturation, each mature pair begets another pair of rabbits each month. How many pairs of rabbits will we have after one month, two months, and so on? Starting at time zero, there are no pairs of rabbits. Just after time zero, however, we have a newborn pair, which gives us one (mature) pair at the end of the first month. At the end of the second month, we still only have one pair. This pair did its thing, however, and we have a newly arrived pair at the beginning of the third month, giving us two pairs at the end of the third month. At the end of the fourth month, we have three pairs—the original, their firstborns, and their secondborns. In the fifth month, we have two newly arrived pairs, one pair from the original pair (the still-at-it grandparents), and the other pair from the firstborns. This gives us five pairs at the end of five months. The story continues, giving us the sequence of Fibonacci numbers 0, 1, 1, 2, 3, 5, 8, 13, 21, . . . Do you see a pattern? Each number (starting with the third) is the sum of the immediately preceding two numbers. Interestingly, it turns out that these numbers have uses other than animal husbandry, particularly in algorithms that search for optimal solutions in applied mathematics and in stock market cycles called Elliot Waves. We will not get that esoteric, so try your hand at a program that inputs the starting and ending positions in the sequence and prints the corresponding Fibonacci numbers. For example, if we input positions 6 through 8, then we print the following output.

Position	Fibonacci Number
6	5
7	8
8	13

Try a run for each of the following position ranges: 1 to 20; 6 to 8; 1 to 2; 2 to 5.

19. **Quadratic roots.** A quadratic equation is defined by

$$y = ax^2 + bx + c$$

where a, b, and c are its coefficients. Many mathematical applications require the "roots" of this equation. By definition, a root is a value of x that when substituted into the equation yields a value of zero for y. The following familiar *quadratic formula* determines the appropriate roots.

---

[2] The data for S and r are Center for Disease Control estimates of the number of current (at the end of 1987) diagnosed AIDS cases in the United States. You might want to compare these predictions to those based on Public Health Service data: $S = 63{,}726$, $r = 0.418$. By the way, don't take the predictions seriously here; our models are far too simplistic for predicting the diffusion of AIDS.

$$x = \frac{-b \pm (b^2 - 4ac)^{1/2}}{2a}$$

Run a program to calculate and print quadratic roots for the following input values of a, b, and c.

a	b	c
5.00	6.00	1.35
1.00	10.00	−1.00
1.00	2.00	1.00
7.00	4.00	2.00

Use a DO-loop to process these values. Your program should have three separate branches within the loop, depending on the value of the expression $b^2 - 4ac$. If this expression is negative, have the computer print "No real roots"; if the expression equals zero exactly, evaluate the single root using $x = -b/(2a)$; if the expression is positive, use the above quadratic formula to calculate the two roots.

20. **Factorials.** The factorial of a number n (written $n!$) is a useful calculation in many problems in mathematics and statistics. By definition $n!$ is given by the product

$$n \cdot (n - 1) \cdot (n - 2) \cdots \cdots 2 \cdot 1$$

For example, if the value of n is 5, then

$$5! = 5 \cdot 4 \cdot 3 \cdot 2 \cdot 1 = 120$$

Note that $0!$ is defined to have a value of 1 and $n!$ is undefined if $n < 0$.
   a. Run a program that inputs n and calculates and prints $n!$ What are the factorials of 1, 5, 10, 25, 50, and 100?
   b. Did you get overflow in part a? By trial and error determine the maximum value of n whose factorial your computer can process. Then design your program to check each input of n to make sure it's within the allowable range of zero to the maximum value. If it's not, print a message to the user to this effect and then process the next input value.
   c. Ensure that your program is capable of printing out the correct value of $0!$ should a user input zero for n.
   d. Design an "outer" loop in your program for the purpose of processing k different values of n. For example, the data in part a would require six iterations of this loop.
   e. Instead of the outer loop in part d, design an outer loop that processes values of n from some initial value ($N1$) to some terminal value ($N2$) in increments of $N3$. Print a table of n values and their factorials. Try two test runs: the first processes n from 1 to 10 in increments of 1; the second processes n from 10 to 50 in increments of 5.

21. **Linear regression.** Linear regression is a curve-fitting procedure for linearly associating a dependent variable (the y-variable) with one or more independent

variables (the x-variables). In the two-variable case, we express this association by the linear equation

$$y = a + bx$$

where y = dependent or criterion variable
x = independent or predictor variable
a = regression coefficient (intercept)
b = regression coefficient (slope)

Given a set of (x, y) observations, the following least squares equations determine the coefficients that minimize the sum of squared deviations of observed y-values from predicted y-values (as predicted by the regression line).

$$b = \frac{n \Sigma yx - (\Sigma y)(\Sigma x)}{n \Sigma x^2 - (\Sigma x)^2}$$

$$a = \frac{\Sigma y - b \Sigma x}{n}$$

where n = number of observations and summation is taken over all observations—for example,

$$\Sigma x \quad \text{is equivalent to} \quad \sum_{i=1}^{n} x_i$$

The coefficient of correlation is one of many measures of how well the linear model fits the observed data, as follows.

$$r = \frac{n \Sigma yx - (\Sigma y)(\Sigma x)}{\sqrt{[n \Sigma y^2 - (\Sigma y)^2][n \Sigma x^2 - (\Sigma x)^2]}}$$

where the sign on r is the same as the sign on b, negative when y and x move inversely, and positive otherwise.

a. Write and debug a program that processes the following data file.

Stock Market Data File

Observation[a]	Magellan Fund[b]	Wall Street Week Index[c]	Dow Jones Industrials Index[d]
1	$40.10	+3	1939
2	40.14	+2	1911
3	40.90	+4	1956
4	40.40	+5	1904
5	41.69	+4	1958
6	41.26	+4	1910
7	42.39	+6	1903
8	42.94	+3	2015
9	43.53	+1	2023
10	44.65	+1	2058

Observation[a]	Magellan Fund[b]	Wall Street Week Index[c]	Dow Jones Industrials Index[d]
11	44.54	+1	2035
12	45.47	0	2087
13	43.97	−1	1979
14	44.10	0	1988
15	45.72	+2	2090

[a]Actual week-ending readings for first 15 weeks in 1988.
[b]A popular stock mutual fund managed by Fidelity Investments.
[c]Popular predictor of stock market behavior, as announced every Friday evening on the PBS
 show *Wall Street Week*.
[d]Stock market index of 30 large ("blue chip") firms; the most widely quoted index.

Interactively offer the user menus that allow the selection of an independent and a dependent variable, as follows.

    Select Dependent Variable
        1   Magellan Fund
        2   WSW Index
        3   DJI Index

    Select Independent Variable
        1   Magellan Fund
        2   WSW Index
        3   DJI Index

Design an output report that prints a, b, and r. In your test runs, regress Magellan (the dependent variable) against WSW Index in the first run, and Magellan against DJI Index in the second run. Which variable, WSW Index or DJI Index, is more highly correlated to the price behavior of the Magellan Fund? Predict the price of Magellan if the DJI Index hits 3000.

b. We can use the linear two-variable regression model to fit the following exponential model.

$$y = ab^x$$

where a and b are coefficients, as before. If we take the logarithm of both sides, we have

$$\log y = \log a + (\log b)x$$

Rewriting this as

$$y = A + Bx$$

we see that this is the standard linear model with

$$Y = \log y$$
$$A = \log a$$
$$B = \log b$$

Taking antilogs of Y, A, and B gets us back to the respective representations for y, a, and b. Although we can use either base 10 or natural logarithms, we prefer natural logs, since the antilog is simply given by the exponential intrinsic function, EXP.

Modify the program in part a to offer the user the choice between the linear and exponential models. If the latter is chosen, then the same formulas work with the logarithms of actual y-values (the x-values are not transformed). Include both sets of coefficients in the output: A, B, a, and b. Answer the same questions as in part a. Which fit is best for these data, the linear model or the exponential model?

5

REPETITION STRUCTURES

We defined the repetition structure in Chapter 3, and introduced a popular loop called the DO-loop. This chapter completes the treatment of loops by defining and illustrating variations of pretest loops and post-test loops, including the eof loops that detect "end-of-file" or "out-of-data" conditions.

5.1 PRETEST LOOPS

A **pretest loop** is the repetition structure defined in Figure 5.1. Note that the loop control test condition precedes the loop body, hence the term pretest. If the test condition is formulated so that the body is repeated while the condition tests true, then the pretest loop is called a **while structure.** The while structure thus says repeat while true.

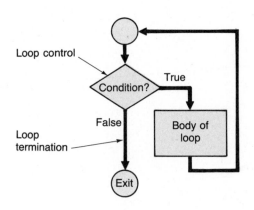

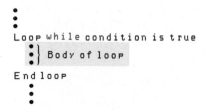

FIGURE 5.1   Pretest loop as while structure

GO TO STATEMENT

To implement the while structure in ANSI FORTRAN 77, we need to use the GO TO statement, as follows.

GO TO Statement

Syntax:

   GO TO *statement label*

Example:

    GO TO 100

The statement label is either a one- to five-digit statement label, as in the example, or an integer variable assigned through an ASSIGN statement, as described in Module B on page 509. In the example above, execution of the GO TO statement transfers control to the statement labeled 100.

WHILE STRUCTURE IMPLEMENTATION

The while structure in FORTRAN 77 is implemented as follows.

While Structure

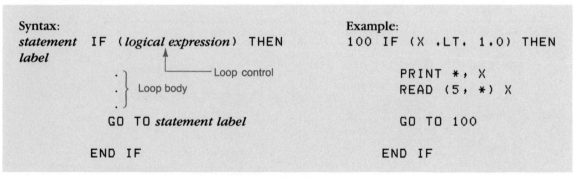

Syntax:

statement label   IF (*logical expression*) THEN

 .   Loop control
 . } Loop body
 .

  GO TO *statement label*

 END IF

Example:

100 IF (X .LT. 1.0) THEN

  PRINT *, X
  READ (5, *) X

  GO TO 100

 END IF

Note that the while structure does not have an explicit implementation in FORTRAN 77, although some FORTRAN implementations do (see Exercise 11). Thus, we simulate the while structure by using the block IF statement, GO TO statement, and END IF statement. The test condition is expressed in the logical expression. While the logical expression tests true, the loop body gets executed; however, when the logical expression tests false, the loop body is bypassed and execution continues at the first executable statement following the END IF statement. In the example, the body gets repeated (X is printed and read) while X stores less than 1.0. As soon as X stores 1.0 or above, the test condition is false and looping terminates (the next executable statement after END IF is executed).

```
          PROGRAM TEMP3
     * * * * * * * * * * * * * * * * * * * * * * * * * * * * * * * * *
     *                                                               *
     *        Temperature Conversions:   Version 3.0                 *
     *                                                               *
     *          Inputs degrees Fahrenheit while desired              *
     *          Calculates degrees Celsius                           *
     *          Outputs degrees Fahrenheit and Celsius               *
     *                                                               *
     *          Key:                                                 *
     *              C........ Degrees Celsius                        *
     *              F........ Degrees Fahrenheit                     *
     *              LINE..... Output double line                     *
     *              SPACE.... Output space                           *
     *                                                               *
     * * * * * * * * * * * * * * * * * * * * * * * * * * * * * * * * *
     *————————
     *  Type names
     *————————
          CHARACTER LINE*50, SPACE*30
          REAL C,F
     *————————
     *  Initialize
     *————————
          LINE   = '============================='
          SPACE  = ' '
     *————————
     *  Print title/message and input first F
     *————————
          PRINT *, 'TEMPERATURE CONVERSIONS'
          PRINT *, LINE
          PRINT *, 'Enter -999 to end program'
          PRINT *, LINE
          PRINT *
          PRINT *, 'Enter degrees Fahrenheit'          <————— Read-in just before loop
          READ *,  F
     *————————
     *  Loop while nearest integer part in F not equal -999
     *————————
     100  IF ( .NOT. (NINT( F ) .EQ. -999) ) THEN      <————— While structure
                                                              └── Sentinel
              C = 5.0/9.0 * (F - 32.0)

              PRINT *, SPACE, LINE
              PRINT *, SPACE, 'Fahrenheit......', NINT( F )
              PRINT *, SPACE, 'Celsius.........', NINT( C )
              PRINT *, SPACE, LINE

              PRINT *, 'Enter degrees Fahrenheit'      <————— Read-in at end of loop body
              READ *,  F

              GO TO 100

          END IF
     *————————
     *  End while loop
     *————————
     *  Print farewell
     *————————
          PRINT *
          PRINT *, SPACE, 'Stay kool...'
     *————————
          END
```

FIGURE 5.2   **Temperature program with while structure**

```
TEMPERATURE CONVERSIONS
════════════════════════════════
Enter -999 to end program
════════════════════════════════

Enter degrees Fahrenheit
32
                                    ════════════════════════════════
                                    Fahrenheit.....        32
                                    Celsius........         0
                                    ════════════════════════════════

Enter degrees Fahrenheit
212
                                    ════════════════════════════════
                                    Fahrenheit.....       212
                                    Celsius........       100
                                    ════════════════════════════════

Enter degrees Fahrenheit
80
                                    ════════════════════════════════
                                    Fahrenheit.....        80
                                    Celsius........        27
                                    ════════════════════════════════

Enter degrees Fahrenheit
-999
          └─── Sentinel            Stay kool...
```

FIGURE 5.2 (*continued*)

NOTE As is true in all *proper* control structures, the flow of execution enters the loop structure through a *single* entry point at the *top* and exits *down* at the bottom through a *single* exit point. The selection structure described in Figure 5.1 clearly shows this top-down structured programming philosophy. In the FOR-TRAN 77 implementation, the single entry point at the top is the block IF statement, and the single exit point at the bottom is the END IF statement.

EXAMPLE 5.1

TEMPERATURE CONVERSIONS AS WHILE STRUCTURE

In Figure 3.8 we illustrated a temperature program that calculated and printed a table of Fahrenheit and Celsius temperatures, where F-temperatures varied systematically over a range entered by the user. The program in Figure 5.2 is a variation where temperatures do not behave systematically. In this case, the user enters F-temperatures "on the fly," in any unsystematic or spontaneous way. The loop repeats the input, calculation, and output of temperatures while the F-temperature does not equal −999. As soon as we input −999, we achieve loop exit, a farewell message is printed, and execution ends.

NOTE 1   The −999 in the program is called a **sentinel;** its purpose is loop termination through a data value that's unique. In general, select a sentinel that would not occur other than by design or choice.

NOTE 2   In words, the logical expression for the loop test reads "Not equal to −999." Since F stores real values, we need to ensure that use of the .EQ. operator does not give us a false result due to an inexact real value when F stores −999. We accomplish this by using the NINT intrinsic function, which returns the nearest integer part in F. (See the discussion on the ".EQ. hazard" in Section 4.5.)

NOTE 3   This type of loop design often requires read-in just before the loop and an identical read-in at the end of the loop body. In the TEMP3 program, the first F-value is read in just before the loop; subsequent F-values are read in at the end of the loop body. This is necessary because the first action on entering the while structure is the loop test based on the value in F; hence, we need to read in the first F-value just before the loop. All other F-values are read at the end of the loop body, which further ensures that the sentinel will not be processed as a "normal" value. In other words, when the sentinel is entered, the next action is the loop test, which immediately gives us loop exit. See Exercise 1b for a traditional, more intuitive but less desirable approach. A posttest loop design is another alternative, which we illustrate in the next section.   ◼

5.2 POSTTEST LOOPS

A **posttest loop** is the repetition structure defined in Figure 5.3. Note that the loop control test condition follows the loop body, hence the term posttest. If the test condition is formulated so that the body is repeated until the condition tests true, then the posttest loop is called an **until structure.** The until structure thus says repeat until true

LOGICAL IF STATEMENT

The following statement is used to implement posttest loops in FORTRAN 77.

Logical IF Statement

Syntax:

     IF (*logical expression*) *executable statement*

Example:

     IF (X .LT. 1.0) GO TO 100

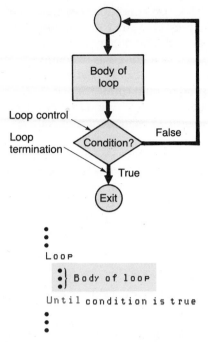

FIGURE 5.3   **Posttest loop as until structure**

If the logical expression is true, then the executable statement immediately to the right of the parentheses is executed; else the executable statement is bypassed and the next executable statement following the logical IF statement is executed. In the example, if the logical expression X .LT. 1.0 tests true, then the next statement executed is the one labeled 100; otherwise, execution of GO TO 100 is bypassed, and execution continues below the logical IF statement.

POSTTEST LOOP IMPLEMENTATION

A posttest loop in FORTRAN 77 is implemented as follows.

Posttest Loop

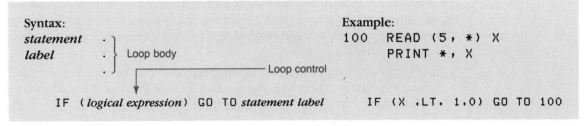

The test condition is expressed in the logical expression. As long as the logical expression tests true, the loop body starting at the statement label gets executed via the GO TO statement; however, when the logical expression tests false, loop exit is achieved as execution "drops" to the next executable statement following the logical IF statement. In the example, the body gets repeated (X is read and printed) until X stores 1.0 or more. As soon as X stores 1.0 or above, the test condition is false and looping terminates (the next executable statement after the logical IF statement is executed).

NOTE   The until structure does not have an explicit implementation in FORTRAN 77, although some FORTRAN implementations do (see Exercise 12). Strictly speaking, the example above is simply a posttest loop, not an until structure, since loop exit is achieved when the test condition is *false.* The until structure achieves loop exit when the test condition is *true.*

EXAMPLE 5.2

TEMPERATURE CONVERSIONS AS POSTTEST LOOP

The temperature program in Figure 5.4 illustrates a posttest loop implementation. Note the following.

1. The program continues looping until the user responds no to the question "More temperatures?" The use of yes/no responses is very common in commercial interactive programs.

2. The character variable MORE stores the user's yes/no response. Note that we declared this variable with a length of 1. In effect we're only interested in the first letter typed in by the user. In the illustrated run, the full response yes actually got stored as y (the characters es were ignored on input). Thus, responses like y, yes, yep, and yo are interpreted as "yes" by the program.

3. The READ statement that inputs the response uses the A edit descriptor for editing the value that gets stored in MORE. Format-directed character input allows character-value input without the surrounding quotation marks. See Table C.1 in Module C.

4. Take a look at the logical expression in the program. Both upper- and lowercase "yes" responses are allowed, which bypasses the capitalization problem of incorrectly interpreting a response solely based on capitalization. In our sample run we entered both uppercase and lowercase letters, to illustrate our point.

5. Any response other than Y or y is interpreted as "No" by the program (the logical expression is false), giving us a loop exit. In Exercise 8 we ask you to implement an error routine that traps incorrect y/n responses. ■

```
      PROGRAM TEMP4
* * * * * * * * * * * * * * * * * * * * * * * * * * * * * * * * * * *
*                                                                   *
*        Temperature Conversions:   Version 4.0                     *
*                                                                   *
*          Inputs degrees Fahrenheit until no more desired          *
*          Calculates degrees Celsius                               *
*          Outputs degrees Fahrenheit and Celsius                   *
*                                                                   *
*          Key:                                                     *
*             C........ Degrees Celsius                             *
*             F........ Degrees Fahrenheit                          *
*             LINE..... Output double line                          *
*             MORE..... Stores y/n to question "More temperatures?" *
*             SPACE.... Output space                                *
*                                                                   *
* * * * * * * * * * * * * * * * * * * * * * * * * * * * * * * * * * *
*
*  Type names
*
      CHARACTER LINE*50, MORE, SPACE*30
      REAL C,F
*
*  Initialize
*
      LINE  = '=================================='
      SPACE = ' '
*
*  Print title
*
      PRINT *, LINE
      PRINT *, 'TEMPERATURE CONVERSIONS'
      PRINT *, LINE
      PRINT *
*
*  Loop
*
100   PRINT *, 'Enter degrees Fahrenheit'
      READ *,  F

      C = 5.0/9.0 * (F - 32.0)

      PRINT *, SPACE, LINE
      PRINT *, SPACE, 'Fahrenheit.....', NINT( F )
      PRINT *, SPACE, 'Celsius........', NINT( C )
      PRINT *, SPACE, LINE

      PRINT *
      PRINT *, 'More temperatures? (y/n)'
      READ '( A )', MORE
      PRINT *

   IF ( MORE .EQ. 'Y'  .OR.  MORE .EQ. 'y' ) GO TO 100
*
*  Until response is no
*
*  Print farewell
*
      PRINT *
      PRINT *, SPACE, 'Stay kool...'
*
      END
```

— Posttest loop

FIGURE 5.4   **Temperature program with posttest loop (*continued on next page*)**

```
═══════════════════════════════════
TEMPERATURE CONVERSIONS
═══════════════════════════════════

 Enter degrees Fahrenheit
32
                              ═══════════════════════════
                              Fahrenheit.....        32
                              Celsius........         0
                              ═══════════════════════════

 More temperatures? (y/n)
Y

 Enter degrees Fahrenheit
212
                              ═══════════════════════════
                              Fahrenheit.....       212
                              Celsius........       100
                              ═══════════════════════════

 More temperatures? (y/n)
yes

 Enter degrees Fahrenheit
80
                              ═══════════════════════════
                              Fahrenheit.....        80
                              Celsius........        27
                              ═══════════════════════════

 More temperatures? (y/n)
n

                              Stay kool...
```

FIGURE 5.4   *(continued)*

5.3 END-OF-FILE (EOF) LOOPS

An **end-of-file (eof) loop** is a pretest loop that detects an "out-of-data" condition, thereby terminating repetitions of the loop. Generally, it's the preferred design for the batch processing of data files, as we illustrate shortly.

READ STATEMENT WITH ADDITIONAL SPECIFIERS

Eof loops in FORTRAN 77 are implemented with the following form of the READ statement.

READ Statement: More Specifiers

Syntax:

READ ⟨ *external unit identifier, format identifier, other specifiers* ⟩ *input list*

Example:

```
READ (5, *, END = 200) NAME, VALUE
```

The external unit identifier is an integer expression for one of the system's input units (terminal, disk drive, and so on) or an * for the system's standard input unit (usually the keyboard). The example uses 5 as the external unit identifier, which is a disk drive on our system. The format identifier identifies an input format (Module C) or is an * for list-directed input. The example uses list-directed input. Other specifiers is a list of additional specifiers delimited by commas. In Chapter 9 we give a complete list of other specifiers in FORTRAN 77. For now, however, let's consider two relevant specifiers for eof loops (Exercise 9 considers a third specifier).

Eof Specifier

Syntax:

END = *statement label*

Example:

```
END = 200
```

I/O Status Specifier

Syntax:

IOSTAT = *integer name*

Example:

```
IOSTAT = STATUS
```

The **eof specifier** is used to exit the loop structure when the processor encounters an eof condition during read-in. An eof condition means that an attempted read-in of data finds an end-of-file condition, as follows:

In a data file. Execution of the READ statement encounters either no more data or an endfile record (Chapter 9).

During interactive input. The user enters a special keyboard sequence that signals the eof condition (often the Control key in combination with some other key). What key sequence signals an eof condition on your system?

In the example, the eof specifier $END = 200$ means that statement 200 is executed immediately after an eof condition.

The **input/output status specifier** works as follows:

- The integer name is a variable or array element name (**Chapter 7**) that is assigned a zero value if neither an error condition nor an eof condition is encountered by the processor during read-in.
- The integer name is assigned a processor-dependent positive integer value if an error condition is encountered during read-in. For example, a character value in a numeric field would give an error condition during read-in.
- The integer name is assigned a processor-dependent negative integer value if an eof condition is encountered, and no error condition is encountered.

For example, the I/O status specifier $IOSTAT = STATUS$ would result in the following assignments to STATUS while the READ statement is executed: 0 if no error or eof condition; positive value if error condition; negative value if eof condition and no error condition.

EOF LOOP IMPLEMENTATIONS

We show two eof loop implementations in FORTRAN 77, depending on whether we use the $END =$ specifier or the $IOSTAT =$ specifier.

Eof Loop with END =

Syntax:

```
First
statement      READ (..., END = second statement label) input list
label          .
               .                                    Loop control
               .
               GO TO first statement label
Second
statement   CONTINUE
label
```

Loop body

Example:

```
100 READ (5, *, END = 200) X
       PRINT *, X
       GO TO 100
200 CONTINUE
```

This eof loop version repeats the body while no eof condition is encountered. As soon as the eof condition is encountered, loop exit is achieved at the `CONTINUE` statement. Note that the `CONTINUE` statement has the same statement label as that used in the `END =` specifier. In the example, values in `X` are repeatedly input from a data file and printed while there's no eof condition. When the eof condition is encountered, loop exit is achieved at statement 200, the `CONTINUE` statement.

NOTE 1 We use the `CONTINUE` statement as the first statement following the loop, or the statement to which control is transferred at loop exit. This is a matter of preference since we can use any executable statement. We prefer the `CONTINUE` statement because it's more general in the sense that future changes to the program could affect the statements immediately after the loop structure, thereby requiring a change in the statement to which control is transferred. By using a `CONTINUE` statement, we decouple loop exit from what follows the loop structure.

NOTE 2 The `READ` statement includes both the action of reading data and the loop control test through the `END =` specifier. This means the eof loop is like a pretest loop, since the test condition for loop exit is at the beginning of the repetition structure; however, since the `READ` statement performs two functions, it's also part of the loop body. We indent the `READ` statement as part of the loop body, although that's a matter of preference.

Eof Loop with IOSTAT =

Syntax:

```
Statement   READ (..., IOSTAT = integer variable) input list
label       IF (integer variable .EQ. 0) THEN          ← Loop control
            .
            .                                     } Main loop body
            .
            ELSE IF (integer variable .LT. 0) THEN
            .
            .                                     } Exit routine
            .
            STOP  ← Stops execution
            ELSE
            .
            .                                     } Error routine
            .
            END IF
            GO TO statement label
```

Example:

```
100 READ (5, *, IOSTAT = CODE) X
    IF (CODE .EQ. 0) THEN
        PRINT *, X
    ELSE IF (CODE .LT. 0) THEN
        PRINT *, 'End of file'
        STOP
    ELSE
        PRINT *, 'Input error'
    END IF
    GO TO 100
```

This eof loop operates as follows when the READ statement is executed.

- If there is no eof or error condition, then the main loop body is executed. We say "main" because the READ statement itself and the entire else-if structure are technically part of the loop body. The next statement executed is the GO TO statement, which repeats the process. In our example, the read-in of a value into X would give a processor-assigned zero value in CODE. Thus, the IF-block would be entered, the value in X would be printed, GO TO 100 would be executed, and the process would repeat.

- If there's an eof condition, then the exit routine within the ELSE-IF block is executed. The exit routine is the set of statements that normally would be executed following an eof loop like that given by the END = design. In our example, the processor assigns a negative value to CODE when the eof condition is encountered, thus printing the message "End of file" within the ELSE-IF block, followed by execution of the STOP statement.

- If there's an error condition, the processor assigns a positive value in CODE, which means the error routine within the ELSE-block is executed. In our example, the message "Input error" would be printed if an error condition is encountered, as in having a text value in the input field when a numeric value is expected. The GO TO 100 statement is executed following the ELSE- block, and the process repeats.

NOTE   The eof loop with an IOSTAT = specifier has the advantage of a built-in input error routine, but at the expense of loop structure complexity. Moreover, loop exit is not achieved at a point following the loop structure; rather "loop exit" is within the *exit routine* that technically resides within the loop body. Thus, it's a technical violation of the top-down-one-entry-one-exit philosophy expressed in the NOTE on page •••. From the point of view of structured programming, the second (IOSTAT =) eof design is somewhat (but not totally) corrupt. For a really corrupt alternative that's commonly used, check out the approach in Exercise 9.

WARNING   Make sure that the exit routine includes the STOP statement; otherwise, we have an infinite loop.

EXAMPLE 5.3

MINIMUM VALUE WITH EOF LOOP USING END =

In Figure 4.4 we illustrated a program that processed a data file and printed the minimum value and its associated description. The data file was processed using a DO-loop. Figure 5.5 illustrates the eof loop variation based on the eof specifier. Note the following differences.

```
      PROGRAM MIN2
* * * * * * * * * * * * * * * * * * * * * * * * * * * * * * * * *
*                                                               *
*        Minimum Value With EOF Loop Using END =                *
*                                                               *
*          Inputs data set title, names and associated real values *
*          Determines minimum value and its associated name     *
*          Outputs minimum value, associated name, records processed *
*                                                               *
*          Data file structure:                                 *
*            Title in quotes                                    *
*            1st name in quotes          value                  *
*            2nd name in quotes          value                  *
*            ...                                                *
*                                                               *
*          Key:                                                 *
*            MINNAM... Name of item whose value is the minimum  *
*            MINVAL... Minimum value                            *
*            NAME..... Descriptive name of item                 *
*            RECORD... Record number                            *
*            TITLE.... Title of data set                        *
*            VALUE.... Value of item                            *
*                                                               *
* * * * * * * * * * * * * * * * * * * * * * * * * * * * * * * * *
```

```
* Type names
*————————
      CHARACTER MINNAM*40, NAME*40, TITLE*80
      INTEGER   RECORD
      REAL      MINVAL, VALUE
```

```
* Initialize
*————————
      RECORD = 1
```

```
* Read title and first record
*————————————————
      READ (5,*) TITLE
      READ (5,*) MINNAM, MINVAL
```

```
* Loop while not eof
*————————————————
```

```
  100   READ (5, *, END = 200 ) NAME, VALUE        ←———— Eof loop

        RECORD = RECORD + 1                        ←———— END = loop control

        IF (VALUE .LT. MINVAL) THEN
          MINVAL = VALUE
          MINNAM = NAME
        END IF

        GO TO 100

  200 CONTINUE ←                                   ———— Loop exit
```

```
* End loop
*————————
* Print results
*————————
      PRINT *, TITLE
      PRINT *,
      PRINT *, ' Minimum value............',      MINVAL
      PRINT *, ' Associated description...  ', MINNAM
      PRINT *
      PRINT *, ' Records processed........',       RECORD
```

```
      END
```

FIGURE 5.5   **Minimum value with eof loop using END = (*continued on next page*)**

```
                                         ┌────── Data file
                                    ╱─────┘
'Benchmork test speeds in seconds, PC Magazine, 10/13/87, p. 332'
'IBM PC AT (8 MHz)'              35.60
'Mitsubishi MP 286'             28.12
'FiveStar FS-286'               27.98
'Wang 280'                      28.01
'IndTech 5191'                  22.23
'ARC Turbo 12'                  23.56
'PC Designs GV-286'             18.82
'Standard 286/12'               23.16
'Compaq Deskpro 386 (16 MHz)'   15.50

                                         ┌────── Output
                                    ╱─────┘
Benchmork test speeds in seconds, PC Magazine, 10/13/87, p. 332

    Minimum value............     15.5000
    Associated description...     Compaq Deskpro 386 (16 MHz)

    Records processed........        9
```

FIGURE 5.5   (*continued*)

_____

1. Compare the current data file with the original on page 130. See the difference? The current data file does not need the number of microcomputer
   records that follow (9 in the original data file).

2. The number of records in the data file is equivalent to the number of loop
   repetitions, except for preliminary records like titles and initialization
   records. Thus, if we wish a record count, we include a record counter in the
   loop body, as illustrated in program MIN2 by the statement

   ```
   RECORD = RECORD + 1
   ```

   We initialized RECORD to 1 (rather than zero) because we used the first
   record (the PC AT record) to initialize MINNAM and MINVAL.

3. In Figure 5.5 when the loop iterates for the 9th time, an eof condition is
   encountered and execution control is transferred out of the loop structure
   to statement 200.   ■

NOTE   The eof loop is the method of choice in commercial applications that use data
       files. The DO-loop approach requires record keeping within the data file for the
       number of records that the DO-loop is to process, since this value is the *DO-limit*
       in the DO statement. The eof approach does not require preknowledge of the
       number of records in the file. In applications where the number of records
       changes often (perhaps even real time in applications like airline reservation sys-

tems and laboratory experiments) the eof approach bypasses the error-prone need to include the number of records in the file.

EXAMPLE 5.4

MINIMUM VALUE WITH EOF LOOP USING IOSTAT =

Figure 5.6 shows the second eof loop approach. Note the following.

1. At each execution of the READ statement, the integer variable STATUS will store a zero (when read-in processes an error-free record), a negative value (when read-in encounters an eof condition), or a positive value (when read-in encounters an error condition). In our sample run, records 2–6 (excluding the title record and first or initialization record, which do not get processed by the loop) are processed error free, giving zero in STATUS, with subsequent executions of the main loop body within the IF-block. At the 7th record, an input error is encountered (missing quotes surrounding the string), thus giving a positive value in STATUS, and subsequent execution of the error routine in the ELSE-block. The 8th and 9th records are processed normally. The next repetition encounters an eof condition, thus storing a negative value in STATUS, followed by execution of the exit routine within the ELSE-IF block.

2. The exit routine prints the minimum value report, the number of records processed, and stops processing via the STOP statement.

3. The error routine rings a bell by using the intrinsic function **CHAR (7)**, which "prints" the 7th ASCII character (bell sound) in the collating sequence. Audio responses are common in commercial error routines as another means (besides visual) of alerting the user. The error routine also prints the record number where the error occurred, and a description of the most recent value stored in NAME, which identifies the record that precedes the incorrect record. This feature is useful in large data files, particularly if some poor guy (women included) is trying to find incorrect records by reading a listing of thousands of unnumbered records.

   We could also place a STOP statement at the end of the error routine, as we did in the exit routine. This means that execution would terminate whenever a data file error is encountered. We could then fix the error and rerun the program. This approach would be cumbersome for large files and more than one error.

   Another interesting variation would be the placement of a PAUSE statement at the end of the error routine. This statement has the following syntax.

```
PROGRAM MIN3
• • • • • • • • • • • • • • • • • • • • • • • • • • • • • • • • •
•                                                               •
•      Minimum Value With EOF Loop Using IOSTAT =               •
•                                                               •
•      Inputs data set title, names and associated real values  •
•      Determines minimum value and its associated name         •
•      Outputs minimum value, associated name, records processed •
•      Includes error routine that identifies faulty record     •
•                                                               •
•      Data file structure:                                     •
•        Title in quotes                                        •
•        1st name in quotes             value                   •
•        2nd name in quotes             value                   •
•        ...                                                    •
•                                                               •
•      Key:                                                     •
•        MINNAM... Name of item whose value is the minimum      •
•        MINVAL... Minimum value                                •
•        NAME..... Descriptive name of item                     •
•        RECORD... Record number                                •
•        STATUS... Status code for I/O Status Specifier         •
•        TITLE.... Title of data set                            •
•        VALUE.... Value of item                                •
•                                                               •
• • • • • • • • • • • • • • • • • • • • • • • • • • • • • • • • •
```

```
•  Type names
•————
    CHARACTER MINNAM*40, NAME*40, TITLE*80
    INTEGER   RECORD, STATUS
    REAL      MINVAL, VALUE
•————
•  Initialize
•————
    RECORD = 1
•————
•  Read title and first record
•————
    READ (5,*) TITLE
    READ (5,*) MINNAM, MINVAL
•————
•  Loop while not eof
•————
```

```
    100    READ (5, *, IOSTAT = STATUS ) NAME, VALUE          ◄—— Eof loop

           IF ( STATUS .EQ. 0 ) THEN                          ◄—— Loop control
                                                                  with IOSTAT =
              RECORD = RECORD + 1

              IF (VALUE .LT. MINVAL) THEN                     ◄—— Main loop body
                 MINVAL = VALUE
                 MINNAM = NAME
              END IF

           ELSE IF ( STATUS .LT. 0 ) THEN

              PRINT *, TITLE
              PRINT *
              PRINT *, ' Minimum value.............',     MINVAL   ◄—— Exit routine
              PRINT *, ' Associated description...    ',  MINNAM
              PRINT *
              PRINT *, ' Records processed........',       RECORD

              STOP

           ELSE

              RECORD = RECORD + 1                            ◄—— Error routine

              PRINT *, CHAR(7)                              ◄—— Ding! (Bell sound)
              PRINT *, '*** Error in record number....',     RECORD
              PRINT *, '     Most recent description...   ', NAME
              PRINT *

           END IF

           GO TO 100
•————
•  End loop
•————
    END
```

FIGURE 5.6   **Minimum value with eof loop using IOSTAT =**

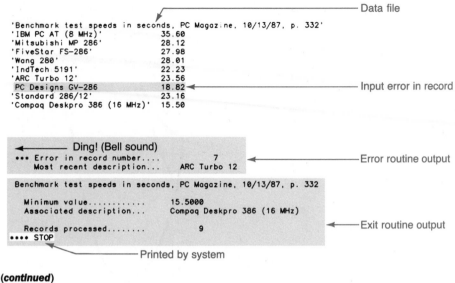

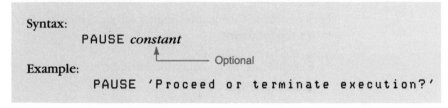

FIGURE 5.6   (*continued*)

PAUSE Statement

The *constant* can be an integer up to five digits or a character string, as illustrated. Execution of this statement interrupts or pauses execution of the program. Typically, the constant is printed. At this point we would either press a key to resume execution with the next executable statement or press another key to terminate execution. The particular keys used are implementation dependent. In general, the PAUSE statement is useful for debugging programs. See Exercise 3c.

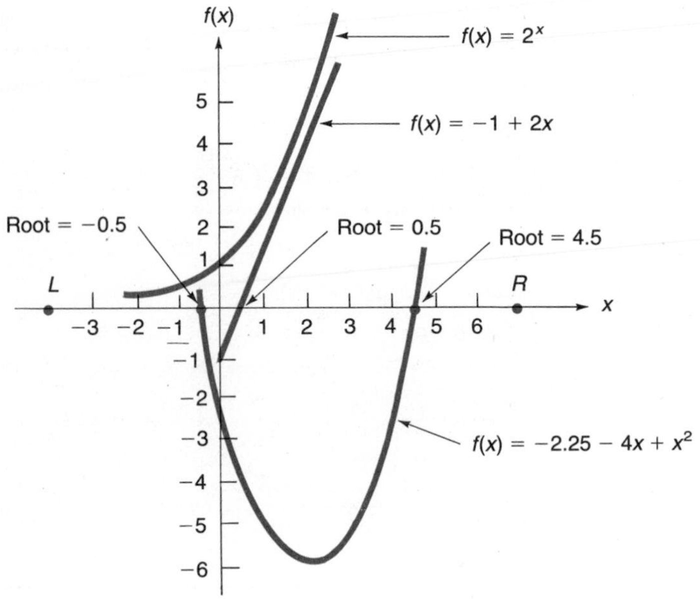

FIGURE 5.7   **Sketches of sample functions**

5.4 ROOT BISECTION PROGRAM WITH MENU

Let's conclude this chapter with a rather elaborate interactive program that illustrates the following.

- FORTRAN's capability for intricate algorithmic logic
- Menu design
- Screen design
- Statement function

PROBLEM ANALYSIS

Many mathematical applications, particularly in calculus, require values for the root(s) of a mathematical function. Given a general mathematical function of x, $f(x)$, a root of the function is a value of x that yields a value of zero for $f(x)$. For example, the linear function

$$f(x) = -1 + 2x$$

TABLE 5.1   **Root Bisection Method for the Function $f(x) = -1 + 2x$ (also see Figure 5.8)**

Iteration	Interval from Left to Right (L)	(R)	Midpoint (M) or Root Estimate	Function Values $f(L)$	$f(R)$	$f(M)$	Half-interval or Max. Error	Comment
1	−3.0	1.0	−1.0	−7.0	1.0	−3.0	2.0	Root in right half-interval since $f(L)$ and $f(M)$ have same sign (both negative). Thus, set $L = M = -1.0$ to create new interval at iteration 2.
2	−1.0	1.0	0.0	−3.0	1.0	−1.0	1.0	Again root in right half-interval, so set $L = M = 0.0$ at iteration 3.
3	0.0	1.0	0.5	−1.0	1.0	0.0	0.5	Root found at $x = M = 0.5$ since $f(M) = 0.0$.

has a root at $x = 0.5$, since this value for x yields $f(0.5) = 0$. The quadratic function

$$f(x) = -2.25 - 4x + x^2$$

has two roots, one at $x = -0.5$ and another at $x = 4.5$. Figure 5.7 illustrates sketches of these functions. Note from the figure that real roots for the function

$$f(x) = 2^x$$

are not defined, since this function approaches the x-axis asymptotically (gets closer and closer to it but does not cross it).

A number of analytic procedures have been developed for finding the roots of functions. In this section we illustrate the bisection method for finding a real root (if it exists) of any function; Exercise 33 at the end of the chapter describes another procedure.

To illustrate the root bisection procedure for the linear function in Figure 5.7, study Table 5.1 and Figure 5.8 together.

Make sure you understand the bisection procedure by reworking Table 5.1 and Figure 5.8 starting with, say, $L = -1$ and $R = 5$.

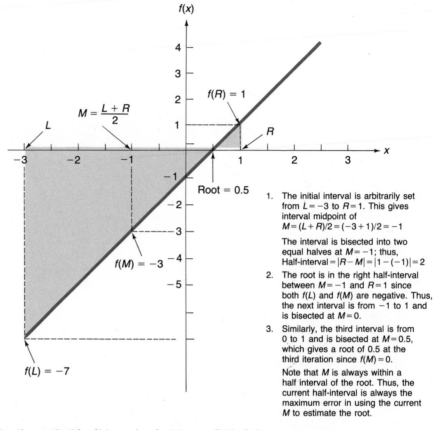

1. The initial interval is arbitrarily set from $L = -3$ to $R = 1$. This gives interval midpoint of $M = (L + R)/2 = (-3 + 1)/2 = -1$

   The interval is bisected into two equal halves at $M = -1$; thus, Half-interval $= |R - M| = |1 - (-1)| = 2$

2. The root is in the right half-interval between $M = -1$ and $R = 1$ since both $f(L)$ and $f(M)$ are negative. Thus, the next interval is from -1 to 1 and is bisected at $M = 0$.

3. Similarly, the third interval is from 0 to 1 and is bisected at $M = 0.5$, which gives a root of 0.5 at the third iteration since $f(M) = 0$.

   Note that M is always within a half interval of the root. Thus, the current half-interval is always the maximum error in using the current M to estimate the root.

FIGURE 5.8   **Bisection method for $f(x) = -1 + 2x$ (also see Table 5.1)**

The root bisection program calculates a real root of a function, if it exists within the interval specified. Output, input, and parameters are defined as follows:

Output Data
A root (if it exists) or a message stating that a root can't be found for the given interval.

Input Data
Menu item selection
F   Function change
R   Root search
    Left end of interval ⎫
    Right end of interval ⎬ If R is selected
    Error tolerance ⎭
S   Stop processing

```
Loop
  Clear screen
  Print menu, input choice
  Select based on menu choice
Until choice is Stop

Clear screen
Print farewell message
End
```

```
If choice is Function change then

  Clear screen
  Print function-change message
  Stop

Else if choice is Root search
  Clear screen
  Input data
  Clear screen
  Store initial interval
  Search for root

Else if choice is Stop
  Continue

Else
  Clear screen
  Print error message
  Pause screen
Endif
```

```
If can't find root in interval then

  Print can't-find message
  Pause screen

Else

  Find root
  Print results

Endif
```

```
Print interval,
  error tolerance,
  iterations

If f(M) = 0 then

  Print exact root

Else

  Print estimated root,
  max error

Endif
Pause screen
```

```
Calculate M, half-interval
Initialize iteration count
While half-interval ≥ error tolerance
                    and f(M) <> 0
  Determine new interval
  Calculate new M, half-interval
  Update iteration count
End while
```

```
If sign f(M) = sign f(R) then
  Root in left half-interval (R = M)
Else
  Root in right half-interval (L = M)
End if
```

FIGURE 5.9   **Stepwise-refined pseudocode for root bisection program**

Parameters
Within the statement function (see Module A) given by

$$f(x) = -1.0 + 2.0x$$

PROGRAM DESIGN

Figure 5.9 shows stepwise-refined pseudocode for the bisection algorithm. Try following the logic by relating the steps in Table 5.1, the graph in Figure 5.8, and the pseudocode in Figure 5.9.

PROGRAM CODE AND TEST

The FORTRAN code for the bisection algorithm is shown in Figure 5.10, and its test run in Figure 5.11. Try following the execution logic by tracing the given input through to its corresponding output. Also, try roleplaying the program by solving Exercise 13.

The following notes relate to the pseudocode in Figure 5.9, the program in Figure 5.10, and the sample run in Figure 5.11.

1. **Screen design.** This program pays attention to the following ideas in interactive screen design.

   a. **Screen clear.** Take the perspective of individual screens, where each screen contains a "chunk" of related information. For example, Screen 1 in Figure 5.11 is a "Menu screen," Screen 2 is an "Input screen," and so on. Each new screen, therefore, requires a screen clear of the previous screen. We accomplish this in the program by printing 25 blank lines using a format-directed PRINT statement with an embedded slash edit descriptor (see Section B.3).

   ```
   PRINT '(25(/))'
   ```

   Some FORTRAN implementations have special statements for screen clears. Does yours?

   b. **Screen pause.**   noninput screen like Screen 3 in Figure 5.11 would scroll off the top immediately without a screen pause. The statements

   ```
   PRINT *, 'Press enter to continue...'
   READ '(A)', PAUSE
   ```

   implement a screen pause. Do you see why? The processor pauses as it awaits input for the character variable PAUSE. After viewing the screen, we simply press the enter key, and the program continues execution. Note that we used the A edit descriptor (Module C) to input a character value without surrounding quotes (which is why we can just press the enter key).

   c. **Screen features.** As usual, screens should communicate concisely, clearly, and without clutter. It's best to use a screen title to identify screens, as done in Figure 5.11. Also, it's best to center material within the screen, to give it a sense of balance. We also use an audio alert in Screen 8 by ringing the bell whenever the user incorrectly selects a menu item. In addition, we can use color effectively for implementations that support it. For example, we can print error messages in red (what else?), prompt for input in one color and make the actual input another color, use different background and foreground colors for each type of screen, and so on.

```
      PROGRAM ROOT
• • • • • • • • • • • • • • • • • • • • • • • • • • • • • • • • • • •
•                                                                    •
•         Root Bisection                                             •
•                                                                    •
•            Inputs menu choice; for choice R inputs interval end points •
•               and error tolerance                                  •
•            Calculates root using bisection method                  •
•            Outputs root search results, or "Can't find root message", •
•               or "Change function message"                         •
•                                                                    •
•            Key:                                                    •
•               CHOICE... Menu choice:  F  Function change           •
•                                       R  Root search               •
•                                       S  Stop                      •
•               ERRTOL... Error tolerance                            •
•               F(X)..... Statement function reference               •
•               HALF..... Width of half-interval                     •
•               INLEFT... Initial left end of interval               •
•               INRITE... Initial right end of interval              •
•               ITER..... Iteration count                            •
•               LEFTC.... Left end of current interval               •
•               LINE1.... Short output line                          •
•               LINE2.... Long output line                           •
•               MIDC..... Middle of current interval                 •
•               PAUSE.... Input variable for pausing screen          •
•               RIGHTC... Right end of current interval              •
•               SPACE.... Output space                               •
•               X........ Argument in statement function (The abscissa) •
•                                                                    •
• • • • • • • • • • • • • • • • • • • • • • • • • • • • • • • • • • •
•────────
•  Type names
•────────
      CHARACTER CHOICE, LINE1*40, LINE2*57, PAUSE, SPACE*10
      INTEGER   ITER
      REAL      ERRTOL, F, HALF, INLEFT, INRITE, LEFTC, MIDC, RIGHTC, X
•────────
•  Statement function
•────────
      F(X) = -1.0 + 2.0*X
•────────
•  Initialize
•────────
      LINE1 = '=======================================′
      LINE2 = '=========================================================′
      SPACE = ' '
•────────
•  Loop
•────────
•        Clear screen
•        ────────
 100     PRINT '( 25(/) )'
•
•
•        Print menu and input menu choice
•        ────────
      PRINT *, SPACE, 'MENU SCREEN'
      PRINT *, SPACE, LINE1
      PRINT *
      PRINT *, SPACE, SPACE, 'F   Function change'
      PRINT *, SPACE, SPACE, 'R   Root search'
      PRINT *, SPACE, SPACE, 'S   Stop'
      PRINT *
      PRINT *, SPACE, LINE1
      PRINT *, SPACE, 'Choice?'
      PRINT '( 8(/) )'
      READ  '( A )', CHOICE
```

FIGURE 5.10   **Listing of Program ROOT (continued on next pages)**

- Start menu choice structure
-

- Choice Function change
-

```
IF ( CHOICE .EQ. 'F'  .OR.  CHOICE .EQ. 'f' ) THEN
```

- Clear screen

```
PRINT '( 25(/) )'
```

- Print function—change message

```
PRINT *, '                 CHANGE FUNCTION SCREEN'
PRINT *
PRINT *, '* * * * * * * * * * * * * * * * * * * * * *'
PRINT *, '*                                        *'
PRINT *, '*  To change function type the following in   *'
PRINT *, '*  statement function section of program:     *'
PRINT *, '*                                        *'
PRINT *, '*     F(X) = real expression              *'
PRINT *, '*                                        *'
PRINT *, '*  Example:                              *'
PRINT *, '*                                        *'
PRINT *, '*     F(X) = -1.0 + 2.0*X                 *'
PRINT *, '*                                        *'
PRINT *, '*  Then run the program again.           *'
PRINT *, '*                                        *'
PRINT *, '* * * * * * * * * * * * * * * * * * * * * *'
PRINT '( 4(/) )'
```

```
STOP
```

-

- Choice Root search
-

```
ELSE IF ( CHOICE .EQ. 'R'  .OR.  CHOICE .EQ. 'r') THEN
```

- Clear screen

```
PRINT '( 25(/) )'
```

- Input interval end points and error tolerance

```
PRINT *, 'ROOT SEARCH INPUT SCREEN'
PRINT *,  LINE1
PRINT *
PRINT *, ' Enter left and right end of interval in'
PRINT *, ' the form xx, xx'
PRINT *
READ *, LEFTC, RIGHTC
PRINT *
PRINT *, ' Enter error tolerance'
PRINT *
READ *, ERRTOL
```

-

- Clear screen

```
PRINT '( 25(/) )'
```

- Assign initial interval end points

```
INLEFT = LEFTC
INRITE = RIGHTC
```

-

FIGURE 5.10   *(continued)*

```
•          Search for root
•          ────────────────────────────────────────────────
           IF ( F(LEFTC) * F(RIGHTC) .GT.  0.0 ) THEN

•             Can't find root
•             ────────────────────────────────────────────────
              PRINT *, 'NO ROOT SCREEN'
              PRINT *, LINE2
              PRINT *
              PRINT *, 'Root can''t be found within interval:'
              PRINT *, LEFTC, '===>', RIGHTC
              PRINT *
              PRINT *, 'Possible reasons:'
              PRINT *, '  1.  No roots exist'
              PRINT *, '  2.  Root outside interval.............',
           +                                     ' Expand interval'
              PRINT *, '  3.  Multiple roots within interval...',
           +                                     ' Shrink interval'
              PRINT *
              PRINT *, LINE2
              PRINT '( 6(/) )'
•          ────────────────────────────────────────────────

•             Pause screen
•             ────────────────────────────────────────────────
              PRINT *
              PRINT *, 'Press enter to continue...'
              READ '( A )', PAUSE
•          ────────────────────────────────────────────────

           ELSE

•             Find root by bisection method
•             ────────────────────────────────────────────────
              MIDC = (LEFTC + RIGHTC) / 2.0
              HALF = ABS(RIGHTC - MIDC)
              ITER = 1

•             While half-interval >= error tolerance and F(x) <> 0
•             ────────────────────────────────────────────────
     200      IF (HALF.GE.ERRTOL .AND. ABS(F(MIDC)-0.0) .GT. 1.0E-06) THEN
                                                          ──── .NE. hazard
                 IF ( F(MIDC) * F(RIGHTC) .GT. 0.0 ) THEN

•                   Root in left half-interval
•                   ────────────────────────────────
                    RIGHTC = MIDC

                 ELSE

•                   Root in right half-interval
•                   ────────────────────────────────
                    LEFTC  = MIDC

                 END IF

•                Calculate new midpoint, half-interval
•                ────────────────────────────────────────
                 MIDC = (LEFTC + RIGHTC) / 2.0
                 HALF = ABS( RIGHTC - MIDC )
•                ────────────────────────────────────────

•                Update iteration count
•                ────────────────────────────────
                 ITER = ITER + 1
•                ────────────────────────────────

                 GO TO 200

              END IF

•             End loop
•             ────────────────────────────────────────────────
```

FIGURE 5.10   *(continued)*

```
•       Print results
•     ─────────────────────────────────────────────
      PRINT *, SPACE, 'ROOT SEARCH OUTPUT SCREEN'
      PRINT *, SPACE, LINE2
      PRINT *
      PRINT *, SPACE, ' Initial interval:',INLEFT,'===>',INRITE
      PRINT *, SPACE, ' Error tolerance :', ERRTOL
      PRINT *, SPACE, ' Iterations      :', ITER
      PRINT *                                          ──── .EQ. hazard

      IF ( ABS ( F(MIDC) - 0.0 ) .LT. 1.0E-06 ) THEN

         PRINT *, SPACE, ' Exact root       :', MIDC
         PRINT *

      ELSE

         PRINT *, SPACE, ' Estimated root   :', MIDC
         PRINT *, SPACE, ' Maximum error    :', HALF

      END IF

      PRINT *
      PRINT *, SPACE, LINE2
      PRINT '( 6(/) )'
•     ─────────────────────────────────────────────

•       Pause screen
•     ─────────────────────────────────────────────
      PRINT *
      PRINT *, 'Press enter to continue...'
      READ '( A )', PAUSE
•     ─────────────────────────────────────────────

      END IF
•       End search for root
•     ─────────────────────────────────────────────

•   Choice Stop
•     ─────────────────────────────────────────────
    ELSE IF ( CHOICE .EQ. 'S'  .OR.  CHOICE .EQ. 's' ) THEN

      CONTINUE
•     ─────────────────────────────────────────────

•   Error routine for wrong choice
•     ─────────────────────────────────────────────
    ELSE

•     Clear screen
•     ──────────────────
      PRINT '( 25(/) )'
•     ──────────────────


•     Print error message
•     ─────────────────────────────────────────────
      PRINT *, SPACE, 'WRONG MENU CHOICE SCREEN', CHAR(7)
      PRINT *, SPACE, LINE1
      PRINT *                                          ──── Bell
      PRINT *, SPACE, ' Please enter F, R, or S'
      PRINT *, SPACE, '    ... in upper or lower case letters'
      PRINT *
      PRINT *, SPACE, LINE1
      PRINT '( 9(/) )'
•     ─────────────────────────────────────────────
```

FIGURE 5.10   (*continued*)

```
  •        Pause screen
  •        _____
           PRINT •
           PRINT •, 'Press enter to continue...'
           READ '( A )', PAUSE
  •        _____

           END IF

  •        End menu choice structure
  •        _____

           IF ( .NOT. ( CHOICE .EQ. 'S' .OR. CHOICE .EQ. 's' ) ) GO TO 100
  •                                                                        ↖
           Until menu choice is Stop                                        ────── End of main loop
  •       ─────────────────────────────────────────────────────────────

  •        Clear screen
  •        _____
           PRINT '( 25(/) )'
  •        _____

  •        Print farewell message
  •        _____
           PRINT •, SPACE, 'FAREWELL SCREEN'
           PRINT •, SPACE, LINE1
           PRINT •
           PRINT •, SPACE, '  You have just terminated me...'
           PRINT •, SPACE, '  I''ve been ROOTing for you...'
           PRINT •, SPACE, '  I hope you found your ROOTs...'
           PRINT •
           PRINT •, SPACE, LINE1
           PRINT '( 9(/) )'
  •        _____
           END
```

FIGURE 5.10   **(continued)**

2. **Menu structure.** The program is controlled by a posttest loop where the loop control test is based on the Stop menu choice. Note that the else-if structure for menu choices accounts for the Stop choice, but does nothing with it by continuing with program execution out the bottom of the else-if structure. We include the Stop choice within the else-if structure because it's a legitimate menu choice that otherwise would be flagged within the error routine in the ELSE-block. Try Exercise 17 for a design that uses the while structure.

3. **Statement function.** The statement function (Module A) named F considerably simplifies the programming statements that reference it. For example, the logical expression

```
    F(MIDC) * F(RIGHTC) .GT. 0.0
```

would have to be written as

```
    (-1.0 + 2.0*MIDC) * (-1.0 + 2.0*RIGHTC) .GT. 0.0
```

without the statement function. The former is more readable as well. Note that we must edit the program to find the root of a function different from

Screen 1

```
          MENU  SCREEN
          ════════════════════════════════════════

                    F    Function change
                    R    Root search
                    S    Stop

          ════════════════════════════════════════
          Choice?

R
```

Screen 2

```
   ROOT  SEARCH  INPUT  SCREEN
   ════════════════════════════════════════

    Enter  left  and  right  end  of  interval  in
    the  form  xx, xx

 -3, 1

    Enter  error  tolerance

 .01
```

Screen 3

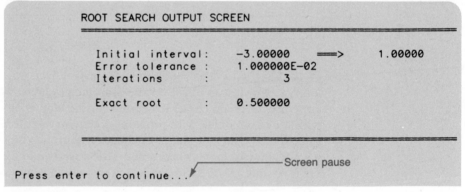

```
          ROOT  SEARCH  OUTPUT  SCREEN
          ════════════════════════════════════════

               Initial  interval:    -3.00000    ===>      1.00000
               Error  tolerance  :    1.000000E-02
               Iterations        :         3

               Exact  root        :    0.500000

          ════════════════════════════════════════
                                        ┌──── Screen pause
 Press  enter  to  continue...✎
```

Screen 4

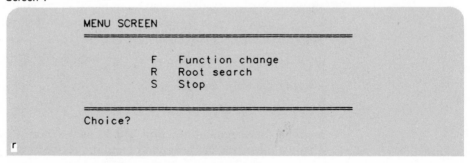

```
          MENU  SCREEN
          ════════════════════════════════════════

                    F    Function change
                    R    Root search
                    S    Stop

          ════════════════════════════════════════
          Choice?

r
```

FIGURE 5.11   **Test run of Program ROOT (*continued on next pages*)**

Screen 5

```
ROOT SEARCH INPUT SCREEN
═══════════════════════════════════════════════

  Enter left and right end of interval in
  the form xx, xx

-50, 50

  Enter error tolerance

.01
```

Screen 6

```
        ROOT SEARCH OUTPUT SCREEN
        ═════════════════════════════════════════

        Initial interval:   -50.0000   ==>    50.0000
        Error tolerance :   1.000000E-02
        Iterations      :        14

        Estimated root  :   0.494385
        Maximum error   :   6.103516E-03

        ═════════════════════════════════════════

 Press enter to continue...
```

Screen 7

```
        MENU SCREEN
        ═════════════════════════════════════════

              F    Function change
              R    Root search
              S    Stop

        ═════════════════════════════════════════

 Choice?

D
```

Screen 8

```
      WRONG MENU CHOICE SCREEN◄──────────Ding!
      ═══════════════════════════════════════════

        Please enter F, R, or S
          ... in upper or lower case letters

      ═══════════════════════════════════════════

 Press enter to continue...
```

FIGURE 5.11   *(continued)*

Screen 9

```
          MENU  SCREEN
          ══════════════════════════════

                    F    Function change
                    R    Root search
                    S    Stop


          ══════════════════════════════
          Choice?

R
```

Screen 10

```
    ROOT  SEARCH  INPUT  SCREEN
    ══════════════════════════════════════

      Enter  left  and  right  end  of  interval  in
      the  form  xx,  xx

   100,  200

      Enter  error  tolerance

   .01
```

Screen 11

```
    NO  ROOT  SCREEN
    ══════════════════════════════════════════════

    Root  can't  be  found  within  interval:
         100.000    ═══>      200.000

    Possible  reasons:
       1.   No  roots  exist
       2.   Root  outside  interval............ Expand  interval
       3.   Multiple  roots  within  interval... Shrink  interval


    ══════════════════════════════════════════════


    Press  enter  to  continue...
```

Screen 12

```
          MENU  SCREEN
          ══════════════════════════════

                    F    Function change
                    R    Root search
                    S    Stop


          ══════════════════════════════
          Choice?

S
```

FIGURE 5.11   (*continued*)

Screen 13

```
              FAREWELL SCREEN
              ═══════════════════════════════════════

        You have just terminated me...
        I've been ROOTing for you...
        I hope you found your ROOTs...


              ═══════════════════════════════════════
```

Screen 1, second run

```
          MENU  SCREEN
          ═══════════════════════════════════════

                      F    Function change
                      R    Root search
                      S    Stop


          ═══════════════════════════════════════

          Choice?

F
```

Screen 2, second run

```
                CHANGE FUNCTION SCREEN

  * * * * * * * * * * * * * * * * * * * * * * * *
  *                                            *
  *   To change function type the following in *
  *   statement function section of program:   *
  *                                            *
  *     F(X) = real expression                 *
  *                                            *
  *   Example:                                 *
  *                                            *
  *     F(X) = -1.0 + 2.0*X                     *
  *                                            *
  *   Then run the program again.              *
  *                                            *
  * * * * * * * * * * * * * * * * * * * * * * * *

  **** STOP
```

FIGURE 5.11   (*continued*)

the one used in the example. See Screens 1 and 2 in the second run, and Exercises 14 and 15.

4. **.EQ. or .NE. hazard.** As discussed earlier, we have to be careful with logical expressions that use the .EQ. (and .NE.) operators to compare real expressions. For example, the statement labeled 200 includes the expression

```
ABS (F(MIDC) - 0.0) .GT. 1.0E-06
```

as a replacement for

```
F(MIDC) .NE. 0.0
```

Approximate representations of real values and roundoff error may render the second expression true instead of false when the function actually equals zero; that would not be the case with the first expression, providing the approximate value is within a certain precision (10^{-6} in the example) of its theoretical value.

5. The program can't find a root if the product `F(LEFTC) * F(RIGHTC)` is positive. This can happen if:

   a. No root exists, as in the 2^x function in Figure 5.7. In this case, the interval from L to R gives $f(L) > 0$ and $f(R) > 0$, so that $f(L) * f(R) > 0$.

   b. The root is outside the interval. For example, the interval $L = -3$ to $L = 0$ in Figure 5.8 does not contain the root. In this case, $f(L) < 0$ and $f(R) < 0$, so that $f(L) * f(R) > 0$. See Screens 10 and 11 in Figure 5.11.

   c. Multiple roots are within the interval, as in Figure 5.7 for the function $f(x) = -2.25 - 4x + x^2$. Here we have $f(L) > 0$ and $f(R) > 0$, so that $f(L) * f(R) > 0$. In these cases, the "Root can't be found" message is printed.

6. The while structure implements the bisection procedure for finding the root. This loop continues iterating until either the half-interval drops below the error tolerance or the exact root is found, that is, `F(MIDC)` is zero within a precision of 10^{-6}.

7. The test `F(MIDC) * F(RIGHTC) .GT. 0.0` is a slick way of determining whether the root lies in the left half-interval or the right half-interval. Take a look at Figure 5.8 again, which shows the root in the right half of the interval that runs from -3 to 1. In this case, we have `F(MIDC)` $= -3$ and `F(RIGHTC)` $= 1$. Thus the test is false, so `LEFTC` gets set to `MIDC`. In general, if `F(MIDC)` and `F(RIGHTC)` have the same sign (both negative or both positive), then the root is in the left half-interval; else, the root is in the right half-interval. You should confirm the generality of this approach by working Exercise 18.

8. The algorithm is not likely to find an exact root as in Table 5.1 for one of two reasons: either roundoff error may prevent locating the exact value or the root may be an irrational number such as one-third (0.3333 . . .). For these reasons, we need to specify a certain error tolerance within which the precision of the computed root is acceptable. For example, we could terminate the algorithm and print the root whenever the half-interval is less than 0.01. The while test and the if-then-else output logic handle both situations: an exact root (within precision 10^{-6}) and an approximate root (within the error tolerance input for `ERRTOL`).

5.5 PROGRAMMING TIPS

DESIGN AND STYLE

1. **Indentation.** Improve the readability of a repetition structure by indenting the loop body and identifying the beginning and end of the structure through the program's documentation.

2. **Structure of Loop.** Be conscious of correct loop structures in structured programming. It's best to use pretest or posttest designs exclusively, since they simplify the identification of the loop structure (its control and body). Loop structures that embed the loop control within the body (see Exercise 1b) are unstructured, or inconsistent with the definition of structured loops as either pretest or posttest. Our eof loop designs are somewhat murky structurally, since the loop test is built into the READ statement, and the READ statement is also the beginning of the loop body. Still, the eof loop is a pretest loop, in *spirit* if not exactly by *the letter of the law*. Some language dialects build the eof condition into the logical expression of a while loop, thus giving us pure pretest eof loops. The repetition structure in structured programming also uses a single entry point at the top and a single exit point at the bottom. A structured loop thus adheres to this concept of **top-down execution,** where a program always executes in a top-to-bottom manner. All of our selection structures in the last chapter and our repetition structures in this chapter adhere to this principle, with one exception: the eof loop that uses the IOSTAT = specifier. In this case, loop exit is achieved within the exit routine, rather than through the bottom of the loop structure.

3. **Pretest Versus Posttest Loops.** The choice of a pretest versus a posttest design is often based on the preferences of the programmer, since many problems are solvable by either approach. For example, compare the two approaches for the temperature problem in Figures 5.2 and 5.4, and see Exercise 2b. The eof loop is essentially a pretest loop.

4. **Eof Versus DO-Loops.** We should use an eof loop whenever a loop is to process many records of data, particularly if the number of records changes often. This approach is convenient and reliable, since it avoids the potentially error-prone activity of having to specify beforehand the exact number of loop iterations. This is the key reason why the eof loop is the method of choice in data file processing applications like payrolls, billings, and large amounts of experimental data. Alternatively, the DO-loop is best in applications where a variable changes systematically (see Exercise 5).

5. **Error Routines.** The design of error routines takes on rather rich dimensions in interactive minicomputer and microcomputer environments. For example, we can design error routines on some systems that alert the user by a combination of sound, color, blinking, and reverse video (hopefully not all at once!). At a minimum, we should print clearly distinguishable error

messages that alert users to the exact nature of the problem (as in Figure 5.11).

6. **Screen Designs.** The I/O design of interactive programs takes special care. Input requests should be stated concisely and clearly, without clutter. Likewise, output should be designed to enhance readability. It's also best to segregate input from output visually, as in Figure 5.4. The screen clear is commonly used to eliminate clutter, as in Figures 5.10 and 5.11. Some dialects have special statements for clearing the screen. Does yours? Another consideration is the screen pause Program ROOT in Figure 5.10 uses a screen pause after each output report (see Figure 5.11); otherwise, the report would be cleared immediately in preparation for the menu. Screen pauses are also useful for long table output. For example, if we need to print a 30-line table and the screen only holds 25 lines at one time, then the first 5 lines of the table would scroll off the top of the screen. To view the first 25 lines of the table we would have to pause the screen by either a special system-dependent keyboard sequence (What's the pause key on your system?) or a selection structure that specifically pauses the screen (see Exercise 10).

7. **Documentation.** Documentation within programs becomes increasingly important as programs get longer and/or more complex. Program ROOT in Figure 5.10 includes more documentation within the algorithmic section than earlier programs. In practice, documentation can be quite elaborate. For example, many of our explanations of the bisection method and program in Section 5.4 are best included within the program's documentation. Try paying greater attention to documentation from now on . . . Yes, it does mean more typing! Lack of program documentation in the "real world" has been very costly in terms of program updates. By one account in a large programming shop of 200 programmers and about 1.3 million lines of FORTRAN code, no program was unrevised over a five-year period.[1] Thorough documentation greatly facilitates program maintenance.

8. **Portability.** Standard-conforming FORTRAN 77 programs are those whose statements strictly adhere to the officially approved version of FORTRAN 77, as described by the American National Standards Institute in the document labeled ANSI X3.9-1978. Theoretically, standard-conforming programs are **portable** from one computer system to another, providing standard-conforming compilers are used. Programmers need to keep portability in mind if a program is to be used in different systems; otherwise, the expense of rewriting programs may prove prohibitive. The downside of portability is that we can't use special features of the local system that are meant to enhance programs. Examples include names with more than six characters,

---

[1] *Fortran Forum, SIGPLAN Special Interest Publication on Fortran,* ACM Press, April 1988, p. 19.

direct implementation of while and until structures (see Exercises 11 and 12), and special screen features like color, clears, and pauses.

9. **Optimization Note: Excessive Computer Time.** A poorly designed algorithm is an important factor that contributes to excessive computer time. This factor is so important in certain applications that professionals in applied mathematics, statistics, and computer science have devoted extensive research efforts to improving the time efficiency of many algorithms. More often than not, this involves the development of entirely new algorithms. For example, the bisection method of finding roots (Figure 5.10) is often more efficient than Newton's approximation method in Exercise 33; integer programming algorithms of the type described in Chapter 7 (see Exercise 52) are the subject of intense research efforts in practice, since solutions to some realistic problems still require many days of computer time; and sorting algorithms have been developed that significantly lower the time it takes to sort large data files (we take these up in Chapter 7).

10. **Write Structured Programs.** A **structured program** exclusively uses the following control structures.

- Sequence structure
- Selection structures
  If-then-else structure
  If-then structure
  Else-if structure
- Repetition structures
  Pretest loop
  Posttest loop

If we view a control structure as a building block (kind of like the ones we played with as kids), then we can conceptualize a program as a stack of building blocks, with some building blocks inside others. Execution enters each building block at the top, flows within the building block as strictly defined by that control structure, and exits out the bottom of the building block (and into the top of the next building block). Thus, the execution flow in a structured program is *well behaved*—from top to bottom, precisely defined, with no surprises. GOTOless programming is often associated with structured programming because the incorrect (unstructured) use of GO TO statements can wreak havoc with the execution flow. In this context, GO TO statements are dangerous and should be used only as shown in the pretest, posttest, and eof loop designs. While structure and until structure enhancements to FORTRAN 77 (see Exercises 11 and 12) are provided as a means of entirely avoiding GO TO statements, although at the expense of portability.

11. **Why Structured Programming?** To underscore the importance of structured programming, consider the following quotations from Steve Olson's article "Sage of Software," which appeared in *Science*.

> Very large software systems consist of millions of separate instructions . . . written by hundreds of different people. Yet these instructions must dovetail with perfect accuracy. If even a single instruction is wrong, the software system can fail. . . .
>
> Then, 20 minutes before launch time [of the Columbia space shuttle], warning lights at mission control began to flash. Something was wrong with the computer system . . . [but] nothing was physically wrong with the computers. The software on board the space shuttle consists of nearly 500,000 elaborately interwoven instructions. Finding . . . a bug in that web would be like finding a single misspelled word in an encyclopedia. The maiden flight of the space shuttle would have to be delayed.
>
> The operating system for IBM's large 360 computer, the most important new computer of the decade, had cost hundreds of millions of dollars, was over a year late, and still contained thousands of errors. . . . In 1968 . . . NATO held a global conference on the "software crisis."
>
> In the early 1970s a team of programmers at IBM . . . used structured programming to build an information bank for the *New York Times*. They finished in record time and then shocked the computing community when the system proved to contain almost no errors. Software developers scrambled to learn the new techniques . . . [yet] even now many programmers are staunch holdouts.[2]

A prominent computer consultant says the following about the value of structured programming and modular programming (Chapter 6):

> the new techniques *do* work—they *do* double the productivity of the average programmer, increase the reliability of his code by an order of magnitude, and decrease the difficulty of maintenance by a factor of two to ten.[3]

In short, structured programming (and modular programming in the next chapter) pays off especially in the development, debugging, reliability, and subsequent maintenance of complex programs. Moreover, in our years of teaching this course, we have seen dramatic improvements in the correctness and sophistication of student programming as we switched from unstructured to structured approaches in our presentation.

---

[2] Steve Olson, "Sage of Software," *Science,* January/February 1984, pp. 75–80.
[3] Edward Yourdon, *Managing the Structured Techniques* (New York: Yourdon Press, 1979), p. 4.

COMMON ERRORS

1. **Loop Repetitions.** Programming an incorrect number of loop repetitions is a very common mistake. One cause of this error is an incorrect boundary description in the logical expression of a pretest or posttest loop. In particular, pay attention to ₊GE₊ versus ₊GT₊ and ₊LE₊ versus ₊LT₊ relational operators. Moreover, watch out for the "₊EQ₊ hazard" when using non-integer values (see item 6 on page 151). This is why we used the NINT function in Program TEMP3 on page 166.

2. **Infinite Loop.** In designing repetition structures, take care that the loop control test satisfies the exit condition sometime during execution of the repetition structure. If the exit condition is never met, or if we don't use a STOP statement in an exit routine, then we have a logic error called an **infinite loop.** In this case, looping continues indefinitely, until we or the sysop (system operator) "pull the plug" by breaking execution. What's the break key on your system? You wouldn't really turn off the machine, would you?

3. **Don't Punt.** If we can't find fault with our algorithm (after roleplaying it thoroughly), yet output does not validate our (correct!) hand-calculated results, then we should look at the possibility of faulty input data. If the input data are part of the output data (a practice we generally recommend), then check to make sure that they are correct; otherwise echo the input data by printing them immediately after they are input. If the problem remains, try whatever relaxes you, get a good night's sleep, and try again in the morning.

FOLLOW-UP EXERCISES

---

1. With respect to Program TEMP3 in Figure 5.2:
   a. Rewrite the loop control test without using the ₊NOT₊ logical operator. Which approach do you prefer?
   b. Rewrite the loop structure so that only one READ statement is used for F-input. Use the same block IF statement. Is this a "structured" repetition structure?
   *c. Rewrite the loop structure to use the END = specifier. Repetitions now terminate with your system's interactive eof condition, instead of the sentinel −999. Which approach do you prefer?
   *d. Rewrite the loop structure to use the IOSTAT = specifier. Repetitions now terminate with your system's interactive eof condition, instead of the sentinel −999. Which approach do you prefer?

2. With respect to Program TEMP4 in Figure 5.4:
   a. Rewrite the loop structure as a while structure. Initialize the response to yes. Which approach do you prefer?

    b. Rewrite the loop structure as a posttest loop with a −999 sentinel for degrees Fahrenheit. Which approach to you prefer?

3. Consider Program MIN3 in Figure 5.6.

    a. How would the output change in the sample run if we were to replace the two record counters with a single record counter just after the READ statement?

   *b. What would happen during execution if the first record (the PC AT record) had missing apostrophes? How might you correct this problem?

   *c. Insert a PAUSE statement in the error routine and run the program.

4. **Sentinel record.** Rewrite Program MIN2 in Figure 5.5 so that the loop terminates with a sentinel instead of with an eof condition. Use a while structure and add a sentinel record to the data file. Use `eof` as the sentinel for NAME. Which approach do you prefer?

5. **DO-Loop Versus Pretest Loop.** Consider the following DO-loop.

```
      DO 500 TIME = 100, 300, 50
         SPEED = START + ACCEL * TIME
         PRINT *, TIME, SPEED
  500 CONTINUE
```

Rewrite this loop based on the while structure in this chapter. Which approach do you prefer?

 *6. With respect to Program TEMP2 in Figure 3.8:

    a. Add an outer loop that asks the user if another table is desired.

    b. Replace the DO-loop with the while structure used in this chapter. Which approach do you prefer?

 *7. **HC ENGINEering.** Rewrite the following programs and data files to use an eof loop.

    a. Program ENG2 on page 96 using the END = specifier.

    b. Program ENG2 on page 96 using the IOSTAT = specifier.

    c. Program ENG4 on page 540 using the END = specifier.

    d. Program ENG4 on page 540 using the IOSTAT = specifier.

 *8. **Y/n error routine.** Add an error routine to Program TEMP4 in Figure 5.4 that captures incorrect y/n responses. Use the following design for the error routine.

```
While response not correct
  Print error message
  Input response
End while
```

The only correct responses are Y, y, N, or n. Illustrate sample runs with incorrect responses.

9. **ERR = specifier.** The **error specifier** has the following form.

Error Specifier

Syntax:

ERR = *statement label*

Example:

ERR = 150

If the error specifier is present in a READ statement, then an error condition during execution of the input statement results in the continuation of execution with the statement whose label is in the specifier. In our example, execution would continue with statement 150.

   a. Rewrite Program TEMP3 in Figure 5.2 to include the error specifier. Show a sample run. Do we still have a structured program?

  ***b.** Rewrite Program MIN2 in Figure 5.5 to include the error specifier. Try duplicating the features of Program MIN3 in Figure 5.6. Show a sample run. Do we still have a structured program?

*10.   **Table screen pause.** Design a routine that pauses table output every 24 lines, and prints the following message on the 25th line:

Press the ENTER key to continue . . .

Apply this routine by writing and debugging a program that prints the numbers 1 to 60, one per line.

*11.   **Explicit while structure.** Does your compiler include an enhancement to FORTRAN 77 that explicitly models the while structure? If so, rewrite Program TEMP3 in Figure 5.2 accordingly. Discuss advantages and disadvantages of using this enhancement.

*12.   **Explicit until structure.** Does your compiler include an enhancement to FORTRAN 77 that explicitly models the until structure? If so, rewrite Program TEMP4 in Figure 5.4 accordingly. Discuss advantages and disadvantages of using this enhancement.

13.   Roleplay computer by processing the following data through Program ROOT in Figure 5.10.

	INLEFT	INRIGHT	ERRTOL	
a.	0.0	1.0	0.01	← Note that midpoint = root
b.	0.5	1.0	0.01	← Note that left endpoint = root
c.	0.0	0.5	0.01	← Note that right endpoint = root

You might want to fill in a table similar to Table 5.1 as you roleplay.

14.   How would you change Program ROOT to process the function

$$f(x) = 2^x$$

See Figure 5.7. Roleplay this function through the program, assuming the input data −3, 1 for the interval and 0.01 for error tolerance. You might want to fill in a table similar to Table 5.1 as you roleplay.

*15. How would you change Program ROOT to process the function

$$f(x) = -2.25 - 4x + x^2$$

See Figure 5.7. Roleplay this function through the program, assuming the following input data.

	INLEFT	INRIGHT	ERRTOL
a.	4.0	6.0	0.005
b.	−2.0	1.0	0.005
c.	1.0	3.0	0.005
d.	−3.0	6.0	0.005

You might want to fill in a table similar to Table 5.1 as you roleplay.

*16. Implement Program ROOT on your system, using the following input data.
   a. Figure 5.11
   b. Exercise 13
   c. Exercise 14
   d. Exercise 15

17. Describe changes in Program ROOT if we were to use a while structure instead of the posttest loop that was used.

*18. In Program ROOT, convince yourself that the test

```
F(MIDC) * F(RIGHTC) .GT. 0.0
```

for the location of the root in the left or right half-interval is perfectly general. Pick an interval in Figure 5.8 that locates the root in the left half-interval and evaluate the test. Next, sketch a negatively sloped linear function and repeat the test for two different intervals, one that locates the root in the left half-interval and one that locates it in the right half-interval.

*19. Improve the computational efficiency of Program ROOT by accounting for the possibility (as in Exercise 13b,c) that one of the input end points of the interval is at the root. *Hint:* Convert an if-then-else structure to an else-if structure that includes new selections.

<hr>

ADDITIONAL EXERCISES

<hr>

20. **Revisit: Microcomputer price quotations.** Replace the DO-loop in Program MICRO in Figure 4.2 with an appropriate loop design from this chapter.

21. **Revisit: Synchronous satellite orbits.** Add a proper loop structure to Program ORBIT in Figure 4.7.

22. **Revisit: SAT report.** Use an eof loop to process the data file in Exercise 15 in Chapter 4.

23. **Revisit: Quality control.** Use an eof loop to process the data file in Exercise 16 in Chapter 4.

24. **Revisit: Epidemiological forecasting.** Use a proper loop design that reoffers the menu in Exercise 17 in Chapter 4.

25. **Revisit: Quadratic roots.** Use an interactive loop design from this chapter in Exercise 19 in Chapter 4.

26. **Revisit: Factorials.** Use an interactive loop design from this chapter for the outer loop in Exercise 20 in Chapter 4.

27. **Revisit: Linear regression.** Use an eof loop to process the data file in Exercise 21 in Chapter 4.

28. **Forecasting population growth.** In recent years, the prediction of world population levels into the next century has been a concern of many political, environmental, and agricultural planners. The following equation can be used to predict future levels of world population:

$$p = c \cdot [1 + (b - d)]^n$$

where p = predicted level of future population
   b = birth rate
   c = current level of population
   d = death rate
   n = number of years into the future

For example, estimated data for the year 1986 show $c = 4.944$ (billions), $b = 0.025$ (2.5%), and $d = 0.006$ (0.9%). If b and d essentially remain constant over a 10-year period ($n = 10$), then we can predict the world population in 1996 as

$$p = 4.944[1 + (0.025 - 0.006)]^{10}$$
$$= 4.944(1.019)^{10}$$
$$= 4.944(1.2071)$$
$$= 5.968 \text{ billions}$$

a. Develop an interactive program that processes input data for c, b, d, and n using a yes/no loop. Calculate and print the predicted level of future population. Use the following test data:

c	b	d	n
4.944	0.025	0.006	10
4.944	0.025	0.006	20
4.944	0.025	0.006	30
4.944	0.020	0.006	30

Does a drop in the birthrate to 0.020 make much difference?

Repeatedly change the value of n to determine the number of years it would take for the population to double. Try different values for n and observe the output values for p. Answer this question for both the 0.025 and the 0.020 birthrates.

b. Let N be a counter for "years into future" in an "inner" loop that lies entirely within the outer loop in part **a.** This inner loop increments N by 1, calculates predicted population, and prints N, corresponding year, and predicted population. Initialize N by defining an input variable called N1. Exit from the loop when the ratio of predicted population to current population exceeds a desired ratio (R). Run the program for the following three sets of input values.

Current Population	Base Year	b	d	N1	R
4.944	1986	0.025	0.006	10	2
4.944	1986	0.025	0.006	25	3
4.944	1986	0.020	0.006	30	3

For example, your output for the first run should look like this:

Years into Future	Corresponding Year	Predicted Population
10	1996	5.968
11	1997	6.081
.	.	.
.	.	.
.	.	.
36	2022	9.735
37	2023	9.921

Note that the counter is initialized by N1 and that this loop terminates when the predicted population *exceeds* (not equals) double (R has a value of 2) the current population. Comment on the number of years it takes the current world population to double and triple relative to changes in the birthrate.

29. **Electric shock.**[4] Ohm's law gives the relationship between current, voltage, and resistance as follows.

$$I = \frac{V}{R}$$

where I = current in amperes (A)
$\quad V$ = voltage in volts (V)
$\quad R$ = resistance in ohms (Ω)

Resistance of the human body to electric shock is very much a function of whether the skin is wet or dry. On average, resistance is 10^5 Ω when the skin is

---

[4] Adapted from Jerry B. Marion, *General Physics with Bioscience Essays* (New York: Wiley, 1979), p. 299.

TABLE 5.2   **Effects on Human Body of Different Currents**

Current (mA)[a]		
Greater Than	No More Than	Effect
0.0	0.5	None
0.5	2.0	Threshold of feeling
2.0	10.0	Pain; muscular contractions
10.0	20.0	Some injury
20.0	100.0	Respiratory paralysis
100.0	3000.0	Fatal, unless immediate resuscitation
3000.0		Cardiac arrest; severe burns

[a]mA = milliAmpere = 0.001A.

dry and 1500 Ω when the skin is wet. The effect on the human body of different alternating currents for 1 second at 60 hertz (Hz), where 1 Hz = 1 cycle per second, is given in Table 5.2. For example, contact with a current at 120 V with dry skin is barely noticeable ($I = 120/10^5 = 1.2$ mA). Contact with the same current with wet skin, however, could result in respiratory paralysis ($I = 120/1500 = 80$ mA). Design, code, and test a program that interactively inputs voltage and whether or not the skin is wet, and outputs current in mA and its effect based on the categories in Table 5.2. Use a repetition structure that terminates based on the y/n response. Include error routines that trap y/n and dry/wet responses while they are incorrect (see Exercise 8). In your test runs, try the following voltages with both wet and dry skin: 120 V, 240 V, and 1000 V.

30. **Police car replacement.** Captain Joseph Friday, the police administrator in Gotham City, would like to estimate the mileage at which a police cruiser should be replaced. Data analyses show that the *cost of operation* (gasoline, maintenance, and so on) is approximated by

$$c = f + v \cdot m + s \cdot m^2$$

where f, v, and s are coefficients, and m is the mileage reading (in thousands) on the odometer. For example, a cruiser that is driven for 30,000 miles and is characterized by $f = 1000$, $v = 200$, and $s = 2$ incurs an operating cost of approximately

$$c = 1000 + (200) \cdot (30) + (2) \cdot (30)^2$$
$$= \$8800.$$

The police department has an arrangement with Generous Motors (GM) for trade-ins of used police cruisers. The automaker has agreed to reduce the price of a new cruiser by the following amount

$$r = pd^m$$

where r is the trade-in (salvage) value of a used cruiser, p is the original (new) car price, d is some depreciation factor, and m is defined as before. For example, if $p = \$10,000$, $d = 0.95$, and $m = 30$, then

$$r = (10,000) \cdot (0.95)^{30}$$
$$= \$2146.$$

This means that the police department pays $10,000 for a new cruiser, drives it for 30,000 miles, and gets $2146 on a trade-in. The *depreciation cost* in this case is $7854, or the difference between the new car price and the salvage price.

Thus, a cruiser driven for 30,000 miles costs $8800 to operate and $7854 in depreciation cost, for a total cost of $16,654. If this type of cruiser is replaced by a new cruiser of the same type at 30,000-mile intervals, then the total cost per 1000-miles (K-miles) is approximately $555 (that is, $16,654 ÷ 30).

a. Design, write, and run a program that determines the mileage (to the nearest thousand) at which cruisers should be replaced. Input for each cruiser should include the following.

1. Cruiser name
2. f, v, s, p, d

Output for each cruiser should appear as follows:

Analysis for Cruiser . . .   Print cruiser name here

Thousands Miles (1)	Operating Cost (2)	Operating Cost per K-Miles (3)	Depreciation Cost (4)	Dept. Cost per K-Miles (5)	Total Cost per K-Miles (6)
1					
2					
3					
.					
.					
.					
100					

Thus the best mileage at which to replace a cruiser is that which gives the smallest value in column (6). Note that 100,000 miles is the maximum replacement mileage that Captain Friday is willing to consider. He is evaluating several types of cruisers, one of which must be selected. The following characteristics are provided courtesy of GM.

Cruiser Name	f	v	s	p	d
Buster	1000	200	2.0	10,000	0.95
Truster	800	300	2.5	8,000	0.93
Terminator	1200	225	1.6	13,000	0.98

At what mileage should each type be replaced and what is the total cost per K-miles? Which cruiser is the cheapest on the basis of total cost per K-miles?

b. Design your program so that the program itself determines and outputs the best cruiser type and its associated total cost per K-miles.

c. As you go down column (6) in this type of table, costs typically begin high, decrease to a minimum, and begin increasing again. Design your program to exit from the table loop either once total cost begins to increase or when mileage exceeds 100K.

31. **Algebraic series.** Consider the following algebraic series.

Arithmetic: $a + (a + d) + (a + 2d) + (a + 3d) + \ldots$

where a = 1st term
d = common difference

Geometric: $a + ar + ar^2 + ar^3 + \ldots$

where a = 1st term
r = common ratio

Harmonic: $1 + 1/2 + 1/3 + 1/4 + \ldots$

a. Design, write, and debug a program that offers a menu for the above three series. Input a and d if the arithmetic series is selected; a and r if the geometric series is selected. Print the first k terms of the selected series, and the nth partial sum (sum of the first n terms). Values for k and n are input for each series. In your test run, select each series once, select an incorrect menu choice, and select the Quit choice. Use k = 10 and n = 20 for all series; a = 5 for the first two series; d = 7 for the arithmetic series; and r = 0.5 for the geometric series.

b. Add the exponential series to the menu.

$$\frac{1}{0!} + \frac{1}{1!} + \frac{1}{2!} + \frac{1}{3!} + \ldots$$

where ! reads factorial
$0! = 1$
$k! = 1 \cdot 2 \cdot 3 \cdot 4 \cdot \ldots \cdot k$

and the series converges to the logarithmic constant e = 2.71828 . . . , the base of natural logarithms. Input k = 5 for this series, and try the following values for n: 5, 10, 50.

32. **Computer dating.** The Sure Thing Dating Service has a data file of clients with the following record layout.

Record Layout

Field	Values	Description
Name	. . .	Last name, first middle
Sex	1	Female
	2	Male
Age	1	Less than 20
	2	20–29
	3	30–39
	4	Over the hill
Height	1	Less than 5'0"
	2	5'0" but less than 5'7"
	3	5'7" but less than 6'0"
	4	Tall
Weight	1	Less than 100
	2	100 but less than 120
	3	120 but less than 160
	4	160 but less than 200
	5	Big
Education	1	Elementary
	2	High school
	3	College
	4	Overeducated
	5	Streetwise
Occupation	1	Professional
	2	Skilled
	3	Student
	4	Surfer
Income	1	Less than $20K
	2	$20K but less than $30K
	3	$30K but less than $50K
	4	$50K but less than $100K
	5	Loaded

The first 10 records in the data file are listed next.

Mark "Copter" Furcolo	2	2	2	3	4	4	2
Charlotte "Char" Manni	1	3	2	2	5	2	2
Mary Jane "MJ" Gesmondi	1	2	2	3	4	1	1
Yarta "Yo" Morfella	1	1	2	1	2	3	1
John "JKD" Dunn	2	4	1	5	3	1	5
Cynthia "Amor" Mello	1	3	3	3	5	2	1
Joshua "Mapper" Clay	2	1	2	2	1	3	1

Rick "Chiro" Jardon	2	2	2	3	4	1	4
Meg "Bev Francis" Carroll	1	2	2	2	4	1	3
Harvey CORE	2	4	4	4	5	1	5

Harvey CORE, Jr., the Head Date at Sure Thing, wants you to develop a program that services walk-in and telephone clients who request dates. The program inputs the data file and interactively inputs a date request. The date request is a series of interactive inputs of a person's (requestor's) preferences for each of the fields (except name) in the data file. For example, input for the first two preferences might appear as follows:

    Enter sex preference
    1

    Enter age preference
    2

A preference of zero indicates "no preference." The program then prints a list of names (possible dates) and their Desirability Index. The desirability index (DI) is the number of matches between preferences in all but the first two fields in the data file. For example, a perfect match between preferences and characteristics is 6. Sex is not used in the DI; rather it is the basis for whether a name is printed or not (unless the requestor enters zero for this preference, in which case all names are printed). Each match adds a point to the DI, unless the preference is zero, in which case we add a half point. Consider the following three date requests.

Request	Sex	Age	Height	Weight	Education	Occupation	Income
First	2	3	3	3	0	4	5
Second	0	1	2	1	2	3	0
Third	1	3	3	3	5	2	1

Output for the first request might appear as follows.

Name	Desirability Index
Mark "Copter" Furcolo	2.5
John "JKD" Dunn	1.5
Joshua "Mapper" Clay	0.5
Rick "Chiro" Jardon	1.5
Harvey CORE	1.5

Note that only males are output, since the sex preference was 2. Confirm the DI output, and do a "hand-run" for the other two requests.

a. Design, write, and debug the program described. Use the given data in your test run.

b. Include field descriptions for each person's last six fields in the output report. For example, the output line for "Copter" would include 20–29 for age, 5'0" to 5'7" for height, 120–160 for weight, Overeducated for education, Surfer for Occupation, and $20,000–$30,000 for income.

Have fun! If you do a good job, HC Jr. might fix you up . . .

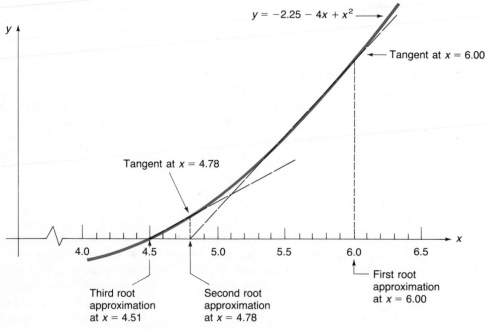

FIGURE 5.12   **Newton's approximation method (Exercise 33)**

33.   **Newton's approximation method.** This method describes a procedure for approximating the root of a function. Consider Figure 5.12, which reproduces a blown-up portion of the quadratic function in Figure 5.7. If we arbitrarily select the first root approximation at $x = 6.00$, then the second approximation is at $x = 4.78$. Graphically, the second approximation is found by constructing a tangent line on the function at $x = 6.00$ and extending this line to the x-axis. The intersection of the tangent line with the x-axis gives the next root approximation, which is 4.78 approximately. Next we construct a tangent at $x = 4.78$, and it intersects the x-axis at roughly 4.51. This process continues until a desired precision is achieved. Note that each successive approximation gets closer and closer to the root at $x = 4.50$.

   Analytically, a tangent line is determined as the first derivative of the function, which we label y' (y prime). For the function

$$y = -2.25 - 4x + x^2$$

the first derivative is

$$y' = -4 + 2x$$

The next root approximation is determined from the following formula.

$$\text{Next } x = \text{Current } x - \frac{y}{y'}$$

The table below illustrates three iterations of this procedure.

Current x	$y = -2.25 - 4x + x^2$	$y' = -4 + 2x$	Next x
6.000000	9.750000	8.000000	4.781250
4.781250	1.485351	5.562500	4.514220
4.514220	0.0713022	5.028440	4.500040
.	.	.	.
.	.	.	.
.	.	.	.

a. Design and run a program that approximates roots by this method. Terminate iterations when the difference between two successive x's is less than an error tolerance that's input by the user. Use the following test data.

y	y'	Initial x-Values	Error Tolerance	Maximum Iterations
$-2.25 - 4x + x^2$	$-4 + 2x$	1,000; 4.0; −3.0	0.001	20 Then 5
$-1 + 2x$	2	3.0; −2.0	0.010	10
2^x	$(2^x) \cdot (\ln 2)^a$	10	0.001	100
$-20 + 108x^2 - 4x^3$	$216x - 12x^2$	Make up your own; try to find multiple roots.	0.010	20

[a] In 2 stands for the natural (base e) logarithm of 2 (see Module A).

b. Incorporate logic for finding multiple roots (if any).

6

MODULAR PROGRAMMING

Behavioral research, not to mention our own experiences, clearly shows that the human brain best solves elaborate problems by a "divide and conquer" strategy. That is, we divide a large problem into distinct and manageable major portions, or tasks. Then we separately work on each task, generally completing one before going on to the next. Finally, when all major tasks are complete, we have a solution to the overall problem. This chapter shows how *modular programming* implements these ideas.

6.1 THE MODULAR CONCEPT

Table 6.1 illustrates the breakdown of specific problems into major tasks. Note that the major tasks in writing a book, building a house, and writing a program are easily identified.

MODULES

As programs increase in length and complexity, it's best to view the major processing tasks as groups of related statements called **modules.** The act of designing and developing a program as a set of modules is called **modular programming.**

As illustrated by the third example in Table 6.1, a module represents a processing task. But exactly what is a module and how is it implemented? Unfortunately, there is no unique definition of a module, nor is there just one way to implement modules. Moreover, the selection of good modules based on processing tasks requires study, experience, talent, and insight. So, rather than answering these questions directly, let's list some key properties of a module and then illustrate their selection and implementation through a series of examples.

Properties of a Module

1. **A module has a single entry point and a single exit point.** In essence, a module is like a "black box" that is activated (entered through the top), performs some assigned function, and is deactivated (exited through the bottom).

2. **A module is independent of other modules.** Essentially this means that we can design, develop, change, or modify a module without affecting other

TABLE 6.1   Sample Major Tasks

Problem	Major Tasks
Write book	Frontmatter
	Chapter 1
	.
	.
	.
	Chapter 9
	Appendix A
	Appendix B
	Index
Build house	Excavation
	Foundation
	First floor
	Second floor
	Plumbing
	Electrical work
	Finish work
	Landscaping
Write Program ORBIT	Print menu/input choice
(see Figure 4.7)	Selection based on menu choice
	Output report
	Other planet input

modules. In reality, absolute independence may not be achievable in many cases; however, modules should at least exhibit the type of functional independence described in the four modules of the Program ORBIT example in Table 6.1.

3. **A module is not too large.** The industry rule of thumb says that a module should not exceed 50 to 100 lines of code, which is one or two pages of listing. The basic idea is that the size of a module should not become so unwieldy that the programmer loses intimacy (understanding in depth) with this portion of the code. Needless to say, this property is subjective but well meaning.

STRUCTURE OF MODULAR PROGRAMS

A module in FORTRAN is called a **program unit,** an independently compiled sequence of statements and comment lines. Figure 6.1 illustrates the types of program units. A **modular program** is a program with two or more program units.

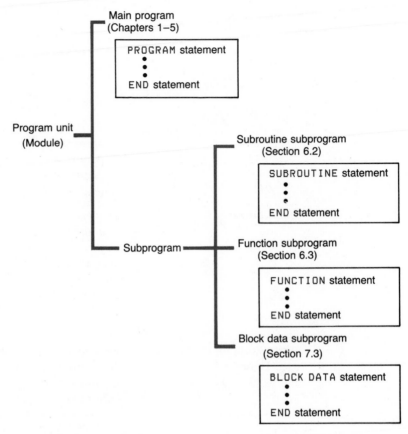

Types of program units or modules

A **main program** is the type of program we have been writing until this chapter. It begins with the PROGRAM statement and ends with the END statement. In a modular program, the main program controls execution in the overall program. For this reason, it's sometimes called the **control module.**

A **subprogram** is any one of the three program units defined in Figure 6.1: **subroutine subprogram, function subprogram,** and **block data subprogram.** Typically, a subprogram is designed to solve a part of the overall programming problem, such as menu selection, output report, error routine, and specialized computations.

The structure of a modular program is illustrated in Figure 6.2. Its compilation and execution are accomplished in one of two ways.

Modular Program

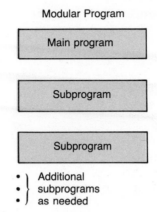

| **FIGURE 6.2** | **Structure of the modular program** |

- The main program and its subprograms are stored in a single program file and compiled/executed in the usual way. Each program unit is still independently compiled.

- The main program and one or more subprograms are stored in separate program files and independently compiled. The program file containing the main program is then executed. Ask your instructor about this procedure on your system.

NOTE We now visualize a program as having major "building blocks" or modules, where each module accomplishes a specialized task. In this context, the control structures (sequence, selection, and repetition) are smaller building blocks within the modules.

6.2 SUBROUTINE SUBPROGRAMS

Let's start the discussion of subprograms with the subroutine subprogram—its structure and how we get it to execute.

SUBROUTINE STRUCTURE

A program unit is a **subroutine subprogram,** or simply a **subroutine,** if it has the following structure.

Subroutine Subprogram

Syntax:

```
SUBROUTINE name (dummy argument list)
                                    Optional
  •  ]  Statements
  •  }  and
  •  ]  comment lines

END
```

Example:

```
SUBROUTINE DIF (X, Y, DACT, DABS)

REAL X, Y, DACT, DABS
DACT = X - Y
DABS = ABS (X - Y)
PRINT *, 'Actual difference   :', DACT
PRINT *, 'Absolute difference:', DABS

END
```

The name of a subroutine is any legitimate FORTRAN name. The subroutine name in the example is DIF. The dummy argument list is a list of variable names, arrays, procedures, or asterisks, separated by commas.[1] In our example, the dummy argument list contains the dummy variables X, Y, DACT, and DABS. The purpose or task of this subroutine is to calculate, store, and print the actual and absolute differences of the values in X and Y. The **END statement** has a double purpose in the subprogram: It defines the physical end of the subprogram, and it returns execution control to the program unit that referenced (caused execution of) the subprogram.

SUBROUTINE REFERENCE

The subroutine is executed whenever it is referenced or called by another program unit. A **subroutine reference** is implemented by the execution of a **CALL statement** within the calling program unit, as follows.

---

[1] We illustrate dummy arrays in Chapter 7, discuss dummy procedures in Section 6.5, and skip asterisks altogether since their function violates top-down execution principles.

Subroutine Reference (CALL Statement)

Syntax:

CALL *name* (*actual argument list*)

Optional

Example:

CALL DIF (A, B, DIFAB1, DIFAB2)

The subroutine name identifies a particular subroutine. Our example references a subroutine called DIF. The usual rules in selecting names apply to subroutines as well (six characters maximum, and so on). The actual argument list is a list of variable names, expressions, named constants, function references (Section 6.5), array names (Chapter 7), array element names (Chapter 7), and substring names (Chapter 8). The actual argument list in the example has four variable names, separated by commas. Execution of the CALL statement has the effect described by the call/return process in Figure 6.3. Note the following points on page 224.

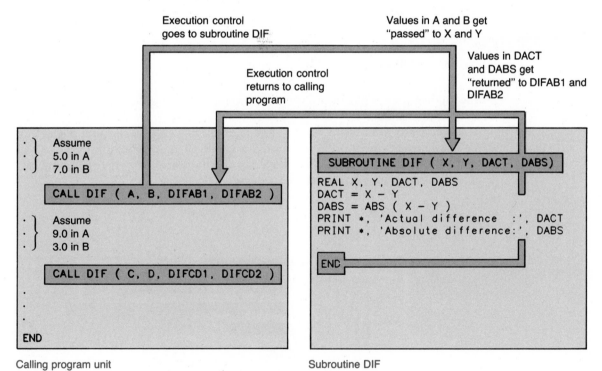

FIGURE 6.3   The call/return process for the first subroutine call

The Call. Execution of the CALL statement associates actual arguments with *corresponding* dummy arguments. In Figure 6.3, A is matched with X and B is matched with Y. Thus, X uses the value 5.0 (as stored in A) and Y uses the value 7.0 (as stored in B). Execution control goes to the subroutine.

Subroutine Execution. Execution of the subroutine now proceeds in the usual manner. DACT stores −2.0 and DABS stores 2.0. (Note that the intrinsic function ABS is defined in Module A.) These values are also printed from within the subroutine.

The Return. Execution of the END statement in the subroutine returns execution control to the calling program unit. The next statement executed is the first executable statement following the CALL statement. In Figure 6.3, the dummy variables DACT and DABS are associated with the corresponding actual variables DIFAB1 and DIFAB2. Thus, back in the calling program unit, DIFAB1 stores −2.0 and DIFAB2 stores 2.0.

Subsequent Calls. Figure 6.3 also shows a second call to subroutine DIF. In this case, make sure you understand that the call/return process gives 6.0 in DIFCD1 and 6.0 in DIFCD2.

EXAMPLE 6.1

BAR CHART SUBROUTINE

The following steps illustrate a program with just two modules, the main program and one subroutine.

Program Analysis. Let's develop a noninteractive program that reads data for a frequency distribution and prints a graphical representation called a bar chart. Figure 6.4 shows a sample frequency distribution and its corresponding bar chart for final grades in an academic course.

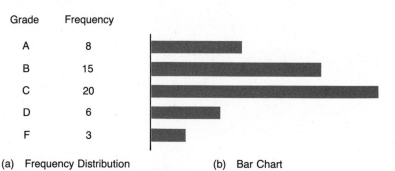

	Grade	Frequency
	A	8
	B	15
	C	20
	D	6
	F	3

(a) Frequency Distribution   (b) Bar Chart

FIGURE 6.4   **Frequency distribution and bar chart of final grades for HC101**

The data requirements are as follows:

Output
Title of bar chart, head, and foot
Label for each bar
Length of each bar
Bars

Input
Title of bar chart
Label for each bar ⎱
Length of each bar ⎰ Frequency distribution

Program Design. The first step in the design is a top-down look at the overall modular structure. Typically, a module has either a specialized task or a set of related tasks within the overall purpose of the program. In our example, let's design a subroutine or module that prints the elements of a bar chart as in Figure 6.4. Thus our subroutine will specialize in printing each bar in a bar chart, together with its label (grade) and length (frequency). The main program (control module), then, must carry out the other tasks, as described below.

Main program (Control module)	Reads all data.
	Prints title and head.
	Establishes a loop that processes a complete bar chart.
	Prints foot.
	Stops processing.
Subroutine bar chart (Module)	Prints a label, length, and bar.

The pseudocode in Figure 6.5 reflects the program's design.

Program Code and Test. Figure 6.6 shows the code and test run for the bar chart program. Note the following.

The call. After reading the grade and frequency for a specific grade category, the main program calls the subroutine. The actual argument GRADE gets paired with the dummy argument LABEL, and the actual argument FREQ gets paired with the dummy argument LENGTH. For example, in the first call, the letter grade A and the frequency 8 get "passed" or "sent" to the subroutine.

Subroutine execution. Subroutine BCHART initializes the bar to all blanks, fills in the first part of the bar with equal signs according to its length, and prints the label, length, and bar. Note that the character variable BAR has 50 positions to fill. The assignment statement

```
BAR = ' '
```

effectively stores all blanks in BAR (the assignment statement stores the first blank and the system fills the remaining positions with blanks). The DO-loop then fills in positions 1, 2, . . . , *length* (1 through 8 in the first call) in BAR with the

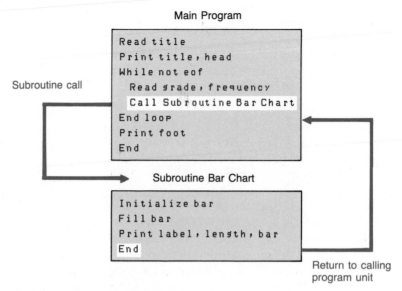

Main Program

```
Read title
Print title, head
While not eof
  Read grade, frequency
  Call Subroutine Bar Chart
End loop
Print foot
End
```

Subroutine call

Subroutine Bar Chart

```
Initialize bar
Fill bar
Print label, length, bar
End
```

Return to calling
program unit

FIGURE 6.5   **Pseudocode design for Bar Chart Program**

equal sign. We do this by using a **substring name** in the body of the DO-loop, as follows.

```
DO 100 POS = 1, LENGTH
   BAR (POS:POS) = '='
100 CONTINUE          Substring name
```

For example, when LENGTH stores 8, the DO-loop successively stores the character = in positions 1, 2, . . . , 8 in BAR. Chapter 8 treats substring names in detail.

The return. Execution of the END statement in the subroutine returns execution control to just after the "point of call" in the main program; that is, the GO TO statement in the main program is executed next.   ∎

ADDITIONAL CONSIDERATIONS

Implications of Independent Compilation.   Since program units are independently compiled, we have wide latitude in the use of variable names and statement labels. For example, the bar chart program in Figure 6.6 uses the statement number 100 in both the main program and the subroutine. The names of main programs and subprograms are called **global names** in the sense that they are unique for all modules in a particular modular program. Global names cannot be used more than once in a modular program. The names of variables, constants,

```
          PROGRAM CHART
     * * * * * * * * * * * * * * * * * * * * * * * * * * * * * * *
     *                                                           *
     *        Bar Chart Demo                                     *
     *                                                           *
     *        Inputs title and frequency distribution of grades  *
     *        Outputs bar chart with the help of Subroutine BCHART *
     *                                                           *
     *        Modular structure:                                 *
     *                                                           *
     *           Main program... Reads title and frequency distribution; *
     *                           calls BCHART for each grade category. *
     *                                                           *
     *              Sub. BCHART.... Prints grade, frequency, and bar for *
     *                           a grade category.               *
     *                                                           *
     *        Data file structure:                               *
     *                                                           *
     *           Title in quotes                                 *
     *           1st label in quotes        length               *
     *           2nd label in quotes        length               *
     *           ...                                             *
     *                                                           *
     *        Key (main program):                                *
     *                                                           *
     *           FREQ..... Frequency of grade                    *
     *           GRADE.... Letter grade                          *
     *           TITLE.... Title of frequency distribution       *
     *                                                           *
     * * * * * * * * * * * * * * * * * * * * * * * * * * * * * * *
     *---------------------------------------------------------------
     * Type names
     *------------
          CHARACTER GRADE*3, TITLE*70
          INTEGER   FREQ
     *---------------------------------------------------------------
     * Input distribution and print bar chart
     *----------------------------------------
          READ (5,*) TITLE
          PRINT *,   TITLE
          PRINT '( 50(''-'') )'
          PRINT *, 'Grade    Frequency'
          PRINT '( 50(''-'') )'

     100  READ (5,*, END = 200) GRADE, FREQ

          CALL BCHART ( GRADE, FREQ )  ◄——————— Subroutine call

          GO TO 100

     200 CONTINUE

          PRINT '( 50(''-'') )'
     *---------------------------------------------------------------
          END
```

FIGURE 6.6   **Bar chart program and run (*continued on next page*)**

Subroutine statement

```
SUBROUTINE BCHART ( LABEL, LENGTH )
* * * * * * * * * * * * * * * * * * * * * * * * * * * * * * * * * * *
*                                                                   *
*        Bar chart subroutine                                       *
*                                                                   *
*          Receives LABEL, LENGTH                                   *
*          Prints LABEL, LENGTH, BAR                                *
*          Returns nothing                                          *
*                                                                   *
*          Key:                                                     *
*                                                                   *
*            BAR...... Bar made up of = signs based on length       *
*            LABEL.... Descriptive label for bar                    *
*            LENGTH... Length of bar (frequency)                    *
*            POS...... Position in BAR (DO-variable)                *
*                                                                   *
* * * * * * * * * * * * * * * * * * * * * * * * * * * * * * * * * * *
*————————————————————————————————————————————————————————————————————
*  Type names
*————————
      CHARACTER BAR*50, LABEL*(*)
      INTEGER   LENGTH, POS
*————————————————————————————————————————————————————————————————————
*  Initialize bar to all blank characters
*————————————————————————————————————————
      BAR = ' '
*————————————————————————————————————————————————————————————————————
*  Fill in = signs in bar, position by position up to length
*————————————————————————————————————————————————————————————
      DO 100 POS = 1, LENGTH

         BAR ( POS:POS ) = '='

  100 CONTINUE
*————————————————————————————————————————————————————————————————————
*  Print label, length, and bar
*——————————————————————————————
      PRINT *, LABEL, LENGTH, '   |', BAR
*————————————————————————————————————————————————————————————————————
      END
```

Return to calling program unit

Data file

```
'Distribution of Final Grades in HC101'
'  A'   8
'  B'  15
'  C'  20
'  D'   6
'  F'   3
```

Output

```
Distribution of Final Grades in HC101
————————————————————————————————————————
Grade    Frequency
————————————————————————————————————————
  A          8     |=======
  B         15     |==============
  C         20     |===================
  D          6     |=====
  F          3     |==
————————————————————————————————————————
```

FIGURE 6.6   *(continued)*

statement functions, intrinsic functions, dummy procedures (Section 6.5), and arrays (Chapter 7) within program units are called **local names.** We can use the same local name in more than one program unit. This also means that we *don't* have to use the same names for corresponding actual and dummy arguments. For example, the actual arguments in Program CHART of Figure 6.6 are GRADE and FREQ, and the corresponding dummy arguments are LABEL and LENGTH. Taking a general perspective, we would not want to name the dummy arguments GRADE and FREQ (although we could as far as the FORTRAN language is concerned), since this particular bar chart subroutine could be used by another program (see Exercise 2e) whose actual arguments have an altogether different meaning (for example, SEX and INCOME).

Argument List Correspondence.   Actual and dummy argument lists must agree with respect to type correspondence (actual integer with dummy integer, actual real with dummy real, and so on). They should also agree with respect to number of arguments. For example, if the dummy argument list has five variables, then the actual argument list should have five variables. If a dummy argument does not have a corresponding actual argument, then it is undefined, and the results may be unpredictable, depending on the system.

If the dummy argument is type character, then its length must be less than or equal to the length of its corresponding actual argument. To avoid this length correspondence problem, it's best to use the assumed length declarator (∗) for the dummy argument in the CHARACTER statement. In this case, the dummy argument assumes the same length as the corresponding actual argument. For example, the dummy argument LABEL in the subroutine within Figure 6.6 is declared with length (∗). This means its assumed length for the calls in Figure 6.6 is 3, or the length of the corresponding actual argument GRADE. This also generalizes the subroutine in that we don't have to be concerned about different lengths for actual arguments in other program units that might reference Subroutine BCHART.

Optional Argument Lists.   We can altogether omit the argument lists in CALL and SUBROUTINE statements if there is no need to associate arguments. For example, a subroutine that simply pauses a screen could be called by the statement

```
CALL PAUSE
```

since argument lists are unnecessary for this task.

RETURN Statement.   The END statement in a subprogram has a dual function: It defines the physical end of the subprogram and returns execution to the referencing program unit. The point of return in a subprogram represents its logical end The RETURN statement also returns execution to the calling program unit.

RETURN Statement

> RETURN

This is used by some programmers when they need to return to the calling program unit at a point other than the end of the subprogram; that is, the subprogram's physical end and logical end are different. We generally don't recommend use of this statement, as it violates the single-entry/single-exit philosophy of top-down, structured, modular programming. Generally, we can design subprograms so that physical and logical ends correspond.[2]

Argument Association.   In our earlier descriptions of argument association we were purposely vague about the actual mechanics of how values are "passed" and "returned" for corresponding arguments. (We decided to spare you the agony at that point, but no longer . . .) A particular system will implement argument association in one of two ways.

Argument association by value/result. In this case, dummy names have storage locations separate from corresponding actual names. For example, in the first call and return in Figure 6.3, values are associated as described in Figure 6.7.

Argument association by location/address. In this case, separate storage locations are not used for dummy names; rather dummy names share the storage locations of corresponding actual names. Thus, rather than a flow of values or contents between corresponding memory locations, there is a transfer or association of addresses, so that the dummy name can use the same storage location as its corresponding actual name. The association of arrays (Chapter 7) is always by location/address, because this can save considerable storage.

---

[2] If you're unlucky enough to run into a modular FORTRAN program that predates FORTRAN 77 (late 1970s), then it must use the RETURN statement, because the END statement did not return control to the calling program unit. Old habits die hard, and so we still see FORTRAN 77 programs written with RETURN statements just before END statements. Check out an old FORTRAN book in the library (this is where *they* go when they die . . . try to find one from the 1960s). While you're at it, note the common use of GO TO statements for selection structures (block IF, ELSE IF, ELSE, and END IF statements are new to FORTRAN 77), and the attendant greater difficulty in following the programming logic. Check out the index. Are any of the following terms defined in the book: modular programming, structured programming, top-down design, if-then-else structure?

Value/Result Association: The Call

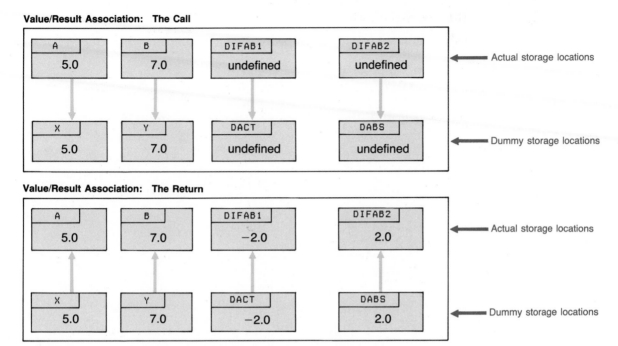

Value/Result Association: The Return

FIGURE 6.7	**Argument association for first call in Figure 6.3**

WARNING   If a dummy argument is assigned a new value in the subprogram, then the value of its corresponding actual argument also changes. Be aware of inadvertently changing dummy values.

6.3 FUNCTION SUBPROGRAMS

So far we have used two types of functions: the intrinsic functions in the FORTRAN Library (Table A.1) and the one-line statement functions written by the programmer (Section A.2). Function subprograms extend the use of functions by providing multiline functions as subprograms. Thus, not only can we write a function whose value is determined by more than one line of code, but also we can make this function easily available to other program units as a subprogram.

FUNCTION STRUCTURE

A program unit is a **function subprogram** if it has the following structure.

Function Subprogram

Syntax:

Type statement FUNCTION *name* (*dummy argument list*)

—————— Optional   Optional

```
. ⎤
. ⎬  Statements
. ⎭  and
       comment lines

END
```

Example:
```
      FUNCTION FACT (NUM)

      INTEGER FACT, K, NUM
      FACT = 1
      IF (NUM .GE. 2) THEN
         DO 100 K = 2, NUM
            FACT = FACT * K
 100     CONTINUE
      END IF

      END
```

A type statement (CHARACTER, INTEGER, REAL, DOUBLE PRECI-SION, COMPLEX) optionally precedes the keyword FUNCTION. If the type statement is present, it types the function. Alternatively, we can type the function within the function subprogram itself, as done in the example (FACT is in the list of typed names in the INTEGER statement). The name identifies the function subprogram. The function name in the example is FACT. The usual rules in selecting names also apply to naming functions. The dummy argument list is a list of variable names, arrays (Chapter 7), or procedures (Section 6.5), separated by commas. In our example, the dummy argument list contains the dummy variable NUM. The purpose of this function is to calculate the factorial of the value in NUM, that is, the product $1 \cdot 2 \cdot 3 \cdot \ldots \cdot$ *value in* NUM. The **END statement** has a double purpose in the subprogram: It defines the physical end of the subprogram, and it returns execution control to the program unit that referenced (caused execution of) the subprogram.

NOTE   The function name must be assigned a value within the function subprogram. In the example, FACT is assigned values through the assignment statements. Its final value (the factorial) is returned when the END statement is executed.

FUNCTION REFERENCE

The function subprogram is executed whenever it is referenced by another program unit. A **function reference** is implemented in the usual way, as follows.

Function Reference

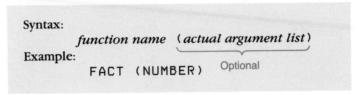

Syntax:

function name (actual argument list)

Example:

FACT (NUMBER)   Optional

The function name is a legitimate FORTRAN name, as illustrated by FACT. The actual argument list is a list of variable names, expressions, named constants, function references (Section 6.5), array names (Chapter 7), array element names (Chapter 7), and substring names (Chapter 8), separated by commas. The actual argument list in the example has the single variable name NUMBER. Execution of a statement that contains the function reference is described in Figure 6.8.

The Reference.   The function reference associates actual arguments with *corresponding* dummy arguments. In Figure 6.8, the actual variable NUMBER is matched with the dummy variable NUM. If NUMBER stores 5, then 5 is used in place of NUM in the function subprogram. Execution control goes to the function subprogram.

Function Execution.   Execution of the function subprogram now proceeds in the usual manner. FACT stores 120 following execution of the DO-loop.

The Return.   Execution of the END statement in the function subprogram returns execution control to the referencing program unit. In Figure 6.8, the PRINT statement outputs the following.

Factorial...   120

EXAMPLE 6.2

FACTORIAL FUNCTION SUBPROGRAM

Figure 6.9 shows a modular program that demonstrates Function Subprogram FACT. Study the program and its output, and relate it to the referencing process described in Figure 6.8.

```
                                                    ┌─── Function reference
                                                    ↓
  PRINT *, ' Factorial...', FACT ( NUMBER )

  PRINT *, ' Factorial...', FACT (  5   )
                                                 Argument passed to Function FACT
```

```
                              FUNCTION FACT ( NUM )

                              INTEGER FACT, K, NUM
                              FACT = 1
                              IF (NUM .GE. 2 ) THEN
                                 DO 100 K = 2, NUM
                                    FACT = FACT * K
                          100     CONTINUE
                              END IF

                              END
```

Value in FACT
returned

```
  PRINT *, ' Factorial...', 120
```

FIGURE 6.8   **Function reference of Function Subprogram FACT**

ADDITIONAL CONSIDERATIONS

Function Type.   Don't forget that we need to specify the type of the function, both in the calling program and the function subprogram (see the integer typing of FACT in Figure 6.9). Within the subprogram, we have a typing alternative. Instead of using the statements

```
     FUNCTION FACT (NUM)
     INTEGER FACT, K, NUM
```
—————— FACT in type list

as in Figure 6.9, we could have used the statements

—————— Type statement placed in front of keyword FUNCTION
```
     INTEGER FUNCTION FACT (NUM)
     INTEGER K, NUM
```
—————— Now FACT not needed in type list

We prefer the former, but it *is* a matter of preference.

```
      PROGRAM FACTOR
* * * * * * * * * * * * * * * * * * * * * * * * * * * * * * *
*                                                           *
*        Factorials Demo                                    *
*                                                           *
*         Inputs numbers                                    *
*         Outputs factorials with references to Function FACT *
*                                                           *
*         Modular structure:                                *
*                                                           *
*            Main program... Reads number while zero or more; prints *
*                            factorial of number by referencing *
*                            Function FACT.                  *
*                                                           *
*            Funct. FACT.... Calculates factorial of number  *
*                                                           *
*         Key (main program):        ———— Describe in Key    *
*                                                           *
*         FACT..... Factorial function                       *
*         NUMBER... Number whose factorial is to be calculated *
*                                                           *
* * * * * * * * * * * * * * * * * * * * * * * * * * * * * * *
*———————————————————————————————————————————————————————————
* Type names                ——— Type function name
*——————————
      INTEGER   FACT, NUMBER
*———————————————————————————————————————————————————————————
* Preliminary I/O
*——————————————
      PRINT *, 'FACTORIAL DEMO'
      PRINT *
      PRINT *, '  Enter negative number to terminate...'
      PRINT *
*———————————————————————————————————————————————————————————
*  Input numbers and print factorials
*——————————————————————————————————
      PRINT *, 'Enter number'
      READ  *, NUMBER

  100 IF ( NUMBER .GE. 0 ) THEN

      PRINT *                              ——— Function reference
      PRINT *, '  Number......', NUMBER
      PRINT *, '  Factorial...', FACT ( NUMBER )

      PRINT *
      PRINT *, 'Enter number'
      READ  *, NUMBER

      GO TO 100

      END IF
*———————————————————————————————————————————————————————————
*  Print farewell
*——————————————
      PRINT *
      PRINT *, '   Life is one big FACTorial...'
*———————————————————————————————————————————————————————————
      END
```

FIGURE 6.9   **Demonstration of Factorial Subprogram FACT (*continued on next page*)**

```
                                       ┌─ Function statement
    FUNCTION FACT ( NUM )
  * * * * * * * * * * * * * * * * * * * * * * * * * * * * *
  *                                                       *
  *     Factorial function                                *
  *                                                       *
  *       Receives NUM                                    *
  *       Calculates factorial based on the product 1*2*3*...*NUM *
  *       Returns factorial                               *
  *                                                       *
  *       Key:                        ┌─ Best to describe in Key *
  *                                                       *
  *       FACT..... Factorial of number                   *
  *       K........ Items in the factorial product (DO-variable) *
  *       NUM...... Number whose factorial is to be calculated *
  *                                                       *
  * * * * * * * * * * * * * * * * * * * * * * * * * * * * *
  *──────────────────────────────────────────────────────
  *  Type names           ┌─ Type function name
  *─────────
        INTEGER  FACT, K, NUM
  *──────────────────────────────────────────────────────
  *  Calculate factorial
  *─────────────────
        FACT = 1 ◄────────────── Assign function initial value
        IF ( NUM .GE. 2 ) THEN

           DO 100 K = 2, NUM

              FACT = FACT * K ◄──────── Assign function subsequent values

    100    CONTINUE

           END IF
  *──────────────────────────────────────────────────────
        END ◄────── Function ends


    FACTORIAL DEMO

        Enter negative number to terminate...

    Enter number
    5

        Number......         5
        Factorial...       120

    Enter number
    10

        Number......        10
        Factorial...    3628800

    Enter number
    -1

        Life is one big FACTorial...
```

FIGURE 6.9   *(continued)*

Optional Argument List. If we don't need to pass values to a function, then the argument list is omitted, *but not the set of parentheses following the function name.* For example, the following function does not have an argument list.

```
                         ┌─No argument list
                         ▼
FUNCTION PI  ( )
DOUBLE PRECISION PI
PI = 3.1415926536D+00
END
```

The function reference is simply PI ( ).

As in Subroutines. Other issues regarding function subprograms are identical to those regarding subroutine subprograms: implications of independent compilation (page 226), argument list correspondence (page 229), and argument association (page 230). Also, the same warning given on page 231 applies here as well.

6.4 COMBINATIONS PROGRAM WITH MENU

Let's put it all together in this section by working with a program that features:

- A more elaborate modular structure
  —Several modules
  —Subprograms calling other subprograms
  —The same subprogram called by different program units
- An alternative treatment of menus from that shown in the last chapter
- A screen orientation at the user interface

PROBLEM ANALYSIS

The number of combinations of n objects taken k at a time (where $n \geq k$) is a common calculation in many statistical and mathematical applications. The formula is given by

$$C = \frac{n!}{(n - k)!k!}$$

where the exclamation point represents "factorial." For example, 5! reads "the factorial of 5" or "5 factorial," which is defined by the product $1 \cdot 2 \cdot 3 \cdot 4 \cdot 5$, or 120. The number of combinations of 5 taken 2 at a time ($n = 5$ and $k = 2$) is calculated from

$$C = \frac{5!}{(5 - 2)!2!} = \frac{5!}{3!2!} = \frac{1 \cdot 2 \cdot 3 \cdot 4 \cdot 5}{(1 \cdot 2 \cdot 3)(1 \cdot 2)} = \frac{120}{6 \cdot 2} = \frac{120}{12} = 10$$

Combinations are defined only if $n \geq k$, $n > 0$, and $k \geq 0$. Moreover, 0! is defined as 1. You should confirm that the number of combinations of 10 taken 4 at a time is 210.

Let's design an interactive program that offers the user a menu of three choices:

C   Combinations
F   Factorials
S   Stop

If C is selected, then let's ask the user to enter values for n and k, calculate and print combinations, and reoffer the menu. If F is selected, then let's enter a number, calculate and print its factorial, and reoffer the menu. Let's also print a farewell message when S is selected, and an error message when an illegitimate menu selection is made. Finally, let's stress a screen orientation in the program's interaction with the user. This means, for example, that we clear and pause screens when appropriate (as done in Program ROOT in Chapter 5).

Input Data
Menu choice
n and k when C is selected
Number when F is selected

Output Data
Menu description
Combinations report when C is selected
Factorial report when F is selected
Farewell message when S is selected
Error message when an incorrect menu choice is selected

PROGRAM DESIGN

Let's modularize this program into the following eight modules.

Control Module (Main program)	Main processing loop; calls Menu module; calls Combinations Print Module, Factorial Print Module, or Error Module, depending on choice; calls Bye Module.

Menu Module (Sub. MENU)	Prints menu; inputs choice.

| **Error Module (Sub. ERROR)** | Prints menu choice error message; calls Pause Module. |

| **Combinations Print Module (Sub. CPRINT)** | Inputs *n* and *k;* calculates combinations referencing Factorials Module; prints combinations report; calls Pause Module. |

| **Factorial Print Module (Sub. FPRINT)** | Inputs number; prints factorial report referencing Factorial Module; calls Pause Module. |

| **Bye Module (Sub. BYE)** | Prints farewell message. |

| **Pause Module (Sub. PAUSE)** | Pauses screen. |

| **Factorial Module (Function FACT)** | Calculates factorial of number. |

The **hierarchy chart** (also called a **structure chart** or **top-down chart**) in Figure 6.10 is a diagram that shows the modular structure of a program, including the relationships among modules. For example, the Factorial Module (FACT) is referenced by both the Combinations Print Module (CPRINT) and the Factorial Print Module (FPRINT); the Pause Module (PAUSE) is called by the Error Module (ERROR), the Combinations Print Module (CPRINT), and the Factorial Print Module (FPRINT). Complex modular programs are best designed and described by hierarchy charts.

Let's take a look at some of the reasoning behind our selection of these particular modules, keeping in mind that there are no set rules in this process other than the characteristics of modules described on page 218.

The offering of the menu and the input of choice suggest related tasks that are easily conceptualized as a module. Moreover, we plan to use a while structure

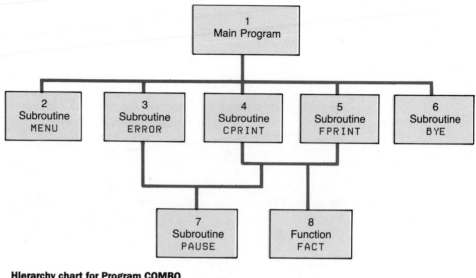

FIGURE 6.10   **Hierarchy chart for Program COMBO**

for the main processing loop in the control module, which means we would call the Menu Module both just before the loop and within the loop at the end of the loop body (we show pseudocode for this later). Given that we need to offer the menu at two different points in the program, the use of a Menu Module saves programming code.

The error and farewell messages also suggest separate modules, since these are clearly defined tasks.

We usually conceptualize output reports as modules. In this case, we have two output reports, one for combinations and one for factorials. We specify these as modules, and include their relevant input as well, since input requirements are modest. If a program requires elaborate input, then its input is best treated as a separate module.

Each of the report modules requires the calculation of factorials, so it's efficient to relegate the calculation of a factorial to its own module. This module is then referenced by the two report (print) modules. An added advantage of a separate Factorial Module is its potential place as a utility module in a computer library; that is, if we store it as a separate program file, other programs that require factorials can reference this module (much like referencing an intrinsic function).

The screen pause is required by three modules, so it's more efficient and readable to make this function its own module.

That leaves the rest for the control module. The key function of the control module is its *control* of the overall execution flow (it lives up to its name). In particular, it sets up the main processing loop that reoffers the menu *while* the choice is not Stop, and *selects* the proper module based on the menu choice. Putting these needs together brings us to the following pseudocode for the control module.

Control Module

```
Call Menu Module
While choice is not Stop
   If choice is Combinations then
      Call Combinations Print Module
   Else if choice is Factorial then
      Call Factorial Print Module
   Else
      Call Error Module
   End if
   Call Menu Module
End while loop
Call Bye Module
End
```

As in the past (see Program ORBIT in Figure 4.7 and Program ROOT in Figure 5.10), we use an else-if structure for menu selection control. Unlike Program ROOT, however, this design uses a while structure as the main processing loop. In this case, the menu is offered at two separate points, just before the loop and last in the loop body. This design bypasses our having to include an ELSE-IF block for the Stop choice, as done on page 192. We prefer this approach, although "beauty is in the eye of the beholder . . ."

PROGRAM CODE AND TEST

Figure 6.11 shows the code for Program COMBO, and Figure 6.12 its sample run. To really understand the program well, try roleplaying the test run through the program. Also check out Exercise 5.

NOTE   A subprogram can reference another subprogram, but may not reference itself. In Program COMBO, Subroutine CPRINT calls Subroutine PAUSE and references Function FACT; Subroutine FPRINT also references the same two subprograms; and Subroutine ERROR references Subroutine PAUSE. Note that Subroutine PAUSE is referenced by three separate subprograms; Function Subprogram FACT is referenced by two separate subprograms. The hierarchy chart in Figure 6.10 clearly summarizes these intermodule relationships.

```
PROGRAM  COMBO
• • • • • • • • • • • • • • • • • • • • • • • • • • • • • • • • • •
•                                                                  •
•      Factorials and Combinations                                 •
•                                                                  •
•        Inputs menu choice, formula terms                         •
•        Calls combinations or factorial modules                   •
•        Outputs factorials or combinations                        •
•                                                                  •
•      Modular structure:                                          •
•                                                                  •
•        Main program... Establishes processing loop, calls MENU,  •
•                        calls CPRINT or FPRINT or ERROR based on   •
•                        menu choice, calls BYE.                    •
•                                                                  •
•          Sub. MENU...... Prints menu and inputs choice.          •
•                                                                  •
•          Sub. ERROR..... Prints menu choice error message,       •
•                          calls PAUSE.                             •
•                                                                  •
•          Sub. CPRINT.... Inputs N and K, calculates combina-     •
•                          tions by referencing Function FACT,      •
•                          prints combinations report, calls        •
•                          PAUSE.                                   •
•                                                                  •
•          Sub. FPRINT.... Inputs number, prints factorial by      •
•                          referencing Function FACT, calls PAUSE.  •
•                                                                  •
•          Sub. BYE....... Prints farewell message.                •
•                                                                  •
•            Sub. PAUSE..... Pauses screen.                        •
•                                                                  •
•            Funct. FACT.... Calculates factorial of number.       •
•                                                                  •
•      Key (main program):                                         •
•                                                                  •
•        CHOICE... Menu choice:  C  Combinations                   •
•                                F  Factorials                     •
•                                S  Stop                           •
•                                                                  •
• • • • • • • • • • • • • • • • • • • • • • • • • • • • • • • • • •
•  Type names
•———————————
•      CHARACTER CHOICE
•————————————————————————————————————————————————————————————————
•  Loop while choice is not Stop
•————————————————————————————————
•      CALL MENU ( CHOICE )

   100 IF ( .NOT. ( CHOICE .EQ. 'S'  .OR.  CHOICE .EQ. 's' ) ) THEN

          IF ( CHOICE .EQ. 'C'  .OR.  CHOICE .EQ. 'c' ) THEN

             CALL CPRINT

          ELSE IF ( CHOICE .EQ. 'F'  .OR.  CHOICE .EQ. 'f' ) THEN

             CALL FPRINT

          ELSE

             CALL ERROR

          END IF

             CALL MENU ( CHOICE )

          GO TO 100

       END IF
•————————————————————————————————————————————————————————————————
•  End while loop
•————————————————————————————————————————————————————————————————
•  Print farewell
•———————————————
       CALL BYE
•————————————————————————————————————————————————————————————————
       END
```

FIGURE 6.11   **Listing of Program COMBO (*continued on next page*)**

```
          SUBROUTINE MENU ( CHOICE )
. . . . . . . . . . . . . . . . . . . . . . . . . . . . . . . . .
.                                                               .
.       Menu subroutine                                         .
.                                                               .
.          Receives nothing                                     .
.          Prints menu and inputs choice                        .
.          Returns choice                                       .
.                                                               .
.          Key:                                                 .
.                                                               .
.             CHOICE... Menu choice                             .
.                                                               .
. . . . . . . . . . . . . . . . . . . . . . . . . . . . . . . . .
.
. Type names
.
          CHARACTER CHOICE*(*)
.
. Print menu and input choice
.
          PRINT '( 25(/) )'
          PRINT *,'             MENU SCREEN            '
          PRINT *,'                                    '
          PRINT *,'        _____       '
          PRINT *,'       |                     |      '
          PRINT *,'       |   C  .Combinations  |      '
          PRINT *,'       |   F   Factorials    |      '
          PRINT *,'       |   S   Stop          |      '
          PRINT *,'       |_____|      '
          PRINT *
          PRINT *,'          Enter choice...           '

          READ '( A )', CHOICE
.
          END


          SUBROUTINE ERROR
. . . . . . . . . . . . . . . . . . . . . . . . . . . . . . . . .
.                                                               .
.        Menu choice error subroutine                           .
.                                                               .
.          Receives nothing                                     .
.          Prints error message and calls Subroutine PAUSE      .
.          Returns nothing                                      .
.                                                               .
. . . . . . . . . . . . . . . . . . . . . . . . . . . . . . . . .
.
. Print error message and call PAUSE
.
          PRINT '( 25(/) )'
          PRINT *, CHAR(7)
          PRINT *,'              ERROR SCREEN            '
          PRINT *,'         _____ '
          PRINT *,'        |                            |'
          PRINT *,'        |  Please enter...           |'
          PRINT *,'        |     C                      |'
          PRINT *,'        |     F                      |'
          PRINT *,'        |     S                      |'
          PRINT *,'        |        ...Upper or lower case |'
          PRINT *,'        |_____|'

          CALL PAUSE
.
          END
```

FIGURE 6.11   *(continued)*

```
              SUBROUTINE CPRINT
  • • • • • • • • • • • • • • • • • • • • • • • • • • • • • • • • • •
  •                                                                 •
  •       Combinations subroutine                                   •
  •                                                                 •
  •         Receives nothing                                        •
  •         Inputs N and K                                          •
  •         Calculates combinations by referencing Function FACT    •
  •         Prints combinations report and calls Subroutine PAUSE   •
  •         Returns nothing                                         •
  •                                                                 •
  •         Key:                                                    •
  •                                                                 •
  •            COMBO.... Combinations of N taken K at a time        •
  •            FACT..... Factorial function                         •
  •            K........ Variable in combinations formula           •
  •            N........ Variable in combinations formula           •
  •                                                                 •
  • • • • • • • • • • • • • • • • • • • • • • • • • • • • • • • • • •
  • Type names
  •─────────
          INTEGER COMBO, FACT, K, N
  ───────────────────────────────────────────────────────────────────
  • Input N and K
  •──────────────
          PRINT '( 25(/) )'
          PRINT •,'  COMBINATIONS INPUT SCREEN'
          PRINT •,'  ════════════════════════'
          PRINT •
          PRINT •,'  Enter N...'
          READ •, N
          PRINT •
          PRINT •,'  Enter K...'                ──── First reference
          READ •, K
  ───────────────────────────────────────────────────────────────────
  • Calculate combinations                      ──── Second reference
  •───────────────────────
          COMBO = FACT ( N ) / ( FACT ( N − K ) * FACT ( K ) )
  ───────────────────────────────────────────────────────────────────
  • Print report and call PAUSE                 ──── Third reference
  •────────────────────────────
          PRINT '( 25(/) )'
          PRINT •,'         COMBINATIONS OUTPUT SCREEN    '
          PRINT •,'         ══════════════════════════════'
          PRINT •
          PRINT •,'         N..............', N
          PRINT •,'         K..............', K
          PRINT •
          PRINT •,'         Combinations...', COMBO
          PRINT •
          PRINT •,'         ══════════════════════════════'

          CALL PAUSE
  ───────────────────────────────────────────────────────────────────
          END
```

FIGURE 6.11   (*continued*)

```
            SUBROUTINE FPRINT
• • • • • • • • • • • • • • • • • • • • • • • • • • • • • • • • •
•                                                               •
•          Factorial subroutine                                •
•                                                               •
•             Receives nothing                                 •
•             Inputs NUMBER                                    •
•             Prints factorial referencing Function FACT and calls •
•                Subroutine PAUSE                              •
•             Returns nothing                                  •
•                                                               •
•          Key:                                                •
•                                                               •
•             FACT..... Factorial function                     •
•             NUMBER... Number whose factorial is to be calculated •
•                                                               •
• • • • • • • • • • • • • • • • • • • • • • • • • • • • • • • • •
•——————————————————————————————————————————————————————————————
•  Type names
•——————————————————————————————————————————————————————————————
            INTEGER FACT, NUMBER
•——————————————————————————————————————————————————————————————
•  Input number
•——————————————————————————————————————————————————————————————
            PRINT '( 25(/) )'
            PRINT •,'   FACTORIAL INPUT SCREEN'
            PRINT •,'   ═══════════════════'
            PRINT •
            PRINT •,'  Enter number...'
            READ  •, NUMBER
•——————————————————————————————————————————————————————————————
•  Print factorial and call PAUSE
•——————————————————————————————————————————————————————————————
            PRINT '( 25(/) )'
            PRINT •,'          FACTORIAL OUTPUT SCREEN    '
            PRINT •,'          ════════════════════════'
            PRINT •
            PRINT •,'          Number.........', NUMBER
            PRINT •
            PRINT •,'          Factorial......', FACT ( NUMBER )
            PRINT •
            PRINT •,'          ════════════════════════'

            CALL PAUSE
•——————————————————————————————————————————————————————————————
            END


            SUBROUTINE BYE
• • • • • • • • • • • • • • • • • • • • • • • • • • • • • • • • •
•                                                               •
•          Farewell Subroutine                                 •
•                                                               •
•             Receives nothing                                 •
•             Prints farewell message                          •
•             Returns nothing                                  •
•                                                               •
• • • • • • • • • • • • • • • • • • • • • • • • • • • • • • • • •
•——————————————————————————————————————————————————————————————
•  Print farewell
•——————————————————————————————————————————————————————————————
            PRINT '( 25(/) )'
            PRINT •,'            FAREWELL SCREEN              '
            PRINT •,'          ─────────────────────────     '
            PRINT •,'          |                       |     '
            PRINT •,'          |  We make a great COMBO...  | '
            PRINT •,'          |                       |     '
            PRINT •,'          |  Looking forward to next time... | '
            PRINT •,'          |                       |     '
            PRINT •,'          ─────────────────────────     '
•——————————————————————————————————————————————————————————————
            END
```

FIGURE 6.11   *(continued)*

```
              SUBROUTINE PAUSE
      · · · · · · · · · · · · · · · · · · · · · · · · · · · · · · · · · ·
      ·                                                                ·
      ·      Pause subroutine                                          ·
      ·                                                                ·
      ·         Receives nothing                                       ·
      ·         Pauses screen                                          ·
      ·         Returns nothing                                        ·
      ·                                                                ·
      ·         Key:                                                   ·
      ·                                                                ·
      ·             ENTER.... Input variable for pausing screen        ·
      ·                                                                ·
      · · · · · · · · · · · · · · · · · · · · · · · · · · · · · · · · · ·
      ·
      ·  Type names
      ·──────────
           CHARACTER ENTER
      ·
      ·  Pause screen
      ·─────────────
           PRINT *
           PRINT *, '  Press ENTER key to continue...'
           READ '( A )', ENTER
      ·─────────────────────────────────────────────────────────────
           END


              FUNCTION FACT ( NUM )
      · · · · · · · · · · · · · · · · · · · · · · · · · · · · · · · · · ·
      ·                                                                ·
      ·      Factorial function                                       ·
      ·                                                                ·
      ·         Receives NUM                                           ·
      ·         Calculates factorial based on the product 1*2*3*...*NUM·
      ·         Returns factorial                                      ·
      ·                                                                ·
      ·         Key:                                                   ·
      ·                                                                ·
      ·             FACT..... Factorial of number                      ·
      ·             K........ Items in the factorial product (DO-variable)
      ·             NUM...... Number whose factorial is to be calculated
      ·                                                                ·
      · · · · · · · · · · · · · · · · · · · · · · · · · · · · · · · · · ·
      ·
      ·  Type names
      ·──────────
           INTEGER  FACT, K, NUM
      ·
      ·  Calculate factorial
      ·──────────────────
           FACT = 1
           IF ( NUM .GE. 2 ) THEN

               DO 100 K = 2, NUM

                   FACT = FACT * K

      100      CONTINUE

           END IF
      ·─────────────────────────────────────────────────────────────
           END
```

FIGURE 6.11   *(continued)*

Screen 1

```
                    MENU  SCREEN

             ┌──────────────────────┐
             │   C    Combinations  │
             │   F    Factorials    │
             │   S    Stop          │
             └──────────────────────┘

                Enter choice...
  F
```

Screen 2

```
  FACTORIAL  INPUT  SCREEN
  ══════════════════════════

  Enter number...
  6
```

Screen 3

```
                FACTORIAL  OUTPUT  SCREEN
                ═════════════════════════

             Number.........        6

             Factorial......       720


                ═════════════════════════

  Press ENTER key to continue...
```

Screen 4

```
                    MENU  SCREEN

             ┌──────────────────────┐
             │   C    Combinations  │
             │   F    Factorials    │
             │   S    Stop          │
             └──────────────────────┘

                Enter choice...
  X
```

Screen 5

```
                    ERROR  SCREEN

             ┌──────────────────────┐
             │  Please enter...     │
             │       C              │
             │       F              │
             │       S              │
             │        ...Upper or lower case │
             └──────────────────────┘

  Press ENTER key to continue...
```

FIGURE 6.12   **Test run of Program COMBO** (*continued on next page*)

Screen 6

```
                    MENU  SCREEN

            ┌──────────────────────────┐
            │  C    Combinations       │
            │  F    Factorials         │
            │  S    Stop               │
            └──────────────────────────┘

              Enter choice...
    C
```

Screen 7

```
      COMBINATIONS  INPUT  SCREEN
      ════════════════════════════

         Enter N...
    5

         Enter K...
    2
```

Screen 8

```
              COMBINATIONS  OUTPUT  SCREEN
              ════════════════════════════

            N..............       5
            K..............       2

            Combinations...      10

              ════════════════════════════

      Press ENTER key to continue...
```

Screen 9

```
                    MENU  SCREEN

            ┌──────────────────────────┐
            │  C    Combinations       │
            │  F    Factorials         │
            │  S    Stop               │
            └──────────────────────────┘

              Enter choice...
    C
```

Screen 10

```
      COMBINATIONS  INPUT  SCREEN
      ════════════════════════════

         Enter N...
    10

         Enter K...
    4
```

FIGURE 6.12   **(continued)**

Screen 11

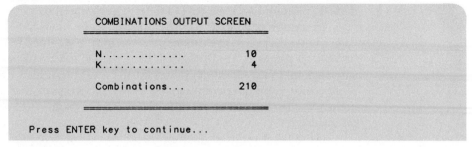

```
            COMBINATIONS  OUTPUT  SCREEN
            ═══════════════════════════════

            N.............        10
            K.............         4

            Combinations...       210
            ═══════════════════════════════


    Press ENTER key to continue...
```

Screen 12

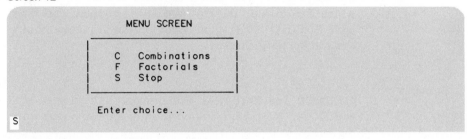

```
                     MENU  SCREEN
            ┌──────────────────────────┐
            │                          │
            │    C    Combinations     │
            │    F    Factorials       │
            │    S    Stop             │
            │                          │
            └──────────────────────────┘

              Enter choice...
  S
```

Screen 13

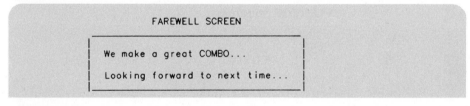

```
                  FAREWELL  SCREEN
            ┌──────────────────────────────┐
            │                              │
            │  We make a great COMBO...    │
            │                              │
            │  Looking forward to next time... │
            │                              │
            └──────────────────────────────┘
```

FIGURE 6.12   **(continued)**

6.5 OTHER TOPICS

Some applications of subprograms require certain statements not yet presented. In this section we provide three such statements, introduce FORTRAN libraries, and discuss the important modeling technique known as simulation

OTHER STATEMENTS

SAVE Statement.   The SAVE statement has the following syntax.

SAVE Statement

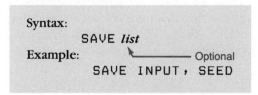

Syntax:
>   SAVE *list*
Example: ↖──────── Optional
>   SAVE INPUT, SEED

where the optional list is a list of variable names, array names (Chapter 7) and/or named common block names (Chapter 7), separated by commas.

Execution of an END statement in a subprogram usually *undefines* the local values not returned to the calling program unit. If we need to retain or *save* some or all local values in a subprogram, then we use the SAVE statement within the subprogram. In the example, values for the local variables INPUT and SEED are retained for subsequent references to the subprogram that contains this statement. (We use this statement in Function Subprogram RAND in Figure 6.13; more on this later.)

If the list is omitted, then *all* local values are saved for subsequent calls to the subprogram. The SAVE statement is one of the specification statements, which also include the PARAMETER statement and type statements. See the table FORTRAN 77 Program Composition inside the book's covers for its placement in the program unit.

INTRINSIC and EXTERNAL Statements.   These specification statements (see FORTRAN 77 Program Composition inside the book's covers) have the following form.

INTRINSIC Statement

Syntax:

     INTRINSIC *list of intrinsic function names*

Example:

     INTRINSIC COS, LEN, TAN

This statement identifies a name in its list as an intrinsic function. Some programmers prefer to use this statement as a matter of programming style, since it clearly shows the names of intrinsic functions used in the program unit. Also, we *must* use the INTRINSIC statement if a *specific* intrinsic function is to be used as an actual argument in a subprogram reference.

Specific intrinsic functions specifically dictate data types in *both* the argument lists and returned values. For example, function DPROD in Table A.1 is a specific intrinsic function with real arguments and a double-precision returned value. The specific intrinsic functions in Table A.1 are DPROD, all the character functions, and all the logical functions. All other functions, called generic intrinsic functions, return a data type that's based on the data type in the argument list. Older FORTRAN programs that predate FORTRAN 77 use specific intrinsic functions not shown in Table A.1 (these are no longer needed in FORTRAN 77 programs). The following intrinsic functions are not allowed in actual argument lists: type conversion like INT, REAL, ICHAR, CHAR; largest and smallest value like MAX, MIN; and logical functions.

EXTERNAL Statement

Syntax:

      EXTERNAL *list*

Example:

      EXTERNAL FUN, ROOT

This statement identifies names in its list as external procedures, intrinsic functions, dummy procedures, and/or block data subprograms (Chapter 7).

A **procedure** is an external procedure, an intrinsic function, or a statement function. An **external procedure** is a subroutine or an external function. An **external function** is a function subprogram or a function specified by means other than FORTRAN (for example, an assembly language external function). **Dummy procedures** are procedure names that appear in dummy argument lists.

So why use the EXTERNAL statement? For the same reasons outlined under the INTRINSIC statement. First, some programmers prefer its use from a style viewpoint, as it clearly identifies external procedures. Second, it *must* be used within a program unit if an external procedure name or a dummy procedure name is used as an actual argument within that program unit.

FORTRAN LIBRARIES

Why would we want to use an external procedure name within an actual argument list? FORTRAN environments usually include libraries of "off-the-shelf" external functions that are available to referencing program units. Three popular commercial FORTRAN libraries are Calcomp Graphics Software Library, International Mathematical and Statistical Library (IMSL), and Numerical Algorithms Group (NAG). These libraries include thousands of FORTRAN subprograms for graphics (x–y line plots, bar graphs, and so forth), statistical algorithms (regression analysis, random number generation, and so on), numerical analysis (roots, solutions to simultaneous equations, integration, solutions to partial differential equations, and so forth), and other specialized algorithms in applied mathematics (like linear programming and other optimization algorithms). References to these external procedures sometimes require the name of another external procedure within an actual argument list, as seen in the following example.

EXAMPLE 6.3

ACCESSING EXTERNAL PROCEDURES IN FORTRAN LIBRARIES

To illustrate a reference to an external procedure in a FORTRAN library, suppose our local computer library has an external function called ROOT that finds the root of a mathematical function (if it exists). Also, suppose the mathematical function itself is a function subprogram, within our modular program, called F U N. The program unit within our modular program that requires the root of this mathematical function would include the following statements.

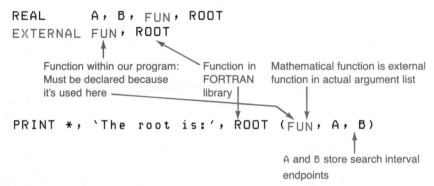

```
REAL        A, B, FUN, ROOT
EXTERNAL FUN, ROOT
```

Function within our program: Function in   Mathematical function is external
Must be declared because   FORTRAN   function in actual argument list
it's used here   library

```
PRINT *, 'The root is:', ROOT (FUN, A, B)
```

A and B store search interval
endpoints

Note that the external function F U N appears as an actual argument in the argument list of the function reference for R O O T; hence, F U N *must* be declared in the E X T E R N A L statement. R O O T need not be declared, except as a matter of programming style.

Alternatively, suppose the mathematical function of interest were the intrinsic function for the cosine (C O S). Now we could use the following statements.

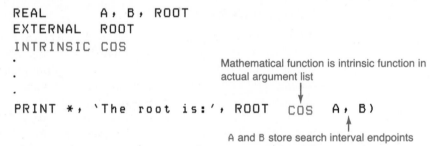

```
REAL        A, B, ROOT
EXTERNAL    ROOT
INTRINSIC COS
      .
      .
      .
```

Mathematical function is intrinsic function in
actual argument list

```
PRINT *, 'The root is:', ROOT  COS  A, B)
```

A and B store search interval endpoints

Since C O S is a generic intrinsic function, we don't have to use the I N T R I N S I C statement. If we insisted on using the specific intrinsic function D C O S (for double-precision values), however, then the I N T R I N S I C statement would be necessary and D C O S would replace C O S in the example.

Do you have access to FORTRAN libraries? If so, give Exercise 6 a try. ■

SIMULATION

Simulation is a methodology for conducting experiments using models of real or proposed systems. In practice, simulation is an extensively used tool in the sciences, engineering, and business. For example, it's been applied to military war (and business) gaming strategies, studying air pollution and air traffic control systems, space defense systems, scheduling computer jobs, studying the replication behavior of biological populations, and analyzing aircraft metal fatigue.

In FORTRAN we can view simulation as a numerical technique for modeling systems on a digital computer. Our interest in this section is in what is variously called Monte Carlo, stochastic, or probabilistic simulation. In this type of simulation, the computer is used to numerically generate random numbers (called pseudorandom numbers) that replicate the probabilistic behavior of some process. Let's illustrate this type of simulation by example.

EXAMPLE 6.4

SIMULATION OF DICE TOSSES

Consider the probability distribution in Table 6.2 for the toss of a single die. For example, the probability of tossing a die and getting a face value of 3 is 1/6. In the absence of a die we could simulate the process of tossing a die in any of several ways. For example, we could individually label 6 poker chips (we're into games in this example) with the numbers 1 through 6, insert them in a container, shake, and pick one out. This replicates the experiment of throwing a die, since the probability (1/6) of getting a chip with a specific number (say, 3) is identical to the probability of rolling a die and coming up with that specific face value (3).

Now, suppose we can use the computer to generate uniformly distributed, real, pseudorandom numbers in the interval 0.0–1.0. By uniformly distributed numbers we mean that the chance of any one number falling at any one point in the interval is the same as the chance of its falling on any other point in the interval. By pseudorandom numbers we mean that the numbers are generated by a numerical (algorithmic) process rather than by a real random process like that generated by "white" electronic noise. To simplify our terminology, we will take random number to mean a uniformly distributed, real, pseudorandom number in the interval 0.0–1.0.

Take a look at the probabilities in Table 6.2 again. The chance of generating a random number between 0 and 1/6 is precisely 1/6, which (we can decide) is equivalent to the simulated event "face value of 1." The chance of generating a

TABLE 6.2   Probability Distribution for Toss of a Die

Face Value	Probability	Cumulative Probability
1	1/6	1/6
2	1/6	2/6
3	1/6	3/6
4	1/6	4/6
5	1/6	5/6
6	1/6	6/6

random number between 1/6 and 2/6 is also 1/6. We say that this is equivalent to having rolled a "face value of 2," since it has a probability of 1/6 . . . and so on.

Now take a look at the cumulative probabilities in Table 6.2. These values mark the class boundaries in a table lookup problem. For example, suppose 0.4 is the generated random number. This is equivalent to a roll with "face value 3," right? Looking down the last column of Table 6.2, we test "Is 0.4 ≤ 1/6?" False. "Is 0.4 ≤ 2/6?" False. "Is 0.4 ≤ 3/6?" True. Thus, the simulated toss is "face value 3." Note that the probability of a random number in the interval 2/6 to 3/6 is precisely 1/6, or the probability of rolling a 3.

This method of simulating experimental events is called the inverse transformation method, since it starts with the probability (the random number) and then finds the event. This is the inverse of the usual process, where we first state the event and then calculate its probability.

Figure 6.13 shows the listing and Figure 6.14 the runs of a modular program that simulates throws of two dice. Try roleplaying the test runs through the program, noting the following.

1. Function RAND uses what's called a multiplicative generator to generate random numbers based on the computer's word size in bits. This methodology is well beyond the scope of this book, but you should understand certain elements in this function.

    a. The function requires a seed value to get it going. We accomplish this by initializing the logical variable INPUT to T, which ensures we enter the if-then structure at the first reference. Thereafter, INPUT stores F. Note that INPUT stores a local value; hence, we need to save its F-value for subsequent calls by including it in the list of the SAVE statement. This guarantees that we enter the initial seed just once.

    b. Each time the function is referenced it requires the preceding seed value (see the assignment statement for RAND). Since SEED stores a local value, it also must be included in the SAVE statement.

    c. The first two runs show two different initial seed values, which gave us two different simulations of five tosses. Thus, we can use different initial seed values to *probabilistically replicate* the process. With different initial seeds, differences in the output are due to the probabilistic (random) behavior of the process. The third run enters the same initial seed as the first run. Thus, the first and third simulations are *exact replications* of one another, as the identical sequence of random numbers was generated. The use of identical random number sequences is an important feature in simulation, as it allows us to judge effects of system variables without the intervening effect of randomness. We ask you to explore these ideas in some of the simulation exercises at the end of the chapter.

2. Subroutine DIESIM selects face value using the table lookup logic described earlier.

```
      PROGRAM DICE
* * * * * * * * * * * * * * * * * * * * * * * * * * * * * * * * * * * *
*                                                                     *
*        Simulation of dice tosses                                    *
*                                                                     *
*         Inputs number of tosses, seed                               *
*         Simulates roll of two dice using Function RAND              *
*         Outputs roll                                                *
*                                                                     *
*         Modular structure:                                          *
*                                                                     *
*           Main program...  Inputs number of tosses; references      *
*                            RAND and DIESIM to simulate each of      *
*                            two dice; outputs roll number, face      *
*                            value of each die, sum of dice.          *
*                                                                     *
*               Sub. DIESIM..... Determines face value of a die based *
*                                on its pseudorandom number.          *
*                                                                     *
*               Function RAND... Inputs seed; generates pseudorandom  *
*                                number.                              *
*                                                                     *
*                                                                     *
*           Key (main program):                                       *
*                                                                     *
*           DIE1..... Face value of first die                         *
*           DIE2..... Face value of second die                        *
*           HEAD..... Print head                                      *
*           LINE..... Print line                                      *
*           RAND..... Pseudorandom number function                    *
*           RN1...... Pseudorandom number for first die               *
*           RN2...... Pseudorandom number for second die              *
*           SPACE.... Print space                                     *
*           SUM...... Sum of two dice                                 *
*           TOSS..... Toss number (DO-variable)                       *
*           TOSSES... Number of tosses (DO-limit)                     *
*                                                                     *
* * * * * * * * * * * * * * * * * * * * * * * * * * * * * * * * * * * *
* ---------
*   Type names
* ---------
      CHARACTER  HEAD*50, LINE*50, SPACE*14
      INTEGER    DIE1, DIE2, SUM, TOSS, TOSSES
      REAL       RAND, RN1, RN2
* ---------
*   Initialize
* ---------
      HEAD = '          Toss    First Die  Second Die    Roll '
      LINE = '================================================'
      SPACE = '   '
* ---------
*   Simulate tosses
* ---------
      PRINT *, 'DICE SIMULATOR'
      PRINT *
      PRINT *, 'Enter number of tosses'
      READ  *, TOSSES

      DO 100 TOSS = 1, TOSSES

        RN1 = RAND ()
        RN2 = RAND ()          ←——— External function references

        IF ( TOSS .EQ. 1 ) THEN

          PRINT *
          PRINT *, SPACE, LINE
          PRINT *, SPACE, HEAD
          PRINT *, SPACE, LINE

        END IF
```

FIGURE 6.13   **Program that simulates dice throws (*continued on next page*)**

```
      CALL DIESIM ( RN1, DIE1 )                    ──── Subroutine references
      CALL DIESIM ( RN2, DIE2 )  ◄────

    SUM = DIE1 + DIE2

    PRINT *, SPACE, TOSS, DIE1, DIE2, SUM

100 CONTINUE

    PRINT *, SPACE, LINE

    END


    SUBROUTINE DIESIM ( RN, DIE )
* * * * * * * * * * * * * * * * * * * * * * * * * * * * * * * *
*                                                             *
*    Simulates single die                                     *
*                                                             *
*        Receives pseudorandom number                         *
*        Selects face value of die by inverse transformation method *
*        Returns face value of die                            *
*                                                             *
*        Key:                                                 *
*                                                             *
*           DIE.................. Face value of die           *
*           ONE, TWO, ..., SIX... Cumulative probability parameters *
*           RN................... Pseudorandom number in interval 0-1 *
*                                                             *
* * * * * * * * * * * * * * * * * * * * * * * * * * * * * * * *
*  Type names
*
      INTEGER  DIE
      REAL     ONE, TWO, THREE, FOUR, FIVE, SIX, RN
*
*  Set cumulative probabilities
*
      PARAMETER ( ONE   = 1.0 / 6.0,
     +            TWO   = 2.0 / 6.0,
     +            THREE = 3.0 / 6.0,
     +            FOUR  = 4.0 / 6.0,
     +            FIVE  = 5.0 / 6.0,
     +            SIX   = 6.0 / 6.0 )
*
*  Select face value
*
      IF ( RN .LE. ONE ) THEN
         DIE = 1

      ELSE IF ( RN .LE. TWO   ) THEN
         DIE = 2

      ELSE IF ( RN .LE. THREE ) THEN
         DIE = 3

      ELSE IF ( RN .LE. FOUR  ) THEN
         DIE = 4

      ELSE IF ( RN .LE. FIVE  ) THEN
         DIE = 5

      ELSE IF ( RN .LE. SIX   ) THEN
         DIE = 6

      END IF

      END
```

FIGURE 6.13   *(continued)*

```
           FUNCTION RAND ()
  • • • • • • • • • • • • • • • • • • • • • • • • • • • • • • • • • • • •
  •                                                                      •
  •        Pseudorandom Number Generator                                •
  •                                                                      •
  •           Receives nothing                                          •
  •           Inputs initial seed                                       •
  •           Calculates uniformly-distributed pseudorandom real number •
  •              in the range 0-1                                       •
  •           Returns pseudorandom number                               •
  •                                                                      •
  •           Key:                                                       •
  •                                                                      •
  •              INPUT.... Input seed?  True or False                   •
  •              PARM1.... First parameter                              •
  •              PARM2.... Second parameter (See Note)                  •
  •              PARM3.... Third parameter                              •
  •              RAND..... Pseudorandom number                          •
  •              SEED..... Seed, or number used to generate next pseudo-•
  •                        random number                                •
  •                                                                      •
  •           Note:                                                      •
  •                                                                      •
  •           PARM2 is based on 32-bit word machines.  If your machine  •
  •           is not 32-bit, then replace the given value for this      •
  •           parameter with the value given by 2**(bits - 1).          •
  •                                                                      •
  • • • • • • • • • • • • • • • • • • • • • • • • • • • • • • • • • • • • •
  •━━━━━━━━━━━━━━━━━━━━━━━━━━━━━━━━━━━━━━━━━━━━━━━━━━━━━━━━━━━━━━━━━━━━━━━━━
  • Type names
  •━━━━━━━━━━━━━
  •        LOGICAL    INPUT
  •        INTEGER    PARM1, PARM2, SEED
  •        REAL       PARM3, RAND
  •━━━━━━━━━━━━━━━━━━━━━━━━━━━━━━━━━━━━━━━━━━━━━━━━━━━━━━━━━━━━━━━━━━━━━━━━━
  • Save values for next function reference
  •━━━━━━━━━━━━━━━━━━━━━━━━━━━━━━━━━━━━━━━━━━━
  •        SAVE   INPUT, SEED
  •━━━━━━━━━━━━━━━━━━━━━━━━━━━━━━━━━━━━━━━━━━━━━━━━━━━━━━━━━━━━━━━━━━━━━━━━━
  • Assign parameters
  •━━━━━━━━━━━━━━━━━━━━
  •        PARAMETER (PARM1 = 65539, PARM2 = 2147483647, PARM3 = 1.0 / PARM2)
  •━━━━━━━━━━━━━━━━━━━━━━━━━━━━━━━━━━━━━━━━━━━━━━━━━━━━━━━━━━━━━━━━━━━━━━━━━
  • Initialize to ensure initial seed is entered
  •━━━━━━━━━━━━━━━━━━━━━━━━━━━━━━━━━━━━━━━━━━━━━━━━━
  •        DATA   INPUT / .TRUE. /
  •━━━━━━━━━━━━━━━━━━━━━━━━━━━━━━━━━━━━━━━━━━━━━━━━━━━━━━━━━━━━━━━━━━━━━━━━━
  • Generate pseudorandom number
  •━━━━━━━━━━━━━━━━━━━━━━━━━━━━━━━━━
  •        IF ( INPUT ) THEN
  •━━━━━━━━━━━━━━━━━━━━━━━━━━━━━━━━━━━━━━━━━━━━━━━━━━━━━━━━━━━━━━━━━━━━━━━━━
  •           Enter initial seed and reset INPUT to False
  •           ━━━━━━━━━━━━━━━━━━━━━━━━━━━━━━━━━━━━━━━━━━━━━
  •           PRINT *
  •           PRINT *, 'Enter random number seed as odd integer'
  •           READ  *, SEED
  •
  •           INPUT = .FALSE.
  •━━━━━━━━━━━━━━━━━━━━━━━━━━━━━━━━━━━━━━━━━━━━━━━━━━━━━━━━━━━━━━━━━━━━━━━━━
  •        END IF
  •
  •        SEED = SEED * PARM1
  •
  •        IF ( SEED .LT. 0 ) THEN
  •           SEED = ( SEED + 1 ) + PARM2
  •        END IF
  •
  •        RAND = REAL ( SEED ) * PARM3
  •━━━━━━━━━━━━━━━━━━━━━━━━━━━━━━━━━━━━━━━━━━━━━━━━━━━━━━━━━━━━━━━━━━━━━━━━━
  •        END
```

— Word size on your machine?

FIGURE 6.13   *(continued)*

```
DICE SIMULATOR                          First run

Enter number of tosses
5                                                            ──── Initial seed
Enter random number seed as odd integer                      ──── Simulation
2001

            Toss      First Die   Second Die     Roll

             1            1           3            4
             2            4           4            8
             3            5           1            6
             4            4           3            7
             5            6           4           10
```

```
DICE SIMULATOR                          Second run

Enter number of tosses
5                                                      ──── Different initial seed gives
                                                            different output (probabilistic
Enter random number seed as odd integer                ──── rather than exact replication)
12345

            Toss      First Die   Second Die     Roll

             1            3           2            5
             2            2           5            7
             3            4           2            6
             4            4           3            7
             5            2           6            8
```

```
DICE SIMULATOR                          Third run

Enter number of tosses
5                                                            ──── Initial seed same as first run
Enter random number seed as odd integer                      ──── Simulation exactly replicates
2001                                                              first simulation

            Toss      First Die   Second Die     Roll

             1            1           3            4
             2            4           4            8
             3            5           1            6
             4            4           3            7
             5            6           4           10
```

FIGURE 6.14   **Simulations of dice tosses**

3. We can use the external random number function as is for other simulations. See Exercises 21–27 at the end of the chapter. ∎

6.6 PROGRAMMING TIPS

DESIGN AND STYLE

1. On Using Modular Programming. The *bottom line* in using modular programming is lower software development and maintenance costs. Therefore, we take the perspective here that we are dealing with the development, testing, and maintenance of large commercial programs.

   a. The assignment of sets of related tasks to modules makes large programs more manageable (the divide-and-conquer strategy).

   b. Tasks that need to be repeated at different points in a program are best implemented as modules, since this reduces the amount of coding. Our factorial module is a good example of this.

   c. A program may use a task that has already been programmed. Assigning this task to a utility module makes it unnecessary to "*reinvent the wheel.*" The IMSL, Calcomp Graphics, and NAG Libraries make a living on this idea.

   d. The development of large programs requires a team of programmers. The use of modules facilitates the management of the project: one can assign specific modules to specific programmers. This specialization and division of labor is an established principle of managerial economics.

   e. Modular programming is a form of stepwise refinement, in which we need not refine a particular task at the point of call. For example, suppose the control module requires the use of five separate, elaborate tasks, among other things. As we design the control module (that is, write pseudocode), we need not provide the details for those tasks at that time. Rather, we simply indicate five calls to those modules. Later we can refine each module in turn.

   f. Modular programming facilitates the debugging process, since bugs are more easily isolated in modules for diagnosis and correction. Moreover, modules can be debugged one at a time by a procedure called **top-down testing.** To illustrate, open the book to the hierarchy chart in Figure 6.10 (without losing this page). We could first code and debug the main program before coding the other modules. In this case dummy modules (also called program stubs) are used in place of Modules 2–8. Each dummy module might be nothing more than a PRINT statement that gives a message like "Module 3 is not ready yet" and an END statement. Once the main program is debugged, we can proceed to the next level of detail: the writing and debugging of Modules 2 and 3 . . . and so on.

g. The subsequent maintenance of modular programs is easier, since tasks are more clearly defined and isolated. For example, adding, dropping, or revising a menu item in Program COMBO simply requires the addition of a new module, the deletion of a module, or changes within a module.

2. **On Designing Modular Programs.** Start with the overall (top-down) modular design of the program. The hierarchy chart is especially useful here. In designing modules, keep in mind the desirable properties of single-entry/single-exit, independence, and manageable size. Don't forget the proper structure for modular programs, as described in Figures 6.1 and 6.2.

3. **Documentation.** Check out the documentation in our modular programs. The main program now includes a description of the modular structure. The description of tasks for each module includes the subprograms called by that module. Including the hierarchy chart within the main program's documentation would be even better. Variable keys are specific to each module. Subprograms include a description of values received and values sent. The increased complexity of modular programs requires increased documentation to enhance understanding.

4. **Function or Subroutine Subprogram?** Once we specify a module we need to answer the question "Should this be a function or a subroutine?" Make it a function subprogram if the purpose of the module is the return of a single value; otherwise, make it a subroutine subprogram.

5. **Optimization Note: Don't Overmodularize.** Don't break up a program into too many small modules. This not only can impair readability, but it also degrades processor time. This is because subprograms increase overhead, or processor time that's devoted to housekeeping chores. Subprograms increase overhead because entry to and exit from subprograms take up processor time.

COMMON ERRORS

1. **Untyped Function.** Don't forget to type the function name in both the calling program unit and the function subprogram. Within the latter, we can do it in either of two ways, as described on page 234. Not typing the function results in implicit typing (see page 30), which can give unintended results (like truncation).

2. **Noncorrespondence of Argument Lists.** Reread the paragraph on "Argument list correspondence" on page 229. Ignoring this issue can lead to syntax errors, execution errors, or unpredictable (system-dependent) results that give logic errors.

3. **Forgetting Assignment of Function Name.** Remember that the name of an external function is also a variable within that function subprogram. Thus, it must be given a value sometime before the return. For example, Function FACT in Figure 6.9 must have the variable FACT within the subprogram; its value is assigned by the assignment statements.

4. **Unintentional Redefinition of Dummy Argument.** Reread the paragraph on "Argument association" and the subsequent warning on pages 230 and 231.

5. **Bugs, Bugs, Bugs.** The following quotations are excerpted from a front-page article in the *Wall Street Journal* (January 28, 1987) titled "As Complexity Rises, Tiny Flaws in Software Pose a Growing Threat":

> The tiniest software bug can fell the mightiest machine—often with disastrous consequences . . . software defects have killed sailors, maimed patients, wounded corporations, and threatened to cause the government-securities market to collapse. Such problems are likely to grow as industry and the military increasingly rely on software to run systems of phenomenal complexity . . .

> "Any software system that is large and has to work perfectly the first time has two strikes against it . . . Star Wars would face a determined adversary—that's strike three."

> Sometimes fixing a small bug can lead to greater problems. Two years before the first launch of the space shuttle, a programmer changed the timing on some shuttle software by one-30th of a second. Unknown to the National Aeronautics and Space Administration, the minuscule change introduced a 1-in-67 chance that the shuttle's five on-board computers wouldn't work in sync. Twenty minutes before the launch in April 1981, the bug appeared, the computers couldn't communicate and NASA scrubbed the flight . . .

> Bank of New York discovered how high the stakes can be in late 1985. A computer error blocked the bank from delivering huge amounts of government securities to customers and accepting payment. As a result, the bank was forced to borrow $23.6 billion overnight from the Federal Reserve Bank of New York to cover the shortfall and pay $5 million interest on the loan.

> The U.S. Defense Department faces a daunting task making its weapons software bug-free, partly because of the sheer size of the job. The Pentagon estimates that it will spend $30 billion in 1990 on weapons software . . . demand for software is growing so rapidly that by 1990 the industry will be short one million programmers and analysts to do the work.

While bugs (computer and otherwise) are a fact of life, we do have fairly effective pesticides in modular and structured programming.

FOLLOW-UP EXERCISES

*1. **Subroutine DIF.** Write and run an interactive program that demonstrates Subroutine DIF in Figure 6.3.

2. **Program CHART.** Modify the program in Figure 6.6 as follows.

a. Input the bar character, instead of forcing the use of =.

b. Suppose the length in GRADE is specified as 30. Any problems? Suppose we wish to restrict the output field for the label to 10 characters. Can we limit the output in LABEL by changing its length to 10 within the subroutine? Can you think of another way of limiting the output field to 10 while still using the assumed length declarator (∗)?

c. What happens if LENGTH stores 60?

∗d. Scaled bar. Scale the length of the bar as follows: If the maximum length is 50 or less, then print the bar as done in the example; else scale the bar length so that the new length is the integer part of

(original length) · (50 / max length)

where the maximum length is an input variable.

∗e. Sex and income. Generate a bar chart for the following frequency distribution.

Sex	Income
Female	$70,000
Male	90,000

∗3.   Plot subroutine. Use some ideas from Subroutine BCHART in Figure 6.6 to create a new subroutine that plots values of the function $y = f(x)$. In other words, this subroutine prints a plot character (say, ∗) based on the y-value instead of a bar. The subroutine prints an x-value, a y-value, and the plot character on a line. The subroutine receives the plot character through its argument list. Note that the plot runs down the screen or page (has a vertical rather than horizontal orientation).

a. Test PLOT by writing a main program that inputs the plot character and the *x-value* range and generates values for the function

$$y = 0.1x^4$$

where x runs from −5 to 5 in increments of 0.5.

b. Suppose x were to run from −10 to 10 in increments of 1? (Hint: See Exercise 2d.)

c. Account for the fact that the function could take on negative values. For example, plot the function

$$y = -20 - 4x + x^2$$

over the x-range −10 to 10 in increments of 1. Input minimum and maximum values for the function. Scale the plot position as follows: The plot position is one for the minimum value and 50 for the maximum value; otherwise the plot position is proportionally based on the range (max y − min y). Develop a formula for the plot position as a function of y, max y, min y, 1, and 50. Plot the ┆ character at the coordinate where $y = 0$. This gives the plot a "horizontal" axis that runs down the screen or page. (Remember that the plot is rotated 90° clockwise from normal plots.)

4. **Program FACTOR.** With respect to the program and run in Figure 6.9:
   a. Roleplay the input of zero for number.
   *b. Try running Program FACTOR on your system and evaluate the factorial of 25. Overflow problem? How might you change the function to handle larger factorials?

5. **Program COMBO.** Modify the program in Figure 6.11 to include an error routine that flags $k > n$, or $k < 0$, or $n < 0$. While any of these conditions is violated, print an appropriate error message and reinput the values for k and n. Test run these errors through your program. Also make sure that negative numbers can't be entered when calculating factorials.

*6. **FORTRAN library.** Solve the root problem in Section 5.4 by using an external procedure from your local computer library. Do you have IMSL or NAG libraries?

*7. **Function RAND.** Write an interactive program that inputs the number of random numbers desired (n) and prints a table of random numbers, as follows.

Random Number

1	0.xxxxxx
2	
3	
.	
.	
.	
n	

ADDITIONAL EXERCISES

8. **Revisit: Microcomputer price quotations.** Modularize Program MICRO in Figure 4.2. Include the pricing structure in Example 4.4. Use a while structure to process quotes. Also see Exercise 8 in Chapter 4.

9. **Revisit: Synchronous satellite orbits.** Modularize Program ORBIT in Figure 4.7. Add a repetition structure to reoffer the menu. Also see Exercise 10 in Chapter 4.

10. **Revisit: Root bisection.** Modularize Program ROOT in Figure 5.10. Make the mathematical function whose root you're finding an external function. Select meaningful modules with respect to tasks.

11. **Revisit:** Modularize the most recent program you were assigned.

12. **Harmonic series function.** Write and test a function subprogram that returns the sum of the first n terms of the harmonic series

$$1 + 1/2 + 1/3 + \ldots + 1/n$$

The function receives n. Design the main program to interactively input values for n until zero is entered. Print n and the sum from the main program. Try the following values for n in your test run: 5, 10, 25, 50, 100, 1000, 1.0E+20, 0.

13. **Substring function.** Write and test a function subprogram that returns a substring starting at position *left* and ending at position *right.* The function receives the *string, left,* and *right.* Design the main program to interactively input the *string, left,* and *right.* Repeat while *left* or *right* is not zero. Print the *string, left, right,* and *substring* from the main program. The main program handles strings up to 70 characters long, but the function has no such restriction. Have the function print an appropriate error message if *left* > *right.* Try the following test data.

String	Left	Right
Harvey CORE	1	6
	8	11
	9	11
	10	10
	10	8
	10	0

14. **Fibonacci function.** Write and test a function subprogram that returns the *n*th Fibonacci number (see Exercise 18 in Chapter 4). The function receives *n.* Design the main program to interactively input values for *n* while zero is not entered. Print *n* and the Fibonacci number from the main program. Try the following values for *n* in your test run: 8, 9, 50, 100, 1000.

15. **Range statistics.** Write and test a subroutine that receives three real values and returns the minimum value, maximum value, and the range (maximum value less minimum value). Design the main program to interactively input three values until one of them is negative. Print from the main program the three values together with the three range statistics. Try the following values in your test run: 6, 7, 8; 6.10, 0.50, 4.75; 15.13, 10.78, 0.00; −1, 1, 1.

16. **Sort: Three values.** Write and test a subroutine that receives four values: three unsorted integer values and a code with value A for ascending (lowest value first) sort or value D for descending sort. The subroutine then sorts the three integer values accordingly, and returns them within the same three memory locations. Design the main program to interactively input the code and the three integer values until the code is X. Print the three sorted values from the main program. Try the following input in your test run: A, 3, 1, 2; d, 3, 1, 2; Z; X. The program should request reinput of a code while it's incorrect. Assign input of the code and its error routine to a subroutine.

17. **Sort: Three strings.** Write a subroutine based on the description in the preceding exercise, except use three strings instead of three integer values. Each of the three strings in the main program has a length of 50, but the subprogram has no such restriction. Try the following input in your test run: D, Mello, CORE, Dunn; A, Mello, CORE, Dunn; c; x. Have the program request reinput of a code while it's incorrect. Assign input of the code and its error routine to a subroutine.

18. **Simple harmonic motion.** Figure 6.15 shows a diagram of the displacement of a particle undergoing simple harmonic motion. The following three functions are important descriptors of the behavior of this particle.

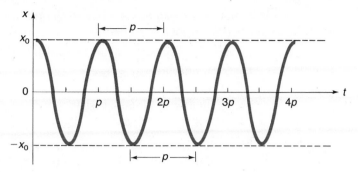

FIGURE 6.15   **Simple harmonic motion**

$$x(t) = x_0 \cos(\sqrt{K/M}t)$$
$$v(t) = -x_0\sqrt{K/M}\sin(\sqrt{K/M}t)$$
$$p = 2\pi\sqrt{M/K}$$

where $x(t)$ = displacement at time t in meters (m)
        $v(t)$ = projected displacement velocity at time t in meters per second (m/s)
         p = period of motion, or time required for one complete cycle, in seconds (s)
        x_0 = displacement at $t = 0$
        K = force constant in newtons per meter (N/m)
       M = mass in kilograms (kg)

a. Write and test a subroutine that receives x_0, K, M, and t and returns x, v, and p. Design the main program to interactively input x_0, K, M, and a range for t (min, max, and increment). Print the following table from the main program.

Simple Harmonic Motion with Period xxxxx.xx

Time	Displacement	Velocity
xx	xxxxx.xx	xxxxx.xx
↓	↓	↓

Use the following test data: $x_0 = 0.1$ m, $K = 8$ N/m (N stands for newton, or kg-m/s^2, a common measure of force), $M = 10$ kg, $t = 1$ s to 20 s in increments of 1 s.

b. Include a subroutine that plots the displacement over time. See the description in Exercise 3c.

19. **Probability functions.** Design, code, and test a modular program that offers the user a menu for calculating probabilities using the following probability functions.

Binomial probability mass function (pmf)

$$f(x) = (_nC_x)(p^x)(1 - p)^{n-x}$$

where $f(x)$ = probability of x "successes"

$\quad x$ = number of "successes"

$\quad _nC_x$ = combinations of n taken x at a time

$\quad n$ = number of binomial trials

$\quad p$ = probability of "success"

Note: A binomial experiment has n trials, two possible outcomes per trial—"success" or "failure"—and a constant probability p of "success" in each trial.

Exponential Cumulative Distribution Function (CDF)

$$F(x) = 1 - e^{-\lambda x}$$

where $F(x)$ = probability that the random variable is x or less

$\quad e$ = exponential constant

$\quad \lambda$ = parameter (inverse of mean)

$\quad x$ = real value of random variable

Poisson pmf

$$f(x) = \frac{(\lambda t)^x e^{-\lambda t}}{x!}$$

where $f(x)$ = probability that the random variable has value x

$\quad x$ = discrete value for random variable

$\quad \lambda$ = parameter (mean per unit time, distance, and so on)

$\quad t$ = number of continuum units (like time, distance, and so forth)

$\quad x!$ = x factorial

Try the following test runs. For n, x, and p in the binomial pmf: 10, 5, 0.5 and 10, 0, 0.5. For λ and x in the exponential CDF: 2, 0.5 and 2, 1.0. For x, λ, and t in the Poisson pmf: 5, 2, 3 and 0, 2, 3.

20. **Queuing models.** A queue is a waiting line of units ("customers") requiring service from a service facility ("servers"). Queuing models have been used for years to study the behavior of existing and proposed queuing systems. Some sample queuing systems: supermarket checkouts, highway toll booths, aircraft landing runways, telephone call switching equipment, hospital rooms, and on and on . . .) Design, code, and test a modular program that offers a menu for calculating selected operating characteristics of the following queuing models.

$M/M/1$ Model: Single queue, one server, Poisson customer arrivals, exponential service times

$$P_0 = 1 - \lambda/\mu$$

$$W_q = \frac{\lambda}{\mu(\mu - \lambda)}$$

$$L_q = \lambda W_q$$

where P_0 = probability of an idle system (zero customers)
W_q = expected steady-state time in queue
L_q = expected steady-state length of queue
λ = mean arrival rate (units per time period)
μ = mean service rate (units per time period) and $\lambda/\mu < 1$

Note: If $\lambda/\mu \geq 1$, then steady-state can't be reached; that is, the system never "settles down" to its long-run expected values for operating characteristics because the number of customers approaches infinity.

$M/M/c$ model: Independent multiqueue, c servers, Poisson customer arrivals, exponential service times

This model is c separate $M/M/1$ models with a queue in front of each server. The formulas for this model are the same as for the $M/M/1$ model, except that λ should be replaced with λ/c.

$M/M/c$ model: Single queue, c servers, Poisson customer arrivals, exponential service times

$$P_0 = \frac{1}{\left(\sum_{i=0}^{c-1} \frac{\rho^i}{i!}\right) + \frac{\rho^c}{c!\left(1 - \frac{\rho}{c}\right)}}$$

$$W_q = \frac{\rho^{c+1}}{\lambda(c-1)!(c-\rho)^2} \cdot P_0$$

$$L_q = \lambda W_q$$

where $\rho = \lambda/\mu$
c = number of servers

and P_0, W_q, L_q, λ, and μ are defined as before, and $\rho < c$.

In the test runs, let's assume a bank queuing system, where servers are tellers. Given

λ = 0.9 customer per minute
μ = 0.4 customer per minute

compare the operating characteristics of the models. Vary the number of servers from 1 to 5. Are the operating characteristics sensitive to variations in c?

SIMULATION EXERCISES
The following exercises use Function RAND

21. **Simulation: State lottery.** Consider a state lottery that generates a three-digit winning number each day. To select a winning number, the state does a nightly

TV thing with a machine that has 10 "whirling" balls numbered 0, 1, 2, . . . , 9. These balls are randomly moved by air streams, so that (supposedly) the selection of any one ball is as likely as any other ball. To generate a three-digit random number, three machines are used. The state is going to can the TV show (but not the daily lottery). They plan to trade in the three machines for a PC (the Lottery Commissioner has one at home). Design, code, and test a modular program that generates an *n*-digit "drawing." Try six test runs to generate separate three- and five-digit drawings using the following seeds: 1, 2001, 1.

22. **Simulation: Coin-flip game.** Sharpie, a long-time resident of Las Vegas, has proposed a game to Harvey CORE on one of his numerous B&P (Business and Pleasure) trips. The conversation, as overheard in the men's room, went something like this:

SHARPIE: (With a gleam in his eye.) I have a game you can't refuse . . .
HARVEY: (Skeptical, but definitely interested.) Oh yeah?
SHARPIE: (Warming up to the occasion.) Yeah. You flip a coin until the difference between the number of heads and the number of tails reaches three.
HARVEY: (Casually, with a subtle smile.) What kind of bread are we talking . . . ?
SHARPIE: (Barely containing his excitement.) You pay me $1 for each flip. When the game ends, I pay you $8. Okay . . . ?
HARVEY: (Feeling the pocket computer in his breast pocket, and figuring his counterproposal will end up paying for this B&P trip . . .) I'll get back to ya in five minutes . . .
SHARPIE: (Somewhat doubtful.) Well, okay . . .

How sharp is Sharpie? Design, code, and test a modular program that simulates this game. (It will probably take you more than five minutes . . .) Simulate 10, 100, and 1000 games. What's Harvey's expected loss per game? What should Harvey propose in place of the $8 if he wishes to pay for his $5,000 B&P trip in 100 games?

23. **Simulation: Craps.** A front-line bet in a game of craps works as follows.

First roll of dice
1. You win what you bet if on the first toss you roll 7 or 11 (a natural).
2. You lose what you bet if on the first toss you roll a 2, 3, or 12 (a crap).
3. If you roll a 4, 5, 6, 8, 9, or 10 on the first toss, then this number becomes your *point* for subsequent rolls.

Subsequent rolls of dice
4. To win, you must roll your point again *before* you roll a 7.
5. If you roll a 7 while trying to get your point, then you lose.
6. If neither your point nor 7 is rolled, then roll again.

a. Write a modular program that simulates the game of craps. Design a loop that simulates a single game of craps as described in items 1 through 6 above. The outcome of this loop is either "won" or "lost."
b. Add a second loop that simulates *n* games. Assume $1 is bet on each game. Keep track of wins and losses. Debug your program by simulating five games.

In your output for each roll, print the point on the first die, the point on the second die, and the overall point (sum of the two dice). At the end of a game print "won" or "lost." At the end of the five games print the following summaries: number of games won, number of games lost, your total dollar winnings (or losses), and the percent (of the total amount bet) dollar winnings (or losses). Use the seeds 1, 3, 5, 7, and 9.

c. Provide an option in the program to suppress the output for each roll and the "won" or "lost" output at the end of each game. For each of the following runs just print the summary statistics:

    (1) $n = 100$
    (2) $n = 500$
    (3) $n = 1000$
    (4) $n = 5000$

Based on your output, estimate the expected (percent) loss by betting the front line in craps.

24. **Simulation: Random walk.** The random walk model has been used to study the probabilistic behavior of radiation emission, chemical reactions, stock market prices, experiments in particle physics and gas dynamics, and many other physical and human-behavioral phenomena. Let's treat the collisions of gas particles as a random walk process, where each gas molecule "takes a random walk" between collisions as follows: After the ith collision, the molecule shoots off at angle θ_i for a distance d_i before the next collision, as illustrated in Figure 6.16. Assume θ_i is uniformly distributed over the interval $0°$–$360°$ and d_i is uniformly distributed over the interval 6×10^{-8} m to 12×10^{-8} m. Design, code, and test a modular program that simulates n collisions of a gas molecule. Print a table that shows the collision number (i), θ_i, d_i, and the coordinate (x_i, y_i). Input the range for d_i and the initial coordinate (x_0, y_0). In your test runs, show two simulations of 25 collisions each. Use the seeds 1999 and 2001, and try a starting coordinate at (0,0). Do the two simulations have a similar walk pattern? Does the particle end up in roughly the same place after 25 simulations? Hint: You need to develop four formulas: the first expresses θ_i as a function of its range and RAND; the second ex-

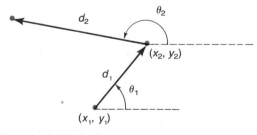

FIGURE 6.16   **Random walks following two collisions**

presses d_i as a function of its range and RAND; the third expresses x_i as a function of x_{i-1}, θ_{i-1}, and d_{i-1}; the last expresses y_i as a function of y_{i-1}, θ_{i-1}, and d_{i-1}.

25. **Simulation: Uniformity chi-square test.** Several tests have been developed to test the "goodness" of a random number generator. Here we describe a relatively simple test for assessing the uniformity of the generator over the interval 0–1. Suppose we generate n pseudorandom numbers over the interval 0–1. If we divide the interval into k equal subintervals, then we would *expect* an equal number of pseudorandom numbers (given by n/k) in each subinterval. For example, if we divide the interval into two equal subintervals, and generate 100 pseudorandom numbers, then we would expect 50 to fall in the first subinterval (0.0 to 0.5) and 50 to fall in the second subinterval (0.5 to 1.0). In practice, randomness and possible nonuniformity of the generator would not give the same number of *observations* in each subinterval. Design, code, and test a modular program with the following features.

   a. Input n and print a frequency distribution of observed pseudorandom numbers for 10 subintervals. For example, output for the first two subintervals might look as follows if we were to generate 500 pseudorandom numbers.

Frequencies		
Interval	Observed, o_i	Expected, e_i
0.0 to 0.1	45	50
0.1 to 0.2	55	50
.		
.		
.		
	500	500

   Use $n = 500$ in your test runs. Try two test runs, one with seed 2001 and the other with a seed of your choosing.

   b. Generate a bar chart of the observed frequencies.

   c. Calculate the chi-square statistic as follows.

   $$s = \sum_{i=1}^{k} \frac{(o_i - e_i)^2}{e_i}$$

   Note that low values for this statistic indicate "good" uniformity. Look up the chi-square test in a statistics text and test the null hypothesis that the observed values are generated from a uniform distribution. Assume 8 degrees of freedom when $k = 10$. Your conclusion? Note: This chi-square statistic is inaccurate if $n < 50$ and $e_i \le 5$.

26. **Simulation: pdf generator.** We can use Function RAND to generate simulated random variates (observations) for a real random variable defined by a **probability density function (pdf)**. Design, code, and test a modular program that offers a menu for generating random variates from the following pdfs.

Exponential pdf

$$x = -(\ln r)/\lambda$$

where x = exponential random variate
r = real pseudorandom number in the interval $0-1$
λ = parameter (inverse of mean)

Normal (Gaussian) pdf

$$x = \mu + \sigma(12/k)^{1/2}\left(\sum_{i=1}^{k} r - 0.5k\right)$$

where x = normal random variate
r = real pseudorandom number in the interval $0-1$
k = number of generated r values
μ = mean of normal pdf
σ = standard deviation of normal pdf

Uniform pdf

$$x = a + (b - a)r$$

where x = uniform random variate
r = real pseudorandom number in the interval $0-1$
a = left endpoint of interval for x
b = right endpoint of interval for x

Try the following test runs. For the exponential pdf: $\lambda = 0.9$. For the normal pdf: $k = 24$, $\mu = 9$, $\sigma = 1.73$. For the uniform pdf: $a = 6$, $b = 12$. Use $n = 10$ for each pdf, where n is input. Print a table for each pdf, as shown here for the exponential pdf.

Exponential pdf	
Number	Random Variate
1	xxxxx.xx
.	
.	
.	
10	

27. **Simulation: Stock market.**[3] Adam Smith, Jr., is an up-and-coming investor. (It runs in the family.) For many trading days he has observed the closing price (per share) behavior of a particular stock that he has taken a fancy to, as shown in Table 6.3.

Adam's parents have just given him 100 shares of this very same stock, which currently closed up $1 at $20 a share. This gift, however, is not without a

---

[3] Adapted from Frank S. Budnick, Dennis McLeavey, and Richard Mojena, *Principles of Operations Research for Management*, 2nd ed. (Homewood, IL: Irwin, 1988), p. 872.

TABLE 6.3   **Conditional Probabilities for Stock Price Behavior** [a]

Price Change Any Given Day to Nearest $1	Price Change the Following Day			
	Down $1	Same	Up $1	Up $2
Down $1	0.4	0.3	0.2	0.1
Same	0.3	0.3	0.3	0.1
Up $1	0.2	0.4	0.2	0.2
Up $2	0.3	0.4	0.2	0.1

[a] Each row in the table is a complete probability distribution given (conditional upon) the row event.

very specific condition: Adam must cash in his shares at the end of 30 days, as the money realized from this sale will become his expense money for his first year in college. Needless to say, Adam is concerned with having a good (extracurricular) time his first year in college, so he has devised an investment strategy that "can't lose," as follows:

(1) Sell all shares owned at the end of a trading day whenever the price of the stock increases.
(2) Buy as many shares as cash allows whenever the price of the stock has declined at the end of a trading day.
(3) Do nothing if price remains the same.

a. Simulate Adam's cash position at the end of 30 days given that 1% of the price of each share goes to the broker as commission whenever shares are bought or sold. Probabilistically replicate this simulation five times, using the seed 2001 for the first simulation.

b. Would Adam have been better off at the end of 30 days if he had just let the shares "ride" while spending his time at the beach? Why should you use the same seeds as part a in this comparison?

c. Can you think of other investment strategies? If so, simulate them and compare.

7

ARRAYS

The use of subscripted variables in algebra is a powerful means to manipulate large amounts of related data. Programming languages use arrays for much of the same reasons, as we demonstrate in this chapter.

7.1 ONE-DIMENSIONAL ARRAYS

Many of our programs until now have used the following execution structure:

```
While more data
   Read data
   Calculate
End loop
Print report
```

For example, if we had to find the mean of 500 temperatures, we would repeat the loop 500 times. For each repetition, we would read a temperature and sum it. Following the loop, we would print the mean. Suppose, however, that we wanted to print all temperatures below the mean, or print all differences from the mean. We would have to find the mean after the first loop is completed, and then add a second loop following the first that *rereads* the same temperatures. Within the second loop, we could print temperatures below the mean, or differences of each temperature from the mean. This approach is *I/O inefficient,* since it requires two complete reads of the same data.

Worse yet, suppose we needed to sort temperatures in ascending order. In this case, we could come up with 500 variable names to store each temperature in memory, and then develop a tedious algorithm that sorts the data. The READ statements alone would have 500 names in their lists! Moreover, program maintenance would be a nightmare, since the need to sort a different number of temperatures, say 600, would require substantial changes to the program itself. This solution would be both *code inefficient* and *maintenance inefficient.*

The solution to our temperature problem is to use an **array,** a sequence of data that's treated as a *related* group of memory locations. This idea borrows the concept from subscripted variables in algebra, as Table 7.1 illustrates. As in al-

TABLE 7.1   The FORTRAN-Array/Algebra-Subscripted-Variable Connection

Subscript i	Algebra: Subscripted Variables F_i	FORTRAN: Array Element Names F(I)	Sample Temperatures °F	Array Elements in Conceptualized Memory
				F
1	F_1	F(1)	62	1 · 62
2	F_2	F(2)	15	2 · 15
3	F_3	F(3)	20	3 · 20
4	F_4	F(4)	32	4 · 32
5	F_5	F(5)	68	5 · 68
· · ·	· · ·	· · ·	· · ·	· · ·
500	F_{500}	F(500)	90	500 · 90

gebra, the use of arrays is notationally convenient and flexible, as we can easily name, store, and manipulate all 500 temperatures.

ARRAY NAMES AND SUBSCRIPTS

An **array name** identifies a group of related memory locations. In Table 7.1 the array name F shows 500 memory locations. Each memory location is called an **array element.** The location of a particular array element is indicated by its subscript. A **subscript** acts as an index or pointer that locates a specific array element. The subscript 5 indicates the array element indexed 5 in Table 7.1.

An array element is referenced by its **array element name** according to the following form.

Array Element Name

> Syntax:
> *Array name (list of subscript expressions)*
> Example:
> F (I)   Subscript

The array name is any legitimate name in FORTRAN, or F in our example. A subscript expression is an *integer* expression. In our example, the subscript expression is I. If I stores 5, then the array element name F(5) references the 5th array element in Table 7.1. Note that the term subscript includes the parentheses surrounding the subscript expressions. If the array element name has a single subscript expression, then the array is a **one-dimensional array,** or vector in matrix algebra. A **two-dimensional array** has two subscript expressions in the subscript, separated by a comma. Its algebraic equivalent is a matrix. A **three-dimensional array** has three subscript expressions separated by commas, and so on. In this section we focus on one-dimensional arrays. In the next section we take up arrays with two or more dimensions, called **multidimensional arrays.**

EXAMPLE 7.1

CODING EFFICIENCY

The following DO-loop prints all 500 elements in array F of Table 7.1.

(Assume N stores 500)	Output (see Table 7.1)
``` DO 200 I = 1, N PRINT *, F(I) 200 CONTINUE ```	62 ← Contents in F(1) 15 ← Contents in F(2) · · · 90 ← Contents in F(500)

Note that the subscript expression I takes on the consecutive values 1, 2, 3, . . . , 500. Thus, the value in array element name F (1) is printed first, followed by the value in F (2), and so on.

This simple example clearly shows the coding efficiency of printing large amounts of stored, related data through an array. Without the array, we would have to have stored the 500 values in 500 different variable names (say, F 1, F 2, . . . , F 5 0 0), and then printed them through a series of PRINT statements with long output lists.

DECLARATION

Arrays must be declared for the compiler to reserve multiple memory locations. The best means to declare arrays is through type statements.

Array Declaration: Type Statements

Syntax:

Type keyword array name (list of dimension declarators), . . .

Example:

```
INTEGER F(1:500), N
```

The type keyword is one of the following: CHARACTER, INTEGER, REAL, DOUBLE PRECISION, LOGICAL or COMPLEX. The example types both the array F and the variable N as integer.

A dimension declarator has the following form.

Dimension Declarator

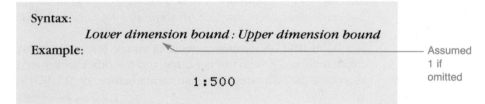

Syntax:

Lower dimension bound : Upper dimension bound

Example:

1:500

Assumed 1 if omitted

The lower dimension bound is a dimension-bound expression whose value determines the reference to the *first* array element. A dimension-bound expression is an integer expression containing constants, named constants (declared in PARAMETER statements), and variables. In our example, the value for the lower dimension bound is 1, so the first array element is F (1). If we omit the lower dimension bound and the colon, as in

```
INTEGER F(500), N
```

then the lower dimension bound is assumed to have a value of 1. The upper dimension bound is either a dimension-bound expression or an asterisk. The value of the upper dimension-bound expression determines the reference to the *last* array element. In our example, the upper dimension bound is 500, so the last array element is F(500). An asterisk as the upper dimension bound is used in subprograms as an assumed-size array declarator (Section 7.3). Integer variables may appear in dimension-bound expressions only as adjustable array declarators (Section 7.3). Dimension bounds may take on positive, zero, or negative values, but the value of the upper dimension bound must be greater than or equal to the value of the lower dimension bound.

The example uses *one dimension declarator* in the list of dimension declarators, since array F is a one-dimensional array. Two-dimensional arrays use *two dimension declarators,* three-dimensional arrays use *three dimension declarators,* and so on.

To summarize, a type statement now identifies which names in its list are array names, their type, the number of dimensions (equals the number of dimension declarators), and their sizes (total number of array elements). As before, we can type other names in the list of the type statement: variables, named constants, functions, and so on. In our example, we have declared an integer array F and an integer variable N. Moreover, array F is one-dimensional and has 500 array elements indexed on the values 1, 2, . . . , 500, as illustrated in Table 7.1. The examples in Table 7.2 show various configurations for dimension bounds.

The DIMENSION statement is an alternative to type statements for declaring arrays, as follows.

Array Declaration: DIMENSION Statement

Syntax:

> DIMENSION *list of array name* (*dimension declarator*)

Example:

DIMENSION DAY(7), F(500), X(-200:100), Y(30:50), Z(-50:-30)

The DIMENSION statement declares arrays, but does not type them. If DAY is a character array, F is an integer array, and the other arrays are real, then we would also place the following type statements before the DIMENSION statement.

TABLE 7.2   **Dimension Declarators and One-Dimensional Array Sizes**

Dimension Declarator $L : U$	Array Element Indices $L, L + 1, . . . , U$	Array Size $U - L + 1$
1 : 500	1, 2, . . . , 500	500
-200 : 100	-200, -199, . . . , 0, 1, . . . , 100	301
30 : 50	30, 31, . . . , 50	21
-50 : -30	-50, -49, . . . , -30	21

```
CHARACTER DAY*10
INTEGER F
REAL    X, Y, Z
```

Since we can use type statements to *both* type and declare arrays, we recommend the use of type statements in place of DIMENSION statements.

WARNING The value of the subscript expression may not fall outside the range given by its dimension bounds. For example, if array F is declared by F(1:500), then J in the array element name F(J) must store values in the range 1 to 500 inclusive; otherwise, we have a run-time error.

INPUT/OUTPUT

Let's assume that we wish to sequentially read and/or print elements in an array. We have a choice among three basic procedures for the efficient I/O of arrays.

1. **DO-loop.** The I/O statement having the array element name is in the body of the loop, the DO-variable is used as the subscript expression in the array element name, the DO-initial value is the index for the *starting* array element, and the DO-limit value is the index for the *ending* array element in the sequence. Each execution of an input statement processes a new input record and each execution of an output statement prints a new output line. Example 7.2 illustrates this approach.

2. **Implied-DO list.** The implied-DO list is an item within the input list of a READ statement or the output list of a PRINT or WRITE statement, as follows.

Implied-DO list

> Syntax:
>
> $(Dlist, DO\text{-}variable = DO\text{-}initial, DO\text{-}limit, DO\text{-}increment)$
>
> Example:
>
> (F(I), I = 1, N)

Dlist is a list of expressions (usually array element names), as in the usual input and output lists of READ, PRINT, and WRITE statements. The other components in the implied-DO list are defined as for the DO statement. Items within dlist are input or output repeatedly according to the repetitions indicated by the DO-initial, DO-limit, and DO-increment values. In the example, given that N stores 5, the values in F(1), F(2), . . . , F(5) are input or output. Example 7.3 shows I/O with implied-DO lists.

3. **Array Name Technique.** If we use the array name in an I/O list, then the *entire* array (as defined by its dimension bounds) is input or output. Example 7.4 shows this technique.

EXAMPLE 7.2

I/O WITH DO-LOOP

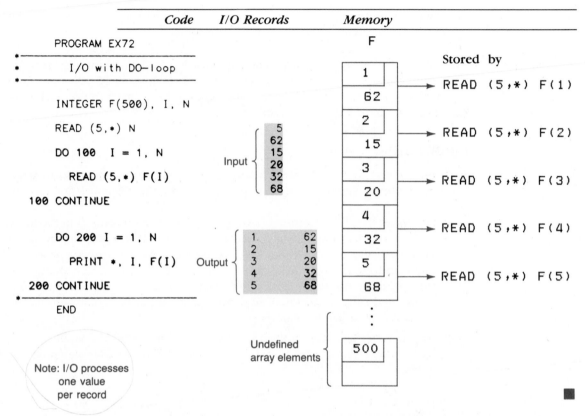

Code	I/O Records	Memory

PROGRAM EX72

* I/O with DO-loop

INTEGER F(500), I, N

READ (5,*) N

DO 100 I = 1, N

    READ (5,*) F(I)

100 CONTINUE

DO 200 I = 1, N

    PRINT *, I, F(I)

200 CONTINUE

END

Input:
```
5
62
15
20
32
68
```

Output:
```
1    62
2    15
3    20
4    32
5    68
```

Memory F:

| 1 |
| 62 | → READ (5,*) F(1) |
| 2 |
| 15 | → READ (5,*) F(2) |
| 3 |
| 20 | → READ (5,*) F(3) |
| 4 |
| 32 | → READ (5,*) F(4) |
| 5 |
| 68 | → READ (5,*) F(5) |

Stored by

Undefined array elements { 500

Note: I/O processes one value per record

Note that each execution of the READ statement in the first DO-loop processes a new input record. Also, the input list in the READ statement only has one item, so each READ operation inputs a single data value from the input record. Since we only input the first five array elements in a 500-element array, array elements 6 through 500 are undefined; that is, the program has not stored values in these array elements (although the compiler may have).

Make sure you understand the following functional equivalences.

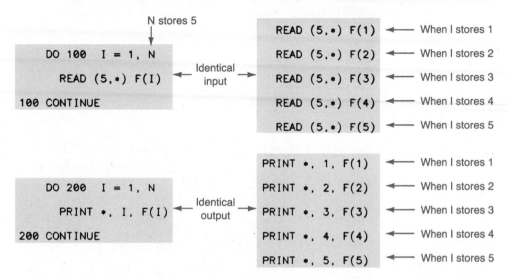

In the output, note that each PRINT statement has two items in its list, the index I and the array element name F(I), so two values are printed per output line. Also, the PRINT statement is executed five times, so five output lines are printed.

EXAMPLE 7.3

I/O WITH IMPLIED-DO LIST

Code	I/O Records	Memory

```
PROGRAM EX73
```

                                                        F

```
*─────────────────────────
*     I/O with Implied-DO List
*─────────────────────────
      INTEGER F(500), I, N
```
                                    Input

```
      READ (5,*) N
```
                             5
                             62 15 20 32 68

```
      READ (5,*) ( F(I), I = 1, N)
```
                                   Output

```
      PRINT *, (I, I = 1, N)
```
                           1   2   3   4   5

```
      PRINT *, (F(I), I = 1, N)
```
                          62   15   20   32   68

```
*─────────────────────────
      END
```

Memory F array:

1	62
2	15
3	20
4	32
5	68
⋮	
500	

Note: I/O processes
multiple values
per record

Undefined
array elements

Note that execution of the second READ statement processes an input record with *multiple* values. In Example 7.2 we had to place *one* value per input record. In the current example, we have more flexibility: We can place either multiple values or single values on input records.

Make sure you understand the following functional equivalences.

```
                                              ———— N stores 5
READ (5,*) ( F(I), I = 1, N )
                                              ———— Identical input
READ (5,*) F(1), F(2), F(3), F(4), F(5)
                                          ———— N stores 5
PRINT *, (I, I = 1, N)
                                          ———— Identical output
PRINT *, 1, 2, 3, 4, 5
                                          ———— N stores 5
PRINT *, (F(I), I = 1, N)
                                          ———— Identical output
PRINT *, F(1), F(2), F(3), F(4), F(5)
```

In the output, note that each PRINT statement has five items in its list, so five values are printed per print line.

If we use an END = specifier in a READ statement with an implied-DO list, then we have an **implied eof loop.** In this case, we eliminate the first input record (the 5) and we rewrite the first part of the sample program as follows.

```
INTEGER    UBOUND
PARAMETER ( UBOUND = 500 )
INTEGER    F(UBOUND), I, N
READ ( 5, *, END = 100 ) ( F(I), I = 1, UBOUND )
100 CONTINUE
    N = I - 1
```

After input of the last data value 68 into F(5), the DO-variable I is incremented to 6. The attempt to input a value for F(6) encounters an eof condition, so control is transferred to the statement labeled 100. The index of the last array element is then stored in N as one less than the value stored in I.

Note that the named constant UBOUND stores the upper dimension bound. This also serves as the DO-limit in the implied-DO list, which ensures that the value in the DO-variable would not exceed the upper dimension bound. ■

I/O WITH ARRAY NAMES

The following examples show some functional equivalences between implied-DO lists and using an array name in an I/O list.

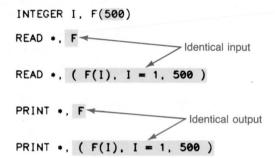

```
INTEGER I, F(500)

READ *, F                          Identical input

READ *, ( F(I), I = 1, 500 )

PRINT *, F                         Identical output

PRINT *, ( F(I), I = 1, 500 )
```

NOTE 1 I/O with a DO-loop that repeats *n* times is functionally equivalent to *n* separate I/O statements (see Example 7.2). I/O with an implied-DO list that repeats *n* times is functionally equivalent to a single I/O statement having *n* items in its list (see Example 7.3).

NOTE 2 We recommend the use of named constants for dimension bounds whenever the same dimension bounds appear in more than one place in the program, as done in Example 7.3. This simplifies program maintenance.

COMMON OPERATIONS

Certain operations on arrays in addition to I/O are common. The following examples illustrate array initialization, sums of array elements, and correspondence among arrays.

ARRAY INITIALIZATION

As with variables, we may need to initialize elements in an array. For example, the following statements perform a run-time initialization by storing zeros in each prescribed array element during execution of the program.

```
                              Can be variable or named constant (or constant)
                              Can be less than upper dimension bound

    DO 100 K = 1, NUMBER

        SUM(K) = 0.0

100 CONTINUE
```

If we only need to initialize the array elements once during any one computer run, then we can specify a compile-time initialization by using the DATA statement.

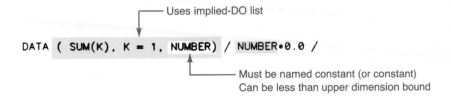

Uses implied-DO list

DATA (SUM(K), K = 1, NUMBER) / NUMBER*0.0 /

Must be named constant (or constant)
Can be less than upper dimension bound

Alternatively, we can compile-time initialize *all* elements in an array by using the array name technique.

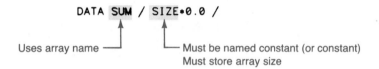

DATA SUM / SIZE*0.0 /

Uses array name ——

Must be named constant (or constant)
Must store array size

Note the following distinctions between these two approaches to initialization.

- The run-time initialization is used whenever the array needs to be reinitialized more than once during any one computer run.
- The run-time initialization is used whenever the number of array elements being initialized is based on the input data. In our example, the array size might be 100 elements (SIZE stores 100), but only elements 1 through 75 need to be initialized in a given computer run (an input statement stores 75 in NUMBER). ■

EXAMPLE 7.6

ARRAY SUM

Suppose we need to find the integer part of mean temperature for the first five elements in our temperature array. The following code does the trick, where SUM and MEAN are typed integer.

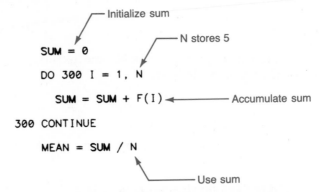

```
        SUM = 0
        DO 300 I = 1, N
            SUM = SUM + F(I)
300 CONTINUE
        MEAN = SUM / N
```

As the DO-loop repeats, values in F(1), F(2), F(3), F(4), and F(5) are successively added to the value in SUM, giving us the "running" sum 62, 77, 97, 129, and 197 based on the array elements in Example 7.2. Following the loop, SUM stores 197, giving 39 in MEAN. ■

EXAMPLE 7.7

ARRAY CORRESPONDENCE

Continuing our temperature problem, suppose we have declared the character array CITY with

```
        CHARACTER CITY(500)*15
```

and input its values for the first five array elements as follows.

Input Data

Memory

```
5
  'Los Angeles'  62
  'Chicago'      15
  'Toronto'      20
  'Boston'       32
  'Miami'        68
```

CITY		F
1		1
Los Angeles		62
2		2
Chicago		15
3		3
Toronto		20
4		4
Boston		32
5		5
Miami		68
⋮		⋮

Code

```
READ (5,*) N

DO 100 I = 1, N

    READ (5,*) CITY(I), F(I)

100 CONTINUE
```

Arrays CITY and F are termed corresponding arrays or parallel arrays, since corresponding array elements based on subscript values store different characteristics for the same entity. In our example, the entity is *city* and the characteristics are *name* and *temperature.*

I/O records for corresponding arrays are best conceptualized as a new record for each entity. In our example, we placed a city's name and temperature on the same input record, one record per city. This gives the input record a tablelike appearance, which is more readable (for us humans). The same idea holds for output.

7.2 MULTIDIMENSIONAL ARRAYS

Multidimensional arrays are useful for processing related data having two or more attributes. For example, if we wish to store °F temperature readings for up to 500 cities at just one point in time, then we have temperatures based on a *single attribute* (city) and the *one*-dimensional array shown earlier and reproduced in Figure 7.1 for five cities. If, however, we wish to classify the temperatures both by city and season (winter, spring, summer, and fall), then we have *two attributes* (city and season) and the *two*-dimensional array shown in Figure 7.1. If we wish to also classify the temperatures by year (three selected years), then we have

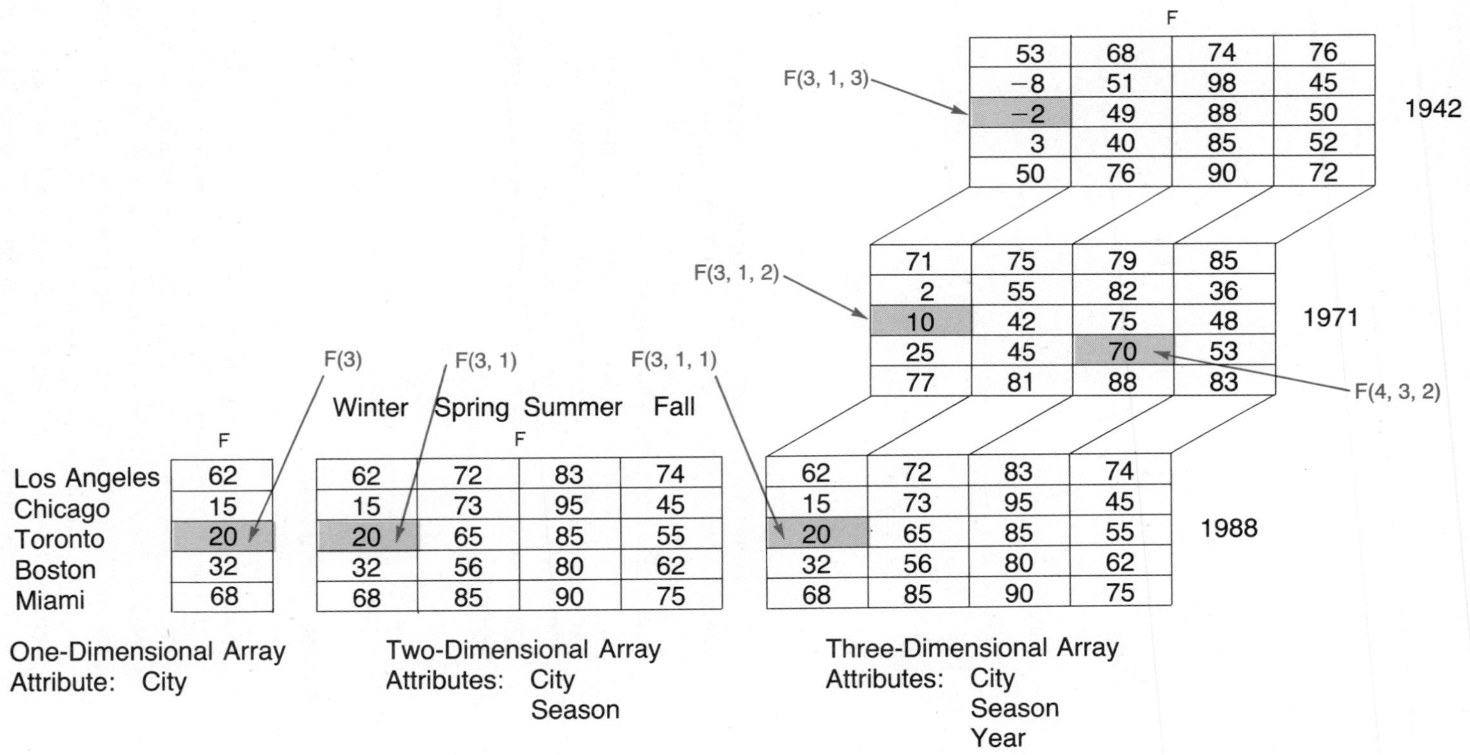

FIGURE 7.1 One-, two-, and three-dimensional temperature arrays

three attributes (city, season, and year) and the *three*-dimensional array illustrated in Figure 7.1.

FORTRAN 77 allows up to seven dimensions, but here we focus on the more common two-dimensional arrays, or matrices in matrix algebra. In Exercises 16 and 41d we ask you to process three-dimensional arrays.

ARRAY NAMES AND SUBSCRIPTS

Array names, subscripts, and array element names are defined for multidimensional arrays as they are for one-dimensional arrays (see page 276). The only difference is the *number* of subscript expressions in the list of subscript expressions.

Two-dimensional arrays have *two* subscript expressions in the array element name, as in F (I , J) for the two-dimensional temperature array in Figure 7.1. In this case, the first subscript expression I represents the *i*th city (1, 2, 3, 4, 5) and the second subscript expression J represents the *j*th season (1, 2, 3, 4). We can picture memory locations for this array as follows (for just five cities).

Array F

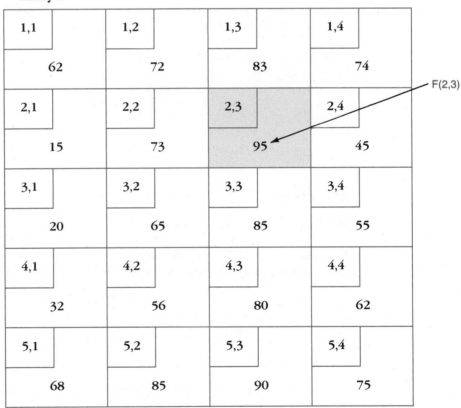

The two-dimensional array is best visualized as a table, where the array element is a cell having a row and column index. In the example, we have a 5×4 array, or a table with 5 rows and 4 columns. The array element indexed on row 2 and column 3 is referenced by the array element name F(2,3), which stores the value 95. Note that FORTRAN uses the algebraic convention of specifying the row subscript followed by the column subscript.

Subscripting Conventions: Two-Dimensional Arrays

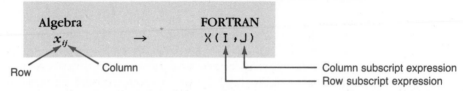

Three-dimensional array element names use three subscript expressions. In this case it's best to visualize the array as a table with depth or layers. In Figure 7.1 the three-dimensional temperature array is a $5 \times 4 \times 3$ array, or a table with 5 rows, 4 columns, and 3 layers. For example, the temperature in Boston (row 4) in the summer (column 3) of 1971 (layer 2) is 70 in Figure 7.1. The corresponding array element name is F(4,3,2).

Subscripting Conventions: Three-Dimensional Arrays

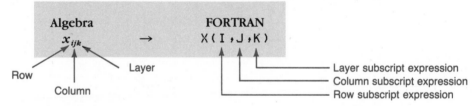

DECLARATION

Multidimensional arrays are declared exactly as one-dimensional arrays are, except the list of dimension declarators has one dimension declarator for each dimension (see page 277). For example, suppose we need to declare F as an integer two-dimensional array, where the first dimension (rows) has dimension bounds from 1 to 500 and the second dimension (columns) has dimension bounds from 1 to 4. The following type statement declares this array.

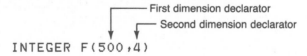

If we wish array F to have a third dimension with three layers, then we would declare as follows.

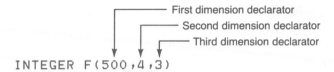

```
INTEGER F(500,4,3)
```

Each of these examples assumes a lower dimension bound of 1. If we want the first dimension for array F to run from a lower dimension bound of -200 to an upper dimension bound of 100, then we could use the following.

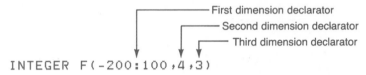

```
INTEGER F(-200:100,4,3)
```

If we wish to store city names up to 15 characters in a 500-element one dimensional array named CITY, season names up to 6 characters in a 4-element one-dimensional array named SEASON, and integer years in a 3-element one-dimensional array named YEAR, then we could use the following type statements.

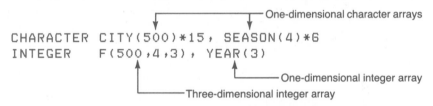

```
CHARACTER CITY(500)*15, SEASON(4)*6
INTEGER   F(500,4,3), YEAR(3)
```

As in one-dimensional arrays, we can use DIMENSION statements to declare multidimensional arrays, but we prefer type statements for the reasons outlined earlier.

INPUT/OUTPUT

The I/O of multidimensional arrays uses the same three approaches as the I/O of one-dimensional arrays: DO-loop, implied-DO list, and array name technique. Of these, we don't recommend the array name technique because multidimensional arrays are not stored in our tablelike, conceptualized order. For example, two-dimensional arrays are usually stored in a column by column manner, which means that I/O using the array name technique would process the first column first, the second column next, and so on. Column-wise I/O is undesirable because the array would not look like a table to our human eyes. It's usually best to use a combination of DO-loops and implied-DO lists to process multidimensional arrays, as the following example illustrates.

EXAMPLE 7.8

I/O OF TWO-DIMENSIONAL ARRAY

The following sample code and I/O process the two-dimensional temperature array in Figure 7.1.

Code	I/O Records

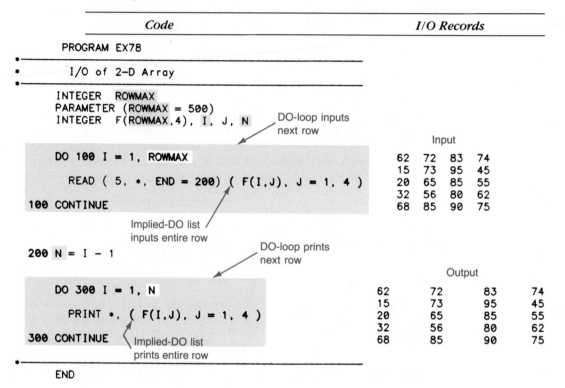

```
PROGRAM EX78

*    I/O of 2-D Array

     INTEGER   ROWMAX
     PARAMETER (ROWMAX = 500)
     INTEGER   F(ROWMAX,4), I, J, N      DO-loop inputs
                                         next row
                                                          Input
     DO 100 I = 1, ROWMAX                            62  72  83  74
                                                     15  73  95  45
        READ ( 5, *, END = 200) ( F(I,J), J = 1, 4 ) 20  65  85  55
                                                     32  56  80  62
100  CONTINUE                                        68  85  90  75

            Implied-DO list
            inputs entire row
                                    DO-loop prints
                                    next row
200  N = I - 1
                                                         Output
     DO 300 I = 1, N                           62      72      83      74
                                               15      73      95      45
        PRINT *, ( F(I,J), J = 1, 4 )          20      65      85      55
                                               32      56      80      62
300  CONTINUE                                  68      85      90      75
            Implied-DO list
            prints entire row

     END
```

Note the following:

1. Each time the DO-loop is incremented, a new row is processed. The DO-variable I is the row subscript expression. For example, when I stores 1 in the first DO-loop, the first row in the array is input; when I is incremented to 2, the second row is input; and so on.

2. Each implied-DO list has four array elements, or an entire row. The DO-variable J is the column subscript expression. For example, when I is 5 in the second DO-loop, the entire last row in the matrix is printed, since J runs from 1 to 4. This is functionally equivalent to the following:

   ```
   PRINT *, F(5,1), F(5,2), F(5,3), F(5,4)
   ```

3. When I is incremented to 6 in the first DO-loop, an eof condition is encountered (there's no sixth row in the input data), so execution control goes to

the statement labeled 200. N thus stores 5, which is the number of rows (out of 500 possible) used in this computer run. N also serves as the DO-limit in the second DO-loop.

4. ROWMAX stores the upper dimension bound for rows, or 500. Since the number of rows utilized (out of 500) depends on the data (5 in our example), we use ROWMAX as the DO-limit for the first DO-loop, and let the eof condition signal when the last row has been input. As a matter of programming style, we use the named constant ROWMAX for the 500, since it appears twice in the program. This simplifies program maintenance should we wish to change the 500 in the future. Assuming we will always process temperatures over four seasons, we simply use the constant 4, rather than specifying a named constant for the upper dimension bound on columns. ■

COMMON OPERATIONS

Operations common to one-dimensional arrays are also common to multidimensional arrays. These include initializations, sums of rows and columns, and array correspondences. We commonly use nested DO-loops in these operations, where each DO-variable is a convenient index that corresponds to a particular subscript expression. The next example shows how we can sum and average the columns in a two-dimensional array. Exercises 14 and 15 extend these operations to rows.

EXAMPLE 7.9

COLUMN AVERAGES FOR TWO-DIMENSIONAL ARRAY

The following program calculates and prints the integer averages for each season (column) in our temperature array from the preceding example. We started with the program of Example 7.8 and made the changes indicated by the screens.

Code	I/O Records

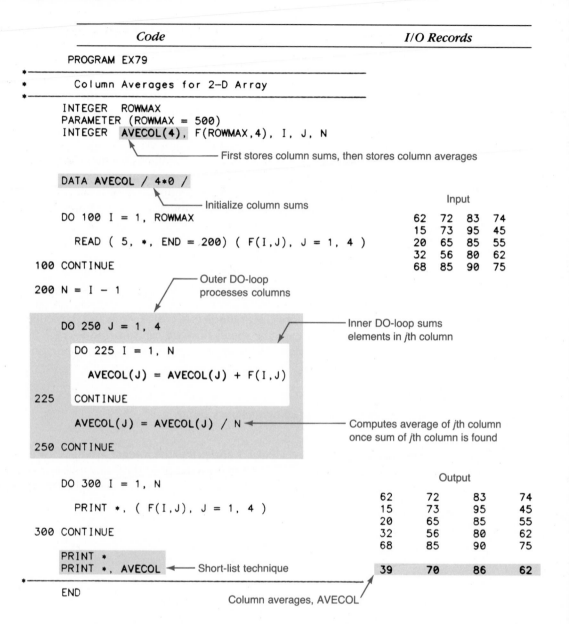

```
PROGRAM EX79
```
*──
*   Column Averages for 2-D Array
*──
```
INTEGER   ROWMAX
PARAMETER (ROWMAX = 500)
INTEGER   AVECOL(4), F(ROWMAX,4), I, J, N
```
— First stores column sums, then stores column averages

```
DATA AVECOL / 4*0 /
```
— Initialize column sums

Input

```
DO 100 I = 1, ROWMAX

    READ ( 5, *, END = 200) ( F(I,J), J = 1, 4 )

100 CONTINUE

200 N = I - 1
```

62	72	83	74
15	73	95	45
20	65	85	55
32	56	80	62
68	85	90	75

— Outer DO-loop processes columns

```
    DO 250 J = 1, 4

        DO 225 I = 1, N

            AVECOL(J) = AVECOL(J) + F(I,J)

225     CONTINUE

        AVECOL(J) = AVECOL(J) / N

250 CONTINUE
```

— Inner DO-loop sums elements in *j*th column

— Computes average of *j*th column once sum of *j*th column is found

```
    DO 300 I = 1, N

        PRINT *, ( F(I,J), J = 1, 4 )

300 CONTINUE

    PRINT *
    PRINT *, AVECOL
```
— Short-list technique

Output

62	72	83	74
15	73	95	45
20	65	85	55
32	56	80	62
68	85	90	75
39	**70**	**86**	**62**

*──
```
END
```
— Column averages, AVECOL

Note the following:

1. Array AVECOL is a one-dimensional array that will end up storing the average of each column. We can visualize this array as a new row following the matrix F. Each element in AVECOL thus stores the average of the column above it. See the output to better visualize this conceptual relationship. In Exercise 15 we ask you to store column averages as a row in F itself.

2. Before calculating averages, we're going to use each element in AVECOL to temporarily store the sum of its respective column. The DATA statement initializes column sums to zero. We could have used another one-dimensional array or a temporary variable to store column sums, but the way we did it is more storage efficient.

3. Two *nested* DO-loops are needed to find column averages. The *outer* DO-loop processes each column; that is, it starts with the first column, sums the elements in that column using the *inner* DO-loop, calculates the average, and then repeats for each subsequent column. Note the convenience of using DO-loops to systematically process array elements. The outer DO-variable J is the index for the *column* subscript expression, and the inner DO-variable I is the index for the *row* subscript expression. We consciously chose I for the row index and J for the column index for consistency with matrix notation in algebra, where F_{ij} refers to the matrix element in row i and column j.

4. Keeping track of the values of subscript expressions is the key to understanding matrix operations. In our example, note that the *row loop is inside the column loop.* This means that each time the outer (column) loop repeats (the value in J increases by 1), the inner (row) loop goes through a complete cycle (the values in I run from 1 to 5). For example, when J stores 2 (the second column), the inner (row) loop systematically changes the value in I from 1 to 5; that is, the five elements in column 2 are summed. Look at the sample program and I/O to confirm the following roleplay.

I	J	F(I,J)	AVECOL(J)	
			0	← Initialized to zero
1	2	72	72	← AVECOL(2) = AVECOL(2) + F(1,2)
2	2	73	145	← AVECOL(2) = AVECOL(2) + F(2,2)
3	2	65	210	← AVECOL(2) = AVECOL(2) + F(3,2)
4	2	56	266	← AVECOL(2) = AVECOL(2) + F(4,2)
5	2	85	351	← AVECOL(2) = AVECOL(2) + F(5,2)

Exit from the inner DO-loop thus gives the sum of the second column, or 351. The integer part of the average is calculated next as follows (look at the program).

```
AVECOL(2) = AVECOL(2) / N
          =    351     / 5
          =     70
```

To make sure you understand the behavior of subscript expressions as DO-variables, try Exercises 14 to 16. ∎

7.3 ARRAYS AND SUBPROGRAMS

We introduced function and subroutine subprograms in the last chapter. We now conclude their treatment by covering the association of arrays among program units.

ARGUMENT LISTS AND DECLARATIONS

The structure of subprograms and their references are unaffected by the use of arrays; that is, the look of a subprogram and the way we invoke it are the same as before. The appearance of an array in an argument list, however, requires some additional considerations and features. In particular we need to look at several alternatives for declaring arrays within subprograms. These are best illustrated by example.

> **EXAMPLE 7.10**
>
> **ARRAY IN ARGUMENT LIST: MEAN OF ONE-DIMENSIONAL ARRAY**

Figure 7.2 illustrates a function subprogram that receives the first N elements in an array and returns the mean of these elements. Study the listing and I/O and note the points below.

1. The main program uses the temperature array from Example 7.3, but the function subprogram is perfectly general in that it will return the real mean of any N-element integer array where elements are indexed 1 through N.

2. The actual argument list contains N (the number of elements used in the array) and F (the array itself). These are passed to the external function.

3. The dummy argument list contains N (the number of elements used in the array) and LIST (the array). LIST is an example of a **dummy array**, since it appears as a dummy argument in the subprogram. In this context F is an example of an **actual array**, since its name is *not* a dummy argument. The argument lists are matched as shown in Figure 7.2: Actual argument N with dummy argument N and actual array F with dummy array LIST. In the sample run, 5 is used in dummy N and 62, 15, 20, 32, and 68 are used as the first five elements in dummy LIST. We can illustrate this argument association as shown in Table 7.3.[1] Note that only the first five elements in LIST are associated with the corresponding elements in F. This is because the array declarator LIST(N) is used in the subprogram, and N stores 5. This is one of three methods for declaring dummy arrays, as discussed next. ■

---

[1] Systems invariably use argument association by location/address (see page 230) for arrays, which means that LIST does not have separate storage locations; otherwise, storage for large arrays would be unnecessarily wasteful.

```
        PROGRAM EX710
*─────────────────────────────────────────────────────────
*          Array in argument list... Mean of 1─D array
*
*          Main program... Inputs 1─D temperature array, references
*                          Function XBAR, prints mean temperature.
*
*          Funct. MEAN.... Returns real mean of 1─D integer array.
*
*          Key:
*             F........ Fahrenheit temperature 1─D array
*             I........ DO─variable / subscript expression
*             MEAN..... Function that returns real mean of 1─D array
*             N........ Number of temperatures
*─────────────────────────────────────────────────────────
        INTEGER F(500), I, N
        REAL    MEAN

        PRINT *, 'How many temperatures?'
        READ *, N
        PRINT *
        PRINT *, 'Please enter temperatures.'
        READ *, ( F(I), I = 1, N )
        PRINT *

        PRINT *, 'Mean temperature...', MEAN ( N, F )
*─────────────────────────────────────────────────────────
        END


        FUNCTION MEAN ( N, LIST )
*─────────────────────────────────────────────────────────
*          Receives number of elements and 1─D integer array
*          Calculates real mean
*          Returns mean
*
*            Key:
*               K........ DO─variable / subscript expression
*               LIST..... 1─D integer array
*               MEAN..... Real mean of elements in LIST
*               N........ Number of elements in LIST
*               SUM...... Sum of N elements in LIST
*─────────────────────────────────────────────────────────
        INTEGER K, LIST(N), N, SUM
        REAL    MEAN

        SUM = 0
        DO 100 K = 1, N
           SUM = SUM + LIST(K)
    100 CONTINUE

        MEAN = REAL( SUM ) / REAL( N )
*─────────────────────────────────────────────────────────
        END


 How many temperatures?
 5

 Please enter temperatures.
 62 15 20 32 68

 Mean temperature...     39.4000
```

FIGURE 7.2   **Arrays in argument lists**

TABLE 7.3   **Argument Associations in Figure 7.2**

Actual Arguments	Values	Dummy Arguments
N	5	N
F(1)	62	LIST(1)
F(2)	15	LIST(2)
F(3)	20	LIST(3)
F(4)	32	LIST(4)
F(5)	68	LIST(5)
F(6)	Undefined	
.	.	
.	.	
.	.	
F(500)	Undefined	

Dummy arrays must be declared in subprograms, since subprograms are independently compiled and the compiler must identify arrays. We have three methods for declaring dummy arrays.

1. **Constant Array Declarator.** Each dimension-bound expression is an integer constant expression. This is the only method we have used for actual arrays. The following shows a constant array declarator for LIST in Figure 7.2.

   ```
   INTEGER K, LIST(500), N, SUM
                    ↑
                    └──── Constant array declarator
   ```

   In this case, the last column in Table 7.3 would show entries for LIST(6),..., LIST(500). This approach presents a maintenance problem if Function MEAN were to be used by other program units with arrays of varying sizes. For example, if a program unit has an array with 1000 elements, then we would change the 500 to 1000 in the subprogram to achieve array-size consistency. The next two approaches are better alternatives for overcoming this problem.

2. **Adjustable Array Declarator.** Dimension-bound expressions contain one or more integer variables. This is the approach we used in Figure 7.2.

   ```
   INTEGER K, LIST(N), N, SUM
                  ↑
                  └──── Adjustable array declarator
   ```

   The dummy variable N is an example of an **adjustable dimension bound,** which means that the dummy array LIST is taken to have an upper dimension bound whose value is given in N (5 in our example). Table 7.3 shows the proper associations. This approach illustrates good design from a maintenance point of view, since this subprogram will handle arrays of any size, so long as the lower dimension bound is 1 (see Exercise 17 for adjustable upper *and* lower dimension bounds).

Note in Figure 7.2 that the adjustable dimension bound N within the subprogram is part of the dummy argument list. In other words, the adjustable dimension 5 is necessarily passed to the subprogram by the referencing program unit.

When using adjustable dimension bounds for dummy arrays with two or more dimensions, the value in each adjustable dimension bound should *equal* the corresponding actual dimension; otherwise the conceptual relationship of array elements (as in a table of numbers) is not maintained. For example, consider the following.

```
PROGRAM MAIN
 . . .
INTEGER COLS, ROWS
PARAMETER (ROWS = 10, COLS = 5)
REAL MATRIX(ROWS,COLS)
 . . .
CALL SUB (ROWS, COLS, MATRIX)
 . . .
END
SUBROUTINE SUB (M, N, TABLE)
 . . .
INTEGER M,N
REAL TABLE(M,N)
 . . .
END
```

Actual array MATRIX and dummy array TABLE are conceptually identical in the sense that the first row in MATRIX corresponds to the first row in TABLE, the second row in MATRIX corresponds to the second row in TABLE, and so on. This is because the actual arguments in the CALL statement pass the actual upper dimension bounds (10 rows and 5 columns) to the subroutine. The subroutine uses these as the adjustable upper dimension bounds M and N for TABLE. The reference

```
CALL SUB (4, 3, MATRIX)
```

would not preserve our conceptual row-by-row association.

NOTE Don't forget to include adjustable dimension bounds in dummy argument lists. In multidimensional arrays, use adjustable dimension bounds that equal the corresponding actual dimensions to maintain conceptual associations.

3. **Assumed-Size Array Declarator.** An asterisk is used as the upper dimension bound of the last dimension. This is the third approach to declaring dummy arrays. In this case the asterisk indicates that the upper dimension bound of the dummy array is identical to the upper dimension bound of its corresponding actual array. In Figure 7.2 we could have declared the dummy array L I S T as follows.

```
INTEGER K, LIST(*), N, SUM
```
——————— Assumed-size array declarator

The dummy array L I S T is assumed to have an upper dimension bound of 500, as established by the declaration for its corresponding actual array F. In Table 7.3, the last column would include L I S T (6) to L I S T (500). This approach also reduces subprogram maintenance, since it automatically establishes upper-dimension-bound consistency between the dummy array and its corresponding actual array. Assumed-size array declarators are convenient for one-dimensional arrays that have lower dimension bounds of 1, as in Figure 7.2. It's not as useful for multidimensional arrays, since *the asterisk only applies to the upper dimension bound of the last dimension.* For example, in our illustration that matches real array MATRIX with dummy array TABLE, we could have used the following.

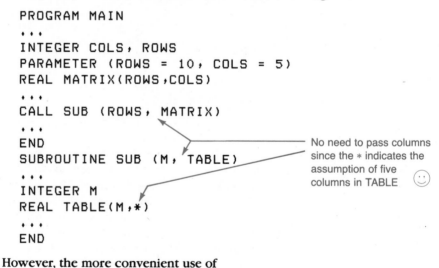

```
PROGRAM MAIN
  . . .
INTEGER COLS, ROWS
PARAMETER (ROWS = 10, COLS = 5)
REAL MATRIX(ROWS,COLS)
  . . .
CALL SUB (ROWS, MATRIX)
  . . .
END
SUBROUTINE SUB (M, TABLE)
  . . .
INTEGER M
REAL TABLE(M,*)
  . . .
END
```
No need to pass columns since the ∗ indicates the assumption of five columns in TABLE ☺

However, the more convenient use of

```
REAL TABLE(*,*)
```
                                                                    ☹

would provoke a compile-time error. It's simpler to use adjustable array declarators for dummy multidimensional arrays.

NOTE 1   If an assumed-size array declarator is used to declare a *character* dummy array, then make sure that the declared length of each dummy array element is identical to the declared length of each actual array element; otherwise, a complicated rule applies for establishing the size of the character dummy array.

NOTE 2 Adjustable and assumed-size array declarators are used only in function and subroutine subprograms.

COMMON STATEMENT

As you know, we use argument lists to associate names among different program units. The COMMON statement provides an alternative means to name association by establishing a common storage area that is used by two or more program units. The COMMON statement allows two types of common storage areas: blank common blocks and named common blocks. Let's look at each of these separately.

COMMON Statement: Blank Common Block

Syntax:
       COMMON *list of names*
Example:
       COMMON N, F

The COMMON statement is a nonexecutable statement that is placed among type statements and other specification statements (see FORTRAN 77 PROGRAM COMPOSITION inside the back cover). The list of names can contain variable names, array names, and array declarators. In our temperature example, we have two names: N is a variable name and F is a 500-element, one-dimensional array. The sample COMMON statement above establishes a **blank common block** with 501 storage locations: one for variable N and 500 for array F, in that order. This blank common block can be shared in *common* by all program units that use this form of the COMMON statement.

EXAMPLE 7.11

BLANK COMMON BLOCK

The program in Figure 7.3 is a revision of the earlier program in Figure 7.2. This version eliminates argument lists altogether by defining a blank common block for the number of elements used in the array and the array itself.

The association in a common block is by *relative position* rather than by name. This means that it's the order of names in COMMON statements that determines how variables and array elements are associated. In Figure 7.3, the blank common block is configured as shown in Table 7.4.

```
PROGRAM EX711
```

```
*--------------------------------------------------------------
*       Blank common block:   Revision of Program EX710
*
*         Main program... Inputs 1-D temperature array, references
*                         Function XBAR, prints mean temperature.
*
*         Funct. MEAN.... Returns real mean of 1-D integer array.
*
*         Key:
*           F........ Fahrenheit temperature 1-D array
*           I........ DO-variable / subscript expression
*           MEAN..... Function that returns real mean of 1-D array
*           N........ Number of temperatures
*--------------------------------------------------------------
      INTEGER F(500), I, N
      REAL    MEAN

      COMMON N, F   ◄──────────── Blank common block

      PRINT *, 'How many temperatures?'
      READ *, N
      PRINT *
      PRINT *, 'Please enter temperatures.'
      READ *, ( F(I), I = 1, N )
      PRINT *

      PRINT *, 'Mean temperature...', MEAN ()
*--------------------------------------------------------------
      END                                        No argument list

      FUNCTION MEAN ()
*--------------------------------------------------------------
*       Receives number of elements and 1-D integer array
*       Calculates real mean
*       Returns mean
*
*         Key:
*           K........ DO-variable / subscript expression
*           LIST..... 1-D integer array
*           MEAN..... Real mean of elements in LIST
*           N........ Number of elements in LIST
*           SUM...... Sum of N elements in LIST
*--------------------------------------------------------------
      INTEGER K, LIST(500), N, SUM
      REAL    MEAN
                                    Constant array declarator
      COMMON N, LIST

      SUM = 0
      DO 100 K = 1, N             Blank common block
        SUM = SUM + LIST(K)
  100 CONTINUE

      MEAN = REAL( SUM ) / REAL( N )
*--------------------------------------------------------------
      END
```

```
How many temperatures?
5

Please enter temperatures.
62 15 20 32 68

Mean temperature...    39.4000
```

FIGURE 7.3   **Blank common block**

TABLE 7.4   **Blank Common Block for Program in Figure 7.3**

		Associated names	
Storage	Main Program	Function MEAN
5	N	N
62	F(1)	LIST(1)
15	F(2)	LIST(2)
20	F(3)	LIST(3)
32	F(4)	LIST(4)
68	F(5)	LIST(5)
	F(6)	LIST(6)
.	.	.
.	.	.
.	.	.
	F(500)	LIST(500)

If we had mistakenly used the statement

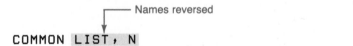

— Names reversed

COMMON LIST, N

in the subprogram, then LIST(1) would be associated with real N, LIST(2) with F(1),..., and dummy N with F(500). Since the last element in F is undefined, we would get a run-time execution error when dummy N is referenced in the subprogram's DO-loop. ∎

We might note the following points regarding blank common blocks.

1. Corresponding names among COMMON statements should be consistent with respect to type: integer with integer, real with real, character with character, and so on.

NOTE   If a character variable or array is in a common block, then all names in that common block must store character values.

2. *Arrays in* COMMON *statements must be declared by constant array declarators;* otherwise, it's a compile-time error. This is why we switched the array declarator for LIST from an adjustable array declarator (in Figure 7.2 we used the adjustable dimension bound N) to a constant array declarator (in Figure 7.3 we used the constant dimension bound 500).

3. We can include constant array declarators in the list of a COMMON statement. For example, in the main program we could have written the following.

```
INTEGER F, I, N
```
⬆ —————— Array name instead of constant array declarator
```
COMMON N, F(500)
```
⬆ ————— Constant array declarator

It's a matter of preference whether we declare arrays in common blocks or in type statements.

NOTE   Associations through common blocks are often preferred to associations through argument lists whenever many of the same names are to be associated across many program units. Argument lists are thus simplified or entirely eliminated, and the likelihood of errors is reduced by copying the same COMMON statements among the different program units.

It's also possible to create common blocks with separate identities by using the following form of the COMMON statement.

COMMON Statement: Named Common Blocks

Syntax:
       COMMON / *common block name* / *list of names* . . .
Example:
       COMMON / AREA1 / A, B, C / AREA2 / D, E

The common block name is the name of a common block; its syntax is the same as other symbolic names in FORTRAN. The list of names includes variables, arrays, and array declarators, as before. In the example, two named common blocks are created. The first is named AREA1 and its list of associated names is A, B, and C; the second named common block is AREA2, and its list of associated names is D and E.

EXAMPLE 7.12

NAMED COMMON BLOCKS

Figure 7.4 is a demonstration of three common blocks. Blank common shares a single variable among all three program units; common block BLOCK1 shares a character array between the main program and Subroutine ONE; common block BLOCK2 shares a real array between the main program and Subroutine TWO. Tables 7.5 to 7.7 show the configurations of these common blocks.

Note that the main program uses the character intrinsic function CHAR to generate the 65th, 66th, and 67th ASCII characters in the collating sequence (see Table A.1 in Module A). ■

```
        PROGRAM EX712
•————————————————————————————————————————————————————
•      Named common blocks demonstration
•————————————————————————————————————————————————————
        INTEGER    J, N, SIZE
        PARAMETER ( SIZE = 100 )
        CHARACTER LETTER(SIZE)
        REAL      X(SIZE)

        COMMON N ◄————————————————————— Blank common block

        COMMON / BLOCK1 / LETTER ◄————— First named common block

        COMMON / BLOCK2 / X ◄————————— Second named common block

        N = 3                          ┌— Character intrinsic function
        DO 100  J = 1, N               │

           LETTER(J) = CHAR( J + 64 )

           X(J)      = 0.5 * J

   100 CONTINUE

        CALL ONE
        CALL TWO
•————————————————————————————————————————————————————
        END

        SUBROUTINE ONE
•————————————————————————————————————————————————————
•      Shares blank common and BLOCK1 named common with Main Program
•————————————————————————————————————————————————————
        INTEGER    K, NUM, SIZE
        PARAMETER ( SIZE = 100 )
        CHARACTER CODES(SIZE)

        COMMON NUM ◄————————————————— Blank common

        COMMON / BLOCK1 / CODES ◄————— First named common block

        PRINT *, 'Subroutine ONE'
        PRINT *, '  Codes....', ( CODES(K), K = 1, NUM )
        PRINT *
•————————————————————————————————————————————————————
        END

        SUBROUTINE TWO
•————————————————————————————————————————————————————
•      Shares blank common and BLOCK2 named common with Main Program
•————————————————————————————————————————————————————
        INTEGER    I, N, SIZE
        PARAMETER ( SIZE = 100 )
        REAL      VALUES(SIZE)

        COMMON N ◄————————————————————— Blank common

        COMMON / BLOCK2 / VALUES ◄———— Second named common block

        PRINT *, 'Subroutine TWO'
        PRINT *, '  Values...', ( VALUES(I), I = 1, N )
•————————————————————————————————————————————————————
        END


   Subroutine ONE
      Codes.... ABC

   Subroutine TWO
      Values...   0.500000        1.00000         1.50000
```

FIGURE 7.4   **Named common blocks demonstration**

TABLE 7.5   **Blank Common Block in Figure 7.4**

	Associated Names		
Storage	*Main Program*	*Subroutine* ONE	*Subroutine* TWO
3	N	NUM	N

TABLE 7.6   **Named Common Block BLOCK1 in Figure 7.4**

		Associated Names	
	Storage	*Main Program*	*Subroutine* ONE
	A	LETTER(1)	CODES(1)
	B	LETTER(2)	CODES(2)
	C	LETTER(3)	CODES(3)
		LETTER(4)	CODES(4)
	.	.	.
	.	.	.
	.	.	.
		LETTER(100)	CODES(100)

TABLE 7.7   **Named Common Block BLOCK2 in Figure 7.4**

		Associated Names	
	Storage	*Main Program*	*Subroutine* TWO
	0.5	X(1)	VALUES(1)
	1.0	X(2)	VALUES(2)
	1.5	X(3)	VALUES(3)
		X(4)	VALUES(4)
	.	.	.
	.	.	.
	.	.	.
		X(100)	VALUES(100)

We might note the following points regarding named common blocks.

1. Different program units that reference the same *named* common block must be consistent with respect to not only name types but also size of the named common block. In Figure 7.4, the named common block BLOCK1 is referenced in two program units: the main program and Subroutine ONE. Each COMMON statement specifies a common block size of 100 storage locations (see Table 7.6). If we had declared array LETTER as 200 elements,

and left `CODES` at 100 elements, then we would have a syntax error. This is not true for blank common blocks. For example, we could have added a second variable to the `COMMON` statements in the main program and Subroutine `ONE`, but not to the `COMMON` statement in Subroutine `TWO`. This allows partial sharing of blank common blocks.

2. Arrays and variables in blank common blocks cannot be compile-time initialized through `DATA` statements; however, in named common blocks they can be initialized by using a block data subprogram, which we take up next.

NOTE We prefer named common blocks to blank common blocks when some program units need to share data that are of no concern to other program units. We also must use named common blocks if we wish to include both numeric data and character data in common blocks, since a single common block cannot contain both character data and numeric data. For example, in Figure 7.4 we cannot combine arrays `LETTER` and `X` into one common block, since it violates a syntax rule (see our note on page 304).

BLOCK DATA SUBPROGRAMS

As noted earlier, we can compile-time initialize variables and arrays in named common blocks by using a block data subprogram, as follows.

Block Data Subprogram

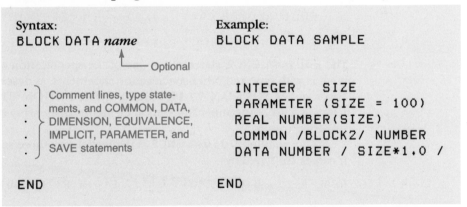

```
Syntax:
BLOCK DATA name
              ↑
              └── Optional

  ·  ⎫ Comment lines, type state-
  ·  ⎬ ments, and COMMON, DATA,
  ·  ⎬ DIMENSION, EQUIVALENCE,
  ·  ⎬ IMPLICIT, PARAMETER, and
  ·  ⎭ SAVE statements

END
```

```
Example:
BLOCK DATA SAMPLE


INTEGER     SIZE
PARAMETER (SIZE = 100)
REAL NUMBER(SIZE)
COMMON /BLOCK2/ NUMBER
DATA NUMBER / SIZE*1.0 /


END
```

The **block data subprogram** is a *nonexecutable* program unit that, like any other subprogram, can be placed anywhere following the main program. The block data subprogram begins with a **BLOCK DATA statement** and ends with an `END` statement. The BLOCK DATA statement includes an optional name for the block data subprogram. Only one *unnamed* block data subprogram is allowed per program. In the example, the block data subprogram called `SAMPLE` specifies the following: the integer named constant `SIZE` with a value of 100; the real array `NUMBER` with elements indexed 1 to 100; named common block `BLOCK2` containing elements in array NUMBER; and the initialization of all elements in NUMBER to 1.0.

EXAMPLE 7.13

BLOCK DATA SUBPROGRAM DEMONSTRATION

Figure 7.5 shows a revision of the program in Figure 7.4. The block data subprogram initializes all elements in the string array to ! and all elements in the numeric array to 1.0. Note that the named common blocks also must be specified within the block data subprogram by using the COMMON statement. ■

EQUIVALENCE STATEMENT

The COMMON statement specifies that storage locations are shared among *different* program units. If we wish to share storage locations within the *same* program unit, then we use the EQUIVALENCE statement.

EQUIVALENCE Statement

Syntax:

    EQUIVALENCE *list of* (*list of associated names*)

Example:

    EQUIVALENCE (A(1),B(1)),(C(2),D,E(3)),(F,G)

The EQUIVALENCE statement is one of the specification statements; its placement is with type and other specification statements, as described inside the back cover under FORTRAN 77 PROGRAM COMPOSITION. The list of associated names is a list of variable names, array element names, array names, and character substring names.

Our sample EQUIVALENCE statement shows three separate equivalences. If names are typed by

REAL A(5), B(5), C(3), D(5), E(4), F(100000), G(100000)

then the arrays share storage locations within the same program unit as follows.

Storage Locations

1	2	3	4	5

A(1) A(2) A(3) A(4) A(5)
B(1) B(2) B(3) B(4) B(5)

A(1) and B(1) share or reference the first storage location in the sequence. The relationships between A(2) and B(2), and so on, are automatically equivalenced since array names imply a sequence of adjacent storage locations. Thus 5 locations instead of 10 are needed.

```
      PROGRAM EX713
*---------------------------------------------------------------
*     Block data subprogram demonstration... Revision of Program EX712
*---------------------------------------------------------------
      INTEGER   N, SIZE
      PARAMETER ( SIZE = 100 )
      CHARACTER LETTER(SIZE)
      REAL      X(SIZE)

      COMMON N

      COMMON / BLOCK1 / LETTER

      COMMON / BLOCK2 / X

      N = 3

      CALL ONE

      CALL TWO
*---------------------------------------------------------------
      END


      SUBROUTINE ONE
*---------------------------------------------------------------
*     Shares blank common and BLOCK1 named common with Main Program
*---------------------------------------------------------------
      INTEGER   K, NUM, SIZE
      PARAMETER ( SIZE = 100 )
      CHARACTER CODES(SIZE)

      COMMON NUM

      COMMON / BLOCK1 / CODES

      PRINT *, 'Subroutine ONE'
      PRINT *, '  Codes....', ( CODES(K), K = 1, NUM )
      PRINT *
*---------------------------------------------------------------
      END


      SUBROUTINE TWO
*---------------------------------------------------------------
*     Shares blank common and BLOCK2 named common with Main Program
*---------------------------------------------------------------
      INTEGER   I, N, SIZE
      PARAMETER ( SIZE = 100 )
      REAL      VALUES(SIZE)

      COMMON N

      COMMON / BLOCK2 / VALUES

      PRINT *, 'Subroutine TWO'
      PRINT *, '  Values...', ( VALUES(I), I = 1, N )
*---------------------------------------------------------------
      END
```

FIGURE 7.5   **Block data subprogram demonstration (*continued on next page*)**

```
     BLOCK DATA
*──────────────────────────────────────────────────
*        Initializes all elements in string and number arrays
*──────────────────────────────────────────────────
     INTEGER    SIZE
     PARAMETER ( SIZE = 100 )
     CHARACTER  STRING(SIZE)
     REAL       NUMBER(SIZE)                        ──── Specification of named common blocks

     COMMON    / BLOCK1 / STRING       / BLOCK2 / NUMBER

     DATA STRING / SIZE * '!' /
                                      ┝ Compile-time initializations
     DATA NUMBER / SIZE * 1.0 /
*──────────────────────────────────────────────────
     END


 Subroutine ONE
    Codes....!!!

 Subroutine TWO
    Values...    1.00000        1.00000        1.00000
```

FIGURE 7.5   **(continued)**

Storage Locations

1	2	3	4	5	6	7

E(2) and C(1) share; E(3), C(2), and D(1) share; E(4), C(3), and D(2) share. Seven instead of 12 locations used, so 5 locations saved.

```
E(1) E(2) E(3) E(4)
     C(1) C(2) C(3)
          D(1) D(2) D(3) D(4) D(5)
```

Storage Locations

1	2	...	100000

F and G totally share corresponding elements. One hundred thousand instead of 200,000 locations used, so 100,000 locations saved.

```
F(1) F(2) ··· F(100000)
G(1) G(2) ··· G(100000)
```

Note the following points.

1. Arrays C, D, and E are said to be *partially associated* where arrays A and B, and F and G, are *totally associated.*

2. Names of type character can be equivalenced only with other names of type character. For example, the statements

```
CHARACTER A*10,B*6
EQUIVALENCE (A,B)
```

equivalence the first 6 (of 10) *character storage units* in A with the 6 character storage units in B.

3. Dummy arguments must not be equivalenced.

4. Two names in one common block or in two different common blocks must not be equivalenced.

5. Names having different numeric type may be equivalenced, but it's not suggested in practice since it may lead to unpredictable logic errors, depending on the hardware.

6. Associations in the list of an EQUIVALENCE statement apply only within the program unit where the EQUIVALENCE statement resides, unless one of the equivalenced names is part of a common block.

The primary justification for using EQUIVALENCE statements is that they can substantially reduce storage requirements. This is particularly desirable when several large arrays are used in one program, as illustrated by the 100,000 storage locations saved by equivalencing arrays F and G in the above example. Assuming F and G have different meanings and purposes within the program unit, then the act of equivalencing them is feasible only if we're through with one of the arrays before we begin manipulating the other. Otherwise logic errors may result.

NOTE   Unless storage is critical, we don't recommend the use of EQUIVALENCE statements, since they reduce program readability and increase the likelihood of syntax, execution, and logic errors.

7.4 SELECTED APPLICATIONS

This section illustrates three array applications that are commonly seen in practice: Table lookup, sorting, and XY-plots.

TABLE LOOKUP

A **table lookup** is an algorithmic procedure for accessing and relating data within a table. We first presented the table lookup problem in the microcomputer price quotation problem (Example 4.4). In that example, the table was a price table that related the price of a microcomputer to the order size. The table lookup problem thus determined the price to charge given the order size. We solved the problem by using a sequence of if-then structures, which theoretically we can use to solve any given table lookup problem. For large tables, however, we prefer the efficiency of the array approach presented next.

Problem Analysis.   Let's consider an insurance application by developing an interactive program that quotes annual premiums for a certain type of life insurance policy based on a person's age and the face value (death benefit) of the insurance. The premium schedule per $1000 of face value is given by the following table.

Premium Schedule

Upper Age Limit	Annual Premium per $1000 Face Value
20	$4.00
25	4.50
30	5.00
35	5.75
40	6.50
45	7.50
50	8.50
55	9.50
60	10.75
65	12.75
70	15.00
75	25.00

For example, a person 28 years old wishing a $100,000 policy would be quoted an annual premium of $500 based on the third row in the table (5.00 × 100). Note that the maximum insurance age is 75, from the last row in the table.

Output data
Quotation number for the day's run (1, 2, 3, . . .)
Annual premium (or uninsurable message if age exceeds 75)

Input data
Premium schedule as two-dimensional matrix (from data file)
Age as variable (from keyboard)
Face value as variable (from keyboard)

Parameters
Rows in premium schedule table (12)
Columns in premium schedule table (2)

Program Design.   Let's work with a modular program that shows a hybrid (batch/interactive) orientation. The program reads in the premium schedule from a data file into a two-dimensional matrix. It inputs a person's age and desired insurance face value interactively. At the user interface, let's have a screen orientation, with appropriate screen clears and screen pauses. Let's take the perspective that the program is to be used by an operator sitting at the terminal (all day!) with a set of headphones giving quotations over a telephone exchange. (It's believed that the

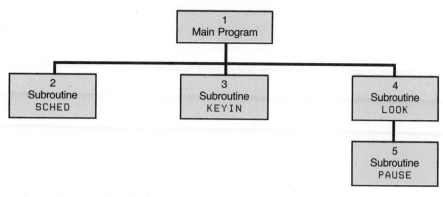

FIGURE 7.6   **Hierarchy chart for Program LOOKUP**

operator flips a switch to radio station WROC during lulls in the action, but no one knows for sure.)

Consider the following modular design, and the hierarchy chart in Figure 7.6.

Main program	Establishes main processing loop that repeats while age exceeds 0. Calls Subroutines SCHED to get premium schedule matrix; KEYIN to get age and face value; and LOOK to send age, face value, and premium schedule.
Subroutine SCHED	Reads premium schedule from data file into two-dimensional matrix. It passes matrix to main program.
Subroutine KEYIN	Inputs age and face value from keyboard, and sends to main program.
Subroutine LOOK	Receives age, face value, and premium schedule matrix from main program. Either prints uninsurable message or does table lookup and prints premium. Calls Subroutine PAUSE.
Subroutine PAUSE	Pauses screen.

Let's consider how we might design the table lookup logic in Subroutine LOOK. In our problem analysis we stated that a person aged 28 wishing a $100,000 life insurance policy would have to pay a $500 annual premium. Did you confirm that? How did you perform your table lookup? Typically, we scan the column of interest (the age column in the table) until we find the proper row. Then we scan across to the related column of interest (the premium column). Our eye/mind algorithm tells us that 28 fits within row 3 of column 1, which gives us an annual premium of $5.00 per $1000 face value. Let's further refine this process for the computer using pseudocode.

Table Lookup Algorithm

```
Initialize row (i) to 1
While age > ith upper age limit in column 1
    We haven't found proper row; try next row:
    i = i + 1
End loop
We found proper row: Premium per $1000 face
                     value is in 2nd column of
                     this (ith) row
```

Table Lookup Example: Age = 28

Row Number (i)	Upper Age Limit	Age > Upper Age Limit?	Action
1	20	True	Wrong row: Repeat
2	25	True	Wrong row: Repeat
3	30	False	Right row: Exit

Thus, our table lookup algorithm is equivalent to the human action of scanning entries in the first column, starting with the first row. While a person's age is greater than the current entry, we proceed to the next row. When we find an entry that's greater than age, we have found the correct row, which terminates our search.

What happens if the age is, say, 105? Try roleplaying the algorithm before reading on. We go through all 12 entries in the premium schedule without finding the correct row. What do you think would happen in the FORTRAN version of the algorithm? The row index i would exceed the row upper dimension bound of the matrix. The following decision structure takes care of this problem.

```
If age > last upper age limit then
   Print uninsurable message
Else
   Use table lookup algorithm
   Print premium
End if
```

Thus, the table lookup algorithm is invoked only if the age is within the last upper age limit in the table (75 in our example).

Program Code and Test.   Figure 7.7 shows the listings of Program LOOKUP and the data file, and Figure 7.8 illustrates a sample run. Study these figures and note the following.

```
        PROGRAM LOOKUP
* * * * * * * * * * * * * * * * * * * * * * * * * * * * * *
*                                                         *
*        Table Lookup:  Life Insurance Premium Quotations *
*                                                         *
*           Inputs premium schedule from data file, age interactively *
*           Looks up premium                              *
*           Outputs premium                               *
*                                                         *
*        Modular structure:                               *
*                                                         *
*           Main program... Repeats while age > 0; calls SCHED, *
*                           KEYIN, LOOK.                  *
*                                                         *
*              Sub. SCHED..... Reads premium schedule from data file. *
*                                                         *
*              Sub. KEYIN..... Inputs age, face value from keyboard. *
*                                                         *
*              Sub. LOOK...... Looks up and prints premium; *
*                              calls PAUSE.               *
*                                                         *
*              Sub. PAUSE..... Pauses screen.             *
*                                                         *
*        Data file structure:                             *
*                                                         *
*           1st age and premium in premium schedule       *
*           2nd age and premium in premium schedule       *
*           ...                                           *
*                                                         *
*        Key (main program):                              *
*                                                         *
*           AGE...... Age of person                       *
*           COLS..... Columns in TABLE                    *
*           FACE..... Insurance face value ($1000)        *
*           ROWS..... Rows in TABLE                       *
*           TABLE.... Premium schedule table              *
*                                                         *
* * * * * * * * * * * * * * * * * * * * * * * * * * * * * *
*----------------------------------------------------------
*  Type names and specify parameters
*----------------------------------------------------------
        INTEGER   COLS, ROWS
        PARAMETER ( ROWS = 12, COLS = 2 )
        REAL      AGE, FACE, TABLE(ROWS,COLS)
*----------------------------------------------------------
*  Input premium schedule
*----------------------------------------------------------
        CALL SCHED ( TABLE )
*----------------------------------------------------------
*  Process quotations
*----------------------------------------------------------
        CALL KEYIN ( AGE, FACE )
    100 IF ( AGE .GT. 0 ) THEN
           CALL LOOK ( AGE, FACE, TABLE )
           CALL KEYIN ( AGE, FACE )
           GO TO 100
        END IF
*----------------------------------------------------------
*  Print farewell
*----------------------------------------------------------
        PRINT *
        PRINT *, '                          Ciao...'
*----------------------------------------------------------
        END
```

FIGURE 7.7   **Listing of Program LOOKUP and data file** (*continued on next page*)

```
          SUBROUTINE SCHED ( TABLE )
* * * * * * * * * * * * * * * * * * * * * * * * * * * * * * * * *
*                                                               *
*          Premium schedule subroutine                         *
*                                                               *
*            Receives nothing                                   *
*            Reads premium schedule from data file             *
*            Returns premium schedule                          *
*                                                               *
*            Data file (TABLE) structure:                       *
*                              Column 1        Column 2         *
*                            _____      *
*                                                               *
*          Record (Row) 1... 1st age limit  1st premium per $1K face *
*          Record (Row) 2... 2nd age limit  2nd premium per $1K face *
*          ...                                                  *
*                                                               *
*            Key:                                               *
*                                                               *
*            COLS..... Columns in TABLE                         *
*            I........ Outer DO-variable / Row index            *
*            J........ Inner DO-variable / Column index         *
*            ROWS..... Rows in TABLE                            *
*            TABLE.... Premium schedule table                   *
*                                                               *
* * * * * * * * * * * * * * * * * * * * * * * * * * * * * * * * *
*_____
*  Type names and specify parameters
*_____
      INTEGER    COLS, I, J, ROWS
      PARAMETER ( ROWS = 12, COLS = 2 )
      REAL      TABLE(ROWS,COLS)
*_____
*  Read table
*_____
      DO 100 I = 1, ROWS
        READ (5, *) ( TABLE(I,J), J = 1, COLS )
  100 CONTINUE
*_____
      END
```

FIGURE 7.7   *(continued)*

---

1. Pay attention to name associations in the argument lists. As specified in the program design step:

   - The main program gets values in the premium schedule matrix from Subroutine SCHED through the following argument list pairings:

$$\text{CALL SCHED (TABLE)} \leftarrow \text{In Main Program}$$
$$\uparrow$$
$$\text{SUBROUTINE SCHED (TABLE)} \leftarrow \text{In Module 2}$$

   - The main program gets values in AGE and FACE from Subroutine KEYIN through the following argument list pairings:

```
        SUBROUTINE KEYIN ( AGE, FACE )
*  *  *  *  *  *  *  *  *  *  *  *  *  *  *  *  *  *  *  *  *  *  *  *  *  *  *  *  *
*                                                                              *
*          Keyboard input subroutine                                           *
*                                                                              *
*          Receives nothing                                                    *
*          Prints quotation number, inputs age and face value                  *
*          Returns age and face value                                          *
*                                                                              *
*          Key:                                                                *
*                                                                              *
*             AGE...... Age of person                                          *
*             FACE..... Insurance face value ($1000)                           *
*             QUOTE.... Quotation number for day                               *
*                                                                              *
*  *  *  *  *  *  *  *  *  *  *  *  *  *  *  *  *  *  *  *  *  *  *  *  *  *  *  *  *
*─────────────────────────────────────────────────────────────────────────────
*    Type names
*─────────────────────────────────────────────────────────────────────────────
        INTEGER QUOTE
        REAL    AGE, FACE
*─────────────────────────────────────────────────────────────────────────────
*    Save, initialize, and update quotation number
*─────────────────────────────────────────────────────────────────────────────
        SAVE QUOTE ◄───────────── Needed to retain value in local variable
        DATA QUOTE / 0 /

        QUOTE =  QUOTE + 1
*─────────────────────────────────────────────────────────────────────────────
*    Clear screen and input
*─────────────────────────────────────────────────────────────────────────────
        PRINT '( 25(/) )'
        PRINT '( /34X,  ''INSURANCE PREMIUM QUOTATIONS'' )'
        PRINT '( /34X,  '' Quotation number...'', I5 / )', QUOTE
        PRINT *, 'Enter age'
        READ  *, AGE
        PRINT *, 'Enter face value'
        READ  *, FACE
*─────────────────────────────────────────────────────────────────────────────
        END
```

FIGURE 7.7   *(continued)*

$$\text{CALL KEYIN (AGE, FACE)} \leftarrow \text{In Main Program}$$
$$\uparrow$$
$$\text{SUBROUTINE KEYIN (AGE, FACE)} \leftarrow \text{In Module 3}$$

- The main program sends values in AGE, FACE, and TABLE to Subroutine LOOK through the following argument list pairings:

$$\text{CALL LOOK (AGE, FACE, TABLE)} \leftarrow \text{In Main}$$
$$\text{Program}$$
$$\downarrow$$
$$\text{SUBROUTINE LOOK (AGE, FACE, TABLE)} \leftarrow \text{In Module 4}$$

Alternatively, we could have used COMMON statements (see Exercise 21).

```
      SUBROUTINE LOOK ( AGE, FACE, TABLE )
* * * * * * * * * * * * * * * * * * * * * * * * * * * * * * * * * *
*                                                                 *
*         Table lookup subroutine                                 *
*                                                                 *
*         Receives age, face value, premium schedule table        *
*         If uninsurable then                                     *
*           Prints message                                        *
*         Else                                                    *
*           Does table lookup, calculates and prints premium      *
*         End if                                                  *
*         Calls PAUSE                                             *
*         Returns nothing                                         *
*                                                                 *
*         Key:                                                    *
*                                                                 *
*           AGE...... Age of person                               *
*           COLS..... Columns in TABLE                            *
*           FACE..... Insurance face value ($1000)               *
*           I........ Row index                                   *
*           ROWS..... Rows in TABLE                               *
*           TABLE.... Insurance premium table                     *
*                                                                 *
* * * * * * * * * * * * * * * * * * * * * * * * * * * * * * * * * *
*—————————————————————————————————————————————————————————————————
* Type names and specify parameters
*—————————————————————————————————————————————————————————————————
      INTEGER   COLS, I, ROWS
      PARAMETER ( ROWS = 12, COLS = 2 )
      REAL      AGE, FACE, TABLE(ROWS,COLS)
*—————————————————————————————————————————————————————————————————
* If uninsurable print message; else do table lookup and print premium
*—————————————————————————————————————————————————————————————————
      IF ( AGE .GT. TABLE(ROWS,1) ) THEN
```
Stores 75
```
          PRINT '( /34X, ''Uninsurable... Age exceeds'', I3 )',
     +                                    INT( TABLE(ROWS,1) )
```
Upper age limit in ith row

Table lookup routine
```
      ELSE

          I = 1

  100     IF ( AGE .GT. TABLE(I,1) ) THEN
```
Proceed to next row
```
              I = I + 1

              GO TO 100

          END IF

          PRINT '(/34X,''Premium.......... $'', F8.2)', FACE * TABLE(I,2)
```
Correct premium
```
      END IF

      CALL PAUSE
*—————————————————————————————————————————————————————————————————
      END
```

FIGURE 7.7   *(continued)*

```
              SUBROUTINE PAUSE
  * * * * * * * * * * * * * * * * * * * * * * * * * * * * * * * * * * * * *
  *                                                                       *
  *        Pause subroutine                                               *
  *                                                                       *
  *          Receives nothing                                            *
  *          Pauses screen                                               *
  *          Returns nothing                                             *
  *                                                                       *
  *          Key:                                                         *
  *                                                                       *
  *              ENTER.... Input variable for pausing screen             *
  *                                                                       *
  * * * * * * * * * * * * * * * * * * * * * * * * * * * * * * * * * * * * *
  *------------------------------------------------------------------------
  *  Type names
  *------------------------------------------------------------------------
           CHARACTER ENTER
  *------------------------------------------------------------------------
  *  Pause screen
  *------------------------------------------------------------------------
           PRINT *
           PRINT *, '  Press ENTER key to continue...'
           READ '( A )', ENTER
  *------------------------------------------------------------------------
           END
                       Data file (Premium Schedule)
       20    4.00
       25    4.50
       30    5.00
       35    5.75
       40    6.50
       45    7.50
       50    8.50
       55    9.50
       60   10.75
       65   12.75
       70   15.00
       75   25.00
```

FIGURE 7.7   *(continued)*

---

2. In Subroutine LOOK, the array element name TABLE(ROWS,1) stores 75, the maximum insurable age, or the last entry in column 1 of the Premium Schedule. Take a look at the PRINT statement for the "Uninsurable" message. Why not use 75 directly in this statement? By using the array element name that corresponds to the last row in column 1 we eliminate program maintenance should the 75 change to, say, 80 in the future. Then why not use TABLE(12,1)? Again we eliminate program maintenance by using the named constant ROWS should the number of rows change in the future. In fact, we used the named constants ROWS and COLS in the first place to reduce maintenance costs should the number of rows and/or columns change. Only the PARAMETER statements would need changes. Check out Exercise 22.

Screen 1

```
                                    INSURANCE PREMIUM QUOTATIONS
                                       Quotation number...    1

  Enter age
28
  Enter face value
100

                                    Premium.......... $  500.00

    Press ENTER key to continue...
```

Screen 2

```
                                    INSURANCE PREMIUM QUOTATIONS
                                       Quotation number...    2

  Enter age
18
  Enter face value
50

                                    Premium.......... $  200.00

    Press ENTER key to continue...
```

Screen 3

```
                                    INSURANCE PREMIUM QUOTATIONS
                                       Quotation number...    3

  Enter age
105  ◄──────────── Nice try!  ☺
  Enter face value
1000 ◄────────────

                                    Uninsurable... Age exceeds 75

    Press ENTER key to continue...
```

Screen 4

```
                                    INSURANCE PREMIUM QUOTATIONS
                                       Quotation number...    4

  Enter age
0
  Enter face value
0

                         Ciao...
```

FIGURE 7.8   **Sample run of Program LOOKUP**

3. In Subroutine LOOK, as the value in the row index I gets incremented, TABLE(I,1) is equivalent to an eye scan down the 1st column (the second subscript expression has a column index of 1) of the premium schedule. When loop exit is achieved, the row index I has the proper value for the correct row. Thus, TABLE(I,2) is the correct premium in the 2nd column of the ith row.

4. The SAVE statement in Subroutine KEYIN is needed to retain successive values for the local variable QUOTE. If you're "rusty" here, reread pages 249–250.

You should roleplay our sample data run through the program to make sure you understand its logic and data associations.

SORTING

Sorting is the act of ordering a list of items, either numerically or alphabetically. It's one of the most common tasks in computing environments. For example, a university administrator might want student records sorted by student names, or by social security numbers, or by state of residence, depending on the objective; the head of a scientific research group might want research projects sorted by granting institution, or by name of principal investigator, or by amount budgeted; an engineer might want stress test data sorted by tensile strength or by test date; and so on.

The development of sorting algorithms is a fertile area of research and experimentation. Depending on the particular algorithm and the nature of the data, sorting performance varies with respect to processing speeds, memory requirements, and other operating characteristics. The algorithms themselves vary from the intuitively obvious to the mathematically abstract; however, sorting algorithms do have one common characteristic: they all use arrays.

Let's illustrate a reasonably fast and easily understood sorting algorithm called the **insertion sort.** In our sample application we work with a one-dimensional integer array and sort in ascending order. See Exercises 25 and 29 for descending sorts and sorts of real arrays, character arrays, and two-dimensional arrays.

Problem Analysis. The following steps describe an insertion sort.

Unsorted set of numbers: 30 50 40 10 20

Step 0 Find the minimum value, which is 10, or the 4th element in the given data.

Step 1 Switch the minimum value with the 1st element in the set. We now have:

Unsorted set
10 50 40 30 20

Step 2 Designate the 1st two elements as the sorted set; the remaining elements are the unsorted set.

Sorted Set   Unsorted Set
10   50   **40** 30 20

We now wish to insert the 1st unsorted element, **40,** into its proper place in the sorted set. Note that elements in positions to the left of **40** are already sorted.

Step 3 Insert the 3rd element, **40.**

Sorted Set   Unsorted Set
10 **40** 50   30 20

Note that 50 is now the 3rd element, and 40 is the 2nd element. In other words, the 50 was moved right one position to make room for the 40. We need to pay attention to position in the sequence when we code the algorithm.

Step 4 Insert the 4th element, **30.**

Sorted Set   Unsorted Set
10 **30** 40 50   20

Note that elements 40 and 50 have been shifted right to make room for 30, and that 30 is now the 2nd element.

Step 5 Insert the 5th element, **20.**

Sorted Set   Unsorted Set
10 **20** 30 40 50

Elements 30, 40, and 50 were each shifted right one position, to make room for the 20. This completes the algorithm.

Data needs include the following.

Output data
Sorted array

Input data
Number of elements to be sorted
One-dimensional integer array

Parameters
Upper dimension bound for the array

Program Design.   Let's work with the following interactive modular program.

Main program . . .   Demonstrates insertion sort: inputs number of elements to be sorted and the array; calls SORT1; prints sorted array elements. To ensure that the input number of elements does not exceed the upper dimension bound, we use the following error routine.

```
Input number of elements
While number of elements > upper
dimension bound
   Print error message
   Input number of elements
End while
```

Note that the while structure repeats while the number of elements is out of bounds. Thus, the program will not continue until a legitimate value is entered for number of elements.

Subroutine SORT1 ... Performs insertion sort. The following pseudocode describes the insertion sort logic in our earlier example.

```
Find minimum element and its
place (position)
   ...Step 0 in example
Switch min and 1st element; two
elements sorted
   ...Steps 1 and 2 in example
Insert remaining elements
   ...Steps 3, 4, 5 in example
End
```

To find the minimum element and its place we refine the pseudocode as follows.

```
Initialize min to 1st element and
place to 1st position
Do each element starting with 2nd
   If element < min then
     Assign new min and place
   End if
End do
```

This step gives min = 10 and place = 4 in the example.

To insert the remaining elements we use the following refined pseudocode, which is based on the sample procedure described earlier starting with Step 3. Note that *k* is equivalent to the step number in our earlier example. It's also equivalent to the position of the element being inserted.

```
Do each element starting with
3rd (k = 3)
   Select kth element as insert
   element
       ...Insert = 40 when k = 3
       (Step 3) in example.
   Initialize possible insert
   position: j = k
       ...j = 3 when k = 3.
   While insert element < element
   in preceding (j-1) position
      Shift sorted element one
      position right
          ...50 moved from 2nd posi-
             tion to 3rd position
             since 40 is less
             than 50.
      Move one position left:
      j = j - 1
          ...Move to 2nd position
             for possible insert;
             the while test will
             next compare 40 to the
             element in position j-1
             (the 10 in the 1st
             position).
   End while
   Place insert element in jth
   position
       ...Exit from while loop
          because 40 > 10; we thus
          insert the 40 in the
          j = 2 position.
End do
```

Program Code and Test. Figure 7.9 shows the listing and test run for the insertion sort program. To understand the algorithm try relating the example, the pseudocode, and the program. Then try Exercises 25 to 30.

```
      PROGRAM SORT
* * * * * * * * * * * * * * * * * * * * * * * * * * * * * * * * * * * * * *
*                                                                         *
*         Demonstration of insertion sort                                 *
*                                                                         *
*         Inputs 1-D integer array                                        *
*         Sorts array in ascending order                                  *
*         Outputs sorted array                                            *
*                                                                         *
*         Modular structure:                                              *
*                                                                         *
*            Main program... Interactively inputs array,                  *
*                            calls Subroutine SORT1, prints sorted        *
*                            array elements.                              *
*                                                                         *
*               Sub. SORT1..... Performs insertion sort on integer,       *
*                               1-D array.                                *
*                                                                         *
*            Key (main program):                                          *
*                                                                         *
*               I........ DO-variable / subscript expression              *
*               N........ Number of elements to be sorted                 *
*               UBOUND... Upper dimension bound on X                      *
*               X........ One-dimensional, integer array                  *
*                                                                         *
* * * * * * * * * * * * * * * * * * * * * * * * * * * * * * * * * * * * * *
*-------------------------------------------------------------------------
*   Type names
*-------------
      INTEGER    I, N, UBOUND
      PARAMETER ( UBOUND = 1000 )
      INTEGER    X(UBOUND)
*-------------------------------------------------------------------------
*   Input array
*-------------
      PRINT *, 'How many elements?'
      READ  *, N

*        ----Error routine for upper dimension bound

  100 IF ( N .GT. UBOUND ) THEN
         PRINT *
         PRINT *, '*** Maximum number of elements is...', UBOUND
         PRINT *
         PRINT *, 'How many elements?'
         READ  *, N
         GO TO 100
      END IF

      PRINT *
      PRINT *, 'Enter array elements.'
      READ  *, ( X(I), I = 1, N )
*-------------------------------------------------------------------------
*   Sort array in ascending order
*-------------------------------
      CALL SORT1 ( N, X )
*-------------------------------------------------------------------------
*   Print sorted array elements
*-----------------------------
      PRINT *
      PRINT *, '   Sorted Array Elements:'
      PRINT *
      PRINT *, ( X(I), I = 1, N )
*-------------------------------------------------------------------------
      END
```

FIGURE 7.9   **Listing and run of Program SORT (*continued on next page*)**

```
SUBROUTINE SORT1 ( SIZE, ARRAY )
* * * * * * * * * * * * * * * * * * * * * * * * * * * * * * * *
*                                                             *
*     Insertion sort subroutine:  Ascending sort             *
*                                  Integer, 1-D array         *
*                                                             *
*     Receives array size and array to be sorted             *
*     Sorts array                                            *
*     Returns sorted array                                   *
*                                                             *
*     Note:  Original array is changed                       *
*                                                             *
*     Key:                                                   *
*                                                             *
*       ARRAY.... Array being sorted                         *
*       INSERT... Array element being inserted into sorted set *
*       J........ Subscript expression                       *
*       K........ DO-variable / subscript expression         *
*       MIN...... Minimum array element                      *
*       PLACE.... Place or index where MIN is found          *
*       SIZE..... Array size, assuming array with element    *
*                 locations 1, 2, ..., SIZE                  *
*                                                             *
*     Example:  Ascending Insertion Sort                     *
*                                                             *
*     | Step |   Sorted Set    |   Unsorted Set    |         |
*                                                             *
*     | 0    |                 | 30 50 40 10 20    | Min = 10 |
*     | 1    | 10              | 50 40 30 20       | Switch 10 30 |
*     | 2    | 10 50           | 40 30 20          | 50  inserted |
*     | 3    | 10 40 50        | 30 20             | 40  inserted |
*     | 4    | 10 30 40 50     | 20                | 30  inserted |
*     | 5    | 10 20 30 40 50  |                   | 20  inserted |
*                                                             *
* * * * * * * * * * * * * * * * * * * * * * * * * * * * * * * *
```

```
*------
* Type names                    ——— Adjustable array declarator
*------
      INTEGER ARRAY(SIZE), INSERT, J, K, MIN, PLACE, SIZE
*------
* Find minimum element:  Step 0 in example shows MIN = 10 and PLACE = 4
*------
      MIN   = ARRAY(1)
      PLACE = 1
      DO 100 K = 2, SIZE
         IF ( ARRAY(K) .LT. MIN ) THEN
            MIN   = ARRAY(K)
            PLACE = K
         END IF
  100 CONTINUE
*------
* Switch minimum element and original first element:  Step 1 in example
* shows switch of elements 10 and 30, automatically giving the sorted
* set 10 and 50 in Step 2
*------
      ARRAY(PLACE) = ARRAY(1)
      ARRAY(1)     = MIN
```

FIGURE 7.9   *(continued)*

```
*----------------------------------------------------------
*   Insert remaining elements starting with leftmost unsorted element:
*   Steps 3-5 in example
*----------------------------------------------------------
        DO 300 K = 3, SIZE

*          ----Select Kth element to insert:  when K = 3, INSERT = 40
*              in example.  Note that elements to left of Kth position
*              are already sorted.

        INSERT = ARRAY(K)

*          ----Scan preceding (sorted) elements to insert; keep scanning
*              while element to be inserted is less than currently
*              scanned element.  First comparison in example is element in
*              3rd position (40) against element in 2nd position (50).

        J = K
200     IF ( INSERT .LT. ARRAY(J-1) ) THEN

*          ----Shift sorted element one position right:  50 moved to 3rd
*              position in Step 3 of example.

        ARRAY(J) = ARRAY(J-1)

*          ----Move to preceding position.

        J = J - 1

*          ----Repeat to scan element located one position left.

        GO TO 200

        END IF

*          ----Location of insert is at position J; insert element in
*              Jth position:  40 placed in 2nd position in Step 3
*              of example.

        ARRAY(J) = INSERT

300 CONTINUE
*----------------------------------------------------------
        END


How many elements?
2001

*** Maximum number of elements is...        1000

How many elements?
1999

*** Maximum number of elements is...        1000

How many elements?
5

Enter array elements.
30 50 40 10 20

    Sorted Array Elements:

        10          20          30          40          50
```

FIGURE 7.9   *(continued)*

If you're having problems understanding the sort subroutine, keep at it. Roleplay the sample data through each step in the program. Pay particular attention to the way we use subscript expressions in moving from one position to the next (as in J and J – 1). Note that the current value in K is the step number in our example *and* the position of the element we're about to insert. Try filling in the following table of memory values when K stores 4 and 5.

Roleplay of Program SORT

K	INSERT	J	INSERT .LT. ARRAY(J-1)	ARRAY(1)	ARRAY(2)	ARRAY(3)	ARRAY(4)	ARRAY(5)
				10	50	40	30	20
3	40	3	T			50		
		2	F		40			
4								
5								

Note that the original array itself is rearranged. If we need to preserve the original positions of items, then check out the approach in Exercise 28. For another sorting algorithm, see Exercise 46.

Most people have to do a lot of roleplaying to understand algorithms that involve a great deal of subscript manipulation. This algorithm is a good example of a problem that's easy to do by hand/eye/mind, but tricky to program.

XY-PLOTS

Graphics software displays "pictures" of data. In recent years, this applications programming area has really taken off commercially, primarily because of the increasing use of desktop computers and reductions in the prices of sophisticated graphics devices like laser printers, color pen plotters, and high-resolution color monitors. Graphics applications include colorful bar charts (Example 6.1); pie charts with and without exploded slices, in color, and in three dimensional perspective; plots of mathematical functions (Exercise 3 in Chapter 6); drawings like electrical engineering diagrams, hierarchy charts, and architectural plans; computer aided design (CAD) applications that scale, rotate, translate (shift), explode, and color engineering drawings like new car designs; and picture processing applications like animation in games and movies, photographic recalls in criminal database queries, and training simulations for pilots and astronauts.

In this section we focus on the use of a high-level language like FORTRAN for the rough plotting of mathematical functions on standard output devices like monochrome monitors and dot matrix printers. Two-variable and three-variable functions are the commonly plotted mathematical functions. The two-variable $y = f(x)$ functions are graphed as xy-plots, with the x-axis either running down the page or screen (the simple approach, as in Exercise 3, Chapter 6), or properly oriented in the horizontal direction (the more difficult approach, which we illustrate in this section). The three-variable $z = f(x,y)$ functions are treated either as surfaces in three-dimensional (30-60-90°) perspective or as contour maps in a two-dimensional graph, where irregularly circular contour lines represent various elevations (values of z), as if looking directly down at a mountain or valley.

The **CalComp Graphics Software Library** is a popular FORTRAN library of programs and external procedures for a variety of graphics applications. The software includes business graphics like bar charts and pie charts; scientific graphics like polynomial curve fitting, line or x-y plots, and contour maps; and drafting, as in drawing arcs, circles, and other geometric figures. Check out Exercise 35 if CalComp or another graphics library is available at your installation.

Problem Analysis. Let's develop a subroutine that plots $y = f(x)$ functions, with the xy-axes in their normal orientation (x-axis horizontal and y-axis vertical). The subroutine should be useful as a utility for plotting any two-variable function. It would require the plot symbol (say, an $*$), the number of coordinates to plot, and the (x,y) coordinates. Figure 7.10 illustrates the desired I/O for a sample of 11 coordinates.

Note that we scale the axes so that each runs from its minimum value to its maximum value. In the sample data, the x-axis runs from -9 to 11, and the y-axis runs from -363 to 21. This approach allows us to plot functions over any range of values.

Let's assume that the plot is primarily for screen viewing, so it must fit on one screen. Accordingly, let's scale the x-axis from print position 0 at the left to print position 50 at the right; that is, we use 51 print positions or columns across the screen, where 0 represents x_{min} and 50 represents x_{max}. Similarly, let's scale the y-axis to run from print line 0 at the bottom of the screen to print line 18 at the top of the screen. The axes and their labeling take up another 4 lines, which means we use up 23 lines on the screen to display the graph.

To scale x and y we use the formulas

$$x\text{-scaled} = \text{nint}\left(\frac{x - x_{min}}{x_{max} - x_{min}} * 50\right)$$

$$y\text{-scaled} = \text{nint}\left(\frac{y - y_{min}}{y_{max} - y_{min}} * 18\right)$$

where *nint* stands for nearest integer. For example, the first coordinate $(-9, -203)$ in Figure 7.10 would be plotted at the *scaled coordinate* $(0,8)$ according to the scaling functions below.

$$x\text{-scaled} = \text{nint}\left(\frac{-9 - (-9)}{11 - (-9)} * 50\right)$$
$$= \text{nint}(0.0 * 50)$$
$$= \text{nint}(0.0)$$
$$= 0$$

```
    Enter plot character
 *
   Print function (Y/N)?
 T

     Please enter yes or no
 WHY?

     Please enter yes or no
 YES
   Enter number of coordinates
 1111

     Enter number no greater than  300
 11
   Enter each coordinate in the form x, y
 -9,-203
 -7,-111
 -5,-43
 -3,1
 -1,21
 1,17
 3,-11
 5,-63
 7,-139
 9,-239
 11,-363
```

XY–DATA

Coordinate	X	Y
1	-9.00000	-203.000
2	-7.00000	-111.000
3	-5.00000	-43.0000
4	-3.00000	1.00000
5	-1.00000	21.0000
6	1.00000	17.0000
7	3.00000	-11.0000
8	5.00000	-63.0000
9	7.00000	-139.000
10	9.00000	-239.000
11	11.0000	-363.000

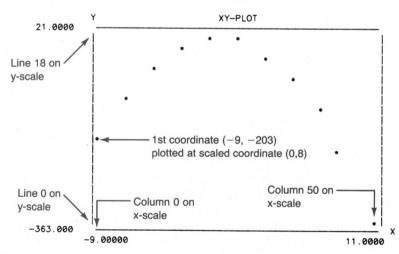

FIGURE 7.10   **Sample run of Program PLOT**

$$y\text{-scaled} = \text{nint}\left(\frac{-203 - (-363)}{21 - (-363)} * 18\right)$$
$$= \text{nint} (0.416667 * 18)$$
$$= \text{nint} (7.50)$$
$$= 8$$

Note that a value at its minimum plots at the scaled value zero, since the numerator term evaluates to zero; a value at its maximum plots at the maximum scaled value (50 for x and 18 for y), since the fraction evaluates to 1.0; a value halfway between its minimum and maximum plots at the halfway point along the scale (25 for x and 9 for y). In effect, a value plots as a proportion of its range along its scale, where the range is the difference between the maximum value and the minimum value (the denominator term in a scaling function).

Program Design.   Let's design an interactive, modular program based on the following ideas. The plot subroutine already described (let's call it XYPLOT) requires the calculations of minimum and maximum values, and their difference the range. These are common calculations in statistical applications, so let's also develop a utility subroutine (STATS) that calculates these statistics.

Let's design a separate subroutine (INPUT) to input the number of coordinates (variable N) and the (x,y) coordinates. The x-coordinates are stored in one-dimensional real array X and the y-coordinates are stored in one-dimensional real array Y. In our example we're going to interactively input specific (x,y) coordinates, as done in Figure 7.10 for 11 coordinates. We could easily redesign INPUT, however, to generate coordinates by filling in elements of X and Y based on a specific function (see Exercise 34).

A common run-time error in array applications is an entry for N that exceeds the declared size of the array. To prevent this, let's develop a utility subroutine (NERR) that alerts the user to this error condition by printing an error message and requesting reinput of the number of array elements *while* it exceeds the declared size. For example, our user in Figure 7.10 mistakenly entered 1111 for the number of coordinates, which flagged an error condition.

Let's also give the user the option of printing the original coordinates in table form, which we accomplish through an output subroutine (OUTPUT). Sample output is shown in Figure 7.10.

The main program inputs the plot symbol and asks whether or not the function's coordinates are to be printed, and expects a yes/no response in its usual allowable forms (Y, N, YES, NO, y, n, yeah, yup, and so on). Incorrect user responses are common here, so let's develop a utility subroutine (YNERR) that flags yes/no response errors: An error message is printed and reinput is requested *while* an incorrect response is entered based on the first letter typed. The sample run in Figure 7.10 shows two incorrect y/n responses.

The hierarchy chart in Figure 7.11 puts together these modules and their relationships. Detailed descriptions of the modules are in the program's documentation.

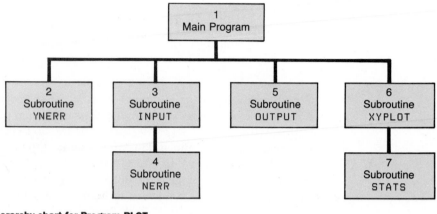

FIGURE 7.11   Hierarchy chart for Program PLOT

Program Code and Test.   Figure 7.12 is a listing of Program PLOT. Try roleplaying the sample run in Figure 7.10 through this program, and note the following.

1. Pay attention to variable associations in argument lists, and to how arrays are declared. For example, values in N, X, and Y are input through Subroutine INPUT, which means that the arrays in this program unit must be declared using constant array declarators. We use X(XYSIZE) and Y(XYSIZE), where the named constant XYSIZE is specified as 300 in the PARAMETER statement. The main program also uses these same array declarators, since adjustable and assumed-size array declarators are only allowed in subroutines. We use a named constant for the array size 300 to slightly simplify program maintenance. Without XYSIZE the 300 would appear at five different points in the program (twice in the main program and three times in INPUT), excluding the PARAMETER statements. By using the named constant we reduce maintenance to the two PARAMETER statements, should we need to change the 300 to some other value. Subroutines OUTPUT, XYPLOT, and RANGE use adjustable array declarators for these arrays, thereby eliminating maintenance problems.

2. The error routines in Subroutines YNERR and NERR use while structures to flag the errors; that is, we wish to repeat *while* an error condition exists. A common mistake here is to use an if-then structure, as in "if error, then print error message and reinput." This would flag one instance of an error (as in the entry of 1111 in Figure 7.10), but not repeated errors (as in entries T and WHY? in Figure 7.10).

```
      PROGRAM PLOT
• • • • • • • • • • • • • • • • • • • • • • • • • • • • •
•
•        Two-variable Plots
•
•          Inputs plot symbol, output choice, and (x,y) coordinates
•          Plots coordinates as XY-plot
•          Outputs coordinates if requested
•
•          Modular structure:
•
•            Main program... Inputs plot symbol, output choice, and
•                            calls YNERR, INPUT, OUTPUT (if desired),
•                            and XYPLOT.
•
•              Sub. YNERR..... Utility that repeats y/n input while
•                              reply is not yes or no.
•
•              Sub. INPUT..... Inputs coordinates; calls NERR.
•
•                Sub. NERR...... Utility that repeats input of number
•                                of elements while greater than max.
•                                array size.
•
•              Sub. OUTPUT.... Displays (x,y) coordinates.
•
•              Sub. XYPLOT.... Plots (x,y) coordinates for display
•                              on a single screen; calls STATS.
•
•                Sub. STATS..... Calculates min., max., and range
•                                for 1-D array.
•
•          Key (main program):
•
•            CHOICE... Yes/no variable for output choice
•            N........ Number of array elements or coordinates
•            SYMBOL... Plot symbol
•            X........ 1-D real array for x-coordinates
•            Y........ 1-D real array for y-coordinates
•            XYSIZE... Size of (upper bound on) X and Y arrays
•
• • • • • • • • • • • • • • • • • • • • • • • • • • • • •
─────────────────────────────────────────────────────────
•  Type names, declare arrays, and specify parameter
  ───────────────────────────────────────────────
      CHARACTER CHOICE, SYMBOL
      INTEGER   N, XYSIZE              ←Named constant
      PARAMETER ( XYSIZE = 300 )       ←Constant array declarators
      REAL      X(XYSIZE), Y(XYSIZE)
─────────────────────────────────────────────────────────
•  Input data
  ──────────
      PRINT *, 'Enter plot character'
      READ '( A )', SYMBOL
      PRINT *, 'Print function (Y/N)?'
      READ '( A )', CHOICE

      CALL YNERR ( CHOICE )

      CALL INPUT ( N, X, Y )
─────────────────────────────────────────────────────────
•  Output (x,y) coordinates if desired
  ─────────────────────────────────
      IF ( CHOICE .EQ. 'Y' .OR. CHOICE .EQ. 'y' ) THEN
        CALL OUTPUT ( N, X, Y )
      END IF
─────────────────────────────────────────────────────────
•  Plot (x,y) coordinates
  ──────────────────────
      CALL XYPLOT ( SYMBOL, N, X, Y )
─────────────────────────────────────────────────────────
      END
```

FIGURE 7.12   **Listing of Program PLOT (*continued on next page*)**

```
        SUBROUTINE YNERR ( REPLY )
. . . . . . . . . . . . . . . . . . . . . . . . . . . . . . . . . . . .
.                                                                      .
.           Utility that ensures correct yes/no reply                 .
.                                                                      .
.              Receives reply                                         .
.              Repeats y/n input while reply incorrect               .
.              Returns revised reply (if initially incorrect)        .
.                                                                      .
.              Key:                                                   .
.                                                                      .
.                  REPLY.... Yes/no reply stored as single character  .
.                                                                      .
. . . . . . . . . . . . . . . . . . . . . . . . . . . . . . . . . . . .
```
```
* Type names
*────────
      CHARACTER REPLY
```
```
* Repeat y/n input while reply is not yes or no
*──────────────────────────────────────────────
  100 IF ( .NOT. ( REPLY .EQ. 'Y'   .OR.   REPLY .EQ. 'y'   .OR.
      +             REPLY .EQ. 'N'   .OR.   REPLY .EQ. 'n'        ) )  THEN

          PRINT *, CHAR(7)
          PRINT *, '  Please enter yes or no'
          READ  '( A )', REPLY

          GO TO 100                                    ←── While structure

      END IF
```
```
      END
```

```
        SUBROUTINE INPUT ( N, X, Y )
. . . . . . . . . . . . . . . . . . . . . . . . . . . . . . . . . . . .
.                                                                      .
.           Input of (x,y) coordinates                               .
.                                                                      .
.              Receives nothing                                      .
.              Inputs N and arrays X and Y                           .
.              Calls NERR to ensure N is within array upper bound    .
.              Returns N, X, and Y                                   .
.                                                                      .
.              Key:                                                   .
.                                                                      .
.                  I........ DO-variable / subscript expression       .
.                  N........ Number of array elements or coordinates  .
.                  X........ 1-D real array for x-coordinates         .
.                  Y........ 1-D real array for y-coordinates         .
.                  XYSIZE... Size of (upper bound on) X and Y arrays  .
.                                                                      .
. . . . . . . . . . . . . . . . . . . . . . . . . . . . . . . . . . . .
```
```
* Type names, declare arrays, and specify parameter
*──────────────────────────────────────────────────
      INTEGER   I, N, XYSIZE
      PARAMETER ( XYSIZE = 300 )          ←── Named constant
      REAL      X(XYSIZE), Y(XYSIZE)      ←── Constant array declarators
```
```
* Input data
*─────────
      PRINT *, 'Enter number of coordinates'
      READ  *, N
```
```
      CALL NERR ( N, XYSIZE )
```
```
      PRINT *, 'Enter each coordinate in the form x, y'
      DO 100 I = 1, N
         READ *, X(I), Y(I)
  100 CONTINUE
```
```
      END
```

FIGURE 7.12   *(continued)*

```
      SUBROUTINE NERR ( N, SIZE )
. . . . . . . . . . . . . . . . . . . . . . . . . . . . . .
.                                                          .
.     Utility that ensures number of array elements is within  .
.     upper bound of array with elements indexed 1, 2, ..., SIZE  .
.                                                          .
.        Receives N and SIZE                               .
.        Repeats input of N while greater than SIZE        .
.        Returns revised N if initially incorrect          .
.                                                          .
.        Key:                                              .
.                                                          .
.           N........ Number of array elements used        .
.           SIZE..... Upper bound on array                 .
.                                                          .
. . . . . . . . . . . . . . . . . . . . . . . . . . . . . .
.——————————————————————————————————————————————————————————
.  Type names
.——————————————————————————————————————————————————————————
      INTEGER N, SIZE
.——————————————————————————————————————————————————————————
.  Repeat input of N while greater than SIZE
.——————————————————————————————————————————————————————————
  100 IF ( N .GT. SIZE ) THEN
          PRINT *, CHAR(7)
          PRINT '( 3X, ''Enter number no greater than '', I4 )', SIZE
          READ *, N

          GO TO 100

      END IF
.——————————————————————————————————————————————————————————
      END
```

↙ While structure

```
      SUBROUTINE OUTPUT ( N, X, Y )
. . . . . . . . . . . . . . . . . . . . . . . . . . . . . .
.                                                          .
.     Output of (x,y) coordinates                          .
.                                                          .
.        Receives N, X, and Y                              .
.        Prints (x,y) coordinates                          .
.        Returns nothing                                   .
.                                                          .
.        Key:                                              .
.                                                          .
.           I........ DO-variable / subscript expression   .
.           N........ Number of array elements or coordinates  .
.           X........ 1-D real array for x-coordinates     .
.           Y........ 1-D real array for y-coordinates     .
.                                                          .
. . . . . . . . . . . . . . . . . . . . . . . . . . . . . .
.——————————————————————————————————————————————————————————
.  Type names and declare arrays
.——————————————————————————————————————————————————————————
      INTEGER   I, N
      REAL      X(N), Y(N)
```

——— Adjustable array declarators

```
.——————————————————————————————————————————————————————————
.  Print (x,y) coordinates
.——————————————————————————————————————————————————————————
      WRITE (*,900)
      WRITE (*,910)
      WRITE (*,920)
      WRITE (*,910)
      DO 100 I = 1, N
         WRITE (*,930) I, X(I), Y(I)
  100 CONTINUE
      WRITE (*,910)
.——————————————————————————————————————————————————————————
.  Specify output formats
.——————————————————————————————————————————————————————————
  900 FORMAT ( //37X, 'XY-DATA' )
  910 FORMAT ( 20X, 42('=') )
  920 FORMAT ( 23X, 'Coordinate        X            Y' )
  930 FORMAT ( 23X, I5, 6X, 2G14.6 )
.——————————————————————————————————————————————————————————
      END
```

FIGURE 7.12   *(continued)*

```
        SUBROUTINE XYPLOT ( SYMBOL, N, X, Y )
* * * * * * * * * * * * * * * * * * * * * * * * * * * * * * * * *
*                                                                *
*         Generates XY-Plot                                      *
*                                                                *
*         Receives SYMBOL, N, X, and Y                           *
*         Calls STATS                                            *
*         Plots (x,y) coordinates                                *
*         Returns nothing                                        *
*                                                                *
*         Key:                                                   *
*                                                                *
*           BLANK.... Blank character                            *
*           COL...... DO-variable/subscript expression for plot col. *
*           ERR...... Error precision tolerance parameter        *
*           LBX...... Lower bound parameter on x-plot range      *
*           LBY...... Lower bound parameter on y-plot range      *
*           LINE..... DO-variable/subscript expression for plot line *
*           N........ Number of array elements or coordinates    *
*           PLOT..... 2-D array that's image of XY-plot          *
*           SYMBOL... Single-character plot symbol               *
*           UBX...... Upper bound parameter on x-plot range      *
*           UBY...... Upper bound parameter on y-plot range      *
*           X........ 1-D real array for x-coordinates           *
*           XMAX..... Maximum x-value                            *
*           XMIN..... Minimum x-value                            *
*           XRANGE... Difference between min. and max. x-values  *
*           XSCALE... Scaled x-value                             *
*           Y........ 1-D real array for y-coordinates           *
*           YMAX..... Maximum y-value                            *
*           YMIN..... Minimum y-value                            *
*           YRANGE... Difference between min. and max. y-values  *
*           YSCALE... Scaled y-value                             *
*                                                                *
* * * * * * * * * * * * * * * * * * * * * * * * * * * * * * * * *
*————————————————————————————————————————————————————————
* Type names, declare arrays, and specify parameters
*————————————————————————————————————————————————————————
      INTEGER   COL, N, LBX, LBY, LINE, UBX, UBY, XSCALE, YSCALE

      PARAMETER ( LBX = 0, UBX = 50, LBY = 0, UBY = 18 )

      CHARACTER BLANK, PLOT(LBY:UBY, LBX:UBX), SYMBOL

      REAL      X(N), Y(N)

      REAL      ERR, XMAX, XMIN, XRANGE, YMAX, YMIN, YRANGE

      PARAMETER ( BLANK = ' ', ERR = 0.000001 )
*————————————————————————————————————————————————————————
* Initialize all plot coordinates to blank
*————————————————————————————————————————————————————————
      DO 200 LINE = LBY, UBY
        DO 100 COL = LBX, UBX

          PLOT(LINE,COL) = BLANK

  100   CONTINUE
  200 CONTINUE
*————————————————————————————————————————————————————————
* Find min. value, max. value, and range for x- and y-values
*————————————————————————————————————————————————————————
      CALL STATS ( N, X, XMAX, XMIN, XRANGE )
      CALL STATS ( N, Y, YMAX, YMIN, YRANGE )
```

← To simplify program maintenance

—— Constant array declarator

——Adjustable array declarators

FIGURE 7.12   *(continued)*

```
*──────────────────────────────────────────────────────
*  Fill plot image with plot symbols
*──────────────────────────────────────────────────────
      DO 300 I = 1, N

         IF ( ABS( XRANGE - 0.0 ) .GE. ERR ) THEN
            XSCALE = NINT( ( ( X(I) - XMIN ) / XRANGE ) * ( UBX - LBX ) )
         ELSE
            XSCALE = ( LBX + UBX ) / 2
         END IF

         IF ( ABS( YRANGE - 0.0 ) .GE. ERR ) THEN
            YSCALE = NINT( ( ( Y(I) - YMIN ) / YRANGE ) * ( UBY - LBY ) )
         ELSE
            YSCALE = ( LBY + UBY ) / 2
         END IF                                    ──── Subscript values transpose of
                                                        scaled coordinate
         PLOT(YSCALE,XSCALE) = SYMBOL

  300 CONTINUE
*──────────────────────────────────────────────────────
*  Display XY-plot
*──────────────────────────────────────────────────────
      WRITE (*,910) YMAX

      DO 400 LINE = UBY, LBY, -1

         WRITE (*,920) ( PLOT(LINE,COL), COL = LBX, UBX )

  400 CONTINUE

      WRITE (*,930) YMIN
      WRITE (*,940) XMIN, XMAX
*──────────────────────────────────────────────────────
*  Specify output formats
*──────────────────────────────────────────────────────
  910 FORMAT ( //14X, 'Y', 22X, 'XY-PLOT' / 2X, G13.6, 51('-') )
  920 FORMAT (    14X, '|', 51A, '|' )
  930 FORMAT (     2X, G13.6, 51('-'), '  X' )
  940 FORMAT (    12X, G13.6, 33X, G13.6 )
*──────────────────────────────────────────────────────
      END


      SUBROUTINE STATS ( N, ARRAY, HIGH, LOW, RANGE )
*  * * * * * * * * * * * * * * * * * * * * * * * * * * * *
*                                                        *
*      Calculates statistics for 1-D array:  Maximum value  *
*                                            Minimum value  *
*                                            Range          *
*                                                        *
*         Receives N and ARRAY                           *
*         Calculates HIGH, LOW, and RANGE                *
*         Returns HIGH, LOW, and RANGE                   *
*                                                        *
*         Key:                                           *
*                                                        *
*            ARRAY.... 1-D real array                    *
*            HIGH..... Highest array element value       *
*            LOW...... Lowest array element value        *
*            N........ Number of array elements used     *
*            RANGE.... Absolute diff. between highest and lowest value *
*                                                        *
*  * * * * * * * * * * * * * * * * * * * * * * * * * * * *
*──────────────────────────────────────────────────────
*  Type names and declare array
*──────────────────────────────────────────────────────
      INTEGER  N
      REAL     ARRAY(N), HIGH, LOW, RANGE
                    ──── Adjustable array declarator
```

FIGURE 7.12   *(continued)*

```
•—————————————————————————————————————————
•   Initialize
•—————————————————————————————————————————
      LOW  = ARRAY(1)
      HIGH = ARRAY(1)
•—————————————————————————————————————————
•   Calculate statistics
•—————————————————————————————————————————
      DO 100 I = 2, N
        LOW  = MIN( LOW,  ARRAY(I) )
        HIGH = MAX( HIGH, ARRAY(I) )
  100 CONTINUE                              ——————————— Intrinsic function names.
                                                        See Module A
      RANGE = HIGH - LOW
•—————————————————————————————————————————
      END
```

FIGURE 7.12   **(continued)**

3. In Subroutine XYPLOT, the following considerations apply.

   a. We use named constants for the plot size parameters (0 to 50 along the x-scale and 0 to 18 up the y-scale). These are used extensively in the subroutine, so program maintenance is simplified should we wish to change the size of the plot.

   b. Two-dimensional character array PLOT is declared with dimension bounds based on the plot size parameters. Thus the first dimension of PLOT runs from a lower bound of 0 to an upper bound of 18; the second dimension runs from 0 to 50. Each element of PLOT has a declared length of one, and stores either a blank or a plot character (* in our example). Can you visualize our conceptual memory for PLOT? This array is like a table whose rows represent lines on the plotted screen and whose columns represent positions or columns on the plotted screen. For our example in Figure 7.10, conceptual memory would appear as follows, where each element stores a single character (blank or *).

PLOT — Northwest corner of screen ... Northeast corner of screen

18,0	18,1	. . .	18,20	. . .	18,25	. . .	18,50
			*		*		
. . .							
8,0	8,1	. . .	18,20	. . .	18,25	. . .	18,50
*							

Represents plotted character for coordinate
(−9,−203) scaled to coordinate (0,8)

0,0	0,1	. . .	0,20	. . .	0,25	. . .	0,50
							*

Southwest corner of screen

Southeast corner of screen

For example, array element name PLOT(8,0) stores the * that gets printed as the first coordinate (−9,−203) in Figure 7.10. In that figure, the scaled coordinate is shown as (0,8). Thus, the *scaled* coordinate is the transpose of the subscript values in PLOT. This is because the first dimension in PLOT represents the y-scale, or lines on the screen; the second dimension represents the x-scale, or columns on the screen. In effect, PLOT(y-scale, x-scale) stores the plotted character for the co-ordinate (x-scale, y-scale). In the subroutine, the values in YSCALE and XSCALE serve as subscript expressions in the array element name PLOT(YSCALE,XSCALE). For instance, the first coordinate (−9,−203) evaluates to 0 in XSCALE and 8 in YSCALE. This means the scaled coordinate is (0,8), and PLOT(8,0) stores * when the assignment statement

PLOT(YSCALE,XSCALE) = SYMBOL

is evaluated.

    c. We use if-then-else structures to calculate scaled values to account for the possibility that the denominator terms XRANGE or YRANGE could be zero (see Exercise 31).

    d. Note that DO-loop 400 prints lines in PLOT in reverse order; that is, high *y*-values are printed before low *y*-values as we print the *y*-axis down the screen. This is why we sketched our conceptual memory for PLOT with row (line) 18 at the top and line 0 at the bottom, which is the reverse from our usual conceptualization. Since lines represent the *y*-scale, it follows that values decrease as we go down the scale or screen. Right?

The transposition of scaled coordinates and subscript values in PLOT is subtle and easily causes confusion. Try Exercise 31 to nail down your understanding here. Exercises 32 to 34 should help you understand other elements in the overall program.

7.5 PROGRAMMING TIPS

DESIGN AND STYLE

    1. Generalized Programming. If the number of elements used in an array is likely to change from run to run, then use an input variable rather than a constant for the number of elements to be processed. This reduces program maintenance. For example, in our temperature problems we used the variable N for number of elements, rather than 5. Similarly, if the dimension bounds appear more than once, then use named constants (PARAMETER statements) to specify the dimension bounds. We illustrate this in Programs LOOKUP, SORT, and PLOT.

    2. Defensive Programming. Use error routines to catch subscript values that exceed dimension bounds. We illustrate this in Programs SORT and PLOT for upper dimension bounds, and ask you to consider lower dimension bounds in Exercise 27.

    3. Matrix Representations. Conceptually visualize a two-dimensional array as a matrix or table with rows and columns. This enhances understanding because we're accustomed to this convention. Thus, we commonly use subscript expressions I and J for rows and columns, respectively, which is consistent with notational conventions in matrix algebra; we place two-dimensional arrays as tables in input storage media by placing a complete row on each line; and we I/O arrays using a combination of an outer DO-loop for rows and an implied-DO list for columns. These are all illustrated in Examples 7.8 and 7.9.

    4. On Data Structures. A **data structure** indicates the relationship, size, and shape of related memory locations. For example, if an array is to store the names of the months, then the data structure suggests a one-dimensional character array with a lower dimension bound of 1 and an upper dimension bound of 12, giving us an array size of 12 that never changes. If we never expect to use more than 500 elements in an array, then we should declare an array size of 500 elements. If the array is to store the temperatures in 500 cities, then it makes sense to index the array starting with a lower dimension bound of 1 and an upper dimension bound of 500. If the array is to store 301 temperatures, where 200 of these are below sea level, 1 is at sea level, and 100 are above sea level, then it may make sense to use dimension bounds of -200 and 100, giving an array of size 301.

To further illustrate relationships and shapes in data structures, consider the data in Example 7.7. City names and temperatures form a data structure of "related" attributes, where each attribute (name and temperature) is stored in the "shape" of parallel one-dimensional arrays. If we visualize these arrays as vertical columns next to each other, then it's like having the shape of a two-dimensional mixed-type array (not allowed in FORTRAN), with rows as cities, the first column as names, and the second column as temperatures.

Shape also refers to how values "fill" an array. For example, a symmetric matrix has elements above the main diagonal that are mirror images of elements below the main diagonal (see Exercise 47). In this case, we don't need to fill the upper triangle of the matrix, since all the necessary data are contained within the diagonal and lower triangle. We can thus describe the shape of a symmetric matrix by its counterpart with the missing upper triangle. Alternatively, we can save storage by describing its shape and size in the form of an equivalent one-dimensional array, as suggested in Exercise 48.

5. **On Memory Management.** Arrays can take up a lot of memory, so a key data-related question we need to ask is, *Do we need to use arrays?* If all we need to do is find the mean of n numbers, then we don't need to store these numbers as an array. If we need to sort these numbers, however, then an array is called for. If we have a choice of playing it either way, then it's usually a matter of the programmer's preference, unless the required amount of memory in using arrays is an issue.

If we need to use arrays and we're concerned about memory limitations, then we have a memory management problem. In this case, we need to answer some questions. *Can we trade off between I/O costs and memory costs?* For example, if we just need to find the sum of n numbers and then the percent of each number, we could read in the numbers twice, first to sum them, and then to find each percent. This would avoid an array (thereby improving memory efficiency) at the expense of additional input (which is I/O inefficient). In very large sorts, as in the nightly sorts performed by banks, large portions of arrays are placed in secondary storage; otherwise, primary memory would be inadequate.

Can we adjust dimension bounds? If we occasionally need to include 300,000 temperatures in an array that normally uses no more than 500 temperatures, then we have to decide on the tradeoff between *storage inefficiency* and *maintenance costs.* For example, we could use an upper dimension bound of 300,000 and never change it, thereby incurring no program maintenance regarding the upper dimension bound, but at the expense of large amounts of unused storage.[2] Alternatively, we could change the array's upper bound to 300,000 whenever we need to process that many temperatures, but keep it at 500 otherwise. This reduces storage needs but increases program maintenance. It just depends on the relative costs between these two tradeoffs.

Can we use COMMON *or* EQUIVALENCE *statements to share memory locations?* Across program units we can save array memory by using COMMON statements under certain circumstances. For example, suppose that three program modules within the same executable program each uses a large local array of 100,000 elements. Further assume that these modules don't communicate with one another, and that once a module finishes executing, its array need not be used by another module. These local arrays take up 300,000 storage locations, which we can reduce to 100,000 storage locations by associating the three arrays through a common block. Within the same program unit, we can save array storage by using EQUIVALENCE statements (see page 308). Its use is error prone, however, as described by the note on page 311.

Very large programs with many lines of code (say, hundreds of thousands) and/or large arrays may require advanced memory management techniques like **overlays,** where modules are loaded into primary memory as they are needed; **virtual memory,** where array storage is swapped between primary memory and high-speed external memory like magnetic disk; and **extended memory,** where additional RAM on cards is swapped with standard RAM.

COMMON ERRORS

1. **Undeclared Array.** If we get a compile-time error like "Undefined function" for each line that has an array element name, then we forgot to declare the array. In declaring an array, remember that the initial declaration by the program unit that first uses the array must be with a constant array declarator. For example, see Subroutine INPUT on page 334.

---

[2] Arrays are memory hogs. If the computer uses 4 bytes to store a value (32-bit words), then 300,000 elements in an array would use up 1.2MB of primary memory. This would exceed available primary memory on many PCs and time-sharing systems.

2. **Subscript Expression Value Out of Bounds.** If we get a run-time error like "Subscript value out of bounds," then the value of a subscript expression falls outside the dimension bounds used in the array declarator. We have two common errors here: We're attempting to input an array that's too large, or we have made a logic error in assigning values to subscript expressions. We can easily handle the former by error routines, as done in Programs SORT and PLOT. In the latter case, we can diagnose the error by using a trace to print values of subscript expressions as they are evaluated. Whenever you use an array element name, ask yourself the question, "Is it possible that subscript expression values could violate dimension bounds?" If the answer is yes, then write code that accounts for this possibility, as in calling an error routine or using a decision structure.

3. **Association Errors.** Arrays that are used across modules must be associated either through argument lists or COMMON statements. Make sure that arrays are properly matched with respect to order, type, and size. If a program uses identical blank common, then type a single COMMON statement and copy it from one module to the other modules. Remember that we can use adjustable and assumed-size array declarators only in subroutines and function subprograms.

4. **Initialization Errors.** We get a run-time error if we attempt to use an un-initialized array element, like one that stores sums or counts. Remember that we can initialize during compilation with DATA statements or during execution with assignment statements. If the array needs to be initialized more than once during any one computer run, then we must use a run-time initialization, or we have a logic error from wrong initial values. Subroutine XYPLOT on page 336 uses a run-time initialization for array PLOT, although we could have used a DATA statement. If we were to plot more than one function in the same computer run (as in Exercise 32), then all plots following the first would be incorrect (the plot symbols from previous plots would not have been blanked out). This is why we used a run-time initialization in that subroutine. Remember that arrays in *blank* common blocks cannot be initialized in DATA statements. We can initialize arrays in *named* common blocks only through block data subprograms, as shown in Example 7.13.

1. Indicate the storage contents of specific array elements for the following, where a value of 4 is input for N.

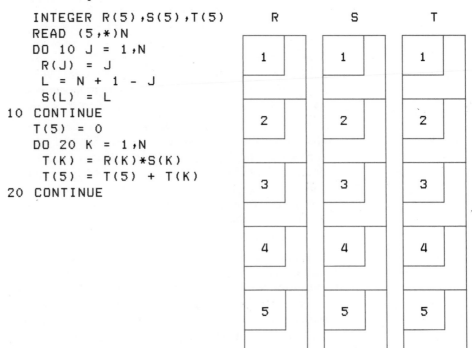

```
      INTEGER R(5),S(5),T(5)
      READ (5,*)N
      DO 10 J = 1,N
       R(J) = J
       L = N + 1 - J
       S(L) = L
10    CONTINUE
      T(5) = 0
      DO 20 K = 1,N
       T(K) = R(K)*S(K)
       T(5) = T(5) + T(K)
20    CONTINUE
```

2. Describe output for the following.

```
      REAL A(100),B(100),SUMA,SUMB,SUMDIF   Input Data
      DATA SUMDIF,SUMA,SUMB/3*0.0/
                                            4
      READ (5,*)M
                                            1,5
      DO 50 J = 1,M
                                            10,4
       READ (5,*)A(J),B(J)
                                            8,1
       SUMA = SUMA + A(J)
                                            2,10
       SUMB = SUMB + B(J)
       SUMDIF = SUMDIF + (A(J) - B(J))
50    CONTINUE
      DO 75 J = 1,M
       PRINT *,A(J),B(J),A(J) - B(J)
75    CONTINUE
      PRINT *,SUMA,SUMB,SUMDIF
      END
```

3. Code a more efficient way of handling each of the following statements.

  a. `READ *,X(1),X(2),X(3),X(4),X(5),X(6),X(7),X(8)`

  b. `READ *,X(1),X(3),X(5),X(7),X(9),X(11)`

  c. `PRINT *,A(1),B(1),A(2),B(2),A(3),B(3)`

  d. `PRINT *,A(1),A(2),A(3),B(1),B(2),B(3),B(4),B(5)`

  e. `PRINT *,X(1,1),X(1,2),X(1,3),X(1,4)`
```
   PRINT *,X(2,1),X(2,2),X(2,3),X(2,4)
   PRINT *,X(3,1),X(3,2),X(3,3),X(3,4)
```

4. Suppose the values 10, 20, 30, and 40 are stored in the four-element integer array YES and the values 5, 10, 15, and 20 are stored in the four-element integer array NO. Indicate output for each case, where N stores a 4.

  a. `PRINT *,(YES(J),J = 1,N),(NO(J),J = 1,N)`

  b. `PRINT *,(YES(J),NO(J),J = 1,N)`

  c.   `PRINT *,(J,YES(J),NO(J),J = 1,N)`

  d.   `DO 50 K = 1,2`
```
        PRINT *,K,(YES(J),J = 1,N)
   50 CONTINUE
```

5. **Input formats.** We wish to store the values 10, 20, 30, and 40 in the first four storage locations of the integer array MONEY. Indicate where you would place the data for each case.

Input Records

1 2 3 4 5 6 7 8 9 10 11 12 13 14 15 16 17 18 19 20

  a.   `READ 1, (MONEY(K), K = 1,4)`
```
   1 FORMAT(4I3)
```

  b.   `READ 1, (MONEY(K), K = 1,4)`
```
   1 FORMAT(I3)
```

  c.   `READ 1, (MONEY(K), K = 1,4)`
```
   1 FORMAT(2I3)
```

  d.   `READ 1, (MONEY(K), K = 1,4)`
```
   1 FORMAT(8I3)
```

  e.   `1 FORMAT(I3)`
```
      DO 10 K = 1,4
        READ 1, MONEY(K)
   10 CONTINUE
```

6. **Output formats.** Suppose we wish to output the contents of MONEY as defined in the preceding exercise. Indicate how output would appear for each case.

a.
```
     PRINT 15,(MONEY(J), J = 1,4)
  15 FORMAT(1X,4I5)
```

b.
```
     PRINT 15,(MONEY(J), J = 1,4)
  15 FORMAT(1X,I5)
```

c.
```
     PRINT 15,(MONEY(J), J = 1,4)
  15 FORMAT(1X,2I5)
```

d.
```
  15 FORMAT(1X,I1,I5)
     DO 20 J = 1,4
       PRINT 15,J,MONEY(J)
  20 CONTINUE
```

e.
```
     PRINT 15,(J,MONEY(J), J = 1,4)
  15 FORMAT(1X,I1,I5)
```

7. Write code for the following manipulations of the 25-element integer array LIST.

a. Input N values in reverse order; that is, the first value gets stored in LIST(N), the second in LIST(N-1), and so on.

b. Find and print the largest value in the array. How might you go about finding the largest and next-to-largest values?

c. Print locations of array elements (values of subscript expressions) that store values of zero.

*d. Create a second array, LIST2, consisting of all nonzero elements in LIST.

*e. Move all values in the array up one position; that is, the value in LIST(1) gets eliminated, LIST(2) gets moved to LIST(1), LIST(3) to LIST(2), and so on. Insert −99 in the last array element.

8. Write a program segment to initialize every element in the (5 × 6) real array D to the value 100 by each of the following approaches.
   a. Compile-time initialization.
   b. Run-time initialization.

9. Write a program segment that initializes the (4 × 4) integer array X in the following manner.

```
1  0  0  0
0  1  0  0
0  0  1  0
0  0  0  1
```

*10. Suppose a 10 × 20 real array X already exists in memory. Write code to
   a. Interchange the values of corresponding array elements in column 3 and column 1.
   b. Print out the smallest value in X and its location (row and column).

11. **Example 7.3 with format-directed I/O.** Modify the code to process all data using the I3 edit descriptor as follows.
   a. Use the input records shown in the example.
   b. Use the output records shown in the example.
   c. Each input value is on a separate line.
   d. Each output line has the array element number and its corresponding temperature.

*12. **Example 7.7.** Write code that prints the following line for each city: city name, temperature, and "Above mean" if temperature is above the mean temperature, or "Equals mean" if at the mean, or "Below mean" if below the mean.

13. **Example 7.8 with format-directed I/O.** Modify the code to process all data using the I4 edit descriptor as follows.
   a. According to the input records shown in the example.
   b. According to the output records shown in the example.

14. **Example 7.9 with row averages.** Modify the example as follows.
   a. Declare and fill a new one-dimensional array called AVEROW that stores the average of each row.
   b. Print AVEROW as a fifth column in the output.
   c. Calculate and print the grand average temperature (mean of all temperatures).
   d. I/O the proper city for each row (see Figure 7.1).
   *e. Test run the revised program.

*15. **Example 7.9 with augmented matrix.** Revise the program as follows.
   a. Include column averages as an extra row in F and row averages as an extra column in F.

    b. Calculate and print the southeast corner element as the grand average temperature (mean of all temperatures).

    c. I/O the proper city for each row (see Figure 7.1).

    d. Test run the revised program.

*16. **Three-dimensional temperature array.** Write and test code to input and output the three-dimensional array shown in Figure 7.1. Store city names and years as one-dimensional character arrays. Do a nice job of labeling the output.

17. **Example 7.10.** Modify the example as follows.

    a. Use an assumed-size array declarator where it's appropriate.

    b. Specify dimension bounds of −200 to 100. Specify these as the named constants LDB and UDB, respectively. Instead of N, input values for the lower and upper array element limits (LOWER and UPPER) for this run.

    *c. Add a subroutine called BOUNDS that detects values in LOWER or UPPER that fall outside their allowable limits.

    *d. Test run the revised program using the same five temperatures and array elements F(−2), F(−1), F(0), F(1), and F(2).

18. **Example 7.11.** Consider the following changes.

    a. Can we replace 500 with N or * in the subprogram's INTEGER statement?

    b. Can we remove N from the common block and use it in the argument lists? Does this change your answer to part (a)?

19. **Example 7.12.** Within each module can we replace multiple COMMON statements with one COMMON statement? If so, try it.

*20. **Example 7.13.** Rewrite the program to perform execution-time initializations.

21. **Table lookup with blank common.** Modify Program LOOKUP to use blank common blocks for all associated values. Which approach do you prefer and why?

*22. **Table lookup with gender.** Modify and test Program LOOKUP to account for a third column in the premium schedule with the following entries: $4.25, 4.75, 5.25, 6.00, 7.00, 8.00, 9.00, 10.00, 12.00, 14.00, 20.00, and 32.00. This column is the proper premiums for males; the second column is the proper premiums for females. Input now includes sex code.

*23. **Table lookup as utility module.** Generalize Subroutine LOOK as a library utility for use by any program unit that requires a table lookup. The subroutine receives values for the following arguments in its dummy argument list.

ROWS . . . . .   Number of rows in table
COLS . . . . .   Number of columns in table
SEARCH . .   Search value (AGE in the example)
KEY . . . . . .   Search key column (= 1 in example)
RESCOL . .   Results column (= 2 in example)
TABLE . . . .   The lookup table

The subroutine performs a table lookup, and returns the proper value in variable RESULT (for example, $5.00 when the age is 28). Test this subroutine by appropriately modifying Program LOOKUP, and duplicating the run in Figure 7.8. Note that generality now dictates that TABLE is declared using an adjustable array declarator.

*24. **Table lookup by traditional method.** The following code describes a traditional method of performing a table lookup.

```
        DO 100 I = 1, ROWS
            IF (AGE .LE. TABLE(I,1)) GO TO 200
    100 CONTINUE
    200 PRINT ...., FACE * TABLE(I,2)
```

This routine would replace the else block in Subroutine LOOK. Do we get the same results as before? Any problems here?

25. **Sorting subroutine variations.** Modify Subroutine SORT1 to create the following new subroutines.

a. SORT2. Sorts real one-dimensional array in ascending order.

b. SORT3. Sorts character one-dimensional array in ascending order. Assume each character array element has a length of 50.

c. SORT4. Sorts integer one-dimensional array in descending order.

*d. SORT5. Sorts integer one-dimensional array in either ascending or descending order. The subroutine receives either the character value A to indicate ascending or D to indicate descending. If the wrong character value is sent, then the subroutine prints an appropriate error message and performs an ascending sort.

*26. **Sorting by different attributes.** Write a program that processes the city name/ temperature data in Example 7.7 and prints two reports. The first report shows a table of city names and temperatures sorted by ascending city names; the second table shows the same table sorted by ascending temperatures.

*27. **Sorting with generalized dimension bounds.** Modify Program SORT to sort an array declared with lower dimension bound LDB and upper dimension bound UDB. Use −200 and 100 for these named constants. In your sample run, use the same five temperatures as the original example, but with array elements that run from −1 to 3. Don't forget to test a revised Subroutine NERR, which might be called BOUNDS (see Exercise 17).

*28. **Sorting without altering original array.** The approach in Program SORT destroys the original ordering of elements once the array is sorted. Modify the calling program unit to retain X as is, and to place the sorted array under the name XSORT.

*29. **Sorting two-dimensional array.** Modify Subroutine SORT1 to sort a two-dimensional integer array. Besides the array dimensions and the array, the subroutine receives the column number (KEY) on which to base an ascending sort. Test the subroutine by processing the temperature matrix in Example 7.8. Try two runs: The first sorts the array using the first column as the key; the second sorts the array using the third column as the key. Note that row integrity must be maintained; that is, a sort based on elements in the *j*th column must rearrange all other columns identically. Put another way, we are actually sorting entire rows. The sort based on the first column as the key gives the following sorted matrix.

```
15  73  95  45
20  65  85  55
32  56  80  62
62  72  83  74
68  85  90  75
```

*30. **Sorting by traditional insertion method.** The following code describes a traditional insertion sort. Note that we don't need to find the minimum value by this method. We also don't need to switch the first element with the minimum. The sorted set begins with the first element, and insertions begin with the second element.

```
    DO 300 K = 2, SIZE
       INSERT = ARRAY(K)
       DO 200 J = K, 2, -1
          IF (INSERT .GE. ARRAY(J-1)) GO TO 250
          ARRAY(J) = ARRAY(J-1)
200    CONTINUE
250    ARRAY(J) = INSERT
300 CONTINUE
```

Roleplay the sample run in Figure 7.9 using this routine. What's the advantage of this approach? The disadvantage? Why did we have to find the minimum value by our original method?

31. **XY-plot questions.** Answer the following questions regarding Program PLOT.
   a. The aspect ratio is the number of vertical print positions divided by the number of horizontal print positions. What's the current aspect ratio in the program? If the typical width of a character is 60% of its height, do aspect ratios other than 0.6 distort the plot? Comment.
   b. What would happen if we were to use the following statement in Subroutine XYPLOT?

   ```
   PLOT(XSCALE,YSCALE) = SYMBOL
   ```

   c. What would be the implication of using a DATA statement to initialize PLOT?
   d. Why do we use variable ERR in Subroutine XYPLOT?
   e. Why do we use the G edit descriptor in Subroutines OUTPUT and XYPLOT?
   f. What's the scaled coordinate for the 11th coordinate in Figure 7.10? Circle this coordinate on the graph. Is it possible that a plot would not show every coordinate? Explain.
   g. Is it possible to get a "subscript value out of bounds" error for array PLOT? Explain.
   h. What are the scaled coordinates given the following three coordinates in a new plot?

```
1, 3
1, 4
1, 5
```

*32. **XY-Plot improvements.** Change Program PLOT as follows.
  a. Input axis labels and a plot title and pass these to XYPLOT. Limit the axis labels to 15 characters and the title to 40 characters.
  b. Process more than one function. After each plot, query the user if another plot is desired.
  c. Print dotted axes that correspond to zero values for x and y.
  In your test run process the following functions:

Title	X-Axis Label	Y-Axis Label	Coordinates
XY-PLOT	X	Y	As in Figure 7.10
Test Plot	Yin	Yang	1, 3
			1, 4
			1, 5

*33. **XY-Plot with Substring.** In Example 6.1 we used a substring to plot characters. Using the same idea, revise Subroutine XYPLOT to work with a one-dimensional array PLOT that has elements with a declared length of 51. Lines in the plot now correspond to elements in PLOT, and print columns correspond to individual characters within each element. Which approach do you prefer, and why?

*34. **XY-Plot of Specific Functions.** Revise Subroutine INPUT to generate X and Y arrays for defined statement functions within the subroutine. The subroutine now inputs initial, final, and incremental values for x. Try the following functions.
  a. $y = 22 - 2x - 3x^2$ over $x = -9$ to 11 in increments of 2.
  b. $y = \cos(x)$ over $x = -10$ to 10 in increments of 0.2.
  c. The three functions in Figure 5.7 over $x = -5$ to 5 in increments of 0.1. How about increments of 0.01?

35. **FORTRAN library.** Is a graphics FORTRAN library like CalComp's available at your installation? If so, check out how to use it and try the following.
  a. Generate a line plot based on our sample illustration in Section 7.4. Try different variations based on scaling, titles, and other options offered by the package.
  b. Generate a bar chart using the data in Example 6.1.
  c. Try other procedures that look interesting to you.

ADDITIONAL EXERCISES

36. **Revisit: Student averages.** Revise the program in Example 3.3 by storing student names in a one-dimensional array and scores in a two-dimensional array. Give the user an interactive option of printing output sorted by either name or average.

37. **Revisit: Microcomputer price quotations.** Apply the table lookup routine to the price table in Example 4.4. Use a generalized lookup subroutine, as described in Exercise 23 of the present chapter.

38. **Revisit: Computer dating.** In Exercise 32 of Chapter 5 use a one-dimensional array for names, a two-dimensional array for the numeric data file fields, and a one-dimensional array for the client's preferences. Print results in decreasing order of desirability. Start a business and make a million with this program . . .

39. **Revisit: Bar chart subroutine.** Rework the program in Example 6.1 by storing the frequency distribution as two one-dimensional arrays. Pass these to a revised Subroutine BCHART, which now prints the entire bar chart in one call.

40. **Revisit: HC ENGINEoil.** Let's get down to serious business with the suggestions in Exercise 18 in Chapter 2, Exercise 9 in Chapter 3, and Exercise 12 in Chapter 4. Store the oil platform coordinates in arrays X and Y. Explore proposed Home Base coordinates as follows: Interactively input a range (low, high, and increment) of x-coordinates and a range of y-coordinates for proposed locations of the Home Base. Use nested DO-loops that vary the proposed ranges. Store the resulting total distances in a two-dimensional array called D. A printout of array D is similar to a geographic contour plot. We're looking for the minimum value (the "valley floor") as the best proposed Home Base location (of those considered). High values indicate "ridges overlooking the valley floor." The selected range of coordinates should bracket the minimum value somewhere in the center of the matrix ("the valley floor should be surrounded by higher ridges"). Otherwise, the minimum may be a local minimum (the lowest "ridge" considered) instead of the global minimum (the "lowest spot on the valley floor"). Include an outer loop that asks the user if another set of ranges is desired. Typically, we start the search for the best location with wide ranges and large increments. When we bracket a minimum, we refine the "map" with a narrower range and smaller increment. Visual search procedures of this type are fun. Enjoy . . . ! You might even win that case of motor oil from Harvey.

41. **Crime Data.** The data below represent the number of arrests for felony crimes in a state over a three-year period.

	Arrest Data by Year		
Felony	*1987*	*1988*	*1989*
Homicide	1,000	1,000	1,000
Robbery	10,000	9,000	11,000
Burglary	27,000	24,000	28,000
Assault	13,000	15,000	16,000
Theft	19,000	20,000	23,000
Forgery	10,000	9,000	10,000

a. Design and write a program to read the arrest data into a two-dimensional integer array. Print out the data in a table format that includes a new row for total arrests in each year and a new column for average arrests for each crime over the past three years.

b. In the output of part **a,** label your columns 1987, 1988, 1989, and AVERAGE. Label your rows according to the felony names in the above table, the last row being TOTALS. Store felony names in a one-dimensional character array, and years in a one-dimensional integer array.

c. Print a second table that projects arrests over the next three years. Interactively input the annual percent increases in arrests for each felony. Use the following percents for the six felonies: 2, 2, 5, 4, 8, 6. For example, we would expect 29,400 burglaries in 1991 (28,000 × 1.05). Store the percents in a one-dimensional real array and all projections in a two-dimensional integer array.

d. Instead of using 2 two-dimensional arrays for the actual and projected arrest data, use a single three-dimensional array.

42. Grade table lookup. Students are assigned final grades according to the following grade table.

Grade Table

Average	Grade
Below 60	F
60 but less than 70	D
70 but less than 80	C
80 but less than 90	B
90 or above	A

The instructor's grade book shows the following.

Grade Book: Computers 101

	Weights				
	0.2	*0.3*	*0.5*		
Name	*Grade 1*	*Grade 2*	*Grade 3*	*Average*	*Grade*
Clay, Josh	85	90	95	91.5	A
Dunn, J. K.	80	60	60	64.0	D
Furc, Mark	90	80	85	84.5	B
Mello, Cynthia	50	60	90	73.0	C
Morfella, Yarta	70	50	40	49.0	F
For the class				72.4	C

a. Design, write, and test a program that electronically reproduces the manual system. Store names, weights, and numeric grades in a data file. The program should handle up to 100 students and 5 grades. It should also ensure that the weights sum to 1.

b. Include the interactive option of printing a frequency distribution of grades. In our sample problem we would have the following.

Frequency Distribution

Grade	Frequency
A	1
B	1
C	1
D	1
F	1
	——
	5

c. Include the interactive option of printing reports of names and grades sorted by grades from high to low.

43. **Polynomial plot.** An n-degree polynomial function is described as follows.

$$y = b_0 + b_1 x + b_2 x^2 + \ldots + b_n x^n$$

a. Design, write, and test an interactive program that inputs n, the coefficients b_i, and a range of values for x (low, high, and increment). Store the coefficients in a one-dimensional array, fill the one-dimensional array X, and use the function to generate the one-dimensional array Y. Print a table of x-y values. Allow up to 10th-degree polynomials. Limit the number of elements in X and Y to 1000. In one computer run, process the following polynomial functions over the range $x = -5$ to 5 in increments of 0.5.

$$y = -2.25 - 4x$$
$$y = -2.25 - 4x + x^2$$
$$y = -2.25 - 4x + x^2 - 0.01x^3$$

After finishing with a function, ask the user if another function is desired. *Hint:* Use a DO-loop to find an element in Y as the sum of terms in the polynomial function.

b. Include the option of plotting a function.

44. **Pascal's triangle.** The French mathematician and philosopher Blaise Pascal (1623–1662) proposed the following triangular array for investigating certain mathematical properties and proving some theorems.

```
1
1  1
1  2  1
1  3  3  1
1  4  6  4  1
. . .
```

Pascal's triangle is constructed according to the following properties: Each row and column begins with 1; each succeeding number is the sum of two numbers, the one directly above it and the one to the left of the upper number. The sixth row, for example, would have the elements 1, 5, 10, 10, 5, 1.

a. Design, write, and test an interactive program that inputs the size of the triangle (number of rows or columns) and prints Pascal's triangle. Print a triangle of size 10 in your test run. Label each row with its row number followed by a separator, as in 3 ¦ for the third row. Allow triangles up to size 100.

b. A binomial expansion to the nth power is given by the following expression.

$$(a + b)^n$$

For example, if $n = 2$, then we have the three terms

$$a^2 + 2ab + b^2$$

Note that the third row in Pascal's triangle includes the three coefficients (1 2 1) in this binomial expansion. In general, the elements in row $(n + 1)$ in Pascal's triangle are the coefficients in a binomial expansion to the nth power.

Include an option in the program for printing coefficients in a binomial expansion. For example, if the user inputs 5 for power, then the program should print the sixth row of Pascal's triangle as follows.

Binomial Expansion to 5th power

Term	Coefficient
1	1
2	5
3	10
4	10
5	5
6	1

45. **Simulation: Screen pattern.** The following procedure is a visual test of the goodness of a pseudorandom number generator.

1. Initialize an $m \times n$ matrix SCREEN to blanks, where m is the number of lines on the screen and n is the number of columns. The typical matrix is 25×80. This two-dimensional character array, where each element has a declared length of 1, is a "picture" of the screen.

2. Generate a pseudorandom integer number in the range 1 to m, and another in the range 1 to n. This gives the coordinates of a position on the screen, or element in the matrix. Fill this element with the dot or period character. Note that we can use Function RAND from Chapter 6 to generate a pseudorandom real number r in the interval $0-1$. A pseudorandom integer number k in the range a to b follows:

$$k = \text{int}[a + (b - a)r]$$

For example, if $a = 1$, $b = 80$, and $r = 0.5$, then $k = 40$; if $a = 1$, $b = 25$, and $r = 0.1$, then $k = 3$. This would be equivalent to placing a dot at screen coordinate $(3, 40)$.

3. Repeat Step 2 a total of $m \times n$ times.

4. Print the matrix.

If the screen shows a random pattern of dots, without evidence of "banding," then the pseudorandom number generator is doing a good job. A strong pattern would suggest a poorly performing generator. Try it on your system.

46. **Bubble sort.** Another simple, but rather slow, sorting procedure is the bubble sort, or exchange sort. The following describes the first two passes in an ascending sort.

Unsorted:	30 50 40 10 20		
Pass 1:	Swap 30 and 50?	No:	30 50 40 10 20
	Swap 50 and 40?	Yes:	30 40 50 10 20
	Swap 50 and 10?	Yes:	30 40 10 50 20
	Swap 50 and 20?	Yes:	30 40 10 20 50
Pass 2:	Swap 30 and 40?	No:	30 40 10 20 50
	Swap 40 and 10?	Yes:	30 10 40 20 50
	Swap 40 and 20?	Yes:	30 10 20 40 50
	Swap 40 and 50?	No:	30 10 20 40 50

Get the idea? The procedure continues until an entire pass has no swaps. How did the term *bubble sort* come about? Low values rise at each pass, much like "bubbles" in a carbonated drink. No kidding . . . Note how the minimum 10 "rises in the glass."

a. Design, code, and test an ascending bubble sort subroutine (BUB1) for integer one-dimensional arrays. Use the above array as test data, and Program SORT as your test program.

b. Design, code, and test a main program that compares the processing speeds of Subroutines SORT1 and BUB1. Generate a test array by using Function RAND from Chapter 6 to fill in elements with integer values that range from 0 to 100, as follows:

```
X(I) = 100 * RAND ()
```

Then sort this array by each of the two sorting procedures, and record the processing times. Perform your comparisons on three separate arrays with the following number of elements: 100, 500, 1000.

Which sorting procedure is faster?

47. **Symmetric Matrix.** A symmetric matrix is an $n \times n$ (square) matrix such that column i is identical to row i, $i = 1, \ldots, n$. For example, the following matrix is symmetric.

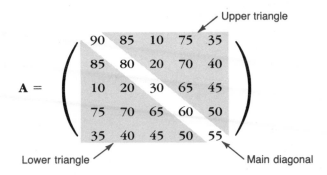

Note that the upper triangle is a "mirror image" of the lower triangle, excluding the main diagonal. Therefore, an input routine would only need to input the lower triangle and the main diagonal, and then fill in the upper triangle accordingly.

Design, write, and code an interactive program that inputs the size and lower part of a symmetric matrix, and prints the entire matrix. Use the above matrix as test data.

48. **Vector as symmetric matrix.** The preceding exercise defined and illustrated a symmetric matrix. Many applications, particularly in applied mathematics and statistics, deal with very large symmetric matrices. Since the lower part of the matrix (lower triangle and main diagonal) contains all the necessary data, we can save memory storage by representing the symmetric matrix as a vector, or one-dimensional array. In other words, instead of working with a two-dimensional array directly, as in the preceding exercise, we work directly with a one-dimensional array whose elements store the lower part of the symmetric matrix. For the symmetric matrix in the preceding exercise, the first six elements of the equivalent vector are 90 85 80 10 20 30. Get the idea?

We can reference element i,j in the symmetric matrix as element k in the vector according to the following transformation scheme.

$$
\begin{array}{llllllll}
i \rightarrow & 1 & 2 & 2 & 3 & 3 & 3 & \ldots & n \\
j \rightarrow & 1 & 1 & 2 & 1 & 2 & 3 & \ldots & n \\
k \rightarrow & 1 & 2 & 3 & 4 & 5 & 6 & \ldots & n(n+1)/2
\end{array}
$$

}Subscripts in lower part of matrix

}Corresponding subscripts in vector

For example, element 3,3 in the matrix is element 6 in the vector. This would be the element whose value is 30 in our sample symmetric matrix.

When $n = 5$, the symmetric matrix requires 25 elements, and the equivalent vector needs 15 elements, or $5(5 + 1)/2$. This saves 10 elements of storage, or 40%; when $n = 500$, the savings is 124,750 elements, or about 50%.

a. Design, write, and code an interactive program that inputs the lower part of an $n \times n$ symmetric matrix directly into a vector. Include the input of n. Print the lower part of the matrix (lower triangle and main diagonal).

b. Include an interactive query feature that could reproduce the following dialogue.

```
            Enter i,j:
        3,2
                    Element    3, 2 is 20
            Enter i,j:
        2,2
                    Element    2, 2 is 80
            Enter i,j:
        1,5
                    Element    1, 5 is 35
            Enter i,j:
        0,0
                        ... Adios
```

49. **Stock portfolio.** Companies, universities, banks, pension funds, and other organizations routinely invest funds in the stock market. The set of stocks in which the organization invests its funds is called a *stock portfolio*. The table below illustrates a sample stock portfolio, including the number of shares owned of each stock, the purchase price per share, and the latest price per share quoted by the stock exchange.

Stock Portfolio

Stock	Number of Shares	Purchase Price ($/share)	Current Price ($/share)
AppleC	40,000	$25\frac{7}{8}$	$39\frac{3}{4}$
Boeing	5,000	$61\frac{1}{2}$	56
EKodk	10,000	60	$54\frac{1}{2}$
HewlPk	15,000	39	50
IBM	2,500	$97\frac{1}{8}$	$120\frac{3}{4}$
Texaco	8,000	$23\frac{1}{2}$	49
TexInst	12,000	80	$45\frac{7}{8}$

a. Design, code, and run a program that calculates the initial (purchase) value of the portfolio, the current value of the portfolio, and the net change in the value. Store number of shares, purchase prices, and current prices in a two-dimensional array. *Hint:* The value of the portfolio is found by multiplying shares by corresponding prices and summing.

b. Output the portfolio before printing the items in part **a**. Store the stock names in a one-dimensional character array.

c. Include a loop in the program for processing more than one portfolio. Find two copies of a newspaper that were published at least two weeks apart. Select a portfolio, make up shares owned, and use the two sets of prices for purchase and current prices. Process the given portfolio and the new portfolio in one run, and include the output of combined value of all portfolios.

50. **Questionnaire analysis.** A university is conducting a survey to determine its undergraduates' "attitudes toward and experiences with the consumption of alcoholic beverages." The following questionnaire has been designed for this survey:

_____1.   What is your sex? 1. male _____ 2. female _____
_____2.   Where do you live? 1. on campus _____ 2. off campus with parents
          _____ 3. off campus alone/with roommates _____
_____3.   What is your class standing? 1. freshman _____ 2. sophomore _____
          3. junior _____ 4. senior _____ 5. other _____
_____4.   How often on the average do you drink alcoholic beverages? 1. never
          _____ 2. less than once a week _____ 3. one to three times per week
          _____ 4. four to five times per week _____ 5. more than five times per
          week _____
_____5.   Do you feel other people's drinking has any adverse effects on your life?
          1. frequently _____ 2. occasionally _____ 3. rarely _____ 4. never _____
_____6.   Do your drinking habits affect your academic life? 1. frequently _____
          2. occasionally _____ 3. rarely _____ 4. never _____
_____7.   Do you ever feel guilty about your drinking? 1. frequently _____ 2. occa-
          sionally _____ 3. rarely _____ 4. never _____
_____8.   Do you feel you drink primarily because of 1. boredom _____ 2. peer
          pressure _____ 3. tension _____ 4. other _____ (specify)

Before conducting the full survey, the questionnaire was pretested on 10 students. The results are shown below.

| | Answer to Question No. | | | | | | | |
Student	1	2	3	4	5	6	7	8
1	1	1	3	3	4	4	2	3
2	1	1	3	1	2	2	1	1
3	2	2	2	2	1	3	3	2
4	2	3	1	4	3	1	3	3
5	1	1	4	4	1	1	2	3
6	1	2	2	2	1	1	2	3
7	2	3	4	1	3	2	1	2
8	2	1	1	2	4	4	2	1
9	1	2	3	3	1	1	1	1
10	2	2	1	4	2	3	2	1

a. Design, code, and write a program that reads questionnaire data into a two-dimensional array and outputs a frequency distribution for each question. For example, the frequency distribution for the first question and the above data would be

	Responses	
Question	1	2
1	5	5

For the second question, we have

	Responses		
Question	*1*	*2*	*3*
2	4	4	2

b. Modify the program to interactively provide cross-tabulation of responses for any two questions that are specified by the user. For example, if we wish to assess differences between the drinking frequencies of men and women, then our output might appear as follows:

		Question 1	
		1	2
	1—	1	1
Question 4	2—	1	2
	3—	2	0
	4—	1	2
	5—	0	0

To make sure you understand this cross-tabulation, confirm the numbers based on the data.

51. **Statistical analysis.** Large programs that give options for various statistical analyses are common in commercial applications. For example, Minitab, UCLA's BMDP, North Carolina State's SAS, and the University of Chicago's SPSS are all widely used packages for implementing a variety of statistical analyses across many disciplines.

  a. Measures of central tendency and dispersion. Design and write a modular program that calculates and prints the statistics described below for analyzing a set of n data items given by $x_1, x_2, \ldots, x_n$. In the descriptions below, assume the following set of values for x: 7, 14, 10, 6, 3.

  1. *Mean,* given by

$$\bar{x} = \frac{x_1 + x_2 + \cdots + x_n}{n} = \frac{\sum\limits_{i=1}^{n} x_i}{n} = \frac{40}{5} = 8$$

  2. *Median,* a value such that one-half of the values are above it and one-half of the values are below it. First sort the data in ascending order, and then find the *position* of the median using the formula $(n + 1)/2$. For example, if the sorted values of x are

  3   6   7   10   14

  ————— Location of median in 3rd position

  then the median is found in position $(5 + 1)/2$, or third position. Thus the median is 7. If n is an even number, however, the median is defined as halfway between the two adjacent positions in the center. For example, in the six-item sequence

3 6 7 10 14 16

— Location of median in 3.5th position

the median is in position 3.5, or midway between the third item (7) and the fourth item (10). Thus the median is 8.5.

3. Minimum value of x, or 3 for the given data.
4. Maximum value of x, or 14 for the given data.
5. *Range,* the difference between max x and min x, or 11 for the given data.
6. *Mean absolute deviation (MAD)*, given by

$$MAD = \frac{\sum_{i=1}^{n} |x_i - \bar{x}|}{n} = \frac{16}{5} = 3.2$$

7. *Variance,* given by

$$s^2 = \frac{\sum_{i=1}^{n} (x_i - \bar{x})^2}{n - 1} = \frac{70}{4} = 17.5$$

8. *Standard deviation,* given by

$$s = \sqrt{s^2} = \sqrt{17.5} = 4.1833$$

b. Frequency distribution. Add a second option to print a frequency distribution. The user enters the number of classes and upper class limits. For example, we might want to group the data into four classes with upper limits 5, 10, and 15 for the first three classes.

In this case, the frequency distribution is given by

Frequency Distribution

Class Limits	Frequency
Under 5	1
5 but under 10	2
10 but under 15	2
15 or above	0
	5

c. Bar chart. Add a third option that prints a bar chart, as illustrated in Example 6.1.

52. **Greedy algorithm: Knapsack problem.**[3] The knapsack problem is an allocation problem with a wide range of applications. In the classical problem a knapsack is to be filled with a selection from n possible items. If $x_j = 1$, then item j is selected for inclusion in the knapsack; otherwise, $x_j = 0$. The available quantity of

[3] Adapted from Frank S. Budnick, Dennis McLeavey, and Richard Mojena, *Principles of Operations Research for Management,* 2nd ed. (Homewood, IL: Irwin, 1988), pp. 393–394.

each item is limited to one unit, and each item has attributes of weight (w_j) and relative benefit (c_j). The problem is to select which of the n items should be packed in the knapsack in order to maximize the total benefit contributed by the items without violating a specified maximum weight (W). We can mathematically formulate the knapsack problem as follows.

$$\text{Maximize} \quad z = c_1x_1 + c_2x_2 + \ldots + c_nx_n$$
$$\text{subject to} \quad w_1x_1 + w_2x_2 + \ldots + w_nx_n \leq W$$

Our friend Harvey CORE not only looks down (for oil) but also looks up (to space), as CEO of CORE Space Express. The company specializes in filling orders for weekly shuttle flights that deliver heavy equipment to scientific laboratories in orbit around the earth. The shuttle vehicle has an overall payload limitation of 30,000 kilograms. Delivery prices are negotiable, depending on such factors as weight, insurance, and specialized handling needs. The accompanying table indicates prices and weights for five items under consideration for the coming flight. CORE Space Express wants to determine the set of items to deliver on its next flight in order to maximize total revenue. Only one unit of each item is offered for delivery.

Shuttle Payload Data

Item	Price per Item	Weight per Item (kg)	Price/Weight ($/kg)
1	$ 50,000	3,750	13.33
2	450,000	15,000	30.00
3	600,000	13,500	44.44
4	650,000	18,000	36.11
5	300,000	7,200	41.67

Algorithms exist for the optimal solution to this problem, but their complexity is beyond the scope of this text. Instead, let's propose a solution by using the following greedy algorithm.

> Load items in the order given by the greedy rule "highest price per unit of weight next," providing capacity is not exceeded; repeat until either all items are loaded or weight capacity is exhausted.

Greedy Algorithm: Weight Capacity = 30,000

Item Selected	Item Price	Item Weight	Loaded Weight	Unused Weight
3	$600,000	13,500	13,500	16,500
5	300,000	7,200	20,700	9,300
1	50,000	3,750	24,450	5,550
	$950,000			

Note that items 3 and 5 were selected first (they have the two highest price/weight ratios), but neither item 4 nor item 2 could be selected next because the weight capacity would have been exhausted. Thus we selected the item having fifth priority (item 1) as the third item to load (its inclusion did not violate the 30,000-kilogram capacity). Our solution reads: Load items 1, 3, and 5, giving total revenue of $950,000 and a loaded weight of 24,450 kilograms.

a. Design, code, and test a program that solves knapsack problems using the described greedy algorithm. The program should handle up to 5000 items. Use our sample problem for test data. Input n, the c_j, the w_j, and W. Output the Greedy Algorithm table illustrated above.

b. Suppose there is a volume limitation as well as a weight limitation. Think up a variation in the greedy algorithm to account for both weight and volume constraints. Solve the sample problem given a volume limitation of 250 cubic meters. Each item respectively takes up 17, 150, 125, 130, and 70 cubic meters.

53. **Matrix multiplication.** Let's define a matrix, **A**, as having dimensions (rows and columns) m_1 by n_1 or ($m_1 \times n_1$). Another matrix, **B**, has dimensions ($m_2 \times n_2$). Two matrices can be multiplied if and only if they are *compatible*, that is, the number of columns in the first matrix equals the number of rows in the second matrix. As an example, the multiplication of matrix **A** times matrix **B**, defined by **AB**, is possible if and only if $n_1 = m_2$. Similarly, the product **BA** is possible if and only if $n_2 = m_1$.

If two matrices are compatible, then the resulting matrix will have dimensions ($m \times n$), where m equals the number of rows in the first matrix, and n equals the number of columns in the second matrix. Referring to the matrices **A** and **B**, we see that if **AB** is possible and

AB = C

then the product matrix, **C**, will have dimensions ($m_1 \times n_2$). Similarly, if **BA** is possible and

BA = D

then **D** will have dimensions ($m_2 \times n_1$).

To compute the product matrix, consider the product

AB = C

Let c_{ij} be a generalized element that is located in row i and column j of the product matrix. To compute any c_{ij}, the elements in row i of matrix **A** are multiplied by the respective elements in column j of matrix **B** and are algebraically summed.

For example, if

$$A = \begin{pmatrix} 1 & 4 \\ 5 & -3 \end{pmatrix}$$

and

$$\mathbf{B} = \begin{pmatrix} 1 \\ 4 \end{pmatrix}$$

then **A** is a (2×2) matrix, and **B** is a (2×1) matrix. If we wish to find the product **AB**, then we must first examine the dimensions of the matrices. The product **AB** involves multiplying matrices with dimensions

Inner dimensions
$$(2 \times 2) \text{ times } (2 \times 1)$$
Outer dimensions

This product is defined because the inner dimensions are equal; that is, the number of columns of **A** equals the number of rows of **B.** The product matrix **C** will have dimensions equal to the outer dimensions indicated above, that is, (2×1). Thus the product will be of the form

$$\mathbf{AB} = \mathbf{C}$$

or

$$\begin{pmatrix} 1 & 4 \\ 5 & -3 \end{pmatrix} \begin{pmatrix} 1 \\ 4 \end{pmatrix} = \begin{pmatrix} c_{11} \\ c_{21} \end{pmatrix}$$

To compute the elements of **C**, we have

$$c_{11} = (1 \quad 4) \begin{pmatrix} 1 \\ 4 \end{pmatrix} = (1)(1) + (4)(4)$$
$$= 17$$

and

$$c_{21} = (5 \quad -3) \begin{pmatrix} 1 \\ 4 \end{pmatrix} = (5)(1) + (-3)(4)$$
$$= -7$$

or

$$\mathbf{C} = \begin{pmatrix} 17 \\ -7 \end{pmatrix}$$

The product **BA** is not defined because the inner dimensions do not match; that is, it involves multiplying a (2×1) matrix times a (2×2) matrix, and the number of columns of **B** *does not equal* the number of rows of **A** $(1 \neq 2)$.

Design an algorithm and write a program to input two matrices and print the two matrices together with their matrix product (if defined).

Process the following to debug your program.

a. Find **AB** given **A** and **B** as in the example.
b. Find **BA** given **A** and **B** as in the example.

c. Find **AB** given

$$A = \begin{pmatrix} 1 & 0 & 6 \\ 2 & -3 & 1 \end{pmatrix}$$

$$B = \begin{pmatrix} 1 & 0 & 0 \\ 0 & 1 & 0 \\ 0 & 0 & 1 \end{pmatrix}$$

54. **Matrix algebra menu.** Let's extend our ideas in the preceding exercise by designing, coding, and testing an interactive program that offers the following menu.

S   Sum of two matrices
D   Difference of two matrices
M   Multiplication of two matrices
T   Transpose of a matrix
X   eXit

Choices S, D, and M start with the input of two arrays. Precede the input of each array by asking whether it's one-dimensional or two-dimensional, and enter the appropriate number of rows and/or columns. Choice T inputs a single array. Here's what we do with the remainder of each choice.

S . . .   Create and print the sum matrix **S**. In our example from the preceding exercise, the sum of **B** and **C** is the matrix whose elements are the sums of corresponding elements in **B** and **C**, or

$$S = B + C$$

$$= \begin{pmatrix} 1 \\ 4 \end{pmatrix} + \begin{pmatrix} 17 \\ -7 \end{pmatrix}$$

$$= \begin{pmatrix} 18 \\ -3 \end{pmatrix}$$

Note that the matrices being summed must be compatible by having identical dimensions.

D . . .   Create and print the difference matrix **D**. Here we subtract corresponding elements. In our example, we would have

$$D = B - C$$

$$= \begin{pmatrix} 1 \\ 4 \end{pmatrix} - \begin{pmatrix} 17 \\ -7 \end{pmatrix}$$

$$= \begin{pmatrix} -16 \\ 11 \end{pmatrix}$$

As in summing, the matrices must be compatible.

M . . .   See the preceding exercise.

T . . .   The transpose matrix **T** of some matrix **A** is the matrix whose rows are identical to the columns in **A** (or whose columns are identical to the rows in **A**). In our example, the transpose of **A** is

$$\mathbf{T} = \begin{pmatrix} 1 & 5 \\ 4 & -3 \end{pmatrix}$$

8

CHARACTER PROCESSING

In earlier chapters we liberally used character constants, variables, and arrays to store, test, and print character data such as names, addresses, descriptions, yes/no replies, and plot symbols. In this chapter we treat additional features of FORTRAN that facilitate more sophisticated character processing applications, like text and linguistic analysis, text editing, and the encoding/decoding of secret messages.

8.1 REVIEW

Let's start with a review of character-processing elements from earlier chapters.

CHARACTER DATA AND NAMES

A **character datum** or **character string** or simply **string** is a sequence of characters, including any blank characters. The **length** of a string is the number of characters in the string. For example, I love FORTRAN 77! is a string of length 18. We process strings as constants, as named constants, and as stored values in variables, array elements, and functions.

The form of a **character constant** is given as follows.

Character Constant

Syntax:

        'string'

Example:

        'I love FORTRAN 77!'

The *value* of the character constant is the string itself, and its length is the length of the string. In our example, the length of the character constant is 18, or the number of characters enclosed within the apostrophes.

NOTE 1   The surrounding apostrophes identify a character constant, but are not part of its value or length.

NOTE 2   The length of a character constant must be greater than zero; that is, the string must be nonempty.

NOTE 3   If an apostrophe is a legitimate character within the string, then we represent it as two successive apostrophes within the character constant. Thus, the string I don't love FORTRAN 77! is expressed by the character constant 'I don"t love FORTRAN 77!', which has a length of 24 (the double apostrophe counts as one).

If a constant has contextual meaning or appears in more than one place in the program, then we can increase readability and reduce maintenance by using a **named constant.** For example, a program that invariably uses the corporate name HC ENGINEering, Inc. in several places might best treat this constant (parameter) as the named constant CORP, specified as follows.

PARAMETER (CORP = 'HC ENGINEering, Inc.')

If strings need to vary within a program's run, then we store these strings within variables or arrays. Variables and arrays, as well as named constants and function subprograms, are specified in CHARACTER statements having the following form.

CHARACTER Statement

Syntax:
       CHARACTER [*dl[,]] item[*dl] [, item[*dl]] . . .
Example:
       CHARACTER*20 COLOR*10, CORP, PHRASE, REPLY*1

Paired brackets [ ] denote optional portions, dl represents the declared length in one of the following forms

- an unsigned, nonzero integer constant
- an integer constant expression *enclosed in parentheses* and with positive value
- an asterisk *enclosed in parentheses* (used when its corresponding argument is a dummy argument, as shown later on page 408),

and item is a named constant, variable name, array name, array declarator, function name, or dummy procedure name.[1]

---

[1] A dummy procedure name is a dummy argument that corresponds to the name of a procedure, as described on page 251.

The **declared length** for a name is the number of character positions available in the storage identified by that name. In our example, CORP and PHRASE store 20-character strings, COLOR stores a 10-character string, and REPLY stores a one-character string. If length is declared just after the keyword CHARACTER, then each item in the list without its own declared length assumes this length. In our example, CORP and PHRASE assumed declared lengths of 20. If the portion *dl* is omitted just after the keyword CHARACTER, then any item in the list without its own declared length assumes a declared length of one. For example, the following statement is equivalent to the above, where REPLY stores one character.

```
CHARACTER COLOR*10, CORP*20, PHRASE*20, REPLY
```

A **character variable** stores a string that's replaceable during the same run. For example, at two different points in the same run we might have the following storage sequence for the character variable PHRASE.

Character positions ——— PHRASE   Declared length in CHARACTER statement

PHRASE

1	2	3	4	5	6	7	8	9	10	11	12	13	14	15	16	17	18	19	20
I		l	o	v	e		F	O	R	T	R	A	N		7	7	!		

PHRASE

1	2	3	4	5	6	7	8	9	10	11	12	13	14	15	16	17	18	19	20
I	'	m		n	o	t		s	o		s	u	r	e		I		l	o

NOTE 1   If the length of the string is less than the declared length of the character variable, then the rightmost unused character positions in storage are "padded" with blanks, as illustrated by the first string in PHRASE.

NOTE 2   If the length of the string is greater than the declared length of the character variable, then the string is "truncated" on the right before storage occurs, as illustrated by the second string in PHRASE.

A **character array** stores a string for each array element, where each array element (storage location) stores the number of character positions specified by the declared length. For example, we might want to store the names of days in the week in a seven-element array DAY, where each element has a declared length of 9 based on the following statement.

```
CHARACTER DAY(7)*9
```

or

```
CHARACTER*9 DAY(7)
```

We can conceptualize memory as follows.

Array elements   Character positions

DAY

	1	2	3	4	5	6	7	8	9
1	M	o	n	d	a	y			
2	T	u	e	s	d	a	y		
3	W	e	d	n	e	s	d	a	y
4	T	h	u	r	s	d	a	y	
5	F	r	i	d	a	y			
6	S	a	t	u	r	d	a	y	
7	S	u	n	d	a	y			

Remember that DAY(3), for example, is called a (**character**) **array element name;** it references the third element in array DAY, and stores the string Wednesday.

Character function names store character values defined in either state-ment functions(Section A.2) or function subprograms(Section 6.3). In Section 8.6 we illustrate character functions.

CHARACTER EXPRESSIONS

A **character expression** evaluates to a string, and has one of the following forms.

- character constant
- character named constant
- character variable name
- character array element name
- character function name
- character substring (Section 8.2)
- concatenated (Section 8.3)

For example, if COLOR is typed character with declared length 10 and stores the string purple as follows

COLOR

1	2	3	4	5	6	7	8	9	10
P	u	r	p	l	e				

then the following relational expression evaluates as false.

```
COLOR .EQ. 'red'
```

Note that the relational expression compares two simple character expressions: a character variable on the left and a character constant on the right. We take up more complicated character expressions starting in the next section.

NOTE   If character expressions of unequal length are compared in a relational expression, then the shorter character expression is treated as if it were extended on the right with blanks to the length of the longer character expression. In our example, COLOR stores the word purple followed by 4 blanks, giving 10 characters; the character constant 'red' has a length of 3, so before the relational expression is evaluated, the processor pads 7 blanks to the right of red.

CHARACTER DATA STORAGE

We store strings in character variables and array element names in any of the following ways.

- DATA statements
- Assignment statements
- Input statements

For example, the following DATA statement compile-time initializes the days of the week shown earlier.

```
DATA DAY / 'Monday', 'Tuesday', 'Wednesday',
+              'Thursday', 'Friday', 'Saturday',
+              'Sunday' /
```

The assignment statement

```
COLOR = 'purple'
```

stores the string purple in COLOR, as shown earlier. We might note that the form of a character assignment statement differs from its numeric counterpart in that a substring name (next section) can appear to the left of the equal sign, besides a variable name or array element name.

The sample input statements in Table 8.1 store the contents in PHRASE shown earlier.

NOTE   List-directed input requires surrounding apostrophes for the string (see the first example above); format-directed input is especially convenient for interactive

TABLE 8.1   **Sample Input Statements for Character Data**

Form	Input Statement	Input
List-directed	READ *, PHRASE	'I love FORTRAN 77!'
Format-directed	READ (*, '(A)') PHRASE	I love FORTRAN 77!
or	READ '(A)', PHRASE	I love FORTRAN 77!

character input, since the user does not enter surrounding quotes (see the second example in Table 8.1).

CHARACTER DATA OUTPUT

As before, we use the WRITE or PRINT statement to output strings as constants, named constants, variables, character expressions, and array element names. Moreover, we can use either list-directed output or format-directed output. The examples in Table 8.2 illustrate these variations.

8.2 SUBSTRINGS

Any contiguous subset of a string is called a **substring.** For example, the string CORE has all of the possible substrings shown in Table 8.3.

We can name substrings, which allows us to reference and redefine portions of strings. This feature is particularly useful in text editing applications. A substring name has the following form.

Substring Name

Syntax:
   Character variable name (*Substring expression for*   *Substring expression for*)
   or array element name   *leftmost character position* : *rightmost character position*)
Example:
        COLOR(1:4)

In the example, the substring name COLOR(1:4) references characters in character positions 1 through 4 in character variable COLOR. If COLOR stores *purple,* then COLOR(1:4) references the substring purp.
   Substring expressions must be integer expressions, and we can omit either substring expression. If the leftmost substring expression is omitted, character

TABLE 8.2   Sample Output Statements for Character Data

Description	Output Statement	Output
Constant and named constant		
. . . list-directed	PRINT *, 'Corporation:', CORP	Corporation: HC ENGINEering, Inc.
. . . format-directed	PRINT '(1X, 'Corporation:', A)', CORP	Corporation: HC ENGINEering, Inc.
or	PRINT '(1X, A13, A)', 'Corporation:', CORP	Corporation: HC ENGINEering, Inc.
Variable		
. . . list-directed	PRINT *, PHRASE	I love FORTRAN 77!
or	WRITE (*,*) PHRASE	I love FORTRAN 77!
. . . format-directed	PRINT '(1X, A)', PHRASE	I love FORTRAN 77!
or	WRITE (*, '(1X, A)') PHRASE	I love FORTRAN 77!
Array element		
. . . list-directed	PRINT *, DAY(3)	Wednesday
. . . format-directed	PRINT '(1X, A)', DAY(3)	Wednesday

TABLE 8.3   **Substrings in String CORE**

Length	Substrings
1	C O R E
2	CO OR RE
3	COR ORE
4	CORE

position 1 is implied; if the rightmost substring expression is omitted, character position *dl* is implied. Moreover, *substring expressions must have values between 1 and dl inclusive, and the value of the leftmost substring expression must not exceed the value of the rightmost substring expression.* If both substring expressions are omitted, then the entire string is referenced.

EXAMPLE 8.1

SUBSTRING EXAMPLES

Assume the following for the illustrations below.

```
CHARACTER  PHRASE*20,SUB*5
INTEGER    L,R
```

PHRASE

1	2	3	4	5	6	7	8	9	10	11	12	13	14	15	16	17	18	19	20
I		l	o	v	e		F	O	R	T	R	A	N		7	7	!		

SUB

1	2	3	4	5

L
2

R
10

Substring Name	Substring	Sample Use	Result
a. PHRASE(3:6)	love	SUB = PHRASE(3:6)	SUB <table><tr><td>1</td><td>2</td><td>3</td><td>4</td><td>5</td></tr><tr><td>l</td><td>o</td><td>v</td><td>e</td><td></td></tr></table>
b. PHRASE(7:11)	ˬFORT	SUB = PHRASE(7:11)	SUB <table><tr><td>1</td><td>2</td><td>3</td><td>4</td><td>5</td></tr><tr><td>F</td><td>O</td><td>R</td><td>T</td><td></td></tr></table>
c. PHRASE(L:R)	ˬloveˬFOR	SUB = PHRASE(L:R)	SUB <table><tr><td>1</td><td>2</td><td>3</td><td>4</td><td>5</td></tr><tr><td>l</td><td>o</td><td>v</td><td>e</td><td></td></tr></table>
d. PHRASE(R + 1:R + 1)	T	PRINT *,PHRASE(R + 1:R + 1)	T
e. PHRASE(1:6)	IˬLOVE	PRINT *,PHRASE(1:6)	IˬLOVE
f. PHRASE(:6)	IˬLOVE	PRINT *,PHRASE(:6)	IˬLOVE
g. PHRASE(8:)	FORTRANˬ	PRINT *,PHRASE(8:)	FORTRANˬ
h. PHRASE(1:1)	I	IF (PHRASE(1:1) .EQ. 'ˬ') THEN	False; IF-block not executed
i. PHRASE(L:30)	Illegal: beyond end of string		Run-time error

EXAMPLE 8.2

DAY-OF-WEEK SUBSTRINGS

In the following program and its output note the following.

1. The blank substring is convenient for spacing list-directed output. In the program, we print the first 8 blanks in a string of 80 blanks.

2. The day substring illustrates substrings based on array element names.

```
      PROGRAM EX82
*------------------------------------------------------------
*       Example 8.2:  Day of week substrings
*------------------------------------------------------------
      CHARACTER BLANK*80, DAY(7)*9
      INTEGER    K

      DATA DAY   / 'Monday', 'Tuesday', 'Wednesday', 'Thursday',
     +             'Friday', 'Saturday', 'Sunday' /
     +      BLANK / ' ' /

      PRINT *, '----------------------------'
      PRINT *, ' Day          Abbreviation  '
      PRINT *, '----------------------------'

      DO 100 K = 1, 7                                          ─── Blank substring

         PRINT *, DAY(K), BLANK(1:8), DAY(K)(1:3)

  100 CONTINUE                                                 ─── Day substring

      PRINT *, '----------------------------'
*------------------------------------------------------------
      END
```

```
----------------------------
 Day          Abbreviation
----------------------------
Monday            Mon
Tuesday           Tue
Wednesday         Wed
Thursday          Thu
Friday            Fri
Saturday          Sat
Sunday            Sun
----------------------------
```

─── Day substrings, first 3 characters
─── Blank substrings, 8 blanks

8.3 CONCATENATION

It's often useful to link or join two or more strings (or substrings) to form a single, longer string. In computer jargon, this task is called **concatenation,** and it's accomplished as follows.

Concatenation

Syntax:

character expression // character expression . . .

Example:

`'Professor ' // FML`

The double slash is called the **character operator;** the processor evaluates the character expressions on each side of the character operator, and links the two resulting strings into one string. For example, if `FML` stores the name initials `HAC`, then the above concatenated expression evaluates as `Professor HAC`.

EXAMPLE 8.3

CONCATENATION EXAMPLES

Try confirming the output below based on the stored strings.

				FIRST					
1	2	3	4	5	6	7	8	9	10
H	a	r	v	e	y				

				MIDDLE					
1	2	3	4	5	6	7	8	9	10
A	b	a	c	u	s				

						LAST								
1	2	3	4	5	6	7	8	9	10	11	12	13	14	15
C	O	R	E											

	FML	
1	2	3
H	A	C

```
PROGRAM EX83
*
*     Example 8.3:  Concatenation examples
*
      CHARACTER*10 FIRST, MIDDLE, LAST*15, FML*3

      FIRST  = 'Harvey'
      MIDDLE = 'Abacus'
      LAST   = 'CORE'

      PRINT *, 'Dr. ' // FIRST // MIDDLE // LAST

      PRINT *, LAST // FIRST // MIDDLE

      PRINT *, LAST // FIRST // MIDDLE(1:1) // '. '

      FML = FIRST(1:1) // MIDDLE(1:1) // LAST(1:1)

      PRINT *, FML

      END
*
```

```
                         Print Positions

            1         2         3         4
   1234567890123456789012345678901234567890

   Dr. Harvey Abacus    CORE

   CORE       Harvey    Abacus

   CORE       Harvey    A.

   HAC
```

EXAMPLE 8.4

CONCATENATED DATE SUBSTRINGS

The following example isolates the month, day, and year substrings in a date substring having the form

2-digit month / 2-digit day / 2-digit year

and prints the substrings in a different order as follows.

2-digit day / 2-digit month / 2-digit year

Specifically, if we enter the date in the North American form

10/19/87

the computer prints the date in the European form

19/10/87

```
PROGRAM EX84
* ─────────────────────────────────────────────
*     Example 8.4:  Date substrings with concatenation
* ─────────────────────────────────────────────
CHARACTER DATE*8

PRINT *, 'Enter date in the form mm/dd/yy'          Day substring and slash
READ '(A)', DATE                                    Month substring and slash
PRINT *                                             Year substring
PRINT *, 'North American form... ',DATE
PRINT *, 'European form........ ',DATE(4:6)//DATE(1:3)//DATE(7:8)
* ─────────────────────────────────────────────
END
```

```
Enter date in the form mm/dd/yy
10/19/87                                            Month and day reversed

North American form... 10/19/87
European form........ 19/10/87
```

8.4 CHARACTER INTRINSIC FUNCTIONS

Table A.1 in Module A includes character-related intrinsic functions. In this section we illustrate these functions in detail.

LEN FUNCTION

Intrinsic function LEN evaluates the length of a string as an *integer* value equal to the number of characters in the string.

Intrinsic Function LEN

Syntax:

LEN (*character expression*)

Example:

LEN('red')

In the example above, the function returns the value 3.

EXAMPLE 8.5

EXAMPLES OF LEN FUNCTION

Note the following in this example.

1. If the argument of the LEN function is a variable (or other name), the function returns the declared length. Thus, LEN(NAME) evalutes as 15, the declared length of NAME; it does not evaluate to the stored length of the string Harvey CORE, which is 11.

NAME

1	2	3	4	5	6	7	8	9	10	11	12	13	14	15
H	a	r	v	e	y		C	O	R	E				

   If we wish to express the length of a variable as the length of its stored string without trailing blanks, then the trailing blanks must be "trimmed," an advanced procedure that we illustrate in Section 8.6.

2. The LEN function is convenient as the upper limit on a DO-variable when we wish to examine a string position by position, as done in the last part of the program.

3. A substring name whose rightmost and leftmost substring expressions are identical is convenient for isolating characters within a string. The substring name NAME(K:K) serves this purpose in the DO-loop. We used the same idea in the bar chart subroutine on page 228.

Program	*Sample Run*

```
PROGRAM EX85
*─────────────────────────────────────────
*     Example 8.5:   Examples of LEN function
*─────────────────────────────────────────
CHARACTER NAME*15
INTEGER    K
```
NAME stores 15 characters, but the stored string is 11 characters

```
NAME = 'Harvey CORE'

PRINT *, LEN( 'Harvey CORE' )                          11

PRINT *, LEN( NAME )                                   15

PRINT *, LEN( 'Dr. ' // NAME )                         19

PRINT *, LEN( NAME(8:11) )                              4

DO 100 K = 1, LEN( NAME )

    PRINT *, NAME(K:K)                                  H
                                                        a
100 CONTINUE                                            r
*─────────────────────────────────────────             v
    END                                                 e
                                                        y

                                                        C
                                                        O
                                                        R
                                                        E
```

4 blanks

INDEX FUNCTION

Intrinsic Function INDEX

Syntax:

    INDEX (*string expression, substring expression*)

Example:

    INDEX (PHRASE, 'love')

The INDEX function searches the evaluated string for the occurrence of the evaluated substring. If the string contains the substring, INDEX returns an *integer* value corresponding to the character position where the substring *begins.* In the example, the value 3 is returned when PHRASE stores I love

FORTRAN 77!. If the substring is not found within the string, or if the length of the substring exceeds the length of the string, then INDEX returns a value of zero. If the substring appears more than once, INDEX returns the starting position of the *leftmost* substring. We can use this function, for example, to find specific characters within words, specific words within phrases, and specific phrases within text.

EXAMPLE 8.6

INDEX FUNCTION EXAMPLES

In the sample run below,

Program	*Sample Run*

```
PROGRAM EX86
*─────────────────────────────────────
*    Example 8.6:   INDEX function examples
*─────────────────────────────────────
CHARACTER PHRASE*20, SEARCH*10

PRINT *, 'Enter phrase'                    Enter phrase
READ (*, '(A)') PHRASE                     I love FORT RAN 77!
PRINT *
PRINT *, 'Enter search substring'          Enter search substring
READ (*, '(A)') SEARCH                     FORTRAN
PRINT *
PRINT *, INDEX( PHRASE, '77' )                        16
PRINT *
PRINT *, INDEX( PHRASE, '7' )                         16
PRINT *
PRINT *, INDEX( PHRASE, 'LOVE' )                       0
PRINT *
PRINT *, INDEX( PHRASE, SEARCH )                       0
PRINT *
PRINT *, INDEX( PHRASE, SEARCH(1:7) )                  8
*─────────────────────────────────────
END
```

storage appears as follows.

PHRASE

1	2	3	4	5	6	7	8	9	10	11	12	13	14	15	16	17	18	19	20
I		l	o	v	e		F	O	R	T	R	A	N		7	7	!		

SEARCH

1	2	3	4	5	6	7	8	9	10
F	O	R	T	R	A	N			

Note the following.

1. The substrings 77 and 7 yield the same results, since it's the first occurrence of 7 that counts.

2. Don't forget to make distinctions between uppercase and lowercase characters. LOVE and love are not the same (in FORTRAN, anyway). Thus, the
INDEX function returns zero in the third example.

3. Does zero in the fourth example surprise you? Note that SEARCH also
stores the three trailing blanks; the substring FORTRAN followed by three
blanks is not found in PHRASE. The next example shows how we can find
FORTRAN within PHRASE. In practice we would want to trim trailing
blanks within SEARCH, since we would expect that the input of FORTRAN
as the search substring would be found within PHRASE. We develop Function TRIM in Section 8.6 for this purpose.   ■

EXAMPLE 8.7

VALID CODES USING INDEX FUNCTION

Suppose valid codes for test samples in a scientific experiment are given by the
following single characters: C, P, R, Y, O. Codes other than these are invalid. In
the program below, the five valid codes are stored as a string in VALID, and the
INDEX function is used to find the existence of a valid input code within VALID.
Also note how we use the character operator to join output strings in the PRINT
statements. It's a matter of preference whether to use the double slash or the
comma . . . we tend to favor //.

```
      PROGRAM EX87
*------------------------------------------------------------
*     Example 8.7:  Valid codes with INDEX function
*------------------------------------------------------------
      CHARACTER VALID*5, CODE

      DATA VALID / 'CPRYO' /  ◄───────────────────── Stores valid codes

100   PRINT *
      PRINT *, 'Enter code... eXit with X'
      READ (*, '(A)') CODE
      PRINT *

      IF ( INDEX( VALID, CODE ) .EQ. 0 ) THEN
        PRINT *, CODE // ' is NOT valid.'
      ELSE                                        ─────────── Note use of //
        PRINT *, CODE // ' is valid.'
      END IF

      IF ( CODE .NE. 'X' ) GO TO 100

      PRINT *
      PRINT *, '... eXit achieved'
*------------------------------------------------------------
      END
```

```
Enter code... eXit with X
P

 P is valid.

Enter code... eXit with X
p

 p is NOT valid.

Enter code... eXit with X
X

 X is NOT valid.

 ... eXit achieved
```

LEXICAL FUNCTIONS

As discussed in the first chapter, characters are encoded by the computer as patterns of bits, where we can think of a bit as a binary digit (0 or 1). For example, a popular coding scheme (ASCII, as described next) encodes the character A as the 7-bit binary 1000001 and the character 1 as the 7-bit binary 0110001.

The most common encoding method on personal computers and minicomputers is the American Standard Code for Information Interchange (**ASCII**, pronounced *ask-key*). It uses 7 bits to code each of 128 characters, as described in Table 8.4.

TABLE 8.4   **Selected ASCII Codes**

Decimals (Positions in Collating Sequence)[a]	Characters
000	Null
007	Bell
032	Space
033–047	! " # $ % & ' ( ) * + , – . /
048–057	0 1 2 3 4 5 6 7 8 9
058–064	: ; < = > ? @
065–090	A B C D E F G H ... X Y Z
091–096	[\ ] ^ – '
097–122	a b c d e f g h ... x y z
123–126	{	} ~
127	Delete

[a]Missing positions are those for control characters like backspace, line feed, and others.

IBM mainframes and compatibles use Extended Binary Coded Decimal Interchange Code (**EBCDIC**, pronounced *ebb-c-dick*). This scheme encodes each of 256 characters with 8 bits, as shown in Table 8.5.

Given that each character is uniquely represented by a binary number, it follows that each character has an associated *integer* value in the decimal numbering system.[2] This means, for example, that the binary representation of the character "1" has a value that's less than the binary representations of the characters "2" through "9." Similarly, we can say, regardless of the particular coding scheme, that "A" is less than "B" and "T" is greater than "K."

The arrangement of characters in ascending numeric order based on the values of their binary representations is called the **collating sequence.** For ex-

---

[2]For example, the 7-bit binary 0110001 for the character 1 is expressed as decimal 49 (see Table 8.4). The rightmost bit represents the unit value (2^0), and it's "on" (1 is in that position); the next bit to the left represents 2 (or 2^1), and it's "off" (0 is in that position); the next bit to the left represents 4 (or 2^2), and it's "off"; the fourth bit from the right represents 8 (or 2^3), and it's "off"; the fifth bit from the right represents 16 (or 2^4), and it's "on"; the sixth bit from the right represents 32 (or 2^5), and it's "on"; finally, the leftmost bit represents 64 (or 2^6), and it's "off." Adding these up from right to left, we get

$1 + 0 + 0 + 0 + 16 + 32 + 0 = 49.$

TABLE 8.5   **Selected EBCDIC Codes**

Decimals (Positions in Collating Sequence)[a]	Characters
000	Null
007	Delete
047	Bell
064	Space
075–078	. < (+
080	&
090–094	! $ *) ;
096–097	– /
106–111	| , % _ > ?
121–127	` : # @ ' = "
129–137	a b c d e f g h i
145–153	j k l m n o p q r
161	~
162–169	s t u v w x y z
192	{
193–201	A B C D E F G H I
208	}
209–217	J K L M N O P Q R
224	\
226–233	S T U V W X Y Z
240–249	0 1 2 3 4 5 6 7 8 9

[a]Missing positions are unassigned, non-ASCII characters like the cent symbol, or control characters like backspace, line feed, and others.

ample, A, B, C, . . . , Z represents the collating sequence for capital letters and 0, 1, 2, . . . , 9 represents the collating sequence for digits. The collating sequence thus represents a lexicographic arrangement (dictionary-type alphabetic ordering) of characters, where characters that precede others in the sequence have a lower decimal value, as seen in the first column of Tables 8.4 and 8.5.

When we make lexicographic comparisons by using character expressions within logical expressions, we necessarily utilize the collating sequence of the computer. For example, the logical expressions

```
       'A' .LT. 'K'
       'B' .NE. 'A'
     'ACE' .EQ. 'ACE'
   'JONES' .LT. 'SMITH'
       '2' .LT. '3'
   'THREE' .LT. 'TWO'
```

all test true, regardless of which method the computer uses to encode characters.

Note that each comparison above is a comparison of either all digits or all uppercase letters. Moreover, a string has a value that implies position in a sequence. For example, the value of THREE is lexically less than the value of TWO, since THREE alphabetically precedes TWO.

Problems arise, however, when we compare strings that include a mixture of upper- and lowercase letters, digits, and special characters. For example, the comparison

```
   '007-Doll' .GT. 'PC-Doll'
```

may be true or false, depending on which scheme the computer uses to collate letters, digits, and special characters. Computers that use ASCII would evaluate this relational expression as false; computers that use EBCDIC would give true.[3]

In general, all encoding schemes are consistent with respect to either "pure" string comparisons (all letters versus all letters of the same case and all digits versus all digits) or .EQ. and .NE. types of comparisons for "mixed" strings. If "less than" or "greater than" types of mixed-string comparisons are required, however, then it's best to use the **lexical intrinsic functions** described in Table

TABLE 8.6 **Lexical Intrinsic Functions**

Function	Value is True if
LGE(s_1 , s_2)	The string s_1 follows or equals (is lexically greater than or equal to) the string s_2 in the ASCII collating sequence.
LGT(s_1 , s_2)	The string s_1 follows (is lexically greater than) the string s_2 in the ASCII collating sequence.
LLE(s_1 , s_2)	The string s_1 precedes or equals (is lexically less than or equal to) the string s_2 in the ASCII collating sequence.
LLT(s_1 , s_2)	The string s_1 precedes (is lexically less than) the string s_2 in the ASCII collating sequence.

[3]You might want to review the discussion in Chapter 4, page 123.

8.6. Note that arguments (s_1 and s_2) are character expressions and the value returned is a logical value (true or false).

EXAMPLE 8.8

EXAMPLES OF LEXICAL INTRINSIC FUNCTIONS

Roleplay the following I/O to make sure you understand the use of lexical functions, noting that numeric characters precede letters in the ASCII collating sequence.

Program	*Sample Run*

```
PROGRAM EX88
*──────────────────────────────────────
*    Examples of lexical intrinsic functions
*──────────────────────────────────────
CHARACTER*10 FIRST, SECOND

PRINT *,'Enter first string'
READ  '(A)', FIRST
PRINT *
PRINT *,'Enter second string'
READ  '(A)', SECOND
PRINT *
PRINT *, LGE( FIRST, SECOND )
PRINT *, LGT( FIRST, SECOND )
PRINT *, LLE( FIRST, SECOND )
PRINT *, LLT( FIRST, SECOND )
*──────────────────────────────────────
END
```

Sample Run:

```
Enter first string
007-Doll

Enter second string
PC-Doll

 F
 F
 T
 T
```

In effect, the lexical intrinsic functions transform the computer's collating sequence to the ASCII collating sequence. Programs using these functions thus give consistent results regardless of the computer used, thereby avoiding potential logic errors and enhancing the portability of programs from computer to computer. These intrinsic functions are especially useful for sorting strings (see Exercise 28).

ICHAR AND CHAR FUNCTIONS

Intrinsic Function ICHAR

Syntax:

    ICHAR (*character expression*)

Example:

    ICHAR (WORD(5:5))

Function ICHAR converts a string of length 1 (a single character) to an *integer* value that corresponds to the *position* of the character in the processor's collating sequence. The first character in the collating sequence corresponds to position zero, and the last character to position $n - 1$, where n is the number of characters represented by the processor. For example, ICHAR(' ') returns 32 by computers using ASCII and 64 by computers using EBCDIC (see Tables 8.4 and 8.5); ICHAR(WORD(5:5)) returns 65 in the ASCII collating sequence and 193 in the EBCDIC collating sequence if A is in the fifth character position in WORD.

Intrinsic Function CHAR

Syntax:
    CHAR   (*integer expression*)
Example:
    CHAR (2*K)

Function CHAR is the inverse of ICHAR; it returns the character in the *i*th position of the processor's collating sequence, where *i* is the value of the integer expression in the range zero to $n - 1$ inclusive. For example, CHAR(0) returns the null (empty) character in the ASCII and EBCDIC coding schemes; CHAR(2*K) returns z in the ASCII scheme and : in the EBCDIC scheme when K stores 61.

The encoding and decoding of cryptograms or writings in code are common uses of these functions, as we illustrate in Section 8.6.

NOTE   Remember that the values returned by functions CHAR and ICHAR are processor dependent according to the coding scheme used by the processor.

EXAMPLE 8.9

EXAMPLES OF FUNCTIONS ICHAR AND CHAR

Note the following in the program and run below.

1. Our particular processor uses the ASCII scheme, although the values returned by ICHAR are offset by +128. It returns position 193 for A. When we use 193 and 65 as arguments in CHAR, the processor returns A, as expected. Try Exercise 17a.

2. We typed CHOICE character instead of integer as a defensive programming technique. Had we typed integer, then inadvertently pressing a nonnumeric key would give a run-time input error. See Exercise 17b for how we might do the same for the input of POS.

```
        PROGRAM EX89
*--------------------------------------------------------------
*       Example 8.9:  ICHAR and CHAR functions examples
*--------------------------------------------------------------
        CHARACTER CHARAC, CHOICE
        INTEGER   POS

100     PRINT *, '===================================='
        PRINT *, 'Enter: 1 to input position and output character'
        PRINT *, '       2 to input character and output position'
        PRINT *, '       ... any other digit to quit.'
        READ (*, '(A)') CHOICE
        PRINT *, '===================================='

        IF ( CHOICE .EQ. '1') THEN
          PRINT *, 'Enter position in collating sequence'
          READ  *, POS
          PRINT *
          PRINT *, ' Character:  ' // CHAR( POS )
        ELSE IF ( CHOICE .EQ. '2') THEN
          PRINT *, 'Enter character'
          READ (*, '(A)') CHARAC
          PRINT *
          PRINT *, ' Position:', ICHAR( CHARAC )
        END IF

        IF ( CHOICE .EQ. '1' .OR.  CHOICE .EQ. '2') GO TO 100

        PRINT *
        PRINT *, '... and just when I was getting warmed up!'
*--------------------------------------------------------------
        END
```

```
================================================
Enter: 1 to input position and output character
       2 to input character and output position
       ... any other digit to quit.
1
================================================
Enter position in collating sequence
0
    Character:
```
— Null character

```
================================================
Enter: 1 to input position and output character
       2 to input character and output position
       ... any other digit to quit.
2
================================================
Enter character
A
    Position:        193
================================================
Enter: 1 to input position and output character
       2 to input character and output position
       ... any other digit to quit.
1
================================================
Enter position in collating sequence
193
    Character:  A
```

```
Enter: 1 to input position and output character
       2 to input character and output position
       ... any other digit to quit.
1

Enter position in collating sequence
65

    Character:   A

Enter: 1 to input position and output character
       2 to input character and output position
       ... any other digit to quit.
2

Enter character
a

    Position:          225

Enter: 1 to input position and output character
       2 to input character and output position
       ... any other digit to quit.
9

... and just when I was getting warmed up!
```

8.5 INTERNAL FILES

Some computer languages have character functions that convert values from numeric form to character form, and vice versa. In FORTRAN 77 we accomplish this by treating a character variable, array, array element, or substring as if it were a data file, called an **internal file.** In this case, we read from or write to the internal file using the character name in place of the external unit identifier, as follows.

Input from and Output to an Internal File

READ (*character name, format identifier*) *input list*
                                    ——————— Identifies internal file
WRITE (*character name, format identifier*) *output list*

We *must* use format-directed I/O statements. If a character variable, array element, or substring is used as the internal file, then the file has one record with length equal to the declared length. If more than one record is needed in the internal file, then we use a character array, where each array element corresponds to a record.

STRING TO NUMERIC DATA CONVERSION WITH INTERNAL FILE

In the program and run below, note the following.

1. The internal file is character variable DATE, which stores the string 10/ 19/87 for the first entry. We can view this string as character data within a single record in a data file.

2. The second READ statement inputs an integer value into NUMBER from this internal file. We use I2 as the edit descriptor, which "picks off" 10 as the integer value. NUMBER thus stores the month in numeric form.

3. The PRINT statement uses the value in NUMBER (the 10) as a pointer to the tenth element in array MONTH, which stores October.

In short, the program illustrates how we can convert a string value (the 10 is part of a string) to a numeric value (integer 10 is used as a subscript expression). In Exercise 19 we ask you to try a numeric-to-string conversion by *writing* to an internal file.

```
      PROGRAM EX810
*————————————————————————————————————————————————————
*       Example 8.10: String to numeric date conversion w/ internal file
*————————————————————————————————————————————————————
      CHARACTER DATE*8, MONTH(12)*10, REPLY
      INTEGER   NUMBER

      DATA MONTH / 'January', 'February', 'March', 'April', 'May',
     +              'June', 'July', 'August', 'September', 'October',
     +              'November', 'December' /
     +     REPLY / 'y' /
  100 IF ( REPLY .EQ. 'y'  .OR.  REPLY .EQ. 'Y' ) THEN

          PRINT *
          PRINT *, 'Enter date in form mm/dd/yy'
          READ (*, '(A)') DATE                        ———— Internal file

          READ (DATE, '(I2)') NUMBER
                                                ———— Stores month in numeric form
          PRINT *
          PRINT *, MONTH(NUMBER) // DATE(4:5) // ', 19' // DATE(7:8)

          PRINT *
          PRINT *, 'Another date?'
          READ (*, '(A)') REPLY
          GO TO 100

      END IF
*————————————————————————————————————————————————————
      END
```

```
 Enter date in form mm/dd/yy
10/19/87

 October   19, 1987

 Another date?
y
 Enter date in form mm/dd/yy
12/07/41

 December  07, 1941

 Another date?
n
```

8.6 SELECTED APPLICATIONS

In this section we illustrate simple applications within two areas of string processing: cryptography and text editing. We let you explore these applications in greater depth in the exercises.

CRYPTOGRAPHY[4]

Cryptography is the science of transforming messages for the purpose of making them unintelligible to all but the intended receiver of the message. A message is transformed either by encoding or decoding. Encoding is the process of transforming a message into code; decoding is the translation of the code into its message form. The encoding and decoding of messages usually includes a transformation algorithm for transforming the messages and a key that controls the process.

Analysis.   One category of secret messages is called ciphers. In this approach the transformation algorithm either rearranges or replaces the letters of each word. Substitution ciphers code messages by replacing one letter with another. The following illustrates a straightforward substitution cipher:

THE ALPHABET SHIFT CIPHER   Encode each letter by replacing it with a letter that falls a given number of positions after the actual letter. The *increment key* provides the number of positions that the letter is shifted. If the shift takes us beyond the end of the alphabet, then wrap around the alphabet by continuing at the beginning.

Example: If the increment key is 10, then A would be replaced by K since K is 10 positions from A. Similarly, B would be replaced by L, C would be replaced by M, and so on. If S is to be encoded, we note that a shift of 10 positions would take us three positions beyond Z. Thus, we would wrap around to C. The following shows the encoding of an entire message. Try confirming each encoded letter.

Actual message: HELP IS ON THE WAY
Encoded message: ROVZ SC YX DRO GKI

Let's design and write a program that encodes messages using the alphabet shift cipher. The data requirements are as follows.

Output
Actual message (in uppercase letters)
Encoded message (in uppercase letters)

Input
Increment key
Actual message (in uppercase letters)

Parameters
Blank character
Position of A in collating sequence
Position of Z in collating sequence

---

[4]It's a good idea to keep handy the ASCII character codes in Table 8.4 for this example. Also look in your system's user manual for the collating sequence that applies to your computer.

Design.   The transformation algorithm expresses the message, one character at a time, to the *ASCII decimal* (position in collating sequence) representing the letter. Then we add the increment key to the ASCII decimal (making sure we keep within the ASCII range 65–90 for the uppercase letters A–Z, as in Table 8.4). This gives us a new or shifted ASCII decimal that we convert back to an encoded letter. Note that our example only encodes uppercase letters. In the follow-up exercises we consider messages that include lowercase letters and punctuation.

The pseudocode below describes the design in more detail.

Control Module

```
Input increment key
Input actual message
Print actual message
Repeat for each character in message
   If character not blank then
      Call Subroutine Encode
   End if
End loop
Print encoded message
End
```

Subroutine Encode

```
Express letter as ASCII decimal (position)
If position out of range then
   Replace letter with *
Else
   Shift position by increment key
   If new position exceeds position for Z then
      Adjust new position to wrap around alphabet
   End if
   Convert position to encoded letter
End if
End
```

To illustrate, consider the actual letter A. Its position in the ASCII collating sequence is 65 (see Table 8.4). If the increment key is 10, then the shifted position is 75, which corresponds to the encoded letter K. Now, suppose the actual letter is S. Its position is 83, which becomes 93 when shifted. Since 93 is beyond the end of the alphabet (greater than 90), we must wrap around the alphabet 3 positions, giving 67 for the new position. This corresponds to the encoded letter C. (Remember that the beginning position, the character A, is 65; wrapping 3 positions beyond Z gives 65 as the first position, 66 as the second position, and 67 as the third and final position.)

Code and Test.   Figure 8.1 illustrates the listing and test run of our cryptography program. We might note the following.

1. The DO-loop in the main program selects one character at a time from the string in TEXT by using the substring TEXT(K:K), where K runs from character position 1 to character position 80. If the character to be encoded is nonblank, then the encoding subroutine is called.

2. Intrinsic function ICHAR is used in the subroutine to express an actual character as its ASCII decimal equivalent, or position in the collating sequence. Normally, for example, ICHAR would return 65 for the letter A. Our processor, however, returns a value that's 128 higher (see page 390). Thus, our low/high parameters are set to range from 193 (or 65 + 128) to 218 (or 90 + 128).

3. If the position of the actual letter is outside the allowable range (193 to 218 for uppercase letters), then the actual character is encoded with an *, which indicates an error in the actual character.

4. Given a legitimate actual character, the position is shifted by the increment key. If this new position exceeds the position that corresponds to Z, then the position is adjusted to properly wrap around the alphabet. The new position is used by the CHAR function to express the encoded letter.

5. Note that the encoded message replaces the actual message one character at a time. For example, the seventh actual letter in our sample message is S, as expressed by the argument TEXT(7:7) in the seventh subroutine call. The subroutine stores S in the variable LETTER, and subsequently encodes it as C, which gets stored in LETTER. Since LETTER and TEXT(7:7) are matched for this call, it follows that TEXT(7:7) now stores C, the encoded letter, instead of S, the actual letter.

To make sure you understand the program, try roleplaying the actual word WAY to its encoded counterpart GKI.

TEXT EDITOR

A text editor is a computer-based tool to create, revise, and display text files. You're either using a text editor or a wordprocessor to create and edit your program files and data files. If you're using a text editor, most likely it's a screen-oriented editor, where a portion of the file is entirely visible on the screen at once. A wordprocessor, essentially, is a screen-oriented editor with enhanced capabilities for displaying and printing text. In the sample program that follows, we illustrate a simple line-oriented editor (line-oriented editors typically operate on one line of text at a time).

```
              PROGRAM CRYPT
  * * * * * * * * * * * * * * * * * * * * * * * * * * * * * *
  *                                                         *
  *         Cryptography:  Message encoding using alphabet shift cipher  *
  *                                                         *
  *            Inputs increment key and actual message      *
  *            Encodes actual message                       *
  *            Outputs actual and encoded messages          *
  *                                                         *
  *            Modular structure:                           *
  *                                                         *
  *            Main program... I/O and calls Sub. ENCODE for nonblank  *
  *                           characters.                   *
  *                                                         *
  *              Sub. ENCODE.... Encodes character.         *
  *                                                         *
  *                                                         *
  *            Key (main program):                          *
  *                                                         *
  *            BLANK.... Blank character                    *
  *            K........ DO-variable, substring character position  *
  *            SHIFT.... Increment key                      *
  *            TEXT..... Message, first actual, then encoded *
  *                                                         *
  * * * * * * * * * * * * * * * * * * * * * * * * * * * * * *
  *
  *  Type names
  *
       CHARACTER BLANK, TEXT*80
       INTEGER   K, SHIFT
  *
  *  Specify parameter
  *
       PARAMETER ( BLANK = ' ' )
  *
  *  Input data and print actual message
  *
       PRINT *, 'Enter increment key'
       READ  *, SHIFT

       PRINT *
       PRINT *, 'Enter actual message'
       READ  '(A)', TEXT

       PRINT *
       PRINT *, 'Actual:   ', TEXT
  *
  *  Encode nonblank characters
  *
       DO 100 K = 1, LEN( TEXT )          ←——— Number of characters in TEXT

          IF ( TEXT(K:K) .NE. BLANK ) THEN

             CALL ENCODE ( SHIFT, TEXT(K:K) )

          END IF                          ←——— Kth character in message

  100 CONTINUE
  *
  *  Print encoded message
  *
       PRINT *, 'Encoded:  ', TEXT
  *
       END
```

FIGURE 8.1   Listing and run of cryptography program (*continued on next page*)

```
      SUBROUTINE ENCODE ( SHIFT, LETTER )
• • • • • • • • • • • • • • • • • • • • • • • • • • • • • • • •
•
•         Encode subroutine for single uppercase letter
•
•            Receives increment key and actual letter
•            Encodes letter
•            Returns encoded letter
•
•            Key:
•
•               HIGH..... Position in collating sequence for Z
•               LETTER... Capital letter
•               LOW...... Position in collating sequence for A
•               POS...... Position in collating sequence
•               SHIFT.... Increment key
•
•
• • • • • • • • • • • • • • • • • • • • • • • • • • • • • • • •
```

```
• Type names
•───────────
      CHARACTER LETTER
      INTEGER   HIGH, LOW, POS, SHIFT
```

```
• Specify parameters ──────────────────────── Position of A in our collating sequence
•───────────────────                          ──── Position of Z
      PARAMETER ( LOW = 193, HIGH = 218 )
```

```
• Encode letter ──────────────────── Actual letter expressed as ASCII decimal
•──────────────
      POS = ICHAR( LETTER )
```

```
•   If position out of range then use *; else encode
•   ─────────────────────────────────────────────────
      IF ( POS .LT. LOW  .OR.   POS .GT. HIGH ) THEN

         LETTER = '*' ──────────────── Unacceptable characters replaced by *

      ELSE ──────────────────── New position for encoded letter

         POS = POS + SHIFT
```

```
•   If necessary, wrap around alphabet
•   ──────────────────────────────────
      IF ( POS  .GT.  HIGH ) THEN

         POS = LOW + ( POS − HIGH ) − 1

      END IF ──────────────── New position for encoded letter
                              that gets wrapped around alphabet
```

```
      LETTER = CHAR( POS )

      END IF ──────────────── Actual letter replaced by encoded letter
•──────────────
      END
```

```
 Enter increment key
 10

 Enter actual message
 HELP IS ON THE WAY

 Actual:   HELP IS ON THE WAY
 Encoded:  ROVZ SC YX DRO GKI
```

FIGURE 8.1   *(continued)*

Analysis. Our line-oriented editor has three functions: to change a portion of an existing text line, delete an existing text line, and insert a new text line.

Our editor inputs up to 1000 lines of text from a file and stores it in a one-dimensional array, in which each element stores one line of text. To correct or otherwise change a text line, we respond to the editor's input prompt (*?) by typing a command line with the following syntax.

Change Command Line

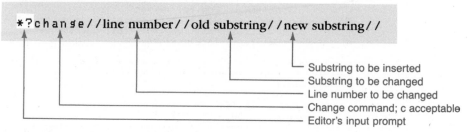

Note that the double slash separates or delimits the four parts of this command line. Also, we can type commands either in all lowercase characters or in all uppercase characters.

Suppose we have the following line-numbered display of a three-line text file.

```
1: Jack or Jill
2: Went up the wall
3: Ta fitch a pail of water
```

Note that the editor displays the line numbers, but the text file itself does not include the line numbers.

To illustrate the change command line, suppose that we wish to replace the old substring o r with the new substring and in the first text line. We would type the change command line as follows.

```
*?c//1//or//and//
```

The changed line would appear as follows.

```
Jack and Jill
```

How would we replace wall with hill? How about Ta fitch with To fetch?

To delete a text line, we would use the following command line.

Delete Command Line

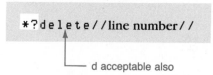

For example, to delete line 2 in our sample text we would type the following command line.

`*?d//2//`

The editor would delete line 2 and move up all succeeding lines by one, giving the following line-numbered text.

```
1:  Jack  and  Jill
2:  Ta  fitch  a  pail  of  water
```

To insert a new line of text we would use the following command line.

Insert Command Line

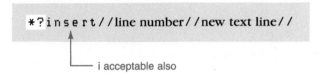

         i acceptable also

For example, to insert the text line we deleted earlier, we would type the following.

`*?i//2//Went up the wall//`

Note that all succeeding lines would be moved down one; in our example, the former line 2 would be moved to line 3.

To exit the editor, we would use the following command line.

Quit Command Line

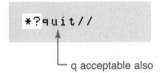

        q acceptable also

Let's define the following data requirements for the program.

Output
Original text with line numbers (optional)
Changed text line following the change command line
Revised text with line numbers (optional)

Input
Original text from file
Yes/no reply for displaying text
Command line

Parameters
Length limit for number of lines (1000 lines)
Width of text (70 characters)

Design.   The following pseudocode gives details of the modular design for our text editor. Note that each command is a module, which simplifies the addition, deletion, and modification of commands in the program. The delete and insert modules are shown as unfinished modules, called **program stubs** or **dummy modules.** Their use is consistent with the ideas behind stepwise refinement and topdown testing **(page 259).** We ask you to finish these modules in Exercise 43.

Main Program

```
Call Subroutine INPUT
Call Subroutine OUTPUT
Repeat
  Input command line
  Call Subroutine PARSE
  If change command then
    Call Subroutine CHANGE
  Else if delete command then
    Call Subroutine DELETE
  Else if insert command then
    Call Subroutine INSERT
  Else if quit command then
    Continue
  Else
    Print error message for illegal command
  End if
Until quit command is entered
Call Subroutine OUTPUT
End
```

Subroutine INPUT

```
Input original text file
Calculate number of lines in file
If lines = length parameter then
  Print warning that file may be too long
End if
End
```

Subroutine OUTPUT

```
Input y/n reply to "Display text?"
Call subroutine YNERR
If reply is yes then
  Print line-numbered text
End if
End
```

Subroutine PARSE

```
Note: This subroutine breaks up the command line into its four parts.
Initialize four command line parts
Do for each character in command line but the last
  If current character and the next are // then
    If 1st part then
      Extract command
    Else if 2nd part then
      Extract line number
    Else if 3rd part then
      Extract string
    Else if 4th part then
      Extract string
    End if
  End if
End do
End
```

Subroutine CHANGE

```
Find first and last character positions in text line for old
substring
Join the following substrings:
  The untouched substring at the left end of the text line
  The new substring
  The untouched substring at the right end of the text line
End
```

Subroutine DELETE

Program Stub

```
Print "Delete function not ready..."
End
```

Subroutine INSERT

←Program Stub

```
Print "Insert function not ready..."
End
```

Function TRIM

Note: This utility function is used by CHANGE to find the **trim length** . . . the length of a string starting with the first character and ending with the last nonblank character. The trim length thus ignores trailing blanks in a string.

```
Find position of 1st nonblank character from right end of
string
If position is 1 and character is blank then
   Trim length = 0
Else
   Trim length = position
End if
End
```

Subroutine YNERR

Note: See utility on page 334.

Code and Test. Figure 8.2 shows a sample text file and editing session and Figure 8.3 the listing of our line editor. To really understand the editor, you need to roleplay the sample run through the program, and solve Exercises 24 to 26. In doing so, note the following.

1. The text file is stored in the 1000-element array TEXT, as declared in the main program. Each element in TEXT has a declared length of 70 characters. Thus, we can store up to 1000 lines of text, where each line is up to 70 characters wide. (*Text continues on page 413*)

Sample Text File
```
Jack or Jill
Went up the wall
Ta fitch a pail of water
```

Sample Editing Session
```
 Display text?
y

     1: Jack or Jill
     2: Went up the wall
     3: Ta fitch a pail of water

 *?
c//2//wall//hill//

     Changed line:  Went up the hill

 *?
c//1//or//and//

     Changed line:  Jack and Jill

 *?
d//3//
```
```
Delete function not ready...
```
```
 *?
i//4//And lived happily ever after...//
```
```
Insert function not ready...
```
```
 *?
x//3//Ta fitch//To fetch//

 *** Unknown command... Use C, D, I, or Q.

 *?
c//3//Ta fitch//To fetch//

     Changed line:  To fetch a pail of water

 *?
q//

 Display text?
y

     1: Jack and Jill
     2: Went up the hill
     3: To fetch a pail of water
```

FIGURE 8.2   **Sample data file and test run for Program ED**

```
PROGRAM ED

*  *  *  *  *  *  *  *  *  *  *  *  *  *  *  *  *  *  *  *  *  *  *  *  *  *  *  *  *  *
*                                                                                    *
*       Text Line Editor                                                             *
*                                                                                    *
*          Inputs lines of text from file and interactive command line               *
*          Edits (changes, deletes, inserts) text                                    *
*          Outputs revised text                                                      *
*                                                                                    *
*          Command line syntax:                                                      *
*                                                                                    *
*             Command... CHANGE or C to change part of text line                     *
*                Command//line number//old substring//new substring//                *
*                                                                                    *
*             Command... DELETE or D to delete entire text line                      *
*                Command//line number//                                              *
*                                                                                    *
*             Command... INSERT or I to insert new text line                         *
*                Command//line number//new text line//                               *
*                                                                                    *
*             Note:  Commands in all upper- or lower-case letters                    *
*                    are acceptable.                                                 *
*                                                                                    *
*          Modular structure:                                                        *
*                                                                                    *
*             Main program... Calls INPUT and OUTPUT; repeats command                *
*                             line input, calls PARSE, and calls                     *
*                             CHANGE, DELETE, or INSERT based on                      *
*                             command, until command is quit; calls                  *
*                             OUTPUT again.                                           *
*                                                                                    *
*                Sub. INPUT..... Reads text file, determines number of               *
*                                lines, and prints warning if file                   *
*                                length limit is reached.                            *
*                                                                                    *
*                Sub. OUTPUT.... Prints line-numbered text if desired;               *
*                                calls YNERR.                                         *
*                                                                                    *
*                Sub. PARSE..... Breaks up command line into its                     *
*                                components.                                         *
*                                                                                    *
*                Sub. CHANGE.... Implements change command; replaces                 *
*                                old substring with new substring for                *
*                                specific text line; uses Function TRIM.             *
*                                                                                    *
*                Sub. DELETE.... Implements delete command; deletes                  *
*                                specific text line.                                 *
*                                                                                    *
*                Sub. INSERT.... Implements insert command; inserts new              *
*                                text line.                                          *
*                                                                                    *
*                Funct. TRIM.... Returns trim length... a utility.                   *
*                                                                                    *
*                Sub. YNERR..... Ensures correct y/n reply... a utility.             *
*                                                                                    *
*          Key (main program):                                                       *
*                                                                                    *
*             CHA...... Change text line?   T or F                                   *
*             COMM..... Entire command line                                          *
*             COMM1.... Command part of command line                                 *
*             COMM3.... Part 3 of command line                                       *
*             COMM4.... Part 4 of command line                                       *
*             DEL...... Delete text line?  T or F                                    *
*             INS...... Insert text line?  T or F                                    *
*             LENGTH... Length limit for number of lines                             *
*             LINE..... Line number                                                  *
*             LINES.... Number of lines in text                                      *
*             QUIT..... Quit editing?  T or F                                        *
*             TEXT..... Text as 1-D array                                            *
*             WIDTH.... Width of text, declared length of TEXT elements              *
*                                                                                    *
*  *  *  *  *  *  *  *  *  *  *  *  *  *  *  *  *  *  *  *  *  *  *  *  *  *  *  *  *  *
```

FIGURE 8.3   **Listing of line editor (*continued on next page*)**

```
*---------------------------------------------------------------
*   Type and specify names
*
        INTEGER              LENGTH, LINE, LINES, WIDTH
        PARAMETER            ( LENGTH = 1000, WIDTH = 70 )
        CHARACTER*(WIDTH) COMM*( 2*WIDTH + 21 ), COMM1*9, COMM3, COMM4,
      +                      TEXT(LENGTH)
        LOGICAL              CHA, DEL, INS, QUIT
*---------------------------------------------------------------
*   Input and output text
*
        CALL INPUT  ( LENGTH, LINES, TEXT )
        CALL OUTPUT ( LINES, TEXT )
*---------------------------------------------------------------
*   Repeat command until quit
*
  100   PRINT *                                              ─────── Input command line
        PRINT *, '*?'
        READ '(A)', COMM                                     ─────── Parse command line

        CALL PARSE ( COMM, COMM1, COMM3, COMM4, LINE )

        CHA  = COMM1 .EQ. 'CHANGE'  .OR. COMM1 .EQ. 'change'  .OR.
      +        COMM1 .EQ. 'C'       .OR. COMM1 .EQ. 'c'

        DEL  = COMM1 .EQ. 'DELETE'  .OR. COMM1 .EQ. 'delete'  .OR.
      +        COMM1 .EQ. 'D'       .OR. COMM1 .EQ. 'd'

        INS  = COMM1 .EQ. 'INSERT'  .OR. COMM1 .EQ. 'insert'  .OR.
      +        COMM1 .EQ. 'I'       .OR. COMM1 .EQ. 'i'

        QUIT = COMM1 .EQ. 'QUIT'    .OR. COMM1 .EQ. 'quit'    .OR.
      +        COMM1 .EQ. 'Q'       .OR. COMM1 .EQ. 'q'

        IF ( CHA ) THEN                                      ─────── Change text line

           CALL CHANGE ( COMM3, COMM4, TEXT(LINE) )
           PRINT *
           PRINT *, '   Changed line:  ', TEXT(LINE)

        ELSE IF ( DEL ) THEN                                 ─────── Delete text line

           CALL DELETE ( LINE, TEXT )

        ELSE IF ( INS ) THEN                                 ─────── Insert text line

           CALL INSERT ( LINE, COMM3, TEXT )

        ELSE IF ( QUIT) THEN

           CONTINUE

        ELSE                                                 ─────── Wrong command error
                                                                     routine
           PRINT *, CHAR(7)
           PRINT *, '*** Unknown command... Use C, D, I, or Q.'
           PRINT *

        END IF

        IF ( .NOT. ( QUIT ) ) GO TO 100
*---------------------------------------------------------------
*   Output revised text if desired
*
        CALL OUTPUT ( LINES, TEXT )
*---------------------------------------------------------------
        END
```

FIGURE 8.3   **(continued)**

```
      SUBROUTINE INPUT ( LENGTH, LINES, TEXT )
• • • • • • • • • • • • • • • • • • • • • • • • • • • • • • • • • •
•                                                                 •
•       Text input subroutine                                     •
•                                                                 •
•          Receives LENGTH                                        •
•          Inputs text, determines number of lines, prints line limit •
•              warning if length limit reached                    •
•          Returns LINES and TEXT                                 •
•                                                                 •
•          Key:                                                   •
•                                                                 •
•              L........ DO-variable for line number              •
•              LENGTH... Length limit for number of lines         •
•              LINES.... Number of lines in text                  •
•              TEXT..... Text as 1-D array                        •
•                                                                 •
• • • • • • • • • • • • • • • • • • • • • • • • • • • • • • • • • •
•—————————————————————————————————————————————————————————————————
•  Type names
•—————————————————————————————————————————————————————————————————
      CHARACTER*(*)  TEXT(LENGTH)
      INTEGER        L, LENGTH, LINES
•—————————————————————————————————————————————————————————————————
•  Read text and determine number of lines
•—————————————————————————————————————————————————————————————————
      READ (5, '(A)', END = 100 ) ( TEXT(L), L = 1, LENGTH )

  100 LINES = L - 1
•—————————————————————————————————————————————————————————————————
•  Print warning if length limit reached
•—————————————————————————————————————————————————————————————————
      IF ( LINES .EQ. LENGTH ) THEN

        PRINT *, CHAR(7)
        PRINT *, 'NOTE:  Text file may exceed line limit of', LENGTH
        PRINT *

      END IF
•—————————————————————————————————————————————————————————————————
      END


      SUBROUTINE OUTPUT ( LINES, TEXT )
• • • • • • • • • • • • • • • • • • • • • • • • • • • • • • • • • •
•                                                                 •
•       Text output subroutine                                    •
•                                                                 •
•          Receives LINES, TEXT                                   •
•          Inputs display y/n option, calls YNERR, and prints     •
•              line-numbered text if desired                      •
•          Returns nothing                                        •
•                                                                 •
•          Key:                                                   •
•                                                                 •
•              L........ DO-variable for line number              •
•              LINES.... Number of lines in text                  •
•              REPLY.... y/n reply to "Display text?"             •
•              TEXT..... Text as 1-D array                        •
•                                                                 •
• • • • • • • • • • • • • • • • • • • • • • • • • • • • • • • • • •
•—————————————————————————————————————————————————————————————————
•  Type names
•—————————————————————————————————————————————————————————————————
      CHARACTER*(*) REPLY*1, TEXT(LINES)
      INTEGER       L, LINES
```

FIGURE 8.3   **(continued)**

```
*------------------------------------------------------------------
*   Input reply and output text if desired
*------------------------------------------------------------------
      PRINT *
      PRINT *, 'Display text?'
      READ  '(A)', REPLY

      CALL YNERR ( REPLY )

      IF ( REPLY .EQ. 'Y'  .OR.  REPLY .EQ. 'y' ) THEN

          PRINT *
          DO 100 L = 1, LINES
             PRINT 900, L, TEXT(L)
  100     CONTINUE

      END IF
*------------------------------------------------------------------
*   Output format
*------------------------------------------------------------------
  900 FORMAT (1X, I4, ': ', A )
*------------------------------------------------------------------
      END


      SUBROUTINE PARSE ( COMM, COMM1, COMM3, COMM4, LINE )
* * * * * * * * * * * * * * * * * * * * * * * * * * * * * * * * * *
*                                                                 *
*          Command line parsing subroutine                        *
*                                                                 *
*          Receives COMM                                          *
*          Parses command line into its constituent parts, and    *
*             converts string line number to integer line number  *
*          Returns COMM1, COMM3, COMM4, LINE                       *
*                                                                 *
*          Key:                                                   *
*                                                                 *
*             COMM..... Entire command line                       *
*             COMM1.... Command part of command line              *
*             COMM2.... Line number part of command line, internal file *
*             COMM3.... Part 3 of command line                    *
*             COMM4.... Part 4 of command line                    *
*             K........ DO-variable for character position        *
*             LINE..... Line number (from COMM2)                  *
*             PART..... Part number for command line parts        *
*             START.... Starting character position for next part *
*                                                                 *
* * * * * * * * * * * * * * * * * * * * * * * * * * * * * * * * * *
*------------------------------------------------------------------
*   Type names
*------------------------------------------------------------------
      CHARACTER*(*)  COMM, COMM1, COMM2*4, COMM3, COMM4
      INTEGER        K, LINE, PART, START
*------------------------------------------------------------------
*   Initialize
*------------------------------------------------------------------
      COMM1 = ' '
      COMM2 = ' '
      COMM3 = ' '
      COMM4 = ' '
```

FIGURE 8.3   (*continued*)

```
*—————————————————————————————————————————
*   Parse command line
*—————————————
        PART = 1

        DO 100 K = 1, LEN( COMM ) - 1
*          Find command separators
*          ————————————————————
           IF ( COMM(K:K+1) .EQ. '//' ) THEN
*              Assign each command part to unique substring
*              ————————————————————————————————————
               IF ( PART .EQ. 1 ) THEN
*                  Extract command (part 1)
*                  ————————————————————
                   COMM1 = COMM(1:K-1)

                   START = K + 2
                   PART  = 2
               ELSE IF ( PART .EQ. 2 ) THEN
*                  Extract line number as string
*                  ————————————————————————
                   COMM2 = COMM(START:K-1)
*                  Convert line number to integer
*                  ————————————————————————
                   READ ( COMM2, '(I4)' ) LINE

                   START = K + 2
                   PART  = 3
               ELSE IF ( PART .EQ. 3 ) THEN

                   COMM3 = COMM(START:K-1)

                   START = K + 2
                   PART  = 4
               ELSE IF ( PART .EQ. 4 ) THEN

                   COMM4 = COMM(START:K-1)

               END IF
*          ————————————————————————————————————
           END IF
*       ————————————————————————————————————————
100    CONTINUE
*—————————————————————————————————————————————
        END
```

FIGURE 8.3 *(continued)*

```
       SUBROUTINE CHANGE ( OLDSUB, NEWSUB, TLINE )
* * * * * * * * * * * * * * * * * * * * * * * * * * * * * * * * * *
*                                                                 *
*        Change command subroutine                                *
*                                                                 *
*          Receives OLDSUB, NEWSUB, and original TLINE            *
*          Replaces OLDSUB with NEWSUB in TLINE; uses Funct. TRIM *
*          Returns revised TLINE                                  *
*                                                                 *
*          Key:                                                   *
*                                                                 *
*            FIRST.... First character position for OLDSUB in TLINE *
*            LAST..... Last  character position for OLDSUB in TLINE *
*            NEWSUB... New substring in TLINE                     *
*            OLDSUB... Old substring in TLINE                     *
*            RIGHT.... Right (untouched) substring in TLINE       *
*            TL....... Trim length                                *
*            TLINE.... Text line undergoing change               *
*            TRIM..... Trim function                             *
*                                                                 *
* * * * * * * * * * * * * * * * * * * * * * * * * * * * * * * * * *
*---------------------------------------------------------------
*  Type names
*---------------------------------------------------------------
       CHARACTER*(*)  NEWSUB, OLDSUB, RIGHT*100, TLINE
       INTEGER        FIRST, LAST, TL, TRIM
*---------------------------------------------------------------
*  Find positions in text line where old substring begins and ends
*---------------------------------------------------------------
       TL    = TRIM ( OLDSUB )   ◄──────────── Trim length of old substring

       FIRST = INDEX( TLINE, OLDSUB(1:TL) )
                                 ──────────── Starting position of old substring
       LAST  = FIRST + TL - 1
*---------------------------------------------------------------
*  Join left substring, new substring, and right substring
*    Left  substring... Left  (untouched) part of TLINE
*    Right substring... Right (untouched) part of TLINE
*---------------------------------------------------------------
       TL    = TRIM( NEWSUB )
       RIGHT = TLINE(LAST+1:LEN(TLINE))
       TLINE = TLINE(1:FIRST-1)//NEWSUB(1:TL)//RIGHT

       END
```

└─Left substring   └─New substring   └─Right substring

└─Revised text line

```
       SUBROUTINE DELETE ( LINE, TEXT )
* * * * * * * * * * * * * * * * * * * * * * * * * * * * * * * * * *
*                                                                 *
*        Program stub:  Module not ready                          *
*                                                                 *
* * * * * * * * * * * * * * * * * * * * * * * * * * * * * * * * * *
*---------------------------------------------------------------
       PRINT *,'════════════════════════════'
       PRINT *,'Delete function not ready...'
       PRINT *,'════════════════════════════'
*---------------------------------------------------------------
       END
```

FIGURE 8.3   **(continued)**

```
                    SUBROUTINE INSERT ( LINE, NEW, TEXT )
      * * * * * * * * * * * * * * * * * * * * * * * * * * * * * * * * *
      *
      *        Program stub:  Module not ready                         *
      *                                                                *
      * * * * * * * * * * * * * * * * * * * * * * * * * * * * * * * * *
      *————————————————————————————————————————————————————————————————
            PRINT *,'═══════════════════════════'
            PRINT *,'Insert function not ready...'
            PRINT *,'═══════════════════════════'
      *————————————————————————————————————————————————————————————————
            END


                    FUNCTION TRIM ( STRING )
      * * * * * * * * * * * * * * * * * * * * * * * * * * * * * * * * *
      *
      *        Trim length utility function                            *
      *                                                                *
      *           Receives string                                      *
      *           Calculates trim length as the length of a string starting *
      *              with the first character and ending with the last *
      *              nonblank character                                *
      *           Returns trim length                                  *
      *                                                                *
      *           Key:                                                 *
      *                                                                *
      *              K........ DO-variable, character position in string *
      *              STRING... String                                  *
      *              TRIM..... Trim length                             *
      *                                                                *
      *           Example:                                             *
      *                                                                *
      *              The following string has a declared length of 10  *
      *                 Harvey                                         *
      *              Its trim length is 6                              *
      *                                                                *
      * * * * * * * * * * * * * * * * * * * * * * * * * * * * * * * * *
      *————————————————————————————————————————————————————————————————
      *  Type names
      *————————————————————————————————————————————————————————————————
            CHARACTER*(*)  STRING
            INTEGER        K, TRIM
      *————————————————————————————————————————————————————————————————
      *  Find position of first nonblank character from right end of string
      *————————————————————————————————————————————————————————————————
            K = LEN( STRING )

        100 IF ( K .GT. 1  .AND.  STRING(K:K) .EQ. ' ' ) THEN
              K = K - 1
              GO TO 100
            END IF
      *————————————————————————————————————————————————————————————————
      *  If K=1 and first character is a blank, then trim length is zero
      *                                         else trim length is K
      *————————————————————————————————————————————————————————————————
            IF ( K .EQ. 1  .AND.  STRING(1:1) .EQ. ' ' ) THEN
              TRIM = 0
            ELSE
              TRIM = K
            END IF
      *————————————————————————————————————————————————————————————————
            END
```

FIGURE 8.3   (*continued*)

```
      SUBROUTINE YNERR ( REPLY )
* * * * * * * * * * * * * * * * * * * * * * * * * * * * * * * * * *
*                                                                 *
*        Utility that ensures correct yes/no reply               *
*                                                                 *
*           Receives reply                                        *
*           Repeats y/n input while reply incorrect               *
*           Returns revised reply (if initially incorrect)        *
*                                                                 *
*           Key:                                                  *
*                                                                 *
*               REPLY.... Yes/no reply stored as single character *
*                                                                 *
* * * * * * * * * * * * * * * * * * * * * * * * * * * * * * * * * *
*_____
*  Type names
*_____
       CHARACTER REPLY
*_____
*  Repeat y/n input while reply is not yes or no
*_____
   100 IF ( .NOT. ( REPLY .EQ. 'Y'  .OR.  REPLY .EQ. 'y'  .OR.
      +              REPLY .EQ. 'N'  .OR.  REPLY .EQ. 'n'      ) )  THEN

          PRINT *, CHAR(7)
          PRINT *, ' Please enter yes or no'
          READ  '( A )', REPLY

          GO TO 100

       END IF
*_____
       END
```

FIGURE 8.3   **(continued)**

---

2. Subroutine PARSE breaks up the command line into its syntactical components, a process called **parsing**.[5] The parsing algorithm examines the command line stored in COMM character by character; it locates the first set of double slashes and assigns the substring in part 1 of the command line (the part to the left of the first set of slashes) to the variable COMM1. In the second command line in Figure 8.2, COMM1 stores c (the change command). When it finds the second set of double slashes, it stores 1 in COMM2; then it reads the 1 (the line number) into integer variable LINE by treating COMM2 as an internal file (see page 392). Similarly, it moves on to the third and fourth sets of slashes, storing o r (the old substring) in COMM3 and an d (the new substring) in COMM4.

---

[5] Parsing plays an important role in the specialization called natural language processing (NLP) in the field of artificial intelligence (AI). The idea is to allow the keyboard (or spoken) entry of commands in our everyday (natural) language. Parsing algorithms then extract the essential nouns, verbs, and objects. Early applications in the field stressed games, as in the original Adventure developed at MIT and its superior successor (from a parsing viewpoint) Zork. "Serious" applications of NLP include database queries like "Display all test results at NASA since 10/5/88", spreadsheet commands like "graph Jan to Mar", and military gaming like "move destroyer to nw quadrant."

3. Subroutine CHANGE conceptualizes three substrings in the revised text line:

a. An untouched substring at the left end of the text line, given by TLINE(1:FIRST - 1) in the program, where FIRST stores the first character position in TLINE where the old substring begins. In the second example of Figure 8.2, we have the following original text line.

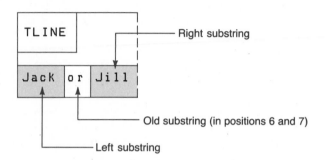

In this case, OLDSUB stores o r, so FIRST stores 6. The untouched substring to the left, therefore, is defined by TLINE(1:5), or Jack⌃.

b. The new substring NEWSUB(1:TL), where TL is the trim length of the new substring. For example, NEWSUB stores a n d followed by 67 blanks in the second edit of Figure 8.2. The declared length in NEWSUB is 70, but its trim length is 3, that is, we wish to insert in TLINE only the first 3 characters in NEWSUB (not the 67 trailing blanks).

c. An untouched substring at the right end of the text line, given by TLINE (LAST+1:LEN(TLINE)), where LAST stores the last character position within TLINE of the old substring and LEN is the intrinsic function for declared length. Continuing our example, LAST stores 7 (the old substring o r is in character positions 6 and 7 within TLINE) and declared length is 70, so TLINE(8:70) stores ⌃Jill followed by 65 blanks.

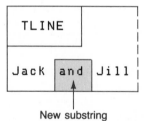

New substring

Putting these three substrings together gives the revised text line shown at left.

NOTE 1   We had to trim OLDSUB to find its occurrence within TLINE; otherwise the INDEX function would return zero, since OLDSUB stores trailing blanks to the right of the old substring. In our second example, the old substring is o r, which is stored with 68 trailing blanks in OLDSUB. If we had used the function call INDEX(TLINE, OLDSUB) to find the first character position of the old substring within TLINE, we would not find the substring, since TLINE doesn't have 68 blanks to the right of o r. Thus, we use the trim length (TL stores 2) for OLDSUB, so INDEX(TLINE, OLDSUB(1:TL)) correctly finds o r starting in character position 6.

NOTE 2   A real text editor would save the revised text to a data file . . . Try out Exercise 14 in the next chapter.

8.7 PROGRAMMING TIPS

DESIGN AND STYLE

Use format-directed interactive input for character data. This defensive programming technique eliminates the need to type surrounding apostrophes for character input, thereby eliminating a potential and common run-time error.

Use LEN function. Use intrinsic function LEN to simplify the tracking of declared lengths and reduce program maintenance. For example, subroutine PARSE on page 410 uses LEN in the DO statement, which eliminates our having to provide the declared length parameter for COMM to this subroutine. Similarly, we use LEN in the DO statement within Program CRYPT on page 398 to avoid directly using the declared length of 80 for TEXT.

Use strings for menu choices. Another defensive programming technique is to use character variables when entering menu choices, since this eliminates the possibility of data input run-time errors. For instance, in Example 8.9 we treated the "numeric" menu choices as strings. If variable CHOICE had been typed integer, then the inadvertent entry of a nonnumeric character would give a run-time error (as in entering a lowercase L instead of the digit 1, a common habit among typewriter users).

COMMON ERRORS

Watch out for logic errors. Logic errors are very common in character processing, possibly because they tend to be subtle and we're less accustomed to string manipulations than to numeric manipulations. This means we need to pay special attention to test data selection and output validation.

Forgetting trim length. Remember that unused character positions in character storage are padded with blanks. When we search for a substring within a string using the INDEX function, we might forget this fact by implicitly using declared length instead of trim length. For example, given the 70-character storage locations

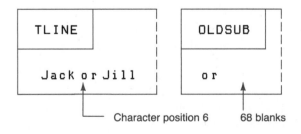

and the statement

```
FIRST = INDEX(TLINE, OLDSUB)
```
⌢‿⌢

————— Entire string used

the INDEX function would return zero, since the search substring in OLDSUB includes the 68 blanks following o r, which is not found in TLINE. If we use Function TRIM (page 412) to trim the length of the string in OLDSUB to 2, as in

```
FIRST = INDEX(TLINE, OLDSUB(1:TRIM(OLDSUB)))
```
☺

————— Substring OLDSUB(1:2) used

then INDEX returns the 6 that we expect. If we always expect INDEX to return a nonzero value, then an error routine should trap the error (as in Exercise 25).

3. **Avoid using character positions in the left member of an assignment statement that are simultaneously referenced in the right member.** For example, the statement

```
STRING(10:27) = STRING(2:19)
```

is not allowed since character positions $10-19$ are simultaneously referenced on both sides of the assignment operator. For a related and subtle logic error, see Exercise 24.

FOLLOW-UP EXERCISES

---

1. Is CRE a substring in the string CORE? Explain.

2. Suppose the character variable REPLY is to store strings like y e s and n o. Design an IF statement that tests whether or not the first character in REPLY is y.

3. State the result given the data in Example 8.1.
   a. PRINT *, PHRASE(R:R)
   b. PRINT *, PHRASE(:)
   c. PRINT *, PHRASE(R:L)
   d. SUB = PHRASE(L+2:2*R-8)
   e.
   ```
        DO 100 K = 1, LEN(PHRASE)
           IF (PHRASE(K:K) .EQ. '!') THEN
              PRINT *, K
           END IF
   100 CONTINUE
   ```

4. Given the character variable STRING with declared length of 30, state code that prints characters in STRING . . .
   a. With a space between each character, all on one line.
   b. Backward, all on one line.

*5. State code that prints the message `Null string` if the character variable `NOTE` contains all blank characters. Assume a declared length of 70.

6. What value is returned in each case?
    a. `INDEX('abcdef', 'x')`
    b. `INDEX('abcdef', 'd')`
    c. `INDEX('abcdef', 'de')`
    d. `INDEX('Mississippi', 's')`

7. Specify the value returned for each of the following.
    a. `LLT('abc', 'abd')`
    b. `LLT('abc', 'ABC')`
    c. `LGE('ABC', '123')`
    d. `LGT('*$**', 'Not nice!')`

8. What gets printed for the following? (Assume ASCII.)
    a. `PRINT *, ICHAR(CHAR(42))`
    b. `PRINT *, CHAR(ICHAR('*'))`

9. Suppose `Newport` is stored in `CITY`, `RI` is stored in `STATE`, and `02840` is stored in `ZIP`. Design a `PRINT` statement that outputs the following.

     `Newport, RI 02840`

Assume the following declared lengths: 15 for `CITY`, 2 for `STATE`, and 5 for `ZIP`.

10. **Day-of-week Substrings.** In Example 8.2, store the dashed line as 80 characters and print substrings of length 26 for the three printed lines.

11. **Concatenation Examples.** Answer the following for Example 8.3.
    a. What gets printed if we use

     `PRINT *, LAST // ',' // FIRST`

    *b. Design a `PRINT` statement that outputs

     `CORE, Harvey A.`
     One blank

12. **Concatenated Date Substrings.** Answer the following for Example 8.4.
    a. Change the program to output the form mm-dd-yy, as in `10-19-87`.
    b. Change the program to output the form mmddyy, as in `101987`.
    c. What happens if we enter the date `1/24/89`? How about the date `12/7/41`?
    *d. Change the program to correct the problem in part **c.**

13. **Examples of LEN function.** In Example 8.5 what's the declared length in `NAME`? What's the trim length? How can we print the trim length?

14. **INDEX function examples.** In Example 8.6 state a `PRINT` statement that finds any nonblank substring in `SEARCH` within `PHRASE`. (Note that the next to last example gave zero, instead of the intended 8.)

*15. **Valid FORTRAN characters.** Suppose `LINE` is a 500-element character array that stores lines in a FORTRAN program. Each element in `LINE` has a declared length of 72. Write code that checks each character in the program. If a character is not a legitimate FORTRAN character (see page 19), then print the character and increment the counter COUNT.

16. **Examples of lexical intrinsic functions.** Suppose we input PC-doll and PC-Doll in Example 8.8. Specify output.

*17. **Examples of functions ICHAR and CHAR.** Answer the following for Example 8.9.
   a. Run Program EX89 on your system. Same results?
   b. Try the following defensive programming technique: Input position as a character value, then convert it to an integer value using an internal file.

*18. **String-to-numeric data conversion with internal file.** Try the following for Example 8.10.
   a. Include an error routine that prints an appropriate error message and reinputs the date while the month is out of range.
   b. Parse the input date string to allow the entry of dates like 12/7/41 and 7/4/76.

*19. **Numeric-to-string conversion.** Suppose that integer variable NUM stores the last two digits in a year (say, 87) and character variable YEAR is to store the string equivalent of this year.
   a. State a WRITE statement that treats YEAR as an internal file to which we write the value in NUM.
   b. State a PRINT statement that prints the following date based on the stored value in YEAR.

   October 19, 1987

20. **Cryptography.** With respect to our cryptography program:
   a. Comment on the use of BLANK = CHAR(32) in the PARAMETER statement from the standpoint of style and portability.
   b. Roleplay the results for the actual message

   Help is on the way!

   c. What happens if we enter the message

   HELP ISN'T ON THE WAY

   Modify the program so any punctuation in the message is ignored (passed through as is).

*21. **Cryptography.** With respect to our cryptography program:
   a. Modify the program to input the day of the week; Monday is 1, Tuesday is 2, and so on. This number is used as the increment key for coding the message. What is the encoded message in our example for Tuesday? For Friday?
   b. Implement this program on your system.

*22. **Cryptography.** With respect to our cryptography program:
   a. Modify the program so an encoded message is entered, decoded, and printed.
   b. Implement this program on your system.

*23. **Cryptography.** With respect to our cryptography program:

   a. Modify the program to allow the encoding of messages with lowercase letters, uppercase letters, and punctuation characters.
   b. Implement this program on your system. Encode the actual message:

   ```
   SS Pierce: Help isn't on the way!
   ```

24. **Text editor.** With respect to our text editor:
   a. What happens if the text file has, say, 1200 lines?
   b. Change the program to handle up to 100 characters in a line.
   c. Change the program to use character variable BELL to ring the bell in Subroutines INPUT and YNERR.
   d. What happens if we omit variable RIGHT in Subroutine CHANGE, and instead use the following?

   ```
TLINE = TLINE(1:FIRST-1) // NEWSUB(1:TL) // TLINE(LAST+1:LEN(TLINE))
   ```

   Roleplay your answer in changing line 1 in our sample run!
   e. What happens in our sample run for changing line 1 if we use variable LEFT as follows?

   ```
   LEFT  = TLINE(1:FIRST-1)
   TLINE = LEFT // NEWSUB(1:TL) // RIGHT
   ```

*25. **Text Editor.** With respect to our text editor:
   a. What happens if we enter an old substring that's not part of the string being edited, as in

   ```
   c//1//ir//and//
   ```

   b. Design a procedure that traps this error and requests a new command line.
   c. Implement and test the revised editor on your system.

*26. **Text Editor.** With respect to our text editor:
   a. What happens if we forget the last pair of slashes in the command line, as in

   ```
   c//1//or//and
   ```

   b. Design a procedure that traps this error and requests a new command line.
   c. Implement and test the revised editor on your system.

ADDITIONAL EXERCISES

27. **Revisit: XY-Plots.** Revise Subroutine XYPLOT on page 336 to work with the one-dimensional array PLOT, where each element has a declared length of 51. Lines in the plot now correspond to elements in PLOT, and print columns correspond to individual characters within each element. Which approach do you prefer and why? Test the revised program on your system.

28. **Revisit: Sorts.** Modify Subroutine SORT1 on page 326 to sort character values in either ascending or descending order. The subroutine receives the character

value A to indicate ascending or the character value D to indicate descending. If the wrong character value is sent, the subroutine prints an appropriate error message and performs an ascending sort. Use lexical functions where appropriate. Test the subroutine on your system by sorting the city names on page 287 both ways.

29. **Collating sequence I.** Write and implement a program that prints the characters corresponding to positions zero through $n - 1$ on your system. Input the value 256 for n, and print a table with two columns: Decimal Value and Character.

30. **Collating sequence II.** Write and implement a program that stores the following characters in the character variable LEGIT: the 10 digits 0 through 9; 26 uppercase letters; 26 lowercase letters; the special characters $+ - * / = ( )$, ' $: . and blank. The program prints a table with two columns: Legitimate Character and Decimal Value

31. **Valid id.** Write a short program that enters *id* as a four-digit string value. Then use the TRIM function to verify that the *id* is valid by being four digits. If the *id* is valid, then print the message *valid;* else print *invalid.* Use the following test data: 1234, 123, 12345.

32. **Name manipulation.** A person's name is stored in a string variable in the format

    first name ⟨space⟩ last name

    Write a short program that manipulates the string and prints the name in the following format:

    last name, ⟨space⟩ first name

    Use the following test data: Harvey CORE
                                H. CORE

33. **Valid numeric data.** Write the code for a routine that inputs numeric data as a string value, confirms that each character in the entered value is numeric (its ASCII code is in the range 48 to 57 inclusive), and converts the string value to a numeric representation. If the string value is not numeric, then print an error message and request reentry while the value is not numeric. Reproduce the following sample run:

    ```
    Enter product code number
    123
    Enter product code number
    i90
       No, dummy! Enter a numeric code
    89o
       No, dummy! Enter a numeric code
    890
    Enter product code number
    000
       End of run.
    ```

    What would happen without a routine that traps this type of error?

34. Case Letter Conversion. Develop a program that:

a. Converts every letter in a text from uppercase to lowercase. The ASCII code for any lowercase letter is 32 greater than the corresponding uppercase letter. If the letter is already lowercase, don't change the letter.

b. Leaves the first letter at the beginning of each sentence in uppercase. *Hint:* The program must identify the beginning of a sentence.

Use the following test text:[6]

```
DEC SENT THIS MACHINE TO MARKET IN 1965. IT
WAS A HIT. IT MADE DEC'S FIRST FORTUNE. THE
PDP-8 ... "ESTABLISHED THE CONCEPT OF
MINICOMPUTERS, LEADING THE WAY TO A
MULTIBILLION DOLLAR INDUSTRY."
```

35. Word Extraction. Write a program that extracts words from a text and prints each on a separate line. A word is defined as a string of characters followed by a space (this is a simplified definition). Include contractions such as *don't* in the definition of a word, which means that the apostrophe is treated as a letter. Also count and print the number of words. Use the following test text:[7]

```
In 1979 Tracy Kidder went underground into the
closely guarded research basement of Data
General to observe a crack team of computer
wizards about to embark on a crash program to
design and build a new computer.
```

36. Course queries. The course numbers at a university are coded as six-character strings, where the first three characters represent the department where the course is offered and the last three characters are digits that signify the academic level. For example, BIO405 is a valid course number. Write a program that answers administrative queries as described below. Use the following data file.

Course Number File

```
BIO405
CSC201
CSC465
HIS101
HIS265
MGS105
MGS207
MGS500
```

---

[6]Tracy Kidder, *The Soul of a New Machine* (Boston: Little, Brown, 1981), p. 15.
[7]Kidder, 1981, jacket cover.

a. Sample run:

```
Department? HIS
                HIS101
                HIS265
Department? BIO
                BIO405
Department? ENG

                ****** No courses in database
Department? END
End of run.
```

b. Use a menu instead of the approach in part **a.** Here's a sample run.

```
Select one:
        1. List of all courses in a department
        2. List of all courses by academic level
        3. List of all graduate courses (500 and above)
        4. Stop processing

Selection?
1
.
:   (Same as part a above)
.
Selection?
2
Enter Level
100
                        H I S 1 0 1
                        M G S 1 0 5
Enter Level
300

                        * * * * * * No courses in
                                    database
Enter Level
0
Selection?
3
                        M G S 5 0 0
Selection?
4
End of run.
```

37. **Form letter.** Write a program that prints the following personalized form letter.

```
Ms. Jane Budwick
10 North Road
Kingston, RI 02881

Dear Ms. Budwick,
     You are indeed one of the fortunate few whom
we have selected for our Gala Prize Drawing. All you
need to do, Jane, is fill in the enclosed handy
magazine order form, which makes you eligible for
one of our many Gala Prizes. Indeed, the Budwick
residence at 10 North Road may be lucky enough to
receive the Most Gala Prize, a free set of
encyclopedias at a maintenance cost of only 10 cents
per day for 30 years.

Good luck!
Hoodwink G. Fox, Manager
Dill Comic Book Co., Inc.
```

In one computer run, print the letter for each of the following.

Name	Address	
Ms. Jane Budwick	10 North Road	Kingston, RI 02881
Mr. Al Bella Bitta	20 Birch St.	Cincinnati, OH 44451
Dr. H. Doolittle	10 Downing	London, UK

Make sure that each letter fits nicely within an $8\frac{1}{2}$-inch width and takes up 11 inches in length.

The following texts are used as test data by Exercises 38 to 41

Text 1

Jack and Jill went up the hill
    To fetch a pail of water;
Jack fell down and broke his crown,
    And Jill came tumbling after.

Text 2

Among other duties, a regional office of the
Environmental Protection Agency (EPA) is charged with
investigating complaints regarding industrial pollution,
when "warranted." A complaint is investigated by
sending a panel of three experts, collectively called the
"proboscis patrol," to the site of the alleged offender.
By consensus, the proboscis patrol then renders one of
three opinions: low level, medium level, or high level of
pollution. (We might note that the human nose has yet
to find an electronic "equal" in detecting offending
odors.) Following an opinion, the regional director of
the EPA then has the option of issuing or not issuing a
citation to the offender. Alternatively, the EPA may
choose not to investigate the complaint and then make
a decision regarding issuance of a citation.

38. **Text analysis I.** Write a program that processes *any number* of separate texts
and prints the following for *each* text.
a. Number of characters
b. Number of letters and proportion of characters that are letters
c. Number of vowels and proportion of letters that are vowels
d. Number of lowercase letters and proportion of letters that are lowercase
Process each text one line at a time (maximum line length is 80 characters) and
ignore trailing blanks in a line. Process the two given texts in your run. It would
be a good idea to output your results in the form of a bar chart, as in Example 6.1.

39. **Text analysis II.** Write a program that processes *any number* of separate texts
and prints the number and proportion of *each* letter in the alphabet for each text.
Make no distinction between lowercase and uppercase letters for purposes of the
count. Process each text one line at a time, where the maximum line length is
80 characters. Process the two given texts in your run. It would be a good idea to
output your results in the form of a bar chart, as in Example 6.1.

40. **Text analysis III.** Write a program that processes *any number* of separate texts and prints the following for each text.
    a. Number of words
    b. Number and proportion of words specified by the user (use *the* or *The* and *and* or *And* as test input)
    c. Number and proportion of words that end in a substring specified by the user (use *ing* as test input)
    d. Number and proportion of words that begin with a letter (or more generally any substring) specified by the user (use the letters *a* or *A* and *e* or *E* as test input)

    Process each text one line at a time, with the maximum line length of 80 characters. Process the two given texts in your run.

41. **Text analysis IV.** A typing textbook contains numerous paragraphs for students to type. These exercises vary in difficulty according to the following criteria.

    1. *Number of strokes* in the exercise. A stroke is any keyboard act, such as typing a letter, typing a space, and returning the carriage to the next line (except for the last line in the exercise), and so on.
    2. *Number of words* in the exercise. Words can include a single letter. For example, the phrase "I love computers" has three words.
    3. *Average word length* in the exercise. This is defined as the number of strokes divided by the number of words.

    The usual approach to developing these exercises is for someone to count strokes, words, and word length for each proposed exercise, to ensure that exercises with various levels of difficulty are selected. This is a tedious task. This is where you come in. You are to computerize this task.

    Write a program that processes *any number* of separate exercises and outputs each line of the exercise followed by a count of the number of strokes and words for that line. For example, the first two lines of Text 1 might be printed as follows:

	Strokes	Words
Jack and Jill went up the hill	31	7
To fetch a pail of water;	28	6

    At the end of each exercise print summary values for the three criteria discussed. Process each exercise one line at a time, with the maximum line length of 70. Use the two given texts as test data.

42. **Cryptography.** Keyword coding is a variation on the increment coding described earlier. Consider a scheme whereby letters in a keyword are used to establish variable increments as illustrated below.

———— First increment = 9 since *I* is 9th letter in alphabet

———— Second increment = 2 since *B* is 2nd letter in alphabet

Keyword: IBM

———— Third increment = 13 since *M* is 13th letter in alphabet

Actual Message	Increment Used	Encoded Message
H	9	Q
E	2	G
L	13	Y
P	9	Y
I	2	K
S	13	F
O	9	X
N	2	P
T	13	G
H	9	Q
E	2	G
W	13	J
A	9	J
Y	2	Δ

Increments are repeated in sequence as often as necessary.

a. Write an encoding program that inputs a keyword of up to 10 characters and an actual message and outputs the actual message together with an encoded message. In your test runs, use the above message and the keywords IBM and DIGITAL.

b. Write a decoding program that inputs an encoded message and keyword and outputs the encoded message together with the decoded message.

43. Text editor. Complete our text editor program as follows.

a. Finish the delete module.

b. Finish the insert module.

c. Add a move module that moves line n1 to line n2.

d. Include the features in Exercises 25 and 26.

To debug your program, use the original three text lines in our example and then insert the following four new lines after the third line:

and jill came tumbling after.
and jill came tumbling after.
Jack fell down and broke his crown,
Up got jack, and home did trot.

Delete the repeated line. Finally, move the next to last line above to its proper place as the fourth line.

9

EXTERNAL
FILE
PROCESSING

Many applications require processing of data files that reside within secondary storage. We have used these files throughout the book for batch processing applications, where interactive input is undesirable. In these cases, we created the data files using our word-processor; indicated the use of a data file by an operating system command or an OPEN statement; and used a READ statement within a loop to input data from the file into primary memory.

This chapter discusses and demonstrates more sophisticated data file approaches: creating and modifying (writing to) files from within programs; multiple processing of the same file within one computer run; processing of multiple files from within one program; and directly accessing data from a file.

9.1 FILE TYPES

Let's start by reviewing and defining some selected file characteristics.

FIELDS, RECORDS, AND FILES

Field.   A fact or attribute (data item) about some entity such as a person, place, thing, or event. For example, an employer might maintain data on employees' attributes such as name, identification number, salary, and sex. Each of these attributes is considered a field. The variables that appear within the lists of input and output statements are used to process fields; that is, each variable in the list corresponds to a field.

Record.   A group of related fields, retrievable as a unit. For example, all of the data items relating to one employee are a record. Typically, the execution of a file input or output statement processes a single record. The fields that make up a record are usually described by a **record layout,** as illustrated in Table 9.1.

File.   A collection of related records. Each record is a logical part of the file, because it contains the same data items (fields, not data values) as all the other records in the file. For example, an *employee file* contains all employee records. Figure 9.1 illustrates this relationship among fields, records, and a file. This file contains three records, and each record contains four fields.

TABLE 9.1   **Record Layout for Employee Record**

Field	Type	Length	Description
Employee Name	Character	25	Last name first
Social Security Number	Character	11	With dashes
Salary	Real	10	Dollars and cents
Sex	Character	1	f or m
Record length		47	

FIGURE 9.1   **External file named EMPLOYEE.DAT**

EXTERNAL VERSUS INTERNAL FILES

What we have called a data file up until now is formally called an external file in FORTRAN. An **external file** is a collection of records (a file) that resides in a storage medium (like tape or disk) that's *external* to primary memory.

The term *external* is also used to distinguish external files from internal files. An **internal file** is a file within primary memory that's referenced by a character variable, substring, character array element, or character array. Internal files are primarily used to convert values from numeric form to character form and vice versa (see Section 8.5). This chapter strictly deals with external files.

UNFORMATTED VERSUS FORMATTED FILES

An **unformatted file** consists strictly of unformatted records. An **unformatted record** contains data in a form that's identical to the machine's internal representation of data (in binary form). Unformatted records are read or written only by *unformatted* input/output statements, as defined in the next section.

A **formatted file** is made up entirely of formatted records. A **formatted record** contains data in "external" form as characters—numeric, alphabetic, or special—that are encoded according to one of the standard coding schemes (like ASCII or EBCDIC). Formatted records are read or written only by *formatted* input/output statements, as defined in the next section.

Unformatted files are processed more rapidly than formatted files because it's not necessary to convert internal/external representations. When the computer inputs a formatted record from an external file into primary memory, it first must convert data from external representation (as stored in the file) to internal representation (as stored within primary memory). Similarly, when the computer writes a formatted record onto an external file, it first must convert data from internal representation to external representation. If the external file is unformatted, however, then there's no need for time-consuming (by computer standards) conversion operations, since all data are represented using the "internal" form.

Unformatted files save storage space on disk and tape, and speed up the processing of data. Unformatted files, however, are processor dependent. Thus, if a particular file is likely to be used by more than one type of computer, it's best to use formatted files.

SEQUENTIAL-ACCESS VERSUS DIRECT-ACCESS FILES

We can process a file in either of two ways—by sequential access or by direct access. File processing by **sequential access** writes or reads records one after the other in serial or "sequential" fashion. For example, if a personnel file contains 10,000 records (employees), sequential processing means that we can read the 9000th record if and only if we first read or process the first 8999 records. All of our file processing, until now, was by sequential access.

Figure 9.2a illustrates the file in Figure 9.1 as a file set up for sequential access. The last record in this file is called an **endfile record.** It signals the processor that the physical end of this file has been reached. An endfile record is used only as the *last* record in a *sequential-access file.*

File processing by **direct access** writes or reads a record without the need to process any other record in the file. For example, if there are 10,000 records in a direct-access personnel file, we can "directly" read the 9000th record without having to read the previous 8999 records.

In direct-access files the record locations are numbered from 1 to n (where n is the maximum number of records in the file). For example, if the direct-access file is to hold 10,000 records, then the record locations on disk use numbers 1 to 10,000. A record location either stores a record or is empty (no record currently stored). The storage and retrieval of a record is based on its **record number,** which is a positive integer that uniquely identifies a record, as seen in Figure 9.2b. By specifying particular record numbers, we can "hop" around this file in a seemingly "random" fashion, which suggests the alternative term random-access file.

By the way, files stored on magnetic tape are processed only by sequential access whereas files stored on magnetic disk are processed by either sequential access or direct access. In general, the access method used depends on both the file medium and the application. Issues regarding which medium to use and which access method to implement relate to factors such as speed, cost, and processing environment. For example, time-shared processing invariably uses magnetic disk and airline reservation inquiry systems process direct-access files.

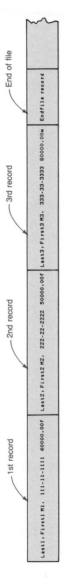

1st record

Last1, First1 MI. 111-11-1111 40000.00f

2nd record

Last2, First2 MI2. 222-22-2222 50000.00f

3rd record

Last3, First3 MI3. 333-33-3333 60000.00m

End of file

Endfile record

File EMPLOYEE · DAT on tape strip or disk track

(a) Sequential-access file

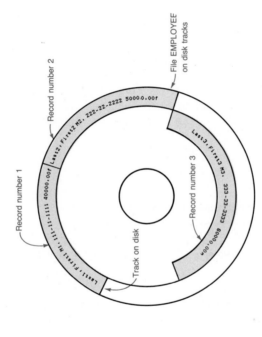

Record number 1

Record number 2

Last1, First1 MI. 111-11-1111 40000.00f

Last2, First2 MI2. 222-22-2222 5000.0.00f

Track on disk

Last3, First3 MI3. 333-33-3333 60000.00m

Record number 3

File EMPLOYEE on disk tracks

(b) Direct-access file

FIGURE 9.2   Conceptual representation of sequential-access and direct-access files

9.2 SEQUENTIAL-ACCESS FILES

We begin by presenting statements that are commonly used for sequential-access processing, followed by the creation, retrieval, and display of files and records.

FILE-PROCESSING STATEMENTS

Statements for file processing are rather detailed, so let's take a "top-down" approach by starting with a simple overview and example of the usual steps in processing a file, as described in Table 9.2. Don't worry about the details just yet; we take these up next. Just focus on the major steps of

1. opening a specific file (for use),
2. writing to or reading from the file, and
3. closing the file.

OPEN Statement. This statement is an executable statement that defines file properties and establishes links among the I/O unit (for example, tape drive or disk drive), the file (stored on tape or disk), and the FORTRAN program.

TABLE 9.2   **Major Steps in File Processing**

Step	Example	Description
Open the file	OPEN (UNIT = 10 , FILE = 'TEST.DAT')	Connects I/O unit 10 to a file named TEST.DAT.
Write to the file	WRITE (10 , *) 'Files are great!'	Writes the note Files are great! to unit 10 (into file TEST.DAT) using list-directed output.
or		
Read from the file	READ (10 , '(A)') NOTE	Reads a note from unit 10 (file TEST.DAT) into variable NOTE using format-directed input.
Close the file	CLOSE (10)	Disconnects unit 10.

OPEN Statement

Syntax:

```
OPEN (list of specifiers)
```

Example:

```
OPEN (UNIT = U, FILE = FNAME, STATUS = STAT,
+      ACCESS = 'SEQUENTIAL', FORM = 'FORMATTED',
+      BLANK = 'NULL')
```

The following specifier *must* be used.

UNIT = *u*

The *unit identifier u* for an external file identifies the specific I/O unit that is to be used (such as tape drive). It must be either an integer expression with a nonnegative value or an asterisk. The asterisk identifies a particular system-determined unit (for example, disk drive) that's preconnected for formatted sequential access. The portion UNIT = can be omitted, but *u* must be present. A value of, say, 10 for *u* might refer to a specific tape drive. The relationship of specific values for *u* to specific I/O units is system-dependent, so ask your instructor or consult your system's manual.

The following specifiers are *optional.*

FILE = *fname*

fname is a character expression whose value (after the removal of trailing blanks) identifies the name of the file to be connected with the specified I/O unit. If this specifier is omitted and the I/O unit is not connected to a file, the I/O unit becomes connected to a system-determined file. In our example, the character variable FNAME stores the name of the file. Later, in Figures 9.4 and 9.5, we input the name of this file.

STATUS = *stat*

stat is a character expression whose value (after the removal of trailing blanks) is OLD, NEW, SCRATCH, or UNKNOWN OLD is specified when the file already exists on the I/O unit, NEW when the file does not exist, SCRATCH when the file is used temporarily and deleted ("scratched") either following the run or following the execution of a CLOSE statement, and UNKNOWN when we wish the status to be system dependent. If OLD or NEW is specified, the specifier FILE = must be given. If SCRATCH is specified, don't use the specifier FILE =. If the specifier STATUS = is omitted, UNKNOWN is assumed. In our example, the character variable STAT stores the proper status. Later, in Figures 9.4 and 9.5, we input the status.

ACCESS = *acc*

acc is a character expression whose value (after the removal of trailing blanks) is SEQUENTIAL or DI-RECT. This specifier establishes the access method. If omitted, sequential is assumed.

FORM = *fm*

fm is a character expression whose value (after the removal of trailing blanks) is FORMATTED or UN-FORMATTED. It specifies whether we have a formatted or an unformatted file. If this specifier is omitted, FORMATTED is assumed for sequential-access files and UNFORMATTED is assumed for direct-access files.

ERR = *slabel*

slabel is the statement label of an executable statement to which control is transferred if an error condition is encountered during execution of the OPEN statement. For example, if we use ERR = 800, then the statement labeled 800 is executed following an error. We can also use this specifier in READ, WRITE, and CLOSE statements.

IOSTAT = *intname*

intname is an integer name that's assigned a positive integer if an error condition is encountered and zero otherwise; it's usually an alternative to the ERR = specifier. We can also use this specifier in a CLOSE statement; another variation exists for READ and WRITE statements (see below).

BLANK = *blnk*

blnk is a character expression whose value (after the removal of trailing blanks) is NULL or ZERO. If we specify NULL, then any blank characters in formatted numeric input fields are ignored. If any field is all blanks, then its value is zero. If we specify ZERO, then all blanks other than leading blanks are edited as zeros. If the BLANK specifier is omitted, then NULL is assumed. This specifier is permitted only for formatted files.

A RECL = specifier is also available for the OPEN statement, which we describe under direct-access files (page 450).

WRITE and READ Statements. The READ statement copies data from a file to primary memory, and the WRITE statement copies data from primary memory to the file.

WRITE and READ Statements for Sequential Access

Syntax:

        WRITE 〈*control list*〉 *output list*
        READ   〈*control list*〉 *input list*
Examples:

    WRITE (UNIT = U, FMT = 920) ENAME, SSN, SALARY, SEX
    READ (U, 920, IOSTAT = IOCODE) ENAME, SSN, SALARY, SEX

As usual, each item in the output list is one of the following: variable name, array element name, array name, implied-DO list, character substring name, or expression. Each item in the input list is a variable name, array element name, array name, implied-DO list, or character substring name.

The control list must include the following specifier.

UNIT = *u*   This specifier identifies an external I/O unit (see page 433). If the portion UNIT = is omitted, then *u* must be the first item in the list, as done in Table 9.2. In our examples above, the unit identifier is stored in the integer variable U (we use these statements in Figures 9.4 and 9.5).

The following specifiers are optional in sequential-access READ/WRITE statements.

FMT = *f*   *f* is a format identifier that identifies the format specification to be used, as follows: an integer constant that's the same as the statement label of a FORMAT statement; an integer variable whose value is the same as the statement label of a FORMAT statement; a character expression or array name that stores the format specification; or an asterisk for list-directed I/O (see pages 507 and 541 if you're "fuzzy" on these terms). If the portion FMT = is omitted, then *f must* be the second item in the control list, where the first item *must* be *u* (see the sample READ statement above that references the FORMAT statement labeled 920, and Figure 9.7).

IOSTAT = *intname*   *intname* is an integer name that's assigned: zero if neither an error condition or end of file is encountered; a positive integer if an error condition is encountered; a negative integer if an end of file is encountered. This specifier is a common alternative to the ERR = and END = specifiers, as illustrated in Section 5.3 and later in Figure 9.7.

ERR = *slabel*   This specifier is the same as that used in the OPEN statement (see page 434); in this case, the error relates to file reads and writes.

END = *s*   *s* is the statement label of an executable statement to which control is transferred if an eof condition or an endfile record is encountered during the execution of a READ statement. This specifier cannot be used in a WRITE statement. It was first presented in Section 5.3. We use it later in Figure 9.4.

A REC = specifier is also available for READ and WRITE statements, as illustrated under direct-access files (see page 451).

NOTE 1   The control list in a READ or WRITE statement must contain exactly one *unit specifier* (UNIT = u) and none or any of the other specifiers. Moreover, we can place these specifiers in any order, unless UNIT = and FMT = portions are omitted, in which case *u* and *f* must be one-two in the control list.

NOTE 2   If the control list contains a *format specifier* (FMT = f), the statement is a **formatted input/output statement;** otherwise it's an **unformatted input/output statement.** If the format identifier *f* is an asterisk, the statement is a **list-directed input/output statement;** otherwise it's a **format-directed input/output statement.**

ENDFILE Statement.   Execution of the following statement places an endfile record as the next record in a sequential-access file.

ENDFILE Statement: Form 1

Syntax:
        ENDFILE *u*
Example:
        ENDFILE 10

ENDFILE Statement: Form 2

Syntax:
        ENDFILE (*list of specifiers*)
Example:
        ENDFILE (10, ERR = 850)

In the first form, u is the unit identifier, which *must* be included. In the second form, the following specifier must be included.

UNIT = *u*

See the description under the OPEN statement (page 433). If the portion UNIT = is omitted, then u must be the first item in the list, as in the example.

The following specifiers are optional, but only one or the other is allowed.

IOSTAT = *intname*

See the description under the OPEN statement (page 434).

ERR = *slabel*

See the description under the OPEN statement (page 434).

We typically use the ENDFILE statement to mark the end of a sequential-access file that we have just created, as illustrated later in Figure 9.4.

REWIND Statement.   If we need to process the same sequential-access file more than once during a given run, then it's necessary to rewind the file back to the beginning. This is equivalent to repositioning a conceptual pointer at the beginning of the first record. We rewind a file as follows.

REWIND Statement: Form 1

Syntax:

        REWIND *u*

Example:

        REWIND 10

REWIND Statement: Form 2

Syntax:

        REWIND (*list of specifiers*)

Example:

        REWIND (UNIT = 10, IOSTAT = CODE)

The specifiers in this statement are identical to those in the ENDFILE statement above. We illustrate the rewinding of a file in Figure 9.4.

CLOSE Statement.   After a file is processed and before execution terminates, it's best to formally disconnect the file from its input/output unit. This is accomplished as follows.

CLOSE Statement

Syntax:

      CLOSE   (*list of specifiers*)

Example:

        CLOSE (U)

As usual the external unit identifier must be included.

UNIT = *u*   See the description under the OPEN statement (page 433).

We can also include *at most one* of the following optional specifiers.

IOSTAT = *intname*   See the description under the OPEN statement (page 434).

ERR = *slabel*   See the description under the OPEN statement (page 434).

STATUS = *sta*   *sta* is a character expression whose value (after the removal of trailing blanks) is KEEP or DELETE. We should specify KEEP to retain the data on the file for later use and DELETE to "wipe out" the data on file. KEEP must not be used if SCRATCH was specified in the OPEN statement. This specifier is optional. If omitted, KEEP is assumed—unless SCRATCH was specified earlier, in which case DELETE is assumed. Got that?

NOTE 1   A unit, once disconnected by the execution of a CLOSE statement, can be reconnected within the same run either to the same file or to a different file.

NOTE 2   A file, once disconnected by the execution of a CLOSE statement, can be reconnected within the same run either to the same unit or to a different unit, provided that the file was not deleted.

NOTE 3   Systems implicitly close all files at termination of execution if CLOSE statements are not used. The effect is as though a CLOSE statement without a STATUS = specifier were executed on each connected unit. As a matter of programming style, however, we recommend the explicit closing of all units.

FILE CREATION AND DISPLAY

As mentioned earlier, up to this point, we have created external files using an editor or wordprocessor. Figure 9.3a shows the process of creating an external file through a FORTRAN program, as follows.

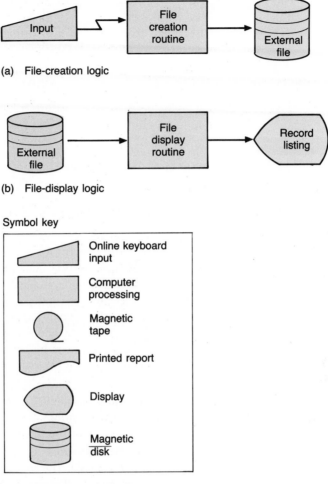

(a)   File-creation logic

(b)   File-display logic

Symbol key

FIGURE 9.3   **Data movement to and from an external file**

File Creation Logic

1. A record is input interactively through the keyboard and placed in primary memory (using a READ statement, as usual).

2. The record is copied to the file from primary memory (using the WRITE statement described earlier).

The process of displaying an existing external file is diagrammed in Figure 9.3b; it's the mirror image of file creation, as follows.

File Display Logic

1. A record is copied from the file into primary memory (using the READ statement described in the preceding section).

2. The record is displayed by taking a copy from its location in primary memory to the screen (using a PRINT or WRITE statement, as usual).

EXAMPLE 9.1

CREATION AND DISPLAY OF A FORMATTED, SEQUENTIAL-ACCESS FILE

Figure 9.4 shows a modular program that creates and displays the employee file first presented in Figures 9.1 and 9.2. Try roleplaying the run of this program in Figure 9.5, noting the following.

1. Subroutine CREATE inputs the file characteristics for unit identifier, file name, and status. This better generalizes the program for file characteristics that commonly vary. We assume in all cases a formatted (FORM = 'FORMATTED'), sequential-access (ACCESS = 'SEQUENTIAL') file, where blanks in numeric fields are ignored (BLANK = 'NULL'). We could have simplified the OPEN statement by leaving out the ACCESS =, FORM =, and BLANK = specifiers, since the parameters we selected (SEQUENTIAL, FORMATTED, and NULL) are default parameters.

2. In the sample run, we entered UNKNOWN for file status, which generalizes the status across the two subroutines. Typically, we would enter NEW for the creation routine and OLD for the display routine.

3. The WRITE statement in Subroutine CREATE copies a record from primary memory to the external file. The record is formatted according to the described record layout. A control character (see page 510 in Module B) is not used within output formats for external files (see the FORMAT statement labeled 920).

4. In Subroutine CREATE, we place an endfile record at the end of the file using the ENDFILE statement. Remember that we use endfile records only for sequential-access files.

5. We rewind the file as our last file act in Subroutine CREATE by using the REWIND statement; this repositions the pointer to the first record in anticipation of the file display routine that follows next. Alternatively, we could have placed the REWIND statement just before statement 200 in Subroutine SHOW.

6. Sequential-access files are typically displayed using an eof loop, as seen in Subroutine SHOW, by using the END = specifier within the READ statement.

```
        PROGRAM SFILE1
 • • • • • • • • • • • • • • • • • • • • • • • • • • • • • • •
 •
 •          Creation/display of formatted, sequential-access file
 •
 •          Inputs file characteristics and employee records
 •          Creates (writes to) file
 •          Outputs (displays) file
 •
 •          Record layout for employee file:
 •          ───────────────────────────────────────────────────
 •          Field                    Type        Length (Bytes)
 •          ───────────────────────────────────────────────────
 •          Employee Name            Character        25
 •          Social Security Number   Character        11
 •          Salary                   Real             10
 •          Sex                      Character         1
 •          ───────────────────────────────────────────────────
 •          Record length.......................... 47
 •
 •          Modular Structure:
 •
 •            Main program... Calls CREATE and SHOW.
 •
 •                Sub. CREATE.... Interactively inputs file characteris-
 •                                tics and records; creates file.
 •
 •                Sub. SHOW...... Displays entire file.
 •
 •          Key (main program):
 •
 •            FNAME.... File name
 •            U........ Unit identifier
 •
 • • • • • • • • • • • • • • • • • • • • • • • • • • • • • • •
──────────────────────────────────────────────────────────────
 • Type names
 •──────────────────────────────────────────────────────────────
       CHARACTER  FNAME*20
       INTEGER    U
──────────────────────────────────────────────────────────────
 • Create file
 •──────────────────────────────────────────────────────────────
       CALL CREATE ( FNAME, U )
──────────────────────────────────────────────────────────────
 • Display file
 •──────────────────────────────────────────────────────────────
       CALL SHOW ( FNAME, U )
──────────────────────────────────────────────────────────────
       END
```

FIGURE 9.4   **Listing of sequential-access file creation and display program (SFILE1) (*continued*)**

---

7. As mentioned in Note 3 on page 438, it's best to close files when finished, as done in Subroutine SHOW.

8. The external file we illustrated in Figure 9.1 is, in fact, a photograph of the file EMPLOYEE.DAT, as created by the run in Figure 9.5. Check it out, noting that the format of each record is described by format 920 in Subroutine CREATE. ∎

```
          SUBROUTINE CREATE ( FNAME, U )
* * * * * * * * * * * * * * * * * * * * * * * * * * * * * * * * *
*                                                               *
*          File creation subroutine                            *
*                                                               *
*          Receives nothing                                    *
*          Inputs data and creates file                        *
*          Returns file name and unit identifier               *
*                                                               *
*          Key:                                                 *
*                                                               *
*            ENAME.... Employee name (last name first)         *
*            FNAME.... File name                               *
*            REPLY.... Y/n reply                               *
*            SALARY... Employee salary                         *
*            SEX...... Sex code (f or m)                       *
*            SSN...... Social security number (with dashes)    *
*            STAT..... Status of file                          *
*            U........ Unit identifier                         *
*                                                               *
* * * * * * * * * * * * * * * * * * * * * * * * * * * * * * * * *
*_____
*  Type names
*_____
      CHARACTER  ENAME*25, FNAME*20, REPLY, SEX, SSN*11, STAT*7
      INTEGER    U
      REAL       SALARY
*_____
*  Input file characteristics and open file
*_____
      PRINT *, 'Enter unit number'
      READ  *,   U
      PRINT *,  'Enter file name'
      READ  900, FNAME
      PRINT *, 'Enter file status'                    ——— Connect external unit to file
      READ  900, STAT

      OPEN ( UNIT = U, FILE = FNAME, STATUS = STAT,
     +       ACCESS = 'SEQUENTIAL', FORM = 'FORMATTED', BLANK = 'NULL' )
*_____
*  Create file:  Interactively input records and write to file
*                until last record
*_____
  100   PRINT *
        PRINT *, 'Enter employee name, last name first'
        READ  900, ENAME
        PRINT *, 'Enter Social Security Number, with dashes'
        READ  900, SSN
        PRINT *, 'Enter salary'
        READ  *,   SALARY
        PRINT *, 'Enter sex code, f or m'         ———Copy record from primary memory to file
        READ  900, SEX

        WRITE ( UNIT = U, FMT = 920 ) ENAME, SSN, SALARY, SEX

        PRINT *
        PRINT *, 'Another record? (y/n)'
        READ  900, REPLY

      IF ( REPLY .EQ. 'y'  .OR.  REPLY .EQ. 'Y' ) GO TO 100
*_____
*  Write endfile record and rewind file
*_____
      ENDFILE U ◄————————————————————— Place endfile record at end of file

      REWIND  U ◄————————————————————————— Rewind file to beginning
*_____
*  Formats
*_____
  900 FORMAT ( A )
  920 FORMAT ( 2A, F10.2, A ) ◄————————————— Control character not used
*_____
      END
```

FIGURE 9.4   **(continued)**

```
      SUBROUTINE SHOW ( FNAME, U )
* * * * * * * * * * * * * * * * * * * * * * * * * * * * * * * * *
*                                                               *
*          File display subroutine                             *
*                                                               *
*          Receives file name and unit identifier             *
*          Reads and displays all records from file           *
*          Returns nothing                                     *
*                                                               *
*          Key:                                                *
*                                                               *
*             ENAME.... Employee name (last name first)       *
*             FNAME.... File name                             *
*             SALARY... Employee salary                       *
*             SEX...... Sex code (f or m)                     *
*             SSN...... Social security number (with dashes)  *
*             U........ Unit identifier                       *
*                                                               *
* * * * * * * * * * * * * * * * * * * * * * * * * * * * * * * * *
*————————————————————————————————————————————————————————————
* Type names
*————————
      CHARACTER  ENAME*25, FNAME*20, SEX, SSN*11
      INTEGER    U
      REAL       SALARY
*————————————————————————————————————————————————————————————
* Display entire file
*——————————————————
      PRINT *
      PRINT *, 'File... ', FNAME
      PRINT 900
      PRINT 910
      PRINT 900                    ———— Copy record from file to primary memory
 200  READ ( UNIT = U, FMT = 920, END = 300 ) ENAME, SSN, SALARY, SEX

      PRINT 930, ENAME, SSN, SALARY, SEX  ——————————— Eof loop control

      GO TO 200

 300 CONTINUE

      PRINT 900
*————————————————————————————————————————————————————————————
* Close file
*——————————
      CLOSE (U) ———————————————————————————— Disconnect external unit and file
*————————————————————————————————————————————————————————————
* Formats
*—————
  900 FORMAT ( 1X, 50('=') )
  910 FORMAT ( 1X, 'Employee Name          SS Number    Salary  Sex')
  920 FORMAT ( 2A, F10.2, A )
  930 FORMAT ( 1X, 2A, F10.2, 2X, A )
*————————————————————————————————————————————————————————————
      END
```

FIGURE 9.4   (*continued*)

NOTE 1 The records in a sequential-access file must either be all formatted or all unformatted. A mixture of the two is not allowed.

NOTE 2 If the ACCESS = specifier is omitted in the OPEN statement, then sequential access is assumed. How is the file processed in Table 9.2?

```
 Enter unit number
6
 Enter file name
employee.dat
 Enter file status
unknown

 Enter employee name, last name first
Last1, First1 M1.
 Enter Social Security Number, with dashes
111-11-1111
 Enter salary
40000
 Enter sex code, f or m
f

 Another record? (y/n)
y

 Enter employee name, last name first
Last2, First2 M2.
 Enter Social Security Number, with dashes
222-22-2222
 Enter salary
50000
 Enter sex code, f or m
f

 Another record? (y/n)
y

 Enter employee name, last name first
Last3, First3 M3.
 Enter Social Security Number, with dashes
333-33-3333
 Enter salary
60000
 Enter sex code, f or m
m

 Another record? (y/n)
n

 File... employee.dat
===============================================
 Employee Name            SS Number    Salary  Sex
===============================================
 Last1, First1 M1.        111-11-1111  40000.00  f
 Last2, First2 M2.        222-22-2222  50000.00  f
 Last3, First3 M3.        333-33-3333  60000.00  m
===============================================
```

Figure 9.1 shows a photograph of the actual file.

FIGURE 9.5   **Creation and display of sequential-access file EMPLOYEE.DAT**

RECORD RETRIEVAL AND DISPLAY

Many applications in file processing require the retrieval and display of a single record based on the value of a desired field. For example, in our employee file, we might wish to retrieve and display the record having the social security number 222-22-2222. Given a desired field value, the procedure reads records from the file until either the desired record is found (based on the desired field value) or an end of file is encountered. The next example illustrates this approach.

EXAMPLE 9.2

RECORD RETRIEVAL AND DISPLAY BY SEQUENTIAL ACCESS

Let's continue the employee file example by developing a procedure that retrieves and displays the first record having a desired social security number. In Exercise 7c we ask you to look at a variation that displays all records satisfying a desired field value.

Figure 9.6 shows pseudocode for our record retrieval/display procedure. Note the following.

1. Outer (first) loop. The outer loop handles multiple requests. For example, if we wish to retrieve and display three separate records, then this loop repeats three times. Note that we open the file before this loop and close it following the loop. Within the loop we need to rewind the file for each request (repetition), since the entire file must be searched anew beginning with the first record. We also initialize a record count because we're going to determine and print the record location of any retrieved record. Finally, we initialize a flag—a true/false loop control variable—for the file loop (discussed next).

2. Inner (second) loop. The inner loop processes the file until either a matching record is found (and displayed) or the end of the file is reached. The body of this loop has an else-if structure with three distinct blocks. If a matching record is found, then it's displayed, the flag is reset to indicate an exit from the file loop, and loop exit is achieved; else if the end of the file is reached, then a message is printed to the effect that a matching record was not found, the flag is reset to exit the loop, and loop exit is achieved; else we have an input error when reading a record, a message to that effect is printed, and file looping continues with the next record.

Figure 9.7 is a listing of a program that follows the described pseudocode design. A sample run is seen in Figure 9.8. Try roleplaying the sample run through the program, and note the following.

1. The IOSTAT = specifier is used as control in the else-if structure. For each execution of the READ statement, IOCODE is assigned one of three values

```
Input file characteristics
Open file
Loop
   Input SS number
   Rewind file
Initialize record count and flag (file loop control) to no exit
Process file until desired record
is found or end of file is encountered ──────────────────┐
Ask if another record is desired                         │
Until another record retrieval/display is not desired    │
Close file                                        Refine │
End                                                      │
        ┌────────────────────────────────────────────────┘
        ▼
```

```
    Loop
        Increment record count
        If no end of file or error then
            If record is a match then
                Display record
                Reset flag to exit
            End if
        Else if end of file then
            Print no match message
            Reset flag to exit
        Else
            Print input error message
        End if
    Until match or end of file is found
```

FIGURE 9.6   **Pseudocode for record retrieval/display procedure when using sequential access**

by the system: if zero (a record is read without encountering an error or end of file), then we check the record for the desired SS number match; else if negative (an end of file is detected by the system), then we print a message that we failed to find the desired record; else (if positive) an error occurred when reading the record, as in trying to read character data into a numeric variable (see Exercise 7a).

2. We control the file processing loop by using the logical variable FLAG. Just before the inner loop, FLAG is set to true, which signifies "repeat the loop" in our loop control test given by

```
IF (FLAG) GO TO 200
```

```
        PROGRAM SFILE2
* * * * * * * * * * * * * * * * * * * * * * * * * * * * * * * * * * *
*                                                                   *
*        Record retrieval and display w/ sequential-access file     *
*                                                                   *
*        Inputs Social Security Number for desired record           *
*        Searches file until desired record found (if any)          *
*        Outputs (displays) desired record (or message if not found)*
*                                                                   *
*        Record layout for employee file:                           *
*       _____        *
*        Field                  Type        Length (Bytes)          *
*       _____        *
*                                                                   *
*        Employee Name          Character        25                 *
*        Social Security Number  Character        11                 *
*        Salary                 Real             10                 *
*        Sex                    Character         1                 *
*       _____        *
*        Record length........................  47                 *
*                                                                   *
*        Key:                                                       *
*                                                                   *
*          ENAME.... Employee name (last name first)                *
*          FNAME.... File name                                      *
*          IOCODE... IOSTAT code: 0 ok; <0 eof; >0 input error      *
*          LINE..... Line in file display table                     *
*          FLAG..... Continue processing file if true               *
*          RECORD... Record number                                  *
*          REPLY.... Y/n reply                                      *
*          SALARY... Employee salary                                *
*          SEX...... Sex code (f or m)                              *
*          SSN...... Social security number (with dashes)           *
*          SSNDES... SSN desired                                    *
*          STAT..... Status of file                                 *
*          U........ Unit identifier                                *
*                                                                   *
* * * * * * * * * * * * * * * * * * * * * * * * * * * * * * * * * * *
*_____
* Type names
*_____
        CHARACTER   ENAME*25, FNAME*20, LINE*60, REPLY, SEX, SSN*11,
       +            SSNDES*11, STAT*7
        INTEGER     IOCODE, RECORD, U
        LOGICAL     FLAG
        REAL        SALARY
*_____
* Initialize
*_____
        LINE = '==========================================='
*_____
* Input file characteristics and open file
*_____
        PRINT *, 'Enter unit number'
        READ  *, U
        PRINT *, 'Enter file name'
        READ  '(A)', FNAME
        PRINT *, 'Enter file status'
        READ  '(A)', STAT

        OPEN ( UNIT = U, FILE = FNAME, STATUS = STAT,
       +       ACCESS = 'SEQUENTIAL', FORM = 'FORMATTED', BLANK = 'NULL' )
```

FIGURE 9.7   **Listing of sequential-access record retrieval and display program (SFILE2) (continued)**

```
*————————————————————————————————————————————————
*   Retrieve/display record until no more desired
*————————————————————————————————————————————————
  100    PRINT *
         PRINT *, 'Enter Social Security Number, with dashes'
         READ  '(A)', SSNDES

         REWIND U
         RECORD = 0
         FLAG = .TRUE.  ◄————————————————— Loop control set to repeat

*       Process file until desired record found or eof condition
*————————————————————————————————————————————————
  200      READ ( U, 920, IOSTAT = IOCODE ) ENAME, SSN, SALARY, SEX

           RECORD = RECORD + 1

           IF (IOCODE .EQ. 0 ) THEN

               Legitimate record processed
               ————————————————————————————————
               IF ( SSN .EQ. SSNDES ) THEN

                   Match found
                   ————————————————————————————
                   PRINT *
                   PRINT *, 'Record number...', RECORD
                   PRINT *, LINE
                   PRINT *, 'Name..... ', ENAME
                   PRINT *, 'SS No.... ', SSN
                   PRINT *, 'Salary...$', INT( SALARY )
                   PRINT *, 'Sex...... ', SEX
                   PRINT *, LINE

                   FLAG = .FALSE.  ◄————————————— Loop control set to exit

               END IF

           ELSE IF ( IOCODE .LT. 0 ) THEN

               Eof condition... matching record not found
               ————————————————————————————————
               PRINT *, CHAR(7)
               PRINT *, LINE
               PRINT *, 'No matching record for SS # ', SSNDES
               PRINT *, LINE

               FLAG = .FALSE.  ◄————————————— Loop control set to exit

           ELSE

               Input error when reading record
               ————————————————————————————————
               PRINT *, CHAR(7)
               PRINT *, LINE
               PRINT *, 'Input error at record number', RECORD
               PRINT *, LINE

           END IF                 ◄————————————— Loop control test
         IF (FLAG) GO TO 200
*————————————————————————————————————————————————

         PRINT *
         PRINT *, 'Another record? (y/n)'
         READ  '(A)', REPLY

      IF ( REPLY .EQ. 'y'  .OR.  REPLY .EQ. 'Y' ) GO TO 100
*————————————————————————————————————————————————
```

FIGURE 9.7   *(continued)*

```
    * Close file
    *─────────
         CLOSE (U)
    *──────────────────────────────────────────────────────
    * Input format
    *─────────────
      920 FORMAT ( 2A, F10.2, A )
    *──────────────────────────────────────────────────────
              END
```

FIGURE 9.7 (*continued*)

```
 Enter unit number
10
 Enter file name
employee.dat
 Enter file status
old

 Enter Social Security Number, with dashes
222-22-2222

 Record number...           2
═══════════════════════════════════════════════
Name..... Last2, First2 M2.
SS No.... 222-22-2222
Salary...$        50000            ◄──Matching record
Sex...... f
═══════════════════════════════════════════════

 Another record? (y/n)
y

 Enter Social Security Number, with dashes
444-44-4444


═══════════════════════════════════════════════
No matching record for SS # 444-44-4444        ◄──No match
═══════════════════════════════════════════════

 Another record? (y/n)
y

 Enter Social Security Number, with dashes
333-33-3333

 Record number...           3
═══════════════════════════════════════════════
Name..... Last3, First3 M3.
SS No.... 333-33-3333
Salary...$        60000            ◄──Matching record
Sex...... m
═══════════════════════════════════════════════

 Another record? (y/n)
n
```

FIGURE 9.8 **Record retrieval and display from sequential-access file EMPLOYEE.DAT**

We wish to terminate file processing either when a matching record is found or the end of the file is reached. In these cases, FLAG is reset to false within the loop. Roleplay our run to really understand this logic! We ask you to consider traditional (but undesirable) loop design alternatives in Exercise 7b. ■

9.3 DIRECT-ACCESS FILES

In Section 9.1 we mentioned that direct-access files allow us to access a record *directly* by its record number, without having to search for the record sequentially. We can also process direct-access files sequentially, should we need to display the entire file, for example.

FILE-PROCESSING STATEMENTS

As with sequential access, the general steps for direct access include the following: opening the file, writing to or reading from the file, and closing the file. As before, we use the OPEN, READ, WRITE, and CLOSE statements, with two additional specifiers (RECL = and REC =). The ENDFILE and REWIND statements are not used for direct access.

OPEN Statement.   This statement is as described under sequential-access files (see page 433), except that the following record length specifier must be used for direct-access files.

RECL = *length*   *length* is an integer expression with positive value that specifies the record length in a direct-access file. *Length* is expressed in number of characters for formatted records and number of processor-dependent units for unformatted records. This specifier *must* be given for direct-access files; it *must* be omitted for sequential-access files.

For example, the statement

```
OPEN (UNIT = 10, FILE = 'EMPLOY.DAT', STATUS
+      = 'NEW', ACCESS = 'DIRECT', FORM =
+      'FORMATTED', RECL = 47)
```

connects unit 10 to a new direct-access file called EMPLOY.DAT having formatted records of length 47.

NOTE   The OPEN statement for direct-access files differs in two respects from its counterpart in sequential-access files: (1) ACCESS = specifies DIRECT instead of SEQUENTIAL; (2) the RECL = specifier must be used.

WRITE and READ Statements. These statements are described under sequential-access files (see page 435). For direct-access we must include the following record specifier in the control list.

REC = *rn*   *rn* is an integer expression whose value is positive. It represents the record number to be processed in a direct-access file. This specifier must be present to process a direct-access file.

For example, the following statements write to and read from record number 999 (RECNUM stores 999) for the file connected to unit 10, using format-directed I/O according to the FORMAT statement labeled 920.

```
WRITE (10, 920, REC = RECNUM) ENAME, SSN, SALARY, SEX
READ  (10, 920, REC = RECNUM) ENAME, SSN, SALARY, SEX
```

NOTE 1   READ/WRITE statements for direct-access files differ in two respects from their counterparts in sequential-access files: (1) the REC = specifier must be used; (2) the END = specifier is not used.

NOTE 2   List-directed formatting is not allowed in direct-access files; that is, the format identifier must not be an asterisk in a READ or WRITE statement that's used to process a direct-access file.

CLOSE Statement.   This statement is identical to that used in sequential access (see page 438).

FILE CREATION AND DISPLAY

The creation and display of an entire direct-access file is conceptually identical to the creation and display of a sequential-access file, as described in Figure 9.3. The next example shows the operational differences.

EXAMPLE 9.3

CREATION AND DISPLAY OF A FORMATTED, DIRECT-ACCESS FILE

Figure 9.9 shows the direct-access version of the program first presented in Figure 9.4. In fact, we created this program by editing the original sequential-access version. Try roleplaying the run in Figure 9.10, noting the following highlighted differences.

1. A record length variable (RLEN) is used to specify the record length 47 in the OPEN statement. The OPEN statement specifies access as DIRECT, and includes the RECL = specifier.

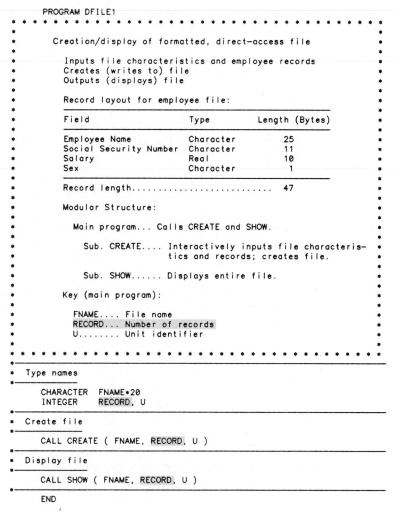

```
        PROGRAM DFILE1
* * * * * * * * * * * * * * * * * * * * * * * * * * * * * * * * * * *
*                                                                   *
*       Creation/display of formatted, direct-access file           *
*                                                                   *
*         Inputs file characteristics and employee records          *
*         Creates (writes to) file                                  *
*         Outputs (displays) file                                   *
*                                                                   *
*         Record layout for employee file:                          *
*       ─────────────────────────────────────────────────────      *
*         Field                   Type         Length (Bytes)        *
*                                                                   *
*         Employee Name           Character        25                *
*         Social Security Number  Character        11                *
*         Salary                  Real             10                *
*         Sex                     Character         1                *
*       ─────────────────────────────────────────────────────      *
*         Record length.......................... 47                 *
*                                                                   *
*         Modular Structure:                                        *
*                                                                   *
*           Main program... Calls CREATE and SHOW.                  *
*                                                                   *
*             Sub. CREATE.... Interactively inputs file characteris-*
*                             tics and records; creates file.       *
*                                                                   *
*             Sub. SHOW...... Displays entire file.                 *
*                                                                   *
*           Key (main program):                                     *
*                                                                   *
*             FNAME.... File name                                   *
*             RECORD... Number of records                           *
*             U........ Unit identifier                             *
*                                                                   *
* * * * * * * * * * * * * * * * * * * * * * * * * * * * * * * * * * *
*──────────────────────────────────────────────────────────────────
*   Type names
*──────────────────────
      CHARACTER  FNAME*20
      INTEGER    RECORD, U
*──────────────────────────────────────────────────────────────────
*   Create file
*──────────────────────
      CALL CREATE ( FNAME, RECORD, U )
*──────────────────────────────────────────────────────────────────
*   Display file
*──────────────────────
      CALL SHOW ( FNAME, RECORD, U )
*──────────────────────────────────────────────────────────────────
        END
```

FIGURE 9.9   **Listing of direct-access file creation and display program (DFILE1)** *(continued)*

2. The record number (RECORD) is a counter within the loop in Subroutine CREATE, and it's used in the WRITE statement with the REC = specifier. For example, at the second repetition of the loop, a record identified as record number 2 is written.

3. The ENDFILE and REWIND statements were eliminated, as these are not relevant for direct-access files.

4. The DO-loop in Subroutine SHOW is convenient for systematically displaying all records in a direct-access file. Note that the DO-variable is used as the record number, and RECORD now stores the number of sequentially numbered records (3 from Subroutine CREATE).

```
      SUBROUTINE CREATE ( FNAME, RECORD, U )
  * * * * * * * * * * * * * * * * * * * * * * * * * * * * * * * *
  *                                                            *
  *         File creation subroutine                           *
  *                                                            *
  *         Receives nothing                                   *
  *         Inputs data and creates file                       *
  *         Returns file name, number of records, and unit identifier *
  *                                                            *
  *         Key:                                               *
  *                                                            *
  *            ENAME.... Employee name (last name first)       *
  *            FNAME.... File name                             *
  *            RECORD... Record number                         *
  *            RLEN..... Record length                         *
  *            REPLY.... Y/n reply                             *
  *            SALARY... Employee salary                       *
  *            SEX...... Sex code (f or m)                     *
  *            SSN...... Social security number (with dashes)  *
  *            STAT..... Status of file                        *
  *            U........ Unit identifier                       *
  *                                                            *
  * * * * * * * * * * * * * * * * * * * * * * * * * * * * * * * *
  *
  *  Type names
  *----------
        CHARACTER  ENAME*25, FNAME*20, REPLY, SEX, SSN*11, STAT*7
        INTEGER    RECORD, RLEN, U
        REAL       SALARY
  *
  *  Initialize
  *-----------
        RECORD = 0                                  ──────────── See record layout
        RLEN   = 47  ◄──────────────────────
  *
  *  Input file characteristics and open file
  *-----------------------------------------
        PRINT *, 'Enter unit number'
        READ *,   U
        PRINT *,  'Enter file name'
        READ  900, FNAME
        PRINT *, 'Enter file status'
        READ  900, STAT

        OPEN ( UNIT = U, FILE = FNAME, STATUS = STAT,
       +       ACCESS = 'DIRECT', FORM = 'FORMATTED', BLANK = 'NULL',
       +       RECL = RLEN )  ◄
                                       ──────── Must specify for direct-access file
  *
  *  Create file:  Interactively input records and write to file
  *                until last record
  *----------------------------------------------------------
   100  PRINT *
        PRINT *, 'Enter employee name, last name first'
        READ  900, ENAME
        PRINT *, 'Enter Social Security Number, with dashes'
        READ  900, SSN
        PRINT *, 'Enter salary'
        READ *,   SALARY
        PRINT *, 'Enter sex code, f or m'
        READ  900, SEX                      ──────── Specifies record number

        RECORD = RECORD + 1

        WRITE ( UNIT = U, FMT = 920, REC = RECORD )
       +                             ENAME, SSN, SALARY, SEX

        PRINT *
        PRINT *, 'Another record? (y/n)'
        READ  900, REPLY

        IF ( REPLY .EQ. 'y' .OR. REPLY .EQ. 'Y' ) GO TO 100
```

FIGURE 9.9   **(continued)**

```
 ←────────────────────────────── ENDFILE and REWIND statements not used in direct access
*
* Formats
*────────
  900 FORMAT ( A )
  920 FORMAT ( 2A, F10.2, A )
*──────────────────────────────────────────────────────────────────────
      END


      SUBROUTINE SHOW ( FNAME, RECORD, U )
* * * * * * * * * * * * * * * * * * * * * * * * * * * * * * * * * * * *
*                                                                     *
*          File display subroutine                                    *
*                                                                     *
*          Receives file name, number of records, and unit identifier *
*          Reads and displays all records from file                   *
*          Returns nothing                                            *
*                                                                     *
*          Key:                                                       *
*                                                                     *
*            ENAME.... Employee name (last name first)               *
*            FNAME.... File name                                      *
*            RECORD... Number of records                             *
*            RN...... Record number (DO-variable)                    *
*            SALARY... Employee salary                               *
*            SEX...... Sex code (f or m)                             *
*            SSN...... Social security number (with dashes)          *
*            U........ Unit identifier                               *
*                                                                     *
* * * * * * * * * * * * * * * * * * * * * * * * * * * * * * * * * * * *
*──────────────────────────────────────────────────────────────────────
* Type names
*───────────
      CHARACTER  ENAME*25, FNAME*20, SEX, SSN*11
      INTEGER    RECORD, RN, U
      REAL       SALARY
*──────────────────────────────────────────────────────────────────────
* Display entire file
*────────────────────
      PRINT *
      PRINT *, 'File... ', FNAME
      PRINT 900
      PRINT 910
      PRINT 900                                  ─── Stores last record number, or number of records

      DO 200 RN = 1, RECORD                      ─── Specifies record number

          READ ( UNIT = U, FMT = 920, REC = RN ) ENAME, SSN, SALARY, SEX

          PRINT 930, ENAME, SSN, SALARY, SEX

  200 CONTINUE

      PRINT 900
*──────────────────────────────────────────────────────────────────────
* Close file
*───────────
      CLOSE (U)
*───────────
* Formats
*────────
  900 FORMAT ( 1X, 50('=') )
  910 FORMAT ( 1X, 'Employee Name              SS Number   Salary  Sex')
  920 FORMAT ( 2A, F10.2, A )
  930 FORMAT ( 1X, 2A, F10.2, 2X, A )
*──────────────────────────────────────────────────────────────────────
      END
```

Stores last record number, or number of records

Specifies record number

DO-loop systematically displays all records

FIGURE 9.9   **(continued)**

```
 Enter unit number
6
 Enter file name
employ.dat
 Enter file status
new

 Enter employee name, last name first
Last2, First2 M2.
 Enter Social Security Number, with dashes
222-22-2222
 Enter salary
50000
 Enter sex code, f or m
f

 Another record? (y/n)
y

 Enter employee name, last name first
Last1, First1 M1.
 Enter Social Security Number, with dashes
111-11-1111
 Enter salary
40000
 Enter sex code, f or m
f

 Another record? (y/n)
y

 Enter employee name, last name first
Last3, First3 M3.
 Enter Social Security Number, with dashes
333-33-3333
 Enter salary
60000
 Enter sex code, f or m
m

 Another record? (y/n)
n

 File... employ.dat
```

Employee Name	SS Number	Salary	Sex	
Last2, First2 M2.	222-22-2222	50000.00	f	◄———— Record number 1
Last1, First1 M1.	111-11-1111	40000.00	f	◄———— Record number 2
Last3, First3 M3.	333-33-3333	60000.00	m	◄———— Record number 3

FIGURE 9.10   **Creation and display of direct-access file EMPLOY.DAT**

NOTE 1   The order of the records in a direct-access file is the order of their record numbers. In our example, this also coincided with the entry sequence (as would be true in a sequential-access file), since we defined the record number using a counter. In many applications, however, record numbers are based on a record ID that is entered along with other input data. We ask you to look at the implications in Exercises 10 and 11.

NOTE 2   We cannot delete records in a direct-access file once they are created; we can only rewrite them (see Exercise 16b).

RECORD RETRIEVAL AND DISPLAY

The retrieval and display of a single record is simpler in direct-access processing in the sense that the record is directly retrieved based on its record number . . . no other records need to be considered, as in sequential-access processing. The complication arises in how we indicate the proper record number. For example, in the file created by the run in Figure 9.10, we can directly access the employee with social security number 222-22-2222 by knowing that this employee is stored in record number 1. How do we know that it's record number 1 in practice? We would have a file, called an **index file,** that indicates the proper record number for each SS number. In other words, SS numbers are indexed on record numbers, much like topics in a textbook are indexed on page numbers.

Index File for Employee File

SS Number	Record Number
222-22-2222	1
111-11-1111	2
333-33-3333	3

In practice a user would know the SS number and not the record number. Since the computer system works directly with the record number and not the SS number, we have a communications problem. The solution is to have the user enter the proper SS number, and have the computer determine the corresponding record number from a sequential index file. Then the system can access the proper record directly from the employee file. The SS number is called the **key,** as its value is like a key that "unlocks" the proper record. The next example illustrates this approach. Alternative approaches are considered in Exercises 9 to 11.

EXAMPLE 9.4

RECORD RETRIEVAL AND DISPLAY BY DIRECT ACCESS

Figures 9.11 and 9.12 illustrate the direct-access alternative to the sequential-access approach in Figures 9.7 and 9.8. Try roleplaying the run, and note the following.

1. We used parameters to declare all file characteristics for both the employee file (File 1) and the index file (File 2). If file characteristics change infrequently in a programming environment, then the use of parameters reduces data entry costs, with little or no increases in maintenance costs.

2. The outer loop processes SS numbers while a blank is not entered. The earlier version used a yes/no reply to control the outer loop. We can use either approach—we just wanted to show an alternative.

3. The inner loop has the same design as the sequential-access alternative, with the following differences.

   a. The READ statement labeled 200 reads from the index file, not the employee file. Our first act is to find the proper record number from the index file, based on the entered SS number. Since the index file is, in fact, a sequential-access file, we have the same fundamental loop design as in Figure 9.7.

   b. Once a match is found, we simply use a direct-access READ statement to "pick off" the proper record from the employee file.

   We ask you to consider in Exercise 10 an alternative design that requires entry of the record number by the user; it's simpler to program (and understand!), but usually less realistic in practice. Exercise 11 describes a hashing algorithm, a sophisticated alternative that's useful (and often used!) in practice, but more difficult to program than our approach in Figure 9.11.

4. Our design is file intensive because each new query (desired SS number) requires reprocessing the index file. This can prove costly in applications that have very large index files, since file I/O is slow compared to data access within primary memory. An alternative is to load index files into arrays in primary memory, and to perform the table lookups from the arrays instead of the index files. This is faster, but memory intensive. We ask you to look at this alternative in Exercise 9c.

5. The direct-access approach in Figure 9.11 is faster in practice than the sequential-access approach in Figure 9.7. Both approaches process a sequential-access file to find a single record, but the index file is smaller (has fewer fields) than the sequential-access employee file (two versus four fields in our example). Index files always have two fields, but the corresponding actual file can have many more fields. The greater the difference in the number and size of fields, the faster it is to process an index file followed by a direct access to the actual file.

```
        PROGRAM DFILE2
  . . . . . . . . . . . . . . . . . . . . . . . . . . . . . . . . . . . . .
  .                                                                       .
  .          Record retrieval and display w/ direct-access file          .
  .                                                                       .
  .                                                                       .
  .          Inputs Social Security Number for desired record            .
  .          Finds record number using index file and directly           .
  .             accesses desired record                                   .
  .          Outputs (displays) desired record (or message if not found) .
  .                                                                       .
  .          Record layout for direct-access employee file (File 1):     .
  .          _____ .
  .                                                                       .
  .          Field                    Type           Length (Bytes)       .
  .          _____ .
  .                                                                       .
  .          Employee Name            Character           25              .
  .          Social Security Number   Character           11              .
  .          Salary                   Real                10              .
  .          Sex                      Character            1              .
  .          _____ .
  .                                                                       .
  .          Record length.........................   47                 .
  .                                                                       .
  .          Record layout for sequential-access index file (File 2):    .
  .          _____ .
  .                                                                       .
  .          Field                    Type           Length (Bytes)       .
  .          _____ .
  .                                                                       .
  .          Social Security Number   Character           11              .
  .          Record Number            Integer              5              .
  .          _____ .
  .                                                                       .
  .          Record length.........................   16                 .
  .                                                                       .
  .          Key:                                                         .
  .                                                                       .
  .            ACC1..... Access for File 1                                .
  .            ACC2..... Access for File 2                                .
  .            BLNK1.... Blank treatment for File 1                       .
  .            BLNK2.... Blank treatment for File 2                       .
  .            FM1...... Format characteristic for File 1                 .
  .            FM2...... Format characteristic for File 2                 .
  .            ENAME.... Employee name (last name first)                  .
  .            FNAME1... File name for File 1                             .
  .            FNAME2... File name for File 2                             .
  .            IOCODE... IOSTAT code: 0 ok; <0 eof; >0 input error        .
  .            LINE..... Line in file display table                       .
  .            FLAG..... Continue processing File 2 if true               .
  .            RECORD... Record number                                    .
  .            REPLY.... Y/n reply                                        .
  .            RLEN1.... Record length for File 1                         .
  .            SALARY... Employee salary                                  .
  .            SEX...... Sex code (f or m)                                .
  .            SSN...... Social security number (with dashes)             .
  .            SSNDES... SSN desired                                      .
  .            STAT1.... Status of File 1                                 .
  .            STAT2.... Status of File 2                                 .
  .            U1....... Unit identifier for File 1                       .
  .            U2....... Unit identifier for File 2                       .
  .                                                                       .
  . . . . . . . . . . . . . . . . . . . . . . . . . . . . . . . . . . . . .
  _____
  . Type names
  _____
        CHARACTER  ACC1*10, ACC2*10, BLNK1*4, BLNK2*4, ENAME*25,
        +          FM1*11, FM2*11, FNAME1*20, FNAME2*20, LINE*60,
        +          REPLY, SEX, SSN*11, SSNDES*11, STAT1*7, STAT2*7
        INTEGER    IOCODE, RECORD, RLEN1, U1, U2
        LOGICAL    FLAG
        REAL       SALARY
```

FIGURE 9.11   **Listing of direct-access record retrieval and display program (DFILE2) (*continued*)**

```
*────────────────────
*  Specify file parameters                                   ──────── Direct-access employee file
*────────────────────
      PARAMETER ( ACC1 = 'DIRECT', BLNK1 = 'NULL', FM1 = 'FORMATTED',
     +            FNAME1 = 'EMPLOY.DAT', STAT1 = 'OLD', U1 = 10,
     +            RLEN1 = 47 )

      PARAMETER ( ACC2 = 'SEQUENTIAL', BLNK2 = 'NULL',FM2 = 'FORMATTED',
     +            FNAME2 = 'EMPLOY.IND', STAT2 = 'OLD', U2 = 20 )
*────────────────────
*  Open files                                                ──────── Sequential-access index file
*────────────────────
      OPEN ( UNIT = U1, FILE = FNAME1, STATUS = STAT1, ACCESS = ACC1,
     +       FORM = FM1, BLANK = BLNK1, RECL = RLEN1 )
                                                             ──────── Needed for
                                                                      direct-access file
      OPEN ( UNIT = U2, FILE = FNAME2, STATUS = STAT2, ACCESS = ACC2,
     +       FORM = FM2, BLANK = BLNK2 )
*────────────────────
*  Initialize
*────────────────────
      LINE = '═══════════════════════════════════════'
*────────────────────
*  Retrieve/display record while SSN not blank
*────────────────────
      PRINT *
      PRINT *, 'Enter SS Number, with dashes... end with blank'
      READ  '(A)', SSNDES

  100 IF ( SSNDES .NE. ' ' ) THEN                            ──────── Rewind index file for each new query

          REWIND U2                                          The index file is sequential
          FLAG = .TRUE.                                      access, so it's processed as
*                                                            in Figure 9.7
*         Find record number from index file
*         ────────────────────────────────────
  200     READ ( U2, 910, IOSTAT = IOCODE ) SSN, RECORD      ──────── Record number that's
                                                                      read from index file is
          IF (IOCODE .EQ. 0 ) THEN                                    used to locate record in
*                                                                     employee file when SS
*             Legitimate record in index file                        numbers match
*             ────────────────────────────────────
              IF ( SSN .EQ. SSNDES ) THEN
*
*                 Match found...read/display employee file record
*                 ────────────────────────────────────
                  READ ( U1, 920, REC = RECORD ) ENAME, SSN, SALARY, SEX

                  PRINT *
                  PRINT *, 'Record number...', RECORD        ──────── Same value in SSN when
                  PRINT *, LINE                                       there's a match
                  PRINT *, 'Name..... ', ENAME
                  PRINT *, 'SS No.... ', SSN
                  PRINT *, 'Salary...$', INT( SALARY )
                  PRINT *, 'Sex...... ', SEX
                  PRINT *, LINE

                  FLAG = .FALSE.

              END IF

          ELSE IF ( IOCODE .LT. 0 ) THEN
*
*             Eof condition... matching record not found
*             ────────────────────────────────────
              PRINT *, CHAR(7)
              PRINT *, LINE
              PRINT *, 'No matching record for SS # ', SSNDES
              PRINT *, LINE

              FLAG = .FALSE.

          ELSE
```

FIGURE 9.11   *(continued)*

```
*       Input error when reading record in index file
*
          PRINT *, CHAR(7)
          PRINT *, LINE
          PRINT *, 'Input error at record number', RECORD
          PRINT *, LINE

       END IF

    IF (FLAG) GO TO 200
*
       PRINT *
       PRINT *, 'Enter SS Number, with dashes... end with blank'
       READ  '(A)', SSNDES

       GO TO 100

    END IF
*
* Close files
*
       CLOSE (U1)
       CLOSE (U2)
*
* Input formats
*
 910 FORMAT ( A, I5 )
 920 FORMAT ( 2A, F10.2, A )

       END
```

FIGURE 9.11   **(continued)**

```
Enter SS Number, with dashes... end with blank
222-22-2222

Record number...            1
============================================
Name..... Last2, First2 M2.
SS No.... 222-22-2222
Salary...$        50000          ◀——Matching record
Sex...... f
============================================

Enter SS Number, with dashes... end with blank
444-44-4444

============================================
No matching record for SS # 444-44-4444 ◀————No match

Enter SS Number, with dashes... end with blank
333-33-3333

Record number...            3
============================================
Name..... Last3, First3 M3.
SS No.... 333-33-3333
Salary...$        60000          ◀——Matching record
Sex...... m
============================================

Enter SS Number, with dashes... end with blank
```

FIGURE 9.12   **Record retrievals and displays for direct-access file EMPLOY.DAT**

9.4 OTHER STATEMENTS

Two other statements round out the external file repertoire of FORTRAN, as presented in this section.

BACKSPACE STATEMENT

The following executable statement positions the file pointer before the preceding record in a *sequential*-access file.

BACKSPACE Statement: Form 1

Syntax:

        BACKSPACE *u*

Example:

        BACKSPACE U2

BACKSPACE Statement: Form 2

Syntax:

        BACKSPACE (*list of specifiers*)

Example:

        BACKSPACE (UNIT = U2, ERR = 800)

The two forms and the specifiers are identical to those used in the ENDFILE and REWIND statements (see page 437). In the examples, the sequential-access file connected to the unit number whose value is stored in variable U2 (for example, unit 10) is repositioned one record back from its present position. For instance, if the pointer currently resides at the beginning of the 50th record, it would be repositioned to the beginning of the 49th record.

INQUIRE STATEMENT

This executable statement is used to query the system about the properties of a specific file or a specific unit, depending on which of the following two forms is used.

INQUIRE Statement: Inquire by File

Syntax:
```
        INQUIRE (FILE = fname, list of inquiry specifiers)
```
Example:
```
        INQUIRE (FILE = 'EMPLOY.DAT', DIRECT = DA, RECL = RL)
```

INQUIRE Statement: Inquire by Unit

Syntax:
```
        INQUIRE (UNIT = u, list of inquiry specifiers)
```
Example:
```
        INQUIRE (UNIT = U2, ACCESS = ACC, FORMATTED = FORM)
```

The FILE = and UNIT = specifiers are as before (see page 433). The inquiry specifiers are described in Table 9.3. By the way, we don't need to place the file name or unit specifier at the beginning of the list, but we recommend doing so to better identify the form of the INQUIRE statement.

In the first example above, assume the INQUIRE statement is placed anywhere after the OPEN statements in Program DFILE2 (page 459). Its execution would place YES in the character variable DA (*yes*, EMPLOY.DAT is a direct-access file) and 47 in the integer variable RL (the record length is 47).

In the second example above, placement of the INQUIRE statement following the OPEN statement for unit U2 in Program DFILE2 (see page 459) would return the value SEQUENTIAL to the character variable ACC (the index file connected to unit U2 is sequential) and the value YES to the character variable FORM (*yes*, the file is formatted).

9.5 COMPUTER-BASED INFORMATION SYSTEMS

Computer-based information system (**CBIS**) is a term that embraces a wide range of computerized information support for an organization. A CBIS can include each of the following computer-based systems.

TRANSACTION PROCESSING SYSTEMS (TPS)

These systems primarily capture, store, maintain, and process data that describe *transactions* within an organization. For example, transactions in a payroll application include the number of hours worked during a given week by each non-

TABLE 9.3   **Inquiry Specifiers for the INQUIRE Statement**

Inquiry Specifiers[a]	*Values Assigned to Variables*[b]
ACCESS = *character variable*	SEQUENTIAL if the file is opened for sequential access and DIRECT if the file is opened for direct access.
BLANK = *character variable*	NULL if blanks in numeric fields are ignored and ZERO if edited as zeros.
DIRECT = *character variable*	YES if the file can be connected for direct access, NO if it cannot, and UNKNOWN if indeterminate.
ERR = *statement label*	No value is assigned; the statement label identifies the beginning of an error routine.
EXIST = *logical variable*	.TRUE. if the file name or unit exists; .FALSE. otherwise.
FORM = *character variable*	FORMATTED if file is opened for formatted I/O; UNFORMATTED if not.
FORMATTED = *character variable*	YES if file is formatted, NO if file is unformatted, and UNKNOWN if indeterminate.
IOSTAT = *integer variable*	Zero if no error, positive value if error.
NAME = *character variable*	Name of the connected file.
NAMED = *logical variable*	.TRUE. if the file has a name, .FALSE. if it does not.
NEXTREC = *integer variable*	1 + most recent record number used in direct access file; undefined if file is not opened for direct access, or if indeterminate.
NUMBER = *integer variable*	Number of connected unit.
OPENED = *logical variable*	.TRUE. if the file and unit are connected; .FALSE. otherwise.
RECL = *integer variable*	Record length of file opened for direct access; undefined if not opened for direct access.
SEQUENTIAL = *character variable*	YES if the file can be connected for sequential access, NO if it cannot, and UNKNOWN if indeterminate.
UNFORMATTED = *character variable*	YES if file is unformatted, NO if file is formatted, and UNKNOWN if indeterminate.

[a]We also can use array elements in place of variables.
[b]Values are defined only if (1) the file name is legitimate and the file exists for inquire by file or if (2) the unit exists and is connected to a file for inquire by unit. Moreover, for inquire by file, the file must have been opened for defined values in ACCESS =, BLANK =, FORM =, NEXTREC =, NUMBER =, and RECL =; otherwise, values are undefined.

salaried employee; monthly transactions in a bank checking-statement application include the processed checks, deposits, and withdrawals from the checking account of each customer; and transactions in an inventory application include the daily shipments and receipts of inventory items.

Transaction processing systems generally accomplish procedural tasks such as payroll, inventory control, reservations (such as airline and hotel), and billing applications. The traditional term for a TPS is **data processing system.** Transaction processing procedures commonly use two file types called master files and transaction files.

A **master file** contains data items that are central to continued operation of the organization. These files are relatively permanent collections of records containing informational, historical, and current-status items. For example, the master file for bank checking accounts might contain a record, for each customer account, that includes the customer's name, account number, address, telephone, and last month's ending balance.

A **transaction file** is a relatively temporary collection of records containing data about transactions that have occurred during the most recent operating period. This type of file is used to process data against the master file. For example, a transaction file for bank checking accounts might contain data on all checks processed during the current month. At the end of the current month, data from both the transaction file and the master file are processed into a new master file that updates the current status of ending balance for each account.

Records in a sequential-access file (transaction or master) are typically organized for easy access through a record key. A **record key** is one or more fields in each record that distinguish it from all others. For example, in the banking illustration, the customer account number might serve as the record key. Data on the bank file would be arranged (sorted) by customer account number; the customer record with the lowest account number is first, followed by the customer with the next account number, and so on until the last record is the customer with the highest account number. These concepts are illustrated in Example 9.5.

MANAGEMENT INFORMATION SYSTEMS (MIS)

An MIS also carries out the functions of capturing, storing, maintaining, and processing data. Unlike transaction processing systems, however, it has the primary task of generating reports and answering queries that provide information to support the traditional management activities of planning, organizing, and controlling. For example, MIS applications might include reports that provide financial information for a corporate merger, sales reports that aid in the reorganization of sales regions, and quality control reports that analyze the performance of work stations in an automated factory. In recent years, MIS applications are increasingly interactive, so that managers themselves sit at a terminal or microcomputer and generate the needed reports. This has the advantage of interactive "What if . . . ?" processing, whereby the information from one query suggests a variation on the query that provides a basis for the next report.

DECISION SUPPORT SYSTEMS (DSS)

In the literature and in practice the distinction between a DSS and an MIS is rather blurred. The distinction is one more of emphasis than of kind. A DSS has a decision rather than an information focus and is more associated with the use of analytic modeling techniques such as forecasting, linear programming, simulation, and other models in statistics and operations research. In some cases, the decision process is automated, as in automated inventory reordering systems and in process control systems such as steelmaking and petroleum blending. These automated systems are sometimes called **programmed decision systems** and are related to the work in artificial intelligence. An **expert system** is another form of decision support system with roots in artificial intelligence research. In this case the software mimics the decision-making behavior of an expert human, as in medical diagnosis.

DATABASE MANAGEMENT SYSTEMS (DBMS)

A **database** is an integrated collection of external files, including various relationships among the files. For example, the database in a video store might include four separate files: a members master file that includes fields like customer ID, name, address, and so on; a movie inventory master file that includes fields like movie ID, title, movie category, and so forth; a rental transaction file that includes customer ID, movie ID, rental date, and due date; and a return transaction file that records rental return transactions like date and movie ID. Note that these files include certain interrelationships. For instance, a rental transaction requires changes in the movie and rental files; a return transaction requires changes in the return and movie files.

A **database management system** (**DBMS**) is a software package that manages a database. Through either a menu system or a fourth-generation programming language, or both, a DBMS might include all or most of the following capabilities.

- Database housekeeping, as in creating, deleting, and merging files.
- File management, as in adding, deleting, and changing records in a file.
- File linkages, as in relating one file to another through a common field like customer ID (these are called relational databases).
- Database security, as in providing file backups and password protection.
- Links to modules written in other computer languages, like BASIC, COBOL, FORTRAN, and Pascal.
- Database queries, as in "What percentage of last month's movie rentals were comedies?"
- Report generation, as in printing a weekly report of rentals by movie categories like comedy, war, horror, and so on.
- Graphics, as in displaying a bar graph of movie rentals by category.
- Statistical and mathematical analyses, as in forecasting next month's rental income based on past rentals.

Note that the described features include elements of TPS, MIS, and DSS systems, which further blurs distinctions among the different CBISs. Popular commercial packages in these areas include Focus, Statistical Analysis System (SAS), Oracle, and dBASE IV.

EXAMPLE 9.5

COMPUTERIZED BLOOD DONOR SYSTEM

A local hospital is developing a computerized blood donor system. This system will be used to contact donors when certain types of blood are needed and to develop statistics about donor usage.

A blood donor master file consisting of one record for each donor has been created, as described by the following record layout.

Record Layout for Blood Donor Master File

Field	Type	Length
Donor ID number	Integer	4
Donor name	Character	20
Address	Character	40
Phone	Character	11
Blood type	Character	3
Date of last donation	Character	8

Let's simplify this example by working strictly with existing donors. In the exercises, we extend the approach to new donors.

Method 1: Batch Processing System

One approach for updating the blood donor file is **periodic (batch) processing.** In this approach, every time a donor gives blood, the donor's ID and date of donation are recorded in a sequential-access transaction file. Periodically, weekly perhaps, the records in the transaction file are used to update the "date of last donation" field in the sequential-access master file.

The process of updating is illustrated by the system flowchart in Figure 9.13a. A **system flowchart** presents a general overview of an entire system, the sequence of major processing operations, and the data flow to and from files. The type of flowchart that we illustrated in other chapters is technically called a **program flowchart.**

In our blood donor illustration, each donor's contribution is recorded by a data entry operator on the same day that the blood is donated. The DATA ENTRY/EDIT program checks the validity of the date and ID before storing the blood donation transaction in a sequential transaction file. A few sample transactions might appear as follows:

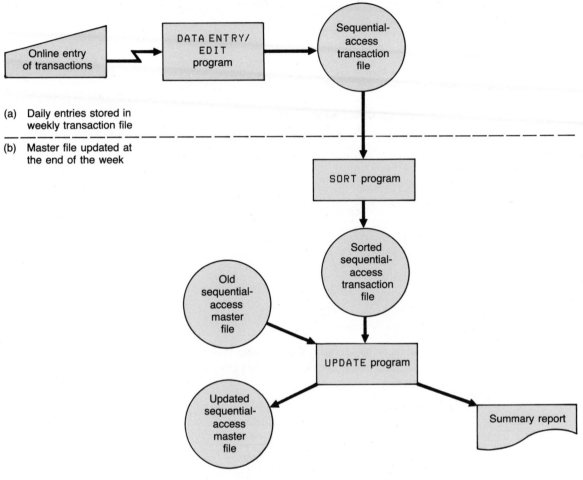

FIGURE 9.13   **Systems flowchart for batch processing blood donor system**

```
Transaction file name?
WEEK24

Today's date...........?
14/06/89  ◄─────────────────────────── This entry would not be needed if
                                         the computer has a date function
                  **Incorrect month. Try again.

Today's date...........?
06/14/89

ID?
4
ID?
2
ID?
-99

Have a nice evening!
```

Transactions are appended to the end of the weekly transaction file every day. At the end of the week the transaction file might contain the following four transactions:

Transaction File

Donor ID	Date of Last Donation
4	06/14/89 ◄──── These are the transactions from
2	06/14/89 the sample run above
3	06/15/89
6	06/16/89
endfile record	

At the end of every week the sequential master file is updated. First, we create a temporary sort file that contains all the records in the transaction file, but in ascending order of ID. Records in this file appear as follows:

Sorted Transaction File

Donor ID	Date of Last Donation
2	06/14/89 ◄──── These are the sorted
3	06/15/89 transactions from the
4	06/14/89 ◄──── sample run above
6	06/16/89
endfile record	

The UPDATE program next uses the sorted transaction file and the *old master file* to create an *updated master file*. The purpose of this program is to update the "date of last donation" field. Additionally, the UPDATE program prints a report showing the donor name, date, and blood type for each donor during that week. If the old master file contains the data shown below before the update,

Old Master File

1	Smith, A.	125 Halpern Ave.	Kingston, RI	792-4091	A+	01/03/87
2	Jones, J.	25 Elmire Rd.	Cranston, RI	731-2067	B+	11/12/85
3	Nagel, T.	Estelle Rd.	Warwick, RI	331-6022	O+	05/22/87
4	Bosworth, B.	106 Broad St.	Westerly, RI	348-9021	A−	10/07/88
5	Bobick, D. D.	1 Main St.	Woonsocket, RI	861-2221	AB+	08/17/88
6	Regae, J.	97 Sinker Dr.	Kingston, RI	401-1111	O+	07/16/86
7	Myer, B.	2 Fort St.	Wakefield, RI	789-1702	O−	03/11/89
8	Fips, B. B.	1036 Indian Rd.	Narragansett, RI	783-2173	B+	02/12/86

Endfile record

then the processing of the transaction file against the master file would result in the following updated master file.

Updated Master File

1	Smith, A.	. . .	A+	01/03/87
2	Jones, J.	. . .	B+	06/14/89
3	Nagel, T.	. . .	O+	06/15/89
4	Bosworth, B.	. . .	A−	06/14/89
5	Bobick, D. D.	. . .	AB+	08/17/86
6	Regae, J.	. . .	O+	06/16/89
7	Myer, B.	. . .	O−	03/11/87
8	Fips, B. B.	. . .	B+	02/12/86

Endfile record   . . .

A program flowchart for the UPDATE program is illustrated in Figure 9.14. The transaction key is the blood donor ID read from a record of the transaction file, and the master key is the blood donor ID from a record of the master file. In the discussion that follows, keep in mind that records in both the transaction and master files are in ascending order according to blood donor ID. Also, we assume that both files are processed by sequential access.

The update program compares the key of the transaction record with the corresponding data item (key) in the master record. If a match occurs (keys of both files are equal), the transaction data are used to update the "date of last donation" field for that master record as illustrated by the middle branch in Figure 9.14.

When the transaction key tests greater than the master key, it follows that processing of the current blood donor on the master file has been completed.

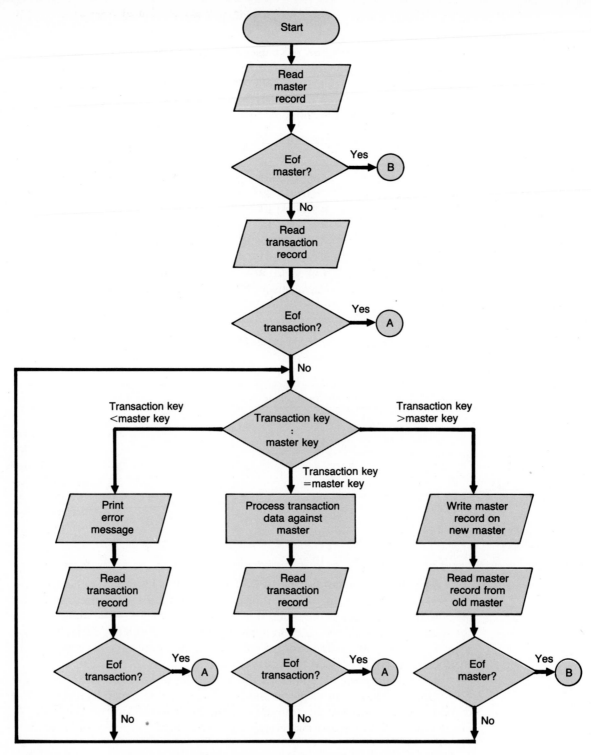

FIGURE 9.14   Program flowchart for sequential access-file update program (*continued*)

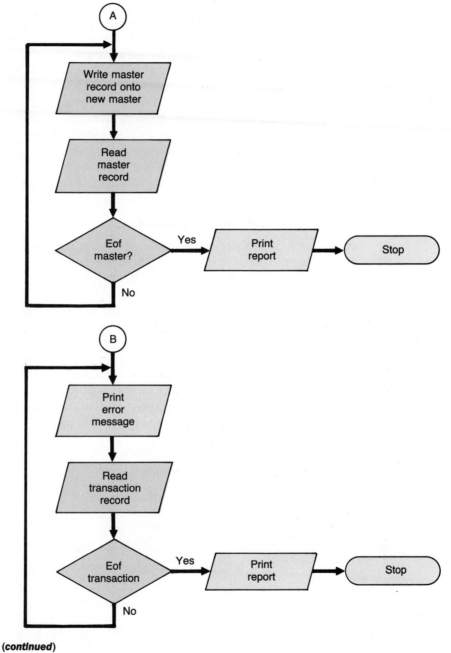

FIGURE 9.14   (*continued*)

Thus, the updated record for this blood donor can now be written onto the new master file. For example, when the second record in the sorted transaction file on page 468 is processed, the transaction key will test greater than the master key ($4 > 3$). At this time the updated record for Nagel (ID = 3) on the new master file can be written, as described in the third (rightmost) branch of Figure 9.14.

A transaction key greater than the master key may also indicate that no transaction (activity) occurred for that record. This is particularly common when master files have many records. In such cases, the master record is copied unchanged onto the new master file, as in the third branch. For example, the first record of the master file is copied unchanged, since the first transaction ID is 2.

Depending on the situation, however, an error may be indicated by the mismatch of keys. In this case, an error message is printed, as illustrated by the first branch in Figure 9.14.

Method 2: Online Processing System

Alternatively, and more simply, we could design an **online processing** system that updates a direct-access master file as transactions are keyed in daily, as illustrated in the system flowchart of Figure 9.15. In this case, transactions are usually entered from a terminal under the control of an EDIT/UPDATE program. This program edits the input data for a valid date and record number (ID). If valid, it then directly updates the proper record in the direct-access master file. If invalid, it prompts the user for a correct entry.

Compared to the batch processing approach, the online system results in a more current master file and facilitates interactive applications such as record queries from the master file. Unlike the batch processing system, however, it does not maintain a separate file of transactions, which can be useful for archiving (maintaining a historical record) and processing by other programs.

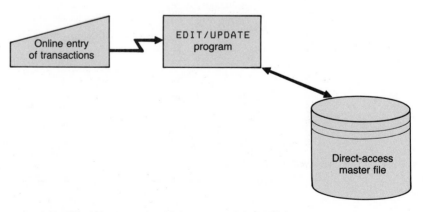

FIGURE 9.15   **Online processing blood donor system (direct-access master file)**

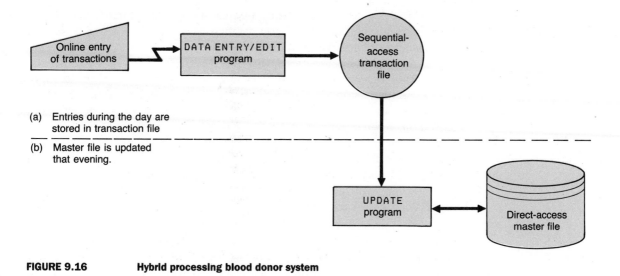

FIGURE 9.16   **Hybrid processing blood donor system**

Method 3: Hybrid Processing System

A third approach to the blood donor system is a combination of batch and online processing. In this case, as transactions occur, they are edited and stored in a sequential-access transaction file by a DATA ENTRY/EDIT program (see Figure 9.16a). Then, at a later date (say, that night) an UPDATE program processes the transaction file against a direct-access master file (see Figure 9.16b).

Note that this approach uses elements of online processing to capture the transactions (compare Figures 9.15 and 9.16a) and features of batch processing to update the master file (compare Figures 9.13b and 9.16b). This approach is less current than the online approach, since the master file is not updated in real time, or immediately; however, it provides a separate transaction file for archiving and use by other programs. We ask you to program these systems in Exercises 21 to 23. (Good luck!)   ■

9.6 PROGRAMMING TIPS

DESIGN AND STYLE

1. **Record layout.** Don't forget to specify the record layout when you analyze the problem and to include this as part of the program's documentation.
2. **Backup files.** The greatest worry in computer installations is the complete loss of a database. The loss of a database through fire, theft, sabotage, or

some other disaster is more damaging than the loss of the hardware system. Hardware is easily replaced, but a database is not easily reconstructed. An integral part of database protection is the backup (duplication) of all existing files. In large organizations, this is not a trivial task. For example, the TWA airline reservation system has 144 magnetic disk spindles for its more than 1 million customer records. Half of these are a backup of the other half. Moreover, on a daily basis, these files are dumped to magnetic tape and stored offsite.[1] For your purposes, it's best either to back up files using your system's copy or save command or to build backup file procedures in programs that manage files (as in Exercises 6e and 8b) and to ensure that you have both backup *data* files and backup *program* files. If you have yet to lose any files, you may not be as nervous as those of us who have been around computers for a while.

3. **Sequential-access versus direct-access files.** Issues regarding which type of file medium and access method to use relate to factors such as speed, cost, the particular application, and the processing environment. For example, a payroll application for a large company within a mainframe environment would typically use sequential-access files on magnetic tape media; an airline reservation inquiry system within a time-shared environment would use direct-access files on magnetic disk media. Generally, we can show that sequential files are best for applications with high file activity, in which all or most records in the file are processed, as in the payroll example; direct-access files are best used for applications requiring low file activity and speedy response, as in airline reservation systems.

4. **Optimization note: Use unformatted I/O whenever possible.** This reduces processor time because there is no conversion from the internal machine representation to characters.

COMMON ERRORS

1. **Mis-opening files.** Make sure that the OPEN statement precedes I/O statements, that file numbers are unique if more than one file is to be open at once, and that you don't inadvertently open an existing file for output (unless you like to see the destruction of file contents). Also, pay attention to the syntax in OPEN statements, especially how they differ with respect to the file types sequential access and relative access.

2. **Specification inconsistency.** Double-check the program for consistency in file/unit characteristics. For example, direct-access processing must have DIRECT for *acc* and a RECL = specifier in the OPEN statement, and a REC = specifier in READ/WRITE statements.

---

[1] David Gifford and Alfred Spector, "The TWA Reservation System," *Communications of the acm*, July 1984, pp. 650–665.

3. Eof errors. Double-check the logic that terminates the processing of sequential-access files. For example, a common error is attempting to read beyond the last record in the file. This execution error is possible when an endfile record is missing from the file. A possible logic error is forgetting to use the END = specifier in a sequential-access READ statement. In this case processing simply stops when the endfile record is encountered, which means that execution never enters any postprocessing logic to which control might have been transferred.

1. Briefly describe the possible makeup of a student grade file for a large (say, 500 students) academic course. What kind of storage medium might be used? Suppose this file is to be used by a menu-driven interactive query program to answer questions such as "What are the current grades for Bob Meyer?" Which type of file would be best, sequential access or direct access? Suppose the application is a program that calculates and assigns final grades and prints a report at the end of each term. Which file type might be best?

2. What file characteristics does the following imply?

   ```
   OPEN (20)
   ```

3. Describe the nature of this statement:

   ```
   WRITE (15)ARC
   ```

   Specify an appropriate OPEN statement such that unit 15 is linked to an existing file called STRESS.

4. Write code to:

   Create a new formatted direct-access file named GRADES that gets connected to unit 20 and has record lengths of 32 characters.

   Interactively input the integer variable student identification (ID), the character variable student name (NAME, with a declared length of 30), and the character variable final letter grade (GRADE, with a declared length of 2).

   Write to the file student name and final grade, using ID as the record number and a FORMAT statement labeled 90.

5. With respect to the examples in Table 9.2:
   a. Write a program that performs the operations described, and run it on your system. Don't forget to place an endfile record on the file. Also, remember to rewind the file before reading in NOTE. Remember to print the contents in NOTE.
   b. Exactly what's on the file? Find out by listing the file TEST.DAT using a system command.
   c. What happens if you try a list-directed read from the file? How would you have to modify the file to accomplish a list-directed read?
   *d. Rework parts a to c using an unformatted file.

6. **Example 9.1.** Change Program `SFILE1` in Figure 9.4 as follows.

    a. Print the number of records processed in the display routine.

    b. Give the option of creating a formatted file or an unformatted file.

    c. Ensure that y/n responses are legitimate.

    d. Can you think of a way to replace the file processing loop in Subroutine `SHOW` with a DO-loop?

    *e. Backup file. Add a subroutine that backs up the employee file under the name `EMPLOYEE.BAK`. Use the following pseudocode.

    ```
    While not eof on original file
        Read record from original file
        Write record to backup file
    End while
    ```

7. **Example 9.2.** Change Program `SFILE2` in Figure 9.7 as follows, or answer the given question.

    a. What would happen if we were to process file `MIN.DAT` on page 130?

    b. Can you think of a loop design that uses `END =` instead of `IOSTAT =`? Any problems with this approach?

    *c. Rewrite the program to display multiple records having the same criterion. Use sex as the criterion. Try a sample run that displays all female records.

    *d. Offer a menu to display records based on the following.

    1. Name
    2. Social security number
    3. Salary upper limit
    4. Sex

*8. **Example 9.3.** Change Program `DFILE1` in Figure 9.9 as follows.

    a. Have the program create the index file for SSN.

    b. Backup File. Create a duplicate file under the name `EMPLOY.BAK`.

*9. **Example 9.4.** Change Program `DFILE2` in Figure 9.11 as follows.

    a. Detect an input error in File 1.

    b. Use `INQUIRE` statements to eliminate as many parameters as you can.

    c. Read the index file into one-dimensional arrays and perform table lookups on the arrays instead of the index file.

*10. **Record number input.** Rewrite the programs in Examples 9.3 and 9.4 using employee ID as record numbers. Interactive input now includes employee ID (up to four digits). Use the following IDs for the three employees in our sample runs: 123, 456, and 789. Does this simplify the programs? Any disadvantage?

*11. **Hashing algorithm.** Hashing is a common technique used to access records in a direct-access file where the record number has more digits than the number of records (storage positions) in the file. For example, the direct use of SS numbers as record numbers would require a file of the order of one billion records, since SS number is a nine-digit number.

    The hashing algorithm converts the record number to a relative record number having a value within the range of the number of records reserved for the file. The location of each record is determined as follows:

1. Convert the record key, via a hashing algorithm, to a relative record number that is within the range 1 to n, where n is the number of records stored in the file. One hashing algorithm divides the record key by the *prime number* [2] closest to n and uses the remainder from the division as the relative record number (the quotient is ignored).[3]

2. Use the relative record number to write the record to (or read the record from) the direct-access file.

Modify the program in Example 9.3 using a hashing algorithm. Assume the employee file contains no more than 100 employees and the social security number is the record number. (*Hint:* Convert the social security number to a two-digit relative record number using the hashing algorithm described above. The prime number closest to 100 is 97.)

ADDITIONAL EXERCISES

12. **Revisit.** Select a program that you have already written and revise it to give the option of output to the screen, line printer (if available), or a file. Make sure you output to a file, then display this file as a report from another program.

13. **Revisit.** Select one of the following applications and appropriately use one or more external files that are opened, processed, and closed within the program.
    a. **Econometric Model.** Exercise 18, Chapter 3.
    b. **SAT Report.** Exercise 15, Chapter 4.
    c. **Quality Control.** Exercise 16, Chapter 4.
    d. **Linear Regression.** Exercise 21, Chapter 4.
    e. **Electric Shock.** Exercise 29, Chapter 5.
    f. **Computer Dating.** Exercise 32, Chapter 5.
    g. **Simulation: pdf Generator.** Exercise 26, Chapter 6.
    h. **Simulation: Stock Market.** Exercise 27, Chapter 6.
    i. **Crime Data.** Exercise 41, Chapter 7.
    j. **Grade Table Lookup.** Exercise 42, Chapter 7.
    k. **Stock Portfolio.** Exercise 49, Chapter 7.
    l. **Questionnaire Analysis.** Exercise 50, Chapter 7.
    m. **Greedy Algorithm: Knapsack Problem.** Exercise 52, Chapter 7.
    n. **Form Letter.** Exercise 37, Chapter 8.

14. **Revisit: Text editor.** Revise the program in Figure 8.3 so that file name is input and the revised text is written to the file. You might also want to take a look at Exercise 43 in Chapter 8.

---

[2] A prime number is a positive integer that is *not* exactly divisible by any positive integer except 1 and itself. For example 2, 3, 5, 7, and 11 are the first five prime numbers.

[3] Remaindering is best accomplished by modulo arithmetic using the MOD function described in Module A. For example, MOD(100,97) would yield the remainder 3.

15. **Alumni file query.** The director of a graduate program wants to compute average salaries of alumni to include in a brochure of past graduates. The director collected the following data on students: name, year graduated, salary on first job after graduation, and prior work experience (y or n).

Alumni File

Name	Year of Graduation	Salary	Work Experience
Dewey	87	29000	y
Epcot	88	43000	y
Farmer	88	0	n
Garner	87	24500	n
Hu	88	30000	n
Jackson	88	34000	y
Kelley	87	32500	y
Moon	88	23000	n
Rodriguez	88	0	y
Silver	88	26000	n
Teller	88	27500	y

a. Develop an interactive query program that computes and prints the average salary for all alumni in a specified graduating year. (*Note:* Not all alumni have submitted salary data; to be part of the average salary computation the salary amount must be greater than 0.) The only input variable is the specified graduating year. Use 87 and 88 as input test data.

b. For graduates of the specified year, also compute and print separate average salaries by work experience versus no work experience.

c. If salary data are unavailable for a given year, print a message to that effect. Use 83 as test input.

d. Offer the following menu.

    D   Display file
    R   Report for given year
    X   eXit program

16. **File maintenance.** Develop a file maintenance program based on one of our employee file examples.

a. **Sequential-access file.** See Examples 9.1 and 9.2.

b. **Direct-access file.** See Examples 9.3 and 9.4.

Offer the following main menu.

    1   Create file
    2   Delete file
    3   Display file or record

4	Modify file
5	Reports
9	Exit program

Provide a submenu under choice 3 that offers a display of the entire file or of selected records. Offer another submenu under choice 4 that gives the following selections.

A	Add record
D	Delete record
C	Change record
X	eXit this menu

Provide a submenu under choice 5 that offers at least two reports. One of these prints average salaries for males and females. Make up the other report(s).

17. **Bond issue.** Write a program that offers the following menu:

C	Create file
A	Append to file
D	Display file
P	Print report
S	Stop processing

a. Create a sequential-access file called BOND with the following records:

County	Yes votes	No votes
Dade	300,000	400,000
Cuyahoga	100,000	75,000
Washington	50,000	30,000

b. Append the following records to the file:

Orange	250,000	100,000
Broward	150,000	75,000

c. Display the revised file.
d. Print a report. You decide what might be nice to include in this report.

18. **Charge card.** Develop a program that prints monthly bills (statements) for Muster Charge, an internationally renowned credit card company. Printout for each person should take up exactly 12 lines in order to conform to the size of the billing statement. Sample input data are described by the table below. A customer's statement should include name, address, previous balance, payments, finance charge, new purchases, new balance, and minimum payment due. Design your own statement, but make sure that it conforms to the 12-line limitation.

Name	Address	Credit Limit	Previous Balance	Payments	New Purchases
Napoleon B.	19 Waterloo St. Paris, France	$ 800	$ 300.00	$ 100.00	$700.00
Duke Welly	1 Thames Ave. London, UK	1500	1350.70	1320.70	645.52
Betsy Ross	1776 Flag St. Boston, MA USA	2000	36.49	36.49	19.15

The following conditions apply to the program.

1. The finance charge is 1.5% of the difference between the previous month's balance and the payments made since the previous month. You should confirm the following new balances for our three sample customers: $903.00, $675.97, and $19.15.

2. The minimum payment due is determined according to one of four results.

   a. If the new balance exceeds the credit limit, then the minimum payment is the difference between the new balance and the credit limit plus 10% of the credit limit. Thus, for the first statement, $(903 - 800) + 10\% \cdot (800)$ gives $183.

   b. If the new balance is $100 or more and does not exceed the credit limit, then the minimum payment is 10% of the new balance. Thus, for the second statement, $10\% \cdot (675.97)$ gives $67.60.

   c. If the new balance is less than $100, then the minimum payment is set to the new balance, or $19.15 for the third statement.

   d. If the new balance is negative, then the minimum payment is zero.

3. A warning is printed if the credit limit is exceeded by the new balance (Muster Charge doesn't fool around). This is the case with the first statement. Use a direct-access master file and a sequential-access transaction file. The master file contains name, address, credit limit, and last billing period's ending (previous) balance for each customer. The transaction file contains name, payments, and new purchases. Think about how you might handle record numbers for the master file. Use the following IDs for the three sample customers: 789, 123, and 456.

   a. Run your program for the data given in the problem so that bills are printed and the master file is updated.

   b. Include the following action codes in the transaction file and program logic.

   1. Change in address
   2. Change in credit limit
   3. Delete customer from master file
   4. Add customer to master file

19. **Electric bill.** Gotham City Electric Company wishes to redesign the computerized bills that it sends to commercial and residential customers. It has announced a citywide contest to determine the best design and FORTRAN program for this purpose.

Input data include the following.

Date data
1. Month (three letters) and day (two digits) for beginning date of monthly billing cycle
2. Month and day for ending date of monthly billing cycle
3. Year (two digits)

Customer data
4. Previous meter reading in kilowatt-hours (up to seven digits)
5. New meter reading in kilowatt-hours
6. Customer rate code (one digit)
7. Past due amount (dollars and cents)
8. Payment since last bill (dollars and cents)
9. Name of customer (up to 20 characters)
10. Street address of customer (up to 20 characters)
11. City, state, and zip code (up to 24 characters)
12. Account number of customer (up to eight digits)

Use a billing cycle from Sep 19 to Oct 18, 1990, and the following sample data per customer.

Previous Reading	New Reading	Rate Code	Past Due Amount	Payment	Name	Street Address	City, State, Zip Code	Account Number
27648	28648	1	60.10	60.10	Make these up	....	....	....
42615	45115	2	45.20	0.00	Make these up	....	....	....
314625	354625	3	3110.00	3110.00	Make these up	....	....	....
615700	695700	3	8000.00	8000.00	Make these up	....	....	....
800500	1025500	3	3000.00	1000.00	Make these up	....	....	....

Rate codes and their corresponding rates per kilowatt-hour (kWh) are explained by the following table.

Rate Code	Rate per kWh (cents)	Comment
1	10.25	Residential, partly electric home
2	9.85	Residential, all electric home
3	8.50	Commercial, usage under 50,000 kWh
3	7.50	Commercial, usage between 50,000 kWh and 100,000 kWh
3	6.50	Commercial, usage above 100,000 kWh

If past due amount less payment is more than zero, then a 1% per month charge on this difference is added to the customer's bill. For example, the last customer in the input data is commercial and used 225,000 kWh (1,025,500 − 800,500).

Thus the customer is charged at 6.5 cents per kWh, which amounts to a current bill of $14,625.00. This customer, however, has a $3000 past due account and payments of only $1000. At an interest rate of 1% per month, the interest charge is $20, that is, $(3000 - 1000) \times 0.01$; hence, the total now due from this customer is $16,645.00, that is, $2000 + 20 + 14,625$.

Output from your program should include the following.

1. Name of customer
2. Street address of customer
3. City, state, and zip code
4. Account number
5. Billing cycle: from (month, day) to (month, day, year)
6. Kilowatt-hours
7. Current amount owed
8. Past due amount
9. Interest charge
10. Total amount due

Label your output and design it to fit within a 3- by 5-inch image, since these statements must fit in a standard size envelope. Use a direct-access master file and a sequential-access transaction file. The master file contains previous reading, rate code, past due amount, name, street address, city, state, zip code, and account number for each customer. In addition to dates, the transaction file contains account number, name, new meter reading, and payments since last bill.

a. Run your program for the data given above so that bills are printed and the master file is updated.

b. Include error detection to ensure that the rate code is 1, 2, or 3 and that the new meter reading is greater than the previous meter reading. If an error is encountered, print an appropriate error message that includes the customer's name, complete address, and account number; bypass the calculations and printout for this customer; space down to the next statement; and go on to the next customer. Add new data to test each of the possible input errors.

c. Include the following action codes in the transaction file and program logic.

1. Change of address
2. Delete customer from master file
3. Add customer to master file

Make up data to test each of these action codes.

Use a modular design for your program. By the way, the winner of the contest gets to ride the Batmobile, which recently was retrofitted with an all-electric turbo power plant.

20. **Airline reservation system.** All major airlines have automated their systems for handling seat reservations. A central computer keeps a record in storage of all relevant information describing the services being sold: flight numbers, flight schedules, seats available, prices, and other data.

A reservation agent can request information on seat availability, can sell seats to passengers (providing seats are available), can cancel reservations (which increases available seats), and, if a flight is full, can put individuals on a waiting list.

a. Design and develop an interactive program to incorporate the following menu options.

1. Update the accompanying flight information table. For example, if a customer requests one tourist reservation on flight number 4, the program should check for available tourist seats. Since one is available, it should then adjust the available tourist seats to zero and print a message such as RESERVATION ALLOWED. If the passenger had requested two seats, however, the program should print RESERVATION DISALLOWED. SORRY, OUR HIGH ETHICAL STANDARDS DO NOT PERMIT US TO OVERBOOK.

2. Retrieve status on a particular flight by printing the appropriate row in the flight information table.

3. Print entire flight information table.

4. Terminate the run.

Use a direct-access file for the current table of flight information. Each table (file) of flight information is based on a specific week for the coming year. Use flight numbers as the record number.

Interactively process the following requests in your computer run.

Option Request	Flight Number	Seat Type	Number of Tickets	Reservation Request
1	4	Tourist	1	Reserve
1	6	Tourist	4	Reserve
2	3	—	—	—
1	9	Tourist	2	Reserve
1	8	1st Class	6	Cancel
1	4	Tourist	2	Reserve
3	—	—	—	—

Current Table of Flight Information

Flight Number	Departing Airport	Arriving Airport	Time of Departure	Time of Arrival	Available Seats First Class	Available Seats Tourist	Seats Sold First Class	Seats Sold Tourist
1	BOS	CHI	0730	0855	20	8	10	75
2	BOS	CHI	1200	1357	20	20	10	50
3	BOS	TOR	0810	1111	30	10	0	120
4	ATL	SF	1145	1604	15	1	25	129
5	CHI	BOS	0645	0948	30	25	5	90
6	CHI	NY	0945	1237	30	8	0	120
7	CHI	LA	1530	1851	20	10	30	60
8	CHI	TOR	1955	2114	5	5	25	85
9	TOR	DEN	1025	1611	10	6	60	60
10	TOR	SF	1435	1556	20	10	10	89

b. Instead of the record numbers in part **a,** use a record number based on the sum of flight number and day code. If the ten flights in the table are numbered 240, 250, 260, 810, 100, 110, 120, 130, 950, and 960 and the days in the week (Monday, Tuesday, . . . , Sunday) are coded 1, 2, . . . , 7, a request for flight 950 on Wednesday would access record number 953, whereas the same flight on Sunday would access record number 957.

c. Besides the options in part **a,** give your program the capability to retrieve and print flight information on all flights between two specified airports. Test your program for flights from Boston to Chicago and Chicago to Los Angeles. In the first case, you should get a printout of the first two rows; in the second case, the seventh row should be printed.

d. Add other useful features. For example, you might want to allow 1% over-booking of seats (a common practice); create a file that stores reservations information such as customer's name, address, and telephone number; create a waiting list file that periodically is processed against the flight table (master) file.

21. Blood donor batch processing system. Write and run the following programs for the batch processing system described in Example 9.5. Use the data given in the example.

a. DATA ENTRY/EDIT. Use the following menu:

C	Create new file
A	Append to existing file
S	Stop processing

Don't forget to design the error routine for valid dates and IDs (max = 999). *Hint:* If you use character values for dates (as shown in the example), then you need to strip off month, date, and year using the methods in Chapter 8; otherwise, use separate numeric values for month, day, and year.

b. SORT. Create the sorted transaction file described earlier. *Hint:* See Section 7.4.

c. UPDATE. Include output of a report of your own choosing. At a minimum, include a summary of transactions by blood type.

d. Add other useful features. For example, UPDATE could include an option to echo print all records in the transaction and master files; DATA ENTRY/ EDIT could include the entry of new donors.

22. Blood donor online processing system. Consider Method 2 in Example 9.5.

a. Write and run the EDIT/UPDATE program. Use the data given in the example. Don't forget to edit the input data for valid dates and record numbers. If an entry is incorrect, prompt the user for a correct entry. See the hint in part **a** of the preceding exercise for the treatment of dates.

b. Include a report as described in part **c** of the preceding exercise.

c. Add other useful features, such as display of the entire master file or selected records or the addition of new donors to the master file.

23. Blood donor hybrid processing system. Consider Method 3 in Example 9.5.

a. Write and run the DATA ENTRY/EDIT program, as in Exercise 21a.

b. Write and run the UPDATE program. Include the report described in Exercise 21c.

c. Add other useful features, such as display of either the entire master file or selected records or the addition of new donors to the master file.

24. **Payroll.** Each week a small firm processes its weekly payroll for hourly employees. The following file input is necessary to process the payroll.

Master Employee File Record Description

Employee ID
Name
Hourly rate of pay
Number of dependents
Cumulative gross pay thus far this year
Cumulative FICA tax thus far this year
Cumulative withholding (income) tax thus far this year
Cumulative group health contribution thus far this year

Master File

1	Bella Bitta, Al	2.50	4	1500.00	112.65	240.00	180.00
2	Budget, Frank	8.25	5	50000.00	3379.50	3900.00	195.00
61	Manicotti, Diane	6.00	1	12300.00	923.73	2706.00	75.00
92	Saintvi, Arun	8.00	3	44800.00	3364.48	5328.00	153.00

Transaction File Record Description

Employee ID
Date
Number of hours worked

Develop a program that

a. Generates a "wage summary report" consisting of a line for each employee: the line contains employee name, employee number, hourly rate, hours worked, gross pay, FICA, income tax, group health, and net pay. After individual figures are printed, the program is to print totals for gross pay, each deduction, and net pay. Include appropriate report and column headings.

To determine the pay for each employee, the following facts must be included in your program:

1. Gross pay is defined as pay for regular time plus pay for overtime. Overtime pay is 1.5 times the regular rate for each hour above 40.

2. Social Security tax (FICA) is 7.51% of gross pay. The deduction is made until the employee's cumulative earnings are above $45,000, after which there is no deduction.

3. Deduction for withholding tax and group health plan are tied to the number of dependents as follows.

Dependents	Income Tax (% of gross pay)	Group Health ($ per week)
1	22	2.50
2	20	3.60
3	18	5.10
4	16	6.00
5 or more	13	6.50

4. Net pay is defined as gross pay less FICA deduction less income tax deduction less group health deduction. Use the data below to test your program.

Transaction File for (date, which you supply)

1	60
2	40
61	45
92	35

b. Updates cumulative gross pay, cumulative FICA tax, cumulative withholding tax, and cumulative group health contribution for each employee in the master file.

c. Run parts **a** and **b** again for the next week using the data below.

Transaction file for (date one week after preceding transaction file)

1	32
2	45
61	35
92	42

d. Design a routine that edits the data for errors. Specifically it ensures that the
   1. Numbers of dependents is greater than zero and less than 15.
   2. Rate of pay is greater than $3.30 and less than $10.00.
   3. Number of hours worked is greater than zero and less than 65.
   4. Total earnings thus far this year is zero or greater or less than $60,000.
   If an error is detected, print an appropriate error message that includes the employee's name and number, bypass the calculations and printout for this employee, and go on to the next employee. Add new data to test each of these four possible input errors.

e. Design your program to include the following menu.

1	Change in hourly rate of pay
2	Change in number of dependents
3	Delete employee from master file
4	Add employee to master file
5	Wage summary report
6	Print transaction file
7	Print master file
8	Stop processing

Make up data to test each of these action codes.

25. **Grades.** Design a comprehensive program that maintains and processes student grades for an academic course. You might include features such as file creation, file modifications (for example, change a grade, add a grade, delete a grade, delete a record, add a record), file display, record display, calculation of final numeric grade based on weights for individual grades (including the assignment of a letter grade if applicable). . . . If a student is added to the file, make sure this student is placed in the correct alphabetic position. Once your program is debugged, hire yourself a marketing major and pedal your program to faculty members for an exorbitant software fee.

A*

INTRINSIC AND STATEMENT FUNCTIONS

This module defines and illustrates intrinsic functions and statement functions.

---

*Study this module anytime after Section 2.6.

A.1 INTRINSIC FUNCTIONS

Suppose we wish to determine the square root of the real arithmetic expression

```
B**2 - 4.0*A*C
```

and to store it in the address labeled Y. The following assignment statement would do this for us, where the exponent on the original arithmetic expression takes the square root.

```
Y = (B**2 - 4.0*A*C)**0.5
```

An alternative approach is to use the following SQRT function:

```
Y = SQRT (B**2 - 4.0*A*C)
```

The right member of this statement is called an **intrinsic function**[1] and has the following general form.

Intrinsic Function

Syntax:
> *Function name (argument list)*

Example:
```
SQRT (B**2 - 4.0*A*C)
```

The **function name** is a keyword that suggests the purpose of the function. In our example, SQRT is the function name, which is an abbreviation for SQuare RooT. The **argument list** is either a single expression or a list of expressions separated by commas. Expressions in the argument list can be character or any of the four numerics, depending on the function. Each expression in the argument list is called an **argument.** In our example, we have a single, real argument given by

```
B**2 - 4.0*A*C
```

Functions operate on their arguments; in this case, the function evaluates the square root of its argument.

---

[1]Another commonly used term is **library function.**

NOTE   The argument list of an intrinsic function is *always* enclosed in parentheses; multiple arguments are *always* separated by commas.

Table A.1 shows intrinsic functions in FORTRAN 77, which we group into three categories for greater simplicity: numeric, character or logical. We use numeric functions throughout the book, and illustrate character and logical functions in Chapter 8.

First, take a look at the intrinsic functions in Table A.1, their descriptions, number of arguments, and the types of arguments and functions. Then note the following points, and try Exercise 1.

1. **Function Call.** The intrinsic function is referenced, or called, by using its function name followed by the parenthetically enclosed argument list. For example, if A stores 10.0, B stores 7.0, and C stores 1.0 in the function call

   ```
   SQRT (B**2 - 4.0*A*C)
   ```

   then the argument is evaluated as 9.0, and the SQRT function evaluates to or returns the value 3.0. Intrinsic functions typically appear ("make their calls") in expressions (character, logical, numeric) and output lists.

2. **Types.** The type of the arguments (all arguments in the argument list must be the same type) usually determines the type of the value returned by the function. For example, the MAX function returns a *real* value if its arguments are *real*. Exceptions necessarily include the numeric-type conversion functions (INT, REAL, DBLE, and CMPLX), the NINT function (which always returns an integer value), the ABS and AIMAG functions (which return a real value when the argument is complex), the DPROD function, the character functions, and the logical functions.

NOTE   Pay attention to type, as described in the last two columns of Table A.1, and make sure all arguments in the argument list are the same type.

3. **Where did the functions come from?** The instructions for evaluating the function are in the FORTRAN Library, which includes machine language code for standard instructions like READ, PRINT, and all intrinsic functions. For example, to find the natural logarithm of a number, we would use the LOG function. When the compiler processes the LOG function, it flags the location for the proper FORTRAN Library instruction. Before the object program is executed, a program called the linker provides or links the set of prewritten instructions that calculates the natural logarithm of the argument.

4. **Motivation for Use.** The use of intrinsic functions within our programs has several advantages.

   a. For certain standardized tasks, as in calculating logarithms, we save programming effort by not having to "reinvent the wheel" (write these in-

TABLE A.1   Intrinsic Functions[a]

Category	Name	Description/Example/Return Value	Number of Arguments	Type of Arguments	Type of Function
Numeric	ABS	Absolute value of argument ABS(5) ← 5 ABS(-5) ← 5	1	Integer Real Double Complex	Integer Real Double Real
	ACOS	Arccosine (in radians) of argument ACOS(0.5) ← 1.04720 (= π/3)	1	Real Double	Real Double
	AIMAG	Imaginary part of argument AIMAG(-8.30, 3.21) ← 3.21	1	Complex	Real
	AINT	Truncation (whole number part) of argument AINT(7.8) ← 7.0 AINT(-7.8) ← -7.0 AINT(0.6) ← 0.0 AINT(-0.6) ← 0.0	1	Real Double	Real Double
	ANINT	Nearest (within 0.5) whole number of argument ANINT(7.8) ← 8.0 ANINT(-7.8) ← -8.0 ANINT(0.6) ← 1.0 ANINT(-0.6) ← -1.0	1	Real Double	Real Double
	ASIN	Arcsine (in radians) of argument ASIN(0.5) ← 0.523599 (=π/6)	1	Real Double	Real Double
	ATAN	Arctangent (in radians) of argument ATAN(1.0) ← 0.785398 (=π/4)	1	Real Double	Real Double
	ATAN2	Arctangent (in radians) of argument1/argument2 ATAN2(6.0, 3.0) ← 1.10715	2	Real Double	Real Double
	CMPLX	Conversion of argument to complex CMPLX(4) ← (4.0, 0.0) CMPLX(4,3) ← (4.0, 3.0)	1,2	Integer Real Double Complex	Complex Complex Complex Complex
	CONJG	Conjugate of argument CONJG((-8.30, 3.21)) ← (-8.30, -3.21)	1	Complex	Complex
	COS	Cosine of argument (in radians) PI = 3.14159 COS (PI/3.0) ← 0.5	1	Real Double Complex	Real Double Complex
	COSH	Hyperbolic cosine of argument PI = 3.14159 COSH (PI) ← 11.5920	1	Real Double	Real Double
	DBLE	Conversion of argument to double precision DBLE(5) ← 0.5D+01 DBLE((3,4)) ← 0.3D+01	1	Integer Real Double Complex	Double Double Double Double

TABLE A.1   *(continued)*

Category	Name	Description/Example/Return Value	Number of Arguments	Type of Arguments	Type of Function
	DIM	Positive difference of argument1 less argument2 DIM(5,3) ← 2 DIM(3,5) ← 0	2	Integer Real Double	Integer Real Double
	DPROD	Double-precision product of real arguments DPROD(5.0,3.0) ← 0.15D+02	2	Real	Double
	EXP	Exponential $e^{argument}$ EXP(-2.0) ← 0.1353353	1	Real Double Complex	Real Double Complex
	INT	Type conversion and truncation of argument INT(7.8) ← 7 INT(-7.8) ← -7 INT(0.6) ← 0 INT(-0.6) ← 0 INT((-8.30,3.21)) ← -8	1	Integer Real Double Complex	Integer Integer Integer Integer
	LOG	Natural (base e) logarithm of argument LOG(0.1353353) ← -2.0	1	Real Double Complex	Real Double Complex
	LOG10	Common (base 10) logarithm of argument LOG10(10.0) ← 1.0	1	Real Double	Real Double
	MAX	Maximum value in argument list MAX(3,6,4) ← 6	≥2	Integer Real Double	Integer Real Double
	MIN	Minimum value in argument list MIN(3,6,4) ← 3	≥2	Integer Real Double	Integer Real Double
	MOD	Modulo arithmetic, or remaindering of arguments mod(arg1,arg2) = arg1 − int(arg1/arg2)*arg2 MOD(5,3) ← 2	2	Integer Real Double	Integer Real Double
	NINT	Nearest (within 0.5) integer of argument NINT(7.8) ← 8 NINT(-7.8) ← -8 NINT(0.6) ← 1 NINT(-0.6) ← -1	1	Real Double	Integer Integer
	REAL	Type conversion of argument to real REAL(7) ← 7.0 REAL((-8.3,3.21)) ← -8.3	1	Integer Real Double Complex	Real Real Real Real
	SIGN	Transfer of sign: abs(arg1) if arg2 ≥ 0 −abs(arg1) if arg2 < 0 SIGN(-4,8) ← 4 SIGN(-4,-8) ← -4	2	Integer Real Double	Integer Real Double
	SIN	Sine of argument (in radians) PI = 3.14159 SIN(PI/6.0) ← 0.5	1	Real Double Complex	Real Double Complex

TABLE A.1   *(continued)*

Category	Name	Description/Example/Return Value	Number of Arguments	Type of Arguments	Type of Function

	SINH	Hyperbolic sine of argument
		
		`PI = 3.14159`
		`SINH(PI) ← 11.5487`
			1	Real
				Double
					Real
					Double

	SQRT	Square root of argument `SQRT(9.0) ← 3.0`	1	Real Double Complex	Real Double Complex

	TAN	Tangent of argument (in radians)
		
		`PI = 3.14159`
		`TAN(PI/4.0) ← 1.0`
			1	Real
				Double
					Real
					Double

	TANH	Hyperbolic tangent of argument
		
		`PI = 3.14159`
		`TANH(PI) ← 0.996272`
			1	Real
				Double
					Real
					Double

Character	CHAR	Character in position of collating sequence given by argument
		
		`CHAR(65) ← A   CHAR(66) ← B`
		`CHAR(97) ← a   CHAR(98) ← b`
			1	Integer	Character

	ICHAR	Position of argument in collating sequence
		
		`ICHAR('A') ← 65   ICHAR('B') ← 66`
		`ICHAR('a') ← 97   ICHAR('b') ← 98`
			1	Character	Integer

	INDEX	Starting position of argument2 within argument1
		
		`INDEX('I love FORTRAN', 'FORTRAN') ← 8`
		`INDEX('I love FORTRAN', 'forever') ← 0`
			2	Character	Integer

	LEN	Length of character value in argument `LEN('I love FORTRAN') ← 14`	1	Character	Integer

Logical	LGE	True if argument1 follows or equals argument2 in the ASCII collating sequence; false otherwise
		
		`LGE('A','A') ← T   LGE('A','B') ← F`
		`LGE('B','A') ← T`
			2	Character	Logical

	LGT	True if argument1 follows argument2 in the ASCII collating sequence; false otherwise
		
		`LGT('A','A') ← F   LGT('A','B') ← F`
		`LGT('B','A') ← T`
			2	Character	Logical

TABLE A.1   (continued)

Category	Name	Description/Example/Return Value	Number of Arguments	Type of Arguments	Type of Function
	LLE	True if argument1 precedes or equals argument2 in the ASCII collating sequence; false otherwise	2	Character	Logical
		LLE('A','A') ← T LLE('A','B') ← T LLE('B','A') ← F			
	LLT	True if argument1 precedes argument2 in the ASCII collating sequence; false otherwise	2	Character	Logical
		LLT('A','A') ← F LLT('A','B') ← T LLT('B','A') ← F			

[a]All intrinsic functions have the form name (argument list), where arguments in the argument list are separated by commas. All arguments within an argument list are of the same type.

structions ourselves) each time we wish to perform the same standardized task.

b. Prewritten systems instructions for evaluating intrinsic functions are most likely more computationally efficient and accurate than those that might be written by the programmer in a high-level language like FORTRAN. For example, a SQRT function requires less processing time than raising an expression to the 0.5 power.

c. The use of an intrinsic function is stylistically preferred, since the task usually suggested by the function name is well understood by a programmer reading its listing.

A.2 STATEMENT FUNCTIONS

At times we need access to a function that is not included in the computer's set of intrinsic functions, in which case we can define our own function. Functions defined by programmers are called **statement functions.**

EXAMPLE A.1

ROUNDING FUNCTION

A procedure for rounding a numeric value to any number of decimal places is useful in list-directed output[2] A general arithmetic expression for rounding a real or double-precision numeric value is

---

[2]Module B shows another approach for format-directed output

```
ANINT (VALUE * 10.0**PLACES) / 10.00**PLACES
```

where VALUE = value to be rounded

PLACES = number of places to right of decimal point

If VALUE stores 5.916 and PLACES stores 2, then the arithmetic expression is evaluated as follows.

1. The value 5.916 is multiplied by 100.0 (or 10^2), giving 591.6. We now have

```
ANINT (591.6) / 10.0**PLACES
```

2. The denominator is evaluated as 100.0, leaving

```
ANINT (591.6) / 100.0
```

3. The intrinsic function ANINT rounds the argument to the nearest whole number expressed as a *real* value, giving

```
592.0 / 100.0
```

4. The value 592.0 is divided by 100.0, giving

```
5.92
```

Thus, the original value 5.916 has been rounded (not truncated) to two decimal places, as required.

To better understand this rounding procedure, go through each step for each of the following: round 5.912 to two places, giving 5.91; round −6.7 to zero places, giving −7.0.

Figure A.1 illustrates this rounding procedure through a statement function. Note that the statement function named ROUND is defined early in the program and referenced nine times in the PRINT statements. At this time, don't worry about the exact details of how this function works, since we discuss this next. Note, however, that its use in the PRINT statements is identical to our use of intrinsic functions. ■

The **statement function statement** has the general form

Statement Function Statement

Syntax:

       Function name (dummy argument list) = expression

Example:

```
ROUND (VALUE,PLACES) = ANINT (VALUE * 10.0**PLACES) / 10.0**PLACES
```

The function name is any legitimate FORTRAN name. ROUND is the function name in the example. The dummy argument list enclosed in parentheses is a list

```
        PROGRAM PLACE
* * * * * * * * * * * * * * * * * * * * * * * * * * * * * * * * * * *
*                                                                   *
*        Statement Function Demo:  Decimal Place Rounding           *
*                                                                   *
*          Inputs number                                            *
*          Calculates natural, common logs and square root          *
*          Outputs rounded calculations                             *
*                                                                   *
*          Key:                                                     *
*                                                                   *
*             HEAD..... Table heading                               *
*             LINE..... Table line                                  *
*             LOGC..... Common log of input number                  *
*             LOGN..... Natural log of input number                 *
*             NUMBER... Input number                                *
*             PLACES... Number of places to right of decimal point  *
*             ROUND.... Statement function name                     *
*             ROOT..... Square root of input number                 *
*             VALUE.... Value being rounded                         *
*                                                                   *
* * * * * * * * * * * * * * * * * * * * * * * * * * * * * * * * * * *
*————————————————————————————————————————————————————————————————————
*  Type names
*————————
        CHARACTER HEAD*70, LINE*70
        INTEGER   PLACES
        REAL      LOGC, LOGN, NUMBER, ROUND, ROOT, VALUE
*————————————————————————————————————————————————————————————————————
*  Statement function
*———————————————————
        ROUND (VALUE,PLACES) = ANINT (VALUE * 10.0**PLACES) / 10.0**PLACES
*————————————————————————————————————————————————————————————————————
*  Initialize table parts
*———————————————————————
        HEAD = '              Zero Places    One Place    Two Places'
        LINE = '—————————————————————————————————————————————————————'
*————————————————————————————————————————————————————————————————————
*  Input data
*————————
        PRINT *,'Enter number'
        READ *, NUMBER
*————————————————————————————————————————————————————————————————————
*  Calculations
*————————————
        LOGC = LOG10 (NUMBER)
        LOGN = LOG   (NUMBER)
        ROOT = SQRT  (NUMBER)
*————————————————————————————————————————————————————————————————————
*  Output table
*————————————
        PRINT *, LINE
        PRINT *, HEAD
        PRINT *, LINE
        PRINT *,'Common log ', ROUND(LOGC,0), ROUND(LOGC,1), ROUND(LOGC,2)
        PRINT *,'Natural log', ROUND(LOGN,0), ROUND(LOGN,1), ROUND(LOGN,2)
        PRINT *,'Square root', ROUND(ROOT,0), ROUND(ROOT,1), ROUND(ROOT,2)
        PRINT *, LINE
*————————————————————————————————————————————————————————————————————
        END


Enter number
35
```

	Zero Places	One Place	Two Places
Common log	2.00000	1.50000	1.54000
Natural log	4.00000	3.60000	3.56000
Square root	6.00000	5.90000	5.92000

FIGURE A.1   Listing and run of statement function demo

of variable names delimited by commas. Variables in the dummy argument list, called dummy variables , act as placeholders for the actual values supplied each time the function is used. The dummy variables in the example are VALUE and PLACES . When the function is referenced or called , values for the dummy variables are supplied to the function (we'll explain just how in a moment). These values are then used to evaluate the expression to the right of the assignment operator. The expression is any valid expression, character, logical, or numeric. This expression includes dummy arguments, and it may also use other names, intrinsic functions, and statement functions in the program. Our sample expression is a real arithmetic expression, and uses the dummy variables VALUE and PLACES, the intrinsic function ANINT, and the real constant 10.0.

Once the statement function is defined, it can be used (called or referenced) anywhere in the program. The following describes the **function call** or **function reference**.

Function Reference or Call

Syntax:
> *Function name (actual argument list)*

Example:
> ROUND (ROOT, 2)

The actual argument list is a list of names, expressions, and other function calls separated by commas. The actual arguments describe the values that get "passed" to the statement function; that is, the statement function uses the corresponding actual arguments in place of its own dummy arguments. In the example, if ROOT stores 5.916080, then the function reference works as follows.

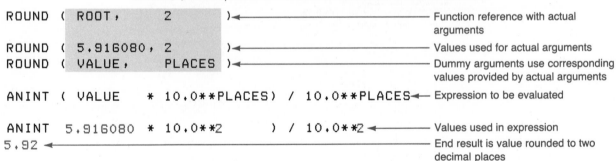

```
ROUND ( ROOT,        2      )◄──────────────────────── Function reference with actual
                                                        arguments
ROUND ( 5.916080, 2         )◄──────────────────────── Values used for actual arguments
ROUND ( VALUE,       PLACES )◄──────────────────────── Dummy arguments use corresponding
                                                        values provided by actual arguments

ANINT ( VALUE   * 10.0**PLACES) / 10.0**PLACES◄──────── Expression to be evaluated

ANINT  5.916080 * 10.0**2        ) / 10.0**2 ◄───────── Values used in expression
5.92 ◄────────────────────────────────────────────────End result is value rounded to two
                                                        decimal places
```

Take a look at the output in Figure A.1. This is the last printed value in the table, 5.92, or the square root of 35 rounded to two decimal places.

The following points should further help you understand statement functions.

1. Placement of statement function. Statement functions follow PARAME-TER, type, and other specification statements, and precede all executable statements. (See the general program composition described inside the book's covers.)

2. **Argument lists correspondence.** Actual arguments must agree in order, number, and type with corresponding dummy arguments. For example, if the dummy argument list has five real variables, then the actual argument list must have five real arguments. If the dummy argument list has a real variable followed by an integer variable, then the actual argument list must have a real argument followed by an integer argument, as in function ROUND. Also, don't forget to pay attention to order. For example, when we call function ROUND we want to make sure that the value is first and the number of decimal places is second in our actual argument list, since that's the ordering in the dummy argument list of function ROUND.

3. **Optional argument lists.** Argument lists are optional, and can be omitted if not needed. For example,

```
PI () = 3.14159
```

defines a function whose value is π. We prefer PI as a named constant that is specified in a PARAMETER statement.

4. **Type function names.** Don't forget to type the name of the function and names in the dummy argument list.

5. **Name scope.** The scope of dummy argument names is restricted to the statement function itself. In other words, dummy arguments have meaning only within the statement function itself, and have no relevance elsewhere in the program. In the program of Figure A.1, for example, we could have used the name VALUE elsewhere in the program to mean something else. We don't recommend this practice, however, since it degrades program readability. Are you ready for this? The scope of names elsewhere in the program includes the statement function. For instance, in the program of Figure A.1 we could take the variable VALUE out of the dummy argument list, keep it in the function statement expression, and assign its value elsewhere in the program. In other words, we don't need to pass the value in VALUE through the argument lists. Indeed, in many applications, we could do the same with PLACES, altogether eliminating the dummy arguments in the rounding function (see item 3 above). This practice also degrades program readability, so we don't recommend it.

6. **Why statement functions?** Coding efficiency is the main motivation for using statement functions. For example, function ROUND is referenced nine times in Figure A.1. Without the function statement, we would have to repeat that rather elaborate rounding expression nine times within the PRINT statements. A secondary motivation is style. It's easier to read program listings with multiple function calls than program listings that otherwise would have complicated expressions in place of every call.

A.3 PROGRAMMING TIPS

DESIGN AND STYLE

1. **Use intrinsic functions.** Don't write your own code to accomplish what an intrinsic function can accomplish. For example, we could easily write our own code for taking square roots, evaluating exponentials, and (with the material in Chapter 4) finding our own absolute values, maximum values, and minimum values. The use of intrinsic functions, however, improves readability, simplifies coding, increases computational efficiency, and increases the likelihood of accurate results.

2. **Naming dummy arguments.** To prevent confusion, variables used as dummy arguments should not appear elsewhere in the program.

3. **Documentation.** Improve the readability of programs by documenting the names of function statements and their dummy variables. Also, clearly set off function statements from surrounding statements, as done in Figure A.1.

COMMON ERRORS

1. **Function statement placement.** Remember that function statements follow PARAMETER and type statements, and precede all executable statements. Function statements themselves are nonexecutable. They are evaluated by the executable statements that invoke the function calls.

2. **Nonconcurrence of arguments.** Make sure that the number, order, and type of actual arguments in a function call correspond to the number, order, and type of dummy arguments in the function statement. Also, don't forget to type dummy variables and function names.

FOLLOW-UP EXERCISES

*1.   **Table A.1.** Write a program that confirms the following examples in Table A.1.
   a. The rounding functions AINT, ANINT, INT, and NINT.
   b. The arithmetic functions EXP, LOG, LOG10, and SQRT.
   c. The miscellaneous functions DIM, DPROD, MAX, MIN, MOD, and SIGN.
   d. The type functions DBLE and REAL.
   e. The trigonometric functions COS, SIN, TAN, ACOS, ASIN, ATAN, and ATAN2.
   f. The character functions CHAR, ICHAR, INDEX, and LEN. (Don't forget to enclose character values in quotes.)
   g. The logical functions LGE, LGT, LLE, and LLT. (Don't forget to enclose character values in quotes.)

   h. The complex functions AIMAG, CMPLX, and CONJG.

   i. The hyperbolic functions COSH, SINH, and TANH.

2. **Rounding Function.** Modify the program in Figure A.1 as follows.

   a. Discuss the implications of using NINT in place of ANINT. How about using INT? AINT?

   b. Eliminate the variables LOGC, LOGN, and ROOT by incorporating their calculation in the call of function ROUND. Which approach do you prefer, and why?

ADDITIONAL EXERCISES

3. **HC ENGINEoil.** Modify Program EUCLID on page 60 to round all distance output to two decimal places. Run the revised program.

4. **Polynomial.** Consider the third-degree polynomial function

$$f(x) = b_0 + b_1 x + b_2 x^2 + b_3 x^3$$

   a. Write a program that interactively inputs the coefficients of this function, and the endpoints (left and right) over an x-interval. The program then outputs an x–y table of coordinates for the left point, the midpoint, and the right point of the interval. Use a statement function for $f(x)$, and try the following test data.

$$f(x) = 250 - 6x^2 + x^3$$

	x	y
Left point	18.0	4138.00
Midpoint	20.0	5850.00
Right point	22.0	7994.00

   b. Include function ROUND in this program. Output all values to one decimal place. In addition to the above test data, try the function

$$f(x) = 1.25 + 3.12x - 0.55x^2$$

over the x-interval with endpoints 2 and 5.

B*

OUTPUT FORMATS

The style of output called list-directed output first described in Section 2.5 is convenient for beginning programmers and for problems requiring simple or "quick-and-dirty" output. Many applications, however, require more elaborate and precise output designs, or **output formats.** Examples include the printing of real numbers to two decimal places (without trailing zeros), the proper alignment of decimals in columns of numbers, the printing of invoices, and the output of graphics with annotated text.

This module describes methods that precisely position output data according to output formats designed by the programmer. This style of output is called **format-directed output.** Let's start with a familiar example.

---

*Study this module anytime after Section 3.3.

EXAMPLE B.1

HC ENGINEERING WITH OUTPUT FORMATS

Program ENG3 in Figure B.1 is a rewrite of Program ENG2 in Figure 3.9, based on the following changes.

- The output is redesigned as a standard table, with head, body, and foot. The head and foot are printed through format-directed output, thereby eliminating the use of the character variables TITLE and LINE in the original program.

- The body of the table is printed by a single PRINT statement that uses format-directed output. Note the precise alignment of numeric output, particularly the readability of engine size expressed to one decimal place.

- Check out the PRINT statements in the program. Each uses a statement label that identifies the specific FORMAT statement that describes the exact placement of output for that PRINT statement. These nonexecutable FORMAT statements are grouped together at the end of the program.

At this time, don't be concerned with the specifics of format-directed output, since the rest of this module describes FORMAT statements in detail. Just focus on the "overall picture" described above, note how this program differs visually from its predecessor, and realize that we now control the exact placement of data on the printed line (through those tedious-looking FORMAT statements). ■

```
      PROGRAM ENG3
* * * * * * * * * * * * * * * * * * * * * * * * * * * * * * * *
*                                                             *
*        Harvey CORE ENGINEering Corporation:   Version 3.0   *
*                                                             *
*          Inputs engine name, size (cc), price, units from data file *
*          Calculates engine size (ci), sales, total sales   *
*          Outputs engine name, size (ci), sales, total sales using *
*            output formats                                   *
*          Uses DO-loop to process all data in one run        *
*                                                             *
*          Data file structure:                               *
*            Number of engine types                           *
*            Name  size(cc)  price   units   <=== 1st engine type *
*            Name  size(cc)  price   units   <=== 2nd engine type *
*            ...                                               *
*                                                             *
*          Key:                                               *
*            METCON... Metric conversion parameter (cc = 0.06102 ci) *
*            NAME..... Engine name                            *
*            NUMBER... Number of engine types processed       *
*            PRICE.... Engine price in $ per unit             *
*            SALES.... Sales in $                             *
*            SIZECC... Engine size in cubic centimeters (cc)  *
*            SIZECI... Engine size in cubic inches (ci)       *
*            TOTAL.... Total sales in $                       *
*            TYPE..... Engine type DO-variable                *
*            UNITS.... Number of engines sold in units        *
*                                                             *
* * * * * * * * * * * * * * * * * * * * * * * * * * * * * * * *
*------------------------------------------------------------
*  Type variables
*------------------------------------------------------------
      CHARACTER NAME*20
      INTEGER   NUMBER, PRICE, SALES, TOTAL, TYPE, UNITS
      REAL      METCON, SIZECC, SIZECI
*------------------------------------------------------------
*  Declare parameters
*------------------------------------------------------------
      PARAMETER (METCON = 0.06102)
*------------------------------------------------------------
*  Initialize
*------------------------------------------------------------
      TOTAL = 0
*------------------------------------------------------------
```

FIGURE B.1   **HC ENGINEering with output formats (*continued on next page*)**

```
*   Print table head
*────────────────────
        PRINT 900
        PRINT 910  ◄──────────────────────── Print table head; see
        PRINT 920                             output below
        PRINT 910
*──────────────────────────────────────────
*   Process data file and print table body
*────────────────────────────────────────────
        READ (5,*) NUMBER

        DO 100 TYPE = 1, NUMBER

          READ (5,*) NAME, SIZECC, PRICE, UNITS

          SIZECI = METCON * SIZECC

          SALES  = PRICE  * UNITS

          TOTAL  = TOTAL  + SALES

          PRINT 930, NAME, SIZECI, SALES  ◄──── Print table body;
                                                 see output below
    100 CONTINUE
*──────────────────────────────────────────
*   Print table foot
*────────────────────
        PRINT 910  ◄──────────────────────── Print table foot;
        PRINT 940, TOTAL                      see output below
*──────────────────────────────────────────
*   Output formats                           Used by PRINT statements to
*────────────────                            position output

    900 FORMAT ( ' ', 20X, '          SALES REPORT' )

    910 FORMAT ( ' ', 20X, '══════════════════════════════')

    920 FORMAT ( ' ', 20X, ' Name              Size (ci)      Sales ')

    930 FORMAT ( ' ', 21X, A20, F8.1, I14 )

    940 FORMAT ( ' ', 20X, '          Total sales.......... $', I9 )
*──────────────────────────────────────────
        END
```

```
3
'Baby Two'     7000   3000   1500
'Momma Four'   8500   4000   2000
'Poppa Six'   10000   5500   1000
```

		SALES REPORT	
Head	Name	Size (ci)	Sales
Body	Baby Two	427.1	4500000
	Momma Four	518.7	8000000
	Poppa Six	610.2	5500000
Foot	Total sales..........		$ 18000000

FIGURE B.1   *(continued)*

B.1 PRINT, WRITE, AND FORMAT STATEMENTS

The precise control of printing[1] is usually accomplished by pairing a PRINT or WRITE statement with a FORMAT statement. The general syntax of PRINT and WRITE[2] statements is now given by the following.

PRINT Statement: Format Directed

Syntax:

    PRINT *format identifier , output list*

Example:

    PRINT 930, NAME, SIZECI, SALES

WRITE Statement: Format Directed

Syntax:

    WRITE (*external unit identifier , format identifier*) *output list*

Example:

    WRITE (*, 930) NAME, SIZECI, SALES

The external unit identifier in the WRITE statement is either an integer expression (usually a numeric constant) for one of the system's output units (terminal, printer, and so on) or an * for the system's standard output unit (usually the terminal). The PRINT statement assumes use of the system's standard output unit. The format identifier identifies a format as a statement label, an integer variable that stores a statement label, a character expression, or a character array name (Chapter 7). The example uses 930 as the format identifier, which is the statement label for one of the formats at the end of Program ENG3 in Figure B.1. As before, the output list is one or more of the following items separated by commas: constant, variable, expression, array name (Chapter 7), array element name (Chapter 7), or character substring name (Chapter 8). To summarize the given example, we wish to print the values in NAME, SIZECI, and SALES through the standard output unit according to the format described by the FORMAT statement labeled 930.

The FORMAT statement is used to describe the output format, or exactly how printed output is to appear.

---

[1] We will use the term print in a general sense to mean output to an output device, as does the ANSI standard. Thus, we not only print to a printer, but also "print" to a video screen, disk drive, or plotter.

[2] A more elaborate (and final) version of the WRITE statement is given in Chapter 9.

FORMAT Statement

Syntax:

> *statement label* FORMAT *format specification*

Example:

> 930 FORMAT (' ', 21X, A20, F8.1, I14)

The statement label is an unsigned, nonzero integer constant up to five digits that uniquely identifies the FORMAT statement. It *must* be placed in positions 1–5 of the program line. In the example, the statement label is 930. This is the FORMAT statement used by the PRINT 930 statement in the earlier example and in Program ENG3 in Figure B.1. Note that the statement label is what *links* a particular PRINT or WRITE statement to its format. The format specification is the parenthetical expression following the keyword FORMAT. It specifies the necessary editing for printed output. For example, we can specify the type, positioning, and length of output values, among other things. The items inside the parentheses in the sample format specification are called edit descriptors, which we take up in the next section. Note that commas are used to delimit the edit descriptors.

NOTE   FORMAT statements are *nonexecutable,* so we have wide latitude on their placement within programs. (See the composition of programs inside the text cover.) We prefer to place all FORMAT statements in a group at the end of the program, as done in Figure B.1. This improves the readability of programs in several ways: The FORMAT statements are easy to find; they are "out of the way" of a visual reading of the execution logic; and we can align our output better, since related format specifications are right under each other (see the first three FORMAT statements that describe the table head in Figure B.1).

The format specification need not be supplied through the FORMAT statement. As mentioned earlier (did you catch it?), the format identifier in the PRINT or WRITE statement can be a character expression. In our example, we could have written the format specification directly into the PRINT statement using a character constant for the format identifier, as follows.

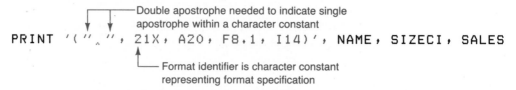

Except for simple output, we generally don't prefer this approach, since it degrades the readability of PRINT statements.

We can also use a character variable to store the format specification, as the following illustrates.

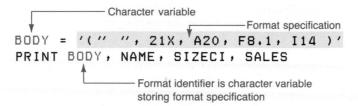

Stylistically, this is a nice approach because the PRINT statement now suggests what it's printing (the BODY of the table). Moreover, all character variables storing format specifications can be grouped in the same place (early in the program) for better readability. (See Exercise 14.)

We also mentioned earlier that format identifiers can be integer variables. The ASSIGN statement is an *executable* statement that assigns a statement label to an integer variable, as follows.

ASSIGN Statement

Syntax:
          ASSIGN *statement label* TO *integer variable*
Example:
          ASSIGN   930   TO   BODY

The PRINT statement in our example thus would be rewritten as

          PRINT BODY, NAME, SIZECI, SALES

                    └──── Integer variable as format identifier

which better describes the purpose of this PRINT statement as the printing of the table body.

NOTE   The distinction between the integer variable BODY and its use in the earlier example as a character variable is important. The *integer variable* BODY stores a statement label that references the FORMAT statement containing the format specification; the *character variable* BODY stores the format specification itself, thereby eliminating the need for the FORMAT statement. We prefer the character-variable approach because of its simplicity and readability. (We ask you to reconsider this issue in Exercise 14.)

B.2 SELECTED EDIT DESCRIPTORS

Edit descriptors are used in format specifications to edit the output. In this section we present the more commonly used edit descriptors.

APOSTROPHE EDIT DESCRIPTOR: CONTROL AND TEXTUAL OUTPUT

The apostrophe edit descriptor is a character constant that's used as either vertical spacing control for an output device or output of textual matter like table heads. It has the following form.

Apostrophe Edit Descriptor

Syntax:
        'character string'
Example:
        `'Turbo computer:'`

Control Character.   The first edit descriptor in the format specification is used by printers and other output devices to control vertical spacing, or movement of the carriage in the case of a printer. In using the apostrophe edit descriptor to control printer movement, we enclose a **control character** within the apostrophes. Table B.1 describes the common control characters. To illustrate, consider the two versions below of the first FORMAT statement in Figure B.1.

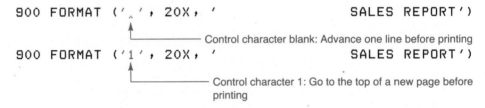

```
900 FORMAT (' ', 20X, '          SALES REPORT')
```
—— Control character blank: Advance one line before printing
```
900 FORMAT ('1', 20X, '          SALES REPORT')
```
—— Control character 1: Go to the top of a new page before printing

NOTE   Systems differ in their treatment of control characters, depending on the system and the output device. For example, output to a terminal may ignore printer control characters altogether, or interpret them as textual matter to be printed. Output to other devices (like a robot arm or a plotter) may use altogether different control characters. Our format specifications will *always* account for output device control as the first descriptor in the format specification, for greater gener-

TABLE B.1   **Control Characters**

Control Character	Output Device Effect
+	Do not advance before printing (hold the line)
Blank space	Advance one line before printing (single or normal spacing)
0	Advance two lines before printing (double spacing)
1	Go to the top of a new page before printing

ality and awareness. Check with your instructor or system's manual for the control character treatment on your system.

Textual Matter.   The apostrophe edit descriptor is most commonly used to output textual matter like report titles, table heads, and labeling. The character string within the apostrophes is printed exactly as it appears. For example, the apostrophe edit descriptor

```
'Turbo computer:'
```

within a format specification would output Turbo computer: as a label. Check out FORMATs 900, 910, 920, and 940 in Program ENG3 on page 506 and the corresponding output for other examples of the apostrophe edit descriptor.

X EDIT DESCRIPTOR: BLANK OUTPUT AND CONTROL

The X edit descriptor inserts blank characters in the printed line. Its general form is

X Edit Descriptor

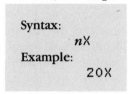

Syntax:
$$nX$$
Example:
$$20X$$

where n is the number of inserted blanks. In the example, 20 blanks get printed. In Program ENG3 of Figure B.1 we used the following statement.

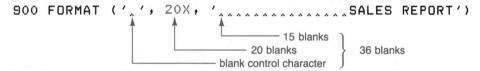

```
900 FORMAT ('.', 20X, '...............SALES REPORT')
```

— 15 blanks
— 20 blanks   } 36 blanks
— blank control character

Implementation of this format specification proceeds as follows, reading from left to right. First, a blank control character is used for single-spaced output device control. Next, 20 blank characters are printed, starting at the left margin. Finally, 15 blank characters followed by the title SALES REPORT are printed. Since the descriptor 1X is equivalent to a blank character, we could have written the following equivalent format specification.

```
900 FORMAT (36X, 'SALES REPORT')
```

— Equivalent to the 36 blanks specified in preceding example

In this example, an output device like a printer would take the "1st X" to mean blank control character, and use the remaining "35 Xs" to print 35 blanks.

NOTE The descriptors 1X and ' ' at the beginning of a format specification are alternative ways of indicating a **blank control character** for the output device.

A EDIT DESCRIPTOR: CHARACTER OUTPUT

The A edit descriptor is used to output character values (strings). It has two alternative forms.

A Edit Descriptor

Syntax:
    A or A*w*

Example:
    A   A20

where *w* is the **field width** or number of print positions used for the output string. In general, the portion of a print line allocated to a printed value is called a **field.** In the examples, the descriptor A indicates a field width equivalent to the declared length of a character variable (based on the declaration in the CHARACTER statement); the descriptor A20 specifies a field width of 20 characters for the printed string. The string would be printed **right-justified** in, or at the extreme right of, the field.

Table B.2 illustrates the A edit descriptor.

TABLE B.2   A Edit Descriptor

Program	Output	Description
PROGRAM AEDIT		
*--------------------------------		Field width = declared length; string printed in field as stored. Trailing blank stored within STRING. We can use A in place of A5, since w = 1.
* A Edit Descriptor Examples		
*--------------------------------		
CHARACTER STRING*5		
STRING = 'abcd'		
PRINT '(1X, A5)', STRING	abcd	Field width > declared length; string printed right-justified as stored, giving one padded blank at start of field.
PRINT '(1X, A6)', STRING	abcd	
PRINT '(1X, A3)', STRING	abc	Field width < declared length; truncated string printed in field.
*--------------------------------		
END		

In general, the field width w may differ from the declared length l of the character variable. In some instances (as in right-justifying character output) we might find it desirable to select a field width different from the declared length, in which cases the following rules apply.

Rule 1 If the field width w is less than or equal to the declared length l of the character variable ($w \leq l$), then the leftmost w characters in storage are output. The rightmost ($l - w$) characters are truncated.

Rule 2 If $w > l$ then all l characters in storage are printed right-justified within the field. The unused or leftmost ($w - l$) part of the field is padded with blanks.

The three examples in Table B.2 illustrate these rules. Note that the descriptor 1X is used in the examples as an output device control character.

I EDIT DESCRIPTOR: INTEGER OUTPUT

The I edit descriptor edits the output of integer values. Its form is given by

I Edit Descriptor

Syntax:
     I w

Example:
     I 14

where again w is the field width. In the example, the integer value would be printed right-justified in a field 14 positions wide.

Table B.3 illustrates the I edit descriptor.

NOTE Integer output is automatically *right-justified* in the field. If the number of significant digits in the value is less than the field width, then the unused (leftmost) portion of the field is padded with blanks. If the value is negative, the field width must account for the output of the negative sign. If the number of significant digits (and a negative sign for negative values) exceeds the field width, then we have a **format overflow condition.** In this case, the processor prints substitute characters in the field (like asterisks) or otherwise indicates a format overflow condition (it depends on the processor). The examples in Table B.3 illustrate these situations.

F EDIT DESCRIPTOR: REAL OUTPUT

The F edit descriptor edits the output of real and complex values. It has the following form.

TABLE B.3   **I Edit Descriptor**

Program	Output
PROGRAM IEDIT	
*--------------------------------	
* I Edit Descriptor Examples	
*--------------------------------	
INTEGER NUMBER	
NUMBER = 705	
PRINT '(1X, I4)', NUMBER	705
NUMBER = 7050	
PRINT '(1X, I4)', NUMBER	7050
NUMBER = -7050	
PRINT '(1X, I4)', NUMBER	****
PRINT '(1X, I5)', NUMBER	-7050
*--------------------------------	
END	

F Edit Descriptor

Syntax:

   F*w.d*

Example:

   F8.1

where w is the field width and d is the number of decimal digits, or the number of digits to the right of the decimal point. In the example, the real value is printed right-justified in a field 8 positions wide, with one digit to the right of the decimal point.

Table B.4 illustrates the F edit descriptor.

NOTE   Take care with format overflow for real values. Keep in mind that we need to account for the decimal point and a possible negative sign when we specify a field of sufficient width. Also note from the examples in Table B.4 that the d-part of the descriptor *rounds* the decimal part of the value whenever more significant digits are stored in the decimal part than are specified in the descriptor.

Description

Value printed right-justified in field. First field position is a blank character.

Value fits exactly in field.

Value does not fit in field, giving format overflow. System prints asterisks.

Value fits exactly in field.

ALL TOGETHER NOW

Let's put it together now by taking a look at a complete PRINT/FORMAT pair. Program ENG3 in Figure B.1 uses the following pair.

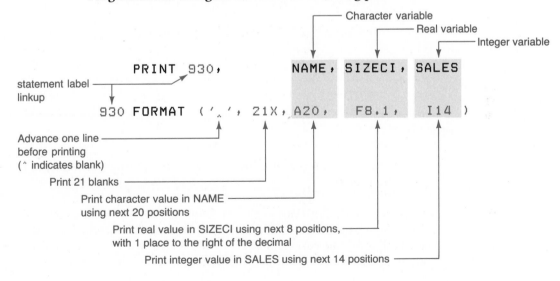

TABLE B.4   **F Edit Descriptor**

Program	Output
`PROGRAM FEDIT`	
`*-----------------------------------`	
`*    F Edit Descriptor Examples`	
`*-----------------------------------`	
`REAL VALUE`	
`VALUE = 735.0`	
`PRINT '(1X, F6.0)', VALUE`	`   735.`
`PRINT '(1X, F6.2)', VALUE`	`735.00`
`PRINT '(1X, F5.2)', VALUE`	`*****`
`VALUE = 66.318`	
`PRINT '(1X, F8.3)', VALUE`	`  66.318`
`PRINT '(1X, F8.2)', VALUE`	`   66.32`
`PRINT '(1X, F8.1)', VALUE`	`    66.3`
`VALUE = -0.14`	
`PRINT '(1X, F5.2)', VALUE`	`-0.14`
`PRINT '(1X, F4.2)', VALUE`	`-.14`
`PRINT '(1X, F3.2)', VALUE`	`***`
`*-----------------------------------`	
`END`	

Check it out in Figure B.1! This is exactly the way printed values in the table body were printed.

NOTE 1   Corresponding output values and their edit descriptors must match with respect to type. In our example, the character variable NAME is matched with the character descriptor A; the real variable SIZECI is matched with the real descriptor F; and the integer variable SALES is matched with the integer descriptor I.

Description

Value printed right-justified in field, to 0 decimal places; unused portion of field padded with 2 blanks.

Value exactly fits in field; 2 decimal places printed. Note that decimal point uses one field position.

Value does not fit in field, giving format overflow.

Value to 3 decimal places printed right-justified in field; two padded blanks in leftmost part of field.

Rounded value to 2 decimal places printed right-justified in field; three blanks in leftmost part of field.

Rounded value to 1 decimal place printed right-justified in field; four padded blanks in leftmost part of field.

Value to 2 decimal places exactly fits in field.

Same value to 2 decimal places exactly fits in smaller field, because this system suppressed the leading 0.

Now we have format overflow.

NOTE 2   Use commas to separate edit descriptors within the format specification. (We illustrate exceptions to this rule in Section B.3.)

OTHER EDIT DESCRIPTORS

The examples in Table B.5 illustrate other common descriptors in addition to those we have already described.

TABLE B.5   **Other Edit Descriptors**

Program	Output
PROGRAM OTHER	
*---	
* Other Edit Descriptor Examples	
*---	
INTEGER NUMBER	
REAL VALUE	
DOUBLE PRECISION DOUBLE	
COMPLEX COMP	
LOGICAL TRUTH	
VALUE = -123.45	
PRINT '(1X, E12.5)', VALUE	-0.12345E+03
PRINT '(1X, E10.5)', VALUE	**********
PRINT '(1X, E13.5E3)', VALUE	-0.12345E+003
PRINT '(1X, G12.5)', VALUE	-123.45
PRINT '(1X, G12.2)', VALUE	-0.12E+03
DOUBLE = -123.45	
PRINT '(1X, D12.5)', DOUBLE	-0.12345D+03
NUMBER = 12345	
PRINT '(5X, ''Number ='', I6)', NUMBER	Number = 12345
PRINT '(T6, ''Number ='', I6)', NUMBER	Number = 12345
PRINT '(3X, ''Time'', 5X, ''Temp'')'	Time Temp
PRINT '(T4, ''Time'', T13, ''Temp'')'	Time Temp
COMP = (-8.30, 3.21)	
PRINT '(1X, F6.2, F6.2)', COMP	-8.30 3.21
TRUTH = .TRUE.	
PRINT '(1X, L5)', TRUTH	T
*---	
END	

Description

E descriptor prints real value followed by E±two-digit exponent.

Format overflow. We need 4 print positions just for the exponential part.

Adding E3 to end of E descriptor prints 3-digit exponent.

G descriptor works like F descriptor in this example. Note 4 blanks at right that account for the missing exponential part.
G descriptor works like E descriptor in this example.

D descriptor prints double-precision value as E descriptor prints real value.

Positioning using X descriptor.

Same positioning using T descriptor.

Positioning using X descriptors.

Same positioning using T descriptors.

Two F descriptors print complex value.

L descriptor prints logical value.

E Edit Descriptor.   The descriptor $Ew.d$ edits real and complex values using exponential notation. As before, w is the field width and d is the decimal digits. Output is right-justified, and two-digit exponents are printed. See the first two examples in Table B.5. Very large values might require an exponent greater than 99. In this case, we can modify the E descriptor with the suffix Ee, as in $Ew.dEe$, where e is the number of digits we wish printed in the exponent. See the third example in Table B.5.

G Edit Descriptor.   The descriptor $Gw.d$ generalizes the output of real and complex values by using E-descriptor editing for "very large" or "very small" values, and F-descriptor editing for "in-between" values. Specifically, if the exponent of the value is between 0 and d inclusive, the value is printed with d significant digits followed by four spaces (see the fourth example in Table B.5); if the exponent of the value is negative or greater than d, the descriptor $Ew.d$ is used (see the fifth example in Table B.5).

D Edit Descriptor.   The descriptor $Dw.d$ edits double-precision or complex values using the same style as the E descriptor, except for substituting D for E in the output format. See the sixth example in Table B.5.

T Edit Descriptor.   The descriptor Tn controls positioning by tabbing to the nth position in the print line. Whereas the nX descriptor controls positioning by skipping the next n positions, the Tn descriptor controls positioning by moving to the nth position. Four examples in Table B.5 demonstrate the X- and T-descriptor approaches to positioning output. Note that a printer would "rob" the first space in the X descriptor and the first tab position in the T descriptor for carriage control. For example, a printer would print the label T i m e starting in position 3 (as shown in Table B.5), but a video screen might print starting in position 4.

L Edit Descriptor.   The descriptor Lw edits logical values, where w is the field width. The logical value T or F is printed right-justified in the field. See the last example in Table B.5.

NOTE   Let's summarize the matchup of descriptors to data types.

A descriptor	Use for character output.
Apostrophe descriptor . . .	Use for textual output and output device control.
D descriptor	Use for double-precision output.
E descriptor	Use for real and complex output.
F descriptor	Use for real and complex output.
G descriptor	Use for real and complex output.
I descriptor	Use for integer output.
L descriptor	Use for logical output.
T descriptor	Use for positioning output.
X descriptor	Use for positioning output and output device control.

The output of complex values is accomplished by any of the D, E, F, or G descriptors. The example in Table B.5 shows F-descriptor output for a complex value. Note that two descriptors are needed, one for the real part and the other for the imaginary part of the complex number.

B.3 OTHER FORMAT SPECIFICATIONS

This section defines and illustrates additional features of format specifications.

REPEATABLE EDIT DESCRIPTORS

A **repeat specification** is a nonzero, unsigned, integer constant that appears in front of a repeatable edit descriptor. A **repeatable edit descriptor** (are ya ready for this?) is an edit descriptor that can be repeated using the following form.

> Syntax:
> > *Repeat specificationRepeatable edit descriptor*
> Example:
> > `2F4.1`

The repeatable edit descriptors are A, D, E, F, G, I, and L. Other edit descriptors are termed nonrepeatable. In the example, the form `2F4.1` is an equivalent shortened version of `F4.1, F4.1`. If we had to print five integer values in a row using the edit descriptor `I10`, then either we could use the long form `I10, I10, I10, I10, I10` or we could use the short form `5I10`.

SLASH EDIT DESCRIPTOR

The **slash edit descriptor** is a nonrepeatable descriptor that terminates a print line or record. This descriptor simply has the form `/`. Slash descriptors are useful for the vertical spacing of output since they have the same effect as printing blank lines. Table B.6 shows examples of the slash descriptor.

NOTE 1   When n slashes are used at the beginning or end of a format specification, n blank lines are printed. When n slashes are used other than at the beginning or end, $n - 1$ blank lines are printed. In all cases, the first slash returns the carriage or cursor to the beginning of the present print line. Subsequent slashes terminate additional print lines. The right parenthesis in a format specification has the same effect as a slash. See the examples in Table B.6.

NOTE 2   Commas are not used to delimit slashes.

TABLE B.6   **Slash Edit Descriptor**

Program	Output
PROGRAM SLASH	
* ———————————————————————————	
* Slash Edit Descriptor Examples	
* ———————————————————————————	
REAL X, Y	
DATA X, Y / 1.1, 1.2 /	
PRINT '(1X, F4.1 / 1X, F4.1)', X, Y	1.1
PRINT *	1.2
PRINT '(1X, F4.1 // 1X, F4.1)', X, Y	1.1
	1.2
PRINT '(// 1X, 2F4.1 /)', X, Y	
	1.1 1.2
PRINT '(3X, ''X'', 3X, ''Y'' / 1X, 2F4.1)', X, Y	X Y
* ———————————————————————————	1.1 1.2
END	

EMBEDDED FORMAT SPECIFICATIONS

A format specification may be embedded within another format specification for greater coding efficiency. This is typically combined with the repeat specification, giving us an **embedded format specification**.

Embedded Format Specification

Syntax:
        (. . . *Repeat specification*(. . .). . .)
Example:
        (1X, 3(I5, F8.2))

The embedded format specification in the example is equivalent to the format specification (1X, I5, F8.2, I5, F8.2, I5, F8.2). The three identical groupings I5, F8.2 thus are rewritten in the embedded form as 3(I5, F8.2).

Table B.7 illustrates some embedded format specifications.

Description

Slash ends 1st print line; 1X control advances to second line; value in Y printed on second line. Single-spaced output.

First slash terminates first print line; second slash terminates second print line; value in Y printed on third line. Double-spaced output.

First two slashes terminate two print lines. Values printed on third line. Last slash ends third print line. Right parenthesis moves cursor or carriage to fourth print line.

Vertically aligned labels and values are easily printed in one format specification using slash.

UNBALANCED FORMAT SPECIFICATIONS

In our work thus far, the number of items in the output list of a PRINT or WRITE statement has equaled or balanced the number of repeatable edit descriptors in the format specification. For greater flexibility (or confusion, depending on your point of view), we can design an **unbalanced format specification** as follows.

- **More Repeatable Descriptors Than Items in Output List.** In this case, the processor uses the following procedure: Each item in the output list is edited according to its corresponding repeatable edit descriptor; format control terminates at the *first* repeatable descriptor not having a corresponding item in the output list. The first example in Table B.8 illustrates this case.

- **Less Repeatable Descriptors Than Items in Output List.** The processor now acts as follows: Items in the output list are edited until the descriptors in the format specification are exhausted (the processor "bumps" into the right parenthesis), which terminates the record; the scan of the format specification is repeated as many times as needed, until all items in the list are processed. If inner parentheses are present within an embedded format

TABLE B.7   **Embedded Format Specifications**

Program	Output
PROGRAM EMBED	
*—————————————————————	
* . Embedded Format Specification Examples	
*—————————————————————	
REAL X, Y	
DATA X, Y / 1.1, 1.2 /	
PRINT '(2(1X, F4.1))', X, Y	1.1 1.2
PRINT *	
PRINT '(2(1X, F4.1 /))', X, Y	1.1
	1.2
PRINT '(3X, ''X'', 3X, ''Y'' / 1X, 8(''='') / 1X, 2F4.1)', X, Y	X Y
*—————————————————————	═══════
END	1.1 1.2

TABLE B.8   **Unbalanced Format Specifications**

Program	Output
PROGRAM UNBAL	
*—————————————————————	
* Unbalanced Format Specification Examples	
*—————————————————————	
REAL X, Y	
DATA X, Y / 1.1, 1.2 /	
PRINT '(1X, 2F4.1)', X	1.1
PRINT *	
PRINT '(1X, F4.1)', X, Y	1.1
PRINT *	1.2
PRINT '('' Value'', F4.1)', X, Y	Value 1.1
PRINT *	Value 1.2
PRINT '('' Value'' / (1X, F4.1))', X, Y	Value
*—————————————————————	1.1
END	1.2

Description

Equivalent to (1 X , F 4 , 1 , 1 X , F 4 , 1).

Equivalent to (1 X , F 4 , 1 / 1 X , F 4 , 1 /).

Form 8 (' = ') equivalent to ' = = = = = = = = '.

Description

The second F 4 , 1 is ignored and the record is terminated.

First scan prints value in X; right parenthesis ends record; second scan (color) prints value in Y, after advancing one line according to blank (1 X) control.

Same procedure as preceding; second scan shown in color. Blank first character in ' V a l u e ' is the blank (advance one line) control character.

Note how second scan (shown in color) resets to inner set of parentheses. The slash ends first print line; 1 X control advances to second line; F 4 , 1 edits value in X; rightmost parenthesis ends second line; 1 X advances to third line; F 4 , 1 edits value in Y; rightmost parenthesis ends third line.

---

specification, repeat scans begin with the *rightmost* set of parentheses. The remaining examples in Table B.8 illustrate this case.

B.4 PROGRAMMING TIPS

DESIGN AND STYLE

1. **Format Specification Methods.** As illustrated in Section B.1, format specifications are provided in any of the following ways:

   a. **FORMAT Statement.** This approach provides the format specification to the immediate right of the keyword FORMAT. Advantages include the grouping of format specifications for easy lookup and better visual alignment of related output parts like table heads and labeled output. Disadvantages include the need for additional statements and linkups between PRINT/WRITE statements and their corresponding FORMAT statements (which open up the possibilities of linkup errors, as described in the next section).

   Character Constant. In this case the format specification is incorporated within the PRINT statement, thereby eliminating its use in a FORMAT statement. This approach is fine for "quick-and-dirty" formatted output. It also avoids the need to link up statements, thereby eliminating a source of error. For elaborate output, however, this method lacks the grouping advantages described under FORMAT statements.

   c. **Character Variable.** Here the format specification is stored in a character variable. The character variable is then used as a format identifier in the PRINT or WRITE statement. This means, of course, that a FORMAT statement is not needed. The advantages and disadvantages of this approach are similar to those when using FORMAT statements. An added advantage of using character variables is that the PRINT/WRITE statements are more descriptive, as in

   ```
   CHARACTER TITLE*70
   TITLE = ' List of Hot FORTRAN Programmers'
   PRINT TITLE
   ```

   Moreover, the use of character variables instead of statement numbers reduces the likelihood of linkup errors like using the wrong format specification. Note that this approach defines the format specifications through *executable* assignment statements, so we need to place these statements in a group before the corresponding PRINT/WRITE statements are executed. We would suggest their placement just before the otherwise first executable statement in the program.

By the way, FORMAT statements are the common and traditional approach to providing format specifications, because other approaches were unavailable before the FORTRAN 77 standard. We suspect, however, that the character-variable approach will become more popular over time. In Exercise 14 we ask you to think some more about these issues.

2. **Treatment of FORMAT Statements.** Place FORMAT statements in a group either at the beginning or end of the program. We prefer end placement simply because too many "other things" go in the beginning of programs (introductory documentation, type statements, and so on). Grouping the formats in one place simplifies our finding formats; gets them out of the way of execution logic when we read listings; and facilitates the visual alignment of table heads, labels with their corresponding output, and so on. It's also best to sequentially number FORMAT statements according to their chronological use within the program. Pick a numbering level (like 900s or 9000s) that's different from any other in the program.

COMMON ERRORS

1. **Unaligned Output.** Elaborate formatted output requires careful planning before we start writing format specifications. First lay out the output design on a sheet of plain paper, quadrille paper (better), or commercially available forms called print chart (best, since they show row and column numbers in a quadrille format, as seen in Exercise 4). In the output sketch, include the desired alignments, the exact form of real output, and so on. Once we're satisfied with the design, then we can start writing down the format specifications. Practice this approach to improve output designs (not to mention your grade) and reduce debugging effort.

2. **Ignoring Control Characters.** Most output devices expect a control character as the first descriptor in the format specification. If we forget to specify a control character, then the processor might "rip it off" from the first descriptor. For example, if NUMBER stores 123 and we use the statement

```
PRINT '(I3)', NUMBER
```

then the processor may take the first digit in NUMBER (the 1) and use it as a control character to skip to the top of a new page. In this case, the remaining digits in NUMBER (the 23) will get printed in the first two positions of the print line. If we simply wish to print the value in NUMBER in the next print line, then we should use

```
PRINT '(1X, I3)', NUMBER
```

3. **Correspondence Errors.** Make sure that the types (integer, real, and so on) of items in the output list correspond to the proper edit descriptors in the format specification (integer with I descriptor, real with E, F, or G descriptor, and so forth); otherwise, we may have unpredictable errors. For

example, some systems may identify correspondence errors as compile-time errors, others may flag them as run-time errors, and still others may just print incorrect values.

4. **Linkup Errors.** If the format specification is not part of the output statement, then it must be linked to the output statement through the format identifier. If the format identifier is a statement label, then make sure that the statement label in the PRINT/WRITE statement corresponds to the statement label that labels the corresponding FORMAT statement. If it doesn't, then we have: a compile-time error when the statement label is nonexistent; a compile-time error, run-time error, or logic error (depending on the system) if the wrong FORMAT statement is referenced and the output list and edit descriptors don't correspond; and a logic error if the wrong FORMAT statement is referenced and the output list and edit descriptors do correspond. The likelihood of this error is reduced if we use either a character variable or an integer variable as the format identifier, as illustrated in Section B.1.

5. **Incorrect Character Output.** Pay careful attention to Rules 1 and 2 on page 513 when the field width in the A descriptor differs from the declared length of the character variable. The last example in Table B.2 shows the common truncation error.

6. **Memory Lapses.** Pay careful attention to edit descriptor syntax, particularly the descriptors that specify both field width w and decimal digits d, as in F$w.d$. Common mistakes include insufficient field width, giving format overflow (see the third example in Table B.4); or compile-time errors like F8 instead of F8.0 to print zero decimal digits.

7. **"Falling Off" the Print Line.** Video screens and printers have defined line lengths. For instance, typical line lengths are 80 characters for video terminals and 132 characters for wide printer paper. If our format specification dictates a print line greater than that defined for the output device, then the current print line typically wraps to the next print line, thereby messing up our (carefully designed!) output format. If this happens, then we have to change our format design, our format specification, or the output device's line length. Can you change the line length for the output device on your system?

FOLLOW-UP EXERCISES

1.   Suppose that the printer has just finished printing line 20 and that the statement

    PRINT 15

is to be executed next. Write the appropriate FORMAT statement to print the label HAL Speaks

   a. At the beginning of line 20.
   b. At the beginning of line 21.
   c. At the beginning of line 22.
   d. Starting in the fifth print position (column) of line 22.
   e. Starting at the beginning of the first line on the next page.

2. Assume the character constant `'RHODE ISLAND'` is stored in the character variable `STATE` as follows:

```
CHARACTER STATE*20
STATE = 'RHODE ISLAND'
```

How would the output appear in each of the following situations?

a.
```
    PRINT 50,STATE
50 FORMAT('      ',A20)
```
b.
```
    PRINT 50,STATE
50 FORMAT(' THE OCEAN STATE IS ',A20)
```
c.
```
    PRINT 50,STATE
50 FORMAT(' ',A10)
```
d.
```
    PRINT 50,STATE
50 FORMAT(' ',A25)
```
e.
```
    PRINT 50,STATE
50 FORMAT(' ',A20,'IS THE SMALLEST STATE')
```
f.
```
    PRINT 50,STATE,'IS THE SMALLEST STATE'
50 FORMAT(' ',A20,A21)
```
g.
```
    PRINT 50,STATE,'IS THE SMALLEST STATE'
50 FORMAT(' ',A,A)
```

3. Indicate the exact output for the following program.

```
INTEGER L,M,N
   .
   .
   .
   PRINT 90,M,N
   PRINT 95,L
90 FORMAT ('1','M=',I4,' N=',I5)
95 FORMAT ('0','    L=',I3)
   END
```

L	M	N
10	756	−401

	1	2	3	4	5	6	7	8	9	10	11	12	13	14	15	16	17	18	19	20
1																				
2																				
3																				
4																				
5																				
6																				
7																				

4. Indicate the appropriate WRITE and FORMAT statements for the following desired output. The carriage or cursor is currently in the "home" position, or row 1 and column 1.

	1	2	3	4	5	6	7	8	9	10	11	12	13	14	15	16	17	18	19	20	21	22	23	24	25	26	27	28	29	30	31	32	33	34	35	36
1																									Contents of character											
2																									variable TYPE											
3				B	L	O	O	D			T	Y	P	E			A	+																		
4																									Contents of integer											
5										P	I	N	T	S	:		X	X	X	X					variable PINTS											
6											C	O	S	T	:		$	X	X																	
7																									Contents of integer											
8																									variable COST											
9																																				

5. Fill in the following table for the output of a real variable.

	Contents	F w.d	Printed Output 1 2 3 4 5 6 7 8 9
a.	3.105		3 . 1
b.	3.105		3 . 1 0 5 0
c.	−.1074	F6.4	
d.	−.1074	F7.4	
e.	−.1074	F9.4	
f.	.1074	F6.4	
g.	3764.	F9.1	
h.	3764.16	F9.1	
i.	3764.16	F9.0	
j.	3764.16	F9.3	
k.	3764.16	F6.3	

6. Fill in the following table for the output of a real variable.

	Contents	E$w.d$	Printed Output (positions 1–15)
a.	3.105		0.3105E+01
b.	3.105		0.31E+01
c.	−.1074	E15.5	
d.	−.1074	E15.4	
e.	−.1074	E15.2	
f.	−.1074	E15.9	
g.	3764.	E14.5	
h.	3764.16	E14.5	
i.	3764.16	E14.6	
j.	3764.16	E10.4	
k.	3764.16	E12.3	

***7.** Indicate appropriate statements for the following desired output. Use the X descriptor for four or more consecutive blanks. The cursor or carriage is in the home position.

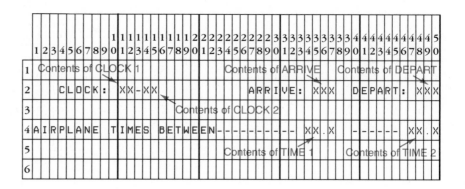

8. Specify exact output for each of the following, where NUM1 stores 75 and NUM2 stores 50. Both variables are typed integer. The cursor or print head currently resides in the home position.

```
PRINT 90, NUM1, NUM2
```

FORMAT Statement | Output

a. 90 FORMAT(1X,I5,///1X,I5)

	1	2	3	4	5	6	7	8	9	10	11	12	13	14	15	16	17	18	19	20	21	22	23	24	25
1																									
2																									
3																									
4																									
5																									

b. 90 FORMAT(///1X,2I5)

	1	2	3	4	5	6	7	8	9	10	11	12	13	14	15	16	17	18	19	20	21	22	23	24	25
1																									
2																									
3																									
4																									
5																									

c. 90 FORMAT(1X,2I5,///)

	1	2	3	4	5	6	7	8	9	10	11	12	13	14	15	16	17	18	19	20	21	22	23	24	25
1																									
2																									
3																									
4																									
5																									

d. 90 FORMAT(1X,6('*'),2I5,2X,6('*'))

	1	2	3	4	5	6	7	8	9	10	11	12	13	14	15	16	17	18	19	20	21	22	23	24	25
1																									
2																									
3																									
4																									
5																									

e. `90 FORMAT(3(/)1X,2I5)`

	1	2	3	4	5	6	7	8	9	10	11	12	13	14	15	16	17	18	19	20	21	22	23	24	25
1																									
2																									
3																									
4																									
5																									

*9. Fill in the output, given that the cursor or print head are in the home position.

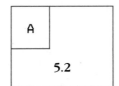

A
5.2

B
7.1

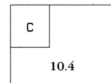

C
10.4

D
6.3

`PRINT 90, A, B, C, D`

FORMAT *Statement*	*Output*

a. `90 FORMAT)'0',2F5.1)`

	1	2	3	4	5	6	7	8	9	10	11	12	13	14	15	16	17	18	19	20	21	22	23	24	25
1																									
2																									
3																									
4																									
5																									

b. `90 FORMAT(1X,F5.1)`

	1	2	3	4	5	6	7	8	9	10	11	12	13	14	15	16	17	18	19	20	21	22	23	24	25
1																									
2																									
3																									
4																									
5																									

c. 90 FORMAT(2(5X,F5.1))

	1	2	3	4	5	6	7	8	9	10	11	12	13	14	15	16	17	18	19	20	21	22	23	24	25
1																									
2																									
3																									
4																									
5																									

d. 90 FORMAT(1X,2(5X,F5.1))

	1	2	3	4	5	6	7	8	9	10	11	12	13	14	15	16	17	18	19	20	21	22	23	24	25
1																									
2																									
3																									
4																									
5																									

e. 90 FORMAT(1X,(5X,F5.1))

	1	2	3	4	5	6	7	8	9	10	11	12	13	14	15	16	17	18	19	20	21	22	23	24	25
1																									
2																									
3																									
4																									
5																									

10. Write necessary statements to print the following label and its value stored in the real variable DROP, starting at the next print line in print position 10.
   a. Pressure drop = ±xxxxx.xxx
   b. Same as part (a), except underline (underscore) the label.

11. Can you think of two reasonably efficient ways of printing, say, 15 blank lines?

*12. Check out how format overflow works on your system by running a short program that purposely commits an overflow error. While you're at it, print an integer, character, and real value using one PRINT statement, and purposely mismatch type between the output list and the format specification.

13. **HC ENGINEering.** Revise Program ENG3 in Figure B.1 as follows.
   a. Explain why the output of names appears left-justified. Use A instead of A20 in FORMAT 930. Same output? What if we were to change the declared length in NAME from 20 to 50 while still using A20? What if we use A instead of A20?
   b. Print the table head with just one format specification; that is, replace FORMATs 900, 910, and 920 with a new FORMAT statement. Take care with the

table line. Code it more efficiently, and don't forget to account for its use in the table foot.

*c. Revise the new output format in part (b) by printing the table at the top of a new page and underscoring the title.

*d. Redesign Program ENG3 so the output table includes columns for size in cc, units, and price. In the table foot, include the sum of units.

*e. Run the revised program on your system.

*14. **Alternative format identifiers.** Rework Program ENG3 in Figure B.1 as follows.

    a. Use character constants for all format specifications.

    b. Use character variables for all format specifications.

    c. Use integer variables for all format identifiers.

    d. Run one or more of these versions on your system.

    Compare the pros and cons of each approach. Which do you prefer, and why?

ADDITIONAL EXERCISES

---

15. **Revisit.** Revise an end-of-chapter program you have already written by using output formats. Improve the output design from the original.

16. **HC ENGINEoil.** Rework Program EUCLID in Figure 2.3 as follows.

    a. Clean up the output of real values in Figure 2.4 by expressing all distances to two decimal places.

    b. Make any other output format changes that you feel improve the program.

C*

INPUT FORMATS

The style of input called list-directed input first described in Section 2.5 is convenient for beginning programmers and uncomplicated input data needs. Many applications, however, include preformatted and precisely positioned input data described by **input formats.** For example, suppose that airfoil stress data generated by wind tunnel experiments is output to a data file on hard disk. A FORTRAN program then can analyze this preformatted data, where input formats precisely describe its positioning in the data file. Input formats are also useful in mass data typing, since it's unnecessary to type decimal points for real values or apostrophes for character values (more on this later).

This module describes methods that precisely position input data according to input formats designed by the programmer. This style of input is called **format-directed input.** Let's start with a familiar example.

---

*Study this module anytime after Section 3.3 and Module B.

EXAMPLE C.1

HC ENGINEERING WITH INPUT/OUTPUT FORMATS

Program ENG4 in Figure C.1 is a rewrite of Program ENG3 in Figure B.1. Changes are shown by the color screens. Essentially, we reworked the input from list-directed input to format-directed input, and necessarily changed the data file. The output of this version is identical to that of its predecessor.

At this time, don't be concerned with the specifics of format-directed input, since the rest of this module describes this in detail. Note, however, that the input data is repositioned in the data file and apostrophes do not surround engine names. (Compare the two data files in Figures B.1 and C.1.) ■

C.1 ON FIELDS, RECORDS, AND FILES

Data files are designed or structured in ways that are best described using the following terminology.

FIELD

A field is a fact or attribute about some entity such as a person, place, thing, or event. For example, the attributes of an automobile might be described in terms of its name, color, body style, engine type, transmission type, EPA gas mileage, wind drag coefficient, and quarter-mile time. Each of these attributes is a field. The variables in input lists are used to process fields; that is, each variable in the input list corresponds to a field.

```
      PROGRAM ENG4
* * * * * * * * * * * * * * * * * * * * * * * * * * * * * * *
*
*         Harvey CORE ENGINEering Corporation:  Version 4.0
*
*           Inputs engine name, size (cc), price, units from data file
*             using input formats
*           Calculates engine size (ci), sales, total sales
*           Outputs engine name, size (ci), sales, total sales using
*             output formats
*           Uses DO-loop to process all data in one run
*
*         Data file structure:
*
*                   Field     Type         Columns        Descriptor
*
*  1st record——> NUMBER    Integer       1 -  3            I3
*
*  2nd+ record——> NAME      Character     1 - 20            A
*                 SIZECC    Real         21 - 30            F10.0
*                 PRICE     Integer      31 - 40            I10
*                 UNITS     Integer      41 - 50            I10
*
*         Key:
*           METCON... Metric conversion parameter (cc = 0.06102 ci)
*           NAME..... Engine name
*           NUMBER... Number of engine types processed
*           PRICE.... Engine price in $ per unit
*           SALES.... Sales in $
*           SIZECC... Engine size in cubic centimeters (cc)
*           SIZECI... Engine size in cubic inches (ci)
*           TOTAL.... Total sales in $
*           TYPE..... Engine type DO-variable
*           UNITS.... Number of engines sold in units
*
* * * * * * * * * * * * * * * * * * * * * * * * * * * * * * *
*———————————————————————————————————————————————————————————
*  Type variables
*———————————————————————————————————————————————————————————
      CHARACTER NAME*20
      INTEGER   NUMBER, PRICE, SALES, TOTAL, TYPE, UNITS
      REAL      METCON, SIZECC, SIZECI
*———————————————————————————————————————————————————————————
*  Declare parameters
*———————————————————————————————————————————————————————————
      PARAMETER (METCON = 0.06102)
*———————————————————————————————————————————————————————————
*  Initialize
*———————————————————————————————————————————————————————————
      TOTAL = 0
*———————————————————————————————————————————————————————————
```

FIGURE C.1   **HC ENGINEering with Input/output formats (*continued on next page*)**

RECORD

A record is a group of related fields, retrievable as a unit. For instance, all of the data items describing the attributes of a particular automobile constitute a record for that automobile. Typically, the execution of an input statement processes an entire record. The fields that make up a record are often described by a **record layout** or **data file structure.** The documentation in Figure C.1 describes the file structure for the data file processed by the program. The record layout thus includes for each field the (variable) name, its type, its positioning in the record, and its edit descriptor.

```
*  Print table head
*———————————
      PRINT 900
      PRINT 910
      PRINT 920
      PRINT 910
*———————————————————————————————————————
*  Process data file and print table body
*———————————————————————————————————————
      READ (5,800) NUMBER

      DO 100 TYPE = 1, NUMBER

        READ (5,810) NAME, SIZECC, PRICE, UNITS

        SIZECI = METCON * SIZECC

        SALES  = PRICE  * UNITS

        TOTAL  = TOTAL  + SALES

        PRINT 930, NAME, SIZECI, SALES

  100 CONTINUE
*———————————————————————————————————————
*  Print table foot
*————————————
      PRINT 910
      PRINT 940, TOTAL
*———————————————————————————————————————
*  Input formats
*————————————

  800 FORMAT ( I3 )

  810 FORMAT ( A, F10.0, 2I10 )
*———————————————————————————————————————
*  Output formats
*————————————

  900 FORMAT ( ' ', 20X, '              SALES REPORT' )

  910 FORMAT ( ' ', 20X, '══════════════════════════════════')

  920 FORMAT ( ' ', 20X, ' Name               Size (ci)     Sales ')

  930 FORMAT ( ' ', 21X, A20, F8.1, I14 )

  940 FORMAT ( ' ', 20X, '              Total sales.......... $', I9 )
*———————————————————————————————————————
      END
```

```
0         1         2         3         4         5
123456789012345678901234567890123456789012345678901234567890   ──Data file

  3
Baby Two               7000      3000      1500   ╮
Momma Four             8500      4000      2000   ├──Records
Poppa Six             10000      5500      1000   ╯
```

Fields

SALES REPORT

Name	Size (ci)	Sales
Baby Two	427.1	4500000
Momma Four	518.7	8000000
Poppa Six	610.2	5500000

Total sales.......... $ 18000000

FIGURE C.1   (*continued*)

FILE

A file or data file is a collection of related records. Usually, each record is a logical part of the file in the sense that it contains the same fields (not data values) as all the other records in the file. For example, an *automobile file* contains all the automobile records described earlier. The file in Figure C.1 is an exception to this idea because the first record is unlike the other records. (We live in a world of exceptions, don't we?) This is because we're using a DO-loop to process the file, requiring a first record as the number of records that follow next. In Chapter 5 we show a way of eliminating this first record. Ignoring the first record, the file in Figure C.1 shows three records, and each record contains four fields.

C.2 READ STATEMENT

The precise control of input is accomplished by a READ statement that uses a format specification. The syntax of the READ statement[1] is now given by the following alternatives.

READ Statement: Format Directed, Form 1

Syntax:

> READ *format identifier , input list*

Example:

> READ 810, NAME, SIZECC, PRICE, UNITS

READ Statement: Format Directed, Form 2

Syntax:

> READ (*external unit identifier , format identifier*) *input list*

Example:

> READ (5, 810) NAME, SIZECC, PRICE, UNITS

The external unit identifier is either an integer expression (usually a numeric constant) for one of the system's input units (terminal, disk file, and so on) or an * for the system's standard input unit (usually the terminal). The first version of the READ statement assumes the system's standard input unit. The example in the second version uses 5 as the external unit identifier, which refers to a hard disk drive on most systems. As in output statements, the format identifier identifies a format as a statement label, an integer variable that stores a statement label, a character expression, or a character array name (Chapter 7). The example uses 810 as the format identifier, which is the statement label for one of the for-

---

[1] A more elaborate (and final) version of the READ statement is given in Chapter 9.

mats at the end of Program ENG4 in Figure C.1. As before, the input list is one or more of the following items separated by commas: variable, array name (Chapter 7), array element name (Chapter 7), or character substring name (Chapter 8). To summarize the given example, we wish to input values for NAME, SIZECC, PRICE, and UNITS through the standard input unit (first version) or a hard disk drive (second version) according to the format specification in FORMAT 810.

As in output formats (see page 508), the format specification describes data editing. In the input format case, we can specify the type, positioning, and length of input values, among other things. For example, the format specification

```
(A, F10.0, 2I10)
```

in Figure C.1 edits the input of a character variable, a real variable, and two integer variables. Edit descriptors and format specification variations as they relate to input formats are described in the next two sections.

NOTE 1   Format specifications for input don't use *control characters* or *apostrophe edit descriptors,* since these have unique functions in output formats.

In Figure C.1, the format specifications are provided by FORMAT statements, which have the same syntax described earlier in Module B on page 508.

NOTE 2   As in output formats, we have three ways of providing format specifications.[2] (See pages 508–509 to review the specifics.)

1. FORMAT statement
2. Character constant
3. Character variable

Also, the format identifier can be an integer variable assigned by an ASSIGN statement (see page 509).

C.3 SELECTED EDIT DESCRIPTORS

Edit descriptors are used in format specifications to edit input as well as output. In this section we present commonly used edit descriptors for input.

A EDIT DESCRIPTOR

The descriptor A or Aw is used to edit strings, where w is the field width or number of positions used to input the string. The descriptor A indicates a field width equivalent to the declared length of a character variable (based on the declara-

---

[2]We can also use a character array name (Chapter 7), but there's no advantage to doing so over a character variable.

tion in the CHARACTER statement); the descriptor A20 specifies a field width of 20 characters for the input string. Typically we left-justify the string within the input field. Table C.1 illustrates some A-descriptor examples.

In general, the field width w may differ from the declared length l of the character variable, in which cases the following rules apply.

Rule 1   If $w \leq l$, then the internal representation will be w characters left-justified followed by $l - w$ trailing blanks. See the first, second, and fourth examples in Table C.1.

Rule 2   If $w > l$ then the internal representation will consist of the rightmost l characters in the input field. See the third example in Table C.1.

NOTE 1   It's more natural for us to *left-justify* strings within input fields, as shown in the input examples of Table C.1. Rule 2, however, may give us unintended results (see the third example in Table C.1), and Rule 1 with $w < l$ may give us unwanted results (see the fourth example in Table C.1). Thus, we recommend setting the field width equal to the declared length. The simplest way to do this is by using the descriptor A (without its field width), as in the second example in Table C.1.

NOTE 2   Did you notice in Table C.1 that we don't enclose input strings in quotes when using input formats? (Not ZZZzzzing again, were ya?) This feature significantly reduces key strokes in large character data files and is more natural in interactive string input.

I EDIT DESCRIPTOR

The descriptor I w edits integer values, where again w is the field width. For example, the descriptor I10 would process an integer value in a field 10 positions wide. Table C.2 illustrates the I edit descriptor.

NOTE 3   Embedded and trailing blanks within numeric input fields are either ignored or converted to zeros, depending on the system's implementation. The second example in Table C.2 illustrates two trailing blanks following the digits 123 in an input field of width 5. Our system ignored these blanks; however, some systems may edit the blanks as zeros, thereby storing 12300 in NUMBER! To be safe, *right-justify* numeric input, as done in the first example. (An alternative that uses the BN and BZ edit descriptors is shown in Table C.4.)

F EDIT DESCRIPTOR

The descriptor F$w.d$ edits real and complex values, where w is the field width and d is the number of decimal digits, or the number of digits to the right of the decimal point. For example, the descriptor F10.0 edits a numeric value in a field 10 positions wide, with zero digits to the right of the decimal point. Table C.3 illustrates the F edit descriptor.

TABLE C.1 **A Edit Descriptor**

Program	Input/Output
``` PROGRAM AINPUT ```	
```*--```	
```* A Descriptor Input Examples```	
```*--```	
``` CHARACTER STRING*5```	123456789
``` PRINT *, 'Input:'```	Input:
``` READ '(A5)', STRING```	abcd
``` PRINT '('' Output:'' / 1X, A /)', STRING```	Output:
	abcd
	^
``` PRINT *, 'Input:'```	Input:
``` READ '(A)', STRING```	abcd
``` PRINT '('' Output:'' / 1X, A /)', STRING```	Output:
	abcd
	^
``` PRINT *, 'Input:'```	Input:
``` READ '(A6)', STRING```	abcd
``` PRINT '('' Output:'' / 1X, A /)', STRING```	Output:
	bcd
	^^
``` PRINT *, 'Input:'```	Input:
``` READ '(A3)', STRING```	abcd
``` PRINT '('' Output:'' / 1X, A /)', STRING```	Output:
```*--```	abc
``` END```	^^

TABLE C.2 **I Edit Descriptor**

Program	Input/Output
``` PROGRAM IINPUT```	
```*--```	
```* I Descriptor Input Examples```	
```*--```	
``` INTEGER NUMBER```	123456789
``` PRINT *, 'Input:'```	Input:
``` READ '(I5)', NUMBER```	123
``` PRINT '('' Output:'' / 1X, I5 /)', NUMBER```	Output:
	123
``` PRINT *, 'Input:'```	Input:
``` READ '(I5)', NUMBER```	123
``` PRINT '('' Output:'' / 1X, I5 /)', NUMBER```	Output:
	123
``` PRINT *, 'Input:'```	Input:
``` READ '(I5)', NUMBER```	123456
``` PRINT '('' Output:'' / 1X, I5 /)', NUMBER```	Output:
```*--```	12345
``` END```	

$w = l$ or field width 5 same as declared length 5; string stored as abcd␣; 5th character in string is the blank character.

A same as A5; equivalent to preceding example.

$w > l$ or $6 > 5$; string assumed right-justified in a field 6 characters wide; thus, bcd␣␣ stored, as seen in output.
See Rule 2.

$w < l$ or $3 < 5$; field width only 3 characters wide, so abc␣␣ stored; in our input, d is not processed since it's past the input field.
See Rule 1.

Input right-justified in field 5 positions wide; NUMBER stores 123.

Input left-justified in field 5 positions wide; NUMBER again stores 123.
See NOTE 3.

Input exceeds field width; the digit 6 is not processed; NUMBER stores 12345.

TABLE C.3   **F Edit Descriptor**

Program	Input/Output
PROGRAM FINPUT	
*	
* F Descriptor Input Examples	
*	
REAL VALUE	
	123456789
PRINT *, 'Input:'	Input:
READ '(F5.1)', VALUE	−123
PRINT '('' Output:'' / 1X, F6.2 /)', VALUE	Output:
	−12.30
PRINT *, 'Input:'	Input:
READ '(F5.1)', VALUE	−123
PRINT '('' Output:'' / 1X, F6.2 /)', VALUE	Output:
	−12.30
PRINT *, 'Input:'	Input:
READ '(F5.1)', VALUE	−1.23
PRINT '('' Output:'' / 1X, F6.2 /)', VALUE	Output:
	−1.23
PRINT *, 'Input:'	Input:
READ '(F5.1)', VALUE	−1.23
PRINT '('' Output:'' / 1X, F6.2 /)', VALUE	Output:
*	−1.00
END	

NOTE 4 Real values can be input with or without a decimal point. If the decimal point is used (as in the last two examples in Table C.3), then the *d* part of the F *w.d* specification is ignored, and the value is stored as entered (providing it fits within the field). If the decimal point is not used, then the last *d* digits in the value are the decimal digits, as illustrated by the first two examples in Table C.3.

NOTE 5 As in integer input, it's best to *right-justify* real values that are entered without the decimal point. Again, this is because some systems might interpret trailing blanks as zeros instead of blanks. For example, some systems would store −123.0 for VALUE in the first example of Table C.3 (the entry would be taken as −1230 if the blank in position 5 is interpreted as zero, giving zero as the single decimal digit). In Table C.4 we illustrate how the BN and BZ descriptors explicitly tell the system how to interpret blanks.

ALL TOGETHER NOW

Let's put it together now by taking a look at a complete READ/FORMAT pair. Program ENG4 in Figure C.1 uses the following pair.

Description

Input left-justified in field 5 positions wide; decimal point not used in input field; −12.3 stored in VALUE. See NOTE 5.

Input right-justified in field; decimal point not used in field. −12.3 stored in VALUE.

Decimal point used in field; −1.23 stored in VALUE as typed.

Value not placed in field given by positions 1−5 (the digits 23 are in positions 6 and 7); thus, −1.0 incorrectly stored in VALUE.

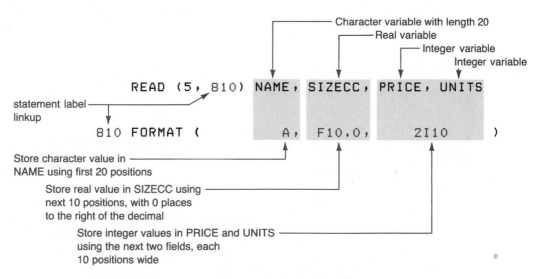

Check it out in Figure C.1! This is exactly the way input values were placed in the records of the data file. Also note how the format specification is consistent with the file structure described in the program's documentation.

NOTE 6   As in format specifications for output, use commas to separate edit descriptors; make sure that the variable type matches the proper descriptor (character variable with A descriptor, integer variable with I descriptor, and so on); and use *repeat specifications* with *repeatable edit descriptors* when warranted (as in 2I10 above).

MORE EDIT DESCRIPTORS

The examples in Table C.4 illustrate other common input descriptors, in addition to those we have already described.

E Edit Descriptor.   The descriptor Ew.d edits real and complex values using exponential notation. As before, w is the field width and d is the decimal digits. It's best to right-justify input when not using decimal points, for the same reasons discussed earlier under I and F descriptor editing. See the first example in Table C.4.

D Edit Descriptor.   The descriptor Dw.d edits double-precision or complex values using the same style as the E descriptor, except for substituting D for E. See the second example in Table C.4. Note that complex values are input with D, E, F, or G descriptors, as shown in the third example of Table C.4 using the F descriptor. We omit a discussion of the G descriptor for input formats because there's no advantage to its use as there was in output formats (see page 520).

L Edit Descriptor.   The descriptor Lw edits logical values, where w is the field width. The fourth example in Table C.4 illustrates the use of this descriptor. We would place the input values T, .TRUE., F, .FALSE. anywhere within the field.

X Edit Descriptor.   The descriptor *n*X skips *n* positions in an input record. It's often used to skip fields containing values not needed for that particular run, as illustrated in the fifth example in Table C.4.

T Edit Descriptor.   The descriptor T*n* skips positions by tabbing to the *n*th position in the input record. It's an alternative to the X descriptor, as shown by the sixth example in Table C.4.

BN and BZ Edit Descriptors.   These descriptors specify the interpretation of embedded and trailing (not leading) blanks in numeric input fields. The descriptor BN specifies that **B**lanks are to be edited as **N**ulls (as if they weren't there, ignored); the descriptor BZ indicates that **B**lanks are to be edited as **Z**eros (as if we had typed zeros instead of blanks). The BN or BZ descriptor is in effect for all succeeding numeric fields, until a different BN or BZ descriptor or the end of the format specification is encountered. The last three examples in Table C.4 illustrate the use of these descriptors.

NOTE 7   Let's summarize the matchup of descriptors to data types when using format-directed input.

Character data .... Use A descriptor.
Integer data .... Use I descriptor.
Real data .... Use D, E, F, or G descriptors.
Double-precision data ... Use D, E, F, or G descriptors.
Complex data .... Use D, E, F, or G descriptors.
Logical data .... Use L descriptor.

C.4 OTHER FORMAT SPECIFICATIONS

This section defines and illustrates additional features of input formats, including run-time input formats.

ADDITIONAL INPUT FORMAT SPECIFICATIONS

The features slash edit descriptor, embedded format specifications, and unbalanced format specifications first presented in Module B also have applications in input formats.

Slash Edit Descriptor.   The nonrepeatable descriptor / terminates the input record. The first example in Table C.5 illustrates the slash descriptor in input formats. Its use allows the processing of multiple records with one READ statement.

Embedded Format Specifications.   The use of inner parentheses within format specifications combined with the repeat specification allows more efficient format representations, as illustrated by the second example in Table C.5.

Unbalanced Format Specifications.   As before, these are format specifications where the number of repeatable edit descriptors is unequal to the number of items in the I/O list. We have two cases, as before.

- More Repeatable Descriptors Than Items in Input List. In this case, the processor uses the following procedure: Each item in the input list is edited according to its corresponding repeatable edit descriptor; format control terminates at the *first* repeatable descriptor not having a corresponding item in the input list. The third example in Table C.5 illustrates this case.
- Less Repeatable Descriptors Than Items in Input List. The processor now acts as follows: Items in the input list are edited until the descriptors in the format specification are exhausted (the processor "bumps" into the right parenthesis), which terminates the record; the scan of the format specification is repeated as many times as needed, until all items in the list are processed. The last example in Table C.5 illustrates this case. If inner paren-

TABLE C.4 **More Edit Descriptors**

Program	Input/Output

```
      PROGRAM MORE
*------------------------------------------------
*     More Descriptor Input Examples
*------------------------------------------------
      INTEGER          NUMBER
      REAL             VALUE
      DOUBLE PRECISION DOUBLE
      COMPLEX          COMP
      LOGICAL          TRUTH

      PRINT *, 'Input:'
      READ '( E10.3 )', VALUE
      PRINT '( '' Output:'' / 1X, E10.3 / )', VALUE


      PRINT *, 'Input:'
      READ '( D10.3 )', DOUBLE
      PRINT '( '' Output:'' / 1X, D10.3 / )', DOUBLE


      PRINT *, 'Input:'
      READ '( 2F5.2 )', COMP
      PRINT '( '' Output:'' / 1X, 2F5.2 / )', COMP


      PRINT *, 'Input:'
      READ '( L7 )', TRUTH
      PRINT '( '' Output:'' / 1X, L3 / )', TRUTH


      PRINT *, 'Input:'
      READ '( 5X, F5.1 )', VALUE
      PRINT '( '' Output:'' / 1X, F5.1 / )', VALUE


      PRINT *, 'Input:'
      READ '( T6, F5.1 )', VALUE
      PRINT '( '' Output:'' / 1X, F5.1 / )', VALUE


      PRINT *, 'Input:'
      READ '( BN, I5, F5.1 )', NUMBER, VALUE
      PRINT '( '' Output:'' / 1X, I5, F5.1 / )', NUMBER, VALUE


      PRINT *, 'Input:'
      READ '( BZ, I5, F5.1 )', NUMBER, VALUE
      PRINT '( '' Output:'' / 1X, I5, F5.1 / )', NUMBER, VALUE


      PRINT *, 'Input:'
      READ '( BZ, I5, BN, F5.1 )', NUMBER, VALUE
      PRINT '( '' Output:'' / 1X, I5, F5.1 / )', NUMBER, VALUE
*------------------------------------------------
      END
```

Input/Output column:

```
1234567890
Input:
  -123E+15
Output:
-0.123E+15


Input:
  -123D+15
Output:
-0.123D+15


Input:
-830 321
Output:
-8.30 3.21


Input:
T
Output:
 T


Input:
123    456
Output:
45.6


Input:
123    456
Output:
45.6


Input:
123  456
Output:
  123 45.6


Input:
123   456
Output:
12300456.0


Input:
123   456
Output:
12300 45.6
```

Description

E descriptor edits real value in exponential form.

D descriptor edits double-precision value in exponential form.

Two F descriptors edit complex value; can also use D, E, and G descriptors.

L descriptor edits logical value; can also input in form ∙TRUE∙ (F or ∙FALSE∙ for false values).

X descriptor used to skip field; input in second field gets stored in VALUE.

T descriptor is alternative to X descriptor for skipping positions; same effect as preceding example.

BN descriptor ignores blanks within input field.

BZ descriptor edits blanks as zeros within input field. Note how identical input as preceding example now stores in NUMBER 12300 instead of 123. Also, 10th position in 2nd field now 0, so VALUE stores 456.0.

We can mix BN and BZ descriptors to interpret blanks differently in different fields. Compare output to preceding two examples; input is identical.

TABLE C.5   **Additional Input Format Specifications**

Program	Input/Output
`PROGRAM ADDIN`	
`*————————————————————————————`	
`*    Additional Input Format Specifications`	
`*————————————————————————————`	
`INTEGER          NUM1, NUM2`	`1234567890`
`PRINT *, 'Input:'`	`Input:`
`READ '( I5 / I5 )', NUM1, NUM2`	`123`
	`456`
`PRINT '( '' Output:'' / 1X, 2I5 / )', NUM1, NUM2`	`Output:`
	`123   456`
`PRINT *, 'Input:'`	`Input:`
`READ '( 2(2X, I3) )', NUM1, NUM2`	`123   456`
`PRINT '( '' Output:'' / 1X, 2I5 / )', NUM1, NUM2`	`Output:`
	`123   456`
`PRINT *, 'Input:'`	`Input:`
`READ '( 2I5 )', NUM1`	`123`
`PRINT '( '' Output:'' / 1X, I5 / )', NUM1`	`Output:`
	`123`
`PRINT *, 'Input:'`	`Input:`
`READ '( I5 )', NUM1, NUM2`	`123`
	`456`
`PRINT '( '' Output:'' / 1X, 2I5 / )', NUM1, NUM2`	`Output:`
`END`	`123   456`

theses are present within an embedded format specification, repeat scans begin with the *rightmost* set of parentheses.

RUN-TIME INPUT FORMATS

A **run-time input format** is a format specification that's input along with the data whose editing it describes; that is, the format specification is stored in the data file instead of the program file.

The general approach is to store the format specification within a character variable whose value (the format specification itself) is input. The character variable is then used as the format identifier in the READ statement that processes the input data that's to be edited by the run-time input format. Did you follow that? (*You* should try writing it!) Run-time input formats are best described by example, so let's get on with it.

Description

Slash descriptor ends 1st record. NUM2 stores value in 2nd record.

Embedded format specification equivalent to (2X , I3 , 2X , I3).

Unbalanced format specification: two repeatable edit descriptors (2I5) and one item in input list (NUM1); 2nd descriptor ignored.

Unbalanced format specification: one repeatable edit descriptor (I5) and two items in input list (NUM1 , NUM2). Right parenthesis "bump" ends 1st record; value in next record used for NUM2 ,

---

EXAMPLE C.2

DESCRIPTIVE STATISTICS WITH RUN-TIME INPUT FORMATS

Consider the program, data file, and output in Figure C.2. The program essentially inputs sets of experimental data (samples) and prints the mean (arithmetic average) and unbiased standard deviation (a measure of variability about the mean . . . see page 109).

The run-time input format is stored in the character variable XINPUT. It's read in from the data file by the following statement.

```
READ(5, 800) XINPUT
```

The data file contains data for two samples. The run-time input format for the first sample is (F10.3), as provided in the fifth record. This means that the remain-

```
      PROGRAM STAT
* * * * * * * * * * * * * * * * * * * * * * * * * * * * * * * * * * * *
*                                                                     *
*        Descriptive Statistics:  Version 1.0                         *
*                                                                     *
*        Inputs number of samples, names, format specs, sample data   *
*        Calculates mean and standard deviation for each sample       *
*        Outputs name, mean, and standard deviation for each sample   *
*                                                                     *
*        Data file structure:                                         *
*                                                                     *
*           Record  Field   Type      Columns    Descriptor           *
*           ───────────────────────────────────────────────          *
*              1     TABLE   Character  1 - 80       A                 *
*              2     NUMBER  Integer    1 -  3       I3                *
*              3     NAME    Character  1 - 80       A                 *
*              4     SIZE    Integer    1 - 10       I10               *
*              5     XINPUT  Character  1 - 80       A                 *
*              6     X       Real      ...Based on XINPUT..            *
*           ......Remaining X-data for 1st sample........             *
*           ......NAME   for 2nd sample.................              *
*           ......SIZE   for 2nd sample.................              *
*           ......XINPUT for 2nd sample.................              *
*           ......X-data for 2nd sample.................              *
*           ......Additional samples.....................             *
*           ───────────────────────────────────────────────          *
*                                                                     *
*        Key:                                                         *
*        BODY..... Table body format specification                    *
*        HEAD..... Table head format specification                    *
*        LINE..... Table line format specification                    *
*        MEAN..... Mean of Xs                                         *
*        NAME..... Name of sample                                     *
*        NUMBER... Number of samples                                  *
*        OBSERV... Observation number (Inner DO-variable)             *
*        SAMPLE... Sample number (Outer DO-variable)                  *
*        SIZE..... Size of sample                                     *
*        STD...... Standard deviation (unbiased) of Xs                *
*        SUM...... Sum of Xs                                          *
*        SUMSQ.... Sum of Xs-Squared                                  *
*        TABLE.... Table title                                        *
*        TITLE.... Table title format specification                   *
*        X........ Sample observation                                 *
*        XINPUT... Run-time format specification for X-input          *
*                                                                     *
* * * * * * * * * * * * * * * * * * * * * * * * * * * * * * * * * * * *
*─────────────
*  Type data
*─────────────
      CHARACTER*80 BODY, HEAD, LINE, NAME, TABLE, TITLE, XINPUT
      INTEGER      NUMBER, OBSERV, SAMPLE, SIZE
      REAL         MEAN, STD, SUM, SUMSQ, X
*─────────────────────────────
*  Output format specifications
*─────────────────────────────
      BODY  = '( 1X, I4, 3X, 2F15.3, 3X, A40 )'
      HEAD  = '('' Sample        Mean       Std. Dev.   Name'')'
      LINE  = '( 1X, 70(''='') )'
      TITLE = '( 1X, A )'
*─────────────────
*  Process samples
*─────────────────
      READ( 5, 800 ) TABLE
      READ( 5, 810 ) NUMBER

      PRINT TITLE, TABLE
      PRINT LINE
      PRINT HEAD
      PRINT LINE
```

FIGURE C.2   **Descriptive statistics with run-time input formats** (*continued on next page*)

```
          DO 200 SAMPLE = 1, NUMBER

            READ( 5, 800 ) NAME
            READ( 5, 810 ) SIZE
            READ( 5, 800 ) XINPUT    ←──────────────── Input of run-time input format

            SUM  = 0.0
            SUMSQ = 0.0

            DO 100 OBSERV = 1, SIZE ──────────────── Use of run-time input format

              READ( 5, XINPUT ) X

              SUM  = SUM  + X
              SUMSQ = SUMSQ + X**2

  100     CONTINUE

            MEAN = SUM / SIZE
            STD  = SQRT( ( SIZE*SUMSQ - SUM**2 ) / ( SIZE*(SIZE - 1) ) )
            PRINT BODY, SAMPLE, MEAN, STD, NAME

  200   CONTINUE

          PRINT LINE
```

```
 •──────────────────────────
 •  Input formats                    ←──────────── Note how each format is used
 •──────────────────────────              by more than one READ statement
    800 FORMAT( A  )
    810 FORMAT( I5 )
 •──────────────────────────

          END
```

```
                                              ── Data file with two sets of
                                                 sample data
STRESS TESTS (PSI)... April 1, 1999
     2
Prototype Terminator 2001
     5
(F10.3) ◄────────────────────────────── Run-time input format for
    5000756                                 first sample
    5099108
    4793112 ◄────────────────────────── X-data for 1st sample
    5234623
    5143987
Prototype Terminator 2010
     3                                    Run-time input format for
(F15.2) ◄────────────────────────────── second sample
        986543
       1276832 ◄─────────────────────── X-data for 2nd sample
       1165266
```

Output

```
STRESS TESTS (PSI)... April 1, 1999
════════════════════════════════════════════════════════════════════
Sample        Mean        Std. Dev.   Name
════════════════════════════════════════════════════════════════════
   1        5054.316       168.570    Prototype Terminator 2001
   2       11428.801      1464.339    Prototype Terminator 2010
════════════════════════════════════════════════════════════════════
```

FIGURE C.2   *(continued)*

ing input data for this sample is to be edited according to this format specification. The input data are input by the following statement.

```
READ(5, XINPUT) X
```

Thus, X-data input is edited by whatever is stored within X I N P U T, or (F 1 0 . 3) for the first sample. You should confirm that the input data for the second sample is edited by the format specification (F 1 5 . 2)

Program S T A T is a heavy user of input/output formats, and thus serves as a good review for putting a number of varied formats together. Try Exercise 15 to make sure you understand the formats in this program.   ■

The flexibility of providing format specifications as part of the input data is quite important in certain applications, because it allows complete independence between the program and the user with respect to input format requirements. Statistical and mathematical packages widely available in the software libraries of computer installations commonly use run-time input formats. In most commercial and research environments, input data usually reside in input media like magnetic disk and tape. If these data are to be analyzed by more than one program (or by an unknown program at the time the data file was created), then either each program would have to have input formats consistent with the data file or the data file would have to be modified for consistency with each program. Either approach would be costly, which is why FORTRAN has the run-time input format feature.

C.5 PROGRAMMING TIPS

DESIGN AND STYLE

1. **Format Specification Methods.** As in output formats, we can provide format specifications in F O R M A T statements, character constants, and character variables. Run-time input formats are necessarily provided through character variables. Note that the program in Figure C.2 makes heavy use of character variables for storing format specifications. Advantages and disadvantages of each approach are described on pages 526–527.

2. **Treatment of FORMAT Statements.** As in output formats, place F O R M A T statements in a group either at the beginning or end of the program. It's also more readable to separate the input formats from the output formats, as done in Figure C.2.

3. **List-Directed Versus Format-Directed Input.** List-directed input is more convenient for simple input data needs than format-directed input; however, in applications with large, preformatted data files, input formats pro-

vide the often-needed flexibility to edit varying data formats. Moreover, input formats can process unquoted character data and real data without decimal points. This reduces typing costs in mass data entry environments typical of large corporations and research organizations.

4. **Documentation of Data File Structure.** Formatted data files are best described in the program's documentation, to reduce the likelihood of data input errors from faulty format specifications. See the descriptions in Figures C.1 and C.2.

COMMON ERRORS

1. **Correspondence Errors.** Make sure that the types (integer, real, and so on) of items in the input list correspond to the proper edit descriptors in the format specification (integer with I descriptor, real with E, F, or G descriptor, and so forth). These in turn should correspond to data types within the fields of the input record. Note that we have a three-way correspondence here: the input list item, the edit descriptor, and the field value. example, we might properly match up a real variable in the input list with an F descriptor in the format specification, but then fail to match these up with the corresponding data item by, say, entering a string in the corresponding field of the input record.

2. **Field Errors.** In this case, we incorrectly place values in the fields of an input record. Examples include the type of correspondence error mentioned in item 1 above, left-justification of numeric input when right-justification is expected by the system (see Note 5, page 546), inattention to character input rules (see page 543), and not fitting a value within its field (see Table C.2, page 544). Remember that the decimal point in an input field for real data overrides the decimal digit specification (the d) in descriptors that edit real data (D, E, F, and G). Also, don't use quoted strings within the fields for character data, unless you want to store the quotes also.

3. **Linkup Errors.** If the format specification is not part of the input statement, then it must be linked to the input statement through the format identifier. If the format identifier is a statement label, then make sure that the statement label in the READ statement corresponds to the statement label that labels the corresponding FORMAT statement.

4. **Maximum Record Length Errors.** The maximum record length allowed depends on the input device and the system. A good rule of thumb is to limit the length to 80 positions, since this is consistent with the "ancient" use of 80-column punched cards (and with the default width of most video screens). Find out if there's a maximum record length for disk data files on your system. Is there a maximum on the video screen? (See Exercise 13.)

1. Suppose an input record contains a principal investigator's first name in columns 1–8, second name in columns 9–16, and last name in columns 17–28. Using

   ```
   CHARACTER FIRST*8, MIDDLE*8, LAST*12
   ```

   a. Specify READ/FORMAT statements to enter these data.
   b. Specify PRINT/FORMAT statements to give an output line at the top of a new page having last name in columns 50–61 followed by a comma, blank space, first name in columns 64–71, blank space, and middle name in columns 73–80.

2. Given the input record

1	2	3	4	5	6	7	8	9	10	11	12	13	14	15	16	17	...
C	A	P	T	A	I	N		N	E	M	O		S	U	B		

   and the statements

   ```
   CHARACTER SHIP*dl
   READ 100,SHIP
   100 FORMAT(Aw)
   ```

   specify storage contents for each variation below.

Part	Declared Length, dl	Field Width, w	Contents in SHIP
a.	20	20	
b.	20	10	
c.	20	25	
d.	15	20	
e.	15	10	

3. For the statements

   ```
   CHARACTER RESULT*80
   INTEGER NUM1,NUM2,NUM3,NUM4
   READ RESULT,NUM1,NUM2,NUM3,NUM4
   ```

   and the input record

1	2	3	4	5	6	7	8	9	10	11	12	13	14	...
5			6	2	4	1	9	8	4		7	5		

   determine the stored values for each case below.
   a. RESULT = '(I1,I3,I4,I2)'
   b. RESULT = '(I1,I8,I2,I3)'

4. Given the input record

1	2	3	4	5	6	7	8	9	...
6	1	3	0	4	2		1		

write the appropriate statements that result in the storage of 613 for K, 42 for M, and 1 for N. Each variable is typed integer.

5. Appropriately fill in the input record below if 35 for L, 600 for M, and -3 for N are to be stored using the statements below. All variables are typed integer.

```
READ 25,L,M,N
25 FORMAT(3I4)
```

1	2	3	4	5	6	7	8	9	10	11	12	13	14	...

6. For the statements

```
CHARACTER RESULT*80
REAL VAL1,VAL2,VAL3,VAL4
READ RESULT,VAL1,VAL2,VAL3,VAL4
```

and the input record

1	2	3	4	5	6	7	8	9	10	11	12	13	14	...
5					6	2	4	1	9	8	4		7	5

← Note: Same input record as Exercise 3.

determine the stored values for each case below.
a. RESULT = '(F1.0,F3.0,F4.1,F2.2)'
b. RESULT = '(F1.0,F8.3,F2.0,F3.3)'

7. Given the input record

1	2	3	4	5	6	7	8	9	...
6	1	3	0	4	2		1		

write appropriate statements that result in the storage of 6.13 for X, 42.0 for Y, and 0.1 for Z.

8. Appropriately fill in the input records below for storage of the indicated values using

```
READ 1,COST,NUM,QUANT
1 FORMAT(F5.2,I5,F5.0)
```

	Values Stored in		Columns in Input Record
COST	NUM	QUANT	1 2 3 4 5 6 7 8 9 10 11 12 13 14 15 16 17 18 19 20
a. 15.25	45	507.0	
b. 152.50	450	5070.0	
c. 1525.00	50	507.4	
d. 105.0	5	−300.0	

*9.   Consider an input record with the following layout.

Description	Variable	Type	Positions
Social security number	SSN	Integer	1−9
Name	NAME	Character	22−45
Age	AGE	Integer	46−47
Marital status	MAR	Character	48
Sex	SEX	Character	49
Salary (to two decimal places)	SALARY	Real	50−57
Blank			58−80

Write down statements that read AGE, SEX, and SALARY.

*10.   Indicate an appropriate FORMAT statement for

    READ 25,A,B,C,D,E

where three input fields for A, B, and C of ten columns each are on the first input record and two input fields for D and E of five columns each are on the next input record. Each real value is to be entered to two decimal places.

*11.   Specify input records for the following

    READ 10,A,B,L,C,D
    10 FORMAT(2F5.0,I10)

where A is to store 1.1, B is to store 1.2, C is to store 1.3, D is store 1.4, and L is to store 100.

*12.   How are trailing blanks in numeric input fields interpreted on your system? Find out by running the sample program in
    a. Table C.2.
    b. Table C.3.

*13.   **Maximum input record length.** Write an interactive program that checks maximum input line length for the video screens in your system, as follows: Declare, input, and print a character variable that has a declared length of 90. Then try other lengths, like 180. Most likely, you can "wrap" the input line on your screen to any length up to the maximum length of the character variable itself. Results?

14.   **HC ENGINEering.** Regarding Program ENG4 in Figure C.1:
    a. How would the data file change if we were to use A20 in FORMAT 810? If we were to use A30?
    *b. Revise the program to use character constants for the input format specifications. Do you prefer this approach? Why or why not?
    *c. Revise the program to use character variables for the input format specifications. Do you prefer this approach? Why or why not?

15. **Descriptive statistics.** Regarding Program STAT in Figure C.2:
     a. As the program stands, what's the maximum number of samples that can be processed? Maximum number of observations?
     b. Describe the difference between the variables TABLE and TITLE. What's the maximum length of the table title on input? On output?
     c. What's the maximum length of the sample name on input? On output?
     ***d.** Add the following third sample to the data set:
        Name . . . .   Prototype Human
        Observations 70.1, 95.33, 52.4, 85.167
        Place the data in positions 21−25. Do we need to make any changes in the program?
     ***e.** Process the revised data file on your system.

ADDITIONAL EXERCISES

16. **Revisit.** Revise an end-of-chapter program you have already written by using input formats.

17. **Descriptive statistics.** Revise and run Program STAT to include the calculation and output of the following additional descriptive statistics: minimum, maximum range (maximum − minimum). Redesign the output table to fit the additional statistics. *Hint:* Use the MAX and MIN intrinsic functions. The argument list has two variables.

ANSWERS TO SELECTED FOLLOW-UP EXERCISES

NOTE In this section we include answers to the follow-up exercises that are not marked with an asterisk. Answers to exercises marked * are given in the Instructor's Manual.

CHAPTER 1

1. No answer; implementation dependent.

2. No answer; implementation dependent. Does your compiler allow lowercase letters for keywords and/or variable names? Does it allow more than six characters in a variable name?

CHAPTER 2

1. (a) Acceptable. (b) Unacceptable in ANSI FORTRAN 77; implementation may allow lowercase names. (c) Unacceptable; begins with number. (d) Acceptable. (e) Unacceptable; special character. (f) Unacceptable in ANSI FORTRAN 77; implementation may allow more than six characters. (g) Acceptable. (h) Unacceptable; special character, more than six characters. (i) Acceptable. (j) Acceptable.

2. (a) Unacceptable constant; comma. (b) Integer constant. (c) Real constant. (d) Real constant. (e) Real constant. (f) Real constant. (g) Real constant. (h) Unacceptable; comma. (i) Integer constant.

3. (a) $-6.142E15$ or $-0.6142E16$ etc. (b) $-6142E12$ or $-0.6142E16$ etc. (c) $0.7E-9$ or $7E-10$ etc. (d) $7E-10$ etc. (e) $0.167E125$ *Note:* May exceed maximum value of the machine.

4. (a) Missing right apostrophe.
   (b) Quotation marks not part of the ANSI standard; use apostrophes.
   (c) Use double apostrophes for apostrophes embedded within outer apostrophes: `'YOU''RE OK, I''M OK'`. Otherwise the computer can't distinguish between legitimate apostrophes within the character constant and the outer apostrophes that enclose the character constant. The double apostrophe is internally represented (stored) correctly as a single apostrophe.

5. `LATHE` and `PRESS` must be typed explicitly before the `PARAMETER` statement; the `PARAMETER` statement has missing parentheses; the `INTEGER` statement must precede executable statements; the length specification on `FOIL` cannot precede `FOIL` as shown. The following is correct.

```
CHARACTER FOIL*15,LEVEL*5
INTEGER   I,PRESS
REAL      LATHE,COST,X
PARAMETER (LATHE = 4.178,PRESS = 7042)
  .
  .
  .
END
```

Note: We could also write the CHARACTER statement as

CHARACTER*15 FOIL,LEVEL*5

In this case the length specification immediately following the key word CHARACTER specifies the length of each variable in the list not having its own length specification.

6. CHARACTER NAME*20
   NAME = 'CLARK S. KENT'

If we had used

CHARACTER NAME*15

there would be only two trailing blanks in storage instead of seven. If the length specification had been ten, storage would appear as follows.

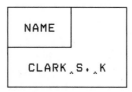

7. (a) Variable must appear to left of the equal sign.

   A = B + C

(b) Two operation symbols next to each other; Rewrite as

   D = 4.0*(-X)

or

   D = -4.0*X

(c) Variable must appear to left of the equal sign.

   AGE = 5.0

(d) Incorrect assignments. Change to

   X = 5.3
   Y = 5.3
   Z = 5.3

(e) Not permissible to raise a negative value to a decimal (real) power since the computer attempts to take the logarithm of a negative number.

(f) OK to raise a negative integer value to an integer power since integer arithmetic in this example is performed as follows.

   J*J*J

8.

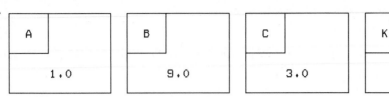

A	B	C	K
1.0	9.0	3.0	20

9. (a) Integer result; 0 (b) Real result; 0.4 (c) Integer result; will cause integer overflow. (d) Real result; 8E120 (May cause real overflow.) (e) Double-precision result; 6.2831853072D+05 (Note that the expression here is mixed type, since A is double precision and B is real; the pairwise computation upgrades the result to double precision.

10. (a) 85.77778 (b) 100 (c) 0

11. (a) 116.0 (b) 28.0 (c) 28.0 (d) 8.5 (e) 4.0 (f) 4.0

12. (a) X**(K + 1)   (e) SQRT(7.0 - X)
    (b) X**K + 1   (f) (Y - 3.0**(X - 1.0) + 2.0)**3
    (c) (X - A)**2/(S + 4.0)   (g) (X - Y)/100.0/(A + B)
    (d) SQRT((X - A)**2/(S + 4.0))   + (Y - 5.0/(X*T) + 2.0)*(-4.0)

13. (a) DATA A, B, C, D, E, F, R1, R2, R3 / 5*0.0, 100.0, 3 * 'YES' /
        or
        DATA A, B, C, D, E / 5 * 0.0 / F / 100.0 / R1, R2, R3 / 3 * 'YES' /
    (b) A   =   0.0
        B   =   0.0
        C   =   0.0
        D   =   0.0
        E   =   0.0
        F   =   100.0
        R1 = 'YES'
        R2 = 'YES'
        R3 = 'YES'

     The DATA statement initializes during *compilation,* whereas the assignment statement initializes during *execution.* If variables need to be reinitialized during the same computer run, we must use assignment statements, as we will show in Exercise 5a of the next chapter.

CHAPTER 3

1. (a) 2 } 2 iterations
         5

    (b) 2 } 1 iteration
    (c) no iterations
    (d) 10.0 }
         12.5
         15.0 } 5 iterations
         17.5
         20.0

    (e) 1   4 }
         1   3
         1   2
         2   4 } 6 (or 2 × 3) iterations
         2   3
         2   2

(f)

1	4	1	
1	4	3	
1	4	5	
1	4	7	
1	3	1	
1	3	3	
1	3	5	
1	3	7	
1	2	1	24 (or 2 × 3 × 4) iterations
1	2	3	
1	2	5	
1	2	7	
2	4	1	
.			
	.		
		.	
2	2	7	

2.

STU	SCO	NAME	SCORE	SUM	AVE
1	1	Joshua Clay	95.0	95.0	? (undefined)
1	2	Joshua Clay	90.0	185.0	? (undefined)
1	3	Joshua Clay	100.0	285.0	? (undefined)
2	1	J. K. Dunn	50.0	50.0	95.0
2	2	J. K. Dunn	90.0	140.0	95.0
2	3	J. K. Dunn	68.0	208.0	95.0
3	1	Rick Jardon	88.0	88.0	69.3333
3	2	Rick Jardon	72.0	160.0	69.3333
3	3	Rick Jardon	87.0	247.0	69.3333
4	1	Cynthia Mello	85.0	85.0	82.3333
4	2	Cynthia Mello	92.0	177.0	82.3333
4	3	Cynthia Mello	95.0	272.0	82.3333

3. (a) Replace INT with NINT.

4. (a) Add AVE to the list in the REAL statement. Just after the CONTINUE statement insert the following:

AVE = TOTAL / NUMBER

Add the following PRINT statement in the report foot section:

PRINT *, 'Average sales...........$', AVE

5. (a) Now SUM cannot be reinitialized for each new student, since the DATA statement initializes during compilation. In the run, the average for the first student is correct, but not for subsequent students. For example, the sum for the second student (J. K. Dunn) starts with the sum of the first student (285.0). After accumulation of this student's three scores, SUM would store 493.0 (or 285.0 + 50.0 + 90.0 + 68.0), giving 164.333 in AVE . . . a fortunate mistake for Mr. Dunn, Mr. Jardon, and Ms. Mello.

NOTE Don't use DATA statements for variables that need to be reinitialized.

CHAPTER 4

1. (a) True   (d) True
    (b) False   (e) False
    (c) True   (f) True

2. (a) False   (d) False
    (b) True   (e) False
    (c) False

3. (a)
```
IF (CREDIT .GE. 12) THEN
    TUIT   = 1200
    SUMFUL = SUMFUL + TUIT
    KOUNTF = KOUNTF + 1
ELSE
    TUIT   = 100 * CREDIT
    SUMPAR = SUMPAR + TUIT
    KOUNTP = KOUNTP + 1
END IF
```
    (b)
```
IF (LAST .EQ. 'CORE') THEN
    PRINT *, 'Harvey is my kind of guy.'
ELSE
    COUNT = COUNT + 1
END IF                          or LAST .NE. 'CORE'
```
    (c)
```
IF (.NOT. (LAST .EQ. 'CORE')) THEN
    PRINT *, 'Where''s Harvey?'
END IF
```
    (d)
```
DISCRI = B**2 - 4.0 * A * C      To improve computational efficiency and simplify
                                 To avoid .EQ. hazard
IF (ABS (DISCRI) .LT. 1.0E-06) THEN
    PRINT *, 'One repeated real root exists'
ELSE
    IF (DISCRI .GT. 0.0) THEN
      PRINT *, 'Two real roots exist'
    ELSE
      PRINT *, 'No real roots exist'
    END IF
END IF
```

4. (a)
```
TEST1 = ABS (DISCRI) .LT. 1.0E-06
TEST2 = DISCRI .GT. 0.0

IF (TEST1) THEN
    PRINT *, 'One repeated real root exists'
ELSE
    IF (TEST2) THEN
      PRINT *, 'Two real roots exist'
    ELSE
      PRINT *, 'No real roots exist'
    END IF
END IF
```

7. (a) If we had no need to find the name of the item whose value is the minimum, then we could simplify by replacing the if-then structure with:

```
MINVAL = MIN (MINVAL, VALUE)
```

9. If order size is always zero or more, then we can simplify the logical expressions on page 139 as follows:

```
IF (SIZE .LT. BREAK1) THEN
   COST = PRICE1 * SIZE
ELSE IF (SIZE .LT. BREAK2) THEN
   COST = PRICE2 * SIZE
ELSE IF (SIZE .LT. BREAK3) THEN
   COST = PRICE3 * SIZE
ELSE
   COST = PRICE4 * SIZE
END IF
```

☺

Also note that the else-block now simply reflects the fourth price, instead of our earlier need to detect an order size less than zero. These simplified logical expressions would not work in the following revised Example 4.5.

```
IF (SIZE .LT. BREAK1) THEN
   COST = PRICE1 * SIZE
END IF

IF (SIZE .LT. BREAK2) THEN
   COST = PRICE2 * SIZE
END IF

IF (SIZE .LT. BREAK3) THEN
   COST = PRICE3 * SIZE
ELSE
   COST = PRICE4 * SIZE
END IF
```

☹   Note, for example, that an order size of 50 would be incorrectly classified in the `PRICE3` block.

We would have to use the original version in Example 4.5, although we would delete the wrong order size logic.

The approach in Example 4.6 would work correctly as follows.

```
IF (SIZE .LT. BREAK1) THEN
   COST = PRICE1 * SIZE
ELSE
   IF (SIZE .LT. BREAK2) THEN
     COST = PRICE2 * SIZE
   ELSE
     IF (SIZE .LT. BREAK3) THEN
       COST = PRICE3 * SIZE
     ELSE
       COST = PRICE4 * SIZE
     END IF
   END IF
END IF
```

We prefer the else-if approach, as it's more readable than the nested-if approach.

10. (a) Modify the logical expressions as follows:

```
IF (CHOICE .EQ. 'E' .OR. CHOICE .EQ. 'e') THEN
ELSE IF (CHOICE .EQ. 'M' .OR. CHOICE .EQ. 'm') THEN
ELSE IF (CHOICE .EQ. 'O' .OR. CHOICE .EQ. 'o') THEN
ELSE IF (CHOICE .EQ. 'Q' .OR. CHOICE .EQ. 'q') THEN
```

(b) Type CHOICE as an integer variable instead of a character variable. Modify the statements that print the menu to reflect numeric choices. Revise the logical expressions as follows:

```
IF (CHOICE .EQ. 1) THEN
ELSE IF (CHOICE .EQ. 2) THEN
ELSE IF (CHOICE .EQ. 3) THEN
ELSE IF (CHOICE .EQ. 9) THEN
```

Revise the error message to reflect the proper numeric choices.

CHAPTER 5

1. (a) NINT (F) .NE. -999

We're neutral in our preference.

(b)
```
100 PRINT *, 'Enter degrees Fahrenheit'
    READ *, F
    IF (NINT(F) .NE. -999) THEN
       C = 5.0/9.0 * (F - 32.0)
       PRINT *, SPACE, LINE
       PRINT *, SPACE, 'Fahrenheit......', NINT(F)
       PRINT *, SPACE, 'Celsius.........', NINT(C)
       PRINT *, SPACE, LINE

       GO TO 100

    END IF
```

This is a traditional approach. It does eliminate a PRINT/READ set, but at the expense of loop readability. The loop exit test is now buried in the loop body, which hampers identification and indentation of the body. Moreover, the loop structure is murky from a structured programming standpoint. Strictly speaking, we have neither a pretest nor a posttest loop, although we could argue that it's essentially a pretest loop. Our original approach is cleaner. The following approach is often suggested by students:

```
    F = 0
100 IF (NINT(F) .NE. -999) THEN
       PRINT *, 'Enter degrees Fahrenheit'
       READ *, F
       C = 5.0/9.0 * (F - 32.0)
       PRINT *, SPACE, LINE
       PRINT *, SPACE, 'Fahrenheit......', NINT(F)
       PRINT *, SPACE, 'Celsius.........', NINT(C)
       PRINT *, SPACE, LINE

       GO TO 100

    END IF
```

Do you see a problem? The sentinel is wrongly processed as a legitimate temperature before loop exit is achieved.

2. (a)
```
      MORE = 'y'
100 IF (MORE .EQ. 'Y' .OR. MORE .EQ. 'y') THEN
        PRINT *, 'Enter degrees Fahrenheit'
        .  ⎫
        .  ⎬ As before
        .  ⎭
        GO TO 100
      END IF
```

The original approach is somewhat simpler.

(b) If we delete the PRINT/READ sequence for MORE and rewrite the logical IF statement as

```
IF (NINT(F) .NE. -999) GO TO 100
```

then we have a posttest loop based on the given sentinel; however, this would wrongly process the sentinel as a legitimate temperature before achieving loop exit. We prefer the TEMP3 approach in Figure 5.2.

3. (a) In the output, records processed would show 10. This is because the record counter gets incremented just after the eof condition is detected by the READ statement. We could simply decrement the record count by one within the print list in the exit routine.

4. Make the following changes in Program MIN2:
Initialize RECORD to zero.
Just after the second READ statement, add the following:

```
NAME  = MINNAM
VALUE = MINVAL
```

Rewrite the repetition structure as follows:

```
100 IF (.NOT. (NAME .EQ. 'eof')) THEN

      RECORD = RECORD + 1

      IF (VALUE .LT. MINVAL) THEN
        MINVAL = VALUE
        MINNAM = NAME
      END IF

      READ (5,*) NAME, VALUE

      GO TO 100

    END IF
```

Try a run based on these changes. Don't forget to add a sentinel record to the data file. For example, try

```
'eof', 0
```

We prefer the simplicity of the original version.

5.
```
      TIME = 100
  500 IF (TIME .LE. 300) THEN
          SPEED = START + ACCEL * TIME
          PRINT *, TIME, SPEED
          TIME = TIME + 50
          GO TO 500
      END IF
```

The DO-loop lives for this type of loop control.

9. (a) Replace the READ statements with:

```
READ (*,*, ERR = 150) F
```

Just after the farewell message add the following error routine:

```
    STOP
150 PRINT *, CHAR(7), 'Input error...please rerun the program.'
```

The loop is not a proper control structure because it shows two different loop controls. It also typifies the kind of "jumping around" that characterized early approaches to programming. If we wish to detect an input error condition, we would use the IOSTAT = approach.

13.

Iter.	LEFTC	RIGHTC	MIDC	F(LEFTC)	F(RIGHTC)	F(MIDC)	HALF	Test at 200
(a) 1	0.0	1.0	0.5	-1.0	1.0	0.0	0.5	F

... Exact root at MIDC

Iter.	LEFTC	RIGHTC	MIDC	F(LEFTC)	F(RIGHTC)	F(MIDC)	HALF	Test at 200
(b) 1	0.5	1.0	0.75	0.0	1.0	0.5	0.25	T
2	0.5	0.75	0.625	0.0	0.5	0.25	0.125	T
3	0.5	0.625	0.5625	0.0	0.25	0.125	0.0625	T
4	0.5	0.5625	0.53125	0.0	0.125	0.0625	0.03125	T
5	0.5	0.53125	0.515625	0.0	0.0625	0.03125	0.015625	T
6	0.5	0.515625	0.507812	0.0	0.03125	0.015625	0.0078125	F

... Estimated root at MIDC, with maximum error in HALF

Iter.	LEFTC	RIGHTC	MIDC	F(LEFTC)	F(RIGHTC)	F(MIDC)	HALF	Test at 200
(c) 1	0.0	0.5	0.25	-1.0	0.0	-0.5	0.25	T
2	0.25	0.5	0.375	-0.5	0.0	-0.25	0.125	T
3	0.375	0.5	0.4375	-0.25	0.0	-0.125	0.0625	T
4	0.4375	0.5	0.46875	-0.125	0.0	-0.0625	0.03125	T
5	0.46875	0.5	0.484375	-0.0625	0.0	-0.03125	0.015625	T
6	0.484375	0.5	0.492188	-0.03125	0.0	-0.015625	0.0078125	F

... Estimated root at MIDC, with maximum error in HALF

Our results should suggest a more efficient algorithm . . . See Exercise 19.

14. Change the statement function to:

```
F(X) = 2.0**X
```

Iter.	LEFTC	RIGHTC	MIDC	F(LEFTC)	F(RIGHTC)	F(MIDC)	HALF	Test at 200
	-3.0	1.0		0.125	2.0			

... The test

```
F(LEFTC) * F(RIGHTC) .GT. 0.0
```

evaluates as true and the NO ROOT SCREEN is displayed.

17. We would have to repeat the printing of the menu, once before the loop and once at the end of the loop body. This is code inefficient, although in the next chapter we will show a way around this problem. Just before the screen clear we would insert the loop control as:

```
100 IF (.NOT. (CHOICE .EQ. 'S' .OR. CHOICE .EQ. 's') THEN
```

At the end of the old loop we would eliminate the logical IF statement and insert:

```
  GO TO 100
END IF
```

We would also eliminate the else-if block labeled 'Choice Stop.'

CHAPTER 6

2. (a) In the control module:

Add the character variable SYMBOL to the CHARACTER statement.

Insert the following READ statement just before the one that reads in the title:

```
READ (5,*) SYMBOL
```

Note: In the data file we would enclose the desired bar character within apostrophes as the first line.

Add SYMBOL to the actual argument list in the CALL statement.

In the subroutine:

Add SYMBOL to the dummy argument list in the SUBROUTINE statement.

Add SYMBOL to the list in the CHARACTER statement.

Within the DO-loop replace ' = ' with SYMBOL.

Try running the revised program using * as the bar character.

(b) Assuming a screen display that's 80 characters wide, a specification of 30 for GRADE (which gives a length of 30 for LABEL in the subroutine) will result in wrapped bars on the screen (the output from the subroutine doesn't fit on an 80-character screen line since we are also printing the integer variable LENGTH, the character constant !, and the character variable BAR having a length of 50). Yes, we can use LABEL*10 in the CHARACTER statement within the subroutine. The declared length in the subroutine for LABEL can be any number up to 30.

The best approach is to use the assumed length declarator (*), and to limit the output in LABEL by using an A10 edit descriptor, as in

```
    PRINT 200, LABEL, LENGTH, BAR
200 FORMAT (1X, A10, I10, '   !', A50)
```

The output line thus takes up 74 characters on the screen.

> **NOTE**   See Module B if you're rusty on the A edit descriptor.

(c) We would have a run-time error when POS stores 51 and the assignment statement for BAR is executed, as the specified length in BAR is 50. Part d addresses this problem.

4. (a) The function subprogram is referenced as usual, FACT is initialized to 1 in the function, the IF-test is false, and 1 (or 0!) is returned as the factorial.

5. In subroutine CPRINT:

Move the input of N and K to a new subroutine called INPUT. In its place use the following:

```
      CALL INPUT (N, K)
100 IF (K .GT. N .OR. K .LT. 0 .OR. N .LT. 0) THEN
      PRINT '(25(/))'
      PRINT *,' INPUT ERROR SCREEN'
      PRINT *,' =================='
      PRINT *
      PRINT *,'One of the following conditions is violated:'
      PRINT *,'  N must be greater than or equal to K'
      PRINT *,'  N and K must be nonnegative'
      PRINT *
      CALL PAUSE
      CALL INPUT (N, K)
      GO TO 100
    END IF
```

NOTE This error routine continues to trap these errors while (as long as) they're committed. The while structure thus insists on reinput while the error condition is present.

Similarly modify Subroutine FPRINT to trap the entry of a negative number. Try running the modified program, and include input that activates each of these traps.

CHAPTER 7

1.

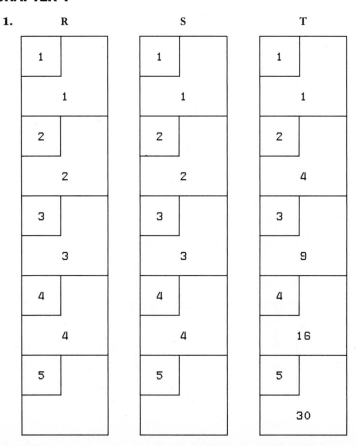

2.

1	5	−4
10	4	6
8	1	7
2	10	−8
21	20	1

3. (a) `READ  *, (X(J), J = 1,8)`
  (b) `READ  *, (X(J), J = 1,11,2)`
  (c) `PRINT *, (A(J), B(J), J = 1,3)`
  (d) `PRINT *, (A(J), J = 1,3), (B(J), J = 1,5)`
  (e) ```
       DO 50 I = 1, 3
          PRINT *, (X(I,J), J = 1,4)
    50 CONTINUE
```

**4.** (a) `10 20 30 40  5 10 15 20`
  (b) `10  5 20 10 30 15 40 20`
  (c) ` 1 10  5  2 20 10  3 30 15  4 40 20`
  (d) ` 1 10 20 30 40`
      ` 2 10 20 30 40`

**5.**

| | 1 2 3 4 5 6 7 8 9 10 11 12 13 14 15 16 17 18 19 20 ... |
|---|---|
| (a) and (d) | 1 0    2 0    3 0    4 0 |
| (b) and (e) | 1 0 |
| | 2 0 |
| | 3 0 |
| | 4 0 |
| (c) | 1 0    2 0 |
| | 3 0    4 0 |

**6.** (a)

|   | 1 | 2 | 3 | 4 | 5 | 6 | 7 | 8 | 9 | 10 | 11 | 12 | 13 | 14 | 15 | 16 | 17 | 18 | 19 | 20 |
|---|---|---|---|---|---|---|---|---|---|----|----|----|----|----|----|----|----|----|----|----|
| 1 |   |   |   |   |   |   |   |   |   |   |   |   |   |   |   |   |   |   |   |   |
| 2 |   |   |   | 1 | 0 |   |   | 2 | 0 |   |   |   | 3 | 0 |   |   |   |   | 4 | 0 |
| 3 |   |   |   |   |   |   |   |   |   |   |   |   |   |   |   |   |   |   |   |   |

(b)

|   | 1 | 2 | 3 | 4 | 5 | 6 | 7 | 8 | 9 | 10 | 11 | 12 | 13 | 14 | 15 | 16 | 17 | 18 | 19 | 20 |
|---|---|---|---|---|---|---|---|---|---|----|----|----|----|----|----|----|----|----|----|----|
| 1 |   |   |   |   |   |   |   |   |   |   |   |   |   |   |   |   |   |   |   |   |
| 2 |   |   |   | 1 | 0 |   |   |   |   |   |   |   |   |   |   |   |   |   |   |   |
| 3 |   |   |   | 2 | 0 |   |   |   |   |   |   |   |   |   |   |   |   |   |   |   |
| 4 |   |   |   | 3 | 0 |   |   |   |   |   |   |   |   |   |   |   |   |   |   |   |
| 5 |   |   |   | 4 | 0 |   |   |   |   |   |   |   |   |   |   |   |   |   |   |   |
| 6 |   |   |   |   |   |   |   |   |   |   |   |   |   |   |   |   |   |   |   |   |
```

(c)

	1	2	3	4	5	6	7	8	9	10	11	12	13	14	15	16	17	18	19	20
1																				
2				1	0				2	0										
3				3	0				4	0										
4																				

(d) and (e)

	1	2	3	4	5	6	7	8	9	10	11	12	13	14	15	16	17	18	19	20
1																				
2	1				1	0														
3	2				2	0														
4	3				3	0														
5	4				4	0														
6																				

7. (a)
```
     INTEGER LIST(25)
     READ *, N
     DO 10 J = N,1,-1
       READ *, LIST(J)
  10 CONTINUE
```

(b)
```
     BIG = LIST(1)
     DO 20 J = 2, N
       BIG = MAX(BIG, LIST(J))  ◄──────── See intrinsic functions in Module A
  20 CONTINUE
```

We would find the two largest values by first sorting the array in descending order, and then referencing LIST(1) and LIST(2).

(c)
```
     DO 30 J = 1, N
       IF (LIST(J) .EQ. 0) THEN
         PRINT *, J
       END IF
  30 CONTINUE
```

8. (a) Using an implied-DO list:

```
DATA ((D(I,J), I = 1,5), J = 1,6) / 30 * 100.0 /
```

Using the array name technique:

```
DATA D / 30 * 100.0 /
```

(b)
```
        DO 200 I = 1,5
           DO 100 J = 1,6
              D(I,J) = 100.0
100        CONTINUE
200 CONTINUE
```

9.
```
        DO 50 I = 1,4
           DO 25 J = 1,4

           IF (I .EQ. J) THEN
              X(I,J) = 1
           ELSE
              X(I,J) = 0
           END IF
25         CONTINUE
50 CONTINUE
```

Alternatively, we could first initialize all array elements to zero using one of the methods in Exercise 8, followed by:

```
     DO 50 K = 1,4
        X(K,K) = 1
50 CONTINUE
```

11. (a)
```
        READ (5,900) N
        READ (5,900) (F(I), I=1,N)

900 FORMAT (50I3)
```

(b)
```
        PRINT 910, (I, I=1,N)
        PRINT 910, (F(I), I=1,N)

910 FORMAT (1X, 16( 2X, I3))
```

> **NOTE**   We assume an 80-character line display; if the array uses more than 16 elements, then we might try the approach in part d.

(c) As in part a, except use

```
900 FORMAT (I3)
```

(d)
```
        DO 100 I = 1, N
           PRINT 910, I, F(I)
100 CONTINUE
910 FORMAT (1X, 2I3)
```

13. (a) Replace * in the READ statement with 900.
Add the following just before END:

```
900 FORMAT (4I4)
```

(b) Replace * in the PRINT statement with 910.
Add the following just before END:

```
910 FORMAT (1X, 4(4X, I4))
```

14. (a) Add AVEROW(ROWMAX) to the list in the INTEGER statement.
Add AVEROW / ROWMAX*0 / to the DATA statement.
Insert the following just before the CONTINUE statement labeled 225:

```
AVEROW(I) = AVEROW(I) + F(I,J)
```

Insert the following just before the CONTINUE statement labeled 300:

```
AVEROW(I) = AVEROW(I)/4
```

(b) Revise the PRINT statement in DO-loop 300:

```
PRINT *, (F(I,J), J=1,4), AVEROW(I)
```

(c) Add GRAND to the list in the INTEGER statement.
Add GRAND / 0 / to the DATA statement.
Insert the following just before the CONTINUE statement labeled 225:

```
GRAND = GRAND + F(I,J)
```

Insert the following just after the CONTINUE statement labeled 250:

```
GRAND = GRAND / (4*N)
```

Add GRAND to the print list in the last PRINT statement.

(d) Insert the following after the PARAMETER statement:

```
CHARACTER CITY(ROWMAX)*15
```

Revise the READ statement as follows:

```
READ (5, *, END = 200) CITY(I), (F(I,J), J=1,4)
```

> **NOTE**   In the data file insert
> 'Los Angeles', at the beginning of record 1
> 'Chicago',   at the beginning of record 2
> and so on. . . .

Revise the PRINT statement in DO-loop 300 as follows:

```
PRINT *, CITY(I), (F(I,J), J=1,4)
```

17. (a) We could replace LIST(N) with LIST(*) within the INTEGER statement in the function subprogram, although there's no advantage to doing so here since we need to pass N anyway.

(b) In the control module . . .
Delete the INTEGER statement and insert in its place:

```
INTEGER   LDB, UDB, LOWER, UPPER
PARAMETER (LDB = -200, UDB = 100)
INTEGER   F(LDB:UDB), I, N
```

Replace the PRINT/READ input sequence with the following:

```
PRINT *, 'Enter lower array element limit'
READ  *, LOWER
PRINT *, 'Enter upper array element limit'
READ  *, UPPER
PRINT *
PRINT *, 'Please enter temperatures,'
READ  *, (F(I), I = LOWER, UPPER)
PRINT *
```

Calculate N just before the PRINT statement that references the function.

```
N = UPPER - LOWER + 1
```

Revise the function reference as follows:

```
MEAN (LOWER, UPPER, N, F)
```

In the function subprogram . . .
Revise the dummy argument list as shown:

```
FUNCTION MEAN (LOWER, UPPER, N, LIST)
```

Use the following specifications:

```
INTEGER   LDB, UDB, LOWER, UPPER
PARAMETER (LDB = -200, UDB = 100)
INTEGER   K, LIST(LDB:UDB), N, SUM
REAL      MEAN
```

Replace the DO statement with:

```
DO 100 K = LOWER, UPPER
```

18. (a) No. FORTRAN does not allow adjustable or assumed-size array declarators in COMMON statements.
    (b) Yes. No.

19. Yes, as follows:
    In the main program . . .

```
COMMON N /BLOCK1/ LETTER /BLOCK2/ X
```

In the first subroutine . . .

```
COMMON NUM /BLOCK1/ CODES
```

In the second subroutine . . .

```
COMMON N /BLOCK2/ VALUES
```

21. In the main program . . .
    Insert the following after the REAL statement:

```
COMMON AGE, FACE, TABLE
```

Replace the given subroutine calls with the following:

```
CALL SCHED
CALL KEYIN
CALL LOOK
```

In subroutine `SCHED` . . .

Add `AGE` and `FACE` to the `REAL` statement. Note that these variables are not used in the subroutine. We need them to properly match `TABLE`.

Use the same `COMMON` statement as the main program.

In subroutine `KEYIN` . . .

Insert the following just after the `REAL` statement:

```
COMMON AGE, FACE
```

Note that we don't need `TABLE`

In subroutine `LOOK` . . .

Use the same `COMMON` statement as the main program.

Our preference? Six of one and half a dozen of the other.

25. (a) Type as follows:

```
INTEGER J, K, PLACE, SIZE
REAL    ARRAY(SIZE), INSERT, MIN
```

(b) Type as follows:

```
INTEGER J, K, PLACE, SIZE
CHARACTER*50  ARRAY(SIZE), INSERT, MIN
```

To ensure ASCII sorts we could replace the `.LT.` operator with the intrinsic function `LLT` (see the last part of Table A.1). We would rewrite the two `IF` statements as follows:

```
IF (LLT(ARRAY(K), MIN)) THEN
IF (LLT(INSERT, ARRAY(J-1))) THEN
```

(c) Replace `MIN` with `MAX`
Replace `.LT.` with `.GT.`

31. (a) The current aspect ratio is 0.37, or 19/51. Yes, aspect ratios other than 0.6 emphasize one scale over another. For example, an aspect ratio of 1.0 distorts the y-scale by overemphasizing it. Aspect ratios above 0.6 effectively expand the y-scale relative to the x-scale; aspect ratios below 0.6 (as in Figure 7.10) compress the y-scale relative to the x-scale.

(b) The scales would be reversed, with the x-scale running up and down the screen.

(c) We could only print one plot per run, since `PLOT` could not be reinitialized within the same run. This would cause incorrect results in a version that allows multiple plots (as in Exercise 32b).

(d) To avoid the `.EQ.` hazard described on page 151.

(e) To accommodate very large, very small, and in-between values in labeling the scales. Extreme values would be expressed in scientific notation and "normal" values would be expressed as if an F edit descriptor were used. See Module B.

(f) The *actual* 11th coordinate is $(11, -363)$.
Using the scaling formulas, we get

$$x\text{-scaled} = 50$$
$$y\text{-scaled} = 0$$

Thus, the *scaled* 11th coordinate is $(50, 0)$. This means `PLOT(0,50)` stores `*`, as shown in the southeast corner in the plot of Figure 7.10. Yes, a plot could have fewer stars (plot symbols) than actual coordinates. Two actual coordinates may be different, yet have the same scaled coordinate. Computationally, calculations of the scaled values to the nearest integer (*x-scaled* and *y-scaled*) would be identical. Visually, we're saying that two actual coordinates that are visually close in actuality would appear on top of one another in a scaled (unrefined) graph. If we could zoom in to that segment of the graph by refining the scales, then we should see two separately plotted points. In practice, we can refine the scale by redefining maxima and minima to the range of the graph we wish to zoom or explode.

(g) No. The calculations for XSCALE and YSCALE ensure that subscript expression values are within the bounds of 0 to 50 for the first subscript and 0 to 18 for the second subscript. These bounds are defined as the named constants LBX, UBX, LBY, and UBY within Subroutine XYPLOT in the PARAMETER statement. Subsequently, they are used in the array declaration for PLOT and in the calculation of the subscripts XSCALE and YSCALE within DO-loop 300.

(h)

Actual Coordinate	Scaled Coordinate	Element in PLOT having *
(1,3)	(25, 0)	(0,25)
(1,4)	(25, 9)	(9,25)
(1,5)	(25,18)	(18,25)

Try executing the program with these actual coordinates to confirm our results.

CHAPTER 8

1. No. Substrings are subsets of strings, where the characters within the subset remain adjacent (as in the original string). Thus, COR is a substring of CORE, but not CRE.

2. IF (REPLY(1:1) .EQ. 'y') THEN

3. (a) R
   (b) I˄love˄FORTRAN˄77!˄˄
   (c) Run-time error; the value in R exceeds the value in L.
   (d) ove˄FORTR
   (e) 18

4. (a) Using an implied DO-list:

    PRINT *, (STRING(K:K) // '˄', K = 1, LEN(STRING))

   (b) Using an implied DO-list:

    PRINT *, (STRING(K:K) , K = LEN(STRING), 1, -1)

6. (a) 0   (c) 4
   (b) 4   (d) 3

7. (a) T   (c) T
   (b) F   (d) F

8. (a) 42   (b) *

9. PRINT *, CITY(1:TRIM(CITY)) // ',˄' // STATE // '˄˄' // ZIP
                        └── Utility function; see Program ED

10. Add LINE*80 to list in CHARACTER statement.
    After the DATA statement insert:

    DO 50 K = 1,80
       LINE(K:K) = '-'
    50 CONTINUE

Replace the three PRINT statements that print the line with:

```
PRINT *, LINE(1:26)
```

11. (a) CORE⌃⌃⌃⌃⌃⌃⌃⌃⌃⌃⌃⌃,Harvey⌃⌃⌃⌃
    — We could use the TRIM function to eliminate these blanks

12. (a) PRINT *, 'Alternative N. Amer... ',
     +   DATE(1:2)//'-'//DATE(4:5)//'-'//DATE(7:8)
    (b) PRINT *, 'Compressed form....... ',
     +   DATE(1:2)//DATE(4:5)//DATE(7:8)
    (c) The program assumes two digits each for month, day, and year. Entry of 1/24/89 would give the output:

```
North American form....1/24/89
European form..........4/81/29.
```

    Entry of 12/7/41 would give the output:

```
North American form....12/7/41
European form..........7/412/1.
```

    The next part corrects this problem. Try it!

13. The declared length is 15, based on the boxed diagram. The trim length is 11, or the position of the last nonblank character in NAME. To print the trim length, we would use the TRIM function shown in Program ED, and available in the Examples Diskette (see inside the front cover):

```
PRINT *, TRIM(NAME)
```

14. PRINT *, INDEX (PHRASE, SEARCH(1:TRIM(SEARCH)))
    Utility function in Program ED
    and Program Diskette

16. T
    T
    F
    F

20. (a) The use of '⌃' instead of CHAR(32) for the blank character is both more readable and portable. Note that CHAR(32) is the blank character in the ASCII code, not in the EBCDIC code.
    (b) Actual: Help is on the way!
        Encoded: R*** **_** *** ****
        Program doesn't handle lowercase letters or punctuation. Code values outside the range defined in LOW and HIGH are assigned *. See exercise 23.
    (c) Actual: HELP ISN'T ON THE WAY
        Encoded: ROVZ SCX*D YX DRO GKI

    To pass through punctuation as is (in our example above, the apostrophe would get printed instead of an * in the encoded message), we would make the following changes in the main program:
    Add PUNC*33 to the CHARACTER statement.
    We're using 33 punctuation (special) characters.
    Add the logical variable PASS (T if a character is to be passed through; F otherwise):

```
LOGICAL PASS
```

    To store all of the special punctuation, use:

```
PARAMETER (PUNC = '⌃!"#$%&''()*+,-./:;<=>?@[\]^_`{|}~')
```

    Double apostrophe for apostrophe.
    We included blank in the 33 special characters.

To pass through special punctuation and blanks, rework the body in DO-loop 100 as follows:

```
PASS = .FALSE.
DO 50 J = 1, 33
   IF (TEXT(K:K) .EQ. PUNC(J:J) THEN
      PASS = .TRUE.
   END IF                    ——— This character in TEXT is a special character.
50 CONTINUE
                             ——— Encode is called only if this character in TEXT is not a special character.
   IF (.NOT. PASS) THEN
      CALL ENCODE (SHIFT, TEXT(K:K))
   END IF
```

24. (a) Subroutine INPUT prints the warning; the last 200 lines in the file get cutoff within TEXT.
   (b) Change 70 to 100 in the PARAMETER statement within the main program. Use of the named constant WIDTH and the assumed length declarator (*) considerably simplify this type of program maintenance.
   (c) Add BELL*1 to the CHARACTER statements.
       Replace CHAR(7) with BELL.
       Insert

       `PARAMETER (BELL = CHAR(7))`

   (d) We get

       `Changed line: Jack anddJill`

       See common error 3 on page 416.
   (e) We get

       `Changed line: Jackand Jill`
                            ——— Missing blank

CHAPTER 9

1. Possible record layout:

Field	Type	Length
Student ID	Character	11
Student name	Character	30
Course code	Character	6
Section	Integer	2
Date enrolled	Character	8
Grade	Character	2
		59

The likely storage medium would be hard (fixed) magnetic disk.

A direct-access file is best for query-type programs, since the few records required would be accessed directly.

A sequential-access file is best when a high percentage of records in the file are processed, as in an end-of-term grade report.

2. Open I/O unit 20 for a sequential-access, formatted file of unknown status and unspecified name.

3. It's an unformatted (no format specifier) output statement that transfers the value in ARC to a sequential-access (no record specifier) file.

```
OPEN (UNIT = 15,FILE = 'STRESS',STATUS = 'OLD',
+       ACCESS = 'SEQUENTIAL',FORM = 'UNFORMATTED')
```

4.
```
        CHARACTER NAME*30, GRADE*2
        INTEGER ID
        .
        .
        .
        OPEN (UNIT = 20,FILE = 'GRADES',STATUS = 'NEW',
+            ACCESS = 'DIRECT',FORM = 'FORMATTED',RECL = 32)
        .
        .
        PRINT *, 'Enter ID'
        READ *, ID
        PRINT *, 'Enter name'
        READ 90, NAME
        PRINT *, 'Enter grade'
        READ 90, GRADE
        WRITE (UNIT = 20,FMT = 90,REC = ID) NAME,GRADE
        .
        .
    90 FORMAT (2A)
        .
        .
        END
```

Note (pointing to CHARACTER/INTEGER declarations and OPEN statement)

Note (pointing to READ ID and READ GRADE)

5. (a) and (b)

```
        PROGRAM T92
*-----------------------------------------------------------------
*       Table 9.2 example... See Exercise 5 in Chapter 9
*-----------------------------------------------------------------
        CHARACTER*80 NOTE
        OPEN (UNIT = 10, FILE = 'TEST.DAT')
        WRITE (10, *) 'Files are great!'
        ENDFILE 10
        REWIND 10
        READ (10, '(A)') NOTE
        PRINT *, NOTE
        CLOSE (10)
*-----------------------------------------------------------------
        END
```

Compilation/execution of program

```
Go F77! FTN77 T92 -LGO
[FTN77 VER 228 Copyright (c) University of Salford 1987]
    NO ERRORS [<T92      >FTN77-VER 228]
    PROGRAM ENTERED
 Files are great!
Go F77! SLIST TEST.DAT
 Files are great!
```

Output (pointing to first "Files are great!")

Listing of file (pointing to second "Files are great!")

(c) Using

```
READ (10, *) NOTE
```

we get an I/O error on unit 10. Within the file, the character value to be stored in NOTE would have to be enclosed in apostrophes.

6. (a) In Subroutine SHOW . . .
Add RECORD to list in INTEGER statement.
Just before the first PRINT statement insert:

```
RECORD = 0
```

Just after the READ statement insert:

```
RECORD = RECORD + 1
```

Just after PRINT 900 insert:

```
PRINT *, 'Number of records processed...', RECORD
```

(b) In the main program . . .
Add FM to the list in the CHARACTER statement.
Add FM to the two actual argument lists.
In Subroutine CREATE . . .
Add FM to the dummy argument list.
Add FM to the list in the CHARACTER statement.
Just before the OPEN statement insert:

```
PRINT *, Enter F if file is Formatted; U if Unformatted'
READ 900, FM
```

> **NOTE** To trap the error of entries other than F or U we could design a routine similar to that which traps yes/no errors (see part c below).

In the OPEN statement replace `FORMATTED` with FM.
Replace the WRITE statement with the following:

```
IF (FM .EQ. 'F' .OR. FM .EQ. 'f') THEN
   WRITE (UNIT = U, FMT = 920) ENAME, SSN, SALARY, SEX
ELSE
   WRITE (UNIT = U) ENAME, SSN, SALARY, SEX
END IF
```

In Subroutine SHOW . . .
Add FM to the dummy argument list.
Add FM to the list in the CHARACTER statement.
Replace the READ statement with the following:

```
200 IF (FM .EQ. 'F' .OR. FM .EQ. 'f') THEN
       READ (UNIT = U, FMT = 920, END = 300)ENAME, SSN, SALARY, SEX
    ELSE
       READ (UNIT = U, END = 300)ENAME, SSN, SALARY, SEX
    END IF
```

(c) In Subroutine CREATE insert just before the logical IF statement:

```
CALL YNERR (REPLY)
```

Utility subroutine in Examples Diskette; also see inside the front cover of the book.

(d) We could use a straightforward DO-loop if we knew the number of records in the file. We generally don't recommend this practice, however, for the reasons outlined in item 4 in Chapter 5 on page 199. When the number of records is unknown, we see the following approach commonly used in practice:

```
      DO 200 RECORD = 1, 99999
         READ (UNIT = U, FMT = 920, END = 300)ENAME, SSN, SALARY, SEX
         PRINT 930, ENAME, SSN, SALARY, SEX
  200 CONTINUE
  300 CONTINUE
```

This design unnecessarily complicates the loop structure, since two loop control tests are used. The test given by the terminal value 99999 is inactive, as this number is picked to well exceed the potential number of records in the file . . . it's a loop pseudocontrol. The real loop control is END = 300. Moreover, execution enters the top of the loop, but does not exit through the bottom at statement 200. Thus it violates the top-down execution principle for control structures. It conveniently gives a record count, if needed, but we prefer the approach described in part a of this exercise, since the integrity of the loop structure is maintained.

7. (a) This would be a file having a record layout that's inconsistent with that assumed by program SFILE2. The read operation at statement 200 would store a positive value in IOCODE, giving an input error message.

   (b) A loop design having both END = and ERR = would require convoluted jumping around with GO TO statements. See our answer to Exercise 9a in Chapter 5.

MODULE A

2. (a) The use of NINT would yield the same results. The main difference is style: ANINT gives a real expression in the function; NINT gives a mixed mode expression (integer divided by real). Since both approaches are equally convenient, we prefer ANINT stylistically. INT and AINT would give incorrect results, since these functions truncate rather than round.

   (b) Eliminate variables LOGC, LOGN, and ROOT from the REAL statement. Eliminate the three assignment statements for these variables. Replace the PRINT statements that round as follows:

```
      PRINT *,'Common log ',ROUND(LOG10(NUMBER),0),
     +       ROUND(LOG10(NUMBER),1), ROUND(LOG10(NUMBER),2)

      PRINT *,'Natural log',ROUND(LOG(NUMBER),0),
     +       ROUND(LOG(NUMBER),1),    ROUND(LOG(NUMBER),2)

      PRINT *,'Square root',ROUND(SQRT(NUMBER),0),
     +       ROUND(SQRT(NUMBER),1),    ROUND(SQRT(NUMBER),2)
```

> **NOTE** We can have functions as arguments to other functions. For example, the intrinsic function LOG is an argument in the statement function ROUND.

Stylistically, we're neutral on the two approaches. From the standpoint of computational efficiency, we prefer the original approach, since the method in this exercise evaluates each intrinsic function twice more than need be. For example, the common log of 35 in our sample run is computed three times by the above method, but only once in Figure A.1.

MODULE B

1. (a) 15 FORMAT('+','HAL Speaks')   (d) 15 FORMAT('0','ˆˆˆHAL Speaks')
   (b) 15 FORMAT('ˆ','HAL Speaks')   (e) 15 FORMAT('1','HAL Speaks')
   (c) 15 FORMAT('0','HAL Speaks')

2.

(a)   RHODE ISLAND

(b) THE OCEAN STATE IS RHODE ISLAND

(c) RHODE ISLA

(d)   RHODE ISLAND

(e) RHODE ISLAND   IS THE SMALLEST STATE

(f) RHODE ISLAND   IS THE SMALLEST STATE

(g) RHODE ISLAND   IS THE SMALLEST STATE

3.

```
1  M =   756  N =   -401
2
3       L =   10
4
5
6
```

4.
```
      PRINT 900, TYPE
      PRINT 905, PINTS
      PRINT 910, COST
```

900 FORMAT ('0∧∧∧∧BLOOD TYPE∧')

    or   ('0', 4X,'BLOOD TYPE∧')

905 FORMAT ('0∧∧∧∧∧∧∧∧PINTS:∧', I4)

    or   ('0', 8X, 'PINTS:∧', I4)

910 FORMAT ('∧∧∧∧∧∧∧∧∧∧COST:∧$', I2)

    or   (10X, 'COST:∧$', I2)

5. (a) F5.1   (b) F8.4

	1	2	3	4	5	6	7	8	9	10
(c) 1	-	.	1	0	7	4				
(d) 2	-	0	.	1	0	7	4			
(e) 3			-	0	.	1	0	7	4	
(f) 4	0	.	1	0	7	4				
(g) 5			3	7	6	4	.	0		
(h) 6			3	7	6	4	.	2		
(i) 7				3	7	6	4	.		
(j) 8		3	7	6	4	.	1	6	0	
(k) 9	*	*	*	*	*	*				

(Overflow if computer inserts leading zero.)

6.

```
                          1 1 1 1 1 1
        1 2 3 4 5 6 7 8 9 0 1 2 3 4 5
(a) E12.4
(b) E12.2
(c)               - 0 . 1 0 7 4 0 E + 0 0
(d)               - 0 . 1 0 7 4 E + 0 0
(e)                   - 0 . 1 1 E + 0 0
(f)     - . 1 0 7 4 0 0 0 0 0 E + 0 0
(g)               0 . 3 7 6 4 0 E + 0 4
(h)               0 . 3 7 6 4 2 E + 0 4
(i)             0 . 3 7 6 4 1 6 E + 0 4
(j)       0 . 3 7 6 4 E + 0 4
(k)               0 . 3 7 6 E + 0 4
```

← (Overflow if computer inserts leading zero)

8.

(a)

	1	2	3	4	5	6	7	8	9	10	11	12	13	14	15	16	17	18	19	20	21	22	23	24	25
1																									
2				7	5																				
3																									
4																									
5				5	0																				

(b)

	1	2	3	4	5	6	7	8	9	10	11	12	13	14	15	16	17	18	19	20	21	22	23	24	25
1																									
2																									
3																									
4																									
5				7	5			5	0																

(c)

	1	2	3	4	5	6	7	8	9	10	11	12	13	14	15	16	17	18	19	20	21	22	23	24	25
1																									
2				7	5			5	0																
3																									
4																									
5																									

Cursor or print head ends up in row 5, column 1

(d)

	1	2	3	4	5	6	7	8	9	10	11	12	13	14	15	16	17	18	19	20	21	22	23	24	25
1																									
2	*	*	*	*	*	*				7	5				5	0				*	*	*	*	*	*
3																									
4																									
5																									

(e)

	1	2	3	4	5	6	7	8	9	10	11	12	13	14	15	16	17	18	19	20	21	22	23	24	25
1																									
2																									
3																									
4																									
5				7	5			5	0																

Same as part b

10. (a)
```
      PRINT 950, DROP
  950 FORMAT(10X, 'Pressure drop =ˏ', F10.3)
```
(b)
```
  950 FORMAT(10X, 'Pressure drop =ˏ', F10.3 / '+', 9X, 15('_'))
```

11. Either

```
   PRINT '(14(/))'
```

   or

```
   DO 500 J = 1, 15
      PRINT *
500 CONTINUE
```

13. (a) The leftmost 20 characters in storage are printed (which is all characters in NAME, since the declared length is 20), according to Rule 1 on page 513. We get the same output using A or A20 in FORMAT 930 because form A uses declared length (which is 20 for NAME) as the field width. A declared length of 50 would not change the output given in Figure B.1 if A20 is used in FORMAT 930 (Rule 1); however, using the edit descriptor A would "push" the output of size and sales 30 positions to the right, since the system assumes a field width of 50 in the output for name (30 additional blanks in storage are printed).

MODULE C

1. (a)
```
      READ 900, FIRST, MIDDLE, LAST
  900 FORMAT(2A8, A12)
```
(b)
```
      PRINT 950, LAST, FIRST, MIDDLE
  950 FORMAT('1', 49X, A12, ',ˏ', A8, 1X, A8)
```

2. Storage in SHIP

```
(a) CAPTAIN NEMO SUBˏˏˏˏˏ
(b) CAPTAIN NEˏˏˏˏˏˏˏˏˏˏˏ
(c) IN NEMO SUBˏˏˏˏˏˏˏˏˏˏ
(d) IN NEMO SUBˏˏˏˏˏ
(e) CAPTAIN NEˏˏˏˏˏˏ
```

3. Storage in . . .

NUM1	NUM2	NUM3	NUM4
----	-----	----	----
(a) 5	0	6241	98
(b) 5	62419	84	75

4.
```
      READ 900, K, M, N
  900 FORMAT(2I3, I2)
```

5.

1	2	3	4	5	6	7	8	9	10	11	12	13	14	15
		3	5		6	0	0				-	3		

6. Storage in . . .

	VAL1	VAL2	VAL3	VAL4
	----	------	-----	-----
(a)	5.0	0.0	624.1	0.98
(b)	5.0	62.419	84.0	0.075

7.
```
      READ 900, X, Y, Z
  900 FORMAT(F3.2, F3.0, F2.1)
      or   (F4.3, F2.0, F2.1)
```

8.

	1	2	3	4	5	6	7	8	9	10	11	12	13	14	15	...
(a)	1	5	.	2	5				4	5		5	0	7	.	
or		1	5	2	5				4	5			5	0	7	
(b)	1	5	2	.	5			4	5	0	5	0	7	0	.	
or	1	5	2	5	0			4	5	0		5	0	7	0	
(c)	1	5	2	5	.			5	0	5	0	7	.	4		

(Need field width of 6 to input COST without decimal point.)

	1	2	3	4	5	6	7	8	9	10	11	12	13	14	15	...
(d)	1	0	5	.					5	-	3	0	0	.		
or	1	0	5	0	0				5		-	3	0	0		
or		1	0	5	.				5	-	3	0	0	.		

14. (a) No change if we use A20, since this is the declared length for NAME (see Rule 1 on page 543). If we were to use A30, then we would have to shift the three records 10 positions to the right, according to Rule 2.

15. (a) The maximum number of samples is equivalent to the maximum value we can store in NUMBER, which according to FORMAT 810 is 5 digits, or 99999 samples. The number of observations in a sample is stored in SIZE, which is edited according to FORMAT 810. Thus, we have 99999 as the maximum number of observations.

(b) TITLE stores the format specification that's used to print the table title stored in TABLE. FORMAT 800 is used to input a table title; thus the maximum length of a title is equivalent to the declared length for TABLE, or 80. On output, the value in TABLE is edited according to the format specification in TITLE, or A. Again, the maximum length is 80, the declared length.

(c) On input it's 80; on output it's based on the format specification stored in BODY, or 40 according to the edit descriptor A40.

I N D E X

PART 2: PROGRAMMING EXERCISES